Routledge Handbook of Adapted Physical Education

This handbook represents the first comprehensive and evidence-based review of theory, research, and practice in the field of adapted physical education (APE). Exploring philosophical and foundational aspects of APE, the book outlines the main conceptual frameworks informing research and teaching in this area, and presents important material that will help shape best practice and future research.

Written by world-leading researchers, the book introduces the key themes in APE, such as historical perspectives on disability, disability and the law, language, and measurement. It examines the most significant theoretical frameworks for understanding APE, from embodiment and social cognitive theory to occupational socialization, and surveys current debates and practical issues in APE, such as teacher training, the use of technology, and physical inactivity and health. Acknowledging the importance of the voices of children, parents and peers, the book also explores research methods and paradigms in APE, with each chapter including directions for further research.

Offering an unprecedented wealth of material, the *Routledge Handbook of Adapted Physical Education* is an essential reference for advanced students, researchers and scholars working in APE, and useful reading for anybody with an interest in disability, physical education, sports coaching, movement science or youth sport.

Justin A. Haegele is an Assistant Professor in the Department of Human Movement Sciences at Old Dominion University, USA. His research focuses within the interdisciplinary field of adapted physical activity, with a primary interest in examining how individuals with disabilities experience physical activity participation. Dr. Haegele has received several awards designated for emerging scholars in physical education and adapted physical activity. He is also Research Fellow with the Research Council of SHAPE and Associate Editor for *Adapted Physical Activity Quarterly* and *Quest*.

Samuel R. Hodge is a Professor in the Department of Human Sciences at The Ohio State University, USA. Professor Hodge is a Fellow in the National Academy of Kinesiology; the National Association of Kinesiology in Higher Education; and the Society of Health and Physical Educators (SHAPE). He is also Editor of *Quest* and an Executive Associate Editor of *Multicultural Learning and Teaching*, and long-time member of *Adapted Physical Activity Quarterly*'s editorial board.

Deborah R. Shapiro is a Professor in the Department of Kinesiology and Health at Georgia State University, USA. Her primary research focus has been in the area of psychosocial factors of sport participation among youth athletes with disabilities and professional preparation. Dr. Shapiro has received several awards for her scholarship and leadership in the field of adapted physical activity, and she serves as Associate Editor of *Adapted Physical Activity Quarterly*.

Routledge Handbook of Adapted Physical Education

Edited by Justin A. Haegele, Samuel R. Hodge, and Deborah R. Shapiro

Routledge
Taylor & Francis Group

LONDON AND NEW YORK

First published 2020 by Routledge

2 Park Square, Milton Park, Abingdon, Oxon OX14 4RN

605 Third Avenue, New York, NY 10017

Routledge is an imprint of the Taylor & Francis Group, an informa business

First issued in paperback 2022

Publisher's Note

The publisher has gone to great lengths to ensure the quality of this reprint but points out that some imperfections in the original copies may be apparent.

British Library Cataloguing-in-Publication Data
A catalogue record for this book is available from the British Library

Library of Congress Cataloging-in-Publication Data
A catalog record has been requested for this book

ISBN: 978-0-367-14611-5 (hbk)
ISBN: 978-1-03-233715-9 (pbk)
DOI: 10.4324/9780429052675

Typeset in Bembo
by Swales & Willis, Exeter, Devon, UK

Contents

Contents

Figures

Tables

Contributors

Jihoun An is an Assistant Professor in the Department of Kinesiology at East Carolina University, USA. Her research and teaching focus on pre-service teacher education in adapted and general physical education, pedagogical approaches of situated learning and critical service-learning in higher education, a school-based mentoring program for inclusion and youth development, and collaborative partnership among home, school, and community. Her scholarship is guided by socioecological, sociocultural, and critical perspectives, so she utilizes qualitative methods to investigate the focused areas of research.

Laura Azzarito is the Program Director of the graduate program in physical education pedagogy and physical culture, and Co-Director of the VRC (Visual Research Center for Education, Art, and Social Change) at Teachers College, Columbia University, USA. Dr. Azzarito strives to understand nuanced conceptualizations of young people's embodiment with attention to the complex articulation of gender/sex, race/ethnicity, and social class. Her research advocates for opening up pedagogical spaces where ethnic minority young people can recognize themselves, resist and counter-narrate negative stereotypes, and self-represent to the public in affirmative ways, finding new positive identity positions in society.

Sheresa Boone Blanchard is an Assistant Professor in the Department of Human Development and Family Science at East Carolina University, USA. Her research and teaching focus on family/community engagement, inclusion, families of color, assessment, and improving teacher preparation competencies through lenses of intersectionality, equity, and social justice. Her scholarly interests emerged fromten years of experience as a teacher, practitioner and consultant in early childhood, special education, and early intervention. Dr. Blanchard currently serves as co-chair of the Division for Early Childhood's Inclusion, Equity, and Social Justice Committee and also serves through other local and state initiatives.

Martin E. Block is a Professor in the Department of Kinesiology at the University of Virginia, USA, where he teaches courses in adapted physical education. He is the author of over 100 peer-reviewed articles, 20 chapters in books, and five books on adapted physical education, including *A Teachers' Guide to Including Students with Disabilities in General Physical Education*. Professor Block is the Editor of the Journal *Palaestra*, past-president of the International Federation of Adapted Physical Activity (IFAPA), and past-president of the National Consortium for Physical Education for Individuals with Disabilities (NCPEID).

Layne Case is currently a doctoral student in Kinesiology with an option in Adapted Physical Activity at Oregon State University, USA. Her primary research interests include gross motor intervention for children with autism spectrum disorder (ASD) and appropriate measurement strategies for unique populations. She has experience with teaching gross motor skills to children with ASD and other developmental disabilities and currently coordinates a large, community-based adapted physical activity program for children with disabilities.

Janine K. Coates is a Lecturer in qualitative research methods in the School of Sport, Exercise and Health Sciences at Loughborough University, UK. Her research focuses on children, specifically those with special educational needs and disabilities, and their experiences of physical activity and sport. Previously, Janine has undertaken research exploring perceptions about physical education, inclusive initial teacher education for physical educators and parent training for attention-deficit disorder. Janine is currently working on research exploring the experiences of parents of young elite para-athletes. In addition to her research, Janine teaches qualitative research methods at undergraduate and postgraduate level. Janine is a member of the British Psychological Society.

Luis Columna is a native of San Juan Puerto Rico and an Associate Professor in the Kinesiology Department at University of Wisconsin at Madison, USA. His research focuses on ways to increase the participation of families (especially Hispanic) of children with disabilities into physical activity with an emphasis on ways to better prepare teachers to work with diverse populations. Dr. Columna developed the Fit Families Program, a physical activity program that brings together children with disabilities, their parents, college students, and in-service professionals in the fields of adapted physical education, special educators, orientation and mobility, psychology, and exercise science, among others. At the national level, Dr. Columna serves on the editorial boards of several journals, including *Disability and Health Journal* and *Palaestra*.

Karen P. DePauw is the Vice President and Dean for Graduate Education and tenured Professor of Sociology and Human Nutrition, Foods & Exercise at Virginia Tech in Blacksburg, Virginia, USA. In her faculty capacity, Dr. DePauw is an internationally recognized scholar in the fields of adapted physical activity and disability sport, focusing on inclusion, equity issues, social construction of disability, and disability sport.

Janice Causgrove Dunn is a Professor in the Faculty of Kinesiology, Sport, and Recreation and Associate Dean in the Faculty of Graduate Studies and Research at the University of Alberta, Canada. Her research interests focus on psychosocial aspects of motivation and participation in physical activity and sport, primarily related to children and youth with disability.

Lindsay Eales recently completed her PhD on Mad performance and mad-accessible trauma informed movement practices, in the Faculty of Kinesiology, Sport, and Recreation at the University of Alberta, Canada. Her work builds on 12 years of experience as an integrated dance choreographer and instructor, as well as a Mad performance and video artist.

Donna Goodwin is a Professor in the Faculty of Kinesiology, Sport, and Recreation at the University of Alberta, Canada. Her research focuses on bringing to light the literal, metaphorical, and political lives of disabled people as they negotiate the social and cultural impediments to engagement in physical activity and community life. Her teaching philosophy is grounded in the need for crucial self-reflexion on taken-for-granted pedagogical practices in teacher education and professional service delivery. Dr. Goodwin has been a visiting professor in China, Hong Kong, Ireland, Japan, Korea, and Norway.

Michelle Grenier is an Associate Professor in the Department of Kinesiology at the University of New Hampshire, USA, where she oversees the adapted physical education concentration at the undergraduate and graduate levels. She is an internationally recognized expert in the field of inclusion and adapted physical education. She served as editor for a Human Kinetics publication entitled *Physical Education for Students with Autism Spectrum Disorders: A Comprehensive Approach* and co-editor for the publication *Physical Education for Students with Moderate to Severe Disabilities.*

Michelle D. Guerrero is a postdoctoral fellow at the Children's Hospital of Eastern Ontario, Canada, working with the Healthy Active Living and Obesity Research Group. Her research focuses on children's outdoor play and learning, sedentary behaviour, disability sport and exercise, and the promotion of physical activity and sport participation via psychological techniques. Dr. Guerrero was one of two winners of the 2017–2018 Governor General's Gold Medals at the University of Windsor in recognition of her academic excellence at the graduate level. In 2018, she was awarded the Reviewer of the Year for *Adapted Physical Activity Quarterly*.

William J. Harvey is an Associate Professor in the Department of Kinesiology and Physical Education at McGill University, Montreal, Canada, and director of the Choices in Health, Action, Motivation, Pedagogy and Skills (CHAMPS) physical activity lab at the Douglas Mental Health University Institute, Montreal, Canada. His research interests include mixed methods research, adapted physical activity, pre-service physical and health education teachers' perspectives about inclusion, disability sport coaching, and the recovery model for children and adults with mental health problems. He has devoted most of his academic life to understanding the physical activity component of attention-deficit hyperactivity for school-aged children.

Damian Haslett is a Doctoral Researcher at Durham University, UK. His research focuses on the intersection of disability activism and disability sport. Damian is a full member of the Division of Sport, Exercise and Performance Psychology (Psychological Society of Ireland) and he serves on the executive committee of Irish Wheelchair Association Sport.

Seán Healy is an Assistant Professor of adapted physical activity in the Department of Behavioral Health and Nutrition at the University of Delaware, USA. Dr. Healy conducts research to understand and promote health among youth, particularly youth with autism spectrum disorder. Dr. Healy's recent research includes examining the effectiveness of web-based interventions to enable teachers and parents to increase physical activity among children with developmental disabilities.

Mary A. Hums was the 2009 NASSM Earle F. Zeigler Lecturer, the 2014 NASSM Diversity Award recipient, an Erasmus Mundus Visiting International Scholar in Adapted Physical Activity at Katholieke Universiteit of Leuvern, Belgium, and was selected by the USOC to represent the United States at the International Olympic Academy in Olympia, Greece. Hums worked the Paralympic Games in Atlanta, Salt Lake City, Athens, and Vancouver, as well as the Olympic Games in Athens, and the Para-Pan American Games in Toronto. She was a co-contributor to Article 30.5 of the United Nations Convention on the Rights of Persons with Disabilities.

Yeshayahu "Shayke" Hutzler is a Professor and Chair of the Graduate School at the Academic College at Windgate, Israel. Between 2007 and 2011, he assumed Presidency of the International Federation of Adapted Physical Activity and, in 2017, was awarded for outstanding contributions to the field of study. Between 2013 and 2016, he served as Editor in Chief of *Adapted Physical Activity Quarterly*. Up to 2019, he has published more than 100 articles in peer-reviewed journals and about 40 book chapters and research reports. Additionally, he has contributed to developing new physical activity programs for persons with disabilities in Israel and other countries.

Leah Ketcheson is the program coordinator for Health and Physical Education at Wayne State University in Detroit, MI, USA. Dr. Ketcheson's primary research interests include the motor behavior of children with autism spectrum disorder. Specifically, Dr. Ketcheson is interested in the examination of health-related outcomes following participation in community-based inventions for preschool-aged children with autism spectrum disorder. The overall goal of her research is to provide a translational approach from research to practice for clinicians and teachers.

Francis M. Kozub is a Professor in the Department of Kinesiology, Sport Studies, and Physical Education at The College at Brockport, State University of New York, USA. He started his career as a public school teacher/coach in New York. Later, Dr. Kozub attended The Ohio State University, USA, where he earned a PhD with a focus in Adapted Physical Activity. Dr Kozub has studied teacher variables, physical activity behavior, and motivational constructs in individuals with disabilities.

Byungmo Ku is an Assistant Professor of Kinesiology at Vanguard University of Southern California, USA. His research focuses on promoting physical activity and motor behaviors of children with disabilities within the context of family. More specifically, he has been investigating the effects of parents on the physical activity and motor behaviors of children with disabilities.

Byron Lai is a postdoctoral researcher within the University of Alabama at Birmingham, USA, Children's of Alabama, and Lakeshore Foundation research collaborative. Dr. Lai currently studies Rehabilitation Science with a specific focus on delivering physical activity as post-rehabilitative care. His research interests focus on physical activity promotion and the development of strategies that increase the reach and sustainability of physical activity trials for both children and adults with disabilities. Dr. Lai is currently serving as the Secretary of the North American Federation of Adapted Physical Activity.

Jihyun Lee is an Assistant Professor of Adapted Physical Activity/Education in the Department of Kinesiology at San Jose State University, USA. She earned her PhD from The Ohio State University, USA and specialized in single-subject experimental designs and motor development. Her research on the improvement of social skills and gross motor skills in children with autism has led to her interest in using single-subject research designs in her studies. She also has a passion for developing physical activity knowledge and skills to improve transition outcomes and quality of life of postsecondary students with developmental disabilities.

Jennifer Leo is the Director of The Steadward Centre for Personal & Physical Achievement in the Faculty of Kinesiology, Sport, and Recreation, University of Alberta, Canada. With over 15 years of research experience, Jennifer has published about experiences of inclusion and participation in adapted physical activity settings. Interested in learning from the perspective of those experiencing disability, Jennifer completed a post doc with the UNESCO Chair in Inclusive Physical Education, Physical Activity, and Sport at the Institute of Technology Tralee in Ireland and is a Researcher with the Family Engaged Sport & Exercise Team in the Canadian Disability Participation Project.

Chunxiao Li is an Assistant Professor at Nanyang Technological University in Singapore. He teaches primarily in the area of adapted physical education/activity, and is currently a board member for the Asian Society of Adapted Physical Education and Exercise. His research interests mainly lie in the areas of teacher preparation for inclusive physical education, mindfulness/motivation and outcomes, and talent development in sport. As a young researcher, he has published over 40 peer-reviewed articles in respected journals such as *Adapted Physical Activity Quarterly*, *Journal of Sports Science*, and *Psychology of Sport and Exercise*. He is a serving board member of several international peer-reviewed journals.

Samuel W. Logan is an Assistant Professor of Kinesiology at Oregon State University, USA. Dr. Logan is the director of the Social Mobility Lab & PlayTech Workshop. The Social Mobility Lab & PlayTech Workshop believes that mobility is a fundamental human right and a radical paradigm shift removing the mobility disparity for children with disabilities is imperative. The mission of the lab is to provide children with disabilities with equitable, equal, and inclusive access to mobility and play. Thus, the lab is dedicated to the design, prototyping, and testing of toy-based technologies and the development and implementation of play-based experiences that promote mobility and play.

Megan MacDonald is an Associate Professor of Kinesiology at Oregon State University, USA. Dr. MacDonald is the Early Childhood Core Director at the Hallie E. Ford Center for Healthy Children and Families. In addition, Dr. MacDonald is the director of the Children and Youth with Disabilities Lab, whose vision is that every child is active and accepted and whose mission is rooted in conducting the best research, teaching, and outreach focused on youthful activity for all people. The Lab aims to positively influence physical activity engagement and motor skill development for all children and, through this work, also aims to provide a gateway to positive influence in other domains of development.

Anthony J. Maher is a Senior Lecturer in Physical Education and Youth Sport at Edge Hill University, UK, where he leads the Pedagogy, Professional Development and Politics in Physical Education and Sport Research Group. Anthony's research interests relate mainly to diversity, equity and inclusion in physical education, teacher education, special education, and disability sport. More specifically, Anthony has contributed to the development of research relating to the role and responsibilities of special educational needs coordinators and teaching assistants; the training of physical education teachers as inclusive educators; whole-school strategies for including pupils with special educational needs and disabilities; and the use of simulation as a form of embodied pedagogy in action. Currently, Anthony is exploring the nature, purpose, and value of physical education and physical activity in special schools and pupil referral units.

Jeffrey J. Martin is a Professor at Wayne State University. He has published over 200 research articles and chapters, as well as the *Handbook of Disability Sport and Exercise Psychology*. His research focuses on the psychosocial aspects of disability sport and physical activity with populations ranging from Paralympians to Wounded Warriors. He has received over seven million dollars of external funding and provided keynote addresses and lectures in Belgium, Czech Republic, Ireland, Italy, Portugal, Sweden, Thailand, China, and Turkey. He was the founding editor of Sport, Exercise, and Performance Psychology, and is the current editor of the *Adapted Physical Activity Quarterly*.

Cathy McKay is an Assistant Professor in the Kinesiology Department at James Madison University, Virginia, USA. Cathy completed her doctoral degree at the University of Virginia. Cathy's scholarly interests focus on changing attitudes and perspectives toward disability and disability sport through Paralympic and disability sport education and awareness programming. Cathy is passionate about contact theory, and applying contact theory in educational settings. Currently, Cathy is exploring the lived experiences of individuals with and without disabilities to inform program planning, access, and diversity initiatives.

Mathieu Michaud is a graduate student in Adapted Physical Education at McGill University, Canada under the supervision of Dr. William J. Harvey and Dr. Gordon Bloom. He received the Fonds de Recherche du Québec—Société et Culture (FRQSC) Master's Award and a Canada Graduate Scholarship from the Social Sciences and Humanities Research Council of Canada (SSHRC) for his research "Teaching Methods and Communication Strategies for the Motor Development of Pre-Verbal and Non-Verbal Children with Autism Spectrum Disorder". His research aims to assist physical education specialists with the practical application of teaching theory directed towards students with disabilities. Mr. Michaud also holds a Master's degree in music and a Bachelor's degree in physical and health education from McGill University, Canada.

Anita M. Moorman is a Professor of Sport Administration at the University of Louisville, USA. She teaches Sport Law and Legal Aspects of Sport. She received her Juris Doctorate from Southern Methodist University and also holds an MS in Sport Management from the University of Oklahoma, USA and a BS in Political Science from Oklahoma State University. Professor Moorman is licensed to practice law in the State of Oklahoma and was admitted to practice before the US Supreme Court when she served as co-counsel for nine disability sport organizations on an *amicus curiae* brief in the landmark Americans with Disabilities Act case involving the professional golfer, Casey Martin (Martin *v.* PGA Tour, 2001). Professor Moorman co-authors—*Sport Law: A Managerial Approach*, published by Routledge, entering its fourth edition in 2020.

Niamh-Elizabeth Mourton is a Lecturer and Researcher at the University of Derby, UK in the discipline of Sport, Outdoor and Exercise Science, where she leads on the areas of adaptive coaching, physical education and physical activity. She is also an inclusion specialist who works with various organizations such as Special Olympics and Youth Sport Trust supporting innovative projects that drive positive meaningful inclusion in and through sport, physical education and physical activity. Niamh is passionate about empowering everyone to take their own personal responsibility for inclusion, so that we can build a more unified generation and inclusive society for everyone.

Iva Obrusnikova is an Associate Professor in the Department of Behavioral Health and Nutrition at the University of Delaware, USA. Dr. Obrusnikova received her PhD in Kinesiology with a focus on Adapted Physical Activity from Palacky University in Olomouc, Czech Republic. Her most recent studies examine how different technology-based strategies promote exercise performance, physical function, independence, and quality of life among individuals with developmental disabilities. For her contribution to research, Dr. Obrusnikova received the G. Lawrence Rarick Research Award from the National Consortium for Physical Education of Individuals with Disabilities. She is an editorial board member of *Adapted Physical Activity Quarterly* and *Palaestra*, as well as the SHAPE of America Research Fellow. She is director of the Health and Disability Laboratory at the University of Delaware's Tower at STAR, USA.

Danielle Peers is a queer crip artist, activist, and academic who is interested in how movement cultures of all kinds – including dance, recreation, and parasport – can deepen or challenge social inequalities. Danielle's work revolves around social structures that disable, and how these structures interact with other forms of structural oppression. Danielle works as an Assistant Professor in the Faculty of Kinesiology, Sport and Recreation at the University of Alberta, Canada.

K. Andrew R. Richards is an Assistant Professor in the Department of Kinesiology and Community Health at the University of Illinois at Urbana-Champaign, USA. Richards completed his PhD and post-doctoral study at Purdue University before serving as a visiting Assistant Professor at Northern Illinois University, USA. Richards' scholarly interests focus on the lives and careers of pre-service and in-service teachers with a focus on socialization and psychosocial factors related to stress, burnout, and resilience. He received the Mabel Lee Award from SHAPE America in 2017 and achieved status as a SHAPE America Research Fellow in 2018.

Terry L. Rizzo is a Professor at CSU San Bernardino, USA. His university leadership includes being former chair of kinesiology and past Associate Vice Provost and Undergraduate Dean. Dr. Rizzo's service includes, but is not limited to, President of the California Association for Health, Physical Education, Recreation and Dance, and President of the National Consortium for Physical Education for Individuals with Disabilities. He is an emeritus editor of the *Adapted Physical Activity Quarterly* and emeritus member of the Board of Directors of the American Kinesiology Association. Dr. Rizzo's research is devoted to attitudes toward individuals with disabilities.

Brett Smith is a Professor in the Department of Sport and Exercise Sciences at Durham University, UK. Working with organizations such as Disability Rights UK and Aspire, his research focuses on disability, sport and physical activity. Brett serves on seven journal editorial boards (e.g., *Disability and Society*), is Associate Editor for two journals, and is the President of the International Society for Qualitative Research in Sport and Exercise.

Erin Snapp is a PhD ccandidate of Exercise and Sport Science at Wayne State University in Detroit, MI, USA. Erin's research interests focus on the engagement of individuals with traumatic brain injuries (TBI) in physical activity (PA) programs. Specifically, Erin's research examines psychological factors, such as cognitive function and social support, which are both predictive of, and impacted by, engagement in various types of PA, including interval training and yoga. This PA research is done with an overall goal of improving quality of life for individuals with TBI.

Nancy L. I. Spencer is an Associate Professor in the Faculty of Kinesiology, Sport, and Recreation at the University of Alberta, Canada. She uses person-centered and participatory-based methodologies to collaborate with participants in exploring experiences of inclusion and exclusion in relation to disability within the contexts of physical activity, recreation, and sport. This work has also led to a deep interest in, and critical questioning of, the taken-for-granted beliefs and practices in adapted physical activity.

Øyvind F. Standal is a Professor of Physical Education at the Faculty of Teacher Education and International Studies, at OsloMet – Oslo Metropolitan University, Norway. In addition to peer-reviewed papers, Standal has published the book *Phenomenology and Pedagogy in Physical Education* (Routledge, 2015) and an edited textbook on inclusive physical education, in Norwegian.

Heidi Stanish is an Associate Professor of Exercise and Health Sciences at the University of Massachusetts (UMass) Boston, USA and holds an adjunct faculty position in the Eunice Kennedy Shriver Center at UMass Medical School, USA. Dr. Stanish is currently serving as Past-President of the North American Federation of Adapted Physical Activity, a Core Committee Member of the Healthy Weight Research Network for Children with Autism Spectrum Disorder, and is on the Editorial Board of the *Adapted Physical Activity Quarterly*.

Jodi Stinson is a graduate of Oregon State University with a Master of Science in Kinesiology, with a focus in adapted physical activity. Her research focuses on motor skill development and challenging behaviors in young children with developmental disabilities. She is currently working at the Children's Hospital of Eastern Ontario, Canada in the Child Development and Rehabilitation department.

E. William Vogler is a Faculty Emeritus of Southern Illinois University, USA, where he served as Chairperson and Professor of Kinesiology. His research interests include teaching and teacher education issues related to adapted physical education. Dr. Vogler has served his profession as President of the North American Federation of Adapted Physical Activity, Vice President and Treasurer of the National Consortium for Individuals with Disability. He has reviewed for multiple journals, and currently serves on the editorial board of the *Adapted Physical Activity Quarterly*.

Phillip Ward is a Professor of Kinesiology at The Ohio State University, USA. He teaches and studies physical education and teacher professional development in both pre-service and continuing education. He is the director of the Learning to Teach Physical Education Research Program that has as its central focus the development of content knowledge and pedagogical content knowledge. He has authored or co-authored more than 120 research papers, five books and book chapters, and has presented over 150 papers. He reviews for 16 journals and is a Research Fellow of SHAPE America and the National Academy of Kinesiology.

Shawn Wilkinson is an Assistant Professor in the Department of Applied Human Sciences at Concordia University, Montreal, Canada. His research interests include developing leisure education programs for persons with mental health problems, children, and older adults living in the community. He is also currently part of a Social Sciences and Humanities Research Council of Canada (SSHRC) funded research team focused on co-creating, implementing, and evaluating a community-based peer-run physical activity program aimed at enhancing the exercise and sport participation of adults with moderate to severe traumatic brain injury.

Wesley J. Wilson is an Assistant Professor in the School of Kinesiology at the University of Louisiana at Lafayette, USA. Wilson completed his PhD at the University of Virginia. Wilson's research focuses on the socialization of adapted physical educators and how teachers understand and implement special education legislation in the physical education setting.

Joonkoo Yun is a Chair and LeRoy T. Walker Distinguished Professor at East Carolina University, USA. Prior to joining ECU, he was a faculty member at Oregon State University, USA for 20 years. As a researcher and scholar, his ultimate goal is the promotion of full participation and active lifestyles to improve health and the quality of life of individuals with disabilities through evidence-based practice. He believes that without appropriate measurement, the research findings are questionable. He has made important contributions to the body of knowledge through a line of studies related to measurement and research-method issues in Adapted Physical Activity.

Xihe Zhu is an Associate Professor of Health & Physical Education at Old Dominion University, Norfolk, Virginia, USA. He has a PhD in Kinesiology from University of Maryland—College Park, USA. Fluent in both quantitative and qualitative methods, his research focuses on epidemiological and psychological variables such as physical activity, health-related fitness, learning, and motivation among populations with and without disabilities. Among other honors, Xihe has been recognized as a Fellow of SHAPE America Research Council, won the Young Scholar Award from AIESEP, and the Mabel Lee Award from SHAPE America.

Chantelle Zimmer recently completed her doctorate at the University of Alberta, Canada in the area of adapted physical activity. Her research explored personal and environmental factors that contributed to experiences of psychological stress in physical education for children at risk for developmental coordination disorder. The theory that guided her research drew on self-determination theory. She is currently a Postdoctoral Associate at the University of Calgary, Canada in the Faculty of Kinesiology.

Introduction

Justin A. Haegele, Samuel R. Hodge, and
Deborah R. Shapiro

We, the editors, are proud to present the *Routledge Handbook of Adapted Physical Education*, the first focused, organized, and evidence-based review of theory, research, and practice specifically focusing on the field of adapted physical education. This handbook highlights the latest research and scholarship in the field and provides in-depth discourse about research and theory related to physical education for individuals with disabilities. To date, adapted physical education has not been a central focus of a comprehensive resource that provides empirically and theoretically driven discourse to contribute to the future of research in the field. Certainly, seminal works by Kirk, Macdonald, and O'Sullivan (2006) as well as Ennis (2017), and their contributing authors, provide significant contributions to scholarly literature in physical education in the form of *The Sage Handbook of Physical Education* and *The Routledge Handbook of Physical Education Pedagogies*. Appropriately, as well, each of these resources provided chapters focused on physical education for individuals with disabilities (Fitzgerald, 2006; Mauerberg-deCastro, 2017; Mauerberg-deCastro, Klavina, Kudlacek, Sit, & Inal, 2017). However, these chapters cannot encompass the complexities and intricacies of the totality of the field of adapted physical education. Thus, we view the *Routledge Handbook of Adapted Physical Education* as an essential reference for graduate students and emerging scholars interested in contributing to research and scholarship in the field of adapted physical education.

Adapted physical education generally refers to school-based programs; and may be conceptualized within adapted physical activity, which refers to physical activity-related content across the lifespan. Because this handbook focuses on school-aged students, the term adapted physical education is used throughout. In addition, it should also be noted that while "inclusion" is discussed throughout the handbook, it is conceptualized as an educational philosophy that can be applied to physical education classes, which requires educators to provide content in ways that encourage diverse learning while taking the burden away from students to have to adapt their learning styles to obtain content (Coates & Vickerman, 2008). "Inclusion", thus, is not described as an education placement, and, rather, the term "integration" (or integrated) or general physical education is used to describe settings or placements in which students receive their education (Haegele, 2019). The handbook provided here is not intended to focus on integrated placements only. Rather, content spans adapted physical education in a number of educational placements that may be appropriate for those with disabilities (Wilson, Haegele, & Kelly, 2019).

The *Routledge Handbook of Adapted Physical Education* is divided into four sections with 29 chapters that explore research and theory in adapted physical education. Each chapter provides an overview of the content area, summary of current research in that area, current trends and issues pertinent to chapter topics, possible implications for practice, and concludes with reflective questions that can be used to develop further thoughts on the topical area. We would be remiss not to extend our sincerest thanks to each of the authors who dedicated time and effort to constructing the chapters housed within this handbook. We believe the collection of authors who contributed to this book represent a collection of emerging and seasoned academics who have active voices in the field of adapted physical education. Thank you.

The handbook begins with a section (I) addressing issues that lay the foundation for theory, research, and practice in the field of adapted physical education. Chapters in this section set the stage for subsequent sections by providing overviews of broadly defined concepts that inform adapted physical education research, scholarship, and practice internationally. This section begins with two chapters, "Historical viewpoint on adapted physical education", by DePauw, and "Legislation internationally", by Hums and Moorman, that provide thorough accounts of the history and legislative influences that have helped establish adapted physical education as a field internationally. Following, Chapters Three through Eight provide overviews of major topics in the field that have broad-reaching implications for research, scholarship, and practice in the field of adapted physical education.

The handbook second section (II), "Research approaches", summarizes basic philosophical and paradigmatic features that guide scholarly research endeavours. Each of the five chapters in this section present information fundamental to understanding assumptions undergirding one of five research methodologies: quantitative research, qualitative research, mixed-methods research, single subject designs, and systematic reviews and meta-analyses. These chapters are viewed as critical to assisting graduate students and emergent scholars in engagement with salient features of research approaches, including theoretical and epistemological foundations, as well as advantages and disadvantages, of each research approach. Each chapter commences with overviews of current research and scholarship in adapted physical education that is situated in, and informed by, the presented research methodologies.

Section III, "Conceptual and theoretical frameworks", was inspired by scholars in adapted physical education who have stressed the importance of using theoretical or conceptual models to drive research and develop hypotheses (Crocker, 1993; Haegele, Lee, & Porretta, 2015; Porretta & Sherrill, 2005; Reid, 2000; Reid & Stanish, 2003; Sherrill & O'Connor, 1999). Prior to the publication of this handbook, a comprehensive resource explicating salient features of theoretical and conceptual frameworks with potential to be utilized in the field of adapted physical education was unavailable. Because adapted physical education is a cross-disciplinary field, it is informed by research in several fields (e.g., physical education, special education, disability studies) and theoretical frameworks. Thus, this section includes overviews, descriptions, and features of a broad variety of frameworks. Each of the ten chapters in this section commences with overviews of research and scholarship in adapted physical education, as well as related disciplines, which have been informed by these frameworks.

Over time, theory, research, and practice-based trends have emerged in the field of adapted physical education that reflect the current needs and philosophies of the field. The final section of this handbook, titled "Research trends", provides descriptions and explanations of several research trends deemed important by the editors that have influenced, and are beginning to influence, the field of adapted physical education.

Our objective, as editors, was to provide a comprehensive resource to help inform future research and scholarship in adapted physical education. Because of this objective, some topics relevant to adapted physical education were omitted from this document. Of note, the editors were mindful to include work that was empirical and/or theoretical in nature, which eliminated many "best-practice" pedagogical practices that are commonly utilized among physical educators of school-aged children. Unlike many competitive and successful texts focusing on adapted physical education (Block, 2016; Hodge, Lieberman, & Murata, 2012; Vickerman & Maher, 2018; Winnick & Porretta, 2017), the handbook is constructed for graduate level students and researchers interested in research and scholarship in the field. Thus, rather than listing practitioner-based content that may be more applicable to pre-service and in-service professionals; this handbook focuses on foundational issues, research approaches, conceptual and theoretical frameworks, and contemporary research trends presented in a sophisticated and organized manner throughout the *Handbook*. We expect that the handbook can be taken and used in a variety of different ways in order to inform and promote research and encourage debate among scholars who wish to use this resource to inform future endeavours and contribute to the field of adapted physical education.

References

Block, M. E. (2016). *A teacher's guide to adapted physical education: Including students with disabilities in sports and recreation* (4th ed.). Baltimore, MD: Brookes.

Coates, J., & Vickerman, P. (2008). Let the children have their say: Children with special education needs and their experiences in physical education – A review. *Support for Learning*, 23(4), 168–175.

Crocker, P. R. (1993). Sport and exercise psychology and research with individuals with physical disabilities: Using theory to advance knowledge. *Adapted Physical Activity Quarterly*, 10(4), 324–335. doi:10.1123/apaq.10.4.324

Ennis, C. (2017). *Routledge handbook of physical education pedagogies*. London, UK: Routledge.

Fitzgerald, H. (2006). Disability and physical education. In D. Kirk, D. Macdonald, & M. O'Sullivan (Eds.), *The handbook of physical education* (pp. 752–766). London, UK: Sage.

Haegele, J. A. (2019). Inclusion illusion: Questioning the inclusiveness of integrated physical education. *Quest*, 71(4), 389–397. doi:10.1080/00336297.2019.1602547

Haegele, J. A., Lee, J., & Porretta, D. L. (2015). Research trends in Adapted Physical Activity Quarterly from 2004 to 2013. *Adapted Physical Activity Quarterly*, 32(3), 184–206. doi:10.1123/apaq.2014-0232

Hodge, S. R., Lieberman, L. J., & Murata, N. M. (2012). *Essentials of teaching adapted physical education: Diversity, culture and inclusion*. Scottsdale, AZ: Holcomb Hathaway.

Kirk, D., Macdonald, D., & O'Sullivan, M. (2006). *The handbook of physical education*. London, UK: Sage.

Mauerberg-deCastro, E. (2017). The Routledge handbook on physical education pedagogies. In C. Ennis (Ed.), *Theory and practice in adapted physical education: The disability rights paradigm in synchrony with complex systems concepts* (pp. 205–222). London, UK: Routledge.

Mauerberg-deCastro, E., Klavina, A., Kudlacek, M., Sit, C., & Inal, S. (2017). An international perspective in physical education and professional preparation in adapted physical education and adapted physical activity. In C. Ennis (Ed.), *The Routledge handbook on physical education pedagogies* (pp. 241–261). London, UK: Routledge.

Porretta, D. L., & Sherrill, C. (2005). APAQ at twenty: A documentary analysis. *Adapted Physical Activity Quarterly*, 22(2), 119–135. doi:10.1123/apaq.22.2.119

Reid, G. (2000). Future directions of inquiry in adapted physical activity. *Quest*, 52(4), 369–381. doi:10.1080/00336297.2000.10491724

Reid, G., & Stanish, H. (2003). Professional and disciplinary status of adapted physical activity. *Adapted Physical Activity Quarterly*, 20(3), 213–229. doi:10.1123/apaq.20.3.213

Sherrill, C., & O'Connor, J. (1999). Guidelines for improving adapted physical activity research. *Adapted Physical Activity Quarterly, 16*(1), 1–8. doi:10.1123/apaq.16.1.1

Vickerman, P., & Maher, A. (2018). *Teaching physical education to children with special educational needs and disabilities* (2nd ed.). London, UK: Routledge.

Wilson, W. J., Haegele, J. A., & Kelly, L. E. (2019). Revisiting the narrative about least restrictive environment in physical education. *Quest.* doi:10.1080/00336297.2019.1602063

Winnick, J. P., & Porretta, D. L. (2017). *Adapted physical education and sport* (6th ed.). Champaign, IL: Human Kinetics.

Part I
Foundational issues in adapted physical education

1

Historical viewpoint on adapted physical education

Karen P. DePauw

Introduction

The evolution of adapted physical education (APE) should be viewed in the historical context of physical activity. Physical activity and movement are integral aspects of life and have long been understood as having curative value dating back to China in 2700 BC. Drew (1922) wrote that

> some sort of exercise for remedial purposes has long been in use from earliest times. Primitive man (sic) seems to have recognized that certain bodily ailments were benefited by physical activity. Records and pictures have been found representing the use of medical gymnastics by the Chinese, at least three thousand years BC.
>
> *(as cited by Stafford, 1947, p. 17)*

This use of physical activity provided the foundation for what now can be called adapted physical activity as the umbrella term in the international context (Sherrill & DePauw, 1997) and the emergence of APE in the education arena in the US. Over the years, the uses of physical activity and terminology have evolved, as shown in Table 1.1, which reveals that the roles of physical activity for individuals with disabilities have ranged from curative to rehabilitative to APE and sport. In addition to the growth in APE, the past 25 years have seen an emphasis on inclusive physical education and the evolution of competitive sport opportunities for athletes with disabilities that have become increasingly available and visible. Although competitive sport, including disability sport and Paralympic sport, has evolved throughout history on a related and parallel track to APE, in this chapter, I focus primarily on physical education for individuals with disabilities commonly known as APE.

A few words about terminology: adapted physical activity/education

The term adapted physical activity was first used in conjunction with the formation of the International Federation of Adapted Physical Activity in 1973 in Quebec, Canada. At that time, adapted physical activity was selected in that it would incorporate movement, physical activity, and sport in which special emphasis was placed on the interests and capabilities of

Table 1.1 Historical periods in adapted physical activity and applications for individuals with disabilities (modified from DePauw & Gavron, 2005)

Historical period	Physical activity applications
Antiquity	• Strength and endurance needed for survival
2700 BC China	• Prevention and alleviation of physical disorders
5th century (Greek)	• Beautiful and harmonious body—balance of mental, social, and physical training
Early 19th (Europe)	• Sound mind and body through medical gymnastics
1850s (U.S)	• Medical gymnastics used by US physicians (curative, corrective)
Early 1900s	• Physical education to improve physical condition of youth corrective physical education, adapted sports (physical education)
Post world wars	• Rehabilitation through physical activity
1960s	• Perceptual and sensory–motor training developmental and remedial physical education
1970s	• US legislation (special education, physical education, sport) • Adapted physical education programs in public schools • Adapted physical activity (Europe)
1980s	• Adapted physical education (APE) and disability sport expansion
1990s	• Competitive sport for athletes with disabilities (e.g., Paralympic sport) accepted and opportunities increased nationally and internationally • Inclusive physical education emerges in US
2000s	• Inclusion in sport and physical education (Europe, Australia)
2010s+	• National and international APE programs strengthened, APE standards and certification

individuals with disabilities. Worldwide, adapted physical activity has become the term of choice for an academic discipline and a professional society over the past 25 years (Sherrill & DePauw, 1997).

In the US context, adapted physical education (commonly abbreviated as APE) is the terminology used to refer to the physical education for individuals with disabilities that occurs primarily in elementary and secondary schools. The terminology originated in the US, as defined by the American Alliance for Health, Physical Education and Recreation (AAHPER, now Society of Health and Physical Educators [SHAPE] of America) in 1952 and became more prominent after the passage of federal laws in the 1970s requiring the education of children with disabilities (e.g., Public Law 94–142, Education of All Handicapped Children Act of 1975). Many definitions have been used and the description of APE has continued to evolve since the original definition and many variations in the programs of APE exist due to the varying needs and abilities of individuals with disabilities (e.g., age, impairment, setting). Perhaps the most informative definition is one offered by Dunn and Leitschuh (2010) as follows: "Adapted physical education programs are those that have the same objectives as the regular physical education program but in which adjustments are made in the regular offerings to meet the needs and abilities of exceptional students" (p. 5). This education can be provided in separate educational settings as well as in general (regular) education settings. Outside of the education system, disability sport (e.g., adapted sport, Paralympic sport) has been used when referring specifically to sport-related activities and therapeutic recreation when referring to recreation and leisure activity that might not be typically found under sport.

History of APE

Beginning in the 19th century

The history of physical education and the foundation for APE can be traced back to the early 19th century in Europe. Through the gymnastics movement developed in Germany and Sweden, gymnastics became a well-known form of physical activity and exercise with therapeutic benefits. In 1811, Friedrich Ludwig Jahn opened the first Turnplatz (open-air gymnasium) in Berlin, which would usher in the gymnastics movement in Germany known as Turnverein (gymnastic association) (Table 1.2). As viewed in the context of the time, the Turnverein (also known as Turners) was not only an athletic initiative, but was also viewed as part of the national identity of Germany.

During this same period, Per Henrik Ling (Sweden), who engaged in daily therapeutic exercises (e.g., calisthenics, fencing), would develop the movement known as "medical gymnastics". In 1813, he founded the Royal Gymnastic Central Institute to advance physical conditioning of adults and youth through gymnastics. In 1840, he published the theory and practice of medical gymnastics, thereby officially launching the medical gymnastics movement. Gymnastic organizations expanded throughout Europe and ultimately to the US. In Europe, these movements, which began as private gymnastics schools (gyms), would evolve into physical education programs in the public schools. In the early 20th century, public schools around the world developed a more formalized physical education curriculum.

Medical gymnastics and the Turnverein movements founded in Europe influenced the development of physical education in the US, including physical education for individuals with disabilities (corrective, developmental, remedial), and laid the groundwork for the future development of APE. These movements were brought to the US in the early to mid-

Table 1.2 Historical milestones (modified from Sherrill & DePauw, 1997)

Year	Milestone
1811	Friedrich Ludwig Jahn opened the first Turnplatz (open-air gymnasium) in Berlin that led to the development of the Turnverein (gymnastics) movement (also known as the Turners)
1838	Gymnastics introduced at Perkins School for the Blind
1840	Theory and practice of medical gymnastics published by Per Henrik Ling which resulted in the medical gymnastics movement
1848	First Turners group formed in Cincinnati that built several gymnasia to serve the German–American populations in the Midwest
1889	Boston Normal School of Gymnastics (Wellesley College Department of Health and Physical Education) founded to train teachers in medical gymnastics
1908	Dudley Allen Sargent, MD, argues that all physical education teachers should have training in remedial and corrective gymnastics
1909	R. Tait McKenzie, MD, wrote about physical education for individuals with sensory impairments (hearing, vision) and mental retardation in his book entitled *Exercise and Education and Medicine*
1918	Increased awareness of disability following the First World War and the need for rehabilitation (physical therapy) of those injured; influenced the development of corrective physical education programs in public schools
1922	Special education in US public schools established
1934	Publication of Josephine Rathbone's book entitled *Corrective Physical Education*, which laid the foundations for physical education programs through the 1960s
1939	*Sports for the Handicapped* by George T. Stafford published, in which he emphasized sport/physical activity over corrective exercise
1952	APE defined by AAHPER and indicated the switch from "correctives" to physical education including teaching of diversified activities
1954	First textbook, entitled *Adapted Physical Education*, by Arthur Daniels, was published
1958	The Adapted Physical Education section of AAHPER was created
1960	First international games for the disabled was held in Rome (would ultimately become Paralympics)
1966	First specialization within Master's degree in Physical Education for individuals with disabilities, UCLA
1967	First federal legislation (PL 90–170) authorizing funding for personnel training and research in physical education and recreation for individuals with disabilities
1968	AAHPER formalized the Unit on Programs for the Handicapped headed by Julian Stein
1969	First Master's degree specialization in APE offered by SUNY Brockport First special feature on APE in JOHPER
1970s	Expansion of APE (remedial, developmental) in Los Angeles (California) City Schools and the development of APE programs in LA County Schools

Year	Event
	First state conference on physical education for individuals with disabilities held in California; now known as the National Conference on Adapted Physical Education and associated with the California Association for Health, Physical Education, Recreation and Dance (CAHPERD)
1973	Founding and first conference of International Federation of Adapted Physical Activity (IFAPA) held in Quebec City, Canada; conferences held every two years internationally
1975	Formation of the National Consortium on Physical Education and Recreation for the Handicapped (NCPERH); now known as the National Consortium for Physical Education for Individuals with Disabilities (NCPEID)
	PL 94–142 Education for All Handicapped Children Act enacted that required physical education as part of special education
	Italy and Norway enacted regulations regarding education of all children, including individuals with disabilities
1978	PL 95–606 the Amateur Sports Act recognized disability sport organizations and their engagement with the United States Olympic Committee; USOC Committee on Sports for the Disabled (COSD) started in 1979
1981	AAHPERD Task Force on Competencies in adapted physical education appointed
1984	Two scholarly journals began publication: *Adapted Physical Activity Quarterly* (*APAQ*) and *Palaestra*
1985	Merger of Therapeutics Council and the Adapted Physical Education Academy into the Adapted Physical Activity Council (APAC) (AAHPERD, now SHAPE)
1989	7th International Symposium of IFAPA held in Berlin; adapted physical activity officially defined, which includes APE; accepted and used internationally
	The first Ellie D. Friedman Award was given to Claudine Sherrill at ISAPA in Berlin
1991	European Master's degree in Adapted Physical Activity established in Leuven, Belgium (continues today)
	Individuals with Disabilities Education Act (IDEA) passed requiring access to physical education in regular school environment and mandating an Individualized Education Program (IEP), including APE
1992	NCPEID took responsibility for establishing standards for APE and receiving funding from US Department of Education
1993	First Young Professional Awards from IFAPA to Harald von Selzam (Germany) and Kazumi Tsukagoshi (Japan) at the ISAPA in Japan
1994	Special Feature of *JOPERD* entitled "Inclusion: Physical education for all"
1995	Eight general textbooks in adapted physical education available worldwide laying the foundation for increasing number of textbooks on APE and inclusion in physical education
1996	NCPERID published position statement on including students with disabilities in physical education
1997	First administration of the Adapted Physical Education Standards (APENS), which provides certification for APE teachers (CAPE)
1999	World Summit on Physical Education, held in Berlin, Germany, issued Berlin Agenda that called for inclusive physical education

(Continued)

Table 1.2 (Cont.)

Year	Milestone
	• First G. Lawrence Rarick Memorial Lecture delivered at ISAPA in Barcelona by Roy Shephard (Canada) entitled "Post modernism and APE: A new gnostic heresy"?
2000	• European Commission issued Nice Declaration on physical education and sport for all European residents, including individuals with disabilities
2001	• World Health Organization endorsed the International Classification of Functioning, Disability and Health (ICF), which focused emphasis on functionality rather than impairment and disability
2005	• Julian Stein received the first Julian Stein lifetime achievement award presented by AAHPERD
2006	• First APE graduate program of the year presented by AAHPERD presented to American Association of Adapted Sports Programs
2007	• First APE doctoral student of the year to Takahiro Sato (The Ohio State University) presented by AAHPERD
	• First APE University graduate program of the year award presented to the University of Wisconsin Osh Kosh Adapted Physical Education Program with Partners (UWOAPEPP) from AAHPERD
2008	• European Commission funded a project entitled European Standards in Adapted Physical Activities (EUSAPA) which included the identification of competencies in APE for Europe
	• *European Journal of Adapted Physical Activity (EUJAPA)* founded; Martin Kudláček served as editor
2010	• Inclusion Club started in UK and Australia
2013	• AAHPERD renamed Society for Health and Physical Educators (SHAPE America) and reorganized into SIG groups including Adapted Physical Education/Activity. Programs and current awards include the following: Julian Stein lifetime achievement award, Claudine Sherrill Breakfast, APE/A workshops, APE Teacher of the Year, APE/A program of the year and APE graduate student of the year

1800s and were accepted as model community-based physical activity programs. One example is the introduction of gymnastics at the Perkins School for the Blind by the School's founder, Samuel Gridley Howe, in 1838 that ultimately would be expanded to include swimming, physical fitness, and physical education for youth with visual impairments, followed also by the development of Sport for the Blind (Buell, 1947). In addition to this specific example with the community of those with visual impairments, the first Turners group built several gymnasia in Cincinnati, Ohio to serve the German–American populations in the Midwest in 1848. Some years later, these programs had been incorporated in the education system and, in 1889, the Boston Normal School of Gymnastics was founded to train teachers in medical gymnastics (see Table 1.2). The medical gymnastics movement of the 19th century would continually evolve and help inform the development of corrective physical education.

In the late 19th century, the primary purpose of physical education in US colleges and universities was based upon the organic health value of exercise and focused on discipline, muscular and organic development, health, and a graceful carriage (posture) (Stafford, 1947). In addition to departments of physical education focusing on healthful exercise and often led by medical doctors (MDs), departments of corrective physical education were developed. In 1908, Dudley Sargent, MD, of Harvard, argued for training in remedial and corrective gymnastics for all physical education teachers. Corrective physical education emphasized correcting "physical defects of a skeletal or bodily type" (Stafford, 1947, p. 19) and the provision of activities through prescribed exercises to remediate specific disorders.

Corrective physical education and sport: the early to mid-20th century

In the early 20th century, physical activity and exercise were used as preventative and as therapeutic (e.g., corrective) to alleviate physical disorders and illnesses. Those programs initially offered at colleges and universities would ultimately influence the development of physical activity programs for individuals with physical impairments in public schools. In addition, R. Tait McKenzie, MD, wrote about physical education for individuals with sensory impairments (hearing, vision) and mental retardation (now known as intellectual disabilities; American Association on Intellectual and Developmental Disabilities, 2010) in his book entitled *Exercise and Education and Medicine* (1909). In this same time period, special education in the public schools was established allowing for physical education for individuals with disabilities (i.e., corrective physical education) to gain some visibility.

As an indicator of the evolving terminology, two books were published in the 1930s that demonstrated the different approaches to physical education. *Corrective Physical Education* (1934), by Josephine Rathbone, continued the emphasis on medical gymnastics and *Sports for the Handicapped* (1939, 1947), by George T. Stafford, would introduce sports as appropriate for the physical education of individuals with disabilities (see Table 1.2).

In the early 20th century, individuals with disabilities were often excused from physical education programs and specific physical education programs for individuals with disabilities were rare in the US or elsewhere in the world until the return of wounded veterans after the world wars of the early 20th century created the need for rehabilitation (Huber, 1984). Historically, physical rehabilitation was made prominent in the UK with the opening of the Spinal Injuries Centre at Stoke Mandeville Hospital. In 1944, Sir Ludwig Guttman introduced competitive sport as an integral part of the rehabilitation program for veterans (DePauw & Gavron, 2005). Rehabilitation through physical activity and sport also found its way into the US and these rehabilitation programs helped promote the use of physical activity and exercises for individuals with disabilities in the public schools. These programs, initially developed in alignment with the medical model, resulted in separate programs focused on the remedial and therapeutic aspects of physical activity. Although corrective physical education was the terminology used through the 1950s, other terms that would emerge included developmental, adapted, remedial, and special physical education.

Emergence of adapted physical education: 1950s and 1960s

In 1952, the American Alliance for Health, Physical Education, and Recreation (AAHPER, later AAHPERD with dance included, and now SHAPE America) defined APE as:

> A diversified program of developmental activities, games, sports and rhythms, suited to the interests, capacities, and limitations of students with disabilities who may not safely or successfully engage in unrestricted participation in vigorous activities of general physical education program.
>
> *(AAHPER, 1952, p. 15)*

This definition expanded the scope of physical education and recreation for individuals with disabilities well beyond the "corrective" emphasis of the time. Although the emphasis was expanded to a diversified program offered to individuals with a variety of physical and cognitive impairments, the predominance of the medical model in the US in the 20th century resulted in physical education, recreation, and sport programs to remain separate for those with disabilities from "regular" physical education and sport. This harks back to 1939, when Stafford wrote one of the first books on adapted sport (*Sports for the Handicapped*) and argued for teaching goals beyond the correction of the physical defect, argued for a program of sports activities (e.g., adapted sports), and even education of "atypical" [sic] students in physical education with normal students (Stafford, 1947).

Shortly after this definition of APE was adopted, the first textbook, entitled *Adapted Physical Education*, by Arthur Daniels (1954), was published and the Adapted Physical Education section of AAHPER was created (1958). Ten years later, the Unit on Programs for the Handicapped was established and Julian Stein was asked to lead the effort. The major physical education professional association of the time (AAHPER) had accepted APE as a part of its organizational structure and the *Journal of Physical Education and Recreation* (*JOPER*) published the first special feature on APE in 1969 (*JOPER*, 1969).

Rapid growth, beginning in the 1970s

Beginning in the 1970s, APE experienced significant growth and development. This growth was aided by federal legislation and realized through the expansion of APE school-based programs, development and expansion of professional training programs in APE (teachers and faculty), development and expansion of professional organizations, emergence of academic journals, and the establishment of professional standards. The growth was seen both nationally and internationally.

In the US, the AAHPER definition helped launch APE and programs of physical activity (physical education and recreation) for individuals with disabilities in the public schools and brought awareness to APE both nationally and internationally. APE for the public schools would be more fully recognized after the passage of three significant federal laws mandating access to education and sport for individuals with disabilities in the 1970s, including (these laws will be more fully discussed in a later chapter):

1. Public Law 93–112 Section 504 of the Rehabilitation Act of 1973.
2. Public Law 94–142 Education of All Handicapped Children Act of 1975.
3. Public Law 95–606 Amateur Sports Act of 1978 (amended and renamed in 1998 as Olympic and Amateur Sports Act).

The Rehabilitation Act of 1973 offered civil rights protection to individuals with disabilities and prohibited discrimination on the basis of disability. Section 504 of the Rehabilitation Act mandated that physical education, athletics and intramurals must be provided to individuals with disabilities when they are provided to individuals who are typically developing. Even more explicit is the mandate of the Amateur Sports Act of 1978 (renamed Olympic and Amateur Sports Act) that mandates that Olympic and amateur sport include athletes with disabilities and to recognize the international Paralympic movement. The Amateur Sports Act created the United States Olympic Committee's (USOC) Committee on Sports for the Disabled (COSD) in 1979.

The Individuals with Disabilities Education Improvement Act (IDEIA) of 2004 and its earlier version the Education of All Handicapped Children Act of 1975 ensured the right of individuals with disabilities to a public education (specifically, to a free and appropriate public education provided in the least restrictive environment), and included an Individualized Education Program (IEP). IDEIA expanded the definition of a child with a disability to include an extensive list of conditions and impairments. These laws have had a significant influence upon the development of APE programs as well as professional preparation in the US

The early laws in the US had implications for physical education and sport, but the later laws and amendments included physical education and sport explicitly. IDEA 1997 had a significant impact upon physical education for individuals with disabilities through its mandate that physical education must be made available to every child through general physical education or as appropriate through APE. By definition, physical education meant the development of physical and motor fitness, fundamental motor skills and patterns, and skills in aquatics, dance, and individual and group games, and sports (including intramural and lifetime sports).

Expansion of APE programs

Although physical education programs for individuals with disabilities existed in some form, the 1970s saw the further development and expansion of APE programs. Significant among the changes was the expansion of the APE programs beyond local school district programs to the development of statewide programs initiated in Pennsylvania (Flanagan, 1969) and in California (Roice, 1973). The rise of statewide programs provided the impetus for strengthening and sustaining APE programs. One such example is the expansion of APE in California and its long-lasting impact in the state and in the nation. Specifically, the confluence of national and state laws, the quality of existing APE programs, and the availability of scholars and practitioners in southern California contributed greatly to the growth of APE. In California, physical education was required of all children, including individuals with disabilities, in 1969. Because physical education programs were required of all "special education" students, physical education programs offered in the public schools and guidelines developed in the 1970s.

The expansion of APE in California began with the existing programs offered by the Los Angeles City Schools and the development of programs in the Los Angeles County Schools in 1972. These programs were initially called corrective physical education, then remedial, developmental, and, finally, adapted physical education. (*Note.* in the 5+ years I taught for Los Angeles City and Los Angeles County Schools, my title changed four times.)

In 1973, the developing cadre of APE teachers from the LA City Schools and LA County Schools would join together with the scholars and practitioners at the "first national conference on physical education techniques and methods for handicapped children and youth" (Roice, 1973, p. 5). The conference was organized by the Division of Special Education of the Los Angeles City Schools (Roice, 1973).

Many of the early researchers/scholars of physical activity and individuals with disabilities (e.g., Daniel Arnheim, Charles Buell, Bryant Cratty, Jack Keogh, Lawrence Rarick), the Bureau of Education for the Handicapped (BEH) funded programs (e.g., Arnheim, Cratty/Keogh) and sensory–motor theorists/practitioners/scholars (e.g., A. Jean Ayers, Ray Barsch, Marianne Frostig, G. N. Getman, Newell Kephart) were working in Southern California at the university level or in private practice in the 1970s. Many of these individuals attended this first national conference and their work would significantly influence the development of APE and future adapted physical activity professionals in California at the time (e.g., Karen DePauw, Ron French, James Rimmer, Janet Seaman).

The annual conference grew from a more regionally attended conference into a national conference and is recognized as a leader in APE in the US. The conference is now known as the National Conference on Adapted Physical Education, officially supported and sponsored by the California Association for Health, Physical Education, Recreation, and Dance (CAHPERD), and continues today. Not only does the Annual Conference stand as an example of the growth of APE, but also serves as a fine example of the value of statewide APE efforts in securing the future of physical education programs for individuals with disabilities.

Training programs

The need for quality professional preparation programs and the funding thereof gained critical attention in the 1960s. In addition, in 1969, BEH funded 15 colleges and universities to develop professional preparation programs (Winnick, 1986). Recognizing the need for training programs and with the assistance of the BEH, two Master's degree specializations in APE were developed by Jack Keogh and Bryant Cratty at the University of California, Los Angeles (UCLA) in 1966 and by Joseph P. Winnick at the College at Brockport, State University of New York (SUNY) in 1968. The program at SUNY-Brockport would ultimately become the first stand-alone, Master's degree program in APE.

As a result of these funded programs and in collaboration with BEH, AAHPER published guidelines for competency-based professional preparation programs in 1973 (Winnick, 1986). A few years later, AAHPERD appointed a task force on APE to develop competencies for APE specialists (Hurley, 1981). Throughout the 20th century, APE programs in the public schools continued to expand, creating the need for well-prepared educators. Since then, over 50 colleges and universities in some 20 states in the US have established APE degree programs offering Master's and Doctoral level degrees.

University degree programs are known to exist in selected countries around the world, although it is sometimes difficult to identify them. A unique program is the European

Master's degree in Adapted Physical Activity established in Leuven, Belgium in 1991. Since its inception, the program has developed further as the APE/activity field has evolved. The most recent degree is offered by APE professionals from several European countries to graduate students from all regions of the world. The program has evolved into the Erasmus Mundus Master in Adapted Physical Activity (EMMAPA) and remains a viable postgraduate university program. EMMAPA is designed to provide education on "research and teaching methodology in Adapted Physical Activity (APA) and the social, pedagogical and technical aspects of physical activity, adapted to the needs of persons with a disability" (www.ecahe.eu).

Professional associations

Several professional associations focused on adapted physical education have been formed over the past 25 years that focus on research, practice, and advocacy in APE.

National Consortium for Physical Education for Individuals with Disabilities

In 1975, the National Consortium for Physical Education and Recreation for the Handicapped (NCPERH) was formed, now known as the National Consortium for Physical Education for Individuals with Disabilities (NCPEID, 2013). The mission of NCPEID is to promote research, professional preparation, service delivery, and advocacy for physical education for individuals with disabilities, which includes APE and general physical education programs (NCPEID, 2013). As stated below, NCPEID played a significant role in the professional preparation of APE specialists and development of professional standards in the US.

International Federation of Adapted Physical Activity and regional associations

Clermont Simard and colleagues founded the International Federation of Adapted Physical Activity (IFAPA) in Quebec City, Canada in 1973. This first gathering of adapted physical activity scholars and practitioners would ultimately become identified as the International Symposium on Adapted Physical Activity (ISAPA). The ISAPA symposia are held every other year throughout the world. Today, IFAPA is described as a cross-disciplinary professional organization of individuals, institutions, and agencies supporting and promoting adapted physical activity, disability sport, and all aspects of sport, movement, and exercise science for individuals with disabilities. The focus is intentionally broad and includes the use of adapted physical activity for instruction, competition, recreation, education, remediation, and research. In recognition of the outstanding contributions of adapted physical activity/ education professionals around world, IFAPA awards include the Ellie D. Friedman Professional Contribution Award (1989), the Young Professional Award in Adapted Physical Activity (1993), and G. Lawrence Rarick Memorial Lecture (1997).

In 1989, the 7th International Symposium of IFAPA was held in Berlin, during which the participants and the IFAPA Board selected and defined adapted physical activity as the umbrella terminology, which includes APE, and is accepted and used around the world. As membership and interest in adapted physical activity/education increased around the world, regional organizations emerged. In 1986, for example, the Asian Society for Adapted Physical Education and Exercise (ASAPE) was formed and officially became the Asian branch of IFAPA in 1989. The purpose of ASAPE is to contribute to the research and education of professionals in APE and exercise of children and adults with disabilities. Two other well-established regional associations affiliated with IFAPA were organized as well: European

Federation of Adapted Physical Activity (EUFAPA) established in 1985, and the North American Federation of Adapted Physical Activity (NAFAPA) in 1994. Though these associations use the terminology of adapted physical activity, the conference sessions and programs incorporate APE and participants often identify themselves as APE professionals.

Society of Health and Physical Educators (SHAPE America)

The US national physical education professional association, SHAPE America (formerly AAHPER, AAHPERD), played a very significant role in the development of APE. From the initial definition of APE (AAHPER, 1952) that gave impetus to the academic discipline and professional field of APE to current support of the APE/activity special interest group (SIG) available to SHAPE America members. Prior to 1985, two primary councils served the professional needs of individuals working in adapted physical activity/education. In 1985, the Therapeutics Council and the Adapted Physical Education merged into the Adapted Physical Activity Council (APAC) (AAHPERD recognized) to strengthen APE. In 2013, AAHPERD was renamed Society of Health and Physical Educators (SHAPE America) and reorganized itself administratively and programmatically around SIGs available to the membership. One of these is dedicated to APE and uses the title of Adapted Physical Education/Activity. Many programs and awards were created since the late 20th century, including the Claudine Sherrill Awards Breakfast and the Julian Stein Lifetime Achievement Award, named after these two leaders of APE (see Table 1.2).

Academic journals

As physical education programs for individuals of varying abilities grew and expanded, professional preparation of educators (e.g., special education teachers and general physical education teachers) and APE specialists was needed. In addition to the development of APE degree programs, interest in, and need for, research about APE resulted in the publication of two scholarly journals in 1984; *Adapted Physical Activity Quarterly (APAQ)* and *Palaestra: Forum for Physical Education and Sport*. Geoffrey Broadhead served as the founding editor of *APAQ* and David Beaver founded and edited *Palaestra*. These journals provided the forum through which significant research was shared with scholars and practitioners. Both of these reached an international audience and, ultimately, *APAQ* would become the official journal of the IFAPA. In 2008, the *European Journal of Adapted Physical Activity* (EUJAPA) was founded and Martin Kudláček has served as the founding editor (Kudláček, 2018). The emphasis on the dissemination of scholarship and professional practices has contributed to the acknowledgement of APE as an academic discipline. APE can be viewed as an academic discipline within exercise and sport science (Sherrill & DePauw, 1997) or a subdiscipline of physical education (Dunn & Leitschuh, 2010).

Professional standards

After the passage of IDEA 1997, the roles of the APE specialist and the academic preparation of specialists became a focus of the profession, especially for the NCPERID (now NCPEID). The effort resulted in the creation of standards for APE specialists known as the Adapted Physical Education National Standards (APENS) and a certification process (Kelly, 2006).

In 1991, NCPEID worked with the National Association of State Directors of Special Education and Special Olympic International in hosting an "action seminar" on APE for state directors of special education and disability advocacy groups. Two goals for the seminar included the identification of barriers preventing the provision of APE services and an action agenda for addressing these barriers. As a result, it was recommended that NCPEID develop professional standards for APE and a means to evaluate these. NCPEID accepted the challenge and responsibility and submitted a proposal to the US Department of Education. Funding was granted for a five-year period, including the following tasks: conducting a national job analysis of roles and responsibilities, developing and validating content standards, developing and evaluating a database of 2000+ test questions, validation of those questions, and creating and administering the national examination held in May 1997. Those who pass the examination are identified as Certified Adapted Physical Education (CAPE) specialists.

The standards (professional competencies) were developed in the following 15 areas: human development, motor behavior, exercise science, measurement and evaluation, history and philosophy, unique attributes of learners, curriculum theory and development, assessment, instruction design and planning, teaching, consultation and staff development, student and program evaluation, continuing education, ethics and communication (Kelly, 2006). The CAPE examination was constructed around the competencies. Details about the criteria, process and examination can be found at APENS.org or from the NCPEID website.

Through the Nice Declaration, the European Council (2000) indicated its strong commitment to inclusive education, including physical education and sport. The European Standards in Adapted Physical Activity (EUSAPA) project was initiated to explore the extent to which EU countries were providing physical education for individuals with disabilities. In 2011, the results of the EUSAPA project were reported by Klavina and Kudláček. Ten partner countries were used to help identify specific recommendations in support of professional preparation of specialists who would deliver physical education to individuals with disabilities, including the following: (a) all physical education teachers should have training in APE; (b) all professional teaching should have training in APE; (c) students with disabilities should be educated by trained teachers; and (d) APE consultants should be employed in all European countries (Klavina & Kudláček, 2011, p. 59).

The inclusion movement: post 20th century

Throughout most of the 20th century, the medical model remained the underlying and predominant approach to the treatment of individuals with disabilities and was reinforced through the earlier definitions by the World Health Organization (WHO) in its International Classification of Impairment, Disability and Handicap (1980). Programs and services for individuals with disabilities relied on categories of "handicapping" conditions (categorical approach) and, initially and frequently, classification by type and severity of impairment. The terms that were used to describe the programs of physical activity and recreation embraced the categorical approach and included remedial, developmental, and APE, along with handicapped or disabled sport, sport for the disabled, disability sport, and therapeutic recreation.

This medical model approach to individuals with disabilities would eventually come into question through the disability rights literature and would ultimately influence and change policy, practice, and programs. By the turn of the 20th century, the WHO offered new definitions with the International Classification of Functioning, Disability and Health (ICF, 2001). The emphasis was placed on functionality and performance rather than specific impairments or categories and applicable to all persons, not just those previously identified as individuals with disabilities. The language used to define and describe individuals with disabilities has evolved worldwide. Less emphasis has been placed on a categorical approach and labels, the "handicapping conditions" and the limitations of one's being and body. Attention has been given to understanding more about the abilities of individuals with disabilities and adaptations to increase access to, and opportunities for, physical activity, fitness, recreation, and sport.

Since the late 20th century, society (e.g., policy, research, programs) has tended to move away from the medical model to a socio-cultural approach which acknowledges and incorporates the social identity(ies) of individuals with disabilities (Shapiro, 1993). This trend was prompted by the emergence of "disability studies" through which scholars have encouraged discourse on disability rights, access, equity, and social justice.

The 21st century ushered in more inclusive language and relied less on categories of impairment and more on ability and performance and a paradigm shift from the medical model and categorical approach to APE to a non-categorical and functionality approach to APE. WHO's shift to the International Classification of Functioning, Disability and Health (International Classification of Functioning, Disability and Health, 2001) proved instrumental to redirecting physical activity, health, and sport away from the deficiency model of disability to consideration of functional ability and health. The non-categorical approach to adapted physical education (e.g., Seaman, DePauw, Morton, & Omoto, 2003) that started in the 1980s was evolving in the US and would ultimately be conceptualized and implemented through an inclusion emphasis to physical education and sport (e.g., DePauw, 1986; DePauw & Doll-Tepper, 2000).

The movement toward inclusive physical education in the US was first highlighted in a Special Feature in *JOPERD*, entitled "Inclusion: Physical education for all", edited by Diane Craft (1994). This feature introduced such topics as inclusion in regular classes, developing successful collaborations, research for inclusion, preparing teachers for inclusion, and more. In 1996, the NCPERID (now NCPEID) published a position statement on including students with disabilities in physical education. These milestones (i.e., publication of *JOPERD*'s special feature and NCPERID's position statement) set the stage for additional scholarship and professional practice of inclusive physical education. Since then, and continuing into the 21st century, professional preparation programs have been implemented, workshops held (Haegele, Hodge, Gutierres Filho, & Gonçalves de Rezende, 2018), numerous articles have been published, research studies have been conducted (e.g., Block & Obrusnikova, 2007; Qi & Ha, 2012), and books have been published (e.g., Block, 2016; Hodge, Lieberman, & Murata, 2012; Lieberman & Houston-Wilson, 2017) in the field of APE.

Clearly there was, and continues to be, an emphasis of serving the physical education needs of individuals with disabilities in general physical education settings as well as in APE. In addition to general physical education programs in the public schools, programs for inclusion in health and fitness have emerged. One such example is the National Center on Health, Physical Activity, and Disability (NCHPAD) founded by James Rimmer in 1999. NCHPAD is an inclusive practice and resource center on health promotion for individuals with disabilities.

Outside of the US, physical education programs have existed for individuals with disabilities and inclusion in general physical education beginning in the late 20th century. These programs vary, depending upon the country and region of the world (e.g., developing, developed); at times, physical activity is provided through physical education and sometimes through after-school sports (disability sport) programs. Separate physical education programs tended to be the primary education option for individuals with disabilities and the terms used to describe these programs were APE (using the US terminology) or terminology specific to the language of the country. In German, for example, sport is an all-encompassing term and utilizes descriptive terms to indicate the type of activity being performed, such as *versehrtensport*—disability sport, *hochleistungssport*—elite (or Olympic) or *freizeitsport*—leisure sport. In German, there is no translation of APE. In Spanish, disability sport is *deporte para personas con discapacidad*, elite sport is *deporte de elite*, and APE is *educación física adaptada*.

In November 1999, in Berlin, the World Summit on Physical Education was held and revealed that many countries around the world were indeed focusing efforts on integrating individuals with disabilities into general physical education. As a result, the "Berlin Agenda called for physical education for all and the development and implementation of inclusive physical education" (Seaman et al., 2003, p. 10). Inasmuch as the agenda was international, the interpretation in the US context would be that APE specialists and general physical education teachers would have responsibility for physical education for individuals with disabilities.

The 1999 World Summit also provided incentive for program development and helped give greater visibility to inclusion and inclusive physical education throughout the world. One particular example of international inclusive physical education is a program called the Inclusion Club, founded by Ken Black (UK) and Peter Downs (Australia). The Inclusion Club is committed to the inclusion of individuals with disabilities in physical activity (e.g., sport, recreation, physical education) and advocates through workshops, publications, and podcasts for inclusive physical education and sport.

During the 1999 World Summit on Physical Education and its support of inclusive physical education, many European countries shared the extent to which they offered inclusive physical education programs. In 2000, the European Commission issued the Nice Declaration, in which it was agreed that physical education and sport should be available to all European residents, including individuals with disabilities (Hardman, 2008). Specifically, the European Commission "recognizes the necessity to move toward an inclusive education where students with and with SEN [special education needs] learn together in a general school system" (Klavina & Kudláček, 2011, p. 58). In conjunction with the EUSAPA Project (Klavina & Kudláček, 2011) and reported on the website of the EUFAPA, selected countries are highlighted below as examples of efforts toward inclusion in physical education:

1. In Belgium, the 2003 Equal Educational Rights policy secured the right of individuals with disabilities to inclusion in general education and the right to enroll in the school of their choosing. Integrated education has been offered since 1983, in which individuals with disabilities are educated in regular school settings with additional services as needed (www.eufapa.edu). There are no specific regulations regarding physical education in integrated and inclusive settings, but all children are required to have at least two hours per week of physical education in special schools as well as regular schools (www.eufapa.edu).

2. In the Czech Republic, integration of individuals with disabilities in education started after the First and Second World Wars and has rapidly increased since 1997. After passage of the governmental support of sport and physical education in 2002, physical education programs for individuals with disabilities include activities found within the regular physical education curriculum combined with the IEP of the student.

3. In Germany, physical education is required of all students, but typically regulated by the different "states". In some states, inclusive physical education is the policy (e.g., Berlin) and in other states, children with disabilities will receive their physical education in special schools.

4. In Norway, inclusion of all children in regular education began in 1975. Physical education is required by the Law on One School in Norway for all children and although sometimes children with disabilities have been exempted from physical education, greater emphasis has been placed on adapted learning in physical education for students with disabilities since 1987.

5. Inclusion in physical education in Italy also dates back to 1975, at which time special schools were abolished and children with disabilities received their education in regular schools with the assistance of specialists.

Concluding comments

The United Nations Convention on the Rights of Persons with Disabilities (2007) addresses the rights of persons with disabilities to participate in physical activity and sport and "to the fullest extent possible in mainstream sporting activities at all levels" (Article 30). In keeping with these rights, programs of physical activity and physical education for individuals with disabilities should be developed and APE specialists called upon to deliver the educational programs. Today, APE programs are offered in special schools and general education schools in separate and integrated settings, and within and across a range of student abilities, APE has developed significantly especially in the last 50 years and yet, the story of APE will continue to evolve.

Summary of key points

1. Physical activity has long been viewed as beneficial to health and wellness.

2. Adapted physical activity is the umbrella term used throughout the world that refers to physical activity, recreation, sports, and physical education for individuals with disabilities.

3. Adapted physical education (APE) is a term developed in the US in reference to programs and research and scholarship in physical education for individuals with disabilities.

4. APE refers specifically to programs offered in school, whereas physical activity and sports programs (e.g., therapeutic recreation, disability sport) occur outside the school in the US system.

5. Physical education programs for students with disabilities exist outside of the US, but are not identified specifically as APE.

6. APE has evolved significantly since being defined in the mid-20th century not only in the US, but also throughout the world, especially European countries.

7. APE programs require trained specialists and generalists to provide quality education for individuals with disabilities and professional preparation programs have increased in the US and around the world.

8. The language used to describe individuals with disabilities has shifted from the medical model and "handicapping conditions" to description of ability and functionality.

9. There has been increased awareness and support for including individuals with disabilities into society, resulting in terminology such as inclusion and inclusive or integrated physical education.

10. National policy and regulations have helped in the development of APE programs not only in the US, but other countries as well.
11. APE is now accepted as an academic discipline within the broader context of exercise and sport science (e.g., kinesiology).
12. National and international professional associations were formed in response to growing need for professional development and advancement of knowledge in APE/activity.

Reflective questions

1. What can we learn from the past to inform the future of APE?
2. What will or should APE look like in 25 years?
3. How has the impact of different cultures and national contexts shaped APE?
4. With the ideology of inclusion and inclusivity, should APE be redesigned to embrace this philosophy? If so, how?
5. With the goal of improving the lives and well-being of individuals with disabilities, how can APE specialists work with others to foster this development?
6. What is so important about what we do that APE needs to be continued?

References

Adapted Physical Education. (1969). Special feature. *Journal of Health, Physical Education, Recreation, 40*(5), 45–46.

American Alliance for Health, Physical Education, and Recreation (AAHPER). (1952). Guiding principles for adapted physical education. *Journal of Health, Physical Education and Recreation, 23*, 15.

American Association on Intellectual and Developmental Disabilities. (2010). *Intellectual disability: Definition, classification, and systems of supports* (11th ed.). American Washington, DC: Association on Intellectual and Developmental Disabilities.

Block, M. E. (2016). *A teacher's guide to adapted physical education: Including students with disabilities in sports and recreation.* Baltimore, MD: Brookes Publishing.

Block, M. E., & Obrusnikova, I. (2007). Inclusion in physical education: A review of the literature from 1995–2005. *Adapted Physical Activity Quarterly, 24*, 103–124.

Buell, C. E. (1947). *Sports for the blind.* Berkeley, CA: Unknown.

Craft, D. H. (Ed.). (1994). Inclusion: Physical education for all. *Journal of Physical Education, Recreation & Dance, 65*(1), 21–55.

Daniel, A. S. (1954). *Adapted physical education.* New York, NY: Harper & Row.

DePauw, K. P. (1986). Towards progressive inclusion: Implications for physical education. *Adapted Physical Activity Quarterly, 3*, 1–5.

DePauw, K. P., & Doll-Tepper, G. (2000). Toward progressive inclusion and acceptance: Myth or reality? The inclusion debate and bandwagon discourse. *Adapted Physical Activity Quarterly, 17*, 135–143.

DePauw, K. P., & Gavron, S. J. (2005). *Disability sport* (2nd ed.). Champaign, IL: Human Kinetics.

Drew, L. C. (1922). *Individual gymnastics.* Philadelphia, PA: Lea and Febiger.

Dunn, J. M., & Leitschuh, C. (2010). *Special physical education.* Dubuque, IA: Kendall Hunt Publishing.

Education of All Handicapped Children Act of 1975, 89 STAT. 773.

European Council. (2000). *Nice declaration: Declaration on the specific characteristics of sport and its social function in Europe.* Nice: Author.

Flanagan, M. E. (1969). Expanding adapted physical education programs on a statewide basis. *Journal of Health, Physical Education, Recreation, 40*(5), 52–55.

Haegele, J. A., Hodge, S. R., Gutierres Filho, P. J. B., & Gonçalves de Rezende, A. L. (2018). Brazilian physical education teachers' attitudes before and after participation in a professional development workshop. *European Physical Education Review, 24*(1), 21–38. doi:10.1177/1356336X16662898

Hardman, K. (2008). The situation of physical education in schools: A European perspective. *Human Movement, 9*(1), 5–18.

Hodge, S. R., Lieberman, L. J., & Murata, N. M. (2012). *Essentials of teaching adapted physical education: Diversity, culture, and inclusion.* Scottsdale, AZ: Holcomb Hathaway (now owned by Taylor & Francis Group).

Huber, C. A. (1984). An overview and perspective on international disabled sport: Past, present, future. *Rehabilitation World, 8,* 8–11.

Hurley, D. (1981). Guidelines for adapted physical education. *Journal of Physical Education, Recreation and Dance, 52*(6), 43–45.

Including Students with Disabilities in Physical Education: A position Statement (Spring, 1996). Advocate (NCPERID), 1–2.

Individuals with Disabilities Education Act of 1997, 20 U.S.C. 1400 et seq.

Individuals with Disabilities Education Act of 2004, Pub. L. No. 108-446, Section 602, 118 Stat. 2657.

International Classification of Functioning, Disability and Health. (2001). Retrieved from www.who.int/classifications/icf/icf_more/en/

Kelly, L. E. (Ed.). (2006). *Adapted physical education national standards* (2nd ed.). Champaign, IL: Human Kinetics.

Klavina, A., & Kudláček, M. (2011). Physical education for students with special needs in Europe: Findings of the EUSAPA project. *European Journal of Adapted Physical Activity, 4*(2), 46–62.

Kudláček, M. (2018). European journal of adapted physical activity in the second decade. *European Journal of Adapted Physical Activity, 11,* 1.

Lieberman, L., & Houston-Wilson, C. (2017). *Strategies for inclusion.* Champaign, IL: Human Kinetics.

McKenzie, R. T. (1909). *Exercise in education and medicine.* Philadelphia, PA: Saunders.

National Consortium for Physical Education for Individuals with Disabilities. (2013). *Welcome to NCPEID.* Available from www.ncpeid.org/

Olympic and Amateur Sports Act of 1998 36 U.S. Code § 220501.

Qi, J., & Ha, A. S. (2012). Inclusion in physical education: A review of literature. *International Journal of Disability Development and Education, 59*(3), 257–281.

Rathbone, J. (1934). *Corrective physical education.* Philadelphia, PA: Saunders.

Roice, G. R. (1973). Developing a county remedial physical education program. In Los Angeles County Superintendent of Schools (Ed.), *Putting it all together: Techniques and methods for handicapped children and youth* (pp. 68–69). ERIC document 102 769. Washington, DC: US Office of Education.

Seaman, J. A., DePauw, K. P., Morton, K., & Omoto, K. (2003). *Making connections: From theory to practice in adapted physical education.* Scottsdale, AZ: Holcomb Hathaway.

Section 504 of the Rehabilitation Act of 1973, as amended 29 U.S.C. § 794.

Shapiro, J. (1993). *No pity: People with disabilities forging a new civil rights movement.* New York: Random House.

Sherrill, C., & DePauw, K. P. (1997). Adapted physical activity and education. In J. D. Massengale & R. A. Swanson (Eds.), *The history of exercise and sport science* (pp. 39–108). Champaign, IL: Human Kinetics.

Stafford, G. T. (1939, 1947). *Sports for the handicapped.* New York: Prentice-Hall.

The Education of All Handicapped Children Act of 1975 20 USC 140.

Winnick, J. P. (1986). History of adapted physical education: Priorities in professional preparation. *Adapted Physical Activity Quarterly, 3,* 112–117.

World Health Organization. (1980). *International classification of impairment, disabilities and handicaps: A manual of classification relating to the consequences of disease.* Geneva, Switzerland: Author.

2

Law and legislation impacting adapted physical education programs

Anita M. Moorman and Mary A. Hums

Introduction to legal foundations of disability rights in physical education and sport

In this chapter, we explore the history of the disability rights movement and how it influenced the development of international and national legal protections for persons with disabilities as they relate to access to physical activity, adapted physical education (APE), recreational, and competitive sports opportunities. We review the emergence of the disability rights movement at the turn of the 20th century and the critical role of international declarations and advocacy initiatives to further this movement. We explore these key international treaties and agreements which created or extended protections for persons with disabilities and the impact of those protections for APE and disability sports programs. We also consider examples of national legislation impacting access and opportunities for persons with disabilities in the United States (US). Last, we identify current trends and issues impacting how the law is developed and applied to APE.

The disability rights movement and physical education and sport

The establishment of protections globally for basic human rights began midway through the 20th century and is illustrated in the Universal Declaration of Human Rights (United Nations, n.d.c). In 1948, the Universal Declaration of Human Rights (UDHR) established that everyone is entitled to certain rights and freedoms without discrimination of any kind, such as discrimination based on race, color, sex, language, religion, political or other opinion, national or social origin, property, birth or other status. Around this same time, a focus on the rights of persons with disabilities as part of the broader human rights declaration also emerged and particularly picked up momentum following the Second World War. Second World War veterans provided a face of disability to many people and sport proved to be an effective platform for advocating for the benefits and needs of the those veterans. Disability sport first emerged in the UK when the National Spinal Injuries Centre at Stoke Mandeville Hospital designed a range of sports and physical activity for the physical and psychological rehabilitation of large numbers of soldiers and civilians with disabilities following the war (Thomas & Smith, 2009). Sir Ludwig Guttmann, a physician at Stoke Mandeville Hospital near London, UK, organized the first Stoke Mandeville Games, initially held for athletes with spinal cord injuries (IPC, n.d). Over the years, a number of disability sport organizations emerged in the UK to meet the needs of people with disabilities, such as British Blind Sports, British Wheelchair Athletics Association, LimbPower, Special Olympics Great Britain, and the English Federation of Disability Sport (British Athletics, 2008).

Since the time after the Second World War, disability sport has developed rapidly from its grassroots beginnings to elite international competition. The growing globalization of these sports for athletes with disabilities and their associated rules reside with numerous national and international sport federations. The establishment of these federations began with the International Committee of Sports for the Deaf, which held the International Silent Games in Paris in 1924 (Fay & Wolff, 2009). The first Paralympic Games were held in Rome in 1960, during which time the International Stoke Mandeville Wheelchair Sports Federation served as the official organizing body. The International Paralympic Committee (IPC) was eventually established in 1989 and took control of international competition for athletes with disabilities with just a few exceptions (Fay & Wolff, 2009). Today, hundreds of national and international disability sport organizations exist which govern youth, recreational, competitive, and elite disability sport. These grassroots disability sport efforts helped make the 2012 London Summer Paralympic Games one of the most successful Paralympic Games in history and that success continued through the 2016 Rio Paralympic Games ("Rio 2016 Paralympic Ticket Sales Exceed 1.8 Million", 2016).

Parallel to the disability sport movement, efforts to increase opportunities for children with disabilities were also developing in schools with a focus on making physical education and physical activity accessible to as many children as possible. International as well as national legal protections and policy initiatives related to physical education, physical activity, and disability sport emerged and developed as the wider political and policy contexts of the disability rights movement expanded within and beyond national borders. The UK, Canada, Sweden, Australia, Israel, New Zealand, the Netherlands, South Africa, and the US all began actively developing policies and laws in response to the political and social movements of persons with disabilities during the 1980s and 1990s. By the end of the 1990s, the European Union had also proposed several recommendations to eliminate all forms of discrimination against people with disabilities. By the late 1990s, worldwide celebrations of the Universal Declaration were also designed to continue to build upon the lofty goals and aspirations established 50 years prior for people with disabilities (Kidd & Donnelly, 2000).

In 2006, the United Nations adopted the Convention on the Rights of Persons with Disabilities (CRPD), urging nation states to ensure and promote the full realization of all civil, cultural, economic, political, and social rights for persons with disabilities. Since this time, global awareness has led to widespread growth of national and international protections for children with disabilities in the context of physical education, physical activity, and sport.

In the context of education, Bines and Lei (2011) reviewed progress toward the United Nations Educational, Scientific and Cultural Organization's (UNESCO) 2008 Education for All (EFA) Global Education Monitoring Report. These researchers noted that about one third of children not enrolled in school had disabilities, and fewer than 10% of children with disabilities in Africa attended school. Bines and Lei also noted several factors contributing toward recent progress. These factors include: (a) a general increase in overall enrollment in EFA has improved awareness of children left behind; (b) acknowledgement that universal education can only be achieved if rights to education are secured; (c) growing recognition of rights of persons with disabilities generally, as well as rights of children with disabilities; (d) changes in attitudes toward people with disabilities and their capabilities; and (e) increasing emphasis on rights and inclusion in relation to disability in northern countries was beginning to influence development in other countries (Bines & Lei, 2011).

Today, a sizeable body of laws and policies includes international treaties and national laws enacted by individual nation states related to disability rights generally and the rights of children with disabilities to education.

Overview of the legal landscape and disability rights legislation

Multiple international treaties and initiatives have recognized the essential nature of physical activity and sport to human development and social inclusion. Particularly, there is greater recognition of the rights of children with disabilities to education due to advocacy at both the national and international levels (Bines & Lei, 2011). Bines and Lei have identified three distinct approaches to policies on disability and education: Charity, Rights–Equity, and Utility. The charitable approach, which is seen historically in a number of societal contexts, views people with disabilities as needing special assistance from the state, such as special schools and benefits in isolation from mainstream society. The more recent rights–equity approach, which is closely linked to a number of international rights declarations, recognizes the essential right of persons with disabilities to access mainstream society, including education, as a basic human right. The rights–equity based approach is then complemented by the utility approach which sees inclusion as an added value to society to improve opportunities for people with disabilities. In so doing, society will experience a number of positive benefits (Bines & Lei, 2011).

Undoubtedly, the recent focus on rights and equity in relation to recognizing legal protections for people with disabilities generally, and specifically for children with disabilities to education, has been framed and guided by multiple international declarations. In the following section, we summarize these key international declarations and initiatives and further explain the complex array of legal protections enacted in the US related to the rights of children with disabilities to education.

International frameworks for inclusion of adapted physical education programs

Binding and non-binding international laws have impacted adapted physical education (APE), physical activity, and disability sport. The UDHR has served as a building block for international human rights advocates since 1948. Several pivotal International Declarations and Conventions have contributed to recognizing the rights of the child, rights to education, and rights for persons with disabilities. All of these international efforts, while addressing universal global principles and ideals, provide a foundation for including physical education for children with disabilities. In this chapter, we address international efforts to recognize universal rights of children with disabilities to be educated and included in society and how these declarations and treaties provide support for the role of physical education and sport in protecting these rights. Specifically, we summarize the history and guiding principles contained in the Convention on the Rights of the Child, the Convention on the Rights of Persons with Disabilities, and UNESCO's Charter on Physical Education, Physical Activity and Sport.

Convention on the Rights of the Child

Numerous documents have addressed the responsibilities of adults for the protection and care of our children, particularly during times of war or economic struggles (Walter, 2003). After the adoption of the UDHR, a Commission on Human Rights was established to help monitor and encourage states to respect the values and principles established in the UDHR. In 1959, the United Nations adopted the Declaration of the Rights of the Child (Humanium, n.d.), which paved the way for the Convention on the Rights of the Child (CRC) in 1989 (United Nations, 2018). The Commission has also issued several texts to complement the UDHR, including the International Covenant for Economical, Social, and Cultural Rights in 1976, which recognized among other rights, the right to be educated. At the United Nations General Assembly of 1976, the year 1979 was designated as the International Year of the Child (The Robinson Library, 2019). In the spring of 1979, the Commission created a working group charged with writing a formal CRC. Finally, in 1989, the General Assembly of the UN adopted the CRC. The Convention opens with this statement: that the General Assembly

> *Proclaims* this Declaration of the Rights of the Child to the end that he may have a happy childhood and enjoy for his own good and for the good of society the rights and freedoms herein set forth, and calls upon parents, upon men and women as individuals, and upon voluntary organizations, local authorities and national Governments to recognize these rights and strive for their observance by legislative and other measures progressively taken in accordance with the following principles ...
>
> *(United Nations, 1959, para. 5)*

Principle 5 expressly addresses children with disabilities, saying "The child who is physically, mentally or socially handicapped shall be given the special treatment, education and care required by his particular condition" (United Nations, 1959, para. 10). The CRC further sets out the civil, political, economic, social, health, and cultural rights of children. Language in the document specifically addresses disability in Article 2:

> 1. States Parties shall respect and ensure the rights set forth in the present Convention to each child within their jurisdiction without discrimination of any kind, irrespective of the child's or his or her parent's or legal guardian's race, colour, sex, language, religion, political or other opinion, national, ethnic or social origin, property, *disability*, birth or other status.
>
> *(United Nations Human Rights Office of High Commissioner, 2018, emphasis added)*

In terms of physical activity, Article 31 addresses leisure, play, and recreational activities (United Nations Human Rights Office of High Commissioner, 2018).

1. States Parties recognize the right of the child to rest and leisure, to engage in play and recreational activities appropriate to the age of the child and to participate freely in cultural life and the arts.
2. States Parties shall respect and promote the right of the child to participate fully in cultural and artistic life and shall encourage the provision of appropriate and equal opportunities for cultural, artistic, recreational and leisure activity (United Nations Human Rights Office of High Commissioner, 2018).

In Article 23, the CRC discusses education for children with disabilities, including recreation opportunities.

> 3. Recognizing the special needs of a disabled child, assistance extended in accordance with paragraph 2 of the present article shall be provided free of charge, whenever possible, taking into account the financial resources of the parents or others caring for the child, and shall be designed to *ensure that the disabled child has effective access to and receives education*, training, health care services, rehabilitation services, preparation for employment and *recreation opportunities* in a manner conducive to the child's achieving the fullest possible social integration and individual development, including his or her cultural and spiritual development.
>
> *(United Nations Human Rights Office of High Commissioner, 2018, emphasis added)*

This language clearly expresses principles recognizing physical activity as an integral part of a child's overall educational development. The next United Nations Convention, which addressed physical activity and physical education for people with disabilities, is the Convention on the Rights of Persons with Disabilities (CRPD).

Convention on the Rights of Persons with Disabilities

The United Nations General Assembly adopted the CRPD on December 13, 2006. It was opened for signature on March 30, 2007 and entered into force on May 3, 2008 (United Nations, 2008b). The CRPD is an international treaty identifying the rights of persons with disabilities as well as the obligations to promote, protect, and ensure those rights and is the first human rights treaty specifically addressing persons with disabilities (Stein & Lord, 2008). The CRPD's comprehensive human rights protections cover a broad spectrum of life activities for persons with disabilities (Schiek, 2015). These fundamental human rights include cultural life, sports, and recreation (Schiek, 2015).

The CRPD states its express purpose is "to promote, protect and ensure the full and equal enjoyment of all human rights and fundamental freedoms by all persons with disabilities, and to promote respect for their inherent dignity" (Stein & Lord, 2008, p. 24). Prior to the adoption of the CRPD, most international and cross-border initiatives aimed at the human rights of persons with disabilities had lacked legally binding character (Stein & Lord, 2008). As of late 2019, 162 countries are signatories to the Convention, and 180 countries have ratified the Convention (United Nations Department of Economic and Social Affairs, n.d). Thus, each of these countries has agreed to implement the provisions of the Convention in accordance with their relevant domestic laws and to adopt legislative, administrative, and other measures including amending existing laws and regulations that constitute discrimination against persons with disabilities (CRPD, 2017; Stein & Lord, 2008).

Article 30 of the Convention addresses both mainstream and disability-specific sport and expressly requires physical education within the school system as follows:

> States Parties shall take appropriate measures to encourage and promote the participation, to the fullest extent possible, of persons with disabilities in mainstream sporting activities at all levels. It also calls upon Governments, States party to the Convention, to ensure that persons with disabilities have access to sport and venues – as spectators and as active participants. This also requires that children with disabilities be included in

physical education within the school system "to the fullest extent possible" and enjoy equal access to "play, recreation and leisure and sporting activities."

(United Nations, n.d.b, para. 7, emphasis added)

Article 30 of the CRPD identifies these rights and calls upon adopting countries to promote participation in cultural life, recreation, leisure, and sports. Article 30, Section 1 provides: "States Parties recognize the right of persons with disabilities to take part on an equal basis with others in cultural life ..." Article 30, Section 5 further provides:

> With a view to enabling persons with disabilities to participate on an equal basis with others in recreational, leisure and sporting activities, States Parties shall take appropriate measures: a) To encourage and promote the participation, to the fullest extent possible, of persons with disabilities in mainstream sporting activities at all levels; b) To ensure that persons with disabilities have an opportunity to organize, develop and participate in disability-specific sporting and recreational activities and, to this end, encourage the provision, on an equal basis with others, of appropriate instruction, training and resources; c) To ensure that persons with disabilities have access to sporting, recreational and tourism venues; d) *To ensure that children with disabilities have equal access with other children to participation in play, recreation and leisure and sporting activities, including those activities in the school system*; (e) To ensure that persons with disabilities have access to services from those involved in the organization of recreational, tourism, leisure and sporting activities.
>
> *(Center for Parent Information and Resources, 2017), emphasis added; (UN, 2008a)*

Article 30 is the first international treaty specifically recognizing the importance of sport and physical activity as a fundamental human right for people with disabilities to experience full inclusion in society and culture and the expectation of providing those experiences within an educational environment. The language used in Article 30 (d), above, reinforces the significance of physical education for children with disabilities as a fundamental human right.

States (nations) that ratify the Convention are legally bound to respect the standards in the Convention, thus representing binding international law. For other States, the Convention represents an international standard they should endeavor to respect and provides lawmakers and advocates a foundation for implementing legal protections at the State (national) level for persons with disabilities (Schulze, 2009). In this instance, the CRPD may be nonbinding, but is still highly influential in developing policies and laws related to disability sport and persons with disabilities more broadly (Cooper & Whittle, 1998).

Prior to the adoption of the CRPD, only about 40 nations had some form of disability rights protections. Now, with 162 signatories and 180 ratifying countries, many more nations will begin to implement express legal protections for persons with disabilities (Stein & Lord, 2008). Even countries yet to ratify the Convention, such as the US, may still have a history of, or be actively pursuing, laws and policies to protect the rights of persons with disabilities. Full implementation presents both opportunities and challenges which will naturally be unique to each nation as it seeks to meet the mandate of the CRPD (Schiek, 2015).

In this relationship, the international standard influences change at the national level. For example, in Canada, sport for people with disabilities received recognition when the Council of Canadians with Disabilities was founded in 1976. People with disabilities in the country wanted to be more fully included in daily society "where people with disabilities had the opportunity to go to school, work, volunteer, have a family, *participate in recreational, sport and cultural activities*" (Council of Canadians with Disabilities, 2013, para. 1, emphasis added). New Zealand also enacted notably progressive domestic disability policies and practices supporting the development of disability sport. New Zealand's first sport participation event for people with disabilities took place in 1962, when an Auckland paraplegic competed in the British Commonwealth Paraplegic Games held in Western Australia. In January 2007, the New Zealand Paraplegic and Physically Disabled Federation changed its name to become Paralympics New Zealand. This was to gain greater public awareness and raise the profile of disability sport by focusing on its most prestigious event—the Paralympic Games (Paralympic New Zealand, 2019). Paralympics New Zealand's mission includes a commitment to equity through sport. Ireland's National Disability Authority's policy document expressly acknowledges

> Ireland has much to learn from the success of umbrella organizations for disability sports in other countries such as the Federation of Disability Sport Wales (FDSW) in Wales, the English Federation of Disability Sport (EFDS) in England and the Australian Sports Commissions Disability Sports Unit (DSU). In these initiatives, while each group retains its identity, united they have a more powerful voice to lobby for funding and support.
>
> *(National Disability Authority, 2005, para. 13)*

UNESCO Charter

An important factor involved in developing international declarations regarding people with disabilities has been the emphasis placed on inclusion. Inclusion as an international policy basis was articulated in the international Salamanca Statement of 1994 by UNESCO, which emphasized the importance of general schools using an inclusive orientation as the best means of achieving education for all (UNESCO, 1994). UNESCO was established in 1945, just as the Second World War ended, and was founded in order to promote global intellectual and moral solidarity with hopes of preventing the outbreak of another world war. Currently, UNESCO works to open dialogue among people and cultures based on respect of commonly held values (UNESCO, 2017).

For example, the UNESCO (2005) Guidelines for Inclusion and UNESCO (2007) Education for All initiative define inclusion as being concerned with the right to non-discriminatory access to education consistent with the fundamental principle that schools have a responsibility to educate all children. Inclusion based on this definition calls upon schools to recognize a diversity of needs among children to achieve full participation and learning, and to identify and actively work to remove barriers arising from attitudes, the environment, or institutional policies and practices (UNESCO, 2005, 2007). UNESCO has also provided guidance regarding the opportunities for children with disabilities to benefit from physical education as part of its advocacy toward education for all.

UNESCO recently updated the Charter on Physical Education, Physical Activity and Sport. Language in the revised UNESCO Charter on Physical Education, Physical Activity and Sport specifically addresses disability in a number of sections (UNESCO, 2015). For example, the Preamble sets the stage in these words:

> 4. *Emphasizing* that resources, authority and responsibility for physical education, physical activity and sport must be allocated without discrimination on the basis of gender, age, disability or any other basis, to overcome the exclusion experienced by vulnerable or marginalized groups ...;

13. *Proclaims* this International Charter that puts physical education, physical activity and sport at the service of human development, and *urges* everyone, especially governments, intergovernmental organizations, sports organizations, non-governmental entities, the business community, the media, educators, researchers, sport professionals and volunteers, participants and their support personnel, referees, families, as well as spectators to commit to and disseminate this Charter, so that its principles can become a reality for all human beings.

The basic premise of the Charter is that the practice of physical education, physical activity, and sport is a fundamental right for all, including people with disabilities. Within the Charter, access to physical education is delineated as follows (UNESCO, 2015):

1.1 Every human being has a fundamental right to physical education, physical activity and sport without discrimination on the basis of ethnicity, gender, sexual orientation, language, religion, political or other opinion, national or social origin, property or any other basis.

1.2 The freedom to develop physical, psychological and social well-being and capabilities through these activities must be supported by all governmental, sport and educational institutions.

1.3 Inclusive, adapted and safe opportunities to participate in physical education, physical activity and sport must be available to all human beings, notably children of preschool age, women and girls, the aged, persons with disabilities and indigenous people.

8.1 Adequate and safe spaces, facilities, equipment, and dress-options must be provided and maintained to meet the needs of participants in physical education, physical activity and sport mindful of different needs associated with climate, culture, gender, age, and disability.

International human rights initiatives and previous efforts by nations with developed or progressive disability rights laws and policies can serve, and have served, as useful guides for how to enable full participation by people with disabilities in physical education, physical activity, and sport. Next, we explore the US model for inclusion of adapted physical education and disability sport as just one example of the varied issues that must be addressed in legislation and policies protecting people with disabilities from discrimination.

The US model for inclusion of adapted physical education and disability sport

The US began recognition of disability rights in the mid 1950s. Since that time, legislators have enacted a number of disability discrimination statutes encompassing education, housing, government services, and public accommodations. The US has a complex and over-lapping legal framework for providing public education to students with disabilities and preventing discrimination against students with disabilities. The US legal framework has also been influential internationally as a guide for other nations to use to enact these vital legal protections. Therefore, we will explore disability laws in the US as they have evolved in the context of education and physical activity as well as in the broader context of disability sport. Advances in the disability sport environment have led to increased awareness and acceptance of the rights of people with disabilities.

Theories underlying legal protections in the US

Similar to how policy and inclusion conversations have evolved from a medical model to a rights based model globally, US laws have primarily framed disability protections using the lens of ensuring rights and addressing inequality. The term "disability" first appeared in US federal law in 1790 to define persons who would receive compensation for injuries sustained in war because they had an incapacity that precluded manual labor (Colker, 2009). This perspective of disability continued until the 1950s–1960s. At that time, attitudes about people with disabilities began to evolve from paternalism, where the government's role was to provide funding to rehabilitate or care for people with disabilities, to inclusion, where the government's role was to eliminate barriers that prevented people with disabilities from seeking full and equal access to society (Weber, 2000).

School age children with disabilities (pre-kindergarten through age 21) have a patchwork of legal protections. Their right to an education is provided for in the *Individuals with Disabilities Education Act* (IDEA) (2004) (an Act to provide federal financial assistance to state and local education agencies to guarantee special education and related services to eligible children with disabilities). In addition, in 1973, federal law prohibited discrimination against persons with disabilities by any recipient of federal financial assistance (such as schools) in *Section 504 of the Rehabilitation Act of 1973* (504 or Section 504) (2015) (a civil rights law prohibiting discrimination on the basis of disability in programs and activities, public and private, that receive federal financial assistance). The federal non-discrimination mandate was expanded even further in 1990 via the *Americans with Disabilities Act* (ADA) (2008) to prohibit discrimination against persons with disabilities by public entities (such as public schools) and private organizations which were defined as places of public accommodation (such as private schools) (a civil rights law prohibiting discrimination solely on the basis of disability in employment, public services, and accommodations).

Despite this breadth of protection, important distinctions exist between the scope of protection afforded under Section 504 and ADA and the rights established in IDEA. First, Section 504 and ADA are both non-discrimination statutes requiring non-discriminatory treatment in covered programs and services, while IDEA is rights based in that it ensures that education is a guaranteed right for students with disabilities and places the responsibility on the educational provider to design and develop programs to meet that mandate. Second, Section 504 and ADA provide for broader coverage than IDEA, but they also afford public and private entities with exceptions and defenses not included in IDEA. Each piece of legislation will be examined in more detail below, with particular emphasis on the key operational features of the legislation and enforcement mechanisms.

Individuals with disabilities in education

The US Congress enacted specific legislation in 1975 to guarantee that children with disabilities could receive an education. Previous to the passage of this legislation, the courts had already introduced the principle that children with disabilities had a civil right to receive an education: see Pennsylvania Ass'n for Retarded Children *v.* Commonwealth of Pennsylvania (1972); and Mills *v.* Board of Education of District of Columbia (1972). Facing pending litigation in multiple states and following a Congressional investigation revealing millions of children with disabilities were not receiving an appropriate education, Congress enacted the *Education of All Handicapped Children Act* in 1975 (Colker, 2009). Now renamed as the *Individuals with Disabilities Education Act* (IDEA), the law's two main purposes were to ensure that children with disabilities (a) received an education that met their unique needs and prepared them for further education, and (b) protected the rights of children with disabilities and their parents to be involved in determining how to meet those needs.

IDEA mandates that each child with disabilities has an "individualized education plan" (IEP) so that he or she can receive a "free appropriate public education" (FAPE). IDEA covers children from age three through 21. IDEA also provides federal funding for educating children with disabilities and is enforced and administered by the Department of Education. As such, the Department of Education has issued regulations to guide implementation of the provisions of IDEA, which expressly includes "instruction in physical education" among the educational instruction required as needed to ensure the unique needs of a child with a disability are being met (Wright & Wright, 2019).

The key operational features include: (a) an operational definition of a "disability"; (b) the establishment of the individualized inquiry standard contained in the IEP; (c) the oversight and accountability imposed by the federal government through the Department of Education; (d) the establishment of a legal right to a FAPE for children with disabilities (i.e., a school cannot refuse to educate a student with disability because it would impose additional costs or other burdens upon the school); and (e) the concept of "least restrictive environment" (Wright & Wright, 2019).

As Block (1996) observed, the US legislation provides a framework for policy and decision making supported by extensive rules and regulations to assist with implementation of the legislation, but also has a long history of court decisions resolving disputes and disagreements as school administrators, teachers, parents and students attempted to implement the legislative mandate. These court cases, both in the context of physical education and disability sport, have played a critical role in defining the duties and responsibilities of schools to comply with IDEA. The key operational features which have been shaped through both regulations and court decisions often related to (a) how FAPE is defined, (b) the reasonableness of the IEP, and (c) the application of the least restrictive environment standard.

FAPE, the IEP, the least restrictive environment

"A FAPE, as the Act defines it, includes both 'special education' and 'related services.' §1401(9). "Special education" is 'specially designed instruction … to meet the unique needs of a child with a disability' (34 C.F.R. § 300.39(a)); 'related services' are the support services 'required to assist a child … to benefit from' that instruction" (34 C.F.R. § 300.34(a)). Special education includes instruction in physical education. It is critical to note that APE is a specially designed instruction, not a related service. In fact, 34 C.F.R. § 300.108 further provides that physical education services, specially designed if necessary, must be made available to every child with a disability receiving FAPE. IDEA defines physical education as the development of:

> Physical and motor skills;
> Fundamental motor skills and patterns;
> Skills in aquatics, dance, and individual and group games and sports (including intramural and lifetime sports);
> Includes special physical education, adapted physical education, movement education, and motor development
> (*Nondiscrimination on the Basis of Handicap in Programs or Activities Receiving Federal Financial Assistant, 34 C.F.R. § 300.39(b)(2))*

Thus, physical education must be made available equally to children with disabilities and children without disabilities. If physical education is provided as part of the general education curriculum for children without disabilities, it must also be available to children with disabilities. Moreover, even if physical education is not part of the general education curriculum, if physical education is specially designed to meet the child's needs and is included in the IEP, those services must be provided whether or not they are provided to other children without disabilities as part of FAPE. A school cannot substitute other academic services for required physical education services and a school cannot substitute extracurricular or non-academic "related or support services" for specially designed physical education. Thus, children with disabilities who can participate in general physical education with or without supplementary aides, services and other supports must be provided that opportunity.

With regard to whether the IEP is reasonable and a school has met its obligations imposed by IDEA, the standard was established in the seminal case decided by the US Supreme Court in Board of Education *v*. Rowley (1982) (hereinafter "Rowley") where the Court held:

> [T]he requirement that a State provide specialized educational services to handicapped children generates no additional requirement that the services so provided be sufficient to maximize each child's potential commensurate with the opportunity provided other children ... The educational opportunities provided by our public school systems undoubtedly differ from student to student, depending upon a myriad of factors that might affect a particular student's ability to assimilate information presented in the classroom.
>
> *458 US at 198–99*

The Rowley decision has been applied to provide that an IEP is reasonable so long as it provides a student some or minimal educational benefit. Thus, if a student is generally progressing from grade to grade, the state has met its burden under IDEA. This has been referred to as the "*de minimis* standard", requiring only minimal educational benefit. Rowley has generally been understood to impose no burden on the school to provide an ideal educational program or to maximize the student's educational potential. A recent Supreme Court decision has narrowed the scope of Rowley in instances where the child with a disability is not fully integrated in the general education classroom. In Endrew F. *v*. Douglas County School District (2017), the Court stated that if a child is not fully integrated in the general education program, the focus shifts even more to the individual needs of the child and the "*de minimis*" progress standard in the non-integrated setting may not satisfy IDEA. Instead, the Court stated "a school must offer an IEP reasonably calculated to enable a child to make progress appropriate in light of the child's circumstances" (p. 999). The Court stated "it cannot be right that the Act [IDEA] typically aims for grade-level advancement for children with disabilities who can be educated in the regular classroom, but is satisfied with barely more than *de minimis* progress for those who cannot" (Endrew F. *v*. Douglas County School District, 2017, p. 1001).

The basic idea of the least restrictive environment is straightforward—make sure that students with disabilities who receive special education instruction are included in the general education classroom as often as possible ("maximum extent appropriate"). The individualized nature of the IEP means a number of scenarios or options may be available when developing annual IEP goals including (a) a child spending most of the day in the general education classroom with support services, (b) a child spending a part of the day in the general education classroom and part of the day receiving special education classes, (c) a child attending full-time special education programs, and (d) a child attending specialized programs outside the school district, such as private schools or residential programs. The physical education regulations stipulate that each child with a disability must be afforded the opportunity to participate in the general physical education program unless the child is enrolled full time in a separate facility or the child needs specially designed physical education as prescribed in the IEP (34 C.F.R. 300.108(b)). Since federal law mandates physical education be included among the special education services provided to children with disabilities, it is imperative that the physical education teacher be actively involved in the IEP development process.

An in-depth discussion of the laws and regulations implementing IDEA is beyond the scope of this chapter. A range of complex issues and interrelationships with other federal laws impact public schools. A number of excellent resources are available for a detailed analysis of special education law in the US and resources for APE standards (APENS, 2008; SHAPE America, 2018; Wright & Wright, 2007)

Section 504 and the Americans with Disabilities Act (ADA)

In addition to IDEA, the ADA and Section 504 impact educational rights for secondary school students with disabilities. Section 504 covers all programs or activities receiving federal financial assistance, which encompasses public school systems receiving federal funding through school lunch programs or other federal school initiatives. The ADA applies to both public and private schools, regardless of whether or not they receive federal funding. While IDEA's purpose is to ensure all children with disabilities receive FAPE, emphasizing special education and related services, the purpose of Section 504 and ADA is to prohibit discrimination against persons with disabilities by both public and private entities.

Section 504 provides:

> No otherwise qualified individual with a disability ... shall solely by reason of her or his disability be excluded from the participation in, be denied the benefits of, or be subjected to discrimination under any *program or activity receiving Federal financial assistance*.
>
> *(Emphasis added)*

ADA provides:

> Title II: No qualified individual with a disability shall, on the basis of disability, be excluded from participation in or be denied the benefits of the services, programs, or activities of a public entity, or be subjected to discrimination by any *public entity*.
>
> *(Emphasis added)*

> Title III: No individual shall be discriminated against on the basis of disability in the full and equal enjoyment of the goods, services, facilities, privileges, advantages, or accommodations of any place of public accommodation by any *private entity* who owns, leases (or leases to), or operates a place of public accommodation.
>
> *(Emphasis added)*

The key operational features shared between Section 504 and the ADA guiding how protections are implemented include: (a) definition of disability; (b) requirement that to be covered, a person must be "otherwise qualified" to access the programs, services, or

opportunities at stake; (c) requirement to make reasonable modifications to policies, practices, or procedures when modifications are necessary, unless modifications would operate as
fundamental alterations or impose an undue burden; (d) prohibition of separate but equal
concept of service delivery, instead requiring services or programs be offered in the most
integrated setting appropriate to the needs of the individual; and (e) that all the aforementioned factors be determined using an individualized inquiry approach.

In the context of education, Section 504 and ADA protect school-age children with disabilities who are "otherwise qualified" regardless of whether they require special educational
instruction or related services. Section 504 and ADA both define a disability as a substantial
impairment which affects one or more major life activities such as learning. Under Section
504 and ADA, the existence of a disability triggers coverage and the coverage extends across
the lifespan. This is in contrast to IDEA, where a disability must trigger a need for special
education or related services and those services must only be provided while the student is
in the public school system (coverage from age three through age 21). For example,
a student with asthma may not need access to any special education or related services under
IDEA but would still be covered under Section 504 and ADA due to her asthma being
a substantial impairment of a major life activity—breathing. She may not be eligible for, or
need, an IEP with an APE program under IDEA, but modifications to the existing physical
education program and services would likely be required as a reasonable accommodation
under Section 504 and ADA.

Similarly, a student may receive special education services while in public school under
IDEA, but find accessing similar services at the university level more challenging. For
example, consider a student with diabetes. The public school system has a duty to identify
students with disabilities such as diabetes and assess any special needs those students may
require while at school. Special needs may include providing appropriate snacks, monitoring
blood glucose levels during school, administering insulin, and granting permission to snack
during classes or exams. A university does not have a duty to identify students with disabilities or to develop individualized plans to assist those students. Most college-aged students
would be expected to monitor and manage their diabetes independently. College-age students would also have to proactively request modifications, such as permission to bring food
into a classroom or to snack during a class, both of which would likely be considered
a reasonable modification and required under Section 504 and the ADA. However,
a student whose blood sugar was particularly troublesome in the morning and who requested
to be required only to take afternoon classes would likely be unable to obtain that modification, since altering the schedule of classes for an academic program planned years in advance
and potentially impacting class schedules of hundreds of other students would be considered
both an undue burden and a fundamental alteration of the university's programs and services.

To be covered by Section 504 and ADA, a student must be a qualified individual with
a disability (Nondiscrimination on the Basis of Disability in State and Local Government Services, 28 C.F.R. § 35.104; 34 C.F.R. § 104.3(l)). Coverage is based on disability, not age,
and would apply beyond the school years for students with disabilities. To be covered, however, the student (person) must be "otherwise qualified", meaning, the student must be
qualified to participate in the program or activity. For example, a student with attention deficit hyperactivity disorder (ADHD) may try out for a basketball team, but lacks the dribbling,
shooting, and passing skills needed to make the team. A coach would not be required to
permit the student to play on the team because the student is not "otherwise qualified."
This is a critical distinction between physical education classes and competitive sports teams.
Physical education classes would not typically have a minimum skills threshold in order for

a student to participate and physical education instruction is required in most general education curriculum; thus, the student with ADHD who may be denied the opportunity to participate on the basketball team could not be denied access to physical education instruction if it was included in the student's IEP and the activities could be adapted to meet his needs.

If a student with a disability is "otherwise qualified" under Section 504 or ADA, these statutes require schools to make reasonable modifications of programs and policies to accommodate the needs of the student. However, unlike IDEA, Section 504 and ADA do not require modifications that would be unduly burdensome or would fundamentally alter the programs or services provided by the schools.

Another unique aspect of Section 504 and ADA in the context of physical education, physical activity, and sport relates to *participation opportunities* in extracurricular activities, which would include recreational after-school physical activity or sports programs as well as the school's competitive sports programs. The ADA's mandate does not stop at the physical structure or physical access to a sport space, nor is it limited only to spectators at stadiums and arenas. Instead, eligibility policies, competition rules, and other operating practices are subject to review if they have the effect of denying equal access to people with disabilities. The ADA expressly provides:

> a public accommodation shall make *reasonable modifications* in policies, practices, or procedures, when the modifications are necessary to afford goods, services, facilities, privileges, advantages, or accommodations to individuals with disabilities, *unless the public accommodation can demonstrate that making the modifications would fundamentally alter* the nature of the goods, services, facilities, privileges, advantages, or accommodations.
>
> *(ADA), 28 C.F.R., Part 36 § 36.302, 2018, emphasis added)*

This statutory framework of reasonable modifications is similarly recognized in Section 504 and is a fundamental feature of US disability discrimination legislation. The principle not only requires a modification be deemed reasonable, but also places the burden of proof on the public accommodation to prove undue hardship or fundamental alteration. This concept has been characterized by Cooper and Whittle (1998) as

> a prerequisite for any type of measure designed to combat both 'direct' and 'indirect' discrimination based on disability and requires a compromise between the disadvantage imposed by the disability and the freedom of the … service provider to treat everybody on equal grounds.
>
> *(p. 13)*

They further state that the principle is balanced by the undue hardship and fundamental alteration limitations, thus preventing overly restrictive application of the principle.

A landmark case in the US confirmed the broad application of the ADA beyond physical structures and also illustrates the reasonable modification principle described above. It is the only US Supreme Court case to date determining whether sport competition rules restricting participation opportunities of an elite athlete with a disability have the effect of denying equal access to that sport. The case involved professional golfer Casey Martin, who requested to use a cart during the Tour competition due to his mobility disability. The Supreme Court held that Martin's requested modification was not a fundamental alteration of the Professional Golfers' Association (PGA) Tour competition, and therefore was a reasonable modification under the ADA. The Supreme Court upheld the district court's conclusion that when evaluating accommodation requests under Title III of the ADA, the court must first conduct an *individualized inquiry*, a fact-specific inquiry relative to the stated purpose of a rule and a person's individual disability and circumstances, to determine whether a requested modification of the rule is reasonable.

The PGA Tour had argued that substantive rules of a competition could not be waived without fundamentally altering the nature of the competition. Thus, in essence the PGA Tour's argument was that once a rule is designated as a substantive rule by the provider, any modification would result in a fundamental alteration. However, § 12182 of the ADA provides that "reasonable modification in policies, practices, or procedures" must be made. The statute does not say that only policies, practices, or procedures that are not substantive are subject to modification. Section 12182(b)(2)(A)(ii) also identifies the elements and evidentiary burdens for a discrimination claim. Martin was required to provide and offered competent evidence that he was an individual with a disability, that a modification was requested, and that the modification requested was reasonable and necessary.

The Supreme Court developed a two-step analysis to determine whether a modification of a substantive rule of competition would result in a fundamental alteration of the competition. First, the requested modification must not fundamentally alter the essence of the sport. Second, the requested modification must not give the athlete with a disability a competitive advantage. The Court held that walking was not a fundamental part of the sport of golf—golf tests one's shot-making skills—not walking skills. The Court concluded that, given Martin's individual circumstances, affording him the use of a cart would not give him a competitive advantage.

Thus, even though the Martin case involved an elite professional sports competition rule, it reaffirmed the breadth of ADA's proscription and reinforced the importance of the individualized inquiry to evaluate modification requests—two important parallels to IDEA and Section 504—as part of the disability discrimination paradigm. The reasonable modification and fundamental alteration framework has been used frequently in the context of recreational and competitive sport for people with disabilities and should be useful to inform how these requirements could be applied in the context of APE, as seen in the following case.

One final example to illustrate the interrelationship between IDEA, Section 504 and the ADA can be found in a federal district court case in California, Meares *v.* Rim of the World Unified School District (2016) (hereinafter "Meares"). Meares is one of the few cases where the courts have been asked to apply the fundamental alteration requirement from Section 504 and ADA to a school's after-school sports team. This case also demonstrates the gaps and overlaps between the student's IEP for physical education and the student's right to access participation opportunities in all school programs, including extracurricular activities.

Meares involved a 21-year old student diagnosed on the autism spectrum who was enrolled in the school's special education program and was expected to continue in that program until he aged out at 22. The student had an IEP providing him specialized academic instruction services for three classes, and three classes in the general education curriculum with supplemental aids and services. The IEP included a full-time one-on-one aide during school as well as behavior intervention therapy and speech therapy. His IEP included participating in basketball and badminton during general physical education. All of his combined services were deemed beneficial to his education and effective at addressing his educational goals identified in his IEP. The student requested to have a one-on-one aide to participate in the school's mountain biking team after school and that the aid must be capable of keeping pace with him. The school had refused to include this request in his new IEP, and his parents appealed that decision through the administrative appeal processes required under

IDEA. The administrative law judge upheld the school district's decision, and his parents appealed to the federal district court.

Meares affirms several important ways the courts have interpreted IDEA with reference to Section 504. First, with regard to FAPE, courts have consistently interpreted IDEA as requiring an IEP that is "appropriate", but does not require an "ideal" or "best" plan (*Rowley*, 1982). Recall that the *Rowley* Test under FAPE is whether the IEP is reasonably calculated to enable the child to garner educational benefits. Second, the court confirmed that IDEA does not provide schools with the defense of undue burden or fundamental alteration contained in Section 504 and ADA, and the burden of proof is always on the public agency to demonstrate either of these defenses under Section 504 or ADA. Third, with regard to the potential defense of undue burden or fundamental alteration, such defenses would rarely prevail in the context of extracurricular activities in education. Since IDEA rejects the notion that cost can be considered and since IDEA requires aids and services as part of FAPE services, it is unlikely providing those same services for extracurricular activities would impose an undue burden or fundamentally alter the educational program.

Consistent with the Supreme Court's Rowley decision, the school district in Meares was held to have met its FAPE obligations under IDEA since the student's educational needs were being met by the physical education activities included in his IEP. However, the additional question in Meares was whether an IEP must include services so that a student can participate in an appropriate but educationally nonessential extracurricular activity to the same extent as his peers without disabilities. This question was not directly addressed in Rowley. Thus, the district court evaluated whether refusing to provide the mountain-biking aid deprived the student of equal access to the school's programs and services in violation of the IDEA equal opportunity implementing regulations (34 C.F.R. § 300.107). The question in this case highlighted the distinction between IDEA's primary FAPE requirement and the more general "equal opportunities" requirements included in IDEA's implementing regulations.

To resolve this question, the court noted the similarity and relatedness between the IDEA implementing regulations and Section 504. IDEA's implementing regulations were originally created by reference to Section 504; the interpretation and implementation of Section 504 directly influences implementation of the equal opportunities regulations added to IDEA. Both IDEA's implementing regulations and Section 504 require public agencies to take steps to provide non-academic and extracurricular services and activities in the manner necessary to afford children with disabilities an equal opportunity for participation in those services and activities. Additionally, Rowley was decided after the implementing regulations were promulgated, thus, at least one circuit has held that Rowley invalidated the regulations with regard to requiring equal opportunity for participation in extracurricular activities. The Meares court, in applying the Rowley standard, emphasized the difference between "strict equality" and "equal access", concluding that Rowley only rejected the notion of IDEA mandating absolute or strict equality. Equal access would not guarantee access, but would require schools to provide the opportunity to access extracurricular activities if they were appropriate to the needs of the child.

This interpretation is also consistent with Section 504 regulations, where the courts have held that the equal opportunity protection included in Section 504 (and incorporated into IDEA's regulations) may impose additional obligations based on a comparison between the manner in which needs of the children with disabilities and those without disabilities are met. The "access" required in the equal opportunity regulations is not contingent on whether it confers an educational or instructional benefit (as the FAPE requires), but only whether the activity is appropriate for the student. Since there was evidence that participating in mountain biking was appropriate for the student (he experienced positive benefits from it and was proficient at it), the court held that once an activity is deemed appropriate, the public agency must ensure that the student has the aids and services appropriate and necessary to participate, which in this case included the one-on-one aid able to assist at the student's riding skill level.

Last, the district court noted that the IDEA implementing regulations do not include any qualifiers or defenses to the public agencies' obligation to provide aids and services such as the undue burden or fundamental alteration defense provided in Section 504 and ADA. The court expressed its reluctance to hold that no such defenses existed under IDEA, given the close relationship between the language of the implementing regulations and Section 504. The court ultimately did not decide that question, however, since the school district had not argued it was not able to provide the services or that it would be difficult to find an aid at the student's biking skill level. Additionally, the court determined permitting the student to apply to be on the mountain biking team would not require a fundamental alteration of the mountain-biking program because he must still be able to earn his spot on the team by having sufficient aptitude and skill for the activity (see, PGA *v.* Martin, 2001). This affords him the equal opportunity to participate on the team, but is not a guarantee of participation. Thus, while the FAPE requirements under IDEA related to direct educational benefits only require services that provide appropriate educational benefits in the IEP, the IDEA's "equal opportunity" regulations suggest a broader scope, similar to Section 504, requiring equal access regardless of educational benefits connected to the IEP so long as the requests are appropriate and necessary for the child to participate.

In this section, we present an overview and some detailed examples of the complexity of the US legal system as it relates to prohibiting discrimination against people with disabilities in physical education, physical activity, and sport. It is important to note that as each nation enacts new legislation as part of global disability awareness initiatives, or continues to create and expand existing national protections, the foundational legal theories and protections will vary greatly from one nation to another. The purpose of this section was to provide some historical context and illustrative legal approaches to creating non-discriminatory school environments and meeting the educational needs of children with disabilities.

Current legal scholarship applicable to APE programs

A great deal of legal scholarship is available to aid scholars and students in understanding the legal obligations to provide inclusive and non-discriminatory extracurricular sport opportunities in their schools and organizations (Boler, 2016; Clement, 2016; Forster, 2015; Lakowski, 2009; McPeters, 2015; Moorman & Masteralexis, 2001). Much of this recent legal scholarship relates to several guidance documents issued by the US Department of Education (DOE) known generally as Dear Colleague Letters. The DOE uses Dear Colleagues Letters to advise schools on their legal responsibilities under Section 504 and ADA. One such guidance, dated August 2011, was in response to the US Government Accountability Office's (GAO) 2010 report revealing that, despite legislation obligating states and schools to provide equal access and opportunities for physical activity for children with disabilities, these opportunities were still very limited (DOE, 2011). The GAO recommended that the DOE provide additional assistance and information to states and schools on ways to provide opportunities in physical education and extracurricular athletics to students with disabilities. The August 2011 guidance provided some general suggestions and information for states and schools, including physical activity guidelines and ways to improve access to physical education for students with disabilities. Then, on January 25, 2013, the DOE's Office of Civil Rights issued another Dear Colleague Letter reaffirming the legal mandate imposed by Section 504 and ADA on schools to provide students with disabilities an equal opportunity to participate not just in physical education, but also in athletics, and non-academic/extra-curricular services and activities (Galanter, 2013). More recently, on October 2, 2017, the DOE, under a new administration, rescinded 72 guidance documents, 63 of which were related to Special Education and Rehabilitative Services creating the potential for uncertainty even though the withdrawn documents should not change the mandate of Section 504 or the ADA.

These DOE guidance documents naturally precipitated legal analysis and inquiry reflected in legal scholarship (Arnhold, Young, & Lakowski, 2013; Davis, 2013; Fristoe, 2018; McPeters, 2014–15; Yell, Losinski, & Katsiyannis, 2014). However, sustained legal scholarship and inquiry specifically focused on legal issues in APE is not as abundant. In a review, Heckman (2007) identified the lack of employment opportunities for people with disabilities in athletic departments includes coaches, physical education teachers, and officials among the positions lacking representation of persons with disabilities. Moreover, Stover (2010) asserted that physical education requirements, together with other factors, are unfairly biased against overweight students who need access to appropriate physical activity, but who lack adequate remedies due to conceptual and legal problems with labeling obesity as a disability. A similar lack of scholarship has been noted in the field of sport management related to people with disabilities. Shapiro and Pitts (2014) conducted a content analysis of sport business management journals between 2002 to 2012 and determined that only 0.016% of the more than 5000 articles published pertained to disability sport, leisure, recreation, or physical activity.

In a recent law review article, Ikram (2018) focused directly on the importance of including students with disabilities in physical education and proposed that physical education be clearly recognized as an integral part of the general education curriculum. Ikram further advocated that students with disabilities must be provided equal access to physical education in public schools and that the goals of IDEA are undermined when local school districts use budget cuts to selectively eliminate curriculum such as physical education (Ikram, 2018). Certainly, many useful compliance guides and legal aids are available from numerous government, educational, and non-profit organizations, but this is an area where more sustained empirical inquiry would be beneficial.

Current legal trends and issues for APE programs

Several ongoing issues continue to challenge educators and scholars working with APE programs. First is the emphasis placed on inclusion. Inclusion, as an abstract goal of disability rights advocates, gained momentum in the 1990s and is used frequently in the literature surrounding rights of persons with disabilities. In the context of IDEA, the words inclusion or mainstreaming appear nowhere in the statute; however, the least restrictive environment language in the statute has often been interpreted as establishing legal preference for integrated educational settings over separate educational settings. Indeed, UNESCO (2005) emphasized the importance of general schools using an inclusive orientation as the best means of achieving education for all. This advocacy perspective has been influential in the application and implementation of the legal protections available to students with disabilities, but not without controversy or concern. Block (1996) explored litigation related to IDEA's "least restrictive environment" requirement and inclusion, resulting in several cases that, instead of recognizing a continuum of educational settings appropriate for students with disabilities, appear to have adopted a "fail first" approach where schools must initially place all students in general educational settings where they may fail before placing students in separate or special education programs.

Next, an ongoing legal discussion involves a child's eligibility for adapted physical education services. Currently, the IDEA "considers students eligible for special education, including physical education, if they are identified as having one of the 14 disabilities named in the law" (SHAPE America, 2018, para. 3). The most recent amendments to IDEA were in 2004 and some parents' advocacy groups have advocated for expanding IDEA (Center for Parent Information and Resources, 2017). Additionally, the Society of Health and Physical Educators (SHAPE) of America, the nation's leading organization related to physical education generally, advocates for a broader interpretation of the law, stating in their position paper on the topic that "any student who has unique needs for instruction in physical education, regardless of disability, is entitled to receive appropriate accommodations through adapted physical education" (SHAPE America, 2018, para. 3). This broader interpretation could serve to expand opportunities for more students with disabilities to experience the benefits of physical education just like their classmates and in a least restrictive environment.

Additionally, the IDEA extends to people ages 3–21. Some issues arise with IEPs with children who are from 3–5 and when they transition to the 18–21 age range. The Meares case is just one example of challenges faced when providing services for students across an age span of almost 20 years. While there is guidance for both of these groups in the form of Dear Colleague Letters, those guidelines are not always followed consistently. In addition, when children transition from elementary school to middle school and also transition to high school, often times physical education is dropped from their IEPs. One issue here which needs to be addressed is the fact that the current standard IEP software used to help establish a child's IEP does not include physical education, even though APE is considered a direct instructional service and not a related service.

Last, one very recent development, and one which will directly impact the APE setting, relates to the question of the inappropriate use of restraint and seclusion to protect children with disabilities. In early 2019, the US Department of Education announced an initiative to examine the legal ramifications of these actions (NCHPAD, 2019; US Department of Education, 2019). The Office of Civil Rights (OCR) and also the Office of Special Education and Rehabilitation Services (OSERS) are responsible for oversight of the program. According to the US Department of Education (2019, para. 3), this initiative

> will not only include components that help schools and districts understand how federal law applies to the use of restraint and seclusion, but the Department will also support schools seeking resources and information on the appropriate use of interventions and supports to address the behavioral needs of students with disabilities.

Under this initiative, OCR's Regional Offices will perform compliance reviews and work with public schools to correct non-compliance, conduct data quality reviews, and provide assistance to school districts on the legal requirements of Section 504 regarding restraint and seclusion of students with disabilities.

In this chapter, we presented an overview of the development of laws and legislation, internationally and within the US, recognizing the rights of persons with disabilities and prohibiting discrimination against people with disabilities in physical education, physical activity, and sport. The international declarations and initiatives continue to expand awareness and enable nations to design legal protections for persons with disabilities. As each nation enacts new legislation as part of global disability awareness initiatives, or continues to create and expand existing national protections, the foundational legal theories and protections will vary greatly from one nation to another but are likely to also feature shared or common themes using a rights based approach and reinforcing the principles of inclusion.

Summary of key points

1. The disability rights movement began midway through the 20th century and continues to evolve and expand as part of numerous global disability rights and awareness initiatives.
2. Several major international declarations and initiatives have supported expansion of physical education and physical activity as an essential component of the disability rights movement, including the Universal Declaration of Human Rights, the Convention on the Rights of Persons with Disabilities, and the UNESCO Charter on Physical Education.
3. The United Nations also adopted the Declaration of the Rights of the Child. This Declaration specifically addressed education for children with disabilities, including physical education and recreational opportunities.
4. The Convention on the Rights of Persons with Disabilities addresses both mainstream and disability specific sport and requires physical education for children with disabilities.
5. UNESCO recently updated the Charter on Physical Education, Physical Activity and Sport and specifically addresses disability in a number of sections.
6. The US legal framework has provided international guidance for combatting discrimination against children with disabilities in educational settings and includes legislation such as the Individuals with Disabilities Education Act (IDEA), Section 504 of the Rehabilitation Act of 1973, and the Americans with Disabilities Act (ADA). In some areas these laws intersect and in other areas they provide divergent forms of legal protection.
7. Legal disputes related to serving the needs of children with disabilities have occurred in the U.S, focusing primarily on areas including individualized education plans (IEP), (FAPE), and least restrictive environments.
8. While a good deal of legal research is available related to special and general education for students with disabilities and on parameters for providing extracurricular and sport opportunities for students and children with disabilities, sustained legal research specific to issues related to APE is not as prevalent.
9. Recent developments related to APE continue to arise, including appropriate inclusion, eligibility for adapted physical education services, and appropriate use of restraint and exclusion to protect children with disabilities.

Reflection questions

1. The United Nations has issued a number of documents related to the rights of children and people with disabilities. Choose two of these documents and discuss how they inform the rights of children with disabilities to participate in adapted and/or general physical education.
2. Even though the Martin case involved professional sport, how is it instructive for examining legal issues in APE?

3. Where should an APE teacher turn when s/he has questions about the legal rights of children with disabilities? What organizations could provide useful information? Which documents? What questions should a teacher ask to begin to make sure the proper services and opportunities are available to students with disabilities?

4. Research on the legal issues in APE is currently quite limited. Why do you think that is the case? What types of legal questions could be examined in this area?

5. Moving forward, how can school personnel such as superintendents, principals, physical educators, and coaches serve as advocates for children with disabilities who wish to be more physically active and their parents?

References

Americans with Disabilities Act of 1990, 42 U.S.C. § 12101 et seq. (2008).

APENS. (2008). 15 standards of specialized knowledge. Retrieved from https://apens.org/15standards. html

Arnhold, R., Young, L., & Lakowski, T. (2013). Part I—The historical and legal background leading to the Office of Civil Rights "Dear Colleague Letter". *Journal of Physical Education, Recreation & Dance, 84*(8), 20–23.

British Athletics (2008). National disability sport organisations. Englandathletics.org. Retrieved from www.englandathletics.org/disability-athletics/disability-sports-organisations

Bines, H., & Lei, P. (2011). Disability and education: The longest road to inclusion. *International Journal of Educational Development, 31*, 419–424.

Block, M. E. (1996, April). Implications of U.S. federal law and court cases for physical education placement of students with disabilities. *Adapted Physical Activity Quarterly, 13*, 127–152.

Board of Education of Hendrick Hudson Cent. Sch. Dist, Westchester Cty. v. Rowley. 458 U.S. 176 1982.

Boler, A. L. (2016). Comment: Put them in, Coach! They're ready to play: Providing students with intellectual disabilities the right to participate in school sports. *Arkansas Law Review, 69*, 579–608.

Center for Parent Information and Resources. (2017). IDEA—The Individuals with Disabilities Education Act. Retrieved from www.parentcenterhub.org/idea/

Clement, O. (2016). Note: Making the cut: The state of public school athletics for disabled students. *Cardozo Arts & Entertainment Law Journal, 34*, 807–834.

Colker, R. (2009). *The law of disability discrimination* (7th ed.). New York: LEXIS/NEXIS.

Cooper, J., & Whittle, R. (1998). Enforcing the rights and freedoms of disabled people: The role of transnational law. *Mountbatten Journal of Legal Studies, 2*(2), 1–21.

Council of Canadians with Disabilities. (2013). History. Retrieved from www.ccdonline.ca/en/about/history

Davis, R. (2013). Special Section: Helping general physical educators and adapted physical educators address the Office of Civil Rights Dear Colleague Guidance Letter. *Journal of Physical Education, Recreation & Dance, 84*(8), 19–45.

Department of Education. (2011, August). Creating equal opportunities for children and youth with disabilities to participate in physical education and extracurricular activities.

Department of Education. (2019). U.S. Department of Education announces initiative to address the inappropriate use of restraint and seclusion to protect children with disabilities, ensure compliance with federal laws. Retrieved from www.ed.gov/news/press-releases/us-department-education-announces-initiative-address-inappropriate-use-restraint-and-seclusion-protect-children-disabilities-ensure-compliance-federal-laws

Endrew, F. v. (2017). *Douglas County School District*, 137 S. Ct. 988.

Fay, T., & Wolff, E. A. (2009). Disability in sport in the twenty-first century: Creating a new sport opportunity spectrum. *Boston University International Law Journal, 27*, 231–248.

Forster, I. (2015). Comment: Fair play for those who need it most: Athletic opportunities for high school student athletes with disabilities. *Jeffrey S. Moorad Sports Law Journal, 22*, 693–726.

Fristoe, A. (2018). Article: No student left behind? Accommodating students with disabilities in higher education during the Trump administration. *North Carolina Central University Law Review, 40*, 73–83.

Galanter, S. M., Assistant Secretary for Civil Rights, Office for Civil Rights. (2013, January 25). Dear Colleague Letter. U.S. Department of Education.

Heckman, D. (2007, Fall). Educational athletic employment and civil rights: Examining discrimination based on disability, age, and race. *Marquette Sports Law Review*, *18*, 101–167.

Humanium. (n.d.) Declaration of the rights of the Child, 1959. Retrieved from www.humanium.org/en/declaration-rights-child-2/

Individuals with Disabilities Education Act, 20 U.S.C. § 1400 (2004).

Ikram, M. (2018, Spring). When local governments waiver: Giving bite to students with disabilities' federal right to avail physical education. *Rutgers Journal of Law & Public Policy*, *15*, 345–398.

IPC. (n.d.). Paralympics—History of the Movement. Retrieved from www.paralympic.org/the-ipc/history-of-the-movement

Kidd, B., & Donnelly, P. (2000). Human rights in sports. *International Review for the Sociology of Sport*, *35*, 131–148.

Lakowski, T. (2009). Athletes with disabilities in school sports: A critical assessment of the state of sports opportunities for students with disabilities. *Boston University International Law Journal*, *27*, 283–315.

McPeters, T. D. (2015). The Rehabilitation Act of 1973: Why OCR's small reminder will likely spark big change for high school athletics in 2014 and beyond. *Marquette Sports Law Review*, *25*, 413–434.

Meares v. Rim of the World Unified Sch. Dist., 269 F. Supp. 3d 1041 (C.D. Cal. 2016).

Mills v. Board of Education of District of Columbia, 348 F. Sup. 866 (D. DC 1972).

Moorman, A. M., & Masteralexis, L. P. (2001, Fall). Writing an Amicus Curiae brief to the United States Supreme Court, PGA Tour, Inc. v. Martin: The role of the disability sport community in interpreting the Americans with Disabilities Act. *Journal of Legal Aspects of Sport*, *11*, 285–314.

National Disability Authority. (2005). Promoting the participation of people with disabilities in physical activity and sport in Ireland. Retrieved from http://nda.ie/Publications/Health/Health-Publications/Promoting-the-Participation-of-People-with-Disabilities-in-Physical-Activity-and-Sport-in-Ireland1.html

NCHPAD. (2019) U.S. Department of Education to address the inappropriate use of restraint and seclusion to protect children with disabilities. Retrieved from www.ed.gov/news/press-releases/us-department-education-announces-initiative-address-inappropriate-use-restraint-and-seclusion-protect-children-disabilities-ensure-compliance-federal-laws

Nondiscrimination on the Basis of Disability in State and Local Government Services. (2016). 28 C.F.R. Part 35 §§ 35.130, 35.104, & 35.149.

Nondiscrimination on the Basis of Disability in Public Accommodations and Commercial Facilities. (2016). 36 C.F.R. Part 36 §§ 36.201, 36.203, 36.301, & 36.302.

Nondiscrimination on the Basis of Handicap in Programs or Activities Receiving Federal Financial Assistant. (2016). 34 C.F.R. Part 104 §§ 104.3(l), 300.34(a), & 300.39(a).

Paralympics New Zealand. (2019). Retrieved from https://paralympics.org.nz/about/.

Pennsylvania Ass'n for Retarded Children v. Commonwealth of Pennsylvania, 343 F. Sup. 279 (D. Pa. 1972).

PGA Tour, Inc. v. Martin, 532 U.S. 661 (2001).

Rio 2016 Paralympic ticket sales exceed 1.8 million. (2016, August 9). *Paralympic.org*. Retrieved from www.paralympic.org/news/rio-2016-paralympic-ticket-sales-exceed-18-million

Rowley v. Hendrick Hudson School District, 458 U.S. 176, 102 S. Ct. 3034 (1982).

Schiek, D. (2015). Intersectionality and the notion of disability in EU discrimination law. *European (Legal) Studies On-line Paper Series: Center of European and Transnational Legal Studies*, *4*, 1–27.

Schulze, M. (2009, September). Understanding the UN Convention on the Rights of Persons with Disabilities. *A Handbook on the Human Rights of Persons with Disabilities*. Retrieved from https://iddc consortium.net/sites/default/files/resources-tools/files/hi_crpd_manual_sept2009_final.pdf.

Section 504 of the Rehabilitation Act of 1973, 29 U.S.C. § 794 (2015).

Section 504 Implementing Regulations, Title 34 C.F.R. Part 104 (1980).

SHAPE America. (2018). Eligibility criteria for adapted physical education services. Retrieved from www.wrightslaw.com/info/ape.shape.elig.crit.2018.pdf

Shapiro, D. R., & Pitts, B. G. (2014, November). What little do we know: Content analysis of disability sport in sport management literature. *Journal of Sport Management*, *28*, 657–671.

Stein, M. A., & Lord, J. (2008, December 8). Future prospects for the United Nations Convention on the Rights of Persons with Disabilities. *Brill Online*. Retrieved from https://brill.com/abstract/book/edcoll/9789004180802/Bej.9789004169715.i-320_003.xml

Stover, M. (2010). Note: "These scales tell us that there is something wrong with you": How fat students are systematically denied access to fair and equal education and what we can do to stop this. *California Law Review, 83*, 933–983.

The Robinson Library. (2019). International Year of the Child. Retrieved from www.robinsonlibrary.com/social/family/family/childyear.htm

Thomas, N., & Smith, A. (2009). *Disability, sport and society: An introduction*. London: Routledge.

UNESCO. (1994). The Salamanca Statement and Framework for Action on Special Needs Education. Retrieved from www.unesco.org/education/pdf/SALAMA_E.PDF

UNESCO. (2005). Guidelines for Inclusion: Ensuring Access to Education for All. Retrieved from https://unesdoc.unesco.org/ark:/48223/pf0000140224

UNESCO. (2007). EFA Global Monitoring Report Education for All: Strong Foundations. Retrieved from https://unesdoc.unesco.org/ark:/48223/pf0000147794

UNESCO. (2015). International Charter of Physical Education, Physical Activity and Sport. Retrieved from www.unesco.org/education/pdf/SPORT_E.PDF

UNESCO. (2017). Introducing UNESCO: What we are. Retrieved from www.unesco.org/new/en/unesco/about-us/who-we-are/introducing-unesco/

United Nations. (n.d.a). Convention on the Rights of Persons with Disabilities. Retrieved from www.un.org/development/desa/disabilities/convention-on-the-rights-of-persons-with-disabilities/convention-on-the-rights-of-persons-with-disabilities-2.html

United Nations. (n.d.b). Disability and sports. Retrieved from www.un.org/development/desa/disabilities/issues/disability-and-sports.html

United Nations. (n.d.c). Universal Declaration of Human Rights. Retrieved from www.ohchr.org/EN/UDHR/Documents/UDHR_Translations/eng.pdf

United Nations. (1959). Declaration on the Rights of the Child. Retrieved from www.un-documents.net/a14r1386.htm

United Nations. (2008a, December 13). Convention on the Rights of Persons with Disabilities: Article 30. Retrieved from www.un.org/development/desa/disabilities/convention-on-the-rights-of-persons-with-disabilities/article-30-participation-in-cultural-life-recreation-leisure-and-sport.html

United Nations. (2008b). Frequently asked questions regarding the Convention on the Rights of Persons with Disabilities. Retrieved from www.un.org/development/desa/disabilities/convention-on-the-rights-of-persons-with-disabilities/frequently-asked-questions-regarding-the-convention-on-the-rights-of-persons-with-disabilities.html

United Nations Department of Economic and Social Affairs. (n.d.). Convention on the Rights of Persons with Disabilities. Retrieved from www.un.org/development/desa/disabilities/convention-on-the-rights-of-persons-with-disabilities.html

United Nations Human Rights Office of High Commissioner. (2018). Convention on the Rights of the Child. Retrieved from www.ohchr.org/en/professionalinterest/pages/crc.aspx

Walter, S. (2003). Declaration on the Rights of the Child. Retrieved from www.unicef.org/malaysia/1959-Declaration-of-the-Rights-of-the-Child.pdf

Weber, M. C. (2000). Disability and the law of welfare: A post-integrationist examination. *University of Illinois Law Review, 2000*, 889–956.

Wright, P. W. D., & Wright, P. D. (2007). *Special education law* (2nd ed.). Hartfield, VA: Harbor Law Press.

Wright, P. W. D., & Wright, P. D. (2019). Physical education for students with disabilities. *Wrightslaw.com*. Retrieved from www.wrightslaw.com/info/pe.index.htm

Yell, M. L., Losinski, M. L., & Katsiyannis, A. (2014, September). Students with disabilities participation in extracurricular athletics: School district obligations. *Journal of Special Education, 27*(2), 86–96.

3

Viewpoints toward disability

Conceptualizing disability in adapted physical education

Damian Haslett and Brett Smith

Introduction

The purpose of this chapter is to provide an overview of the viewpoints towards disability that are adopted, or might be adopted, in the field of adapted physical education (APE). However, before we explain these viewpoints, first we must address why it is important for people involved in APE to be able to explain and understand disability. One reason is because there is now an increasing variety of ways to conceptualize disability. Thus, these various viewpoints will have implications for disabled children, educators and facilitators, able-bodied classmates of disabled children, as well as society at large. For instance, how disability is viewed will impact how physical education (PE) teachers adapt, implement, and evaluate physical education activities.

Different viewpoints will also influence what is targeted in the pursuit of psychosocial development of disabled children; what is prioritized and what is left out of policy and research; how inclusion and exclusion are understood to influence the educational experiences of children; the importance of equality and equity; the educational experiences of children with disabilities and able-bodied classmates (without disabilities) of children with disabilities in PE; societal attitudes towards disability and impairment; the type and quality of instructions that educators give children; the quality of the training that educators receive; how physical activity contexts can influence and what is perceived as competence and confidence; legislation and policy and programming (Haegele & Hodge, 2016; Winnick & Porretta, 2016).

In this chapter, first we outline four models of disability: the medical model, the United Kingdom (UK) social model, the social relational model (SRM), and the human rights model of disability. We include the medical and social model, as these are historically dominant viewpoints towards disability in fields such as APE. As Aggerholm and Martiny (2017) write, adapted physical activity "is a cross-disciplinary field of study and practice, where interventions have historically been governed by what in disability research is referred to as the medical model, and to a lesser extent a social model of disability" (p. 1). Having problematized these two models, we then explain the SRM and human rights model of disability. These two viewpoints are selected to highlight some emerging conceptualizations of disability that might be productively under-stood within the context of APE. After attending to these four models, we conclude with some progressive ways that APE scholars and practitioners can think about disability. These include a call for APE scholars to connect further with critical disability studies.

Medical model

The medical model, also known as the individual model of disability, has historically been the dominant way of understanding disability. In the medical model, disability is defined as a "medical problem that resides in the individual – a defect in, or a failure of, bodily system that is inherently abnormal and pathological" (Goodley, 2016, p. 7). Here, disability is understood as being "caused" by parts of the body that are lacking or do not work "prop-erly" and it can, therefore, be "solved" by psychological or medical interventions performed by (often "able-bodied") experts. A medical model has often, either knowingly or unknow-ingly, underpinned how disability is perceived, described, and depicted in various APE con-texts. For example, Fitzgerald and Stride (2012) observed that, historically, a medicalized imperative has dominated research focusing on disability and physical education. They write "from this perspective, disability and 'the disabled body' have extensively been treated as an object to be tested, modified and re-tested" (Fitzgerald & Stride, 2012, p. 285). Goodley (2018) suggests the various ways a medical model can undergird practice in fields such as APE. For example, medicalized understandings of disablity influence the language that abounds in APE contexts (e.g., children with special needs), how educators (without disabil-ities) identify the young people that they will work with, what forms of interventions will be used on disabled young people, and, how interventions are shaped by the language and practices of rehabilitation and medicine.

Although the medical model usefully promotes faith in medical intervention, and medical and technological advances will continue to greatly improve the lives of disabled people, this viewpoint has been heavily criticized. These critiques have largely emerged from disability rights activists and academics working within disability studies (Goodley, 2016). One prob-lem with the medical viewpoint is that the highly influential field of medicine has conceptu-alized disability though a pathogenic lens (disability as pathology), rather than adopting a salutogentic position (disability as a continuum) (see Goodley, 2016). In doing so, the medical model has become the "ruling ideology" greatly responsible for the pathologization of disability. For example, Grenier (2007) highlights how this underlying authority can influ-ence teachers, learners, and the knowledge they together produce in APE contexts:

> The term 'cognitive authority' has been used to describe how entrenched attitudes influenced by the medical model of disability-as-illness depicts students with disabilities in the classroom whose challenges are defined in relation to prescribed methods of teaching and learning. The language used and the policies attached to these social condi-tions have the tendency to pathologize differences associated with disability. How this plays out in the schools varies depending on school philosophy, resources, and the gen-eral sentiment towards the treatment of students with disabilities.
>
> *(Grenier, 2007, p. 301)*

Another problem with the medical model is that in reducing disability to biological com-ponents, this viewpoint shrinks the important influence of socio–historical–political–cultural–economic forces that shape the lives of disabled people. The medical model also paints a very negative picture of disability (Smith & Bundon, 2018). For example, the model relies on bio-physical assumptions of "normality", and, in doing so, creates a problematic normal/abnormal binary: the disabled (not normal) become "defective" and lose power and the able (normal) gain power. In addition, the "problem" of disability is located squarely within the body of the individual, problematically deeming disability a personal responsibility. Similarly, disability in the medical model is seen as a personal physical tragedy and a psychological trauma that should be overcome (rather than accommodated).

Medical model discourse can be seen in APE work in different ways (see Haegele & Hodge, 2016). For example, often APE authors do not explicitly state how they conceptualize disability, suggesting that this dominant viewpoint influences their work (e.g., Haegele & Porretta, 2015). As we discuss in this chapter, there are numerous viewpoints to adopt on disability, such as affirmative, social, social–relational, and human rights models. In addition, even if researchers themselves may not view disability from a medical lens, its dominance in contemporary culture often requires the use of the medical model in their research. This can be seen in the form of questionnaires that categorize on the basis of medical labels, or in participant recruitment strategies, such as in recent research by Haegele, Healy, and Zhu (2018) where parents were asked to identify "their children's problem, illness or disability". Also, entrenched medical model discourse can shape the knowledge of APE educators. As Grenier (2007) points out, the literature in inclusive education "clearly illustrates how the medical model populates teachers' thoughts and mediates their preferences, as well as their dispositions, to students with disabilities" (p. 303). Further, research in adapted physical activity often compares some kind of behavior between one medically labelled disability group against their non-disabled peers (Jespersen & McNamee, 2008).

On top of these critiques, it is important to highlight how the field of psychology has also reduced disability to a problem that resides with the individual (Goodley, 2016). Influential perspectives (e.g., evolutionary and cognitive psychology), techniques (e.g., statistical analysis), and philosophies (e.g., post-positivism) that dominate the field of psychology have contributed towards the process of psychologization: the manufacturing of an ideal individual (i.e., the unitary-isolated-cognitively-able-rational-developed-innately-normed-consensual individual) against which we are expected to judge ourselves (Goodley, 2016). Therefore, APE research that frames experience based on cognitivist theories (e.g., Cervantes & Porretta, 2013) can be open to the accusation of reducing social barriers to the level of the individual, and has the potential to be viewed as apolitical, normalizing, and even oppressive (Goodley, 2016). For instance, this type of approach could imply that it is simply the responsibility of the individual to participate in physical activity, and, in so doing, disregard health inequalities that restrict activity (see Smith & Perrier, 2014). In light of such problems with the medical model, and the growing criticisms of it, alternative understandings have been developed. One of those viewpoints can broadly be labelled the social model of disability.

UK social model

Derived from the British disability rights organization—Union of the Physically Impaired Against Segregation (UPIAS), the United Kingdom (UK) social model, often referred to simply as "the social model", understands and explains disabled people as socially oppressed. From this viewpoint, disability is not caused by biological impairment but by the social barriers (structural and attitudinal) that people with impairments (e.g., physical, sensory, cognitive, emotional) encounter daily in society (Owens, 2015). Importantly, in the social model, the concepts of impairment and disability are separated: impairment does not equate to disability. Impairment remains a biological phenomenon but disability becomes a wholly social phenomenon; in other words, people with impairments are (can be) *disabled* by society. Thus, the "solution" to disability does not lie in medical or psychological "cures" (as in the medical model) but lies in the eradication of disabling structural, political, social, economic, cultural, and psychological barriers (Goodley, 2016). As Goodley writes, "the social model approach is classic counter-hegemony: an alternative idea to the medical/individual tragedy that serves the aims of paramedical professions such as rehabilitation, medicine, psychology, special educational needs and social work" (Goodley, 2016, p. 11).

The UK social model is a barriers approach, underpinned by Marxism, rooted in the scholarship of British disabled intellectuals and UPIAS activists in the 1970s, 1980s and 1990s, such as Colin Barnes, Paul Hunt, Mike Oliver, and Vic Finkelstein. However, as Owens (2015) highlights, there are other similar but different social models that scholars and practitioners should be aware of. For example, the North American social model (also known as the minority model) similarly views disability as failure of social environments. However, this approach promotes a political response from an individual level (e.g., identity politics) rather than at a structural level, like the materialist focus on oppression in the UK social model. Likewise, the Nordic social relative model (also known as the Nordic relational model) rejects the medical dichotomy between illness and health, but views disability as a relative, situational, contextual, person–environment mismatch. Disability and impairment, from a Nordic social relative perspective, are explained as interacting with each other along a continuum. Despite these differences, as we discuss in the next paragraph, the social models viewpoint has been useful in a variety of ways.

The social model has, in many instances, been used to successfully challenge discrimination and marginalization, link civil rights and political activism, and enable disabled people to claim their rightful place in society. It has been a powerful tool for producing social and political change, for challenging the material problems experienced by many disabled people, and for driving emancipatory types of research, such as participatory action research. It has also been influential in producing anti-discrimination legislation in the form of various disability discrimination Acts around the world, including in the UK, France, and North America. Although certainly not perfect or always followed, these Acts mean that disabled people in numerous countries should now legally have equal access to education, sports arenas, employment, and so on. In addition, when disabled people encounter the social model, the effect can be revelatory and liberational. Rather than seeing themselves as the "problem" and the "solution" traced to their own individual bodies, disabled people have been empowered by the social model to recognize that society is often the problem and that the removal of social barriers to their inclusion and participation in social life is what is needed (Smith & Bundon, 2018).

In the context of APE, the social model has been drawn upon to explain and understand disability (see Haegele & Hodge, 2016). As Jespersen and McNamee (2008) explain, in adapted physical activity research, there has been a significant trend away from using the medical/individual tradition to understand disability towards connecting with the social model. For example, Grenier, Collins, Wright, and Kearns (2014) used the social model to frame their research. They were interested in how able-bodied young people's perceptions of disability and APE would reflect and advance the social model. For instance, their study illuminated how young people's perceptions of disability shifted from a medical to social model understanding after being introduced to disability sport. Their findings show how PE and school settings offer a useful space to challenge (medical lens) myths around disability. Bredahl (2013) explains that the social model has been predominantly used in APE research to understand teachers, administrators, or able-bodied peers' experiences of participation in APE. For instance, a social model viewpoint is often used to emphasize the importance of addressing societal barriers in order to enhance participation in adapted physical activity.

While, under the umbrella of the social model, important achievements have been made, this model of disability has also been subject to numerous criticisms. Largely emanating from disability studies, critical disability studies, and the sociology of the body (see Owens, 2015; Thomas, 2012, 2014), these include the following. First, the social model has been accused of ignoring embodied experience at the expense of a focus on oppressive barriers. A materialist/Marxist worldview is useful for making political gains but less so for explaining varied embodied identities and a variety of lived disability experiences (e.g., illness, pain, fluctuating impairments). Second, the social model has created an unhelpful dualism between impairment and disability. The focus on disability has resulted in the impaired body being treated as simply biological; in doing so, this "gifts" the body to medical interpretation (Owens, 2015). Third, the social model does not explain disability adequately. For example, defining disability as oppression is simplistic (e.g., the social model makes no attempt to conceptualize the many components of disability). This lack of explanation positions the social model as a straw man argument or as a heuristic, rather than a comprehensive conceptual model. Fourth, oppression is poorly understood in the social model. For example, it says little about the origins of oppressive attitudes. Finally, it is argued that a world free of all physical barriers is idealistic. For instance, prominent disability theorists such as Carol Thomas and Thomas Shakespeare have argued that sometimes restrictions are indeed "caused" by impairment (see Thomas, 2014).

In light of such criticisms, for some (e.g., Shakespeare & Watson, 2001) the social model is an outdated ideology. The critiques, and subsequent conceptual moves to go beyond the social model, are particularly important when considered within the context of APE. This is because, when a disability model is explicitly utilized in APE research, it is often a social model of disability. Accompanying this use is, with rare exceptions, a silence surrounding the problems of a social model. For example, in fields such as the sociology of sport and sport psychology, there have been calls for both a social model understanding of disability and a focus on disabled bodies (see Smith & Perrier, 2014; Smith, Perrier, & Martin, 2016). In addition, although the social model and the medical model are conflicting viewpoints, they have similar limitations when explaining and understanding disability. For example, both models view disability as a problem: either a problem with the body or a problem with society. (However, scholars can also connect with the affirmation model of disability [Cameron, 2014; Swain & French, 2000] that celebrates the positive aspects of the disability community and explains disability as a proud identity.) In addition, both models ignore important experiences of disability (e.g., biological, psychological or social experiences). Thus, it is vital that researchers engage with the limitations of the social and medical models, but also connect with other models that address the concerns raised above. We now turn to two such models.

The social relational model (SRM)

APE scholars and practitioners can also connect with the SRM of disability (Thomas, 1999, 2004a, 2004b, 2007, 2012, 2014): a conceptually progressive understanding of disability that can be employed as an explanatory and analytical device. As described by Thomas (2007), the SRM builds on problems with the social model as well as on the discontent with the individualist tradition (e.g., medical model) that considers the individual mind and bounded/

autonomous self as the fundamental atom of human life (e.g., psychologization) (see Smith & Perrier, 2014). While the social and medical models conceptualize disability, disablism, and impairments as originating in the individual, in the SRM these are reconstituted as manifestations of social relationships (Thomas, 2007).

As Thomas (2007) argues, the study of disability should

> engage both with social structure (order) and social agency (action), and should therefore accommodate an analyses of social relations and social forces that construct, produce, institutionalize, enact and perform disability and disablism. The lived experience of both disablism and impairment should have its place, as should theorizations of impairment, per se.
>
> *(pp. 181–182)*

In other words, what differentiates the SRM and makes it attractive, as we describe in the following paragraphs, is an expansion of how we understand disablism and impairment.

The SRM uniquely encompasses and extends our understating of disablism. Thomas (2014) promotes a focus on understanding of disablism as the term "disability" has acquired a confusing mix of meanings within disability studies and in society. Disablism, as defined by (Thomas, 2012) refers to:

> The *social* imposition of *avoidable* restrictions on the life activities, aspirations and psycho-emotional well-being of people categorized as 'impaired' by those deemed 'normal'. Disablism is social–relational in character and constitutes a form of social oppression in contemporary society – alongside sexism, racism, ageism, and homophobia. As well as enacted in person-to-person interactions, disablism may itself in institutionalized and other socio-structural forms [sic].
>
> *(Thomas, 2012, p. 211)*

In other words, emerging not from an individual's mind, but from oppressive relationships with structures and human beings, in the SRM different people at different times and places can experience different forms of social oppression; namely (a) psycho-emotional disablism, (b) structural disablism, and (c) internalized oppression (see Reeve, 2014). Psycho-emotional disablism can be separated out as emerging from two sources. Indirect psycho-emotional disablism is associated with the experience of structural disablism (e.g., exclusion from opportunities, services, and activities) and recognizes the psycho-emotional consequences of such experiences. For example, feelings of dislocation, humiliation or disrespect resulting from various levels of exclusion, such as inaccessible trains or being made to use the back entrance to access some buildings (Reeve, 2014).

The second source, direct psycho-emotional disablism, recognizes the consequences of discriminatory—often unpredictable—negative social interactions that disabled people can have with others. The looks, words, and actions of others (e.g., family, friends, strangers, professionals, other disabled people) can become pathologizing "acts of invalidation". For example, being stared at or talked over, experiencing patronizing comments ("does she take sugar?") or assumed tragedy ("what happened to you?"), and overhearing thoughtless words ("I'd rather be dead than in a wheelchair") can contribute considerable emotional distress. Importantly, as Reeve (2014) highlights, there is also a concerning link between hate crime (e.g., 25% of people with disabilities report being victimized) and direct psycho-emotional disablism.

Internalized oppression, as described by Reeve (2014), emerges as a result of a relationship that disabled people can have with *themselves* as result of such hostility. Operating at a psychic level—often unconsciously—and common among subordinated groups, internalized oppression is a powerful example of disablism because it has direct influence on what disabled can *become*. Disabled people can devalue disability, lower self-worth and intrinsic value as a consequence of living in a culture that relentlessly views disability as negative. For example, internalizing ablest norms can be seen in behaviors such as disabled people positioning themselves in hierarchies relative to other disabled people (dispersal), hiding impairment to avoid negative reactions of others (emulation), or overachieving in order to prove they are better than "normal" (supercrip stereotype).

As exemplified in the work of Smith and Caddick (2015) and Richardson, Smith, and Papathomas (2017), the effects of psycho-emotional disablism, structural disablism, and internalized oppression can be profound. Self-esteem, confidence, feelings of worth and ontological security can be damaged as a result of negative social interactions, attitudes, and discourse—whether intended or unintended—in a PE lesson, for example. In such social interactions, a disabled person's psycho-emotional well-being is not simply undermined. As a result of such undermining, they may avoid future behaviors such as taking part in PE. Hence, psycho-emotional disablism can damage well-being as well as place limits on what one can do and what one can *become*. Thus, the psycho-emotional register is progressive because it seeks to consider what "disabled people can be" rather than simply what "disabled people can do" (Goodley, 2016; Smith & Bundon, 2018; Smith & Perrier, 2014).

In addition to disablism, the SRM also usefully extends our understating of impairment. Thomas (2014) finds the binary separation of impairment and disability in disability studies unhelpful. Nonetheless, she promotes the analytical separation as a useful explanatory device. She argues that impairment and disablism are thoroughly intermeshed within the social conditions that bring them into being and, therefore, the conceptual focus should be on the relationship between them. In her critique of the materialist social modelist's reluctance to "deal with" impairment, she highlights that there is a "realness" to impaired bodies and that this—material—experience within a social world requires attention; not all restrictions can be explained by wholly social barriers (e.g., physical pain). In other words, the biological entity can be held directly responsible for restricting some activities a person can do and, at times, damage psycho-emotional well-being. And that impairment, like disability, is also a socially constructed, culturally specific, linguistically shaped category (see Thomas, 2014). To help in this regard Thomas (2012) introduces the concept of impairment effects into the SRM, defined as:

> The direct and *unavoidable* impacts that 'impairments' (physical, sensory, intellectual, emotional) have on individuals' embodied functioning in the social world. Impairments and impairment effects are always bio-social and culturally constructed in character, and may occur at any stage in the life course
>
> *(Thomas, 2012, p. 211)*

The concept of "impairment effects" has been highly influential in British disability studies for several reasons (Goodley, 2016). First, it can allow scholars to acknowledge that impairments can have a direct and immediate impact on daily life without undermining the importance of prioritizing the impact of disablism (Thomas, 2014). This is because Carol Thomas argues for a more dialectic, non-reductionist (neither biologically nor culturally) materialist ontology of the body as opposed to, for example, Thomas Shakespeare's biological realities of the body (Goodley, 2016). Second, by centralizing impairment, the SRM can allow scholars to distinguish between restrictions in society due to the effects of impairment (impairment effects) and socially imposed restrictions (disablism) (Townsend, Cushion, & Smith, 2017). For example, when impairment effects are just corporeal, disablism is absent (i.e., social oppression is not engendered because it is the biological "realness" of having an impaired body that simply affects activity and well-being) (see Smith & Perrier, 2014). Third, it can allow scholars to view the body as biological, experienced, socially constructed, culturally fashioned, and agentic, thereby viewing impaired bodies as simultaneously biological, lived, social, and cultural (Smith & Perrier, 2014). Finally, connecting with impairment effects can allow scholars to understand that the biological reality of impairment can harm psycho-emotional well-being, and, at the same time, impairments can become a site for social oppression. For example, the effects of impairment can spread beyond restrictions caused just by biology to the socially engendered undermining of participation in activities and well-being (Smith & Bundon, 2018).

Although few APE scholars have explicitly connected with the SRM, combined recent research from the fields of disability sport, education, and psychology (Martin, 2013; Reindal, 2008; Simpson, McMillan, & Reeve, 2013; Smith & Perrier, 2014; Townsend et al., 2017) provide several reasons why explaining disability as a social relation is attractive. For example, connecting with the SRM can allow APE researchers to analyse and understand disability in APE at individual, social, cultural, and political levels; foreground disability as an experience of socialized impairment; understand that the experience of social oppression, inequality and cultural stereotypes of disability can be synonymous with the personal experience of physical impairment; show how stigmatizing attitudes contribute to the experience of physical, cognitive, or emotional restriction; draw upon a theoretical framework that accounts for individual differences as well as the experience of oppression in educational settings; understand how physical, social, and environmental barriers to APE are inextricably linked; understand the various social mechanisms that constitute oppression, othering, disablement, and, indeed, *enablement* in APE settings; critically attend to the influence of dominant discourses and practices in APE; expand how disability is positioned, understood, and translated in the formation and expression of APE knowledge, disablism, and impairment; think differently about disability; consider conventions, assumptions, and aspirations of research, theory, and activism; and, analyse disability in micro-contexts.

Let us pause here to give an example of how the SRM can be used to view behavior in an APE context. Imagine that a young person living with a condition labelled osteogenesis imperfecta (brittle bones disease) willingly attends PE class and mentions to her able-bodied PE teacher that she is in physical pain from breaking another bone in last week's class—her second break this year. Her teacher instructs her that she cannot participate in this week's session. Certainly, in this scenario, the biological reality of the body (e.g., pain from impairment) plays a role in preventing this particular physical activity. However, because the teacher imposes upon the young person what she can or cannot do, this social interaction becomes a potential site for oppression, and can damage her psycho-emotional well-being at a number of levels. For example, the young person is potentially reminded that her biological impairment can, at times, prevent social participation (impartment effect). Also, if the teacher is drawing on a set of misinformed cultural assumptions about what people with osteogenesis imperfecta can and cannot do, then here occurs an epistemic invalidation (i.e., direct psycho-emotional disablism). In addition, if the school steps in to prevent further activity in PE based on insurance grounds, this can be a form of structural disablism. On top of this, indirect psycho-emotional disablism can occur if she receives unintended patronizing remarks from other children, teachers or parents, based on this experience. Furthermore, the social interaction has the potential for the young person to place self-imposed restrictions on what she can *do* and *become* in the future (internalized oppression). Thus, from a viewpoint of the SRM, restrictions can simultaneously occur at an individual, social, and environmental level.

The social relational model is clearly complex. For some, this complexity is a limitation and serves only to overcomplicate an already complicated understanding of disability (see Shakespeare & Watson, 2010). For others, connecting with the SRM produced a concerning analytical task because they struggled to identify where the boundaries of impairment effects and disablism began and ended (and, indeed, the boundaries between direct and indirect psycho-emotional disablism) (see Owens, 2015). However, because impairment, disability, and disablism are so complex, this is exactly what makes the SRM attractive to some scholars in physical activity research (see Martin, 2013; Smith, 2013; Smith & Bundon, 2018). Certainly, the SRM needs to be empirically studied much more because it holds various potential benefits. One underused application of the SRM is to utilize this viewpoint to understand the effects of positive social relationships, such as the experience of enabling discourse and structures on psycho-emotional well-being and subsequent "ways of becoming". Evidently, more dialogue with the SRM within the fields similar to APE is needed. The same can be said for the next model that we now attend to.

Human rights model of disability

Unlike the social model and the social relational model, the human rights model of disability is underpinned by rights-based principles. For example, in some parts of the world, rights-based disability discrimination legislation has had a significant influence on the development of APE (Winnick & Porretta, 2016). The *Americans with Disabilities Act* (1990) litigates for physical education so young disabled people can develop skills necessary to participate in recreation and leisure activities in community settings. More recently, also in the United States (US), the *Every Student Succeeds Act* (2015) supports the right to high quality physical education for disabled children (Winnick & Porretta, 2016). However, most countries have no such protection of their citizens with disability. As a result, pressure grew to develop an international convention that would be legally binding on nations to improve and document the position of disabled people in society. To recognize that disabled people have a right to access services from all areas of citizenship, such as PE opportunities, the United Nations' Convention on the Rights of Persons with Disabilities (UNCRPD, United Nations, 2006) was introduced.

In contrast to approaches like that of the World Health Organization (2001) International Classification of Functioning, Disability, and Health (also known as the ICF), which focuses on the health condition of disabled people, the UNCRPD is founded on social approaches that recognize disability as the outcome of social processes. There are eight guiding principles that underlie the Convention and each one of its specific Articles. Together, the principles capture: (a) the human rights viewpoint towards disability; (b) what actions should be taken to undo any damage done to disabled people; and (c) what is needed to ensure that activities such as PE is a basic human right that any person can claim. The principles are: (1) respect for inherent dignity, individual autonomy, including the freedom to make one's own choices, and independence of persons; (2) non-discrimination; (3) full and effective participation and inclusion in society; (4) respect for difference and acceptance of disabled people as part of human diversity and humanity; (5) equality of opportunity; (6) accessibility; (7) equality between men and women; and (8) respect for the evolving capacities of disabled children and the right of disabled children to preserve their identities (United Nations, 2006). Grounded on these principles, the UNCRPD has several Articles that pertain to APE. For instance, Article 30 of the Convention recognizes physical activity and sport as important parts of any person's citizenship. Article 24 of the Convention recognizes the right to education, including the rights of persons with disability to develop their physical abilities.

APE scholars who wish to adopt a human rights viewpoint can draw upon the UNESCO (2015) revised International Charter of Physical Education and Sport. This charter is a rights-based reference that understands "disability" in line with the UNCRPD and has several provisions addressing APE, such as stressing that resources for physical education must be allocated without discrimination on disability; adapted, safe opportunities to participate in physical education must be provided for persons with disabilities; safe spaces, facilities, and equipment for APE must be provided to meet the different need associated with disability. In addition, APE scholars can also draw on the recently adopted UNESCO (2017) Kazan Action Plan. This document connects physical education policy development with the United Nations 2030 Agenda for Sustainable Development (United Nations, 2015) and makes provision for disability. For example, this plan advocates that a minimum of 15% of urban areas should be allocated for integrating opportunities, such as sport and physical education, and should be designed to consider the needs of disabled people.

A recent special edition of the *Journal of Sport for Development*, titled "Disability Sport: Changing lives, changing perceptions", provides examples of how APE scholars can use a human rights viewpoint to explore issues such as social change and pedagogy (see Brittain & Wolff, 2015). For example, Devine et al. (2017) used a human rights model to assess the outcomes of a sport for development program. Their research showed how organizations are becoming more socially aware since the introduction of the UNCRPD, citing improved attitudes towards disability and improvements in the quality of life and economic empowerment for disabled people. In another example, Beacom and Golder (2015) adopt a UNCRPD perspective of disability to make a case for a critical pedagogy to help develop APE practitioners. They drew on a human rights model to argue that educators should be nurtured to challenge: established patterns of thinking about disability; established ways of working in APE settings; and, the systemic inequities increasingly characteristic of competitive disability sport in local and global settings (Beacom & Golder, 2015).

Additional future directions

So far, in this chapter, we have used a models approach to suggest some of the ways in which researchers in APE might conceptualize disability. However, the four models we have suggested are not the only ways to explain and understand disability. Scholars could also draw on the revised World Health Organization (2001) ICF while remaining mindful of the numerous critiques of it (see Reindal, 2008). For instance, the ICF is underpinned by a bio-psycho-social model of disability that can imply an understanding of disability as a phenomenon of disadvantage. This is because restrictions of activity in the ICF are viewed in relation to activities that can be considered statistically "normal" or, in other words, can be positively desirable abilities in cultural context (Reindal, 2008). Narrative inquiry can also be a useful lens to make sense of disability in APE research. For example, narratives can illuminate young disabled people's self-identities and socio-cultural contexts (e.g., Svendby &

Dowling, 2013); provide insight into the multiple realities of inclusion and/or exclusion, disability and PE (e.g., Svendby, 2016); and, contribute understandings beyond medically defined notions of disability by capturing complex lived experiences (e.g., Fitzgerald & Stride, 2012). Phenomenological scholars can capture individuals' experiences as well as general structures of experience (Aggerholm & Moltke Martiny, 2017; Bredahl, 2013). For example, Bredahl (2013) used a phenomenological lens to illuminate critical issues in APE (e.g., positive and negative experiences of PE for young disabled people).

A relatively new and exciting way to think about disability comes from the powerful emergence of what has come be called critical disability studies (CDS) (see Goodley, 2013; Shildrick, 2012). CDS can be described as a paradigmatic shift that builds on the foundational perspectives of disability studies (e.g., the social model of disability) while integrating new transformative agendas associated with the recent diversification of critical social theory (e.g., postcolonial, queer, and feminist theories) (Meekosha & Shuttleworth, 2009). The introduction of the word "critical" denotes a sense of self-appraisal: reassessing where we have come from, where we are now, and where we might be going (see Smith & Perrier, 2014). Thus, by connecting disability studies to intersections of class, gender, sexuality, race, and ethnicity, CDS has become a lens that goes beyond understanding disability to understanding society in general. As Goodley (2016) writes, "while critical disability studies might start with disability it never ends with disability" (p. 19). Thus, CDS is a space from which to think through a host of political, theoretical, and practical issues that are relevant to all. Shildrick (2012), for example, describes CDS as the academic site to watch because it is a space that can ask questions of embodiment, identity, and agency, as they affect all living things. Therefore, thinking about disability through a lens of CDS can help stimulate the field of APE, as it calls upon scholars to be open to using an eclectic range of theories and new lines of critical enquiry.

But what exactly are critical disability studies? A useful way to think of CDS is as the result of the emergence of many interrelated perspectives and developments in disability research over the past 20 years. Reflecting on recent writings (Goodley, 2013, 2016; Goodley, Liddiard, & Runswick-Cole, 2017; Meekosha & Shuttleworth, 2009; Shildrick, 2012; Smith & Bundon, 2018), these developments include the influence of disciplines previously on the outskirts of disability studies entering the field (e.g., affect studies); the incorporation of sophisticated social theories to make sense of complex social phenomenon (e.g., austerity, technology, inequality, globalisation, capitalism); a move to view disability as possibility and affirmative (i.e., "cripping" disability); an examination of resistance and agency; a move away from the preoccupation with binary explanations (e.g., disability/impairment and individual/society); a desire for more complex conceptual understandings of disability oppression (e.g., the social relational model); a move to challenge disablism (i.e., the social, political, cultural, and psycho-emotional exclusion of people with impairments) and ableism (i.e., the contemporary "normative" ideals on which the able, healthy, autonomous, productive citizen is based); a desire to theorize the material realities of disability (e.g., biological impairment); and, the merging of Marxist accounts with those from feminism, queer, post-colonial, critical men's health, discourse or narrative studies.

Connecting with CDS also involves respecting the building blocks of disability studies (e.g., the social model of disability); considering the impact of global, national, and local economic contexts on the lives of disabled people; adopting a position of cultural relativism; remaining attuned to the relational qualities of disability (e.g., impairment in relative cultural context); understanding that any analysis of disability should not preclude consideration of other forms of political activism; promoting praxis (i.e., the intertwining of activism and theory); conceptualizing the impaired body as simultaneously cultural, social, biological, fluid, lived, and could be lived; challenging the dogmatic tendencies of some theories and theorists through reference to an eclectic mix of theories; producing new ways that can inform activism and are informed by activism for the purposes of undoing some of the historic damage done to disabled people; throwing the spotlight on the community as the place to address issues of social change and well-being (Goodley, 2016; Meekosha & Shuttleworth, 2009; Smith & Bundon, 2018). Another way to understand what CDS are is to consider what CDS are not. As described by Goodley (2016), connecting with CDS is not a futile exercise that simply adds the word "critical" to disability studies to suggest that all previous examples of disability studies have not been critical; just another approach to sit alongside the traditional individual and social models of disability; a preoccupation with culture, power and structure; a simple study of disability and ability; an academic exercise without political commitment; or a movement away from an emancipatory focus around disability.

One way to frame CDS is by considering some emerging perspectives and analytical themes. Goodley (2016) highlights four emerging perspectives of activism and scholarship. Crip studies scholarship, for example, adopts a subversive position, rejects the view of disability as deficiency, and replaces it as a place of becoming, an affirmative account of being, or a celebratory moment of body politics. Critical studies of ableism (see Campbell, 2008) turns the gaze back to non-disabled people and shines a light on an underpinning prejudice resulting from a societal bias in favor of those who possess certain abilities over those who are believed not to. Global South disability studies remind us that disabled people in the Global South are often excluded from Global North discourses and discussions of disability and that, for example, localized knowledge (e.g., useful indigenous knowledge that can address disablism) are often ignored in favor of interventions devised in the Global North. Dis/ability studies (see Goodley & Runswick-Cole, 2014) captures the ways in which the politics of disability simultaneously disrupts (dis) and desires the norm (ability). This ambiguity recognizes the crip potential of disability to challenge disablism while also acknowledging the inevitable presence of ability and ableism.

Goodley (2016) also suggests three analytical themes that might shape the future of theory and research. First, engagement with CDS allows us to ask questions about how we might understand the human. For example, as we enter an increasingly technological and postmodern landscape, certain (disability) experiences can shift from undesired towards having a "futuristic desire". Second, CDS questions the idea that bodies are biological. For instance, in what ways and when do disabled bodies rearticulate as "bodies that matter" (e.g., developing new positive identities after acquired impairment). Third, CDS allows us to question the differential workings of biopower (i.e., the co-construction of disability and ability, disablism and ableism, and illness and heath through a host of biopolitical discourses, techniques, professions, and institutions).

Although holding many benefits, such as seeking to theorize in diverse ways and challenge marginalization in the name of disablism, viewing disability not necessarily a tragedy but as affirmative, and asking what bodies can do rather than what a body is, few APE researchers have connected explicitly with this way of thinking. However, the contributing authors for a recent special edition of *Adapted Physical Activity Quarterly* focused on themes of interdisciplinary, and provide some examples of how CDS can be applied to APE work (see Goodwin & Causgrove Dunn, 2018). Peer's (2018) work, for example, connects with CDS to argue for the value of axiological reflection within fields such as APE. She shows how "interdisciplinary conversations" with fields such as queer studies can illuminate axiological assumptions (e.g., underlying often unquestioned values) in fields like APE that undermine transdisciplinary research (researching involving stakeholders from outside the academy). For example, the axiological assumption that disability is inherently something bad (an assumption resulting from APE's post positivist parent disciplines such as exercise physiology) rather than affirmative (influenced by connecting disability with queer studies) can influence whether strategies to fund research and adapted physical activity programs involve pitying, charitable giving, and inspirational overcoming rather than opportunity, rights, inclusion, and social justice.

Another recent example published in an APE outlet that connects with CDS can be found in Goodley (2018). He argues that working across disciplinary boundaries can help fields such as APE embrace the complex and often contradictory ways that disability labels (categories) work. He draws on three perspectives—the biopsychological, the biopolitical, and what he terms an in-between-all politics—to theorize about labeling, disability, and the human condition. For example, he draws on feminist and postcolonial theory to call for the usefulness of frictional politics (to simultaneously desire and reject labels). This "in-between-all" space can allow APE educators, researchers, and practitioners to move from questions about disability to questions about humanity; for instance—"in what ways might we learn again about our common humanity through the politics of disability?"

Furthermore, the work of Connolly and Harvey (2018) on preparing future practitioners/teachers in APE connects to CDS by advocating for an "eclectic and interdisciplinary disposition to theories of teaching and learning and adapted physical activity program delivery" (p. 295). These scholars demonstrate how blending knowledge from critical pedagogy (e.g., phenomenology and disability activist-oriented scholarship) and adapted physical activity (e.g., social and natural sciences) can help nurture the pedagogic sensibilities of APE student educators who will work with complex profile individuals in service-learning contexts. For example, Connolly and Harvey highlight that educators in training report experiencing a profound dissonance between their perceived competence and the demands of the placement context. They go on to suggest that integrating knowledge through interdisciplinary work (e.g., in course design, assessment, and evaluation) and connecting with CDS can help address this dissonance. Work by Szostak (2016) and Szostak (2018) also demonstrates the ways that connecting with CDS can add value to APE. They highlight how diverse thinking through interdisciplinary work can enhance research collaborations in a variety of ways, and reduce the perceived need for scholars to adhere to their disciplines particular ontologies, epistemologies, or theories. For example, disciplines can collaborate conceptually (e.g., conceptual resonances or complementarities), critically (tackle a problem or an analysis that involves multiple perspectives on a phenomenon), or instrumentally (develop strategic alliances based on shared goals) (Szostak, 2018).

It might also be said that other APE scholarship connects with CDS themes even though they do not mention critical disability studies. For example, Haycock and Smith (2011) investigate ableism, inclusion, and exclusion in APE. They suggest that including disabled children in mainstream education reduced, rather than enhanced, opportunities offered by the special school sector, due to an emphasis given competitive team sports that retain a strong emphasis on performance, excellence and skills. Sparkes, Martos, and Maher's (2017) work, motivated by a desire to develop a socially just world, drew on various forms of critical pedagogy. Their critical approach challenged how knowledge is constructed and used in APE by, for example, suggesting ways that physical education teacher education (PETE) programmes can be developed to help practitioners to become more inclusive.

Haegele, Yessick, and Zhu (2018) connected with CDS when they explored the intersections between disability and gender among females with visual impairments in APE.

CDS are clearly and necessarily eclectic, and this eclecticism could be considered a limitation. But what brings CDS scholars together, say Meekosha and Shuttleworth (2009), is an agreement that addressing the continuing marginalization, undervaluing, and discrimination of disabled people requires diverse theoretical lenses as these cannot be addressed simply through liberal or neo-liberal policy and legislation. Therefore, we contend that connecting with CDS can contribute to important empirical, conceptual, and theoretical developments that will help APE scholars explain and understand disability.

Summary of key points

- There are an increasing variety of viewpoints towards disability, with no consensus on a way forward.
- Using conceptual models to explain and understand disability has been a popular approach within disability studies.
- A medical–individual model viewpoint remains the dominant way that disability is understood in many parts of academia, as well as in society at large.
- The discipline of psychology has contributed towards the individualization of disability.
- The medical–individual tradition paints a negative picture of disability.
- The UK social model of disability emerged from disability activism as a direct riposte to the medical–individual tradition.
- There are various forms of social models, such as the North American social model, the Nordic relative model, and the affirmative model.
- The UK social model of disability has made a significant contribution to improving the lives of disabled people. However, it is a weak explanation of disability.
- There are many critiques of UK social model. However, these are rarely mentioned by APE scholars.
- The social relational model is a conceptually progressive way to view disability because it accounts for the limitations of the medical and social models and expands how we understand impairment and disablism. For these reasons, it is also a useful analytical device for researchers.
- Carol Thomas's concept of *impairment effects* has been hugely popular in disability studies because it allows researchers to attend to impairment without reverting to the essentialist understandings of the medical model.
- Scholars should be aware of the various international rights conventions and charters that can be drawn upon to advocate for the development of APE.
- The human rights viewpoint towards disability is useful for tracking social change over time, particularly from an international perceptive.
- There are various ways, beyond a models approach, to view disability, such as by drawing on phenomenology and narrative enquiry.
- Critical disability studies (CDS) have become the emerging landscape to think about disability in this century.
- Critical disability studies may start with disability but never end with it. CDS have become an exciting viewpoint to ask questions about life itself.

Reflective questions

1. The medical model underpins the majority of APE research. However, this viewpoint is rarely explicitly mentioned in research papers. Why is this the case?
2. Why is it important for APE scholars to explicitly state their viewpoints toward disability?
3. Is the UK social model "a poor explanation of disability"? Discuss.
4. Why is the social relational model of disability a useful analytical device, and what might be some of the weaknesses of this model?
5. Is "critical disability studies a progressive way to view disability"? Discuss.

References

Aggerholm, K., & Moltke Martiny, K. M. (2017). Yes we can! A phenomenological study of a sports camp for young people with cerebral palsy. *Adapted Physical Activity Quarterly*, *34*(4), 362–381. doi:10.1123/apaq.2015-0135

Beacom, A., & Golder, G. (2015). Developing disability sport: The case for a critical pedagogy. *Journal of Sport for Development*, *3*(5), 71–88.

Bredahl, A.-M. (2013). Sitting and watching the others being active: The experienced difficulties in pe when having a disability. *Adapted Physical Activity Quarterly*, *30*(1), 40–58. doi:10.1123/apaq.30.1.40

Brittain, I., & Wolff, E. (2015). Disability sport: Changing lives, changing perspectives. *Journal of Sport for Development*, *3*(5), 1–3.

Cameron, C. (2014). Developing an affirmative model of disability and impairment. In J. Swain, C. Barnes, & C. Thomas (Eds.), *Disabling barriers – Enabling environments* (3rd ed.), (pp. 22–28). London, UK: Sage.

Campbell, F. A. K. (2008). Exploring internalized ableism using critical race theory. *Disability & Society*, *23*(2), 151–162. doi:10.1080/09687590701841190

Cervantes, C. M., & Porretta, D. L. (2013). Impact of after school programming on physical activity among adolescents with visual impairments. *Adapted Physical Activity Quarterly*, *29*(2), 127–146. doi:10.1123/apaq.30.2.127

Connolly, M., & Harvey, W. J. (2018). Critical pedagogy and apa: A resonant (and timely) interdisciplinary blend. *Adapted Physical Activity Quartler*, *35*(3), 293–307. doi:10.1123/apaq.2017-0106

Devine, A., Carrol, A., Naivalu, S., Seru, S., Baker, S., Bayak-Bush, B., … Marella, M. (2017). 'They don't see my disability anymore' – The outcomes of sport for development programmes in the lives of people in the Pacific. *Journal of Sport for Development*, *5*(8), 4–18.

Fitzgerald, H., & Stride, A. (2012). Stories about physical education from young people with disabilities. *International Journal of Disability, Development and Education*, *59*(3), 283–293. doi:10.1080/1034912x.2012.697743

Goodley, D. (2013). Dis/entangling critical disability studies. *Disability & Society*, *28*(5), 631–644. doi:10.1080/09687599.2012.717884

Goodley, D. (2016). *Disability studies: An interdisciplinary introduction*. London: Sage.

Goodley, D. (2018). Understanding disability: Biopsychology, biopolitics, and an in-between-all politics. *Adapted Physical Activity Quarterly*, *35*(3), 308–319. doi:10.1123/apaq.2017-0092

Goodley, D., Liddiard, K., & Runswick-Cole, K. (2017). Feeling disability: Theories of affect and critical disability studies. *Disability & Society*, *33*(2), 197–217. doi:10.1080/09687599.2017.1402752

Goodley, D., & Runswick-Cole, K. (2014). Becoming dishuman: Thinking about the human through dis/ability. *Discourse: Studies in the Cultural Politics of Education*, *37*(1), 1–15. doi:10.1080/01596306.2014.930021

Goodwin, D. L., & Causgrove Dunn, J. (2018). Revisiting our research assumptions 20 years on: The role of interdisciplinarity. *Adapted Physical Activity Quarterly*, *35*(3), 249–253. doi:10.1123/apaq.2017-0192

Grenier, M. (2007). Inclusion in physical education: From the medical model to social constructionism. *Quest*, *59*(3), 298–310. doi:10.1080/00336297.2007.10483554

Grenier, M., Collins, K., Wright, S., & Kearns, C. (2014). Perceptions of a disability sport unit in general physical education. *Adapted Physical Activity Quarterly*, *31*(1), 49–66. doi:10.1123/apaq.2013-0006

Haegele, J. A., Healy, S., & Zhu, X. (2018). Physical activity and obesity among nine-year-old children with and without chronic health problems, illness, or disabilities in Ireland. *Disability & Health Journal*, *11*(1), 143–148. doi:10.1016/j.dhjo.2017.08.002

Haegele, J. A., & Hodge, S. (2016). Disability discourse: Overview and critiques of the medical and social models. *Quest*, *68*(2), 193–206. doi:10.1080/00336297.2016.1143849

Haegele, J. A., & Porretta, D. (2015). Physical activity and school-age individuals with visual impairments: A literature review. *Adapted Physical Activity Quarterly*, *32*(1), 68–82. doi:10.1123/apaq.2013-0110

Haegele, J. A., Yessick, A., & Zhu, X. (2018). Females with visual impairments in physical education: Exploring the intersection between disability and gender identities. *Research Quartely for Exercise and Sport*, *89*(3), 298–308. doi:10.1080/02701367.2018.1484067

Haycock, D., & Smith, A. (2011). Still 'more of the same for the more able?' Including young disabled people and pupils with special educational needs in extra-curricular physical education. *Sport, Education and Society*, *16*(4), 507–526. doi:10.1080/13573322.2011.589647

Jespersen, E., & McNamee, M. (2008). Philosophy, adapted physical activity and dis/ability. *Sport, Ethics and Philosophy*, *2*(2), 87–96. doi:10.1080/17511320802267672

Martin, J. J. (2013). Benefits and barriers to physical activity for individuals with disabilities: A social-relational model of disability perspective. *Disability and Rehabilitation*, *35*(24), 2030–2037. doi:10.3109/09638288.2013.802377

Meekosha, H., & Shuttleworth, R. (2009). What's so 'critical' about critical disability studies?. *Australian Journal of Human Rights*, *15*(1), 47–75. doi:10.1080/1323238x.2009.11910861

Owens, J. (2015). Exploring the critiques of the social model of disability: The transformative possibility of Arendt's notion of power. *Sociology of Health & Illness*, *37*(3), 385–403. doi:http://dx.doi.org/10.1111/1467-9566.12199

Peers, D. (2018). Engaging axiology: Enabling meaningful transdisciplinary collaboration in adapted physical activity. *Adapted Physical Activity Quarterly*, *35*(3), 267–284. doi:10.1123/apaq.2017-0095

Reeve, D. (2014). Psycho-emotional disablism and internalised oppression. In J. Swain, C. Barnes, & C. Thomas (Eds.), *Disabling barriers – Enabling environments* (3rd ed., pp. 90–96). London, UK: Sage.

Reindal, S. M. (2008). A social relational model of disability: A theoretical framework for special needs education?. *European Journal of Special Needs Education*, *23*(2), 135–146. doi:10.1080/08856250801947812

Richardson, E. V., Smith, B., & Papathomas, A. (2017). Collective stories of exercise: Making sense of gym experiences with disabled peers. *Adapted Physical Activity Quarterly*, *34*(3), 276–294. doi:10.1123/apaq.2016-0126

Shakespeare, T., & Watson, N. (2001). The social model of disability: An outdated ideology? *Exploring Theories and Expanding Methodologies: Where we are and where we need to go*. Series: Research in social science and disability (2) (pp. 9–28). Amsterdam and New York: JAI.

Shakespeare, T., & Watson, N. (2010). Beyond models: Understanding the complexity of disabled people's lives. In G. Scambler & S. Scambler (Eds.), *New directions in the sociology of chronic and disabling conditions: assaults on the lifeworld* (pp. 57–76). Basingstoke: Palgrave Macmillan.

Shildrick, M. (2012). Critical disability studies: Rethinking the conventions for the age of postmodernity. In N. Watson, A. Roulstone, & C. Thomas (Eds.), *Routledge handbook to disability studies* (pp. 30–41). London: Routledge.

Simpson, J., McMillan, H., & Reeve, D. (2013). Reformulating psychological difficulties in people with Parkinson's disease: The potential of a social relational approach to disablism. *Parkinsons Disease, 2013*, 1–8. Article ID 608562, doi:10.1155/2013/608562

Smith, B. (2013). Disability sport and mens narratives of health a qualitative study. *Health Psychology*, *32*(1), 110–119. doi:10.1037/a0029187

Smith, B., & Bundon, A. (2018). Disability models: Explaining and understanding disability sport in different ways. In I. Brittain (Ed.), *The Palgrave handbook of paralympic studies* (pp. 15–34). London: Palgrave Macmillan.

Smith, B., & Caddick, N. (2015). The impact of living in a care home on the health and wellbeing of spinal cord injured people. *International Journal of Environmental Research and Public Health*, *12*(4), 4185–4202. doi:10.3390/ijerph120404185

Smith, B., & Perrier, M.-J. (2014). Disability, sport, and impaired bodies: A critical approach. In R. J. Schinke & K. R. McGannon (Eds.), *The psychology of sub-culture in sport and physical activity: Critical perspectives* (pp. 107–118). London: Routledge.

Smith, B., Perrier, M.-J., & Martin, J. J. (2016). Disability sport: A partial overview and some thoughts about the future. In R. Schinke, K. R. McGannon, & B. Smith (Eds.), *Routledge international handbook of sport psychology* (pp. 296–303). London: Routledge.

Sparkes, A. C., Martos, D., & Maher, A. J. (2017). Me, osteogenesis imperfecta, and my classmates in physical education lessons: A case study of embodied pedagogy in action. *Sport, Education and Society*, 1–11. doi:10.1080/13573322.2017.1392939

Svendby, E. B. (2016). (Re)Telling lived experiences in different tales: A potential pathway in working towards an inclusive PE. *Sport Education and Society*, *21*(1), 62–81. doi:10.1080/ 13573322.2015.1113166

Svendby, E. B., & Dowling, F. (2013). Negotiating the discursive spaces of inclusive education: Narratives of experience from contemporary physical education. *Scandinavian Journal of Disability Research*, *15*(4), 361–378. doi:10.1080/15017419.2012.735200

Swain, J., & French, S. (2000). Towards an affirmation model of disability. *Disability & Society*, *15*(4), 569–582. doi:10.1080/09687590050058189

Szostak, R. (2016). Interdisciplinary best practices for adapted physical activity. *Quest*, *68*(1), 69–90. doi:10.1080/00336297.2015.1117001

Szostak, R. (2018). Interdisciplinarity and adapted physical activity. *Adapted Physical Activity Quarterly*, *35* (3), 254–266. doi:10.1123/apaq.2017-0079

Thomas, C. (1999). *Female forms: Experiencing and understanding disability*. London: McGraw-Hill Education (UK).

Thomas, C. (2004a). How is disability understood? An examination of sociological approaches. *Disability & Society*, *19*(6), 569–583. doi:10.1080/0968759042000252506

Thomas, C. (2004b). Rescuing a social relational understanding of disability. *Scandinavian Journal of Disability Research*, *6*(1), 22–36.

Thomas, C. (2007). *Sociologies of disability and illness: Contested ideas in disability studies and medical sociology*. London: Palgrave Macmillan.

Thomas, C. (2012). Theorising disability and chronic illness: Where next for perspectives in medical sociology?. *Social Theory & Health*, *10*(3), 209–228. doi:10.1057/sth.2012.7

Thomas, C. (2014). Disability and impairment. In J. Swain, C. Barnes, & C. Thomas (Eds.), *Disabling barriers – Enabling environments* (3rd ed.) (pp. 9–16). London, UK: Sage.

Townsend, R., Cushion, C. J., & Smith, B. (2017). A social relational analysis of an impairment-specific mode of disability coach education. *Qualitative Research in Sport, Exercise and Health*, *10*(3), 346–361. doi:10.1080/2159676x.2017.1407355

UNESCO. (2015). Revised international charter of physical education, physical activity and sport. Retrieved from http://unesdoc.unesco.org/images/0023/002323/232325e.pdf

UNESCO. (2017). Kazan action plan. Retrieved from https://en.unesco.org/mineps6/kazan-action-plan

United Nations. (2006). Convention on the rights of persons with disabilities. Retrieved from www.un. org/development/desa/disabilities/convention-on-the-rights-of-persons-with-disabilities.html

United Nations. (2015). Transforming our world: The 2030 agenda for sustainable development. Retrieved from https://sustainabledevelopment.un.org/post2015/transformingourworld

Winnick, J., & Porretta, D. (2016). *Adapted physical education and sport* (6th ed.). Champaign, IL: Human Kinetics.

World Health Organization. (2001). *International classification of functioning*. Retrieved from www.who.int/ classifications/icf/en/

4

Historical context and definition of inclusion

Iva Obrusnikova and Martin E. Block

Introduction

The right of all children to education is noted in numerous international treaties and texts, and has been affirmed by both legally binding and non-binding instruments (UNESCO, 2017). This commitment arose in the context of the UNESCO World Conference on Education for All held in Jomtien, Thailand, in 1990 (Inter-Agency Commission, 1990). By educating all children together, persons with disabilities have the opportunity to prepare for life in the community, teachers have the opportunity to improve their professional skills, and society makes the conscious decision to operate according to the social value of equity for all people, with the consequent results of enhanced social peace (Karagiannis, Stainback, & Stainback, 1996). However, including all learners and ensuring that all individuals have equitable and personalized opportunity for educational progress is still a challenge in almost every country (UNESCO, 2017). Despite commendable progress made over the past three decades to expand access to basic education, including physical education, for children with disabilities, further efforts are needed to minimize barriers to learning and ensure that all learners in schools and other learning settings experience a genuine inclusive environment. Prior to defining inclusion and exploring the current status of inclusive practices in general physical education (GPE), it is essential to understand the history of inclusion in general, and then provide an example of inclusive practices employed in the United States (US).

The role of special education in the early years

Inclusion has grown out of a long history of how individuals with disabilities are viewed. The biggest hurdle for children with disabilities in the first part of the 20th century worldwide was simply to receive any special education (David, 1970; Odom, 1976). During the 1950s, more and more children with mild disabilities were placed in general education classes but often without any special support. As long as they kept up with the other students in the class and did not cause any problems, the teacher and their classmates accepted them. There were no special services and no trained specialists to help children with disabilities or the general education teacher (Lewis & Doorlag, 2011; US Department of Education, 2010). If a child was falling behind, causing problems, or was perceived as having disabilities that were too severe for the child to benefit from education, then the child was simply sent home or to an institution and excluded from the public schools (Beirne-Smith, Patton, & Hill, 2011; Sigmon, 1983). The one exception was special schools for children who were deaf or blind. If students continued to be educated in a general education setting but struggled to participate in physical education classes, they were placed in remedial or corrective classes that primarily focused on health, posture, or fitness problems (Sherrill, 2004).

The humanistic philosophy and civil rights movement around the world brought concerns about social justice (Sherrill, 2004; United Nations, 1948; United; States, 1969). Consequently, much debate and research has focused on the prevention of disabilities and deinstitutionalization from education, habilitation, and rehabilitation programs into communities (e.g., public schools, foster homes, group homes) (Clarke, 1991; Geddes & Summerfield, 1977; Tizard, 1971). With the help of parents of children with disabilities, public schools started to develop special schools and special classes based on the reasoning that children with disabilities needed a highly structured, very intense, and unique teaching environment conducted by a trained specialist (Lewis & Doorlag, 2011; Rodriguez & Garro-Gil, 2015). In the US, these parents formed groups such as the Association for Retarded Citizens (now known as The Arc) to advocate for more educational opportunities for their children (Karagiannis et al., 1996). While the integration of children with disabilities in general education was growing, guidelines on how to integrate children with disabilities (particularly those with intellectual and severe disabilities) in general physical education (GPE) classes were needed. The limited number of studies focusing on integration in GPE show that it was feasible and desirable if such programming was approached with positive attitudes and knowledge on the part of related personnel and if appropriate, flexible program planning and activity modifications were made when necessary (Auxter, 1970; Christensen, 1970; Forman, 1969; Johansen, 1971). However, very little information was published concerning attitudes of children and school personnel toward integration in GPE (Buell, 1972; Seaman, 1970). The creation of Special Olympics in 1968 helped increase physical educators' knowledge and awareness of the needs and capabilities of persons with intellectual disabilities by developing instructional materials such as the one published by Stein & Klappholz (1972). The manual consisted of activities, methods, teaching/coaching hints, drills, devices, and sequenced progressions appropriate for athletes of all ages and at all performance levels in different sports.

The number of students educated in special education classes was on the rise between the 1950s and 1970s, particularly in the US. However, there were a number of reasons why many special education leaders, including adapted physical educators (Auxter, 1970; Buell, 1972; Dewey, 1972; Seaman, 1970; Travena, 1970), began to advocate for the rights of students with disabilities to receive education in general environments alongside their peers without disabilities. First, reports to Congress and the American Alliance for Health, Physical Education, and Recreation guide (Geddes & Summerfield, 1977) in the early 1970s suggested that labeling and separating children with disabilities from their peers without disabilities led to stigma, ridicule, and poor self-image (Geddes & Summerfield, 1977; Kraft, 1972; Lewis & Doorlag, 2011; Odom, 1976). Kraft (1972) stated, "society is not served and neither is the child by labeling a child with a tag which does not enhance his learning" (p. 7). Odom (1976) further argued that it is not surprising that children with disabilities struggle emotionally and behaviorally and underperform academically if a school sees them as an educational challenge and sends them to a class that is out of the child's neighborhood.

Second, without any laws governing education of children with disabilities, these children were placed in special programs without first determining whether they could benefit from general education placement (Seaman, 1970; Stainback, Stainback, & Bunch, 1989a). There was no effort to determine if individually prescribed curricular and instructional adaptations could occur within GPE classes even though evidence started to grow that many children with disabilities were able to successfully participate at least in some of the activities of the general class (Brace, 1966; Seaman, 1970; Stainback, Stainback, & Bunch, 1989b; Stein, 1966). Third, following the United States Supreme Court's ruling in the *Brown v. Board of Education* (1954) school desegregation case, there was evidence suggesting that separate but equal self-contained classrooms tended to be unequal (Karagiannis et al., 1996; Seaman, 1970; Stainback et al., 1989b; Taylor, 1988). Special class placement in the 1960s and early 1970s often meant having the "worst" teacher, the most inferior facilities, limited educational materials, and exclusion from assemblies and other school-wide activities (Lewis & Doorlag, 2011). Fourth, there was a growing concern over the terminal aspects of special education (Turnbull, Turnbull, Stowe, & Wilcox, 2000). When children with disabilities were placed in separate special education programs, many of them would spend the rest of their education in these separate programs (Odom, 1976; Taylor, 1988). It was common to see students with disabilities being placed in special classes without any opportunity to move out of these classes. As noted by Turnbull et al. (2000), the dual system of education prior to 1975 specifically in the US had a variety of effects, one of which was the denial of educational opportunities for children with disabilities.

Education in the least restrictive environment

In the United States, the activism of the 1960s and early 1970s on behalf of children with disabilities culminated in the US Congress passing a landmark law, the *Education for All Handicapped Children Act of 1975* (Public Law 94–142). This law was reauthorized as the *Individuals with Disabilities Education Act of 1990* (IDEA, 1990) and later as *the Individuals with Disabilities Education Improvement Act of 2004* (IDEA, 2004). It mandates that schools that receive federal funding provide a free and appropriate education for all students with disabilities and that they be placed in the least restrictive environment (LRE) (US Department of Education, 2010). According to the law, physical education is recognized as a direct service that should be afforded to all students with disabilities. To ensure that these students receive education that is appropriate to their specific needs, it requires school districts to provide students with disabilities with individualized education programs (IEP) and supplementary aids and services. The LRE refers to the concept that students with disabilities have the right to be educated in general education settings, including GPE settings, unless "the nature or severity of the disability is such that education in regular classes with the use of supplementary aids and services cannot be achieved satisfactorily" (IDEA, 20 U.S.C. § 1412 [5][B], 2004). Applying this to physical education, segregation of adapted physical education (APE) classes from GPE is not prohibited under the law. However, school districts are required to provide evidence and justify that a child with a disability placed in a separate setting cannot be satisfactorily educated within the GPE setting, even after making provisions for supplementary aids and services (such as a paraprofessional, adapted equipment, and modified instruction). Additional changes to the IDEA regulations were made in 2006 that require schools to use scientific, research-based interventions in the process of identifying children with specific learning disabilities, or determining their eligibility for special education.

The principle of the LRE was extremely forward-looking for its time. It emerged in an era in which the vast majority of children with disabilities, especially those with more severe disabilities, were offered segregation or nothing at all (Brace, 1966; Taylor, 1988). Once Public Law 94–142 opened school doors for students with disabilities in 1977, clinical teams started to evaluate, label, and determine, with parental input, the most appropriate educational placement for each student (Connor & Ferri, 2007). The practice of simply placing students in separate programs based on a label or pre-placement evaluation was considered a violation of the intent of the law (Bateman & Chard, 1995; Maloney, 1994; Osborne, 1996). Lawmakers made a clear statement that, regardless of where children with a disability are placed or how severe their disability is, they must receive education (including physical education) that is appropriate and considers their individual abilities and needs (Taylor, 1988).

Soon after the implementation of this law, the courts faced a challenging task of interpreting and applying the LRE principle to a school system that had not yet developed a capacity or a willingness to integrate students with disabilities in general education settings (Turnbull et al., 2000). In some cases, the courts asked school systems to integrate students with a disability into an unprepared and often resistant general education program (Lavay & DePaepe, 1987) while in other cases, the courts ordered students with more severe disabilities to be placed into a special education program, in which the professional staff generally was able and willing to provide an appropriate education (Turnbull et al., 2000). In this process, even when children were educated in segregated programs, they still met the provision of receiving free appropriate public education in the LRE mandate under the Public Law 94–142. Given that parents and professionals did not speak with a unanimous voice regarding integrated placements, the courts more often than not chose the placement that offered the more appropriate education (Turnbull et al., 2000). As a legal concept and policy direction, the LRE principle helped create options and alternatives that continue to be part of IDEA 2004. However, it lacked specificity, which undoubtedly explains much of its appeal.

Mainstreaming and the regular education initiative

In the early years, the LRE principle was expressed in the US through the concept of mainstreaming. Mainstreaming emphasized the setting in which special education of children with disabilities took place (Gartner & Lipsky, 1987; Stainback & Stainback, 1984). The Council for Exceptional Children (CEC) (1975) officially defined mainstreaming as placing students with disabilities in the least restrictive setting based on their assessed educational needs rather than clinical labels. Additionally, CEC made it clear that students with disabilities must receive individually determined supplementary aids and services when mainstreamed. With CEC operationalizing LRE through the concept of mainstreaming, more students with disabilities were moved from special schools to special classes within general schools, and more efforts were made to mainstream children with disabilities into general education classes (including GPE) (Lavay & DePaepe, 1987; Sherrill, 2004).

Despite the CEC's efforts and clear call for support and accommodations, children with disabilities who were mainstreamed into general education classes (including GPE classes) were asked to follow the same curricular content, using the same materials and instruction, and following the same pace as the other students in the class. There were no regulations for administrators and educators to determine when children with disabilities should be placed in general education programs and how to support these children within those programs (Hocutt, Martin, & McKinney, 1991). Even special educators, who originally endorsed the concept, were worried about the integration of children with and without disabilities without full recognition of the barriers that they wanted to address first. Mainstreaming, including mainstreaming in GPE, became associated with unsuccessful "dumping" of students into general education classes with no support or accommodations (DePaepe, 1984; Grosse, 1991; Lavay & DePaepe, 1987). Unsurprisingly, many children with disabilities failed in such settings. The term mainstreaming was misused to the point that nowadays it is rarely used in special education literature.

Recognizing the failure of mainstreaming, in 1986, Madeleine Will (then Assistant Secretary for the Office of Special Education and Rehabilitative Services, US Department of Education) called for a regular education initiative (REI). In her article, "Educating students with learning problems: A shared responsibility," Will (1986) suggested merging special and general education into an integrated system and returning children with high incidence disabilities to the general education classroom, with appropriate support. Furthermore, Will proposed increased instructional time, empowerment of principals to control all programs and resources at the building level, provision of support systems for general education teachers, and the use of new approaches such as curriculum-based assessment, cooperative learning, and personalized curricula (Will, 1986). Following this article, many schools implemented REI as a method of meeting the new requirements set by IDEA. Proponents of REI encouraged the scaling back of traditional special education classrooms in favor of integration. Opponents of REI, however, found a number of flaws (Kauffman, 1995). First, the REI lacked support from constituencies. As an initiative of a small group of special educators, general educators did not take ownership of the REI agenda. Further, many other special educators did not believe the REI agenda was going to be effective (Singer, 1988). Second, it lacked specificity in the proposed restructuring. Even though it was supposed to provide details regarding critical aspects of how special and general education should be restructured and how and where services would be made available to students, the specifics were unclear to administrators and educators. Moreover, REI did not address students with more severe disabilities, and this exclusion, along with a growing body of research on successful education of students with severe disabilities in the general education setting, led to the subsequent call for a more broad-based inclusive philosophy (Chadsey-Rusch, 1990; Condon, York, Heal, & Fortschneider, 1986; Peck, Donaldson, & Pezzoli, 1990; York et al., 1992).

The shift from integration to inclusion

Integration was established as a goal for educational systems that had already developed a segregated school system for persons with disabilities (Haustätter & Jahnukainen, 2014). Similar to mainstreaming, the goal of integration was to restructure the educational system so that children with disabilities had the right to be educated in local schools (Vislie, 2003). The goal of integration highlighted the role of special education as part of the general educational system and it emphasized the rights of all children to receive sufficient educational support for further life. Inclusion is an outgrowth of the REI, or the integration model of the 1980s. The term reflects a philosophy in which all children, regardless of abilities or disabilities, are educated within the same environment, an environment where each child's individual needs are met (Causton, Theoharis, & Villa, 2014; Downing, 2008; Karagiannis et al., 1996). The philosophy of inclusion is perhaps best summed up by the following statement: "Although some children, especially those with severe and multiple disabilities, may have unique ways of learning, separating them from others who learn in a different way is unnecessary and could prevent them from achieving their full potential" (Downing, 2008, p. xii). An inclusion philosophy goes beyond simply physically placing a child in a general education classroom (Block, 1999; Bricker, 1995; Brown et al., 1989; Downing, 2008; Ferguson, 1995; Stainback & Stainback, 1990). As noted by Stainback and Stainback (1990), "An inclusive school is a place where everyone belongs, is accepted, supports, and is supported by his/her peers and other members of the school community in the course of having his/her educational needs met" (p. 3).

Embedded within this definition is the understanding that children with disabilities receive an individually determined, appropriate program with supplementary services and supports to meet their unique needs (Block, 1994; Stainback & Stainback, 1990). However, these services need to be provided to the child with a disability within the general education environment (Downing, 2008). In terms of physical education services, individually determined goals, objectives, and accommodations are provided within the GPE setting by an APE specialist, trained GPE specialist, trained para-professional, or trained peer tutor (Block, 1999). This notion of bringing services to the general education setting intends to provide continual opportunities for the child with a disability to interact with, learn from, and form friendships with peers while ensuring that the child receives an appropriate, individualized program (Downing, 2008; Stainback & Stainback, 1990).

Another critical tenet of the inclusion philosophy is that children with disabilities are the responsibility of both general and special education staff (Downing, 2008; Giangreco, 1997; Givner & Haager, 1995; Sailor, Gee, & Karasoff, 1993; Stainback & Stainback, 1990). Unlike traditional self-contained programs, in which the special education teacher (with the support of related services personnel) is solely responsible for a child's education, in inclusive programs it is the responsibility of all school personnel to make sure that each child's educational program is carried out appropriately (Downing, 2008; Sailor et al., 1993; Stainback & Stainback, 1990). In terms of physical education, the adapted physical educator serves as a consultant to the GPE teacher (Block & Conatser, 1999; Lytle & Collier, 2002) and, in some cases, even co-teaches with the GPE teacher when children with disabilities are included (Grenier, 2010). The inclusion philosophy suggests that only through the merger of resources, knowledge, and talents of general and special education (including GPE and APE) can both children with and without disabilities receive a comprehensive, appropriate education (Lipsky & Gartner, 1998; Sailor et al., 1993; Stainback & Stainback, 1990). Continual support and training for the general education teacher is certainly required to make such a merged system work. In addition, the use of various co-teaching arrangements (i.e., the general and special education teachers dividing and sharing class instruction) might be an effective way to facilitate inclusive programs (Lipsky & Gartner, 1998). For example, Block and Zeman (1996) and Grenier (2010) noted the effectiveness of having an APE specialist work with students with and without disabilities and co-teach various aspects of the GPE lesson.

Providing services within general education does not necessarily mean that all services for a particular child would always take place within the general education setting (Block, 1994; Brown et al., 1989; Lipsky & Gartner, 1998; Sailor et al., 1993). For limited periods of time during the school day, a child with a disability (as well as any other child in the class) can receive specialized instruction using specialized equipment in specialized environments outside the general education classroom. For example, a high school student with severe intellectual disabilities may need extra time in the locker room with the support of a para-professional getting dressed to go back to class. This student may leave GPE ten minutes early so he can work on these functional dressing skills. However, this student is still perceived as a member of the GPE class (Block, 1994; Lipsky & Gartner, 1998).

Current status of inclusion in physical education

The increasing implementation of national standards, as a result of the *No Child Left Behind* of 2001 provisions (NCLB, 2001) and the increased emphasis on exam performance in the

US has made a commitment to inclusive education in the public schools more challenging. By stipulating transparency and sanctions for schools that failed to close the achievement gap in core academic subjects (e.g., math and reading), NCLB intended to measure whether IDEA was being put into action and students with disabilities were getting access to mainstream curricula and the tools they needed to be successful. Since physical education is not "a core academic subject," school districts started to cut back on physical education and recess time under the mistaken belief that more time needs to be spent in activities that help raise test scores in core academic subjects (Cook & Kohl, 2013; Winter, 2009; Zhu, Boiarskaia, Welk, & Meredith, 2010). This is problematic, considering the accumulating evidence of children with disabilities not engaging in sufficient amounts of physical activity (e.g., Causgrove Dunn & Dunn, 2006; Pan, Tsai, Chu, & Hsieh, 2011).

Based on concerns from national advocacy organizations, the US Government Accounting Office (GAO) was asked in 2010 to examine what is known about physical education and extracurricular athletic opportunities that schools provide and how the US Department of Education assists states and schools in these areas (GAO, 2010). The GAO reviewed federal survey data and relevant federal laws and regulations, as well as conducted interviews with state, district, and school or disability association officials and parents. The GAO reported that schools provided students with and without disabilities with similar opportunities to participate in physical education, but serving students with disabilities was found to be challenging. Many school officials cited limited teacher preparation and budget constraints as key challenges to appropriately serving students with disabilities in GPE. For example, many suggested GPE teachers needed more training opportunities to be better prepared to serve students with disabilities, yet resources for training were not always available.

On December 10, 2015, President Obama signed the *Every Student Succeeds Act* (ESSA) (Public Law 114–95) legislation to rewrite the *Elementary and Secondary Education Act* and replace the NCLB. ESSA provides support to high schools where one-third or more of students do not graduate. It also provides support to schools with groups of traditionally underserved students who consistently demonstrate low performance. The law requires data on student achievement and graduation rates to be reported as well as action in response to those data. Unlike NCLB, states, districts, and schools have the autonomy to determine what support and interventions are implemented particularly for their lowest-performing schools. ESSA requires states to publicly report assessment results and disaggregate them by race, socio-economic, disability, and English language status. It also emphasizes well-rounded education. Much like other content areas (e.g., mathematics, science, or civics), physical education should also be part of the educational experience for all students, rather than being considered an optional subject or one that is eliminated due to budgetary challenges (Turner, Johnson, Calvert, & Chaloupka, 2017). ESSA aims to provide states with greater flexibility to, for example, revise their own accountability systems to empower educators and students to refocus on teaching and learning in the classroom. The decision of whether and how to measure teacher effectiveness is left completely to the states. Thus far, limited research data have been available about the effects of ESSA on nationwide allocation of resources to physical education programs in schools, or the impact of the allocation on the quality of physical education for children with disabilities.

Teachers' beliefs about inclusion in physical education

The GAO findings are consistent with a wealth of research studies conducted in GPE. In general, GPE teachers seem to have ambivalent to favorable attitudes and beliefs, and mostly express a willingness to work with students with disabilities in their GPE classes (Fitzgerald,

2005; Hersman & Hodge, 2010; Hodge, Ammah, Casebolt, Lamaster, & O'Sullivan, 2004; Obrusnikova, 2008). For example, Combs, Elliott, and Whipple (2010) interviewed two GPE teachers with favorable attitudes toward teaching children with mild to moderate disabilities in their classes and found that those teachers incorporated different teaching styles in their lesson plans, had received training in modifying and adapting physical education instruction or activities for students with disabilities, and desired their students to be successful in their classes. Those factors are consistent with the findings in other research studies (Fitzgerald, 2005; Haegele, Zhu, & Davis, 2018). Conversely, most GPE teachers do not perceive their professional preparation, clinical experiences, in-service training, support, and teaching conditions to be adequate to promote successful inclusion in GPE (Ammah & Hodge, 2005; Combs et al., 2010; Fejgin, Talmor, & Erlich, 2005; Hersman & Hodge, 2010; Jerlinder, Danermark, & Gill, 2010; Sato, Hodge, Murata, & Maeda, 2007; Vaz et al., 2015; Vickerman & Coates, 2009). For example, in the study by Hersman and Hodge (2010), GPE teachers called for more and better professional preparation (e.g., more courses on inclusive pedagogy and hands-on experiences teaching students with a wide range of disabilities) at the pre-service level. They also called for more and better professional development opportunities in their current school district to be better prepared to teach students with different disabilities in their GPE classes. Additionally, GPE teachers in Fejgin et al.'s (2005) study complained that they do not receive support and professional help from the other members of the instructional team, such as school counselors, special education teachers, and APE teachers. This situation is problematic, since many studies highlighted the importance of a collaborative approach when working with students with disabilities in GPE (Fejgin et al., 2005; Grenier, 2010; Umhoefer, Vargas, & Beyer, 2015).

Effective communication between GPE teachers and parents is essential to meet the needs of children with disabilities (An & Meaney, 2015; Chaapel, Columna, Lytle, & Bailey, 2013). Unfortunately, researchers have reported a lack of support and undeveloped partnership and communication between parents and physical education teachers (An & Meaney, 2015; Chaapel et al., 2013). Similarly, GPE high school teachers in Hersman & Hodge's (2010) study, while intrinsically motivated to teach students in their GPE classes, did not feel supported by the administration. This was largely attributed to the administration failing to inform the teachers about students with disabilities in their classes (Hersman & Hodge, 2010) and to various contextual issues such as lack of adequate equipment, limited instructional space, and large or overcrowded classes, particularly when working with students with emotional and behavioral disorders (e.g., Ammah & Hodge, 2005; Hersman & Hodge, 2010; Hodge et al., 2009; Sato et al., 2007; Vickerman & Coates, 2009). The contextual issues were perceived to negatively affect the teaching methods the teachers selected, the pace of the lessons, classroom safety, students' level of motivation to participate in activities, and the type of social interaction between students with and without disabilities (Fejgin et al., 2005; Hersman & Hodge, 2010; Suomi, Collier, & Brown, 2003).

Listening to the voices of students in general physical education

Students often internalize teacher attitudes and behaviors (Brillhart, Jay, & Wyers, 1990). Research with students with disabilities published over the past two decades has been mostly qualitative and focused on experiences rather than attitudes or beliefs. While a few researchers report that students with disabilities enjoyed GPE classes with their peers without disabilities (Coates & Vickerman, 2010; Lieberman, Robinson, & Rollheiser, 2006; Spencer-Cavaliere & Watkinson, 2010), most students with disabilities in the same or other qualitative studies expressed less positive experiences (Asbjørnslett & Hemmingsson, 2008; Bredahl, 2013; Fitzgerald, 2005; Fitzgerald & Stride, 2012; Goodwin & Watkinson, 2000; Haegele & Sutherland, 2015; Herold & Dandolo, 2009; Spencer-Cavaliere & Watkinson, 2010). The three common themes in these studies were: (a) feeling different, (b) lack of competence, and (c) not having friends.

If a student's physique, behavior, abilities, or skills do not match the norm or are not compatible with the styles, manners, and routines of the setting, the student will most likely struggle to be accepted and feel treated differently by their peers and even the teacher (Bredahl, 2013; Fitzgerald, 2005; Fitzgerald & Stride, 2012; Herold & Dandolo, 2009; Spencer-Cavaliere & Watkinson, 2010). For example, some students with disabilities voiced their struggles to execute a task or control movements or behaviors due to their disability, which made them feel more noticeable and different and consequently feel embarrassed, incompetent, and inadequate (Asbjørnslett & Hemmingsson, 2008; Bredahl, 2013; Fitzgerald, 2005; Fitzgerald & Stride, 2012; Spencer-Cavaliere & Watkinson, 2010). Such feelings were even more prevalent when peers without disabilities were frustrated with the challenges the students with disabilities faced (e.g., they would get angry when the student did not catch a ball) (Bredahl, 2013). The degree of perceived similarity (in interests and level of social, cognitive, or physical competence) emerged as a critical factor contributing to social relationships between students with and without disabilities in GPE (André, Deneuve, & Louvet, 2011; Kalymon, Gettinger, & Hanley-Maxwell, 2010; Obrusnikova, Block, & Dillon, 2010; Seymour, Reid, & Bloom, 2009). For example, middle-school-aged boys without disabilities who were interviewed in Kalymon et al.'s (2010) study did not view students with a mild disability as having a disability because "… they don't really show learning disabilities or anything like that. They're just like any other kid. I have better time hanging out with them than I would someone with, like, a severe disability" (p. 309). Those boys did not view peers with more severe disabilities as being capable of participating in similar physical activities and sports.

Sometimes even physical educators treated their students with disabilities differently (Bredahl, 2013; Fitzgerald, 2005; Fitzgerald & Stride, 2012; Herold & Dandolo, 2009; Spencer-Cavaliere & Watkinson, 2010). Some examples of preferential treatment as articulated by students with disabilities were being engaged in different types of activities (e.g., Boccia instead of soccer), being given exceptions during activities, or having different social roles or activity positions (e.g., being a spectator, a goalie, a score keeper). Even more problematic, GPE teachers did not always listen to the voices of their students with disabilities (Asbjørnslett & Hemmingsson, 2008; Bredahl, 2013; Fitzgerald, 2005). Students with disabilities complained during interviews that their teachers were either not willing or not knowledgeable enough to adjust the demands of the GPE curriculum to their needs. Most students with disabilities associated the unrealistic demands and the lack of adequate accommodation with their experiences of failing and embarrassment (Bredahl, 2013). Being pushed beyond their individual physical limitations was particularly noted among students with less visible or less comprehensive disabilities, such as being partially sighted or having a minor degree of cerebral palsy (Asbjørnslett & Hemmingsson, 2008; Bredahl, 2013).

To promote more desirable learning experiences in GPE for students with disabilities and ultimately increase their levels of physical activity, GPE teachers need to do a better job of assessing and learning about their students' needs and seek further education or training on how the GPE curriculum can be adequately adapted so that inclusion of students with disabilities in GPE is more successful. Relationships between students with and without disabilities will not be formed merely by grouping students together. The teacher needs to provide students without disabilities with knowledge about, and positive learning experiences with, their peers with a disability in and outside of GPE (Kalymon et al., 2010; Seymour et al., 2009). To facilitate positive learning experiences, the emphasis should be on creating relationships that are equal (i.e., helping one another), mutual (i.e., both sides have similar interest), and voluntary (i.e., peers are peers, not caretakers or teachers) (André et al., 2011; Kalymon et al., 2010; Obrusnikova et al., 2010; Seymour et al., 2009).

Summary

The LRE mandate within the *Education for All Handicapped Children Act* was enacted into law more than 40 years ago. LRE was the first national effort in the US to bring children with disabilities into general education schools, classrooms, and gymnasiums. As a result of LRE, more and more students with disabilities have had the opportunity to receive their education in the general education setting. Nevertheless, LRE and, more specifically, the continuum of support model, has been criticized for perpetuating and justifying segregated placements. This criticism lead to the philosophy of inclusion in which there is no continuum and all children receive their education in the general setting. While there has been research that does show children with disabilities can be successfully included in GPE (e.g., Klavina & Block, 2008; Obrusnikova, Valkova, & Block, 2003), other research shows that there are some chronic issues that ultimately affect the experience of students with disabilities (Bredahl, 2013; Fitzgerald, 2005; Fitzgerald & Stride, 2012; Herold & Dandolo, 2009; Spencer-Cavaliere & Watkinson, 2010).

Perhaps the most glaring problem is the lack of support and preparation of GPE teachers. Without a doubt, GPE teachers are perhaps the most critical element to the success of inclusion in GPE. If GPE teachers are not provided with sufficient parental and administrative support and resources to fulfill the demands, inclusion will not be effective and teachers will not always be in favor of having students with disabilities in their classes. Learning to be patient, taking time for professional training, gaining positive clinical experiences, and getting adequate support and teaching conditions are critical in facilitating a teacher's sense of behavioral control associated with teaching efficacy (Hersman & Hodge, 2010; Sato et al., 2007). Still, the research is clear that most GPE teachers, while agreeing that inclusion is ultimately the right thing to do (e.g., Block & Rizzo, 1995; Haegele & Hodge, 2017; Hersman & Hodge, 2010; Obrusnikova, 2008), do not feel adequately prepared for inclusion and do not feel confident in their ability to successfully include students with disabilities (e.g., Ammah & Hodge, 2005; Combs et al., 2010; Vickerman & Coates, 2009). Unfortunately, research shows that GPE teachers' lack of preparation and confidence can affect the experience of students both with and without disabilities (e.g., Asbjørnslett & Hemmingsson, 2008; Bredahl, 2013; Fitzgerald & Stride, 2012; Haegele & Hodge, 2017; Kalymon et al., 2010; Seymour et al., 2009).

Summary of key points

- Historically, people with disabilities were often placed in hospitals, asylums, or other institutions that provided little, if any, education.
- The important national and international education policy documents strongly emphasize equity and personalized opportunity for children with disabilities to achieve and maintain an acceptable level of learning.
- The least restrictive environment (LRE) principle helped create placement options and educational alternatives that continue to be part of IDEA 2004.
- Mainstreaming, including mainstreaming in GPE, became associated with unsuccessful "dumping" of students into general education classes with no support and accommodations.

- The goal of integration highlights the role of special education as part of the general educational system and it emphasizes the rights of all children to receive sufficient educational support.
- Inclusion reflects a philosophy in which all children, regardless of abilities or disabilities, are educated within the same environment, an environment where each child's individual needs are met. The inclusion philosophy suggested that only through the merger of resources, knowledge, and talents of general and special education (including GPE and APE) could children both with and without disabilities receive a comprehensive, appropriate education.
- Most GPE teachers do not perceive their professional preparation, clinical experiences, in-service training, support, and teaching conditions adequate to promote successful inclusion in GPE.
- Effective communication between GPE teachers and parents and minimal contextual barriers at the gym (e.g., adequate equipment and instructional space) are essential to meet the needs of children with disabilities.
- Most students with disabilities feel less favorable about being part of GPE classes due to three reasons: (a) feeling different, (b) lack of competence, and (c) not having friends.
- Relationships between students with and without disabilities will not be formed in GPE classes merely by grouping students together.
- Teachers need to do a better job of assessing and learning about their students' needs and seek further education or training on how the GPE curriculum can be adequately adapted so that inclusion of students with disabilities in GPE is more successful.
- If GPE teachers are not provided with sufficient parental and administrative support and resources to fulfill the demands, inclusion will not be effective and teachers will not always be in favor of having students with disabilities in their classes.
- All services and institutions involved with learners and their families need to work together in coordinating inclusive and equitable educational policies and practices.

Reflective questions

1. What is the difference between LRE and inclusion?
2. What prompted advocates to call for a shift from LRE to inclusion?
3. What are some the key tenants of inclusion that separate it from integration?
4. Why do you think research shows many students with disabilities have negative experiences when included in general physical education?
5. What can be done to change the pre-service physical education teacher training model to better prepare future physical educators for inclusion?
6. What teaching techniques/accommodations have been found effective when including students with disabilities in general physical education?

References

Ammah, J. O., & Hodge, S. R. (2005). Secondary physical education teachers' beliefs and practices in teaching students with severe disabilities: A descriptive analysis. *High School Journal*, *89*(2), 40–54.

An, J., & Meaney, K. S. (2015). Inclusion practices in elementary physical education: A social-cognitive perspective. *International Journal of Disability, Development and Education*, *62*(2), 143–157. doi:10.1080/1034912X.2014.998176

André, A., Deneuve, P., & Louvet, B. (2011). Cooperative learning in physical education and acceptance of students with learning disabilities. *Journal of Applied Sport Psychology*, *23*(4), 474–485. doi:10.1080/10413200.2011.580826

Asbjørnslett, M., & Hemmingsson, H. (2008). Participation at school as experienced by teenagers with physical disabilities. *Scandinavian Journal of Occupational Therapy*, *15*(3), 153–161. doi:10.1080/11038120802022045

Auxter, D. (1970). Programs for handicapped. *Journal of Health, Physical Education, Recreation*, *41*(7), 61–62. doi:10.1080/00221473.1970.10610636

Bateman, B. D., & Chard, D. J. (1995). Legal demands and constraints on placement decisions. In J. M. Kauffman, J. W. Lloyd, D. P. Hallahan, & T. A. Astuto (Eds.), *Issues in educational placement* (pp. 285–316). Mahwah, NJ: Lawrence Erlbaum Associates.

Beirne-Smith, M., Patton, J. R. & Hill, S. (2011). *An introduction to intellectual disabilities.* Upper Saddle River, NJ: Merrill.

Block, M. E. (1994). Why all students with disabilities should be included in regular physical education. *Palaestra*, *10*(3), 17–24.

Block, M. E. (1999). Did we jump on the wrong bandwagon? Problems with inclusion in physical education. *Palaestra*, *15*(3), 30–38.

Block, M. E., & Conatser, P. (1999). Consultation in adapted physical education. *Adapted Physical Activity Quarterly*, *16*, 9–26.

Block, M. E., & Rizzo, T. L. (1995). Attitudes and attributes of physical educators associated with teaching individuals with severe and profound disabilities. *Journal of the Association for Persons with Severe Handicaps*, *20*(1), 80–87. doi:10.1177/154079699502000108

Block, M. E., & Zeman, R. (1996). Including students with disabilities into regular physical education: Effects on nondisabled children. *Adapted Physical Activity Quarterly*, *13*, 38–49.

Brace, D. K. (1966). *Physical education and recreation for mentally retarded pupils in public schools.* Washington, D.C: American Alliance for Health, Physical Education, and Recreation.

Bredahl, A.-M. (2013). Sitting and watching the others being active: The experienced difficulties in PE when having a disability. *Adapted Physical Activity Quarterly*, *30*(1), 40–58. doi:10.1123/apaq.30.1.40

Bricker, D. (1995). The challenge of inclusion. *Journal of Early Intervention*, *19*, 179–194.

Brillhart, B. A., Jay, H., & Wyers, M. E. (1990). Attitudes toward people with disabilities. *Rehabilitation Nursing*, *15*(2), 80–85. doi:doi:10.1002/j.2048-7940.1990.tb01439.x

Brown, L., Long, E., Udvari-Solner, A., Schwarz, P., VanDeventer, P., Ahlgren, C., … Jorgensen, J. (1989). Should students with severe intellectual disabilities be based in regular or in special education classrooms in home schools? *Journal of the Association for Persons with Severe Handicaps*, *14*(1), 8–12. doi:10.1177/154079698901400102

Buell, C. (1972). How to include blind and partially seeing children in public secondary school vigorous physical education. *The Physical Educator*, *1*(29), 6–8.

Causgrove Dunn, J., & Dunn, J. H. (2006). Psychosocial determinants of physical education behavior in children with movement difficulties. *Adapted Physical Activity Quarterly*, *23*(3), 293–309.

Causton, J., Theoharis, G., & Villa, R. A. (2014). *The principal's handbook for leading inclusive schools* (1st ed.). Baltimore: Brookes Publishing.

Chaapel, H., Columna, L., Lytle, R., & Bailey, J. (2013). Parental expectations about adapted physical education services. *The Journal of Special Education*, *47*(3), 186–196. doi:10.1177/0022466912447661

Chadsey-Rusch, J. (1990). Social interactions of secondary-aged students with severe handicaps: Implications for facilitating the transition from school to work. *Journal of the Association for Persons with Severe Handicaps*, *15*, 69–78.

Christensen, D. (1970). Creativity in teaching physical education to the physically handicapped child. *Journal of Health, Physical Education, Recreation*, *41*(3), 73–74. doi:10.1080/00221473.1970.10619946

Clarke, A. D. B. (1991). A brief history of the International association for the scientific study of mental deficiency. *Journal of Mental Deficiency Research*, *35*, 1–12.

Coates, J., & Vickerman, P. (2010). Empowering children with special educational needs to speak up: Experiences of inclusive physical education. *Disability and Rehabilitation*, *32*(18), 1517–1526. doi:10.3109/09638288.2010.497037

Combs, C., Elliott, S., & Whipple, K. (2010). Elementary physical education teachers' attitudes towards the inclusion of children with special needs: A qualitative investigation. *International Journal of Special Education*, *25*(1), 114–125.

Condon, M. E., York, R., Heal, L. W., & Fortschneider, J. (1986). Acceptance of severely handicapped students by nonhandicapped peers. *Journal of the Association for Persons with Severe Handicaps, 11*, 216–219.

Connor, D. J., & Ferri, B. A. (2007). The conflict within: Resistance to inclusion and other paradoxes in special education. *Disability & Society, 22*(1), 63–77. doi:10.1080/09687590601056717

Cook, H. D., & Kohl, H. W. (2013). *Educating the student body: Taking physical activity and physical education to school.* Washington, DC: National Academies Press.

Council for Exceptional Children. (1975). What is mainstreaming? *Exceptional Children, 42*, 174.

David, H. P. (1970). Mental health and social action programs for children and youth in international perspective. *Mental Hygiene, 54*(4), 503–509.

DePaepe, J. L. (1984). Mainstreaming malpractice. *Physical Educator, 41*, 51–56.

Dewey, M. (1972). The autistic child in a physical education class. *Journal of Health, Physical Education, Recreation, 43*(4), 79–80. doi:10.1080/00221473.1972.10614059

Downing, J. E. (2008). *Including students with severe and multiple disabilities in typical classrooms: Practical strategies for teachers* (3rd ed.). Baltimore: Paul H. Brookes Publishing Co.

Fejgin, N., Talmor, R., & Erlich, I. (2005). Inclusion and burnout in physical education. *European Physical Education Review, 11*(1), 29–50. doi:10.1177/1356336x05049823

Ferguson, D. L. (1995). The real challenge of inclusion: Confessions of a "rabid inclusionist". *Phi Delta Kappan, 77*(4), 281–306.

Fitzgerald, H. (2005). Still feeling like a spare piece of luggage? Embodied experiences of (dis)ability in physical education and school sport. *Physical Education and Sport Pedagogy, 10*(1), 41–59. doi:10.1080/1740898042000334908

Fitzgerald, H., & Stride, A. (2012). Stories about physical education from young people with disabilities. *International Journal of Disability, Development and Education, 59*(3), 283–293. doi:10.1080/1034912X.2012.697743

Forman, E. (1969). Forman and the inclusion of visually limited and blind children in a sighted physical education program. *Education of the Visually Handicapped, 1*(4), 113–115.

Gartner, A., & Lipsky, D. K. (1987). Beyond special education: Toward a quality system for all students. *Harvard Educational Review, 57*(4), 367–396. doi:10.17763/haer.57.4.kj517305m7761218

Geddes, D. M., & Summerfield, L. (1977). *Integrating persons with handicapping conditions into regular physical education and recreation programs. (ED 104 092).* Washington, D.C.: American Association for Health, Physical Education, and Recreation.

Giangreco, M. F. (1997). *Quick-guides to inclusion.* Baltimore, MD: Paul H. Brookes Publishing Co.

Givner, C. C., & Haager, D. (1995). Strategies for effective collaboration. In M. A. Falvey (Ed.), *Inclusive and heterogeneous schooling: Assessment, curriculum, and instruction* (pp. 41–57). Baltimore, MD: Paul H. Brookes Publishing Co.

Goodwin, D. L., & Watkinson, J. E. (2000). Inclusive physical education from the perspective of students with physical disabilities. *Adapted Physical Activity Quarterly, 17*(2), 144–160. doi:10.1123/apaq.17.2.144

Grenier, M. (2010). Moving to inclusion: A socio-cultural analysis of practice. *International Journal of Inclusive Education, 14*(4), 387–400. doi:10.1080/13603110802504598

Grosse, S. (1991). Is the mainstream always a better place to be? *Palaestra, 7*(2), 40–49.

Haegele, J. A., & Hodge, S. R. (2017). Current practices and future directions in reporting disability in school-based physical education research. *Quest, 69*(1), 113–124. doi:10.1080/00336297.2016.1165122

Haegele, J. A., & Sutherland, S. (2015). Perspectives of students with disabilities toward physical education: A qualitative inquiry review. *Quest, 67*(3), 255–273. doi:10.1080/00336297.2015.1050118

Haegele, J. A., Zhu, X., & Davis, S. (2018). Barriers and facilitators of physical education participation for students with disabilities: An exploratory study. *International Journal of Inclusive Education, 22*(2), 130–141. doi:10.1080/13603116.2017.1362046

Haustätter, R. S., & Jahnukainen, M. (2014). From integration to inclusion and the role of special education. In K. Florian & R. S. Haustätter (Eds.), *Inclusive education twenty years after the Salamanca* (pp. 119–132). New York: Peter Lang.

Herold, F., & Dandolo, J. (2009). Including visually impaired students in physical education lessons: A case study of teacher and pupil experiences. *British Journal of Visual Impairment, 27*(1), 75–84. doi:10.1177/0264619608097744

Hersman, B. L., & Hodge, S. R. (2010). High school physical educators' beliefs about teaching differently abled students in an urban public school district. *Education and Urban Society, 42*(6), 730–757. doi:10.1177/0013124510371038

Hocutt, A., Martin, E., & McKinney, J. D. (1991). Historical and legal context of mainstreaming. In J. W. Lloyd, N. N. Singh, & A. C. Repp (Eds.), *The Regular Education Initiative: Alternative perspectives on concepts, issues, and models* (17–28). Sycamore, IL: Sycamore Publishing Company.

Hodge, S., Ammah, J., Casebolt, K., Lamaster, K., & O'Sullivan, M. (2004). High school general physical education teachers' behaviors and beliefs associated with inclusion. *Sport, Education and Society, 9*(3), 395–419. doi:10.1080/13573320412331302458

Hodge, S., Ammah, J. O. A., Casebolt, K. M., LaMaster, K., Hersman, B., Samalot-Rivera, A., & Sato, T. (2009). A Diversity of Voices: Physical education teachers' beliefs about inclusion and teaching students with disabilities. *International Journal of Disability, Development and Education, 56*(4), 401–419. doi:10.1080/10349120903306756

Inter-Agency Commission. (1990). *World Declaration on Education for All and Framework for Action to Meet Basic Learning Needs.* New York: Unicef.

Jerlinder, K., Danermark, B., & Gill, P. (2010). Swedish primary-school teachers' attitudes to inclusion – The case of PE and pupils with physical disabilities. *European Journal of Special Needs Education, 25*(1), 45–57. doi:10.1080/08856250903450830

Johansen, G. (1971). Integrating visually handicapped children into a public elementary school physical education program. *Journal of Health, Physical Education, and Recreation, 42*(4), 61–62.

Kalymon, K., Gettinger, M., & Hanley-Maxwell, C. (2010). Middle school boys' perspectives on social relationships with peers with disabilities. *Remedial and Special Education, 31*(4), 305–316. doi:10.1177/0741932508327470

Karagiannis, A., Stainback, W., & Stainback, S. (1996). Rationale for inclusive schooling. In S. B. E Stainback & W. C. Stainback (Eds.), *Inclusion: A guide for educators* (pp. 3–16). Baltimore, MD: Paul H. Brookes.

Kauffman, J. M. (1995). The regular education initiative as Reagan-Bush education policy: A trickle-down theory of education of the hard-to-teach. In J. M. Kauffman & D. P. Hallahan (Eds.), *The illusion of full inclusion: A comprehensive critique of a current special education bandwagon* (pp. 125–155). Austin, TX: Pro-Ed.

Klavina, A., & Block, M. E. (2008). The effect of peer tutoring on interaction behaviors in inclusive physical education. *Adapted Physical Activity Quarterly, 25*(2), 132–158. doi:10.1123/apaq.25.2.132

Kraft, A. (1972). Down with (most) special education classes! *Academic Therapy, 8*(2), 207–216.

Lavay, B., & DePaepe, J. (1987). The harbinger helper: Why mainstreaming in physical education doesn't always work. *Journal of Health, Physical Education, Recreation, and Dance, 58*(7), 98–103.

Lewis, R. B., & Doorlag, D. H. (2011). *Teaching special students in the mainstream* (8th ed.). New York: Macmillan.

Lieberman, L. J., Robinson, B. L., & Rollheiser, H. (2006). Youth with visual impairments: Experiences in general physical education. *RE:view, 38*(1), 35–48.

Lipsky, D. K., & Gartner, A. (1998). *Inclusion and school reform: Transforming America's classrooms.* Baltimore: Paul H. Brookes Publishing Co.

Lytle, R. K., & Collier, D. (2002). The consultation process: Adapted physical education specialists' perceptions. *Adapted Physical Activity Quarterly, 19*(3), 261–279. doi:10.1123/apaq.19.3.261

Maloney, M. (1994). Courts are redefining LRE requirements under the IDEA. *Inclusive Education Programs, 1*(1), 1–2.

Obrusnikova, I. (2008). Physical educators' beliefs about teaching children with disabilities. *Perceptual and Motor Skills, 106*(2), 637–644. doi:10.2466/pms.106.2.637-644

Obrusnikova, I., Block, M. E., & Dillon, S. R. (2010). Children's beliefs toward cooperative playing with peers with disabilities in physical education. *Adapted Physical Activity Quarterly, 27*(2), 127–142. doi:10.1123/apaq.27.2.127

Obrusnikova, I., Valkova, H., & Block, M. E. (2003). Impact of inclusion in general physical education on students without disabilities. *Adapted Physical Activity Quarterly, 20*(3), 230–245. doi:10.1123/apaq.20.3.230

Odom, M. (1976). Segregated classes for the retarded. *Educational Considerations, 3*(3), 6–8.

Osborne, A. G. (1996). *Legal issues in special education.* Boston, MA: Allyn & Bacon.

Pan, C.-Y., Tsai, C.-L., Chu, C.-H., & Hsieh, K.-W. (2011). Physical activity and self-determined motivation of adolescents with and without autism spectrum disorders in inclusive physical education. *Research in Autism Spectrum Disorders, 5*(2), 733–741.

Peck, C. A., Donaldson, J., & Pezzoli, M. (1990). Some benefits nonhandicapped adolescents perceive for themselves from their social relationships with peers who have severe handicaps. *Journal of the Association for Persons with Severe Handicaps, 15*, 211–230.

Rodriguez, C. C., & Garro-Gil, N. (2015). Inclusion and integration on special education. *Procedia Social and Behavioral Sciences, 191*, 1323–1327. doi:10.1016/j.sbspro.2015.04.488

Sailor, W., Gee, K., & Karasoff, P. (1993). Full inclusion and school restructuring. In M. E. Snell (Ed.), *Instruction of students with severe disabilities* (pp. 1–30). New York: Merrill.

Sato, T., Hodge, S. R., Murata, N. M., & Maeda, J. K. (2007). Japanese physical education teachers' beliefs about teaching students with disabilities. *Sport, Education and Society, 12*(2), 211–230. doi:10.1080/13573320701287536

Seaman, J. A. (1970). Attitudes of physically handicapped children toward physical education. *Research Quarterly, 41*(3), 439–445.

Seymour, H., Reid, G., & Bloom, G. A. (2009). Friendship in inclusive physical education. *Adapted Physical Activity Quarterly, 26*(3), 201–219. doi:10.1123/apaq.26.3.201

Sherrill, C. (2004). *adapted physical activity, recreation, and sport: Crossdisciplinary and Lifespan* (6th ed.). Boston, MA: McGraw-Hill.

Sigmon, S. (1983). The history and future of educational segregation. *Journal for Special Educators, 19*, 1–13.

Singer, J. D. (1988). Should special education merge with regular education? *Educational Policy, 2*, 409–424.

Spencer-Cavaliere, N., & Watkinson, J. E. (2010). Inclusion understood from the perspectives of children with disability. *Adapted Physical Activity Quarterly, 27*(4), 275–293.

Stainback, S., & Stainback, W. (1984). Broadening the research perspective in special education. *Exceptional Children, 50*(5), 400–408. doi:10.1177/001440298405000502

Stainback, S., & Stainback, W. (1990). Inclusive schooling. In W. Stainback & S. Stainback (Eds.), *Support networks for inclusive schooling* (pp. 3–25). Baltimore, MD: Paul H. Brookes.

Stainback, W., Stainback, S., & Bunch, G. (1989a). Introduction and historical background. In S. Stainback, W. Stainback, & M. Forest (Eds.), *Educating all students in the mainstream of regular education* (pp. 3–14). Baltimore, MD: Paul H. Brookes.

Stainback, W., Stainback, S., & Bunch, G. (1989b). A rationale for the merger of regular and special education. In S. Stainback, W. Stainback, & M. Forest (Eds.), *Educating all students in the mainstream of regular education* (pp. 15–26). Baltimore, MD: Paul H. Brookes.

States, U. (1969). *Civil rights acts of 1957, 1960, 1964, 1968, and Voting rights act of 1965*. Washington: U.S. Govt. Print. Off.

Stein, J. U. (1966). *Physical fitness in relation to intelligence qotient, social distance, and physique of intermedfate school mentally retarded boys*. (Doctor's thesis), George Peabody College for Teachers, Memphis, TN.

Stein, J. U., & Klappholz, L. A. (1972). *Special Olympics instructional manual...from beginners to champions*. Washington, D.C: American Alliance for Health, Physical Education, and Recreation and The Joseph P. Kennedy Jr. Foundation.

Suomi, J., Collier, D., & Brown, L. (2003). Factors affecting the social experiences of students in elementary physical education classes. *Journal of Teaching in Physical Education, 22*(2), 186–202.

Taylor, S. J. (1988). Caught in the continuum: A critical analysis of the principle of the least restrictive environment. *Journal of the Association for Persons with Severe Handicaps, 13*, 41–53.

Tizard, J. (1971). National and international studies in mental retardation. *British Journal of Medical Psychology, 44*, 345–354.

Travena, T. (1970). Are physical education programs meeting the needs of students? *Journal of Health, Physical Education, Recreation, 41*, 42–43.

Turnbull, H. R., Turnbull, A. P., Stowe, M. J., & Wilcox, B. (2000). *Free appropriate public education*. Denver, CO: Love.

Turner, L., Johnson, T. G., Calvert, H. G., & Chaloupka, F. J. (2017). Stretched too thin? The relationship between insufficient resource allocation and physical education instructional time and assessment practices. *Teaching and Teacher Education, 68*, 210–219. doi:https://doi.org/10.1016/j.tate.2017.09.007

U.S. Department of Education. (2010). *Free appropriate public education for students with disabilities: Requirements under Section 504 of The Rehabilitation Act of 1973*. Washington, DC: U.S. Department of Education.

Umhoefer, D. L., Vargas, T. M., & Beyer, R. (2015). Adapted physical education service approaches and the effects on the perceived efficacy beliefs of general physical education teachers. *The Physical Educator, 72*(3), 361–381.

UNESCO. (2017). A guide for ensuring inclusion and equity in education. Retrieved from http://unes doc.unesco.org/images/0024/002482/248254e.pdf

United Nations. (1948). *Universal declaration of human rights*. Retrieved from www.ohchr.org/EN/ UDHR/Documents/UDHR_Translations/eng.pdf.

Vaz, S., Wilson, N., Falkmer, M., Sim, A., Scott, M., Cordier, R., & Falkmer, T. (2015). Factors associated with primary school teachers' attitudes towards the inclusion of students with disabilities. *Plos One*, *10*(8), e0137002. doi:10.1371/journal.pone.0137002

Vickerman, P., & Coates, J. K. (2009). Trainee and recently qualified physical education teachers' perspectives on including children with special educational needs. *Physical Education and Sport Pedagogy*, *14*(2), 137–153. doi:10.1080/17408980802400502

Vislie, L. (2003). From integration to inclusion: Focusing global trends and changes in the western European societies. *European Journal of Special Needs Education*, *18*(1), 17–35. doi:10.1080/0885625082000042294

Will, M. C. (1986). Educating children with learning problems: A shared responsibility. *Exceptional Children*, *52*, 411–416.

Winter, S. (2009). Childhood obesity in the testing era: What teachers and schools can do. *Childhood Education*, *85*(5), 283–288.

York, J., Vandercook, T., Macdonald, C., Heise-Neff, C., Caughey, E., Vandercook, T., … Caughey, E. (1992). Feedback about integrating middle-school education students with severe disabilities in general education classes. *Exceptional Children*, *58*(3), 244–258.

Zhu, W., Boiarskaia, E. A., Welk, G. J., & Meredith, M. D. (2010). Physical education and school contextual factors relating to students' achievement and cross-grade differences in aerobic fitness and obesity. *Research Quarterly for Exercise and Sport*, *81*(3), S53-S64.

5

Utilizing theory to drive research in adapted physical education

Anthony J. Maher and Janine K. Coates

Introduction

It would be difficult to pinpoint one, universal reason for, or way of, conducting research. The purposes of research are multifarious but, according Gliner and Morgan (2000), include some, or all, of the following: (1) identifying descriptions and patterns in data, for example the physical education (PE) participation tendencies of children with visual impairments; (2) exploring diversity, such as the ways in which the identity markers of children with disabilities intersect and shape their experiences of adapted physical education (APE); (3) making predictions, perhaps in relation to the physical activity tendencies of children with hearing impairments once they leave compulsory education; and, by no means last, (4) acquiring knowledge and constructing and advancing theory, which can be used to improve the policy, processes and practices associated with APE to, ultimately, make APE more relevant and meaningful for all children. It is in light of the final point that this chapter focuses on the use of theory to drive research in APE.

For the majority of academics in the field of APE, research forms an integral part of their professional identities and activities. In much of Western Europe and North America, the pervasiveness of neo-liberal ideologies has meant that academics are being placed under growing pressure by senior leaders in higher education institutions (HEIs) to increase the "quality" of research processes and, in turn, research outputs. It is important to note here that tensions exist among and between policy makers and academics in many countries when it comes to the criteria used to judge research quality. Nonetheless, it is crucial that those new to academia have the knowledge, skills, and, over time, professional experience to contribute to the research activities and agendas of HEIs. It is with this in mind that we aim to provide a systematic and critical introduction to the use of theory to drive research in APE. To achieve this, we begin by briefly exploring research "theory" in order to provide a foundation. Next, the ontological and epistemological considerations relating to research in APE will be tied to the theories and assumptions that are used to guide decisions about the methodologies researchers working within the field adopt. Then, a brief overview of empirical research relating to APE is offered to shed light on current trends in APE research. The final portion of the chapter summarizes the implications of empirical research for practice in APE, before drawing some conclusions.

Those researching APE have become accustomed to providing rationales for their research topics, methods, and results. As part of this, they are professionally obliged to adhere to existing guidelines relating to specific research procedures and practices; for instance, established ways of gathering data using interviews or surveys, and collectively agreed upon processes of analyzing qualitative and quantitative data. However, researchers in APE are rarely compelled to explain how theoretical frameworks guide and shape their research, nor do they often explain theory-building techniques. This lack of professional challenge, according to Kettley (2010), constitutes a primary cause of a so-called "crisis of theory and theory building" (p. 10) in education research. Throughout this chapter, researchers are encouraged to critically reflect on the ways in which theoretical frameworks can be used to shape their intended and ongoing research projects. Indeed, we are convinced that researchers in the field of APE will benefit significantly from a critical awareness of the main theoretical assumptions underpinning research. It is hoped that such critical awareness will enable researchers to better understand the utility of theory for APE policy and practice and help them to make informed decisions about the different approaches to "knowing" and "doing" that can be drawn upon.

What is "theory"?

When it comes to research, "theory" can be defined and conceptualized in different ways. At a more general level, when we talk about theory we are referring to established and emerging frameworks for conducting research (Ennis, 1999; Wiersma, 1995). Theories are like maps, which help researchers in APE navigate the often bumpy and contested terrain of research processes in that they aid us to make decisions about what to research, how to research, and how to interpret and represent what we have researched. If nothing else, Mouly (1978) suggests that theory is both a convenience and a necessity because it allows us to make manageable and make sense, in a more systematic way, of the interface between what may at first seem like a body of unrelated laws, concepts, and principles that can be used to guide research design and interpretation. Accordingly, theory may also enable researchers to make judgments about future social patterns and behaviors of those who are a part of APE by, as suggested by Kettley (2010), "drawing on the inferences of the explanation" (p. 9).

For Elias (1978), theory can help illuminate certain cherished myths, which are often taken for granted without being tested. What may first appear to be axiomatic or common sense in APE, for example, may instead be no more than the established educational and sporting ideologies and cultural practices of senior leaders in schools or governing bodies. It is only through painstaking study that the researcher can unearth unreliable impressions of common sense and, subsequently, learn more about the social world (Durkheim, 1938; Goudsblom, 1977; Park & Burgess, 1921) of those key stakeholders who are a part of APE, such as teachers, parents, and children. Theory can be useful in so far as it can help to generate new ideas for further study. In this regard, however, a caveat must be noted: theoretical thinking is not antithetical to empirical enquiry; they are interdependently tied. In fact, Auguste Comte (1798–1857)—a French philosopher who is widely regarded as the person who coined the term "sociology" and responsible for its early development—stressed the interdependence of theory and method back in the 19th century (Comte, cited in Elias, 1978, p. 34):

> For, if on the one hand a positive theory must necessarily be based on observations, it is equally true that, in order to make observations, and in consequence to make any sense of them, our minds require a theory of some sort. If, in considering phenomena, we did

not relate them immediately to some principles, not only would it be impossible for us to connect these isolated observations, and in consequence make any sense of them, but we would be quite incapable of remembering them; and, most often, the facts would remain unperceived.

In short, theoretical thinking should always be informed by empirical observations while, at the same time, researchers must employ a theoretical framework so that they know where to look and what to look for. Without a continual interdependence or "an uninterrupted two-way traffic" (Elias, 1987, p. 20) between empirical data and a theoretical model, the collection of detailed knowledge in relation to APE will be of limited use. This is because, to extend Comte's argument, it is only by the use of theoretical models that researchers can generalize from one situation to another, and only by constantly checking against empirical results can researchers test the adequacy of theoretical models. It is, in fact, the interdependence and continuous interchange between theory and data that distinguishes the work of theoretical–empirical social scientists from non-scientific attempts at constructing knowledge (Elias, 1987). In this regard, however, a further caveat should be noted: researchers must never interpret their findings to fit their theoretical framework; rather, they must endeavor to "test" their theories. That is, they must cast their theories into forms that are actually testable, and, if the theories do not correspond with their empirical data, they must either modify or scrap them. It is only through this process that APE researchers can increase the adequacy of theoretical frameworks.

For Macdonald et al. (2009), an exploration of theory cannot and should not be divorced from a discussion about research paradigms in terms of the ontological (i.e., nature of existence) and epistemological (i.e., nature of knowledge, the rules of knowing) theories which inform them. In this respect, Guba (1990) draws on the work of Kuhn (1970) to argue that there is little consensus when it comes to the meanings associated with the term "research paradigm". Over time, many dynamic, fluid and nuanced understandings have developed. Sparkes (1992), for one, considers research paradigms as contrasting perspectives with differing—sometimes compatible, but often not—sets of beliefs, values, and assumptions, all of which are tied to the epistemological, ontological, and methodological foundations that shape social investigation. Accordingly, the paradigmatic allegiance of researchers in APE influences the theoretical frameworks that are used as guiding tools. In the next section, we explore the philosophical foundations of research in APE.

Ontological and epistemological considerations

Philosophical underpinnings form the foundations of all research. It is necessary to acknowledge these foundations because it is through such ontological and epistemological considerations that researchers are better able to make appropriate decisions about their research methodologies and the tools they use to understand phenomena. As purported by Hitchcock and Hughes (1995), ontology, or our understanding of what constitutes reality/truth, gives rise to epistemological assumptions—our understanding of what constitutes knowledge and how it can be obtained. This then gives rise to methodological considerations, which is inextricably linked to considerations about what methods should be used to collect data and how data are interpreted and reported.

Over centuries, ontological and epistemological debates have centered on ideologies of truth. In what has been termed the "classical period of philosophical development", the aim of research in the physical sciences, in particular, was to change process-orientated phenomena into something static and immutable (Elias, 1978). This tradition, according to Elias (1978), obscured the ostensibly obvious point that the scientific study of culture, social groupings, and human behavior makes different demands of their researchers than those studying lifeless matter such as atoms and molecules. Nevertheless, a philosophical theory of science and knowledge subsequently adopted and legitimized this static, immutable, process-reducing tendency as the ideal model for discovering so-called fact-orientated knowledge in the social sciences. This theoretical position—known as positivism—was adopted by social scientists as a way of endeavoring to emulate the prestige associated with physicists and biologists. Nonetheless, the process-reducing approach manifested itself most significantly in the social sciences in the form of ontological and epistemological dichotomies, whereby some aligned with the search for truth and facts, and others embraced the ideology that the social world consists of multiple realities, which can only be understood through interpretation—known as interpretivism.

When talking about research relating to APE, it is important to discuss and justify the ontological and epistemological considerations guiding the study (Bryman, 2016) to ensure that the rationale for choice of theory, aims, methods, and data analysis technique is established (Creswell & Creswell, 2018; Saunders, Lewis, & Thornhill, 2015). Here, ontology refers to a theory of the existence and "nature" of reality or, at least, collectively agreed perceptions of the way things are. For instance, this may involve researchers exploring the culture of APE in schools. According to Crotty (1998), epistemology refers to the methods of procedure leading to knowledge, or the "nature" of knowledge; how we know what we (think we) know about, for example, the inclusivity of regular schools. Historically, there was said to be an unbridgeable chasm between an ontological belief that there is a social world in schools that "exists" and is waiting to be "uncovered" and analyzed through research, independent of social actors such as education policy-makers, head teachers, parents, teachers, and children and the claim that social world(s) in schools are in a continuous process of creation and recreation by all those individuals and groups who are a part of them (Bryman, 2009). Creswell and Creswell (2018) claim that an understanding of the two main philosophical epistemologies—that is, positivism and interpretivism—can help researchers to make a balanced and informed judgement about the most adequate research design and method(s) for answering their research questions. For Sparkes and Smith (2009), researchers need to adopt the role of connoisseur in order to pass judgment on different kinds of study in a fair and ethical manner. If this is to be accepted, it seems axiomatic that all APE researchers should make their philosophical position and ideas explicit within their work in order to further explain and justify their choice(s) of research design, methods, and data analysis techniques. With this in mind, in the next two sections we critically discuss established philosophical positions relating to APE research.

From positivism to post-positivism

Positivism, a philosophy that is often said to have developed out of the work of Auguste Comte (1798–1857) (Scott & Marshall, 2009), is based on the ontological notion that there is an "objective" reality to be investigated in the social world (Bryman, 2016). The aim of this position is said to be the collection of detailed, objective data. That is to say, the data gathered and, indeed, the data collection process *per se*, is said to be value-free because the researcher is nothing more than a neutral "objective analyst" (Remenyi, Williams, Money, & Swartz, 1998, p. 33) of established rituals, customs and representations in APE. Using this approach, conclusions are drawn using deductive reasoning; that is, testing a hypothesis based upon existing theories or models in order to confirm or disprove established understanding.

A positivistic epistemology has been used to research many fields, some compatible, others quite disparate, including medicine, nursing, psychology, sociology, economics, education, and sport. According to Macdonald et al. (2009), operant psychology and behaviorism have been the key focus of researchers in education (and sport) who have ascribed to a positivistic world-view. This is not to say, of course, that behaviorist approaches to education and sport represent the complete assortment of positivist thought, more that they are central tenets that have guided research focusing on the discovery of scientific laws through the objective measurement and systematic manipulation of associated variables that aim to "uncover", through reliable, valid, and generalizable methods, the behaviors of teachers and learners, for example. Thus, positivist research is aligned with quantitative methodologies.

Of course, behaviorism does not represent the entire range of positivist thought, only its central tenet. From this perspective, it is said that scientific laws can be uncovered through the objective measurement and systematic manipulation of relevant variables, applied in this discussion most often to the behaviors of teachers and learners. Accordingly, the overarching goal of this research tradition is to predict and control human behaviors in order to initiate and facilitate quicker, more efficient, and longer lasting changes (Macdonald et al., 2009) relating, for instance, to teaching strategies in APE. In this respect, behaviorism can be said to be more deeply anchored in the scientific study of biology and neurology than, for example, sociology.

Despite once being a dominant force in research relating to APE pedagogy, positivist thought as it relates to theory and practice is being resolutely challenged in education, teacher education, and physical education. Over time, those defending a positivist philosophy of science have attempted to reconcile a number of criticisms, particularly from those academics who once subscribed to the philosophical position. For Crook and Garratt (2011), there are two enduring issues that positivists have difficulty reconciling: (1) the burden of proof, known as the verification of knowledge, and (2) the problem of separating the researcher from what is being researched. By drawing on the work of Popper (1990) to critique the burden of proof, Smith (1993, p. 71) contends:

> Popper convincingly pointed out that, no matter how many confirmation or verification instances have been accumulated for a theory, it is always possible that the next test of prediction will go astray. The problem is that induction does not allow one, with complete certitude, the as yet unknown based on the known, or to predict the future based on what has happened in the past ... A claim to knowledge must always stand as provisional in the sense that one can accept the claim only insofar as no one has been able to refute it or demonstrate it is false.

The point is of perhaps even greater significance when studying the behaviors of those involved in APE, such as policy makers, teachers, parents, children, and support staff. Here, a traditional positivist philosophy would fail to recognize the agency of these individuals and groups. When examining cultural practices and experiences in APE, or any other social phenomena, many have argued that it cannot always be predicted that "X" will always cause "Y", or that "X" is even associated with "Y" because, unlike the subject matter of the natural sciences, all humans have, to varying degrees, the power to act in a number of different ways and to reject attempts to orchestrate their actions (see Elias, 1978; Hargreaves, 1986). In short, a traditional positivist approach has been rejected by some because it is mono-causal, deterministic, and fails to take into account the complexity of human relationships and behaviors, and the power of individual agency.

One outcome of a perceived failure to address such fundamental philosophical questions has been the development of "post-positivism" (Philips & Burbules, 2000), "post-empiricism" (Norris, 2007), "neo-realism" (Smith & Hodkinson, 2009) or "neo-positivism" (Hammersley, 2008) as new ways of thinking that build on the foundations of positivistic thought. While these new ways of thinking are said to challenge hegemonic ideas relating to validity, reliability, and generalizability, they do not render them obsolete. Instead, they are used by researchers in APE to ensure professional accountability. This means they give close consideration to the descriptive tools and frameworks they use in order to try to systemize what is observed. It means critically reflecting on how any systemization resonates with the phenomena researchers wish to understand through research. For Crook and Garratt (2011, p. 215),

> efforts to ensure accountability need not imply epistemological commitment to the belief that some absolute success or truth can be achieved in relation to reliability, validity or generalisation. There is certainly no assumption that numerically-grounded[sic] representations of social or psychological phenomena have some privileged status. The positivist legacy places pressure on researchers to be reflective (rather than prescriptive) about their methods, their relationships with participants in their research, and their conceptualisations of the context in which the research is situated.

From this purview, validity, reliability, and generalizability are tools used in order to systemize what is observed through APE research. However, for some, post and/or neo versions of positivism do not go far enough in emphasizing and exploring the role of individuals and groups in creating and re-creating social worlds, or the ways in which researchers are inextricably bound to research processes. It is for this reason that we now turn to a discussion about interpretivism in order to try to emphasize the significance of these points.

Interpretivism

The work of Wilhelm Dilthy (1961) is widely acknowledged as contributing significantly to the development of interpretivist ontologies. Dilthy (1961) contended that hermeneutics (interpretation) should form a central tenet of research philosophies in order to shed light on the meaning-perspectives of the people being studied. The work of Dilthy has since been developed by, among many others, Merleau-Ponty (1962) and Rorty (1979). While there are a number of epistemologies (e.g., subjectivist and constructivist), theoretical perspectives (e.g., critical and feminist), and methodologies (e.g., action research, ethnography, autoethnography, and life history) that those claiming allegiance to interpretivism have used to guide their research, these have some central, shared, epistemological and methodological features. In this regard, Macdonald et al. (2009, p. 369) suggest that social organizations such as schools and sports clubs are constructed by people through purposeful actions, as individuals "negotiate social roles and define status within collective social groups". From this perspective, the dominant ideologies, traditions, rituals, and experiences of APE are intentionally (and not) shaped and influenced by the key stakeholders involved, such as policy makers, school leaders, teachers, coaches, parents, and pupils as they interact with each other, and individually and collectively engage in meaning-making.

From a research perspective, some interpretivists ascribe to a relativist ontology. From this purview, interpretations of the established ideologies, traditions, rituals, and experiences of

APE will reflect the multiple realities and subjectivities of the people involved in its social organization (Maxwell, 2012). Importantly, these socially constructed realities are dynamic and continuously in flux, making the establishment of positivist-inspired universal laws of human behavior an impossibility. Therefore, even though the teachers who deliver APE may work in the same or similar schools, have experienced similar teacher education programs, have similar career ambitions and share identity markers relating to age, gender, ethnicity, and socioeconomic status, the sense they make of, and meaning given to, their experiences of APE may differ because each individual has her or his own—sometimes compatible, other times not—ideologies, values, intentions, and embodied experiences, all of which can shape experiential interpretation and meaning construction (Sparkes & Smith, 2014). To continue this line of thinking, it is important to acknowledge that we, as researchers, also have our own ideologies and experiences that will inevitably spill into the research process. This point is, according to Creswell and Poth (2018), the axiological assumption that characterizes qualitative research, and a direct challenge to the claim of researcher-as-objective-analyst (Remenyi, Williams, Money, & Swartz, 1998). Here, Sparkes and Smith (2014) invite researchers to reflexively analyse the ways in which they are inextricably bound to research processes.

What this kind of research may be most interested in is, for example, how APE is taught in schools and how these approaches were established, contested, and negotiated by those who are a part of its social formation, such as, but not exclusively, teachers, learners, and school leaders. Often, interpretivist research is qualitative in nature, and the focus is on gathering rich, detailed, thick descriptions of views and experiences of research participants (Sparkes & Smith, 2014). Typically, sample sizes are small, thus making conventional statistical generalizations impossible and, for many interpretivists, undesirable, because of philosophical incompatibility. Instead, researchers who ascribe to this tradition may invite readers—academics, policy makers and practitioners—to reflect upon data and theoretically informed discussions provided to make sense of, and to orientate, their own situations. The making of connections in this way engenders recognizability (see Delmar, 2010) and allows for, according to Sparkes and Smith (2014), the making of naturalistic generalizations that can be utilized to shape the practices of key stakeholders. While positivism is much more tightly bound to biology and psychology, interpretivism is often associated with, for our purposes, the sociology of APE, embodiment, and social constructivist approaches to learning in APE.

Here, it must be acknowledged that the sections provided so far provide only a brief and parochial insight into the philosophical and theoretical complexities of research traditions. Nonetheless, they will serve as a useful basis for the next section of the chapter, where we review current empirical scholarship relating to APE in order to give the reader a sense of the main philosophical and theoretical foundations that have been utilized to guide research in APE.

A review of current trends in APE scholarship

Literature reviews—including systematic reviews, qualitative reviews, and meta-analyses—are a useful starting point for understanding current scholarship in APE research. Through these types of texts, it is possible to gain a broad understanding of what research has been carried out in the field and to begin to explore the existing trends. A good example of this is the review conducted by Haegele, Lee, and Porretta (2015), which sought to examine the trends in research published in *Adapted Physical Activity Quarterly*, an academic, peer-reviewed journal dedicated to adapted physical activity (APA) research. This review highlights some interesting trends in relation to where APA research is conducted (88% coming from institutions in the US, Canada, and Western Europe), research design (the majority are non-intervention studies), and methods used (70% align with quantitative methodologies). What is of interest here, however, are the trends in relation to the theoretical foundations applied and explicitly discussed in these studies. Haegele et al. (2015) show in their review that of 181 articles published in the journal over a ten-year period, only 38% explicitly discuss the theory underpinning their research. This is despite the growing discourse in APA research arguing for the importance of using theory to drive research (Cervantes & Taylor, 2011).

It is worth reinforcing here the ambiguities associated with the term "theory". Depending upon the discipline and approach taken, theory could refer to one of many things. It could be the wider ontological and epistemological paradigm providing the foundation for the research and its design; it might be the philosophical approach adopted which informs the ways in which the research is interpreted (e.g., post-structuralism, phenomenology); or it may relate to an established conceptual framework which informs the variables being measured or tested (e.g., self-determination theory, social–cognitive theory). With this in mind, Haegele et al. (2015) uncover some interesting trends. First, they note that theories often explicitly referred to within quantitative studies are those that denote a conceptual framework. While (post-) positivism is not directly referred to in these studies, the use of conceptual frameworks that identify measurable factors and variables implies a positivist epistemological paradigm. However, fewer than half of the quantitative studies examined included discussion of an underpinning theoretical framework. This is problematic, given that all research is underpinned by distinct ontological and epistemological perspectives and, thus, are, whether the researchers acknowledge it or not, theory driven. Therefore, the values upon which research is built should be made explicit so that journal article reviewers and the wider academic community can judge whether they are compatible with methodological decisions. As stated by Smith and McGannon (2018), "research methods cannot be divorced from their philosophical undercarriage" (p. 104).

By comparison, the majority (68%) of qualitative studies included in this review made reference to a theoretical framework, although the specifics of which theories these include are not discussed. Haegele et al. (2015) explain this difference through the perceived value of adopting explicit theory for different research approaches, where qualitative research might be more appropriately understood through the adoption of specific theoretical frameworks. Indeed, there is often a tendency for qualitative researchers to make their theoretical assumptions more explicit when writing up their research, perhaps in an attempt to legitimize qualitative approaches (and, thus, their own research), which have been, and continue to be, criticized by (post-) positivists for lacking validity, reliability, and generalizability (Bryman, 2016). Perhaps ironically, this raises questions about the taken-for-granted nature of positivist research, whereby the philosophical paradigms underpinning the research are considered implicit. This is possibly due to the perceived primacy of this form of research in the sciences, or it might be that, within interpretive research, there is the understanding that no research can be theory-free (Smith & McGannon, 2018) and that there are multiple ways in which research can be interpreted, thus there is more need to explicitly outline theory. Nevertheless, what is clear is that the theories driving research in APA are not made explicit frequently enough, and this diminishes the ability to make informed judgments about the quality of research in this discipline.

While this provides an overview of the trends in research within APA more broadly, it also stands as a useful basis for understanding current scholarship within APE specifically. A useful way of getting a sense of current empirical scholarship in APE is to use relevant databases, like SPORTDiscuss, Web of Science, PubMed, Academic Search Complete,

Emerald Insight, ERIC, PsycINFO, ProQuest, and/or Physical Education Index, to access the most recent articles in the field of APE. In doing so, it is worthwhile keeping a note of effective search terms and key authors.

In the past five years, a number of articles relating to APE have been published, several of these being literature reviews (e.g., Haegele & Sutherland, 2015; Kalef, Reid, & Mac-Donald, 2013). These literature reviews present syntheses of empirical research within APE in distinct ways. Where Kalef et al. (2013) explore the impact of peer tutoring for children with disabilities in physical education settings with a focus on quantitative outcomes, Haegele and Sutherland (2015) provide a qualitative review of research articles addressing the PE perceptions of students with disabilities. While systematic reviews tend not to report guiding theoretical principles, the ways in which inclusion criteria are developed and how the findings are reported provides insight into the ontologies and epistemologies guiding those pieces of work. For research to be comparable, which is necessary within a review, they must share commonalities in how knowledge production and conceptions of truth and reality are understood. Where ontological and epistemological incompatibilities exist, data cannot be collated, nor can credible conclusions be drawn. Thus, there is the tendency for inclusion criteria to seek common outcomes (e.g., behavioral variables impacted by an intervention, or attitudes toward PE) or common forms of knowledge production (e.g., qualitative or quantitative methods of data collection). For example, the Haegele and Sutherland (2015) review included only those studies that presented qualitative data relating to PE in schools; whereas the Kalef et al. (2013) included only peer-tutoring intervention studies using a single-subject or group-experimental design.

Despite approaching the reviews from different theoretical standpoints, both suggest that peers are significant stakeholders in the PE experiences of children and young people with disabilities. Further, both reviews also indicate that more *quality* research is needed to confirm these conclusions. Where they diverge is in how quality research is defined. For Haegele and Sutherland (2015), quality research is that which is innovative and inclusive, and tailored to the needs of young people with disabilities to encourage meaningful engagement in research. This aligns with the interpretivist paradigm underlying the review, which acknowledges the importance of understanding subjective experience. The Kalef et al. (2013) review, on the other hand, recommends research that addresses specific quality criteria for study design, including the use of reliability and validity testing, and so aligning with a positivist epistemological position. However, determining quality in research is dependent on the researchers carrying out that work having a sound understanding of the ontological and epistemological underpinnings of their studies. Without this, naturally, the quality of the research will be diminished, leaving it open to critique. With this in mind, the remainder of this section will focus on some of the empirical research published in recent years and what it tells us about current trends in relation to how theory is (or is not) used within APE research.

Like the review undertaken by Haegele et al. (2015) about APA research, few of the recently (since 2012) published APE studies explicitly discuss a theoretical (epistemological) position, yet most do highlight the strategies used to ensure "quality" within the research. The epistemological positioning in a study is important when we consider issues relating to rigor and quality (or trustworthiness when considering qualitative research). Through this, it is possible to examine how theory and research quality are closely interlinked by highlighting how some strategies used to determine quality may, in fact, be incongruent with the implied epistemological position taken. A good example of this is considering "member checking", which is a strategy used in qualitative research to determine rigor, whereby interview transcripts are returned to study participants for accuracy checking prior to, or during, data analysis. This method was used in all of the qualitative research articles considered here to affirm trustworthiness in the data (Chaapel et al., 2013; Sato et al., 2017; Sato & Haegele, 2017; Park & Curtner-Smith, 2018). Only one of these studies stated that the philosophical position was interpretivism (Park & Curtner-Smith, 2018), yet little is said about how this underpinned methodological decisions. It can be assumed that the other studies also followed a broad interpretivist design, as implied by the use of qualitative methods and aims to understand participant experiences within these studies. One other study (Chaapel et al., 2012) states that through member checking, feedback was received from several participants, yet no detail is provided about the implications of this feedback on study findings.

Member checking was first suggested as a method for ensuring the trustworthiness of qualitative findings by Lincoln and Guba (1985), and this has become a staple for qualitative researchers for demonstrating rigor. Despite its popularity, concerns have been raised over its "fit" with the ontological and epistemological foundations of qualitative research (Smith & McGannon, 2018), particularly given this strategy was devised at a time when qualitative researchers were forced to appraise and justify their work in light of well-established scientific (positivist) standards—reliability and validity (Birt, Scott, Cavers, Campbell, & Walter, 2016). Since then, several criterion-based checklists have been developed to support qualitative researchers in demonstrating rigor (see, for example, Tracy, 2010), and member checking, or participant validation is a frequently mentioned strategy within these. However, Smith and McGannon (2018) point out that member checking, and criterion-based methods more generally, when used for demonstrating study quality, may in fact conflict with the ontology and epistemology of the studies they are used in. This is explained thus:

> Although Lincoln and Guba accepted a world of multiple and mind-dependent realities (i.e., ontological relativism), they also discussed member checking as informed by epistemological foundationalism. Epistemological foundationalism refers to the assumption that method, like member checking, itself is neutral and can thereby control for bias and be the repository of procedural objectivity to sort out the more or most trustworthy from the less trustworthy. However, a major problem with epistemological foundationalism is that methods are not neutral, objective, or unbiased but rather are dependent on people (Culver et al., 2012; Smith & Deemer, 2000). In the case of member checking, it is the researcher and participant who are the member checkers. Moreover, like all people, researchers and participants alike are unable to step outside of their own experiences and history or rise above and separate themselves from the study of the social world.
>
> (Smith & McGannon, 2018, p. 104)

One of the key problems here is that, from an ontological perspective, qualitative research embraces multiple realities. From an epistemological perspective, it embraces subjective interpretations of experience, opinion and values, and this is dependent on context and situation, both of which are dynamic and in flux. Social contexts, and thus realities, are constantly changing, and so asking a participant to engage with a reality independent of context is problematic. Further, as seen in the studies examined by Haegele et al. (2015) and in this brief review, many researchers are failing to acknowledge the theoretical positioning of their work, and, importantly, also failing to detail how member checking was carried out and what implications this had for the findings reported. While member checking may be a useful tool in some studies, without explanation of the principles underlying the use of the method, or explanation about how the method was employed, it cannot be considered an effective method for enhancing rigor in research (Birt et al., 2016; Smith & McGannon, 2018). This example demonstrates the importance of using theory (ontological and epistemological) to underpin research design. Ontological and epistemological considerations underpin research, providing the foundations for methodological, analytical, and quality control decisions.

Conclusions and implications for practice

At the beginning of this chapter we encouraged you, the reader, to critically reflect on the ways in which theory can and should be used to drive research in APE. In this regard, we have argued that theoretical frameworks should be explicitly stated and justified in the research papers that we, as academics, construct, and that it should be explicitly obvious how theory is tied to our philosophical position; that is, the ways in which we view and attempt to understand "reality" or, depending on your world-view, "realities". In turn, it is important that any discussion relating to philosophical position and theory be inextricably tied to the methods and data analysis and verification techniques used. In other words, there is a need to consider philosophical compatibility and alignment. Interestingly, and perhaps ironically, it seems that (post) positivist, quantitative researchers in the field of APE are less inclined to follow these guidelines. This is perhaps of some surprise given claims that this type of research is more systematic, valid, reliable, and generalizable. Nonetheless, interpretivist, qualitative researchers are not immune to these criticisms. For instance, we offer the example of member checking, which is used frequently in APE research, to highlight potential issues with philosophical compatibility. Either way, the point remains: APE researchers, regardless of their philosophical position, need to be much more explicit in their discussion about how theory informed the development of research questions, data collection, data analysis, and verification techniques. This will assist APE researchers to make informed decisions during the planning and development of research projects. Moreover, it will help journal editors, reviewers, and wider academic communities to make judgments about research quality and the compatibility of research processes. We argue that this should be part of an audit trail that contributes to ensuring transparency and accountability and should be an integral part of our professional standards as researchers of APE.

Before ending, we thought it essential to note that this chapter is written by two authors who have their own beliefs, values, intentions, motivations, and professional and personal experiences, all of which have inevitably shaped its construction. This point perhaps hints at our own views about the nature of "reality", and the extent to which knowledge, or perhaps more appropriately, knowledges, can ever be value-neutral. Indeed, we are both qualitative researchers who are committed in our personal and professional capacities to, among other things, improving the educational experiences and life chances of people with disabilities, which is something that has enviably spilled into our research generally and the development of this chapter specifically. For this, we offer no apologies. However, you should recognize that this chapter would have been written differently by other scholars, especially by those who ascribe to different philosophical positions.

Summary of key points

- Theory underpins research and should be used to inform methodological decisions including the development of research questions, the selection of data collection tools, and the interpretation of data.
- When we refer to theoretical paradigms in research, we most often are making reference to ontological and epistemological positions.

- Ontology refers to our understanding about the nature of existence or what constitutes reality. Epistemology, on the other hand, refers to the existence of knowledge and how knowledge might be constructed and understood.
- Ontology and epistemology indicate the ways in which researchers view the world, and determine the methodological decisions made in research.
- Positivism is the epistemological stance often taken by quantitative researchers. This theoretical position aims to create knowledge that is objective and value-free.
- Interpretivism is one epistemological stance often adopted by qualitative researchers. Researchers adopting this theoretical position perceive the world as constructed through multiple realities, existing in the subjective experiences of humans.
- APE research draws on both of these paradigms, yet APE researchers seldom state the theoretical position of their research, which can be problematic.
- One issue raised in this chapter related to rigor in research. The theoretical position of the research helps researchers to determine the most appropriate strategies to demonstrate rigor.
- Where theory is not explicitly drawn upon, research can be open to critique because methodological decisions are not properly considered or justified.
- APE researchers should, therefore, explicitly consider the ontological and epistemological positioning of their research and use this informed approach to make appropriate methodological decisions.

Reflective questions for discussion

We offer the following questions to help APE researchers to reflect on how theory can and should drive research:

(1) Is there one, universal "truth" that can be measured; or are there multiple "truths" that may differ depending on who you ask?
(2) What theories best help you to understand your research questions; and how do they tie into your answer to question (1)?
(3) What method(s) are most appropriate for gathering data to address your research questions, and how do they relate to your answers for questions (1) and (2)?
(4) What techniques can be used to help you to make sense of your data, and how do they tie into your answers for questions (1), (2) and (3)?
(5) How can you ensure rigor and generalizability in your research, and how does it relate to your answers to questions (1), (2), (3) and (4)?

References

Birt, L., Scott, S., Cavers, D., Campbell, C., & Walter, F. (2016). Member checking: A tool to enhance trustworthiness or merely a nod to validation? *Qualitative Health Research, 26*(13), 1802–1811.
Bryman, A. (2009). The end of the paradigm wars? In P. Alasuutari, L. Bickman, & J. Brannen (Eds.), *The Sage handbook of social research methods* (pp. 13–25). London: Sage.
Bryman, A. (2016). *Social research methods* (5th ed.). Oxford: Oxford University Press.
Chaapel, H., Columna, L., Lytle, R. and Bailey, J., 2013. Parental expectations about adapted physical education services. *The Journal of Special Education, 47*(3), pp. 186–196.
Cervantes, C. M., & Taylor, W. C. (2011). Physical activity interventions in adult populations with disabilities: A review. *Quest, 63*(4), 385–410.

Creswell, J., & Poth, C. (2018). *Qualitative inquiry and research design: Choosing among five approaches* (3rd ed.). London: Sage.

Creswell, J. W., & Creswell, J. D. (2018). *Research design: Qualitative, quantitative and mixed methods approaches* (5th ed.). London: Sage.

Crook, C., & Garratt, D. (2011). The positivist paradigm in contemporary social research: The interface of psychology, method and sociocultural theory. In B. Somekh & C. Lewin (Eds.), *Theory and method in social research* (2nd ed., pp. 212–219). London: Sage.

Crotty, M. (1998). *The foundations of social research*. Sydney: Allen and Unwin.

Delmar, C. (2010). "Generalizability" as recognition: Reflections on a foundational problem in qualitative research. *Qualitative Studies, 1*(2), 115–128.

Dilthy, W. (1961). *Meaning in history*. London: Allen and Unwin.

Durkheim, E. (1938). *The rules of sociological method*. Chicago: University of Chicago Press.

Elias, N. (1978). *What is sociology?* New York: Columbia University Press.

Elias, N. (1987). *Involvement and detachment*. Oxford: Basil Blackwell.

Ennis, C. D. (1999). A theoretical framework: The central piece of a research plan. *Journal of Teaching in Physical Education, 18*(2), 129–140.

Gliner, J. A., & Morgan, G. A. (2000). *Research methods in applied settings: An integrated approach to design and analysis*. Mahwah, NJ: Lawrence Erlbaum.

Goudsblom, J. (1977). *Sociology in the balance*. Oxford: Basil Blackwell.

Guba, E. (1990). *The paradigm dialog*. Newbury Park, CA: Sage.

Haegele, J. A., Lee, J., & Porretta, D. L. (2015). Research trends in adapted physical activity quarterly from 2004 to 2013. *Adapted Physical Activity Quarterly, 32*(3), 187–205.

Haegele, J. A., & Sutherland, S. (2015). Perspectives of students with disabilities toward physical education: A qualitative inquiry review. *Quest, 67*(3), 255–273.

Hammersley, M., 2008. *Questioning qualitative inquiry: Critical essays*. Sage.

Hargreaves, J. (1986). *Sport, power and culture*. Cambridge: Polity Press.

Hitchcock, G. and Hughes, D. (1995) *Research and the teacher: A qualitative introduction to school-based research* (2nd Ed.), London: Routledge.

Kalef, L., Reid, G., & MacDonald, C. (2013). Evidence-based practice: A quality indicator analysis of peer-tutoring in adapted physical education. *Research in Developmental Disabilities, 34*(9), 2514–2522.

Kettley, N. (2010). *Theory building in educational research*. London: Continuum International Publishing Group.

Kuhn, T. (1970). *The structure of scientific revolution* (2nd ed.). Chicago: University of Chicago Press.

Lincoln, Y. S., & Guba, E. G. (1985). *Naturalistic inquiry*. London: Sage.

Macdonald, D., Kirk, D., Metzler, M., Nilges, L., Schempp, P., & Wright, J. (2009). It's all very well, in theory: Theoretical perspectives and their applications in contemporary pedagogical research. In R. Bailey & D. Kirk (Eds.), *The Routledge physical education reader* (pp. 369–392). London: Routledge.

Maxwell, J. (2012). *A realist approach for qualitative inquiry*. London: Sage.

Merleau-Ponty, M. (1962). *The phenomenology of perception*. New York: Humanities Press.

Mouly, G. (1978) *The art and science of investigation*, Boston, MA: Allyn and Bacon.

Norris, C. (2007) *On truth and meaning: language, logic and the grounds of belief*. London: Continuum.

Park, C. W., & Curtner-Smith, M. D. (2018). Influence of occupational socialization on the perspectives and practices of adapted physical education teachers. *Adapted Physical Activity Quarterly, 35*(2), 214–232.

Park, R., & Burgess, E. (1921). *Introduction to the science of sociology*. Chicago: University of Chicago Press.

Phillips, D.C. and Burbules, N.C., 2000. *Postpositivism and educational research*. Rowman & Littlefield.

Popper, K. (1990). *The logic of scientific discovery*. London: Unwin Hyman.

Remenyi, D., Williams, B., Money, A. and Swartz, E. (1998) *Doing research in business and management*, London: Sage.

Rorty, R. (1979). *Philosophy and the mirror of nature*. Princeton, NJ: Princeton University Press.

Sato, T., and Haegele, J. A. (2017). Graduate students' practicum experiences instructing students with severe and profound disabilities in physical education.. *European Physical Education Review, 23* (2), pp. 196–211.

Sato, T., Haegele, J.A. and Foot, R., 2017. In-service physical educators' experiences of online adapted physical education endorsement courses. *Adapted Physical Activity Quarterly, 34*(2), pp. 162–178.

Saunders, M., Lewis, P., & Thornhill, A. (2015). *Research methods for business students* (7th ed.). Harlow: Pearson Education.

Scott, J., & Marshall, G. (2009). *Oxford dictionary of sociology*. Oxford: Oxford University Press.

Smith, B., & McGannon, K. R. (2018). Developing rigor in qualitative research: Problems and opportunities within sport and exercise psychology. *International Review of Sport and Exercise Psychology*, *11*(1), 101–121.

Smith, J. (1993). *After the demise of empiricism – The problem of judging social and educational inquiry*. New Jersey: Ablex.

Smith, J. K., & Hodkinson, P. (2009). Challenging neorealism: A response to Hammersley. *Qualitative inquiry*, *15*(1), 30–39.

Sparkes, A. (1992). The paradigm debate: An extended review and celebration of difference. In A. Sparkes (Ed.), *Research and physical education and sport* (pp. 9–60). London: Falmer.

Sparkes, A., & Smith, B. (2014). *Qualitative research methods in sport, exercise and health: From process to product*. London: Routledge.

Sparkes, A. C., & Smith, B. (2009). Judging the quality of qualitative inquiry: Criteriology and relativism in action. *Psychology of Sport and Exercise*, *10*(5), 491–497.

Tracy, S. J. (2010). Qualitative quality: Eight "big-tent" criteria for excellent qualitative research. *qualitative Inquiry*, *16*(10), 837–851.

Wiersma, W. (1995). *Research methods in education*. Needham Hts, MA: Blackwell.

6

Evidence-based practices in adapted physical education

Yeshayahu "Shayke" Hutzler

Introduction

For education decision makers, evidence-based practice (EBP) is a practice supported by rigorous and high quality scientifically based research studies that utilize appropriate designs and demonstrate meaningful effects on desired student outcomes (Cook, Smith, & Tankersley, 2012; Kvernbekk, 2017; US Department of Education, 2003a). Such evidence may be helpful for policy makers who want to support budget-related decisions. However, the fundamental reason for constructing EBP, also known as "evidence informed practice (EIP)" (Nelson & Campbell, 2017; p. 128), is to make knowledge about "what works" meaningful and accessible for teachers, who are expected to utilize this knowledge within their pedagogical decision making (Cook et al., 2012). Within the complex reality facing a teacher in practice, EBP is among several potential frameworks adding data about the pedagogical context, such as parental support, students' capabilities, and environmental conditions (Kvernbekk, 2017). Educational EBP follows the generic principle outlined in the medical world—the informed and judicious use of current research to guide decision making on individuals (Sackett, Rosenberg, Gray, Haynes, & Richardson, 1996). Within this framework, systematic reviews (with or without meta-analysis) are typically seen as the highest level of evidence, followed by randomized controlled trials (RCTs), controlled studies, cohort studies, systematic reviews of qualitative reports, case studies, and expert viewpoints (e.g., Ackley, Swan, Ladwig, & Tucker, 2008).

In the world of education, decisions about specific interventions to be utilized in order to facilitate a desired student outcome are made every time a teacher faces a situation caused by the interaction of an impairment in the student's functional learning processes, the learning task, and the learning environment—that is, the school and peer students' factors. For example, Jin and Yun (2010) described a case of an adapted physical education (APE) teacher who was teaching a ten-year-old student with Down syndrome (DS) who presented an inadequate level of physical fitness, and the teacher was searching for appropriate and safe EBPs suitable for enhancing fitness. Therefore, Jin and Yun (2010) proposed a model for utilizing EBP in APE, which includes (a) exploring evidence available in the professional and scientific literature; (b) reflecting on this evidence with the practitioner's and service recipient's (e.g., the student) experiences using discourse, (c) discussing alternatives and determining the most compatible alternative, (d) testing the practice alternative, and (e) evaluating the outcomes for subsequent decision making.

While some problems confronted in practice may have received significant scientific attention, such as fitness programming for children with DS (e.g., Dodds & Shields, 2005; Pitetti, Baynard, & Agiovlasitis, 2013), many other physical education (PE) contexts have not received such attention thus far. One such area is skill development. For example, if a primary school-aged student is unable to perform a forward roll after having been given an explanation and demonstration of the skill, the teacher has to decide upon additional means to enable the child to perform the skill, at least to a certain degree of quality, or to find a meaningful alternative motor skill to be performed in the same context. The typical actions an experienced APE teacher would undertake in this case might be (a) utilizing additional instructional strategies (e.g., physical guidance), or a variety of prompting and/or feedback alternatives; (b) introducing an instructional aid (e.g., a peer tutor) to facilitate the student's motivation to engage; (c) using environmental modifications (e.g., an incline to facilitate trunk flexion); or (d) utilizing tools (e.g., a beanbag held between the chin and chest) to facilitate neck flexion. None of these options has been tested to provide evidence of its success or failure. Furthermore, it is plausible that the selection of adaptation strategies would vary across children of different ages and with different disabilities or genders. This is just a brief example illustrating the complexity of challenging PE teachers with informed decision making following the EBP tradition. Furthermore, the need to faithfully construct learning outcomes for all children, with and without disabilities, creates additional decision making challenges. Therefore, APE scholars discourage practitioners from using cookbook style standard recipes for solving each problem or overcoming specific obstacles during pedagogical decision making, and instead recommend analyzing the task and finding tailor-made individualized solutions (e.g., Sherrill, 2004; Van Lent, 2006).

Hutzler and Bar-Eli (2013) adopted a judgment and decision making perspective from the field of economics, and described the physical educators' responses when facing the "real world, where time is short, knowledge lacking, and other resources limited" (Gigerenzer, 2000, p. 125). They used the term labeled by Simon (1956) as "bounded rationality", or the term labeled by Tversky and Kahneman (1974) as "heuristics", for choosing alternatives without a preceding informed process in such cases with many degrees of freedom, where decision time becomes too limited for optimized choices. In APE practice, heuristics may occur when decisions are made according to instances or scenarios that are available for retrieval in the educator's experience, rather than an informed judgment of the complete data set. A common example is the selection of the foam ball to facilitate motor skill acquisition for a child with a disability. However, it should be noted that such a ball is mainly suitable to enable catching, but is quite detrimental when used for bouncing (Hutzler & Bar-Eli, 2013). Therefore, these authors recommended the practice of prioritizing alternatives based on multiple choices, preferable within a cooperative framework of decision makers such as teachers or coaches. The prioritization of alternatives requires as many sources of information as possible, and the decision maker is encouraged to seek knowledge bases exceeding his or her own practical experience—here is where EBP can be extremely helpful.

Given the limited experiential resources available to the teacher, and in line with principles proposed in medical practice and psychological practices, the EBP process can be explained as a three-legged-stool model (Haynes, Devereaux, & Guyatt, 2002; Paynter, 2009; Spring, 2007). This model describes an interaction of practitioner experience, service recipient experience, and best evidence gained from a literature search. Although previous accounts of EBP in APE have not included participants' experience (e.g., Cormack, 2002; Jin & Yun, 2010), it may be useful to include the student in the APE decision making process, given that the experiences this student may have had during his or her schooling are greater than those of the teacher, who may be confronted with the problem for the first time.

The purpose of this chapter is to discuss the pros and cons of utilizing an EBP approach for decision making in APE, and to review evidence relating to selected intervention approaches. A chronology of the discussion in this regard precedes the review. In the sections comprising the review, research evidence in APE referring to self-contained or integrated PE contexts will be synthesized and discussed. Finally, recommendations for further research and implementation of this practice are outlined.

How is EBP constructed?

Describing levels of evidence based on both quantity and quality is the common way of presenting scholarly evidence (e.g., Centre of Evidence Based Medicine, 2018; Guyatt, Cook, & Haynes, 2004; Hutzler, 2011; Jin & Yun, 2010). Research quality is based on quality indicators, where, following Cochrane's medical point of view (Cochrane, 1972), RCTs have been considered as the gold standard in evaluating the effectiveness of interventions, extending from medical to psychological and educational contexts. The desire to establish an EBP for APE (Jin & Yun, 2010) has been met with controversy among scholars. For example, Bouffard and Reid (2012) outlined 10 arguments contrasting the basic arguments in favor of EBP, hoping that the reader would better appreciate the complexities and challenges involved in prioritizing one type of evidence over another that identifies hierarchies of evidence. Furthermore, Reid, Bouffard, and MacDonald (2012) presented several fundamental beliefs challenging EBP in APE, which related to the individualized, system-based, and self-determined contexts of APE. These authors suggested a research model that includes the following eight steps: (a) conceptualize the problem, (b) conduct research on the process of the problem, (c) conceptualize and specify the intervention, (d) evaluate intervention outcomes, (e) evaluate intervention processes, (f) determine person-by-treatment interactions, (g) determine context-dependent limitations, and (h) investigate factors related to intervention adoption maintenance. According to the authors, these processes enable the assessment of a variety of methodological approaches within a systematic review, rather than focusing on RCTs, and consider quality indicators that could be gained through both quantitative and qualitative methods.

Conversely, in special education, a related and parallel field, the Council for Exceptional Children (CEC) (2014) proposed standards for EBP based on a significant amount of preliminary work (e.g., Gersten et al., 2005; Homer et al., 2005), as well as on the recommendations of a panel of special education researchers. The CEC approach includes two major research categories: (a) group comparison research, including randomized, comparative nonrandomized, and discontinuity designs, and (b) single-subject research. A list of quality indicators has been defined for each of these categories, relating to how information was reported in reference to context, participants, the intervention agent, description of practice, implementation fidelity, internal validity (i.e., the degree of control of the independent variables), and appropriateness of the outcome measures (i.e., the dependent variables and the data analysis procedures). Here, the utilization of effect size as a measure of clinically meaningful difference is specifically recommended. Based on *a priori* specified effect sizes (e.g., below or above 0.025), interventions may be classified as having positive, neutral, or negative effects. The level of quality of research supporting such effects should be considered according to the amount of quality standards adhered to and number of studies supporting the effects.

Accounts of EBP in APE

Responding to the challenge of the evidence-based education policy in the beginning of the 21st century (US Department of Education, 2003a), a number of authors summarized accounts of survey and program evaluation evidence within APE or in the broader field of knowledge labeled adapted physical activity (APA), which includes a spectrum of study to non-school-based physical activity and sport instruction of participants with disabilities (Hutzler, 2007; Porretta & Sherrill, 2005; Reid & Stanish, 2003; Zhang, deLisie, & Chen, 2006). These researchers explored research trends (e.g., in population, intervention context) and, to a lesser degree, the level of the quality of conducting and reporting the research outcomes.

So far, we have encountered no study using the CEC method for classifying EBP research in APE. Most accounts of evidence regarding APE follow the medical system, and consider systematic reviews as the major source for evaluating research outcomes. Nevertheless, and in line with the CEC framework, APE researchers rarely use randomized designs, instead establishing their research either using controlled groups or single-subject designs (Hutzler, 2006; Wilhelmsen & Sørensen, 2017). In addition, qualitative inquiry reviews synthesizing child and stakeholder perspectives have also been reported (Haegele & Sutherland, 2015; Pocock & Miyahara, 2018; Rekaa, Hanisch, & Ytterhus, 2018). Figure 6.1 summarizes the categories of evidence common in the APE research accounts that follow.

Motor skill development programs

The development of fundamental motor skills (FMS) of elementary school-aged children and their EBP has been targeted as a research focus, particularly during the recent decade, assuming that motor skill proficiency may increase physical activity participation time during childhood and, thus, reduce adult health risks due to physical inactivity (e.g., Dobbins, Husson, DeCorby, & LaRocca, 2013; Logan, Robinson, Wilson, & Lucas, 2012). FMS refers to

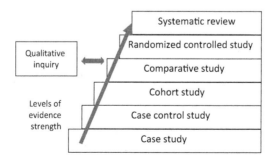

Figure 6.1 Hierarchy of evidence strength common in APE research

building blocks of basic and more complex movement skills represented within the school curriculum to support the development of most sport skills (Payne & Issacs, 2016).

Bishop and Pangelinan (2018) conducted a comprehensive and critical review of fundamental motor skill (FMS) intervention research in children with disabilities aged 3–18 years, which could be replicated in community or school contexts. The authors surveyed electronic databases for articles published from 1984 through 2014 and found only 21 studies, that complied with the inclusion criteria, demonstrating the results of 964 participants. The majority of studies (20 out of 21) indicated an increase in motor performance in locomotor skills (assessed in three studies), object control skills (in five studies), or both locomotor and object control skills (in 13 studies) due to the intervention. However, the authors reported that only one study could be considered an RCT, while the others included non-randomized comparative trials, single-subject designs, or case studies. Furthermore, the studies varied considerably regarding the length of participation time (one to 72 weeks), intensity (one to five sessions per week), and session length (30–120 minutes). The authors suggested that future research is needed with a more rigorous theoretical foundation and greater rigor while conducting and reporting the participants' recruitment, sampling, and assessment (e.g., blinding assessors to group allocation)—that is, research quality indices, which were lacking in several cases.

One particular group of school children that should be targeted for FMS interventions are those with a developmental coordination disorder (DCD), who comprise about 5% of the population internationally (Kirby & Sugden, 2007). Based on a combined systematic review and meta-analysis of the efficacy of interventions to improve the motor performance of children with DCD, Smits-Engelsman and associates (2012) concluded that compared to traditional physical and occupational therapies or process-oriented approaches, task-specific training such as activities performed during school-based sports yields stronger effects. Furthermore, a more recent study by Farhat and associates (2016) indicated that a school-based motor skill training program specifically designed for children with DCD revealed favorable results, with a transfer effect to the performance of skills which had not been trained during the program, including handwriting.

Finally, it should be noted that while an association of FMS and physical activity participation has been conceptualized (Stodden et al., 2008), the actual association of FMS outcomes and habitual physical activity participation has yet to be established. In typically developing children, this association has been found to be weak (Fisher et al., 2005). However, in children with disabilities, the emerging findings vary. In a cross-sectional study of children with visual impairments (VIs), a moderate association was found between motor skill proficiency and camp-based accelerometer activity data (Brian et al., 2018). However, in a study applying an FMS training program to children with cerebral palsy (CP), no significant increases in physical activity participation were reported, in spite of an improvement in skill scores in the training group (Capio, Sit, Eguia, Abernethy, & Masters, 2015).

School- and community-based fitness exercise training programs

The US Ministry of Education (Federal Register, 1977) addressed fitness, in addition to motor skills, as a main content area of APE. For more than two decades, an increased interest in developing the fitness of children with disabilities within a school and/or community framework has been expressed in the scientific health-related literature (e.g., Rimmer & Marques, 2012; Verschuren, Ketelaar, Takken, Helders, & Gorter, 2008; Verschuren,

Peterson, Balemans, & Hurvitz, 2016; Wiart, Darrah, Kelly, & Legg, 2015). However, only a limited number of school exercise and fitness programs for children with disabilities has been reported, mostly supervised by paramedical staff who are not always available at schools (e.g., Unnithan et al., 2007; Verschuren et al., 2007).

While few school-based programs are available for youth with disabilities, more research has been done with community-based fitness exercise training. It should be noted that the majority of reported programs included participants with one type of disability and therefore a relatively restricted range of disability symptoms, such as children with CP who are ambulatory (e.g., Verschuren et al., 2007), or children who are overweight and with intellectual disability (Wu et al., 2017). The published results document a general improvement in the specific fitness variables addressed within the training program, such as performance on shuttle run tests (Verschuren et al., 2007), the six-minute test measuring distance covered (Mylius, Paap, and Takken 2016), and a VO_2 peak test (Unnithan et al., 2007) in children with CP. Circuit training appears to be a preferred modality. For example, Aviram and associates (2017) assessed the effectiveness of a group circuit training program in a comprehensive multi-center, matched pairs study and compared it with treadmill training results in 95 ambulatory adolescents with spastic CP. Their findings suggested greater progress throughout the program and fewer reduced training effects on follow-up in favor of the circuit training group. In spite of these encouraging results, in a recent Cochrane review, which typically utilizes rigorous, medically-based quality criteria (Ryan, Cassidy, Noorduyn, & O'Connell, 2017), the authors concluded that limited evidence exists supporting aerobic exercise in children with CP only on motor function, and no evidence supporting strength training positive outcomes on gait, motor function, participation, or quality of life. Furthermore, very limited information exists regarding the practical effectiveness of school fitness programs for children with autism spectrum disorders (ASD; Srinivasan, Pescatello & Bhat, 2014) or any other specific disability condition.

Applied behavior analysis

Applied behavior analysis (ABA) is one of the classic intervention methods applied in special education. Basically, the principles of ABA are derived from operant conditioning (Skinner, 1953) and are applied to manage socially and pedagogically relevant behaviors (Baer, Wolf, & Risley, 1968). The use of ABA in social and educational practices is common for managing behaviors of persons with autism spectrum disorder (ASD) or intellectual disability (ID) (Virués-Ortega, 2010), and has a history of over 40 years, with a vast body of scientific research attempting to support its responsiveness and effectiveness in children with disabilities (Odom et al., 2005). The ABA approach has also been adopted among many physical educators. Nevertheless, due to the major reliance on single-subject designs and the lack of randomized and controlled research in large groups in ABA, it can only be characterized as probably efficacious (Odom et al., 2005). For example, Ward and Barrett (2002) reported a review of ABA research in PE and listed only six out of the 36 articles reviewed (16.67%) as focusing on students with disabilities, with two of them also implementing peer tutoring as the main strategy. In a viewpoint article, Haegele and Hodge (2015) presented the assumptions underlining the research methodology in ABA, described key aspects of single-subject research designs, and discussed quality criteria in this type of research. Furthermore, Parker, Vannest, Davis, and Sauber (2011) recommended that TAU-U statistics be used for measuring trends and interpreting results. The strong association of ABA research and single-subject designs is also reflected in the descriptive analysis of Zhang and Qi (2015), who provided a review of single-subject designs published in the journal *Adapted Physical Activity Quarterly* since its establishment in 1984 through 2013. They found a total of 26 articles with single-subject designs out of a total of 540 research articles published in *APAQ* issues throughout the review period (4.81%). Most studies involved participants with learning and behavior problems (88.46%), focused on measuring desired behaviors (77.77%), and recruited a sample size of fewer than ten participants (92.31%). Furthermore, the authors reported that the amount of this type of research declined during the second half of the period compared to the first part. It can be concluded that, in spite of the reputation of the ABA approach among APE scholars and professionals, the actual evidence base is scarce and is based on a small number of cases.

Inclusion strategies

One of the main topics within the APE research literature is the study of inclusive outcomes and processes within the PE framework. Complying with the legal definition and the special education frameworks of the 1970s in the USA, APE was directed toward developing specially designed PE services, as prescribed in a child's IEP. However, adapting PE practices to enable the participation of students with disability gradually became a challenge that had to be negotiated by the general physical education teacher, and, by 2016, 95% of children with disabilities were included in regular schools (US Department of Education, National Center for Education Statistics, 2016). This magnitude has been reflected in many other countries and is well suited to the international trend toward inclusive education. Inclusive education is understood as a school culture where all students—including those with disabilities—are given support to fully develop their social and personal competence, and where all students benefit from the diverse backgrounds and abilities (Ainscow & Miles, 2008; Smith, Polloway, Patton, & Dowdy, 2008). Furthermore, according to the Assistant Secretary for Special Education and Rehabilitative Services (U. S. Federal Register, 2013), the main focus of educational practices should be securing community living and participation opportunities for persons with physical as well as intellectual and developmental disabilities. Achieving this goal requires interaction with persons without a disability, such as during PE sessions. Therefore, PE classes are considered an excellent arena for experiencing such interactions, particularly during games and other group activities.

Studying the techniques and outcomes of practicing teachers within inclusive physical education frameworks has flourished throughout the recent two decades, resulting in a series of both more and less established strategies to support inclusion. In the sections that follow, inclusive strategies in PE will be reviewed and the evidence supporting them critically appraised. Systematic reviews will be reported first, followed by individual inclusive strategies, ordered according to the amount of presented evidence.

In a series of systematic reviews, authors generated a variety of themes related to this domain. For example, Block and Obrusnikova (2007) summarized the research on inclusion published between 1995 and 2005 and found 38 studies, representing six focus areas: (a) support (e.g., teacher assistants), (b) impact on performance of peers without disabilities, (c) attitudes and intentions of children without disabilities toward their peers with a disability, (d) social interactions between those with and without disabilities, (e) active learning time (ALT) during the physical education lessons of students with disabilities, and (f) training and attitudes of general physical education teachers. More recently, Qi and Ha (2012) performed a systematic review of the research literature pertaining to inclusion in PE and identified 75 articles, which included stakeholder (educators or parents) and student perspectives. Less than

20% of the studies included in this review addressed inclusive strategies. No adverse effects on students without disability were identified. However, while some favorable outcomes of using inclusive strategies for students with disabilities were observed, some disempowerment from significant others, social isolation, and reduced motor engagement were evident (Coates & Vickerman, 2008b; Hutzler, Fliess, Chacham, & Van den Auweele, 2002; Pocock & Miyahara, 2018; Wilhelmsen & Sørensenm, 2017).

In another review, Tant and Watelane (2016) synthesized several factors from the teachers' perspective that are favorable to inclusion, focusing on professional training quality and volume, exchanges between teachers and other colleagues, and adequacy of the training programs for curriculum modifications supporting the participation of people with disabilities. Most recently, a systematic review on teacher attitudes and student experiences in PE (Rekaa et al., 2018) suggested three steps for addressing qualitative study outcomes, which can be generalized through interpretation: (a) classifying studies, (b) comparing and contrasting their findings, and (c) performing a thematic analysis. Based on these steps, they contrasted the perceptions of possibilities in physical education and the attitudes toward inclusive physical education among physical education teachers and students with disabilities, and found that all shared the positive attitudes and highlighted the opportunities gained within the inclusive environment. These authors also acknowledged the association of teachers' perceived competence and favorable perceptions of inclusion.

Haegele and Sutherland (2015) also synthesized the perspective of students with disability included in physical education, based on 13 qualitative research articles. These authors reported three thematic clusters of evidence: (a) perspectives toward typically developing peers, (b) perspectives toward the physical educators, and (c) perspectives toward inclusion and exclusion. The main message of the authors was that children with disabilities faced significant challenges within integrated classes, such as being bullied and experiencing social isolation. The authors also suggested that educators' positive attitudes are crucial for implementing a favorable inclusion climate and for establishing meaningful learning experiences.

In the following sections, specific practices that are commonly used in integrated physical education are discussed. In these discussions, existing empirical literature is reviewed and EBP status is considered for each practice.

Peer tutoring

Also labeled peer-mediated instruction (PMI) or peer-assisted learning (PAL), these strategies refer to peer-mediated partial or complete teaching activities such as modeling, motivating, and skill instruction (Maheady, Harper, & Mallette, 2001). Peer tutoring has evolved within educational practices over a long period of time (Topping, 2005), and has been utilized within PE frameworks for at least 40 years. Peer tutoring involves one or more students providing a learning experience for other students to learn and master a learning content that the tutee(s) have not yet mastered in class (Mitchell, 2007). For this purpose, tutors may use a variety of strategies to support tutees, including transferring teacher-based information to the tutee (e.g., in cases of hearing or visual impairments or lack of attention); adding explanations when the preliminary information is not sufficient; demonstrating skills the tutee is expected to do; asking practice questions; prompting and providing feedback to support the tutee's active learning; clarifying misunderstandings that may become apparent; and facilitating the tutee's motivation and engagement (Killian, 2016).

There are several modalities that utilize peer tutoring. Class wide peer tutoring (CWPT) is a model where all class students form pairs. Another option is to use cross-age tutoring, with older students providing instruction to junior ones. Another preferred option is to select and train tutors *a priori* in order to be better prepared for the tutorship engagement. There are several factors that were found to particularly support beneficial learning while peer tutoring: (a) teacher-formed pairings ensure that tutors have the adequate levels of skill mastery to enable pairs to cooperate; (b) the interventions should be structured and tutors should be clear about what the tutee is expected to achieve, and what they are expected to do in order to achieve this goal; (c) the curricula tasks and goals should be matched to current levels of students' performance and comprehension; (d) the assessment of the tutee's learning should be individualized and compared to the previous level of performance; and (e) some form of rewards should be earned if the tutee meets the learning goals, in order to foster continuous engagement (Killian, 2016).

Two systematic reviews considered the research evidence on peer tutoring. Ward and Lee (2005) reviewed findings from research studies in general education and in PE settings, where peer tutors were implemented and studied. They did not differentiate between general and separated physical education settings, and described the methods utilized in practice but did not synthesize effectiveness and quality. Later, Kalef, Reid, and MacDonald (2013) investigated peer tutoring for students with disabilities in APE, and conducted a comprehensive electronic search, screening journals in English published between 1960 and November 2012. The quality of 15 research articles meeting the inclusion criteria and employing either group or single-subject designs was assessed, based on CEC criteria. The authors concluded that most articles significantly lacked quality and suggested that claims of peer-tutoring being an EBP were premature.

Self-determined and mastery learning

Self-determined action is a basic human right reflecting individual and community self-governance and autonomous behavior, and has been advocated as the right of people with disabilities to control their lives (Nirje, 1972). Self-determined behavior is characterized by autonomous, self-regulated, empowered, and self-realized action (Wehmeyer, 1996). Researchers suggest that greater autonomous, self-determined, and intrinsic motivation for PE participation is associated with higher participation rates in PE (Standage, Gillison, Ntoumanis, & Treasure, 2012). However, one of the disadvantages observed in students with a developmental disability is their lack of self-determination and autonomy (Wehmeyer, 1996). This lack in self-determination has been reflected in the goal orientation for sport participation in people with ID. When comparing sport motivation scale outcomes, participants with ID increased their external motivation with increasing age, while a reverse pattern was observed in typically developing athletes aged 14–40 years (Hutzler, Oz, & Barak, 2013). The authors suggested that as participants with ID grow out of the educational system, they may become more externally motivated toward sport participation. Therefore, they are less likely to benefit from the health outcomes associated with physical activity and reduce their physical performance as they grow into adulthood (Lahtinen, Rintala, & Malin, 2007).

Self-determined learning is strongly associated with mastery climate, which has been described as a student-centered instructional approach where the primary emphasis is on the autonomy of the child. This autonomy is expected to facilitate motivation for learning and, thereby, the learning outcomes. Valentini and Rudisill (2004) conducted a mastery climate intervention in two randomly distributed groups, where about one-third of the students had disabilities. One group underwent a 12-week mastery climate intervention and the second was a comparative group. The test of gross motor development (TGMD) was assessed in students before and after the intervention, with outcomes indicating that children with and without disabilities who participated in the mastery climate intervention gained significant improvements in motor skill performance during the intervention, while the comparison group did not. While initial evidence is promising for mastery climate and student-centered instructional approaches to enhance self-determined learning among children with disabilities, evidence is not yet sufficient to refer to it as an evidence-based practice.

Co-teaching and teacher consultants

Utilizing supportive educators, such as consultative APE specialists, is a way to reduce the organizational and curricular burden often reported by physical education teachers facing inclusion (Block & Obrusnikova, 2007; Fejgin, Talmor, & Erlich, 2005; Qi & Ha, 2012; Tant & Watelain, 2016). A few studies reported positive evidence for implementing such supports. For example, Obrusníková, Válková, and Block (2003) assessed motor skill performance and student attitudes (CAIPE-R) in two elementary school classes participating in a volleyball unit. A female itinerant APE teacher provided consultative support for a fourth-grade student who was a wheelchair user. She assisted the class teacher by (a) writing the IEP, (b) suggesting adaptations to equipment and activities, (c) directing classmates to assist the student, (d) conducting on-going evaluations of the student, and (e) occasionally assisting the student. The other class did not include any students with disability. The results did not indicate significant differences or a substantial effect size on volleyball skill across classes. Furthermore, the attitudes toward including a student with a disability in physical education in both classes appeared to be positive and stable during the intervention. In both cases, the authors claimed that if proper support services are provided, even students with severe disabilities can be included in regular physical education without resulting in negative effects for students without disabilities. Heikinaro-Johansson and Sherrill (1994), who reported the results of a Finnish survey, addressed in their findings that APE specialists may serve in a consultant role of advisers or may co-teach with the regular class teacher. Thus far, just two studies have provided empirical support for the utilization of consultants in APE. More empirical research is needed to provide more support for this practice to be considered an EBP.

Paraeducators

Paraeducators, also labeled paraprofessionals or teacher assistants, can be used as teacher aids. Their role is specified within educational legislation in many countries, following the American model (US Department of Education, 2003b), to provide instruction only under the direct supervision of a teacher. Block and Zeman (1996) performed a study where one APE teacher and two one-on-one teacher assistants worked together for three months prior to the beginning of the study in one class that included three students with severe disabilities. The authors compared skill acquisitions and attitude changes after a 3.5-week PE basketball unit toward including children with disability, using the Children's Attitude Scale toward Inclusion—Revised (CAIPE-R) instrument ((Block, 1995) between the experimental class and a comparative sixth-grade class. The results indicated no significant differences in skill improvement between the two groups except in dribbling, which favored the non-integrated class. In addition, no differences in gain scores for either general or sport-specific attitudes were observed. Paraeducators are expected to be familiar with educational goals and to help facilitate interaction and desirable social behaviors between students with and without disabilities (Davis, Kotecki, Harvey, & Oliver, 2007). However, the results of the 76 respondents in Davis et al.'s (2007) study to the questionnaire disseminated among 138 paraeducators (55.1% response) revealed very limited sharing of these tasks within the physical education framework. Only 16% of the total respondents reported receiving specific training in physical education; however, only 38% indicated participating in physical education—mostly escorting students, providing cues, and working individually with students. Only 28% had a role in performing assessments, IEP, or ABA program implementation.

In another study (Bryan, McCubbin, & Mars, 2013), the authors utilized a qualitative approach to examine the stakeholders' perception of the role of paraeducators in the general physical education environment. The authors indicated an ambiguity concerning the paraeducators' role and practice in general PE contexts. Similar concerns were addressed in a broader review of the research on paraprofessionals in inclusive schools, which summarized that the collaborative relationships among paraprofessionals and the other educational team members need clarification (Giangreco, Suter, & Doyle, 2007). Unfortunately, no comparative studies of utilizing paraeducators, peer tutors, or co-teachers have been conducted in integrated physical education. Clearly, ethical and organizational barriers might interfere with such a design. However, shedding more light on the relative strengths and weaknesses of each asset within the inclusion framework seems to be an important task for future studies. Based on the current literature, it is unknown if paraeducators' utilization in APE contexts is an effective practice, and should not yet be considered an EBP.

Universal design/universal design for learning

Universal design (UD) is a concept introduced in the early 1990s at the University of North Carolina (Nasar & Evans-Cowley, 2007), suggesting that good design should be pre-planned to accommodate the young, old, able, and disabled users of environments and equipment. Seven guidelines have been conceptualized to fulfill this goal: equitable use, flexibility in use, simple and intuitive in use, perceptible information, tolerance for error, low physical effort, and appropriate size and space for approach and use. These principles have been progressively accepted by designers and by statements such as in the United Nations Convention on the Rights of Persons with Disabilities (UNCRPD) (United Nations, 2006). Since educational institutions target a variety of students with diverse physical, sensory, and information processing capacities, in the early 2000s these principles were adopted into education. Hence, the concept universal design for learning (UDL) soon became common among proactive and progressive education programmers, which suggests not waiting for needs to be served with unique adaptations, but to *a priori* preparation of an inclusive, affording, and enabling environment for all students (Gargiulo & Metcalf, 2013). UDL targets three learning frameworks: (a) the representation of practical and/or theoretical concepts; (b) the expression of learning outcomes; and (c) the engagement of potential participants throughout the learning process. All of these processes are necessary for initiating and maintaining successful learning participation and outcomes. Increasingly, UDL is now included in national and international policies, such as, for example, the *Higher Education Opportunity Act*, 2008 (US Department of Education, 2010).

Several authors have proposed to incorporate the UDL approach into physical education and sport practice (e.g., Lieberman, Lytle, & Clarcq, 2008; Munafo, 2017; Sherlock-Shangraw, 2013). Specifically, these authors illustrated how practitioners could utilize multiple means for (a) recognizing the content and the tasks addressed during practice, (b) expressing knowledge while engaging in sport tasks, and (c) enhancing motivation, engagement, and eventually adherence. However, experience reported on UD and UDL models in PE is still scarce. Grenier, Miller, and Black (2017) reported a case study demonstrating one teacher's use of collaborative practices—UDL across the inclusion spectrum ranging from everyone can play (universal), to modified, parallel, and separate disability sport activities, thereby creating an accessible learning environment benefiting students both with and without disabilities. However, there is very limited empirical support for the utilization of UDL concepts in PE settings. Given the impact of UDL in inclusive pedagogy, empirical support is needed for exploring UDL to be considered an EBP.

Systematic and ecological task analysis

While physical educators typically have relied on lists of task criteria for analyzing the qualitative performance of a student learning a skilled behavior (see Gallahue, 1982), some scholars maintain that the framework for performing physical activity tasks is far more complex, and should be seen with a lens based in the system approach (e.g., Balan & Davis, 1993; Burton & Davis, 1995; Davis & Burton, 1991). The model derived for movement task analysis is based on the dynamic system approach, as articulated by Newell (1986), suggesting that patterns of motor behavior are the result of an interaction of actor (e.g., performer's specific disability, anthropometric and psychosocial factors), environmental (e.g., surface, equipment, and human resources), and task (e.g., complexity) constraints. Based on the interaction between these constraints, curricular adaptations may be provided to facilitate inclusion. Several acronyms have been recommended in order to establish the knowledge base regarding such adaptations, such as ETAT: ecological task analytic teaching (Tripp, Rizzo, & Webbert, 2007). When using this strategy, the educator must consider the performer's age and developmental stage, the cultural context, the environment, and the equipment available for instruction, as well as select task variations and activity choices that may facilitate a student's success. Hutzler (2007) proposed adding the task goal, referring to the International Classification of Function and Disability (ICF) (World Health Organization, 2001), where preservation and improvement of function, activity, and/or participation are to be involved in the decision making process. He recommended selecting a goal within the ICF framework when attempting curricular modification, and labeled it the systematic ecological modification approach (SEMA; Hutzler, 2007). "Tools and tips", published by the Australian Sports Commission (2018), addresses the major elements of adaptation, using the TREE acronym: teaching style, rules, equipment, and environments. The English Sport Federation (Black & Williamson, 2011) uses fairly similar categories, but labeled STEP: space, task, equipment and [eople, while instructing sport skills. In spite of the interest in the task analytic approach to inclusive physical education planning and implementation, no evidence is available thus far in support of this practice within inclusive contexts.

Summary and recommendations

In this review, scientific literature referring to intervention research in APE was summarized and synthesized into several domains, including (a) motor skill development programs, (b) school- and community-based fitness exercise training programs, (c) applied behavior analysis, and (d) inclusion-related practices.

Based on this review, it may be concluded that in all domains of research in this area, both the volume and level of research are unsatisfying. While acknowledging the difficulties in complying with medical or educational standards for EBP, even the more specific guidelines proposed by the CEC for children with special needs or disabilities have mostly not been accessed. Regarding group designs, in most intervention domains research with larger and more representative samples needs to be published. In some of these domains, there is hardly any comparative research available. Regarding single-subject designs, which comprise the majority of research evidence, greater rigor in the conduction and analysis should be exercised (Haegele & Hodge, 2015; Parker et al., 2011). Finally, in some domains of intervention, such as ecological task analysis and universal design, even though recommended, no research evidence has been presented so far to determine the effects of intervention. APE scholars are encouraged to pursue research that enables better support for their practice recommendations. Given the difficulties discussed in this chapter to acquire high-level research evidence (e.g., RCT) in self-contained and inclusive classes, it is recommended to address and multiply case-studies designs. Furthermore, there is a need to develop valid and reliable criteria enabling the identification of interventions, particularly in emerging inclusive practices such as ecological task analysis and universal design.

Key summary points

- Evidence-based practice (EBP) is one of several important assets for practical decision making in adapted physical education.
- EBP can be translated into practice when reflecting on the evidence with the service recipient, discussing alternatives, determining the most compatible alternatives, and evaluating the outcomes.
- EBP can be helpful for widening the practitioner's horizons regarding alternative strategies.
- APE scholars recommend that EBP not be used as a recipe, but rather as task analysis and prioritizing alternatives, and for finding individualized solutions.
- Some APE scholars discourage the use of randomized controlled trials (RCTs) as a high level of evidence, due to the individualized, system-based, and self-determined contexts of APE.
- The utilization of effect size as a measure of clinically meaningful difference is recommended when addressing EBP in APE.
- The accounts of evidence in APE report very few RCTs, and add qualitative inquiry to the evidence perspective.
- Motor skill development programs have mostly been found to increase performance quality in locomotor and object-control skills, but failed to increase physical activity participation.
- School and community-based exercise training programs have improved the targeted fitness components in children with intellectual disability (ID), overweight, developmental coordination disorders (DCD), autism spectrum disorders (ASD), and cerebral palsy (CP). However, evidence is mostly based on controlled, single-subject, and case study designs.
- Applied behavior analysis has been reported to be effective mostly in children with ID and ASD, and based on single-subject designs.
- Inclusive strategies are an increasingly important area of research. However, the evidence supporting these practices is relatively scarce.

- Peer tutoring is probably the most studied inclusive strategy, and evidence based on systematic reviews exposes a variety of contexts and populations, mostly including single-subject designs.
- Paraeducators were targeted in few studies, including survey, qualitative, and case study designs.
- Self-determined and mastery learning, co-teaching, universal design, and ecological task analysis are recommended by scholars but supported with very limited research, and therefore cannot yet be acknowledged as EBP in APE.
- Continued research in support of these and other emerging inclusive strategies is warranted for better establishing the inclusive approach in physical education.

Reflective questions for discussion

1. How can evidence-based practice in APE be defined?
2. Which are the levels of evidence for APE practices?
3. Which APE practices appear to be EBP supported?
4. Which inclusive strategies appear to lack EBP support?
5. What type of research and how much research would be needed to document the use of paraeducators, UDL, and the ecological model as EBP?

References

Ackley, B. J., Swan, B. A., Ladwig, G., & Tucker, S. (2008). *Evidence-based nursing care guidelines: Medical-surgical intervention* (p. 7). St. Louis, MO: Mosby Elsevier.

Ainscow, M., & Miles, S. (2008). Making education for all inclusive: Where next?. *Prospects*, *145*(1), 15–34.

Australian Sports Commission (2018). Adapting and modifying for people with disability – part one. *IDEAS: Information on disability, education, and awareness services*. Retrieved 24/ 10.2018from www.ideas.org.au/r/front/adapting-and-modifying-for-people-with-disability-part-one/4?

Aviram, R., Harries, N., Namourah, I., Amro, A., & Bar-Haim, S. (2017). Effects of a group circuit progressive resistance training program compared with a treadmill training program for adolescents with cerebral palsy. *Developmental Neurorehabilitation*, *20*(6), 347–354. doi:10.1080/17518423.2016.1212946

Baer, D. M., Wolf, M. M., & Risley, T. R. (1968). Some current dimensions of applied behaviour analysis. *Journal of Applied Behavior Analysis*, *1*, 91–97. doi:10.1901/jaba.1968.1-91

Balan, C. M., & Davis, W. E. (1993). Ecological task analysis—An approach to teaching physical education. *Journal of Physical Education, Recreation & Dance*, *64*(9), 54–62. doi:10.1080/07303084.1993.10607352

Bishop, J. C., & Pangelinan, M. (2018). Motor skills intervention research of children with disabilities. *Research in Developmental Disabilities*, *74*, 14–30. doi:10.1016/j.ridd.2017.11.002

Black, K., & Williamson, D. (2011). Designing inclusive physical activities and games. In A. Cereijo-Roibas, E. Stamatakis, & K. Black (Eds.), *Design for sport* (pp. 124–195). Farnham, UK: Gower.

Block, M. E. (1995). Development and validation of the children's attitudes toward integrated physical education-revised (CAIPE-R) Inventory. *Adapted Physical Activity Quarterly*, *12*, 60–77. doi:10.1123/apaq.12.1.60

Block, M. E., & Obrusnikova, I. (2007). Inclusion in physical education: A review of the literature from 1995-2005. *Adapted Physical Activity Quarterly*, *24*(2), 103–124.

Block, M. E., & Zeman, R. (1996). Including students with disabilities in regular physical education: Effects on nondisabled children. *Adapted Physical Activity Quarterly*, *13*(1), 38–49. doi:10.1123/apaq.13.1.38

Bouffard, M., & Reid, G. (2012). The good, the bad, and the ugly of evidence-based practice. *Adapted Physical Activity Quarterly*, *29*(1), 1–24. doi:10.1123/apaq.29.1.1

Brian, A., Pennell, A., Haibach-Beach, P., Foley, J., Taunton, S., & Lieberman, L. J. (2018). Correlates of physical activity among children with visual impairments. *Disability and Health Journal*. doi:10.1016/j.dhjo.2018.10.007

Bryan, R. R., McCubbin, J. A., & Mars, H. V. D. (2013). The ambiguous role of the paraeducator in the general physical education environment. *Adapted Physical Activity Quarterly, 30*(2), 164–183. doi:10.1123/apaq.30.2.164

Burton, A. W., & Davis, W. E. (1995). Ecological task analysis: Utilizing intrinsic measures in research and practice. *Human Movement Science, 15*(2), 285–314. doi:10.1016/0167-9457(95)00047-X

Capio, C. M., Sit, C. H. P., Eguia, K. F., Aberneth, B., & Masters, R. S. W. (2015). Fundamental movement skills training to promote physical activity in children with and without disability: A pilot study. *Journal of Health and Sports Sciences, 4*, 235–243. doi:10.1016/j.jshs.2014.08.001

Centre of Evidence Based Medicine (Oxford). Oxford University, Oxford, England. Retrieved online Aug 13, 2018. www.cebm.net

Coates, J., & Vickerman, P. (2008b). Let the children have their say: Children with special education needs and their experiences of physical education – A review. *Support for Learning, 23*(4), 168–175. doi:10.1111/j.1467-9604.2008.00390.x

Cochrane, A. L. (1972). *Effectiveness and efficiency. Random reflections on health services.* Reprinted in 1989 in association with the BMJ, Reprinted in 1999 for Nuffield Trust by the Royal Society of Medicine Press, London (ISBN 1-85315-394-X). London, UK: Nuffield Provincial Hospitals Trust.

Cook, B. G., Smith, G. J., & Tankersley, M. (2012). Evidence-based practices in education. In K. R. Harris, S. Graham, & T. Urdan (Eds.), *APA educational psychology handbook* (Vol. 1, pp. 495–528). Washington, DC: American Psychological Association. Retrieved 20.10.2018 from www.researchgate.net/publication/232542339_Evidence-based_practices_in_education

Cormack, J. C. (2002). Evidence-based practice…What is it and how do I do it?. *Journal of Orthopedic & Sports Physical Therapy, 32*(10), 484–487.

Council for Exceptional Children. (2014). *Council for exceptional children standards for evidence-based practices in special education.* Arlington, VA: The author. Retrieved online on Aug 22, 2018. from www.cec.sped.org/~/media/Images/Standards/CEC EBP Standards cover/CECsEvidence Based Practice Standards.pdf

Davis, R. W., Kotecki, J. E., Harvey, M. W., & Oliver, A. (2007). Responsibilities and training needs of paraeducators in physical education. *Adapted Physical Activity Quarterly, 24*(1), 70–83. doi:10.1123/apaq.24.1.70

Davis, W. E., & Burton, A. W. (1991). Ecological task analysis: Translating movement behavior theory into practice. *Adapted Physical Activity Quarterly, 8*(2), 154–177. doi:10.1123/apaq.8.2.154

Dobbins, M., Husson, H., DeCorby, K., & LaRocca, R. L. (2013). School-based physical activity programs for promoting physical activity and fitness in children and adolescents aged 6 to 18. *The Cochrane Database of Systematic Reviews, 28*(2), CD007651. doi:10.1002/14651858.CD007651.pub2

Dodds, K. J., & Shields, N. (2005). A systematic review of the outcomes of cardiovascular exercise programs for people with down syndrome. *Archives of Physical Medicine & Rehabilitation, 86*(10), 2051–2058. doi:10.1016/j.apmr.2005.06.003

Farhat, F., Hsairi, I., Baati, H., Smits-Engelsman, B. C. M., Masmoudi, K., Mchirgui, R., … Moalla, W. (2016). The effect of a motor skills training program in the improvement of practiced and non-practiced tasks performance in children with developmental coordination disorder (DCD). *Human Movement Science, 46*, 10–22. doi:10.1016/j.humov.2015.12.001

Fejgin, N., Talmor, R., & Erlich, I. (2005). Inclusion and burnout in physical education. *European Physical Education Review, 11*, 29–50. doi:10.1177/1356336x05049823. from http://unesdoc.unesco.org/images/0023/002354/235409e.pdf

Fisher, A., Reilly, J. J., Kelly, L. A., Montgomery, C., Williamson, A., Paton, J. Y., & Grant, S. (2005). Fundamental movement skills and habitual physical activity in young children. *Medicine & Science in Sports & Exercise, 37*(4), 684–688. doi:10.1249/01.MSS.0000159138.48107.7D

Gallahue, D. L. (1982). *Understanding motor development in children.* New York: John Wiley & Sons.

Gargiulo, R. M., & Metcalf, D. (2013). *Teaching in today's inclusive classrooms: A universal design for learning approach* (2nd ed.). Belmont, CA: Wadsworth, Cengage Learning.

Gersten, R., Fuchs, L. S., Compton, D., Coyne, M., Greenwood, C., & Innocenti, M. S. (2005). Quality indicators for group experimental and quasi-experimental research in special education. *Exceptional Children, 71*, 149–164.

Giangreco, M. F., Suter, J. C., & Doyle, M. B. (2007). Paraprofessionals in inclusive Schools: A review of recent research. *Journal of Educational and Psychological Consultation, 20*(1), 41–57. doi:10.1080/10474410903535356

Gigerenzer, G. (2000). *Adaptive thinking: Rationality in the real world.* New York: Oxford University Press.

Grenier, M., Miller, N., & Black, K. (2017). Applying universal design for learning and the inclusion spectrum for students with severe disabilities in general physical education. *Journal of Physical Education, Recreation & Dance, 88*(6), 51–56. doi:10.1080/07303084.2017.1330167

Guyatt, G. H., Cook, D., & Haynes, B. (2004). Evidence based medicine has come a long way. *British Medical Journal, 329*, 990–991.

Haegele, J. A., & Hodge, S. R. (2015). The applied behavior analysis research paradigm and single-subject designs in adapted physical activity research. *Adapted Physical Activity Quarterly, 32*(4), 285–301. doi:10.1123/APAQ.2014-0211

Haegele, J. A., & Sutherland, S. (2015). Perspectives of students with disabilities toward physical education: A qualitative inquiry review. *Quest, 67*, 255–273. doi:10.1080/00336297.2015.1050118

Haynes, R. B., Devereaux, P. J., & Guyatt, G. H. (2002). Physicians' and patients' choices in evidence based practice: Evidence does not make decisions, people do. *British Medical Journal, 324*, 1350.

Heikinaro-Johansson, P., & Sherrill, C. (1994). Integrating children with special needs in physical education: A school district assessment model from Finland. *Adapted Physical Activity Quarterly, 11*(1), 44–56. doi:10.1123/apaq.11.1.44

Homer, R. H., Carr, E. G., Halle, J., McGee, G., Odom, S., & Wolery, M. (2005). The use of single-subject research to identify evidence-based practice in special education. *Exceptional Children, 71*, 165–179.

Hutzler, Y. (2006). Evidence-based research in adapted physical activity: Theoretical and data-based considerations. *Revista Da Sobama, 11*(1), 13–24.

Hutzler, Y. (2007). A systematic ecological model for adapting physical activities: Theoretical foundations and practical examples. *Adapted Physical Activity Quarterly, 24*(4), 287–304. doi:10.1123/apaq.24.4.287

Hutzler, Y. (2011). Evidence-based practice and research: Challenge to the development of adapted physical activity. *Adapted Physical Activity Quarterly, 28*, 189–209. doi:10.1123/apaq.28.3.189

Hutzler, Y., & Bar-Eli, M. (2013). How to cope with bias while adapting for inclusion in physical education and sports: A judgment and decision making perspective. *Quest, 65*(1), 57–71. doi:10.1080/00336297.2012.727372

Hutzler, Y., Fliess, O., Chacham, A., & Van Den Auweele, Y. (2002). Perspectives of children with disabilities on inclusion and empowerment: Supporting and limiting factors. *Adapted Physical Activity Quarterly, 19*(3), 280–299.

Hutzler, Y., Oz, M., & Barak, S. (2013). Goal perspectives and sport participation motivation of special Olympians and typically developing athletes. *Research in Developmental Disabilities., 34*(7), 2149–2160. doi:10.1016/j.ridd.2013.03.019

Jin, J., & Yun, J. (2010). Evidence-based practice in adapted physical education. *Journal of Physical Education, Recreation & Dance, 81*(4), 50–54.

Kalef, L., Reid, G., & MacDonald, C. (2013). Evidence-based practice: A quality indicator analysis of peer-tutoring in adapted physical education. *Research in Developmental Disabilities, 34*(9), 2514–2522. doi:10.1016/j.ridd.2013.05.004

Killian, S. (2016). 5 keys to successful peer tutoring. The Australian Society for Evidence based Teaching. Downloaded from: www.evidencebasedteaching.org.au/5-keys-successful-peer-tutoring/

Kirby, A., & Sugden, D. A. (2007). Children with developmental coordination disorders. *Journal of the Royal Society of Medicine, 100*(4), 182–186. doi:10.1258/jrsm.100.4.182

Kvernbekk, T. (2017). Evidence-based educational practice. *Oxford Research Encyclopedia of Education.* Online. doi:10.1093/acrefore/9780190264093.013.187

Lahtinen, U., Rintala, P., & Malin, A. (2007). Physical performance of individuals with intellectual disability: A 30 year follow up. *Adapted Physical Activity Quarterly, 24*(2), 125–143.

Lieberman, L., Lytle, R., & Clarcq, J. (2008). Getting it right from the start: Employing the universal design for learning approach to your curriculum. *Journal of Physical Education, Recreation & Dance, 79*(2), 32–39. doi:10.1080/07303084.2008.10598132

Logan, S. W., Robinson, L. E., Wilson, A. E., & Lucas, W. A. (2012). Getting the fundamentals of movement: A meta-analysis of the effectiveness of motor skill interventions in children. *Child Care, Health and Development, 38*(3), 305–315. doi:10.1111/j.1365-2214.2011.01307.x

Maheady, L., Harper, G. F., & Mallette, B. (2001). Peer-mediated instruction and interventions and students with mild disabilities. *Remedial and Special Education, 22*(1), 4–14. doi:10.1177/074193250102200102

Mitchell, D. (2007). *What really works in special and inclusive education: Using evidence-based teaching strategies.* Abingdon Oxford, UK: Routledge.

Munafo, C. (2017). Towards a new culture in physical education with the universal design for learning. *International Journal of Science Culture and Sport, 5*(1), 1–10. Retrieved from www.iscsjournal.com/Maka leler/1378171236_5c1s_1.pdf

Mylius, C. F., Paap, D., & Takken, T. (2016). Reference value for the 6-minute walk test in children and adolescents: A systematic review. *Expert Review of Respiratory Medicine, 10*(12), 1335–1352. doi:10.1080/17476348.2016.1258305

Nasar, J., & Evans-Cowley, J. (2007). *Universal design and visitability: From accessibility to zoning.* Columbus, OH: The John Glenn School of Public Affairs.

Nelson, J., & Campbell, C. (2017). Evidence-informed practice in education: Meanings and applications. *Educational Research, 59*(2), 127–135. doi:10.1080/00131881.2017.1314115

Newell, K. M. (1986). Constraints on the development of coordination. In M. G. Wade & H. T. A. Whiting (Eds.), *Motor development in young children: Aspects of coordination and control* (pp. 341–360). Dordrecht: Martinus Nijhoff.

Nirje, B. (1972). The right to self-determination. In W. Wolfensberger (Ed.), *Normalization: The principle of normalization in human services* (pp. 176–200). Toronto, Canada: National Institute on Mental Retardation.

Obrusníková, I., Válková, H., & Block, M. E. (2003). Impact of inclusion in general physical education on students without disabilities. *Adapted Physical Activity Quarterly, 20*(3), 230–245. doi:10.1123/apaq.20.3.230

Odom, S. L., Brantlinger, E., Gersten, R., Horner, R. H., Thompson, B., & Harris, K. R. (2005). Research in special education: Scientific methods and evidence-based practices. *Exceptional Children, 71*(2), 137–148. doi:10.1177/001440290507100201

Parker, R. I., Vannest, K. J., Davis, J. L., & Sauber, S. B. (2011). Combining nonoverlap and trend for single-case research: Tau-U. *Behavior Therapy, 42*(2), 284–299. doi:10.1016/j.beth.2010.08.006

Payne, V. G., & Issacs, I. (2016). *Human motor development: A lifespan approach.* New York: McGraw Hill.

Paynter, R. A. (2009). Evidence-based research in the applied social sciences. *RSR. Reference Services Review, 37,* 435–450.

Pitetti, K., Baynard, T., & Agiovlasitis, S. (2013). Children and adolescents with down syndrome, physical fitness and physical activity. *Journal of Sport and Health Science, 2,* 47–57. doi:10.1016/j.jshs.2012.10.004

Pocock, T., & Miyahara, M. (2018). Inclusion of students with disability in physical education: A qualitative meta-analysis. *International Journal of Inclusive Education, 22*(7), 751–766. doi:10.1080/13603116.2017.1412508

Porretta, D. L., & Sherrill, C. (2005). APAQ at twenty: A documentary analysis. *Adapted Physical Activity Quarterly, 22,* 119–135.

Qi, J., & Ha, A. S. (2012). Inclusion in physical education: A review of literature. *International Journal of Disability, Development and Education, 59*(3), 257–281. doi:10.1080/1034912X.2012.697737

Register, F. (1977, August 23). Education of Handicapped Children: Implementation of Part B of the Education of the Handicapped Act, Vol. 42. 163, Part II, 42474–42518.

Reid, G., Bouffard, M., & MacDonald, C. (2012). Creating evidence-based research in adapted physical activity. *Adapted Physical Activity Quarterly, 29,* 115–131.

Reid, G., & Stanish, H. (2003). Professional and disciplinary status of adapted physical activity. *Adapted Physical Activity Quarterly, 20,* 213–229.

Rekaa, H., Hanisch, H., & Ytterhus, B. (2018). Inclusion in physical education: Teacher attitudes and student perspectives. A systematic review. *International Journal of Disability, Development and Education,* 1–20. doi:doi/abs/10.1080/1034912X.2018.1435852

Rimmer, J. A., & Marques, A. C. (2012). Physical activity for people with disabilities. *The Lancet.* Published online July 18 doi:10.1016/S0140-6736(12)61028-9.

Ryan, J. M., Cassidy, E. E., Noorduyn, S. G., & O'Connell, N. E. (2017). Exercise interventions for cerebral palsy. *Cochrane Database Systematic Reiviews, Jun, 11:6,* CD011660. doi:10.1002/14651858. CD011660.pub2

Sackett, D. L., Rosenberg, W. M. C., Gray, M. J. A., Haynes, B. R., & Richardson, W. S. (1996). Evidence based medicine: What it is and what it isn't. *British Medical Journal, 312,* 71–72. doi:10.1136/bmj.312.7023.71

Sherlock-Shangraw, R. (2013). Creating inclusive youth sport environments with the universal design for learning. *Journal of Physical Education, Recreation & Dance*, *84*(2), 40–46. doi:10.1080/07303084.2013.757191

Sherrill, C. (2004). *Adapted physical activity, recreation and sport: Crossdisciplinary and lifespan* (6th ed.). Boston, MA: McGraw-Hill Higher Education.

Simon, H. A. (1956). Rational choice and the structure of the environment. *Psychological Review*, *63*, 129–138.

Skinner, B. F. (1953). *Science and human behaviour*. New York: Macmillan.

Smith, T. E. C., Polloway, E. A., Patton, J. R., & Dowdy, C. A. (2008). *Teaching students with special needs in inclusive settings* (5th ed.). Boston, MA: Allyn and Bacon.

Smits-Engelsman, B. C. M., Blank, R., van der Kaay, A.-C., Mosterd-van der Meijs, R., Vlugt-an Den Brand, E., Polatajko, H. J., & Wilson, P. H. (2012). Efficacy of interventions to improve motor performance in children with developmental coordination disorder: A combined systematic review and meta-analysis. *Developmental Medicine & Child Neurology*, *55*(3), 229–237. doi:10.1111/dmcn.12008

Spring, B. (2007). Evidence based practice in clinical psychology: What it is, why it matters, what you need to know? *Journal of Clinical Psychology*, *63*, 611–631.

Srinivasan, S. M., Pescatello, L. S., & Bhat, A. N. (2014). Current perspectives on physical activity and exercise recommendations for children and adolescents with autism spectrum disorders. *Physical Therapy*, *94*(6), 875–889. doi:10.2522/ptj.20130157

Standage, M., Gillison, F. B., Ntoumanis, N., & Treasure, D. C. (2012). Predicting students' physical activity and health-related well-being: A prospective crossdomain investigation of motivation across school physical education and exercise settings. *Journal of Sport and Exercise.Psychology*, *34*(1), 37–60. doi:10.1123/jsep.34.1.37

Stodden, D. F., Goodway, J. D., Langendorfer, S. J., Roberton, M. A., Rudisill, M. E., Garcia, C., & Garcia, L. E. (2008). A developmental perspective on the role of motor skill competence in physical activity: An emergent relationship. *Quest*, *60*(2), 290–306. doi:10.1080/00336297.2008.10483582

Tant, M., & Watelain, E. (2016). Forty years later, a systematic literature review on inclusion in physical education (1975-2015): A teacher perspective. *Educational Research Review*, *19*, 1–7. doi:10.106/j.edurev.2016.04.002

Topping, K. (2005). Trends in peer learning. *Educational Psychology*, *25*(6), 631–645.

Tripp, A., Rizzo, T., & Webbert, L. (2007). Inclusion in physical education: Changing the culture. *Journal of Physical Education, Recreation & Dance*, *78*(2), 32–36. doi:10.1080/07303084.2007.10597971

Tversky, A., & Kahneman, D. (1974). Judgment under uncertainty: Heuristics and biases. *Science*, *185*, 1124–1131.

U.S. Federal Register. (2013). Final priorities; National Institute on Disability and Rehabilitation Research – Rehabilitation Research and Training Centers. *Final Priorities*, *9*, *78*(90), 27038–27044, Office of Special Education and Rehabilitation Services, Department of Education.

U.S. Department of Education. (2003a). *Identifying and implementing educational practices supported by rigorous evidence: A user friendly guide*. Washington, DC: Author. Retrieved from www2.ed.gov/rschstat/research/pubs/rigorousevid/rigorousevid.pdf

U.S. Department of Education (2010). Higher education opportunity act – 2008. Retrieved on 25.10.2018 from: www2.ed.gov/policy/highered/leg/hea08/index.html

U.S. Department of Education, National Center for Education Statistics. (2016). *The digest of education statistics, 2015 (NCES 2016-014)*, Table 204.60. Washington, DC: U.S. Department of Education.

U.S. Department of Education, Office of the Secretary, Office of Public Affairs. (2003b). *No child left behind: A parents' guide*. Washington, DC: Author.

United Nations. (2006). *Convention on the rights of persons with disabilities*. New York: Author. Retrieved on 25.1.2018 from:

Unnithan, V. B., Katsimanis, G., Evangelinou, C., Kosmas, C., Kandrali, I., & Kellis, E. (2007). Effect of strength and aerobic training in children with cerebral palsy. *Medicine & Science in Sports & Exercise*, *39*, 1902–1909.

Valentini, N. C., & Rudisill, M. E. (2004). An inclusive mastery climate intervention and the motor skill development of children with and without disabilities. *Adapted Physical Activity Quarterly*, *21*(4), 330–347. doi:10.1123/apaq.21.4.330

Van Lent, M. (Ed.). (2006). *Count me in: A guide to inclusive physical activity, sport and leisure for children with a disability*. Leuven, Belgium: Acco.

Verschuren, O., Ketelaar, M., Gorter, J. W., Helders, P. J., Uiterwaal, C. S., & Takken, T. (2007). Exercise training program in children and adolescents with cerebral palsy: A randomized controlled trial. *Archives of Pediatrics & Adolescent Medicine, 161*(11), 1075–1081.

Verschuren, O., Ketelaar, M., Takken, T., Helders, P. J., & Gorter, J. W. (2008). Exercise programs for children with cerebral palsy: A systematic review of the literature. *American Journal of Physical Medicine & Rehabilitation, 87*(5), 404–417. doi:10.1097/PHM.0b013e31815b2675

Verschuren, O., Peterson, M. D., Balemans, A. C., & Hurvitz, E. A. (2016). Exercise and physical activity recommendations for people with cerebral palsy. *Developmental Medicine & Child Neurology, 58*, 798–808.

Virués-Ortega, J. (2010). Applied behavior analytic intervention for autism in early childhood: Meta-analysis, meta-regression and dose–Response meta-analysis of multiple outcomes. *Clinical Psychology Review, 30*(4), 387–399. doi:10.1016/j.cpr.2010.01.008

Ward, P., & Barrett, T. (2002). A review of behavior analysis research in physical education. *Journal of Teaching in Physical Education, 21*(3), 242–266.

Ward, P., & Lee, M. A. (2005). Peer-assisted learning in physical education: A review of theory and research. *Journal of Teaching in Physical Education, 24*(3), 205–225. doi:10.1123/jtpe.24.3.205

Wehmeyer, M. L. (1996). Self-determination as an educational outcome: Why is it important to children, youth and adults with disabilities?. In D. J. Sands & M. L. Wehmeyer (Eds.), *Self-determination across the life span: Independence and choice for people with disabilities* (pp. 17–36). Baltimore, MD: Paul H. Brookes.

Wiart, L., Darrah, J., Kelly, M., & Legg, D. (2015). Community fitness programs: What is available for children and youth with motor disabilities and what do parents want? *Physical & Occupational Therapy in Pediatrics, 35*(1), 73–87. doi:10.3109/01942638.2014.990550

Wilhelmsen, T., & Sørensen, M. (2017). Inclusion of children with disabilities in physical education: A systematic review of literature from 2009 to 2015. *Adapted Physical Activity Quarterly, 34*(3), 311–337. doi:10.1123/apaq.2016-0017

World Health Organization (WHO). (2001). International classification of function, disability and health. Geneva: United Nations. Retrieved 28.10.2018 from http://apps.who.int/iris/bitstream/handle/10665/42407/9241545429.pdf;jsessionid=4FE03CC288C3AB688BFA433ACE6BAC61?sequence=1

Wu, W. L., Yang, Y. F., Chu, I. H., Hsu, H. T., Tsai, F. H., & Liang, J. M. (2017). Effectiveness of a cross-circuit exercise training program in improving the fitness of overweight or obese adolescents with intellectual disability enrolled in special education schools. *Research in Developmental Disabilities, 60*, 83–95. doi:10.1016/j.ridd.2016.11.005

Zhang, J., deLisie, L., & Chen, S. (2006). Analysis of AAHPERD research abstracts published under special populations from 1968 to 2004. *Adapted Physical Activity Quarterly, 23*, 203–217.

Zhang, J., & Qi, Y. (2015). Application of single subject experimental designs in adapted physical activity research: A descriptive analysis. *International Journal of Medical and Health Sciences, 9*(6), 475–480.

7

Measurement in adapted physical education research

Joonkoo Yun and Layne Case

Measurement in adapted physical education research

The *term* "measurement" in the context of research is a technical and narrowly defined concept, whereas the *word* "measurement" is part of the basic vocabulary that is commonly used in everyday language. In fact, it is considered as one of 3000 words that are most frequently used in the English language (Education First, n.d). The difference between the use of the word within research settings and everyday vernacular may create confusion and misuse of the term. In this chapter, we define the term measurement within the context of adapted physical education (APE) research. Then, we discuss the process of how to obtain accurate measurement results. Additionally, we introduce three common misconceptions of evaluating the accuracy of measurement within APE research.

Understanding research and the process of research

In order to define the term measurement in the context of scientific research, it is necessary to operationalize research. Like measurement, research can be defined in many different ways and can cover a broad spectrum of meanings. Some suggest that the act of research is simply to gather information and make a sound decision (Berg & Latin, 2008). For example, a sixth-grade physical education teacher may ask students to conduct research on the Paralympics, or newly accepted doctoral students in an APE program may perform research to find available apartments in their new university's town for the upcoming academic year. These activities, however, may not be considered research within science (Leedy & Ormrod, 2019). Research within the context of APE should instead be defined as a systematic process and attempt to find solutions for a well-defined problem. In other words, research is the sequence of activities involved in answering a specific question with a predetermined and systematic process. Research can be conducted in formal laboratory environments or less technical settings, including within public schools, after-school programs, communities, and/ or even the library. Regardless of the location, setting, or sophistication of equipment involved, however, all research must include specific questions and a systematic process to answer the given problem.

Leedy and Ormrod (2019) elaborate on what is *not* scientific research in their popular textbook. Research is neither simply gathering information nor rummaging through information. In other words, a graduate student in APE gathering information about Special Olympics to write a term paper is not a sound example of scientific research. Leedy and Ormrod instead call this activity information discovery. Unlike research, information discovery may not include a specific problem (i.e., research question) to solve and/or may not follow a systematic process. In order for information discovery to be considered research, the included activities should demonstrate five characteristics: (a) systematic, (b) logical, (c) empirical, (d) reductive, and (e) replicable and transmittable (Thomas, Nelson, & Silverman, 2015). Although we acknowledge that all scholars, particularly researchers from postmodernism philosophy, may not fully agree on these exact characteristics, these five characteristics are important properties of research (Tuckman & Harper, 2012).

Many scholars have elaborated upon the process of research, which generally includes identifying the problem, reviewing the literature, setting up a hypothesis, collecting data, analyzing data, and drawing interpretations and conclusions. We would like to modify this commonly suggested research process as (a) gain curiosity in the topic, (b) conduct literature review, (c) define a specific question and develop hypothesis, if appropriate, (d) collect and analyze data, (f) interpret data, (g) find solution(s) for the specific research questions, and (h) become curious about the topic again. Figure 7.1 elaborates on and presents a visual model for this research process. While other chapters in this book have

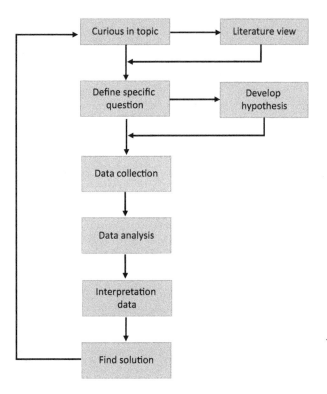

Figure 7.1 Process of research

addressed a more detailed process of different types of research engagement, we continue on to discuss data collection and analysis, as they are both essential parts of quality measurement procedures.

Definition of measurement

Data collection and analysis can be divided into five distinctly different processes including (a) observation, (b) gathering data, (c) data reduction, (d) data analysis, and (e) interpretation of the data analysis. Figure 7.2 provides further detail on these measurement procedures. Historically, traditional psychometrists, as well as those working in the field of kinesiology, define measurement as the process of assigning numbers to objects or events according to a given rule (e.g., Morrow, Mood, Disch, & Kang, 2016; Safrit, 1989). This act may be more closely aligned with the second step (i.e., gathering data) in Figure 7.2. This particular view of measurement is influenced by Stanley Stevens, a mid-20th century Harvard psychologist. Despite his significant impact on current measurement practice, his view on measurement has been criticized by numerous scholars (e.g., Michell, 1986; Velleman & Wilkinson, 1993). For example, Velleman and Wilkinson (1993) summarized one of the major criticisms of his views as being too strict to apply to real-world data. In addition, "the phenomena to be measured may not directly associate with object or events" alone (Carmines & Zeller, 1979, p. 9).

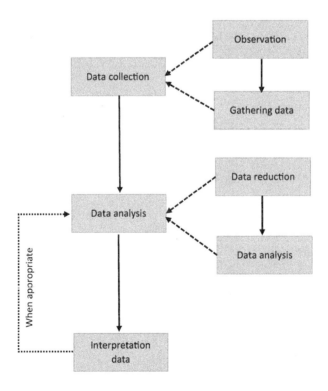

Figure 7.2 Measurement procedure

The concepts and variables we measure in adapted physical education research are often associated with high levels of abstraction. For example, Renia, Hutzler, Iniguez-Santiago, and Moreno-Murcia (2019) studied the ability beliefs and attitudes toward inclusion in physical education of 976 students. In this example, neither ability beliefs nor attitudes are objects or events. The classical definition of measurement, resultantly, may be too narrowly defined for all measurement practice within APE. It is, therefore, our opinion that measurement practice should no longer be viewed as a single act of assigning numbers to our observations, but should instead be updated to include the process of obtaining the appropriate information necessary to interpret and answer a given research question.

It is also necessary to acknowledge that, traditionally, researchers in kinesiology have separated measurement and evaluation. They define measurement as the act of assigning numbers to an event and evaluation as the interpretation of measurement results (Baumgartner, Jackson, Mahar, & Rowe, 2015; Morrow et al., 2016). However, the Task Force of the Standards for Educational and Psychological Testing view that measurement should not only include the collection of data (a simple act of obtaining numbers), but should also pay careful attention to fairness for all test takers and allow for appropriate interpretation of test scores (American Educational Research Association & American Psychological Association, 2014). Given these considerations, we adopt Zeller and Carmine's (1979) definition of measurement in this chapter. Zeller and Carmine suggested that measurement practice should be viewed as the process of linking abstract concepts to empirical indicators. Additionally, as we have argued that measurement practice should also include all five processes (i.e., observation, gathering data, data reduction, etc.) that we previously indicated in Figure 7.2, *measurement* is the *process of obtaining accurate information and making appropriate decisions to answer a given research question*.

Process of obtaining accurate measurement

Observation

All measurement practice starts with observation. Observation not only includes direct observation of a behavior and/or attribute of interest, but also identifies the specific behavior(s) and/or attributes that we want to observe while answering the research questions. In a recent meta-analysis, Case and Yun (2019) pointed out that a large number of studies within gross motor interventions for children with autism spectrum disorder (ASD) may have selected inappropriate outcome measures for the defined research questions. The authors were interested in identifying specific intervention types that have greater effects on gross motor outcomes among children with ASD. They unexpectedly found inconclusive results, however, and suggested that the results may be related to the use of inappropriate dependent variables. In other words, researchers within the included studies may have failed to identify appropriate outcome variables and measurement tools that accurately observed the change in performance specific to the intervention. As this misalignment can create obstacles within the measurement process, researchers should carefully select the variable(s) of interest that match their research question.

A critical first step in ensuring accurate measurement is to identify the appropriate variable to be observed. For example, Ulrich and his colleagues (2001) studied the effects of treadmill practice on the onset of walking for 30 infants with Down syndrome. Under the framework of dynamic systems theory, they hypothesized that in order to facilitate walking behavior, infants must practice walking. However, the challenge was that the infants of interest could not practice walking as they could not yet walk independently. From their previous work, however, Ulrich and his colleagues knew that when infants are placed on a mobilized treadmill, they mimic walking behavior (Ulrich, Ulrich, & Collier, 1992). The authors therefore used this mimicking behavior as an intervention strategy. In this example, the research question, included intervention strategies, and chosen dependent variables (onset of walking) are closely aligned with each other. Alternatively, when researchers are not able to identify closely aligned observed variables, the outcome of the study may be difficult to determine. For example, Pawlowski and her colleagues (n.d) studied the effects of a service-learning program on undergraduate students' self-efficacy through Bayesian analysis. The study unfortunately failed to identify the appropriate observed variable, which may have resulted in the authors' difficulty with publishing the study in a reputable journal. Although the study team discussed the potential dependent variables (observed variables) for examining the effects of the existing service-learning program, the decision to choose the observed variable was influenced more by convenience rather than a strong theoretical or empirical rationale. Despite sophisticated statistical approaches, the authors were not able to draw conclusive results from their study. Failing to identify the appropriate observed variables may have contributed to their insignificant and inconclusive results, as well as the ultimate inability to publish their manuscript.

At the same time, we want to recognize that identifying the appropriate observed variable is not always a straightforward process. It requires extensive literature review and careful consideration, while the authors must also be realistic about their circumstances. For example, Jin and Yun (2013) examined the physical activity levels of 503 adolescent children with and without disabilities in inclusive middle school physical education classes using a pedometer. Since pedometers only measure the number of steps taken, as opposed to all aspects of physical activity (e.g., energy expenditure, heart rate), some may argue that using pedometers, or a number of steps, are not appropriate methods for measuring overall physical activity. It is, therefore, important to recognize the limitation of using a number of steps as a representation of overall physical activity. At the same time, however, the number of steps may be sufficient to summarize the overall levels of physical activity (Tudor-Locke & Bassett, 2004) within this specific context when considering walking is the most common form of physical activity that individuals with intellectual disabilities engage in (Draheim, Williams, & McCubbin, 2002; Stanish & Draheim, 2005). Overall, an assumption of measurement is that the observed variable represents the variable of interest. Therefore, APE researchers should take steps to ensure they select the most appropriate observed variable(s). With that, the observed variable should have theoretical or strong empirical support in order to accurately represent the variable of interest. In fact, the stronger the link between the two, the more confident you can be in the accuracy of the measurement.

Gathering data

The next stage of the measurement process is gathering data. Some believe that direct observations made in research should be viewed as the most accurate measurements. However, this idea misrepresents the central process of measurement. Within the measurement process, all observations must be converted into a numerical value. If this conversion process is inappropriate or inaccurate, the researcher will subsequently have inaccurate data. This process of gathering data may be the most closely aligned with Stevens' (1946) traditional definition of measurement. In order to understand the process of converting observations into a numerical system, there are four different types of numbers that are important to understand. These numerical systems are often referred to as scales. Stevens (1946) divided the types of numbers into four separate categories, including (a) nominal scale, (b) ordinal scale, (c) interval scale, and (d) ratio scale. Table 7.1 summarizes the characteristics of the four different types of numbers.

Nominal scales are types of numbers commonly used for labeling observations. Common examples of nominal variables include gender, race, ethnicity, and group. More specifically, nominal scales differentiate between levels of observations based on their names or classifications. For example, researchers might assign participants in an experimental group as "1" and a control group as "2" in order to label observations by group. It is important to note that all nominal scales are mutually exclusive and discrete variables. In the previously used example of Ulrich and colleagues' (2001), the sample of infants with Down syndrome in the study was divided into experimental and control groups. During the study, the researchers measured locomotor behaviors, including (a) raises self to stand, (b) walks with help, and (c) walks independently three separate times. In this research example, both independent variables were treated as, and serve as examples of, nominal scales. Measurement times were assigned the numbers 1, 2, or 3. The experimental condition was assigned either 1 or 2, with 1 representing the experimental group and 2 representing the control group. Because each of these observations was converted to a numerical system, the assigned numbers could then be used in the statistical analysis to answer their research question.

Ordinal scales assign numbers to represent rank or ordered sequence of relationship. A simplistic example is the order of performance finishes, such as when Paralympic athletes are placed first, second, or third based on their performance. Another example is when a researcher asks the study participants to rank their satisfaction with an APE service-learning program, ordered from very unsatisfied, somewhat unsatisfied, somewhat satisfied, to very satisfied. In this example, the assigned numbers can be between 1 and 4. Ordinal scales are

Table 7.1 Characteristics of different types of numbers

Type of scale	Characteristics/description	Examples
Nominal	Used to name or label variables Mutually exclusive categories No true zero, order, or measurable difference between variables	Gender (male/female/other) Race/ethnicity (White/Asian/etc.) Research group (control/experimental/etc.) Age group (under 18/18 and over)
Ordinal	Used to name or label variables Meaningful order No true zero or measurable difference between variables	Ranked placements Grade levels Likert scale measurements
Interval	Meaningful order Equal and measurable differences between variables No true zero	Temperature Date
Ratio	Meaningful order Equal and measurable differences between values Includes a true, absolute zero	Age Height/weight

discrete variables and identify the order of possible responses. Despite the order, however, we do not know the exact mathematical relationship between the ranked values within these types of scales. In other words, two responses of *satisfied* with participation in a service-learning program do not equal one response of *very satisfied*. In an example from current literature in APE, Li and his colleagues (2019) studied the relationship between mindfulness and attitudes toward students with ASD among 211 pre-service physical education teachers. The participants' dispositional mindfulness was measured using the 20-item, five-facet mindfulness questionnaire. The questionnaire included five 4-item subscales including observing, describing, acting with awareness, non-judging, and non-reactivity. Pre-service teachers were asked to rate each item on a 5-point Likert type scale, ranging from 1 (never), 2 (seldom), 3 (sometimes), 4 (often), to 5 (always). Likert type scales, like the one previously described, are often treated (used) as interval and/or ratio scales in many APE research studies (e.g., Pawlowski & Yun, 2019; Siebert, Hamm, & Yun, 2017). However, traditional psychometrists have argued that Likert type scales should be treated as ordinal variables. The five points of the Likert type scales have a clear order, as 3 (i.e., sometimes) is more frequent than 2 (i.e., seldom), but the mathematical distance between sometimes and seldom is not the same as the distance between often and sometimes.[1]

Interval scales are numeric scales in which both the order and the exact differences between the values are known. Therefore, in contrast to ordinal scales, these scales not only indicate the rank order, but also the distance, or interval, between two numbers is meaningful. Interval scales include continuous variables and can range from negative to positive infinity. Temperature is a common variable used to explain interval scales. For example, when we measure the average low temperatures during the winter months, Ivalo, Finland may be $0°$ F while Honolulu, Hawaii may be $71°F$ at the same time. If the average low temperature of Corvallis, Oregon during the winter months is $35°F$, Corvallis is $35°F$ warmer than Ivalo, but Honolulu is about twice as warm as Corvallis. Interval scales can also contain zero, but zero does not necessarily indicate the absence of value. An average low temperature of $0°$ F in Ivalo, Finland in January does not indicate that the temperature does not exist—instead, zero degrees is a temperature that represents specific characteristics.

Interval scales may be the most common scale used in APE research. When researchers convert observations into normalized and/or standardized data, they become interval scales. For example, Yun and Ulrich (1997) examined the relationship between perceived and actual competence of physical performance among children with intellectual disabilities. Because the unit of each measure was different (e.g., running speed, dribbling count, long-jump distance), the authors converted the raw scores for each test item to a Z score in order to create a total score that represented actual competence. Moreover, running speed was based on seconds, dribbling was measured by counting the frequency, and long-jump distance was measured in meters. In order to create a total score, the researchers converted the raw score measurements into a standardized score. This process creates interval scores for actual physical competence. Two popular motor development tests, the Test of Gross Motor Development (TGMD) and Movement ABC, similarly convert raw observations into interval scales.

Ratio scales are numeric scales that provide rank order or variables, have equal distance between each unit of measurement, and include an absolute zero. Ratio scales are a mutually exclusive representation of our observations. They also have an equal distance value between each unit of measurement. The ratio scale and interval scales share common characteristics of numerical values. The main difference between the interval and ratio scales is that ratio scales include an absolute zero. In ratio scales, zero means the absence of value. For example, a number of new doctoral students in APE want to transfer credits from their Master's degree program. A student may not be able to transfer any credit hours if he or she did not have the appropriate credit hours to transfer, whereas other students may be able to transfer 15 credits. In this situation, the number zero included is the absence of a value. Another example of a ratio scale can be found from Haegele and his colleagues' (2017) study, in which they examined the accuracy of the number of steps measured by Fitbit Zips among 14 adolescents with visual impairments. In order to estimate the measurement accuracy, the authors calculated the absolute error by the square root of differences between the results of the criterion measure (manual step count) and the estimation of step counts from Fitbit Zips. This process created a variable with an absolute zero and an equal interval between each score.

APE researchers should not only know the different types of scale, but also understand specific rules for collecting data. A crucial step in measurement is to ensure accurate measurement. This process requires researchers to understand details about the specific instrument (measurement tool) and have appropriate levels of practice and training for using that instrument. Some instruments may require a minimum level of practice while other instruments require extensive training or certifications. In Breslin and Rudisill's (2013) examination of the relationship between motor skill performance, time on task, and assessment time among children with ASD, assistants were trained to code observations using the Behavior Evaluation Strategy and Taxonomy (BEST) software. As opposed to a sufficient training duration, the authors reported that coder training for the BEST software continued until the coders reached 90% agreement between their data coding. Alternatively, some other instruments used within APE may require an extensive amount of training. For example, the training required to administer the Autism Diagnostic Observation Schedule (ADOS) is often two full-day workshops. Addressing the specific training requirements for different instruments is beyond the scope of this chapter. However, researchers should recognize that, regardless of the extensiveness of training required, researchers should always be familiar with the testing protocols and must follow the appropriate procedures in order to ensure accurate measurement. It is also important to remember that accurate measurement is influenced by multiple additional factors, including the quality of the instrument, adherence to the appropriate administration procedures, efforts of both the examiner and examinee and the testing conditions. If these factors are not appropriately addressed or considered, then the accurate gathering of data may be jeopardized.

Data reduction

Once APE researchers identify the appropriate variable(s) to observe and collect data, the next step is to reduce the data. This step is rarely recognized as a part of measurement practice but is an important step for ensuring accurate measurement results. When a researcher has collected data from a measurement tool with multiple items, it is likely that the researcher will have a large amount of data that may be difficult to make meaning out of as is. Therefore, the researcher will need to reduce the data down to some type of simplified or organized form for it to be meaningful. Data may be reduced by creating a sum of total scores, averaging all scores, rounding scores to two decimal points, or transforming scores into some type of composite score. One example of data reduction can be found from the TGMD. Motor development literature clearly suggests that fundamental motor skills are composed of two subtypes of skills, including locomotor skills and object control skills. As such, the TGMD measures fundamental motor skills with several items and clearly divides the skill measurements into two separate sub-scores (e.g., locomotor and object control) to represent these two different variables. The total measurement score is then summarized by both the sum of the object control skill scores and the sum of locomotor skill scores.

Data reduction can often be a complex process, as it may be difficult for researchers to decide the most appropriate way to simplify or combine their data. For example, Rizzo (1984) developed an instrument that measures physical educator attitudes toward teaching children with disabilities that has since been updated and commonly used in APE research (Hutzler, Meier, Reuker, & Zitomer, 2019). The instrument was based on the theory of reasoned action and later expanded to measure attitudes using the theory of planned behavior. The instrument includes 12 different statements (items) that measure attitudes. In order to reduce the instrument's measurement of the 12 different items, the scores of all items are summed in order to create a total attitude score. Rizzo and Vispoel (1991) have also strongly argued that attitude is a multidimensional construct. However, the way data were reduced using his measurement instrument is not reflective of this view of attitudes. By creating a sum of the different attitudes scores to represent a total score, he assumed that each item is measuring the same construct. In other words, the way Rizzo reduced data within his instrument represented attitudes as a unidimensional construct rather than a multidimensional construct. Instead, a more appropriate way to summarize scores in this and similar examples is to summarize scores based on and within each dimension of the construct of interest. The Children's Assessment of Participation and Enjoyment (CAPE) instrument, which measures multiple factors of participation among children with disabilities, is a quality example of an appropriate summarization of a multidimensional construct (King et al., 2004). In addition to an overall participation score, the CAPE also provides scores for five dimensions of participation, including diversity, intensity, with whom, where, and enjoyment of participation, in order to simplify their data while simultaneously capturing the intricacies of the construct. As many variables within APE may similarly be multidimensional or complex, it is important for researchers to carefully ensure that the way they choose to reduce their data is representative of their variables of interest and research question(s).

Data analysis

The next step in the measurement process is to analyze the data, which often includes employing a statistical analysis technique. In this chapter, we will not be able to address the many different types of statistical techniques. However, readers should understand two different types of statistical analyses that are used to analyze data, including (1) descriptive statistics and (2) inferential statistics. Descriptive statistics is a statistical method that summarizes and analyzes data in order to *describe* the data. The most commonly used descriptive statistics are the mean and standard deviation, while other common examples can include population descriptions such as age range, frequency of gender, and types of disability diagnoses observed within the sample. While there are numerous ways to describe data, researchers should carefully select the appropriate method(s) to describe their data. For example, if the observed variable uses a nominal scale (e.g., gender), describing the data in terms of its mean and standard deviation may not be meaningful or appropriate. Instead, descriptions of the variables' frequency and/or percentage of cases may be more informative. When creating and providing descriptive statistics, researchers should remember the specific characteristics and details of the four different types of numerical scales and use the appropriate descriptive methods in order to most accurately describe the data.

Inferential statistics are the second type of statistical technique that can be used to analyze data. Inferential statistics include numerical summaries from a sample that help researchers to make a conclusion, or *inference*, about the population that goes beyond the available data descriptions. A significance test using a *p*-value (e.g., commonly, α is less than 0.05) is the most common approach of inferential statistics, although confidence intervals may also be used to make the appropriate conclusions about the data.

It is our opinion that the concept of a significance test (i.e., *p*-value) is commonly misunderstood. A significance test does not provide information regarding the magnitude of the relationship (Sutlive & Ulrich, 1998). It is instead a probability statement of the confidence that what the researcher has observed from the sample is likely to happen at a population level. For example, in the previously used example of Ulrich and colleagues' (2001) examination of the effects of treadmill training on the onset of independent walking among infants with Down syndrome, 15 infants with Down syndrome were in the experimental group and the other 15 infants were in the control group. They reported that infants with Down syndrome in the experimental group walked an average of 101 days earlier than infants in the control group ($p = 0.02$). In other words, since the observed *p*-value was less than the predetermined significance level (e.g., $\alpha < 0.05$, $\alpha < 0.01$), there was a significant difference between the two groups in terms of the onset of independent walking. In this example, walking an average of 101 days earlier is a piece of descriptive information about this particular sample. If other researchers were to duplicate the exact sampling protocol used by Ulrich et al. (2001), the differences between the two groups will likely be different than 101 days, such as 90 or 110 days. However, since there is a significant difference between the two groups, Ulrich and his colleagues (2001) can be confident that infants with Down syndrome who receive the treadmill training will walk earlier than infants with Down syndrome who do not receive the specific training. As addressed above, a significance test is not providing information about the strength or magnitude of the differences between the two variables. This information can instead be expressed by effect size. Effect sizes are commonly represented by standardized differences in means, odds ratios, risk ratios, and correlations. Readers can find additional information regarding effect sizes from other sources (e.g., Sutlive & Ulrich, 1998).

Interpretation of data

After collecting and analyzing the data, the next and often final step in the measurement process is to make interpretations. The goal of analyzing data is to make meaning out of the number of data points. In general, when interpreting data, researchers will explain the results uncovered during their data analysis. It is important for researchers to go beyond merely interpreting the descriptive statistics or significance level of their relevant statistical techniques. For example, addressing questions regarding patterns seen in the data, how the data might answer the specific research question of interest, and how the data relate to existing evidence within and outside of APE literature are all important additions and considerations for data interpretation. When interpreting the data and offering any new, resulting perspectives, researchers also should be careful with the amount of subjectivity used in their discussions and interpretations. Subjectivity is often natural during the data interpretation process and may lead to new questions and curiosities within the topics of interest. However, this can also often lead to inconsistencies and may be frowned upon by other researchers during the peer-review process. Researchers should, therefore, use theory or existing empirical evidence to support their interpretations whenever possible.

The ultimate goal of measurement is not only to obtain accurate data, but also to make appropriate interpretations from the collected data. Some readers may perceive measurement practice as a simple act of obtaining data by using a measurement tool and might only focus on the quality of the measurement instrument. As defined earlier in the chapter, however, measurement is the process of linking abstract concepts to empirical indicators. If appropriate and necessary, the researchers may decide to reanalyze and reinterpret the analysis to ensure the accuracy of measurement practice. As mentioned earlier, it is our opinion that measurement should no longer be viewed as a discrete act of obtaining data from our observation, but as a continuous process of the researcher's effort to gather the most appropriate information to make the right decision. APE researchers should consider the following factors to ensure accurate measurement practice:

a) careful identification of variables that closely align with the research interest,
b) potential influences of the quality of the instrument, adherence to the appropriate administration procedures, efforts of the examinee and examiner, and the testing conditions,
c) appropriate preparation and reduction of data for the analysis, and
d) use of appropriate statistical analyses needed to interpret the data.

Ensuring the accuracy of measurement

As addressed previously in this chapter, a major component of the measurement process is the accuracy of the included measurements. As fact, the results of measurement always contain error components. It is the researcher's job to make efforts to minimize this error. APE researchers should specifically be able to examine evidence of the accuracy of the measurement. Historically, the accuracy of measurement is evaluated by examining validity and reliability evidence. In layman's terms, validity is often defined as the degree to which a test measures what it is intended to measure, while reliability refers to the consistency of a measure. Most of the current measurement textbooks in kinesiology present validity and reliability as two separate concepts (e.g., Baumgartner et al., 2015; Morrow et al., 2016), which we briefly elaborate upon in the remainder of this chapter. However, a more contemporary view of measurement theory does not separate these two concepts. According to the Standards for Educational and Psychological Testing (American Educational Research Association, & American Psychological Association, 2014), different components of validity evidence include

> (a) evidence of careful test construction; (b) *adequate score reliability*; (c) appropriate test administration and scoring; (d) accurate score scaling, equating, and standard-setting; and (e) careful attention to fairness for all test takers, as appropriate to the test interpretation in question.
>
> *(p. 22)*

Validity is viewed as a much broader concept than reliability. Reliability evidence is considered a part of validity rather than an entirely separate concept. As part of this chapter, we do not intend to present a great deal of different strategies to evaluate validity and reliability evidence. Instead, we explain a few common misconceptions of the psychometric properties (i.e., validity and reliability) of measurement. However, we encourage readers to review detailed strategies used to evaluate validity and reliability evidence elsewhere (American

Educational Research Association, & American Psychological Association, 2014; Crocker & Algina, 1986; Yun & Ulrich, 2002).

There are three important concepts to understand when ensuring the accuracy of measurement. The first key essential concept is that the properties of validity and reliability do not belong to an instrument and/or research tool. These are, instead, properties of measurements. Moreover, Cronbach (1971) suggests that an instrument cannot be validated—only the results of measurement from a specific procedure can be validated. In other words, while it is inappropriate to say an instrument is a valid and/or reliable test, we can examine validity and reliability evidence of a measurement. Contradictory to this idea, it is common to read that a researcher used a "valid test" within current adapted physical activity literature. For example, Caçola and her colleages (2015) developed the Affordances in the Home Environment for Motor Development-Infant Scale. They conducted three phases of comprehensive development procedures and concluded that the instrument is "a reliable and valid instrument to assess affordances" (p. 910). We believe, however, that such a statement misrepresents this key fundamental concept of measurement.

As we have previously addressed, the results of measurement, and, therefore, the accuracy, are influenced by multiple factors. Of course, the quality of an instrument may have a significant effect on the accuracy of measurement, but it alone does not determine the accuracy of measurement. As a reminder, measurement is a continuous dynamic process of obtaining data and making appropriate interpretations. Other factors of the measurement process, such as interpretation of results, may, therefore, influence the associated psychometric properties. For example, it is commonly reported that children with ASD show deficits in gross motor performance when compared to children without ASD (Berkeley, Zittel, Pitney, & Nichols, 2001; Staples & Reid, 2010). A body of literature, however, challenges this notion of performance deficits among children with ASD and suggests that lower levels of performance may instead be interpreted as inappropriate assessment methods (Breslin & Rudisill, 2011; Case, Schram, & Yun, 2019). For example, Case and her colleagues (2019) argued that without considering the attention and effort of children with ASD, researchers may not be able to accurately capture motor performance within this population. As a result, the authors provide specific strategies, such as making the assessment enjoyable and providing the child choice, to maximize participation and motivation within testing among children with ASD. Additionally, some have suggested that, due to relative strengths in visual processing among children with ASD, the use of visual supports within gross motor assessments may increase measurement accuracy (Allen, Bredero, Van Damme, Ulrich, & Simons, 2017; Breslin & Rudisill, 2011).

The second key concept includes that, although there are many different strategies and methods to demonstrate validity evidence, there are not different *types* of validity. Many textbooks and literature that introduce validity often present three different major types of validity evidence, including content-related evidence, criterion-related evidence and construct-related evidence (Baumgartner et al., 2015; Morrow et al., 2016; Safrit, 1989). These instead represent different strategies in which to demonstrate validity of a measurement. Content validity refers to "the degree to which the samples of items, tasks, or questions on a test represent some defined universe or domain of content" (American Educational Research Association & American Psychological Association, 1985, p. 10). It focuses on the items of the tests that are representative of the domain or construct of interest. Other names of validity evidence, including face validity, curricular validity, and instructional validity, have similar logical approaches to evaluate how closely the items of a measurement tool represent the variables of interest. Since the evaluation of content-related evidence is solely focused on items and/or research tools, pure psychometric theorists have argued that content validity itself should not be accepted as validity evidence. However, content-related evidence is an important and necessary step, as the test content influences the test results (Messick, 1993).

Criterion-related validity evidence is used to draw inferences from test scores from one measure about behavior on a performance criterion. For example, Usera and his colleagues' (2005) study, in which they examined the accuracy of estimating body composition using skinfold measurement, the measure of interest was the estimation of the percentage of body fat from skinfold techniques and the criterion measure was the estimation of percentage of body fat from the BOD POD®. Criterion-related evidence is often evaluated by the magnitude of the relationship between observed test scores and scores from the criterion measures. The terms concurrent, predictive, and convergent validity evidence all use a similar logical approach to evaluate the strength of the relationship between test scores and scores from criterion measures. Yun and Ulrich (2002) described detailed strategies to demonstrate criterion-related validity and pointed out multiple limitations of evaluating validity evidence solely based on criterion-related evidence, including sample selection issues, statistical artifacts, and the conceptual difficulty of identifying a true criterion measure. Due to these potential limitations, researchers may consider using multiple strategies to demonstrate validity evidence.

Construct validity is the collection of empirical evidence to support the existence of the theoretical construct that underlies the measurement and its resulting inferences (Burton & Miller, 1998). Additionally, this concept assumes that the measurement is consistent with its theoretical properties (constructs). The strength of validity is evaluated based on the strength of congruence between test scores and the theoretical rationale. Since the focus on construct validity evidence involves linking theoretical constructs and scores from measurement, the concepts include both content representativeness (content-related evidence) and criterion-related evidence. Although examination of internal test structure using factor analysis may be the most common strategy to demonstrate construct validity evidence (e.g., Yun & Shapiro, 2004), more contemporary psychometrists view construct-related evidence as more of a unified concept. The common and ultimate goal of evaluating validity evidence is to demonstrate that the measurement results accurately capture the variable of interest.

The third key concept to understand involves reliability of measurements. It explains that reliability is not necessarily an evaluation of the consistency of a score, but it is an overall index of "the consistency of such measurements (not the test) when the testing procedure is repeated on a population of individuals or groups" (American Educational Research Association & American Psychological Association, 1999, p. 25). The task of reliability estimation involves separating the error scores and true scores. It is not possible to completely separate the true components of score from the error components of score on a single measure. However, when researchers accept four basic assumptions, including (a) the true score does not change, (b) the true score is independent from error scores, (c) the mean of error scores is zero, and (d) error scores from different distributions of the same test are independent of one another, they can estimate the overall consistency of measurement from a set of test scores.

The reliability coefficient is a ratio between the variance of the true score over the variance of the observed scores. Because it is a ratio, the coefficient may not directly estimate the amount of error components but it can include a percentage of error components within the observed scores. This has an important implication in APE research. Some scholars may interpret the reliability coefficients as the absolute value for estimating error scores and/or the consistency of scores. It is important, however, to remember that even if two sets of scores include the same amounts of error components, the magnitude of reliability coefficients may fluctuate based on the variabilities of observed scores.

In this chapter, we have defined measurement within the context of APE research, introduced the process of how to obtain accurate measurement results, and briefly illustrated the basic concepts of evaluating the accuracy and psychometric properties of measurement. The intention of this chapter is not to duplicate information from other measurement textbooks, but to bring in unique perspectives to improve our measurement practice in APE and, ultimately, the quality of research in our field.

Summary of key points

- Measurement is the continuous process of obtaining appropriate information to make accurate interpretations of the answers to a given research question. It is not merely the act of assigning numbers to observations.
- The measurement process includes (a) observation, (b) gathering data, (c) data reduction, (d) data analysis, and (e) interpretation.
- Researchers should be sure to carefully identify the appropriate variable(s) to observe when answering their research question. Failure to do so can challenge the measurement process.
- The accuracy of measurement is influenced by multiple factors, including the quality of the measurement tool, resulting interpretations, efforts given by those involved, testing environment, and adherence to testing procedures.
- The data reduction process should be closely aligned with the conceptual and/or theoretical frameworks of the study.
- Accurate measurement requires appropriate statistical approaches, including data collection techniques and interpretation of the resulting data.
- Validity and reliability are psychometric properties of measurements, not assessment tools or instruments.
- Significance tests, and a significant test result, do not provide information about the strength of the relationship, effect, or validity and reliability evidence

Reflective questions for discussion

- Why is it important to view measurement as the process and efforts utilized to obtain accurate information and to make the best possible decision, rather than the act of collecting data?
- What is the relationship between research, measurement, and statistics?
- What is the importance of identifying the appropriate variable to observe within measurement?
- What are the potential consequences of misidentifying an appropriate variable or measurement tool?
- What shall we consider when selecting appropriate statistical analyses?
- What are the concerns with statements describing instruments as "valid tests"?

Note

1 There are extensive research studies and discussion on the appropriateness of treating some ordinal scales (e.g., Likert Scale) as interval and/or ratio scales. This discussion, however, is beyond the

scope of this chapter. Readers interested in this topic should please refer to other resources (e.g., Coombs, 1960; Hodge, & Gillespie, 2003; Jakobsson, 2004; Wu & Leung, 2017).

References

Allen, K. A., Bredero, B., Van Damme, T., Ulrich, D. A., & Simons, J. (2017). Test of gross motor development-3 (TGMD-3) with the use of visual supports for children with autism spectrum disorder: Validity and reliability. *Journal of Autism and Developmental Disorders*, doi:10.1007/s10803-016-3005-0

American Educational Research Association, & American Psychological Association. (1985). *Standards for educational and psychological testing*. Washington, DC: American Educational Research Association.

American Educational Research Association, & American Psychological Association. (1999). *Standards for educational and psychological testing*. Washington, DC: American Educational Research Association.

American Educational Research Association, & American Psychological Association. (2014). *Standards for educational and psychological testing*. Washington, DC: American Educational Research Association.

Baumgartner, T. A., Jackson, A. S., Mahar, M. T., & Rowe, D. A. (2015). *Measurement for evaluation in kinesiology*. Burlington, MA: Jones & Bartlett.

Berg, K. E., & Latin, R. W. (2008). *Essentials of research methods in health, physical education, exercise, and recreation* (3rd ed.). Philadelphia, PA: Lippincott Williams & Wilkins.

Berkeley, S. L., Zittel, L. L., Pitney, L. V., & Nichols, S. E. (2001). Locomotor and object control skills of children diagnosed with autism. *Adapted Physical Activity Quarterly*, *18*(4), 405–416.

Breslin, C. M., & Rudisill, M. E. (2011). The effect of visual supports on performance of the TGMD-2 for children with autism spectrum disorder. *Adapted Physical Activity Quarterly*, *28*(4), 342–353.

Breslin, C. M., & Rudisill, M. E. (2013). Relationships among assessment time, time on task, and motor skill performance in children with autism spectrum disorder. *Adapted Physical Activity Quarterly*, *30*(4), 338–350.

Burton, A. W., & Miller, A. (1998). *Movement skill assessment*. Champaign, IL: Human Kinetics.

Cacola, P. M., Gabbard, C., Montebelo, M. I. L., & Santos, D. C. C. (2015). Further development and validation of the affordances in the home environment for motor development-infant scale (AHEMD-IS). *Physical Therapy*, *95*(6), 901–923. doi:10.2522/ptj.20140011

Carmines, E. G., & Zeller, R. A. (1979). *Reliability and validity assessment* (Vol. 17). Newbury Park, CA: Sage.

Case, L., Schram, B., & Yun, J. (2019). Motivating children with autism spectrum disorder in gross motor-skill assessments. *Journal of Physical Education, Recreation & Dance*, *90*(4), 32–38. doi:10.1080/07303084.2019.1568933

Case, L., & Yun, J. (2019). The effect of different intervention approaches on gross motor outcomes of children with autism spectrum disorder: A meta-analysis. *Adapted Physical Activity Quarterly*, *36*(4), 501–526.

Coombs, C. H. (1960). A theory of data. Psychololgy Reviewv. 67, 143–159. doi: 10.1037/h0047773

Crocker, L., & Algina, J. (1986). *Introduction to classical and modern test theory*. Orlando, FL: Holt, Rinehart and Winston.

Cronbach, L. (1971). Test validation. In R. Linn (Ed.), *Educational measurement* (pp. 443–507). Washington, DC: American Council on Education.

Draheim, C., Williams, D., & McCubbin, J. (2002). Prevalence of physical inactivity and recommended physical activity in community-based adults with mental retardation. *Mental Retardation*, *40*(6), 436–444.

Education First. (n.d.). *3000 most common words in English*. Retrieved from www.ef.edu/english-resources/english-vocabulary/top-3000-words/

Haegele, J. A., Brian, A. S., & Wolf, D. (2017). Accuracy of the fitbit zip for measuring steps for adolescents with visual impairments. *Adapted Physical Activity Quarterly*, *34*(2), 195–200. doi:10.1123/apaq.2016-0055

Hodge, D. R., & Gillespie, D. (2003). Phrase completions: An alternative to Likert scales. *Social Work Research*, 27(1), 45–55..

Hutzler, Y., Meier, S., Reuker, S., & Zitomer, M. (2019). Attitudes and self-efficacy of physical education teachers toward inclusion of children with disabilities: A narrative review of international literature. *Physical Education and Sport Pedagogy*, *24*(3), 249–266. doi:10.1080/17408989.2019.1571183

Jakobsson, U. (2004). Statistical Presentation and Analysis of Ordinal Data in Nursing Research, Scandinavian. *Journal of Caring Sciences*, 18, 437–440.

Jin, J., & Yun, J. (2013). Three frameworks to predict physical activity behavior in middle school inclusive physical education: A multilevel analysis. *Adapted Physical Activity Quarterly, 30*(3), 254–270.

King, G., Law, M., King, S., Hurley, P., Hanna, S., Kertoy, M., & Young, N. L. (2004). *Children's assessment of participation and enjoyment and preferences for activities of kids.* San Antonio, TX: PsychCorp.

Leedy, P., & Ormrod, J. (2019). *Practical research: Planning and design* (12th ed.). Saddle River, NJ: Pearson.

Li, C., Wong, N. K., Sum, R. K., & Yu, C. W. (2019). Preservice Teachers' Mindfulness and Attitudes Toward Students With Autism Spectrum Disorder: The Role of Basic Psychological Needs Satisfaction. Adapted Physical Activity Quarterly, 36(1), 150–163.

Messick, S. (1993). Validity. In R. Linn (Ed.), *Educational measurement* (3rd ed., pp. 13–103). Phoenix, AZ: The Oryx Press.

Michell, J. (1986). Measurement scales and statistics: A clash of paradigms. *Psychological Bulletin, 100*(3), 398–407.

Morrow, J. R., Mood, D., Disch, J. G., & Kang, M. (2016). *Measurement and evaluation in human performance* (5th ed.). Champaign, IL: Human Kinetics.

Pawlowski, J., & Yun, J. (2019). Adapted physical educators' beliefs and intentions for promoting out of school physical activity. *European Journal of Adapted Physical Activity, 12*(1), 4. doi:10.5507/euj.2019.003

Pawlowski, J., Yun, J., Beamer, J., Siebert, E., & Hamm, J. (n.d.). *Exploration of the effects of an adapted physical activity service learning program on participant's self-efficacy through bayesian analysis.* Unpublished manuscript.

Reina, R., Hutzler, Y., Iniguez-Santiago, M. C., & Moreno-Murcia, J. A. (2019). Student attitudes toward inclusion in physical education: The impact of ability beliefs, gender, and previous experiences. *Adapted Physical Activity Quarterly, 36*(1), 132–149. doi:10.1123/apaq.2017-0146

Rizzo, T., & Vispoel, W. P. (1991). Physical educators' attributes and attitudes toward teaching students with handicaps. *Adapted Physical Activity Quarterly, 8*(1), 4–11.

Rizzo, T. L. (1984). Attitudes of physical educators toward teaching handicapped pupils. *Adapted Physical Activity Quarterly, 1*(4), 267–274. doi:10.1123/apaq.1.4.267

Safrit, M. (1989). *Measurement concepts in physical education and exercise science.* Champaign, IL: Human Kinetics.

Siebert, E. A., Hamm, J., & Yun, J. (2017). Parental influence on physical activity of children with disabilities. *International Journal of Disability, Development and Education, 64*(4), 378–390. doi:10.1080/1034912X.2016.1245412

Stanish, H., & Draheim, C. (2005). Walking habits of adults with mental retardation. *Mental Retardation, 43*(6), 421–427.

Staples, K. L., & Reid, G. (2010). Fundamental movement skills and autism spectrum disorders. *Journal of Autism and Developmental Disorders, 40*(2), 209–217. doi:10.1007/s10803-009-0854-9

Stevens, S. S. (1946). On the theory of scales of measurement. *Science, New Series, 103*(2684), 677–680.

Sutlive, V. H., & Ulrich, D. A. (1998). Interpreting statistical significance and meaningfulness in adapted physical activity research. *Adapted Physical Activity Quarterly, 15*(2), 103–118. doi:10.1123/apaq.15.2.103

Thomas, J. R., Nelson, J. K., & Silverman, S. J. (2015). *Research methods in physical activity* (7th ed.). Champaign, IL: Human Kinetics.

Tuckman, B. W., & Harper, B. E. (2012). *Conducting educational research* (6th ed.). Lanham, MD: Rowman & Littlefield Publishers.

Tudor-Locke, C., & Bassett, D. R. (2004). How many steps/day are enough?. sports medicine. *Sports Medicine, 1*(34), 1–8.

Ulrich, B. D., Ulrich, D. A., & Collier, D. H. (1992). Alternating stepping patterns: Hidden abilities of 11-month-old infants with down syndrome. *Developmental Medicine & Child Neurology, 2*(34), 233–239.

Ulrich, D. A., Ulrich, B. D., Angulo-Kinzler, R. M., & Yun, J. (2001). Treadmill training of infants with down syndrome: Evidence-based developmental outcomes. *Pediatrics, 108*(5), e84–e84.

Usera, P. C., Foley, J. T., & Yun, J. (2005). Cross-validation of field-based assessments of body composition for individuals with down syndrome. *Adapted Physical Activity Quarterly, 22*(2), 198–206. doi:10.1123/apaq.22.2.198

Velleman, P. F., & Wilkinson, L. (1993). Nominal, ordinal, interval, and ratio typologies are misleading. *The American Statistician, 47*(1), 65–72.

Wu, H., & Leung, S.-O. (2017). Can likert scales be treated as interval scales?—A simulation study. *Journal of Social Service Research, 43*(4), 527–532. https://doi.org/10.1080/01488376.2017.1329775

Yun, J., & Shapiro, D. R. (2004). A quantitative approach to movement skill assessment for children with mental retardation. *Adapted Physical Activity Quarterly, 21*(3), 269–280.

Yun, J., & Ulrich, D. A. (1997). Perceived and actual physical competence in children with mild mental retardation. *Adapted Physical Activity Quarterly, 14*(4), 285–297.

Yun, J., & Ulrich, D. A. (2002). Estimating measurement validity: A tutorial. *Adapted Physical Activity Quarterly, 19*(1), 32–47.

8

Disability language in adapted physical education

What is the story?

Nancy L. I. Spencer, Danielle Peers, and Lindsay Eales

Introduction

The focus of this chapter is to discuss the conceptual frameworks that have contributed to the emergence and use of diverse disability terminologies within the field of adapted physical activity (APA) and, more specifically, within adapted physical education (APE). The purpose of this chapter is to explore different disability languages and terminologies used in research in the field of APE. In essence, we will illustrate the stories (i.e., assumptions and understandings) behind different language usages in order to both inform and contribute to the reader's awareness of the meanings and implications of their own and others' use of disability terminology. This chapter will also bring to the forefront the need for coherence between our theoretical approaches to research and the disability terminology we use. Of critical importance is recognition of the potential for harm in our use of disability language and that the decision of which terminology to use is not simply a matter of picking one over the other. We will also attend specifically to the use of disability language with children in schools and, by extension, within APE.

We join a number of APA scholars who have written on the topic of disability language and terminology (e.g., Block, 2016; Columna, Lieberman, Lytle, & Arndt, 2014; Reid, 1992; Sherrill, 2010). We have written on the topic of disability language formally twice now (Peers, Eales, & Spencer-Cavaliere, 2018; Peers, Spencer-Cavaliere, & Eales, 2014). The first instance was through an article addressing disability language and terminology within an academic journal in our field, the *Adapted Physical Activity Quarterly* (see Peers et al., 2014). This article contributed to a change in the journal's disability language policy which expanded the theoretical possibilities for publication, making it more inclusive to diverse forms of disability research and ways of representing people. In doing so, it also brought to the forefront the need for consistency between the ways in which disability is understood in our work and the language and terminology we use. The second piece was a chapter published in a book focused on people's perceptions of disability (see Peers et al., 2018). In the 2018 chapter, we analyzed cultural, historical, theoretical, and political differences in disability terminology and pressed for diversity in language use. In the end, we argued in both previously published works for the use of respectful language, one of the key mainstays of which is consistency with the ways in which people and communities desire to be represented and identified. We continue to engage with the topic of disability language and terminology from this perspective.

Within both texts described above (Peers et al., 2014, 2018), we also shared a quote from Shakespeare (2006) to foreground the debates around language use and the need to carefully consider the disability languages we employ. We once again return to these words as we challenge ourselves to continually and "consciously consider the meanings of our language and the consequences it may have for particular groups" (Boyd, Ng, & Schryer, 2015, p. 1550). Shakespeare (2006) wrote, "Quibbling over 'disabled people' versus 'people with disabilities' is a diversion from making common cause to promote the inclusion and rights of disabled people" (p. 33). Shakespeare was not discounting the importance of considering disability language use, but, rather, impressing that the underlying values are more important. We argue, however, that disability language usage is, in fact, a reflection of values. That the languages and terminologies we employ are laden with assumptions and understandings of what disability is, who is and is not responsible for it, what it means for rights and access, and, ultimately, how it positions people in society. Here, we foreground our discussion of disability terminology, its history, relevance, and possibilities, with the words of Burton Blatt, who was instrumental in bringing attention to the atrocities and harms committed against people forced to live in institutions. He wrote, "Some stories enhance life and others degrade it so we must be careful about the stories we tell" (Blatt, 1987, p. 142). Our choices of terminology and language tell a particular kind of story about disability and in doing so, a story about people, their value, and our values.

In this chapter, we also highlight terminology that has been used within different research studies conducted within APE. In doing so, our intention is to offer clarity and opportunities to consider the potential consequences of our language use, rather than to reprimand or point fingers. Notably, there is significant incoherence across many studies between the languages used, the disability models employed, how people are represented, and the nature of the research. Often, it is the case that multiple models and languages co-occur. One way to think about this incoherence is to also view disability models and disability language as tools scholars might use to achieve particular research goals and/or convey specific messages. What is considered to be respectful language has also changed over time and this must be acknowledged in the critique of the ways in which researchers have previously used different terminology and language. We aim to open conversations with the hope of continuing to expand the possibilities for work and accompanying terminology and language in our field that tell stories that are life enhancing (Blatt, 1987).

Overview of disability models: what is the story?

The history of disability language is embedded within different models of disability. The languages used to describe disability and, ultimately, people, offer particular understandings and conceptualizations of disability. Although our attempt here is to provide an overview of different disability language and terminology, we focus on different models of disability, including how social and political movements have shaped disability language development and use in general and specific to the field of APE.

The medical model

Disability, understood within the context of the medical model, is recognized today as a pathologizing and often deeply harmful way of describing people, especially when used outside of medical contexts (Peers et al., 2018). Traditionally, medical model understandings of disability are embedded within a correctives approach to non-normative bodies and minds. Disability is viewed as another word for impairment and diagnosis, and something negative that should be fixed, reducing disability to something undesirable and tragic residing within individual bodies and minds (Withers, 2012).

The language that accompanies the medical model approach is one that forefronts the importance of diagnosis in defining the person; for example "a person with muscular dystrophy", or, worse, "a T1 SCI" in reference to the level of thoracic lesion (T1) of an individual with a spinal cord injury (SCI). Medical model language also revolves around differences based on what is considered normal, acceptable, and valued compared to that which is viewed as abnormal, unacceptable, and devalued. "An extension of this conceptualization is the notion of ableism, or the idea that those who are 'more able' are 'more includable' into mainstream educational environments (including physical education [PE]) as well as greater society" (Shyman, 2016, p. 367).

As we noted previously, some of these comparative terms (e.g., typically developing and average) when used within the context of considering statistical averages and norms may be appropriate for researchers to use, yet, can be deeply discrediting, stigmatizing, and harmful when people are judged against normative standards (Peers et al., 2014). Similar terms, such as able-bodied versus disabled, further promote a dichotomy that reinforces the view that disability is an undesirable difference to be corrected, intervened upon, and eradicated. This dichotomy further extends into power relations, where the role of experts (e.g., doctors, teachers, researchers) is to intervene upon those who have been diagnosed (e.g., patients, students, participants). Within the educational setting, having access to additional services such as specialized classrooms, smaller student to teacher ratios, and paraprofessionals is most often dependent on demonstrating medical diagnoses (Haegele & Hodge, 2016). As researchers, medical diagnosis is often how we go about finding and subsequently recruiting students to take part in our research studies. Even when our own APE research questions are embedded within alternative perspectives, the medical model often remains a salient feature.

In their work exploring and deconstructing language practices in individualized education plans (IEPs), Boyd and colleagues (2015) articulate how the negative language practices used to describe children can have damaging impacts on their everyday lives, reaffirm power imbalances, and further perpetuate the ways in which society understands disability. These authors argue that particular, and often unintended, negative language practices may further medical understandings of disability, leading to harmful conceptualizations of children. Examples of these harmful conceptualizations include transformational attributes and passive voice, which reduce children's identity to a disability, an exception to a standardized norm relative to their peers, and, ultimately, powerless.

Although the work of Boyd and colleagues (2015) is nested within deconstructing language practices in IEP resource documents, the transference of these practices are highly relevant to language practices in APE research. This is particularly notable in comparative research and intervention work that distinguishes between typically developing students versus non-typically developing, or students with and without disabilities. An example is a study exploring the daily physical activity levels of elementary children with and without "mental retardation" [sic] in school and out of school (Foley, Bryan, & McCubbin, 2008,

p. 365). Similarly, Pan (2008) examined differences in physical activity in recess between "children with autism spectrum disorders and children without disabilities" (p. 1292). Differentiating among students with different diagnoses is another example of research driven primarily by the medical model. Likewise, Sit et al. (2017) explored differences in physical activity and sedentary time across activity settings, including physical education of children who were categorized into various "disability" groups based on impairment diagnosis.

Similar to a rehabilitation approach, APA and, by extension, APE, has used adaptation to diminish body–mind differences in order to approximate normativity and to integrate people (Phelan, 2011). For example, behavioral intervention approaches (e.g., applied behavior analysis) used with people who are neurodiverse (e.g., autistic; diagnosis of autism) with the aim of normalizing the ways in which they exist (Shyman, 2016). Within the APE literature, it is not uncommon to see articles focusing on how to minimize what are often described as challenging behaviors of children diagnosed with autism (e.g., Lee & Haegele, 2016; Menear & Neumeier, 2015). While much of this work is articulated using person-first language and also emphasizes understanding from the perspective of the child (e.g., Lee & Haegele, 2016), the influence of the medical model is apparent within the discourse of minimizing challenging behaviors. Intervention approaches used with children with different diagnoses in physical education (PE) also reflect normalized ways of thinking about participation in PE. For example, Tzanetakos, Papastergiou, Vernadakis, and Antoniou (2017), measured the improvement in balance performances of "adolescents with deafness" using interactive videogames compared to an APE based program.

In sustaining these ability–disability dichotomies (Phelan, 2011), we also perpetuate normality rather than diversity (Phelan, Wright, & Gibson, 2014), which is antithetical to inclusion, one of the topics central to our field. At the same time, not all studies that employ aspects of medical model understandings of disability are nested within interventions or quantitative methods. Blagrave (2017) used a phenomenological approach to examine how children with "autism spectrum disorder" experienced APE using drawings, observations, and interviews. The children taking part in this study required a diagnosis of autism spectrum disorder in order to be eligible. Despite an interpretivist approach, the use of person-first language, and recognizing barriers external to the children, the medical model was still present: for example, through the recruitment of participants diagnosed with autism spectrum disorder. This example, among others, brings our attention to the challenges associated with identifying the dominant disability discourse, when, for example, medical model research in which person-first language (e.g., children with cerebral palsy) is used. However, we return to the concept of story. While we acknowledge that some stories overlap, we also encourage researchers to attend to other types of language that are present and might signify the dominance of a medical approach (e.g., intervention, comparison disorder).

Social model

The social model of disability emerged in the 1970s in the United Kingdom (UK) and is often positioned as opposite to the approach taken within the medical model. The essence of the social model approach to understanding disability is that people are disabled not by their bodily differences, but by the barriers created by society (Oliver, 2013). The language of the social model is consistent with this understanding and the term "disabled person" is then used to refer to individuals who are actively oppressed by social barriers such as architecture and policies (i.e., they are disabled by society).

"Impairment", within this model, refers to individual and biological differences, while "disability" refers to the ways that society excludes, marginalizes, or discriminates against those with impairments. The social model has been criticized for negating the role of the body (i.e., impairment) in disability (Shakespeare, 2006). As a result, some have argued for using similar terminology within a social relational model (Thomas, 2009), which not only focuses on changing disabling social structures (e.g., widespread disability exclusion from sport), but can also account for "impairment effects," that is, the limitations that impairments put on our activities (e.g., reduced exercise due to pain).

Examples of researchers in APE who have engaged a social model approach include Grenier, Collins, and Wright (2014) who explored children's perceptions of disability sport in the general PE curriculum. Importantly, we also see, in this example, incoherence in disability language (i.e., the use of person-first language) with the conceptual model (i.e., social) underpinning the nature of the research question. Notably, the language policy of the journal at that time required authors to engage with person-first language. Richardson, Smith, and Papathomas (2017) explored the PE experiences of disabled peers revealing their collective experiences of oppression and marginalization. Fitzgerald (2005) sought the insights of disabled youth about their PE experiences to expand social model perspectives through the exploration of embodied identities. Finally, Petrie, Devich, and Fitzgerald (2018) challenged medical model understandings of disability through the use of a social model approach in their work that focused on the experiences of a primary school teacher navigating inclusion within PE. However, we also see incoherent language in the use of person-first in this article. As noted above, it may be difficult to recognize work that is social model in nature when the language used might reflect other approaches. Searching for key words that align with a social model approach (e.g., oppression, marginalization) can help to identify the dominant disability story (i.e., disability model) guiding the research.

Disability rights model—person-first language

A person-first approach to disability language is nested within a rights-based approach to understanding disability. The language of this model, "people with disabilities" or "children with disabilities", is used deliberately to be respectful and to demonstrate support for social inclusion and disability rights (Shakespeare, 2006). Within the education context, it is also common to see the person-first terminology "children with special educational needs (SEN)" to refer to children with specific learning needs associated with different impairments (see Smith, 2004). Using a person-first approach is intended to prioritize a person as a human being first and impairment is considered to be one, among many, attributes of a person. The person-first approach to disability language is the dominant approach to disability language use in North America and Australia (Peers et al., 2014). The use of person-first language in North America may often go unchallenged on the basis that it is assumed to be the most respectful approach to disability language and representative of what people experiencing disability or with impairment diagnoses want (Phelan, 2011). However, some communities in North America have rejected this language, arguing that it reproduces the idea that disability is a characteristic of an individual (i.e., of the person *with* a disability) rather than something socially imposed, and also that it doesn't match other identitarian language (e.g., we do not say "a person with femaleness"). Problems arise, therefore, when person-first language is non-consensually imposed upon communities or individuals who use other terminology to define themselves, or who do not understand themselves through a North American disability rights framework (e.g., deaf/Deaf communities).

The use of person-first language is common to see in the field of APA and, subsequently, APE. However, it is also common to see diagnosis used as a starting point for recruiting and then describing children in these studies. What can help us to differentiate work that is medical versus rights based when the terminology is similar (e.g., child with a disability) and tables of impairment descriptions are provided, is when the research speaks to the issues of rights, inclusion, and social justice specifically (e.g., DePauw & Doll-Tepper, 2000). Attitudinal work in APE often reflects the incorporation of a rights-based model because the investment is oriented toward greater inclusion and the use of strategies that are not centered on changing or intervening upon the child with an impairment. An example is the work of McKay, Block, and Park (2015) on attitudes of students without disabilities toward PE inclusion via the use of a Paralympic school day. Other examples include the work of Wang, Qi, and Wang (2015), who examined the beliefs held by physical educators who taught children with disabilities in general PE, and Taliaferro, Hammond, and Wyant (2015), who explored the impact of coursework and practicums on the self-efficacy beliefs of pre-service PE teachers on inclusion. Additional examples of rights-based work in the field include studies that focus on the importance of the perspectives of children with impairments being heard. Goodwin and Watkinson (2000) were among the first researchers in our field to bring attention to the exclusionary experiences of children with disabilities in inclusive PE. Subsequently, other researchers (e.g., Bredahl, 2013; Fitzgerald & Stride, 2012; Haegele & Zhu, 2017; Healy, Msetfi, & Gallagher, 2013; Spencer-Cavaliere & Watkinson, 2010) have sought to include the perspectives of both children and adults with disabilities about their PE experiences. Balgrave's (2017) work, previously described within the medical model, also sought the perspectives of the children, again highlighting the complexity and incoherence that can exist across disability models and languages.

International Classification of Functioning, Health and Disability

The International Classification of Functioning, Health and Disability (ICF), World Health Organization (WHO) (2013) is an international tool that attempted to create a common set of disability terminology that bridges various cultural and theoretical understandings of disability, and that produces a common framework for describing and enacting cross-national public health interventions. In this model, an individual's level of functioning is the outcome of a complex interaction between a health condition, body functions and structures, activities and participation, environmental factors, and personal factors (Thomas, 2004). Impairment in this model refers to bodily difference, but in a deeply medical and loss-oriented sense: "problems in body function and structure such as significant deviation or loss" (WHO, 2013, p. 5). Disability refers more broadly to "negative aspects" of the dynamic interaction among these various components (WHO, 2013). This dynamic interaction is bidirectional, that is, "changes in one component may influence one or more of the other components" (Hammond & Anttila, 2015, p. 197). Some have argued the ICF moves away from a medical model approach toward a more social model understanding and representation (Kattari, Lavery, & Hasche, 2017). While the approach takes into account various physical and environmental factors, disability scholars and activists have argued its incorporation of the social model is overstated, given that—as the definitions above attest—impairments are still largely conceptualized as entirely negative problems to be fixed, and disability is never conceptualized as an issue of oppression: the fundamental claim of the social model (Thomas, 2004). As such, ICF terminology can be a useful tool for the international public health engagements for which it is designed, but it should not be mobilized as a universal model that reconciles all of the above models and terminology within it.

Examples of the use of the ICF approach within APE appear scarce. Using the ICF approach as a structural framework, Saebu and Sørensen (2011) examined associated physical activity factors among young people with a disability. Leisure time physical activity was the focus of a study by Martin Ginis et al. (2012), where the authors used the ICF framework to identify physical activity predictors among people with spinal cord injury.

Cultural, identity-first, and experiential models

Many communities that would be medically understood as "having" disabilities do not self-identify within any of the models, or with any of the related terminology, covered above. One notable example is how "deaf or hard of hearing" and "people with hearing impairments" can be understood by many whom these terms intend to refer to as deeply disrespectful and inaccurate. Instead, many prefer to be called a Deaf person, where the capital D signifies membership in a cultural-linguistic (rather than medically defined) community, with its deeply valued and valuable languages, world-views, and cultural practices (Gannon, 2011).

Further, numerous disability communities have reclaimed impairments as meaningful aspects of their identities, and sites of powerful community connection, activism, and pride. For example, "an autistic," "a neurodivergent person," and "a neurominority" are examples of self-proclaimed identities by autistic activists and organizations and preferred over "people with autism" (Walker, 2013). Such terms frame the ways their minds work as neutral or positive human variations, and frame their social and medical treatment as forms of oppression, eugenics, and genocide. Sometimes, a community's terminology refers precisely to the forms of oppression people have experienced, or to their desired relationship to the medical systems that they rely on, such as "psychiatric survivors" and "consumers" (Charlton, 2000; Menzies, LeFrancois, & Reaume, 2013). In other instances, communities have pridefully reclaimed terms that have been used against them, in order to define themselves, as well as the ideas, art, and movements that they have generated. Examples include "Mad" and "crip" (Diamond, 2013; Peers, Brittain, & McRuer, 2012). Importantly, not everyone feels comfortable being defined by these terms, and some of these terms are used primarily by insiders about themselves. These words may be offensive or hurtful to some people in some contexts, and they carry with them strong cultural and theoretical understandings that must be grappled with when choosing to adopt them more broadly. If you are not a member of the above communities, it is wise to exercise added caution and consent when choosing to use such community-specific terminology. These community-specific terminologies are, to date, rarely used in APA and APE research, but are far more common in research areas led by these communities (such as critical disability studies). As communities become more involved in research about themselves, expect this usage to increase.

In some contexts, APA and APE practitioners and researchers may be primarily interested in how people understand and experience their own lives, and, yet, need to speak about communities before they get a chance to ask how they identify. In such cases, some have chosen to use experiential language like "people who experience disability" or, if more relevant, "people who have experienced parasport classification" (Peers, 2012; Titchkosky, 2007). Such terminology leaves open the possibility that those they work with might experience and conceptualize their identity through any of the above models, a model not covered herein, or multiple different models in different contexts (e.g., someone with muscular dystrophy at the doctor's office, a person with a disability when negotiating student supports, and Crip when making art with the community). An example from APA is the work of Leo and Goodwin (2016), who explored the reflections of people experiencing disability on the use of simulations in undergraduate courses to introduce students to the concept of disability. Within the PE context, Wang (2019) employed a social-relational model of disability toward understanding the perspectives of students with special needs on inclusion. This is another example of where a researcher might work from a particular disability lens, in this case a social relational theoretical framework, yet, the language "students with special needs" may not be synonymous.

Accountability and representation

In our coverage of different disability models, we have attempted to reveal the assumptions underlying diverse disability language and terminology. In addition, we have offered up examples of research from within the field that demonstrate varied, as well as incoherent, disability language usage, in order to illustrate the ways in which disability models and assumptions are woven into research in the field. In the following section, we further explore issues of accountability and representation, ending with a focus on children in APE.

As researchers, whether we engage directly with participants, write about them or about issues that affect them, we must be accountable to them. A significant part of this account-ability is about representation, and includes both how disability in general and specific groups or individuals are represented and identified in the descriptions we offer as well as the terminology we employ in our writing. We have an ethical "obligation to develop and maintain cultural competence regarding disability and the language used to describe it and the people affected by it" (Dunn & Andrews, 2015, p. 255).

We have a responsibility to represent participants and communities using the words and descriptions they choose, with their consent. APA research has been criticized for lack of participant voice (Bredahl, 2008) and we extend this to also include participants' say in how they are identified and described in our collective research. Detailed in our first article addressing disability language and terminology, we reported several instances where disability language did not resonate with the ways in which people self-identified (Peers et al., 2014). Specifically, one of the authors, Peers, described, in their account of being a study participant in APA research, the feelings of betrayal and non-consensual misrepresentation that emerged from the disregard for how they wished to self-identify (Peers et al., 2014). This also extended to the ways in which they felt their sporting community had been misrepresented. Respecting how people identify requires that we ask how people wish to be described in our research and that we do not decide for them. Deciding how one wishes to be identified can foster agency, choice, and autonomy (Dunn & Andrews, 2015), and may serve to build more trusting, collaborative relationships between disability communities and those of us who research with them (Peers, 2018).

We also have a responsibility to use disability language that promotes, rather than under-mines, inclusion. To illustrate, we draw again from our previous work, where Eales, within the context of dance and in her role as a practitioner–researcher, described how she came to question the relevance of diagnosis and the unintended consequences of the use of binary terms such as "people with and without disabilities" (Peers et al., 2014, p. 269). Specifically, how the use of these terms could actively work against the realization of an inclusive program. In APE research, it is common to see published works that juxtapose the experi-ences, abilities, and attitudes of students described as "with and without disabilities". Rarely do we question how this type of language use and divisive identification might, though unintentionally, reify difference, underemphasize similarities, and reduce possibilities for inclusion rather than enhance them through knowledge generation. The language and terminology we use to describe children with impairments in our research can have significant implications for their inclusion and exclusion (Boyd et al., 2015). Children with impairments have historically been conceptualized from a deficits perspective in research that has problematized and medicalized their lives (Curran & Runswick-Cole, 2014). Curran and Runswick-Cole (2014), and Goodley, Runswick-Cole, and Liddiard (2016) speak to the importance of the voices of disabled children and their allies (e.g., parents, carers) in research. According to these authors, by bringing greater attention to these voices we can challenge disabled children's conceptualization as other, contribute to the disruption of normativity, and further a greater valuing of all childhoods. As researchers in a field that embraces inclusion, recognizing how our disability language and terminologies, and their underlying assumptions contribute to or detract from children's actual inclusion in PE, is paramount.

Research in APE necessarily implicates students (i.e., children and youth) and also their parents or guardians when it comes to disability identification. Phelan (2011) speaks to the tensions parents experience around their child receiving a diagnosis in order to access needed services and the potential negative labeling implications on their child's opportunities to be and feel included. Within the research context, the questions asked by APE scholars often rely on parents' willingness to disclose impairment diagnoses and/or how they identify and talk about their children. We need to consider how to proceed ethically when doctors, researchers, teachers, parents, and children disagree with each other about respectful terminology and disability identity. Further, it is worth noting that many children, and perhaps their parents, may not have ever been offered access to models for understanding their bodies and experiences beyond medical models. What role might APE researchers and practitioners play in offering access to these alternative models, some of which might offer greater resonance, advocacy opportunities, access to communities, and positive self-regard than the model that has defined them to date? How we go about asking for and gathering this type of self-disclosure information is a critical question and one that also reflects the complexities of disability models, terminologies, and experiences. Ideas around how to respectfully ask for consent and information include beginning with phrases such as "If you feel comfortable sharing ...", and using terminology that engages self-identification: for example, "Does your child identify as experiencing disability? If you are comfortable, please explain" leaves greater room for self-expression. Also, not asking questions that require responses on dichotomous questions such as "Does your child have a disability: yes or no" and other approaches that force people into categories is more respectful of their choices and leads to greater accuracy and accountability in the ways in which we write about participants.

We argue there is a critical need to understand the story underlying the disability languages we employ in research so we can not only "say what we mean" (Peers et al., 2014), but do so in a way that offers up the most respectful possibilities and limits the perpetuation of negative stereotypes and stigmas associated with disability. As Ng, Friesen, McLagan, Boyd, and Phelan (2014) explain, it is about our ongoing attention to, and reflection on, the languages we use to describe children rather than locating the one best way of doing so. "As we think, speak, [write], and act, we must consciously consider the meanings of our language and the consequences it may have for particular groups. In doing so, we can uncover and avoid harmful language practices ..." (Boyd et al., 2015, p. 1550). "Some stories enhance life and others degrade it so we must be careful about the stories we tell" (Blatt, 1987, p. 142).

Summary of key points

- Each set of disability terminology emerges from specific histories and theories of disability, thus one should be aware of the stories one is perpetuating by using specific terminology.
- There is a wide range of respectful disability terminology, and this differs by language, culture, geographical region, academic discipline, impairment type, political and community allegiances, self-identity, as well as the specific context that one is referring to (e.g., in a doctor's office or on the playing field).
- Terminology that has emerged from the medical model tends to define people by the abnormalities in their bodies and minds, and constructs these as problems that need to be fixed.
- Social model language emerged in the UK and emphasizes the role of social oppression in disabling individuals who have impairments.
- Social relational models also emphasize how oppression disables people, but also addresses how impairment effects may limit opportunities.
- Person-first language emerged from disability rights models of the United States and emphasizes the need to treat individuals with real or perceived body–mind differences as people with fundamental rights, and to protect them from unwarranted discrimination.
- The International Classification of Functioning, Health and Disability is designed to provide a shared set of terminologies and understandings about disability for the purpose of public health interventions. Although addressing some physiological and contextual criteria, it shares medical perspectives of bodily lack and does not conceptualize disability as a site of oppression.
- Many disability communities have developed their own unique terminologies to represent how their body–mind differences are not problems to be fixed, but, rather, as neutral variations, positive attributes, or valued locus of cultural creation and shared cultural experience.
- Many deaf/Deaf communities and individuals identify themselves as Deaf (rather than deaf or hard of hearing), representing an understanding of Deafness as a shared cultural linguistic community rather than a disability.
- Some communities and individuals have adopted terminology that has historically been used against them (such as crip); because such words are sometimes still used to harm, individuals who are not from the referred to community should use extreme caution and explicit consent when using these terms.
- It is a best practice to ensure that, whenever possible, individuals we are speaking about consent to the language we use to describe them.

Reflective questions

1. Within your own research, practice, or teaching context, what are three different respectful ways that you could ask whether someone identifies with disability and what terminology they would prefer you to use?
2. Think about a key questionnaire, protocol, or form used in your research or practice. What disability model frames the assumptions of this tool? How might this tool look or work differently if it were based on the assumptions of one of the other disability models covered in this chapter?

3. Identify one set of terminology covered in this chapter that you are most comfortable with. In what ways do your assumptions about disability match with, or differ from, the assumptions of the model from which the terminology emerged?

4. Identify two or three different models or sets of terminology you could use in your specific area of research or practice. Identity several aspects of each of these models or terms that you think would be most useful or helpful, and several aspects that you think could be most dangerous or limiting.

5. If you were researching or advising within an APE context, how might you handle a situation where a ten-year-old child, their parent, and their teacher disagree about which terminology to use around the child's disability?

References

Blagrave, J. (2017). Experiences of children with autism spectrum disorders in adapted physical education. *European Journal of Adapted Physical Activity*, *10*(1), 17–27.

Blatt, B. (1987). *The conquest of mental retardation*. Austin, TX: Pro-Ed.

Block, P. (2016). *Occupying disability: Critical approaches to community, justice, and decolonizing disability*. Dordrecht, Germany: Springer. Retrieved from http://login.ezproxy.library.ualberta.ca/login?url=http://search.ebscohost.com/login.aspx?direct=true&db=cat03710a&AN=alb.8108017&site=eds-live&scope=site

Boyd, V. A., Ng, S. L., & Schryer, C. F. (2015). Deconstructing language practices: Discursive constructions of children in individual education plan resource documents. *Disability & Society*, *30*(10), 1537–1553. doi:https://doi.org/10.1080/09687599.2015.1113161

Bredahl, A.-M. (2008). Ethical aspects in research in adapted physical activity. *Sport, Ethics and Philosophy*, *2*, 257–270. doi:10.1080/17511320802223881

Bredahl, A.-M. (2013). Sitting and watching others being active: The experienced difficulties in PE when having a disability. *Adapted Physical Activity Quarterly*, *30*(1), 40–58.

Charlton, J. (2000). *Nothing about us without us*. Berkeley, CA: University of California Press.

Columna, L., Lieberman, L. J., Lytle, R., & Arndt, K. (2014). Special education terminology every physical education teacher should know. *The Journal of Physical Education, Recreation & Dance*, *85*(5), 38–45.

Curran, T., & Runswick-Cole, K. (2014). Disabled children's childhood studies: A distinct approach? *Disability & Society*, *29*(10), 1617–1630. doi:https://doi.org/10.1080/09687599.2014.966187

DePauw, K. P., & Doll-Tepper, G. (2000). Toward progressive inclusion and acceptance: Myth or reality? the inclusion debate and bandwagon discourse. *Adapted Physical Activity Quarterly*, *17*(2), 135–143.

Diamond, S. (2013). What makes us a community? Reflections on building solidarity in anti- sanist praxis. In B. A. LeFrançois, R. Menzies, & G. Reaume (Eds.), *Mad matters: A critical reader in Canadian mad studies* (pp. 64–78). Toronto, ON: Canadian Scholars Press.

Dunn, D. S., & Andrews, E. E. (2015). Person-first and identity-first language: Developing psychologists' cultural competence using disability language. *American Psychologist*, *70*(3), 255–264. doi:http://dx.doi.org/10.1037/a0038636

Fitzgerald, H. (2005). Still feeling like a spare piece of luggage? embodied experiences of (dis)ability in physical education and school sport. *Physical Education & Sport Pedagogy*, *10*(1), 41–59.

Fitzgerald, H., & Stride, A. (2012). Stories about physical education from young people with disabilities. *International Journal of Disability, Development & Education*, *59*(3), 283–293.

Foley, J. T., Bryan, R. R., & McCubbin, J. A. (2008). Daily physical activity levels of elementary school-aged children with and without mental retardation. *Journal of Developmental & Physical Disabilities*, *20*(4), 365–378. doi:10.1007/s10882-008-9103-y

Gannon, J. (2011). *Deaf heritage: A narrative history of Deaf America*. Washington: Gaullaudet University.

Goodley, D., Runswick-Cole, K., & Liddiard, K. (2016). The dishuman child. *Discourse: Studies in the Cultural Politics of Education*, *37*(5), 770–784. doi:https://doi.org/10.1080/01596306.2015.1075731

Goodwin, D. L., & Watkinson, E. J. (2000). Inclusive physical education from the perspective of students with physical disabilities. *Adapted Physical Activity Quarterly*, *17*, 144–160. doi:10.1123/apaq.17.2.144

Grenier, M., Collins, K., & Wright, S. (2014). Perceptions of a disability sport unit in general physical education. *Adapted Physical Activity Quarterly*, *31*(1), 49–66. doi:http://dx.doi.org/10.1123/apaq.2013-0006

Haegele, J. A., & Hodge, S. (2016). Disability discourse: Overview and critiques of the medical and social models. *Quest*, *68*(2), 193–206.

Haegele, J. A., & Zhu, X. (2017). Experiences of individuals with visual impairments in integrated physical education: A retrospective study. *Research Quarterly for Exercise & Sport*, *88*, 425–435. doi:10.1080/02701367.2017.1346781

Hammond, R., & Anttila, H. (2015). Profession's identity challenged by the language it uses. *Physiotherapy Research International*, *20*(4), 197–199. doi:https://doi.org/10.1002/pri.1657

Healy, S., Msetfi, R., & Gallagher, S. (2013). 'Happy and a bit nervous': The experiences of children with autism in physical education. *British Journal of Learning Disabilities*, *41*(3), 222–228. doi:10.1111/bld.12053

Kattari, S. K., Lavery, A., & Hasche, L. (2017). Applying a social model of disability across the lifespan. *Journal of Human Behavior in the Social Environment*, *27*(8), 865–880. doi:https://doi.org/10.1080/10911359.2017.1344175

Lee, J., & Haegele, J. A. (2016). Understanding challenging behaviours of students with autism spectrum disorder in physical education. *Journal of Physical Education, Recreation & Dance*, *87*(7), 27–30.

Leo, J., & Goodwin, D. (2016). Simulating others' realities: Insiders reflect on disability simulations. *Adapted Physical Activity Quarterly*, *33*, 156–175. doi:http://dx.doi.org/10.1123/APAQ.2015-0031

Martin Ginis, K. A., Arbour-Nicitopoulos, K. P., Latimer-Cheung, A. E., Buchholz, A. C., Bray, S. R., Craven, B. C., … Horrocks, J. (2012). Predictors of leisure time physical activity among people with spinal cord injury. *Annals of Behavioral Medicine*, *44*(1), 104–118. doi:10.1007/s12160-012-9370-9

McKay, C., Block, M., & Park, J. Y. (2015). The impact of paralympic school day on student attitudes toward inclusion in physical education. *Adapted Physical Activity Quarterly*, *32*, 331–348. doi:http://dx.doi.org/10.1123/APAQ.2015-0045

Menear, K. S., & Neumeier, W. H. (2015). Promoting physical activity for students with autism spectrum disorder: Barriers, benefits, and strategies for success. *Journal of Physical Education, Recreation & Dance*, *86*(3), 43–48.

Menzies, R., LeFrancois, B. A., & Reaume, G. (2013). Introducing mad studies. In B. A. LeFrancois, R. Menzies, & G. Reaume (Eds.), *Mad matters: A critical reader in Canadian mad studies* (pp. 1–22). Toronto, ON: Canadian Scholars Press.

Ng, S., Friesen, F., McLagan, E., Boyd, V., & Phelan, S. (2014). A critical theory response to empirical challenges in report-writing: Considerations for clinical educators and lifelong learners. *Journal of Educational Audiology*, *20*, 1–11.

Oliver, M. (2013). The social model of disability: Thirty years on. *Disability & Society*, *28*(7), 1024–1026. doi:https://doi.org/10.1080/09687599.2013.818773

Pan, C. Y. (2008). Objectively measured physical activity between children with autism spectrum disorders and children without disabilities during inclusive recess settings in taiwan. *Journal of Autism & Developmental Disorders*, *38*(7), 1292–1301.

Peers, D. (2012). Patients, athletes, freaks: Paralympism and the reproduction of disability. *Journal of Sport & Social Issues*, *36*(3), 295–316.

Peers, D. (2018). Engaging axiology: Engabling meaningful transdisciplinary collaboration in adapted physical activity. *Adapted Physical Activity Quarterly*, *35*, 267–284.

Peers, D., Brittain, M., & McRuer, R. (2012). Crip excess, art, and politics: A conversation with Robert McRuer. *Review of Education, Pedagogy, & Cultural Studies*, *34*, 148–155. doi:http://dx.doi.org/10.1080/10714413.2012.687284

Peers, D., Eales, L., & Spencer-Cavaliere, N. (2018). Narrating ourselves and our movements: Terminology and political possibility. In S. Carraro (Ed.), *Alter-habilitas: Perceptions of disability among people* (pp. 25–40). Verona, Italy: Alteritas.

Peers, D., Spencer-Cavaliere, N., & Eales, L. (2014). Say what you mean: Rethinking disability language in adapted physical activity quarterly. *Adapted Physical Activity Quarterly*, *31*(3), 265–282. doi:10.1123/apaq.2013-0091

Petrie, K., Devich, J., & Fitzgerald, H. (2018). Working towards inclusive physical education in a primary school: 'Some days I just don't get it right'. *Physical Education and Sport Pedagogy*, *23*(4), 345–357.

Phelan, S. K. (2011). Constructions of disability: A call for critical reflexivity in occupational therapy. *Canadian Journal of Occupational Therapy*, *78*, 164–172. doi:10.2182/cjot.2011.78.3.4

Phelan, S. K., Wright, V., & Gibson, B. E. (2014). Representations of disability and normality in rehabilitation technology promotional materials. *Disability & Rehabilitation*, *36*(24), 2072–2079.

Reid, G. (1992). Editorial. *Adapted Physical Activity Quarterly*, *9*, 1–4.

Richardson, E. V., Smith, B., & Papathomas, A. (2017). Collective stories of exercise: Making sense of gym experiences with disabled peers. *Adapted Physical Activity Quarterly*, *34*(3), 276–294. doi:https://doi.org/10.1123/apaq.2016-0126

Saebu, M., & Sørensen, M. (2011). Factors associated with physical activity among young adults with a disability. *Scandinavian Journal of Medicine & Science in Sports*, *21*(5), 730–738. doi:10.1111/j.1600-0838.2010.01097.x

Shakespeare, T. (2006). *Disability rights and wrongs*. Oxon, UK: Routledge.

Sherrill, C. (2010). Language matters: From 'mental retardation' to 'intellectual disabilities'. *Palaestra*, *25*(1), 54–55.

Shyman, E. (2016). The reinforcement of ableism: Normality, the medical model of disability, and humanism in applied behavior analysis and ASD. *Intellectual & Developmental Disabilities*, *54*(5), 366–376.

Sit, C. H. P., McKenzie, T. L., Cerin, E., Chow, B. C., Huang, W. Y., & Yu, J. (2017). Physical activity and sedentary time among children with disabilities at school. *Medicine & Science in Sports & Exercise*, *49*(2), 292–297. doi:10.1249/MSS.0000000000001097

Smith, A. (2004). The inclusion of pupils with special educational needs in secondary school physical education. *Physical Education & Sport Pedagogy*, *9*(1), 37–54. doi:10.1080/1740898042000208115

Spencer-Cavaliere, N., & Watkinson, E. J. (2010). Inclusion understood from the perspectives of children with disability. *Adapted Physical Activity Quarterly*, *27*(4), 275–293.

Taliaferro, A. R., Hammond, L., & Wyant, K. (2015). Preservice physical educators' self-efficacy beliefs toward inclusion: The impact of coursework and practicum. *Adapted Physical Activity Quarterly*, *32*, 49-67. doi:http://dx.doi.org/10.1123/apaq.2013-0112

Thomas, C. (2004). How is disability understood? An examination of sociological approaches. *Disability & Society*, *19*(6), 569–583. doi:10.1080/0968759042000252506

Thomas, C. (2009). Rescuing a social relational understanding of disability. *Scandinavian Journal of Disability Research*, *6*(1), 22–36. doi:https://doi.org/10.1080/15017410409512637

Titchkosky, T. (2007). *Reading and writing disability differently: The textured life of embodiment*. Toronto, ON: University of Toronto Press.

Tzanetakos, N., Papastergiou, M., Vernadakis, N., & Antoniou, P. (2017). Utilizing physically interactive videogames for the balance training of adolescents with deafness within a physical education course. *Journal of Physical Education and Sport*, *17*(2), 614–623.

Walker, N. (2013, August 16). Throw away the master's tools: Liberating ourselves from the pathology paradigm. [web log comment] Retrieved from http://neurocosmopolitanism.com/throw-away-the-masters-tools-liberating-ourselves-from-the-pathology-paradigm/

Wang, L. (2019). Perspectives of students with special needs on inclusion in general physical education: A social-relational model of disability. *Adapted Physical Activity Quarterly*. doi:10.1123/apaq.2018-0068

Wang, L., Qi, J., & Wang, L. (2015). Beliefs of chinese physical educators on teaching students with disabilities in general physical education classes. *Adapted Physical Activity Quarterly*, *32*, 137–155. doi:10.1123/APAQ.2014-0140

Withers, A. J. (2012). *Disability politics and theory*. Black Point, NS: Fernwood.

World Health Organization. (2013). *How to use the ICF: A practical manual for using the International Classification of Functioning, Disability and Health (ICF)*. Retrieved from www.who.int/classifications/drafticf practicalmanual.pdf

Part II
Research approaches

9

Quantitative research

Samuel R. Hodge

Introduction

Adapted physical education researchers commonly use quantitative research designs. Several years ago, Haegele, Lee, and Porretta (2015) conducted a documentary analysis to analyze trends in research published in *Adapted Physical Activity Quarterly* (*APAQ*) over a ten-year span. They analyzed a total of 181 research articles published from 2004 to 2013 and categorized most of those studies as being group design (n = 127, 70%); that is, mostly quantitative studies. Qualitative research made up the second-highest percentage of the studies in the analysis (n = 34, 19%). Only seven (4%) of the studies were categorized as mixed-method studies. Last, single-subject design (n = 5, 3%), other (n = 5, 3%), and case studies (n = 3, 2%) accounted for the remaining design types. Haegele and colleagues' (2015) findings are consistent with earlier patterns. For example, using data from a documentary analysis of 419 studies in *APAQ* and 367 studies in the *Journal of Teaching in Physical Education* (*JTPE*) between the 1980s and 2005, Hodge and Hersman (2007) reported that of 786 studies mostly (66%) quantitative methods were used in those cases where the researcher(s) identified the study design, followed by 24% qualitative methods, and 10% representing a mixed-method approach. Importantly, however, Hodge and Hersman concluded that since "only 32% of the studies analyzed explicitly stated the research designs, nearly two-thirds of the studies' designs are left open to interpretation by the reader" (p. 14).

In this chapter, I identify the basic philosophical foundation that guides researchers who use research designs situated in the quantitative paradigm. I also discuss quality indicators (criteria) for conducting and/or consuming quantitative research. Next, I discuss the fundamental components of different types of quantitative research approaches, and how the approaches have been used in adapted physical education research. Last, I present examples of studies in adapted physical education (APE) that are positioned in different types of quantitative research approaches.

Quantitative research: philosophy of positivism

The quantitative research paradigm is grounded in the philosophy of positivism. Positivism is positioned by an external–realist ontology (of the real nature of whatever is), which presupposes that a hard reality exists (Fraenkel, Wallen, & Hyun, 2012; Haegele & Hodge, 2015; Pringle, 2000). In short, positivist researchers use scientific methods to discover the nature of phenomena in reality and determine how it works (Fraenkel et al., 2012). Moreover, a positivist epistemology (i.e., the nature of knowledge and justification) claims to be free of value and not influenced by social context; in other words, objective and unbiased (Haegele & Hodge, 2015; Pringle, 2000). Positivist researchers espouse that knowledge can be generalized to groups of people across different environments and time. Positivism posits that the natural world is deterministic, which supposes that all events that come about in the world are a result of cause and effect relationships (Haegele & Hodge, 2015; Trochim & Donnelly, 2006).

The reader should consult Haegele and Hodge's (2015) tutorial paper for an easy to understand discussion of the philosophy of positivism and the quantitative research paradigm. They explained that positivism influences the quantitative research paradigm by providing basic assumptions which guide researchers' decisions and actions. Specifically, Fraenkel et al. (2012) identified eight major assumptions of quantitative research, as: (a) a hard reality exists and it is the task of science to discover the nature of reality and how it works; (b) research investigations can result in accurate statements about the way the world really is; (c) researchers may remove themselves from what is being researched; (d) facts are independent of the knower (the person with the knowledge) and can be known in an unbiased way; (e) facts and values are distinct from one another; (f) proper research designs can lead to accurate conclusions about the nature of the world; (g) the purpose of research is to explain and predict relationships; and (h) the goal of research is to develop laws that make prediction possible. Researchers should take these assumptions, as well as quality indicators, into consideration when conceptualizing, designing, and implementing research using the quantitative paradigm (Haegele & Hodge, 2015).

Quality indicators in conducting empirical studies

From early traditional research methodologies to current expanded conceptualizations of scientific research in education, the complexity of conducting research in APE necessitates the need to identify quality indicators across research approaches. In the next section, I present quality indicators for conducting empirical studies in APE situated in the quantitative research paradigm. Specifically, I discuss quality indicators (criteria) for conducting and/or consuming quantitative research, particularly for those interested in quasi- and true experimental designs that represent rigorous application of methodology to questions of interest in APE research.

In 2005, a series of articles was published in a special issue of the journal *Exceptional Children* that focused on quality indicators and guidelines across research paradigms as a result of a task force established by the Council for Exceptional Children's Division for Research (Odom et al., 2005). The Council's task force identified the following methodologies as being common in special education research: (a) experimental group, (b) correlational, (c) single subject, and (d) qualitative designs (Odom et al., 2005). Odom and colleagues explain that the "task force was to establish quality indicators for each methodology and to propose how evidence from each methodology could be used to identify and understand effective practices in special education" (p. 138). Further, Odom et al. (2005) described quality indicators as follows:

> Quality indicators are the feature of research that represents rigorous application of methodology to questions of interest. They may serve as guidelines for (a) researchers who design and conduct research, (b) reviewers who evaluate the "believability" of research findings, and (c) consumers who need to determine the "usability" of research findings. High-quality research is designed to rule out alternative explanations for both

the results of the study and the conclusions that researchers draw. The higher the quality of research methodology, the more confidence the researcher and readers will have in the findings of the study.

(p. 141)

To that end, the authors of the special issue of *Exceptional Children* described quality indicators and provided guidelines for researchers and authors for judging rigor and credibility of studies across research methodologies in special education. More specifically, there were four papers in the special issue wherein the authors identified quality indicators of research in special education as well as proposed the use of research findings as evidence for practice. Of importance for this chapter, Gersten et al. (2005) discussed quality indicators for group experimental designs and proposed guidelines for using the results of group studies for evidence of effective practices. In addition, quality indicators for correlational designs and ways in which results from correlational studies may contribute evidence of effective practices were presented in the paper by Thompson, Diamond, McWilliam, Snyder, and Snyder (2005).

The various quality indicators and guidelines identified by the authors of the *Exceptional Children* special issue 2005 have been adopted and extended by professionals in APE. Furthermore, readers of *APAQ* and other publication outlets continue to have access to a number of published works that describe what criteria are indicative of high-quality research within the quantitative methodological paradigm. For example, Haegele and Hodge's (2015) focus on quantitative research methodology provides informed discourse as to what is quality work in APE research in the quantitative paradigm. Furthermore, Carano (2014) conducted an extensive literature review and used a Delphi study approach to identify categories and criteria in developing taxonomies for use in planning, conducting, and evaluating research across paradigms and methodologies in APE. To extend those discourses, the current work is framed around conducting empirical studies in terms of what criteria are important to consider when conducting APE research or analyzing the quality of published works in the quantitative research paradigm. In this chapter, therefore, I identify and discuss quality indicators (criteria) for conducting and/or consuming quantitative research, in particular for true experimental and quasi-experimental designs.

In regard to the quantitative paradigm, those pursuing group (experimental) designs should consider quality indicators most relevant to those methodologies. For the reader, Petty, Thomson, and Stew (2012) compared criteria for judging quality (or rigor) in quantitative research and qualitative research with accompanying strategies. They assert that criteria for judging quality in quantitative research include: (a) objectivity, which refers to the extent to which the findings are the product of the inquiry and not the bias of the researcher; (b) reliability, which typically concerns instrumentation (consistency of the measures); (c) internal validity, which means the degree to which the results are attributable to the independent variable(s) and not to some other conflicting explanation and typically indicates the researcher's degree of control or manipulation of variables; and (d) external validity, which represents the extent to which the results of a study can be generalized; that is, the extent to which the findings can be applied in other contexts or with other participants (Petty et al., 2012). In general, quantitative methods rely on research questions and hypothesis testing, design controls, and statistical manipulation and interpretation (i.e., deductive reasoning and reductionist logic) to establish a research design *a priori* and to make sample to population generalizations (Haegele & Hodge, 2015).

Descriptive, correlational, and comparative research designs

In this section, I briefly discuss non-experimental research designs, including descriptive, correlational, and comparative research. The main function of descriptive research studies is to describe characteristics of a population (e.g., demography of a group and their beliefs about teaching students with severe disabilities) and/or status of various phenomena with no attempt to manipulate independent variable(s) and no assertion of cause–effect relationships. These designs are commonly used in educational research (Thomas, Nelson, & Silverman, 2015). There is a large range of descriptive studies, including case studies, descriptive surveys, descriptive–observational designs, Delphi method, and developmental studies, as examples.

The main function of correlational studies is to determine whether, and to what degree, a relationship exists between two or more quantifiable variables. But there is no attempt to manipulate or influence the variables. In the most basic approach, the researcher uses a correlational design to analyze the possibility (or probability) of relationships between only two variables. However, correlational research involving multiple variables is more common (Fraenkel et al., 2012).

Typically, researchers use comparative research designs to make group comparisons and to draw conclusions about the groups based on the findings associated with the variables of interest. The main function of these designs is to identify and analyze similarities and differences between groups. For example, a comparative study would be useful to compare the cultural norms of Brazilian compared to Puerto Rican physical education teachers in teaching students with disabilities in general physical education settings. In fact, Richardson (2018) asserts that comparative "studies are most often cross-national, comparing two separate people groups" (para. 1). These types of studies are useful in enhancing our understandings about different cultures, languages, societies, and ways of life among different people groups. Further, comparative research can accommodate either quantitative or qualitative research methods (Richardson, 2018).

Experimental designs

In their classic text, Donald T. Campbell and Julian C. Stanley (1963) discussed the usefulness of sixteen pre-experimental, quasi-experimental, and true experimental designs in controlling common threats to the internal and external validity of these designs. Internal validity is defined as the extent to which a study's results can be credited to the intervention(s) used in the study (Thomas et al., 2015). Types of threats to internal validity are identified and defined in numerous research textbooks (e.g., Cook & Campbell, 1979; Fraenkel et al., 2012; Thomas et al., 2015). Suffice to say here that a goal of the researcher is to control all, or as many as reasonably possible, factors that might influence the study's results. True experimental research designs are designs that include randomly formed experimental and comparison or control groups, which allow the researcher to assume that the groups were reasonably equivalent at the outset of the study. These designs, particularly randomized controlled trials, are considered to have strong internal validity controls for establishing strong, or at least probable, evidence of an intervention's effectiveness (Coalition for Evidence-Based Policy, 2003). In comparison, quasi-experimental research designs do not include randomly formed experimental groups; as such, the researcher must rely on techniques other than randomization to control (or reduce) threats to internal validity. Campbell and Stanley (1963) cautioned that it is with "extreme reluctance that these summary tables are presented because they are apt to be 'too helpful,' and to be depended upon in place of the more complex and qualified presentation in the text"

(p. 8). I also must caution the reader not to rely solely on such checklists, but, rather, to carefully consider each design's implementation in use for a particular purpose and context.

Likewise, educational researchers Jack R. Fraenkel, Norman E. Wallen, and Helen H. Hyun (2012) present a checklist (see p. 280) that identifies the *potential* effectiveness of experimental designs in controlling threats to internal validity. They indicate that several quantitative experimental designs, such as the Solomon Four-Group Design, offer strong control over most threats to internal validity. There are several other designs, such as the Matching-Only Pretest–Posttest Control Group Design, which provide some control over most threats (e.g., participants' characteristics, mortality, testing), but the threats may still occur. In contrast, such designs as the One-Group Pretest–Posttest Design have weak control over the various threats to internal validity and, in fact, the threats are likely to occur (Fraenkel et al., 2012). Paradoxically, Campbell and Stanley's (1963) Separate-Sample Pretest–Posttest (quasi-experimental) Group Design has strong external validity, but weaknesses in internal validity controls. External validity refers to the extent that the results are generalizable (Thomas et al., 2015). Threats to external validity are also identified and defined in various research textbooks (e.g., Cook & Campbell, 1979; Fraenkel et al., 2012; Thomas et al., 2015).

Gersten and colleagues (2005) identified and discussed a host of quality indicators for group experimental and quasi-experimental research proposals in special education. These quality indicators are also applicable to group experimental and quasi-experimental research proposals in APE (see Gersten et al., 2005, p. 151). Further, they presented a set of quality indicators (see p. 152) for appraising the quality of completed experimental or quasi-experimental studies. Likewise, the *Publication Manual of the American Psychological Association* (American Psychological Association, 2010) present journal article reporting standards (JARS) within summary tables (see pages 247–252). These JARS tables present outlined information recommended for inclusion in manuscripts that report: (a) new data collections regardless of research design; (b) studies with an experimental manipulation or intervention; and (c) studies using random and non-random assignment of participants to experimental groups. To date, however, there is an underdeveloped database of experimental studies, particularly true experimental studies, reported in articles appearing in *APAQ* (Haegele et al., 2015).

Again, Haegele and colleagues (2015) conducted a documentary analysis of research studies published in *APAQ* from 2004 to 2013 and reported that only 24 (13%) of the articles published were intervention studies. Of these experimental studies, 18 used group designs, five used single-subject designs, and only one used a mixed-methods design. Haegele and colleagues' findings lend support to Zhang, deLisle, and Chen's (2006) conclusion that adapted physical activity research is primarily descriptive and correlational in nature. Although there have been a few noteworthy true experimental designs (e.g., Casey & Emes, 2011; Mazzoni, Purves, Southward, Rhodes, & Temple, 2009) published in *APAQ*, there is clear need for additional, well-designed, randomized controlled trial studies in APE research. Of course, APE researchers should be cautious to utilize randomized controlled studies in appropriate settings and instances. Unfortunately, randomized control studies may not be feasible in natural environments, such as playgrounds or gymnasiums, which are common to the applied nature of APE research (Haegele & Porretta, 2015). Further, the low number of students with disabilities in schools and the integrated nature of physical education classes make conducting randomized control studies with a sufficient number of participants difficult at best. Haegele and Porretta (2015) suggest that "for researchers to conduct randomized control studies [in schools], they would likely need to create groups

Samuel R. Hodge

of participants, which would affect the ecological validity of the study, as well as the generalization of results to practice" (p. 80).

Typically, though, randomized controlled trials are considered the gold standard for establishing strong evidence of an intervention's effectiveness. In fact, the US Department of Education's Institute of Education Sciences (IES) strongly advocates the use of randomized controlled trials in educational research. Randomized controlled trials are defined as "studies that randomly assign individuals to an intervention group or to a control group, in order to measure the effects of the intervention" (Coalition for Evidence-Based Policy, 2003, p. 1). The Department of Education's IES commissioned the preparation of a user-friendly guide for identifying and implementing educational practices supported by rigorous evidence (i.e., evidence-based interventions), preferably randomized controlled trials (Coalition for Evidence-Based Policy, 2003). Table 9.1 presents the IES quality indicators for evaluating whether an intervention is supported by strong evidence that it will improve educational outcomes. The following resources can be useful also in finding evidence-based educational interventions.

Table 9.1 Quality of evidence needed to establish strong evidence of effectiveness

Key items to look for in the study's description of the intervention and the random assignment process

- The study should clearly describe (i) the intervention, including who administered it, who received it, and what it cost; (ii) how the intervention differed from what the control group received; and (iii) the logic of how the intervention is supposed to affect outcomes.
- Be alert to any indication that the random assignment process may have been compromised.
- The study should provide data showing that there were no systematic differences between the intervention and control groups before the intervention.

Key items to look for in the study's collection of outcome data

- The study should use outcome measures that are "valid"—i.e., that accurately measure the true outcomes that the intervention is designed to affect.
- The percentage of study participants that the study has lost track of when collecting outcome data should be small, and should not differ between the intervention and control groups.
- The study should collect and report outcome data even for those members of the intervention group who don't participate in, or complete, the intervention.
- The study should preferably obtain data on long-term outcomes of the intervention, so that you can judge whether the intervention's effects were sustained over time.

Key items to look for in the study's reporting of results

- If the study claims that the intervention improves one or more outcomes, it should report (i) the size of the effect, and (ii) statistical tests showing the effect is unlikely to be due to chance.
- A study's claim that the intervention's effect on a subgroup (e.g., Hispanic students) is different than its effect on the overall population in the study should be treated with caution.
- The study should report the intervention's effects on all the outcomes that the study measured, not just those for which there is a positive effect.

Note. Constructed from the Coalition for Evidence-Based Policy (2003, pp. 5–9).

> *Campbell Systematic Reviews* [CSR] is the peer-reviewed online monograph series of systematic reviews prepared under the editorial control of the Campbell Collaboration. CSR follow structured guidelines and standards for summarizing the international research evidence on the effects of interventions in crime and justice, education, international development, and social welfare.
>
> *(Campbell Collaboration, 2015)*

The Evidence for Policy and Practice Information and Co-ordinating Centre (EPPI-Centre) is part of the Social Science Research Unit at the UCL Institute of Education. The EPPI-Centre is committed to informing policy and professional practice with sound evidence. As such, it is involved in two main areas of work: (1) systematic reviews: this includes developing methods for systematic reviews and research syntheses, conducting reviews, supporting others to undertake reviews, and providing guidance and training in this area; and (2) research use: this includes studying the use/non-use of research evidence in personal, practice, and political decision-making, supporting those who wish to find and use research to help solve problems, and providing guidance and training in this area (Evidence for Policy and Practice Information Centre, 2006–2009).

The What Works Clearinghouse (WWC) collects, screens, and identifies studies of effectiveness of educational interventions (programs, products, practices, and policies). The WWC regularly updates the WWC Technical Standards and their application to take account of new considerations brought forth by experts and users. Such changes may result in reappraisals of studies and/or interventions previously reviewed and rated. The current WWC Standards offer guidance for those planning or carrying out studies, not only in the design considerations, but also the analysis and reporting stages as well. The WWC Standards, however, may not pertain to every situation, context, or purpose of a study and will evolve (www.w-w-c.org/standards.html).

Given that well-designed and implemented randomized controlled trials are rare in APE research (Haegele et al., 2015); the evidence supporting an intervention usually falls short of meeting all of the quality indicators, as identified in Table 9.1, for *strong* evidence of effectiveness. Relevant to this issue, Carano (2014) developed taxonomies useful in evaluating the strength of quality of research in APE from strong to weak. In other words, she developed matrixes which present a set of quality indicators (criteria) for judging the rigor of experimental (true and quasi), correlational, single-subject, and qualitative research designs, respectively (Carano, 2014). Each matrix presents three levels of strength of quality: Level 1 represents strong evidence of rigor (quality), Level 2 represents moderate evidence of quality, and Level 3 indicates weak evidence of rigor (Carano, 2014; Carano, Silliman-French, French, Nichols, & Rose, 2015). In using the taxonomies, the user first selects the taxonomy that matches the research design (e.g., a quasi-experimental group design) and then completes the review. Next, the user determines the level of recommendation (Sharon L. Carano, personal communication, July 28, 2015). Established scholars, as well as emerging professionals such as early career faculty and graduate students interested in research pertaining to physical education for individuals with disabilities, should use quality indicators such as those appearing in these matrixes in planning, conducting, and analyzing research within the quantitative and qualitative paradigms. The reader should consult Carano's (2014) work to learn more about this process.

Quantitative studies in adapted physical education (APE)

It is clear that in APE research, the quantitative paradigm is the dominant paradigm used (Haegele et al., 2015; Hodge & Hersman, 2007). There are many types of quantitative research designs and approaches used, including: (a) documentary and content analyses, and secondary data analyses; (b) descriptive studies (e.g., descriptive case studies, Delphi method, descriptive surveys, developmental and observational studies); (c) correlational, comparative, and epidemiological studies; and (d) quasi- and true experimental studies (Thomas et al., 2015). For the interested reader, there are chapters in this handbook devoted to other quantitative research designs. Specifically, the chapter "Systematic reviews and meta-analysis", by Xihe Zhu (Chapter 13), and Jihyun Lee and Phillip Ward's chapter, "Single-subject research designs in adapted physical education" (Chapter 12) are excellent resources.

Documentary and content analyses, and secondary data analyses

Documentary and content analysis designs support both quantitative (Bordens & Abbott, 1999) and qualitative applications (Bowen, 2009). In APE, researchers have used these types of designs to quantify variables of interest. For example, Sherrill and O'Conner (1999) used a documentary analysis approach to determine the status quo of *APAQ* research and identify specific areas for improvement. They analyzed 38 databased research articles that were published in *APAQ* during 1997–1998. Sherrill and O'Conner reported that only 14%, 27%, and 14% of the articles during that time frame met the stated criteria for "good" research in regard to identifying and describing the variables race, educational level, and socioeconomic status, respectively. In contrast, they found that contributors to *APAQ* typically had identified and described participants in regard to the variables gender (92%), age (86%), and disability (76%). On the other hand, Bowen (2009) describes documentary analysis in research as "a form of qualitative research in which documents are interpreted by the researcher to give voice and meaning around an assessment topic" (para. 1).

The use of documentary and content analyses is quite common in the adapted physical education literature and related fields (e.g., Haegele et al., 2015; Hodge, Kozub, Robinson, & Hersman, 2007; Táboas-Pais & Rey-Cao, 2012). Haegele and colleagues' (2015) documentary analysis is a fine example. In their study, they analyzed trends in research published in *APAQ* and reported that most of the studies they analyzed were situated in the quantitative paradigm. Specific to physical education, Táboas-Pais and Rey-Cao (2012) used a content analysis design to examine how images of disability are portrayed in physical education textbooks for secondary schools in Spain.

The secondary data analysis method is the statistical analysis of data that was collected previously by the same or different researchers or various entities such as the United States Department of Education's (2018) *40th Annual Report to Congress on the Implementation of the Individuals with Disabilities Education Act* for various educational purposes. Crossman (2019) explained that in using a secondary data analysis approach,

> … the researcher poses questions that are addressed through the analysis of a data set that they were not involved in collecting. The data was not collected to answer the researcher's specific research questions and was instead collected for another purpose. So, the same data set can actually be a primary data set to one researcher and a secondary data set to a different one.
>
> *(Crossman, 2018, para. 1–2)*

Secondary data analyses are rarely conducted in the APE literature (Almasri, O'Neil, & Palisano, 2014). In a broader context, however, Lee (2011) conducted a secondary data analysis using a national data set (National Early Intervention Longitudinal Study, or NEILS) to analyze the World Health Organization's (WHO) International Classification of Functioning, Disability and Health for Children and Youth (ICF-CY) in organizing data to describe children's functioning (including some movement components) through use of a profile of functioning. Lee's (2011) study has relevance for future APE research.

Descriptive studies

Thomas et al. (2015) explained that descriptive research is "a study of status" (p. 285) and descriptive designs are regularly used in educational research. There is a large range of descriptive studies, including case studies (Vogler, Koranda, & Romance, 2000); descriptive surveys (e.g., Columna et al., 2016; Ogu, Umunnah, Nwosu, & Gloria, 2017; Reina, Hutzler, Iniguez-Santiago, & Moreno-Murcia, 2019), which is the most common type of descriptive research method used; (pre-experimental) descriptive–observational designs (Houston, van der Mars, & Lorenz, 2018); Delphi method (Park, Koh, & Block, 2014); and developmental studies (Ericsson & Karlsson, 2014), used in APE research. As a noteworthy example, Park et al. (2014) used a Delphi method and an analytical hierarch process "to identify and prioritize factors believed to contribute to an effective inclusive physical education program for students with disabilities" (p. 42). In using developmental studies, researchers focus on changes in behaviors over a prolonged period of time (years) (Thomas et al., 2015). For example, Ericsson and Karlsson (2014) examined the long-term effects (longitudinal study over nine years) on motor skills and school performance of students with motor delays and neurotypical peers as a function of time duration and frequency (daily versus twice per week) in physical education, and adapted motor skills training (i.e., individualized instruction) in physical education.

Using survey methods, Columna et al. (2016), and Ogu et al. (2017) administered an attitudinal instrument to physical education teachers from Latin American countries and Nigeria, respectively, to examine variables associated with teaching students with disabilities. In comparison, Reina and colleagues (2019) surveyed 976 students (age 11–16 years) to analyze links "between students' ability beliefs and attitudes toward inclusion in physical education, as well as the impact of gender and previous contact/participation with children with disability on these variables" (p. 132). Survey designs are commonly used in much of the attitudinal and psychosocial research conducted in APE.

In the case study method, Vogler et al. (2000) used both quantitative and qualitative strategies to examine the effect of a people resource model in teaching a child with severe cerebral palsy who was integrated in a general physical education class. More recently, Houston et al. (2018) used a descriptive observational design to analyze the physical activity levels of elementary-aged students with physical disabilities in inclusive physical education and recess settings.

Correlational research, comparative analyses, and epidemiological studies

Researchers use correlational research to explore relationships that may exist among variables, whereas comparative research designs are used to make group comparisons. Scholars conducting research in APE settings use correlational (Agiovlasitis, Pitetti, Guerra, & Fernhall, 2011) including psychometric analyses (Hodge, Murata, & Kozub, 2002b; Li, Wang, Block, Sum, & Wu, 2018; Rizzo, 1988) and epidemiological (Lobenius-Palmér, Sjöqvist, Hurtig-Wennlöf, & Lundqvist, 2018; Unsal & Ayranci, 2008) research designs to investigate possible relationships among variables without attempting to manipulate or influence the variables

(Fraenkel et al., 2012). For example, Agiovlasitis et al. (2011) used a correlational design to predict either VO_{2peak} (from 20-meter shuttle-run test) of youth with Down syndrome. Interestingly, Charaśna-Blachucik and Blachucik (2016) used a comparative study to analyze "somatic development and physical fitness of 20 schoolgirls with mild intellectual disabilities and 20 schoolgirls with normal intellectual capacity" from multiple physical education classes. They found no statistically significant differences in somatic development and physical fitness between the two groups of girls (those with mild intellectual disabilities and their peers without disabilities).

The process of instrument development and validation calls for the use of psychometric analyses. Since the 1980s, with the development and validation of Rizzo's "Physical educators' attitude toward teaching the handicapped" attitude survey (Rizzo, 1988), there have been a number of scales developed and validated for different groups in the APE literature (e.g., Hodge et al., 2002, 2015; Hodge, Sato, Mukoyama. & Kozub, 2013; Li et al., 2018; Rizzo, 1984, 1985, 1988).

In an epidemiological study regarding mental health, Unsal and Ayranci (2008) sought to determine variables associated with the prevalence and prevention of depression among high school students. In recent years, there have been epidemiological studies published relevant to APE literature. For example, Lobenius-Palmér et al. (2018) conducted an epidemiological study to compare accelerometer-measured habitual physical activity, sedentary time, and meeting physical activity recommendations among children and adolescents with disabilities in four disability groups (i.e., autism spectrum disorders, intellectual disability, hearing impairment, and physical/visual impairments) and neurotypical children and adolescents.

True and quasi-experimental designs

In recent years, there has been an increase in interventions studies involving children with disabilities and physical activity and/or fundamental motor skill development (Getchell, Liang, Golden, & Logan, 2014; Robinson, Palmer, & Meehan, 2017; Yu et al., 2016); still, APE scholars call for the conduct of more true and quasi-experimental studies in the field (Apache, 2005; Hodge et al., 2002; Hodge & Jansma, 1999; Rizzo & Vispoel, 1992; Slininger, Sherrill, & Jankowski, 2000). True experimental research designs require randomly formed experimental, and comparison or control, groups, which allows the researcher to presume that the groups are equivalent at the start of the study. As a noteworthy example of a true-experimental study, Slininger et al. (2000) used a pretest–posttest randomized groups design to analyze the effects of three physical education settings (i.e., structured contact, non-structured contact, control) on the attitudes of neurotypical elementary-aged students toward schoolmates with severe intellectual disabilities. Much more recently, Pritchard Orr, Keiver, Bertram, and Clarren (2018) used a "crossover (wait-list control) within-subject [group] design" (p. 406) to analyze the effects of a physical activity intervention program on executive function skills of 30 children ages 7–14 years with a diagnosis of fetal alcohol spectrum disorder. They explained that executive function skills "refers to a set of cognitive abilities required to attain goals efficiently in non-routine situations" such as "problem solving, planning, concept formation and conceptual set shifting ..." (p. 404). The FAST Club intervention program was implemented in a school gymnasium, and the researchers reported significant improvements in executive functioning for the children following participation in the FAST Club program. Although Pritchard Orr et al. articulated that they used a wait-list control design, it is unclear whether or not the children were assigned to the intervention and control groups randomly to constitute a true experimental design versus a quasi-experimental design.

Quasi-experimental designs serve essentially the same function as true experimental designs, but with the critical exception that, in these designs, the participants are *not* assigned randomly to the experimental, and comparison or control groups. Therefore, the researcher should *not* presume that the groups are equivalent at the start of the study in using quasi-experimental designs. Nonetheless, researchers in APE and related fields use these designs to do important work. For example, Tzanetakos, Papastergiou, Vernadakis, and Antoniou (2017) used a quasi-experimental group design (two equal-sized groups of three boys and two girls with deafness) to compare two balance training programs: (a) an exergame (i.e., intervention group—Nintendo Wii Fit Plus physically interactive videogames); and (b) a traditional adapted physical education program using traditional balance exercises and equipment on the effectiveness of the two programs "to improve students' balance ability" (p. 620). Statistical analysis revealed that the groups were not statistically significantly different on either the pretest or posttest measures. Tzanetakos et al. (2017) explained that "the two groups did not differ in balance ability. Following intervention, both programs yielded an improvement in balance ability, although this improvement did not reach statistical significance" (p. 619). Apache (2005), as another example of experimentation in physical education, used a nonequivalent pretest–posttest comparison group design to examine the effectiveness of an activity-based intervention versus a direct instruction approach in fundamental motor skill development of preschool children with disabilities.

In a well-established line of attitudinal research, Terry L. Rizzo and Walter P. Vispoel (1992) used a quasi-experimental group design to compare the effects of two courses (Adapted Physical Education versus Physical Education for Children) on undergraduate physical education students' attitudes toward teaching school-age students with intellectual disabilities, behavioral disorders, and learning disabilities. Likewise, Hodge and colleagues have used non-equivalent pretest–posttest comparison group designs to examine attitude change of physical education majors enrolled in APE courses (Hodge et al., 2002a) as well as attitude change of teachers who participate in professional development workshops designed for teaching students with disabilities (Haegele, Hodge, Gutierres Filho, & Gonçalves de Rezende, 2018). For example, Hodge et al. (2002a) used a quasi-experimental group design to compare the effects of two practicum types (off- and on-campus) on physical education teaching majors' attitudes and perceived competence toward teaching students with physical disabilities and intellectual disabilities. More recently, Hodge and colleagues (2018) collected pretest–posttest quantitative data (scale responses) using direct administration of a survey to analyze the attitudes of physical education teachers about inclusion and teaching students with disabilities in Brazil before and after they participated in a professional development workshop focused on inclusive ideology and strategies.

Notwithstanding the many studies cited within this chapter, there are major gaps in the APE research base. Future studies may address such issues as teachers' preparedness in teaching an increasingly diverse student population (including students with disabilities) in school physical education as well as associated issues of access, equity, and social justice (Erwin, Brusseau, Carson, Hodge, & Kang, 2018; Hodge, 2014). In the conception of social justice, for example, more APE-based research is needed to counter the triple jeopardy of intersecting identities where historically marginalized groups (e.g., children of color with disabilities) are minoritized, impoverished, and disabled, placing them at greater health risks. For example, survey method and/or correlational research could be used to ascertain answers to such questions as: "What opportunities exist across school locales [i.e., city, suburb, town, or rural] for school-age students with disabilities to participate in moderate to vigorous physical activity regularly?" "How are such opportunities similar or different across locales such as low-performing, high-poverty schools in comparison to low- to mid-poverty or affluent schools and communities?" There is a need for innovative studies using culturally and geographically relevant programs and experimental interventions to address such issues, as mentioned above in regard to students of color, including those with disabilities (Erwin et al., Hodge, 2014).

Summary and conclusions

Over the years, scholars of APE research have used many different research designs (e.g., descriptive survey studies, pretest–posttest control group designs, and pretest–posttest nonequivalent comparison group designs) and established internal validity in their studies using multiple strategies as indicators of scholarly rigor (Haegele et al., 2015). There is a wealth of APE research (e.g., studies involving pre-service and in-service teachers and/or school-age children/youths) studies situated in the quantitative paradigm. Further, various educational scholars as well as organizations (e.g., National Research Council) have asserted that the enterprise of research is shaped by different types of questions and that different methodologies are needed to address these questions (Haegele & Hodge, 2015; O'Sullivan, 2007). In contrast, other entities (e.g., Coalition for Evidence-Based Policy, 2003) and

> research synthesis organizations (e.g., the What Works Clearinghouse [WWC], 2003) have focused primarily on the question of whether a practice is effective and proposed that the 'gold standard' for addressing this question is a single type of research methodology—randomized experimental group designs (also called randomized clinical trials or RCTs; WWC, 2003).
>
> *(Odom et al., 2005, p. 138)*

Broadly speaking, I believe the enterprise of research is shaped by different types of questions and that different methodologies are needed to address these questions.

In this chapter, therefore, I identified the basic philosophical orientation of positivism, which influences the work of quantitative researchers. What's more, I discussed quality indicators for conducting and/or consuming quantitative research designs that represent rigorous application of methodology to questions of interest in APE research. Established scholars and emerging professionals interested in research pertaining to physical education for individuals with disabilities should use quality indicators such as those appearing in this chapter in evaluating their and others' research.

Summary of key points

- Adapted physical education researchers commonly use quantitative research designs.
- The quantitative research paradigm is grounded in the philosophy of positivism, which is positioned by an external–realist ontology that presupposes a hard reality exists.
- The complexity of conducting research in APE necessitates the need to identify quality indicators across research approaches.
- There are many types of quantitative research designs and approaches used, including: (a) documentary and content analyses, and secondary data analyses; (b) descriptive studies (e.g., descriptive case studies, Delphi method, descriptive surveys, developmental and observational studies); (c) correlational and epidemiological studies; and (d) quasi- and true experimental studies (Thomas et al., 2015).

- Documentary and content analysis designs support both quantitative (Bordens & Abbott, 1999) and qualitative applications (Bowen, 2009).
- Secondary data analysis method is the statistical analysis of data that were collected previously by the same or different researchers or various entities.
- Descriptive research is a study of status and descriptive designs are regularly used in APE research.
- There is a large range of descriptive studies, including case studies, descriptive surveys, descriptive–observational designs, Delphi method, and developmental studies.
- Researchers use correlational research to explore relationships that may exist among variables.
- Scholars conducting research in APE and physical activity settings use correlational, including psychometric analyses and epidemiological research, designs to investigate possible relationships among variables without attempting to manipulate or influence the variables.
- Still, today, APE scholars call for the conduct of more true and quasi-experimental studies in the field.
- True experimental research designs require randomly formed experimental, and comparison or control, groups, which allows the researcher to presume that the groups are equivalent at the start of the study.
- Randomized controlled trials are considered the gold standard for establishing strong evidence of an intervention's effectiveness.
- Quasi-experimental designs serve essentially the same function as true experimental designs, but with the critical exception that in these designs the participants are *not* assigned randomly to the experimental or comparison or control groups, and, therefore, the researcher should *not* presume that the groups are equivalent at the start of the study.
- There remain major gaps in the APE research base. In the conception of social justice, for example, more APE-based research is needed.

Reflective questions

1. What major assumptions are foundational to the quantitative research paradigm?
2. What is the main function of correlational research?
3. What is the main function of descriptive research?
4. What are the main differences and similarities between true experimental and quasi-experimental designs?
5. What major gaps do *you* believe exist in the APE research base, particularly in regard to quantitative research methods?

References

Agiovlasitis, S., Pitetti, K. H., Guerra, M., & Fernhall, B. (2011). Prediction of VO_{2peak} from the 20-m shuttle-run test in youth with down syndrome. *Adapted Physical Activity Quarterly, 28*, 146–156.

Almasri, N. A., O'Neil, M., & Palisano, R. J. (2014). Predictors of needs for families of children with cerebral palsy. *Disability and Rehabilitation, 36*(3), 210–219. doi:10.3109/09638288.2013.783123

American Psychological Association. (2010). *Publication manual of the American* psychological association (6th ed.). Washington, DC: Author.

Apache, R. R. G. (2005). Activity-based intervention in motor skill development. *Perceptual and Motor Skills, 100*, 1011–1020.

Bordens, K. S., & Abbott, B. B. (1999). *Research design and methods: A process approach* (pp. 167–172). Mountain View, CA: Mayfield.

Bowen, G. A. (2009). Document analysis as a qualitative research method. *Qualitative Research Journal, 9*(2), 27–40. doi:10.3316/QRJ0902027 Retrieved from: https://lled500.trubox.ca/2016/244

Campbell Collaboration. (2015). *Campbell systematic reviews*. Retrieved from www.campbellcollaboration.org

Campbell, D. T., & Stanley, J. C. (1963). *Experimental and quasi-experimental design for research*. Chicago, IL: Rand McNally.

Carano, S. L. (2014). *Development of a research taxonomy for adapted physical activity* (order no. 3672826). Available from ProQuest Dissertations & Theses A&I.

Carano, S. L., Silliman-French, L., French, R., Nichols, D., & Rose, K. (2015). *Development of a research taxonomy for adapted physical activity*. Paper presented at the annual meeting of the National Consortium for Physical Education for Individuals with Disabilities, McLean, VA.

Casey, A. F., & Emes, C. (2011). The effects of swim training on respiratory aspects of speech production in adolescents with Down syndrome. *Adapted Physical Activity Quarterly, 28*(4), 326–341.

Charaśna-Blachucik, J., & Blachucik, J. (2016). Somatic development and physical fitness of schoolgirls with mild intellectual disabilities - A comparative study. *Journal of Physical Education & Health, 5*(8), 35–48.

Coalition for Evidence-Based Policy. (2003). *Identifying and implementing educational practices supported by rigorous evidence: A user friendly guide*. U.S. Department of Education Institute of Education Sciences, National Center for Education Evaluation and Regional Assistance, Washington, DC. Retrieved from, http://coalition4evidence.org/468-2/publications/

Columna, L., Hoyos-Cuartas, L. A., Foley, J. T., Prado-Perez, J. R., Chavarro-Bermeo, D. M., Mora, A. L., … Rivero, I. (2016). Latin American physical educators' intention to teach individuals with disabilities. *Adapted Physical Activity Quarterly, 33*, 213–232. doi:10.1123/APAQ.2014-0167

Cook, T. D., & Campbell, D. T. (1979). *Quasi-experimentation: Design & analysis issues for field settings*. Chicago, IL: Rand McNally College Publishing.

Crossman, A. (2019, May 10). Pros and cons of secondary data analysis: A review of the advantages and disadvantages in social science research. *ThoughCo*. Retrieved from, www.thoughtco.com/secondary-data-analysis-3026536.

Ericsson, I., & Karlsson, M. K. (2014). Motor skills and school performance in children with daily physical education in school – A 9-year intervention study. *Scandinavian Journal of Medicine & Science in Sports, 24*, 273–278. doi:*10.1111/j.1600-0838.2012.01458.x*

Erwin, H., Brusseau, T. A., Carson, R., Hodge, S. R., & Kang, M. (2018). SHAPE America's 50 million strong[TM]: Critical research questions related to youth physical activity. *Research Quarterly for Exercise and Sport*, doi:10.1080/02701367.2018.1490607

Evidence for Policy and Practice Information Centre. (2006–2009). *EPPI-Centre introduction*. London: Author. Retrieved from http://eppi.ioe.ac.uk/EPPIWeb/home.aspx

Fraenkel, J. R., Wallen, N. E., & Hyun, H. H. (2012). *How to design and evaluate research in education* (8th ed.). San Francisco, CA: McGraw-Hill.

Gersten, R., Fuchs, L. S., Compton, D., Coyne, M., Greenwood, C., & Innocenti, M. (2005). Quality indicators for group experimental and quasi-experimental research in special education. *Exceptional Children, 71*(2), 149–164.

Getchell, N., Liang, L.-Y., Golden, D., & Logan, S. W. (2014). The effect of auditory pacing on period stability and temporal consistency in children with and without dyslexia co-existing motor dysfunction. *Adapted Physical Activity Quarterly, 31*, 19–34. doi:10.1123/apaq.2013-0023

Haegele, J., & Hodge, S. R. (2015). Quantitative methodology: A guide for emerging physical education and adapted physical education researchers. *The Physical Educator, 72*, 59–75.

Haegele, J. A., Hodge, S. R., Gutierres Filho, P. J. B., & Gonçalves de Rezende, A. L. (2018). Brazilian physical education teachers' attitudes before and after participation in a professional development workshop. *European Physical Education Review, 24*(1), 21–38. doi:10.1177/1356336X16662898

Haegele, J. A., Lee, J., & Porretta, D. L. (2015). Research trends in adapted physical activity quarterly from 2004 to 2013. *Adapted Physical Activity Quarterly, 32*(3), 187–205. doi:10.1123/APAQ.2014-0211

Haegele, J. A., & Porretta, D. L. (2015). Physical activity and school-age individuals with visual impairments: A literature review. *Adapted Physical Activity Quarterly, 32*(1), 68–82. doi:10.1123/apaq.2013-0110

Hodge, S. R. (2014). Ideological repositioning: Race, social justice, and promise. *Quest, 66*, 169–180.

Hodge, S. R., Davis, R., Woodard, R., & Sherrill, C. (2002a). Comparison of practicum types in changing preservice teachers' attitudes and perceived competence. *Adapted Physical Activity Quarterly, 19*, 155–171.

Hodge, S. R., Gutierres Filho, P. J. B., Haegele, J. A., & Kozub, F. M. (2015). Underlying dimensions of the physical educators' judgments about inclusion instrument: Brazilian-version. *Journal of Curriculum and Teaching, 4*(2), 96–103. doi:10.5430/jct.v4n2p

Hodge, S. R., & Hersman, B. L. (2007). Unavoidable politics in physical education research and language: Positivism to social constructionism and beyond. *Chronicle of Kinesiology and Physical Education in Higher Education, 18*(3), 14–15.

Hodge, S. R., & Jansma, P. (1999). Effects of contact time and location of practicum experiences on the attitudes of physical education majors. *Adapted Physical Activity Quarterly, 16*, 48–63.

Hodge, S. R., Kozub, F. M., Robinson, L. E., & Hersman, B. L. (2007). Reporting gender, race, ethnicity, and sociometric status: Guidelines for research and professional practice. *Adapted Physical Activity Quarterly, 24*, 21–37.

Hodge, S. R., Murata, N. M., & Kozub, F. M. (2002b). Physical educators' judgments about inclusion: A new instrument for preservice teachers. *Adapted Physical Activity Quarterly, 19*, 435–452.

Hodge, S. R., Sato, T., Mukoyama, T., & Kozub, F. M. (2013). Development of the physical educators' judgments about inclusion instrument for Japanese physical education majors and an analysis of their judgments. *International Journal of Disability, Development and Education, 60*(4), 332–346.

Houston, J., van der Mars, H., & Lorenz, K. A. (2018). Physical activity patterns in students with physical disabilities in general physical education and inclusive recess settings. *Palaestra, 32*(3), 51–57.

Lee, A. M. (2011). Using the ICF-CY to organize characteristics of children's functioning. *Disability and Rehabilitation, 33*(7), 605–616. doi:10.3109/09638288.2010.505993

Li, C., Wang, L., Block, M. E., Sum, R. K. W., & Wu, Y. (2018). Psychometric properties of the physical educators' self-efficacy toward including students with disabilities—Autism among Chinese preservice physical education teachers. *Adapted Physical Activity Quarterly, 35*, 159–174. doi:10.1123/apaq.2017-0086

Lobenius-Palmér, K., Sjöqvist, B., Hurtig-Wennlöf, A., & Lundqvist, L.-O. (2018). Accelerometer-assessed physical activity and sedentary time in youth with disabilities. *Adapted Physical Activity Quarterly, 35*, 1–19. doi:10.1123/apaq.2015-0065

Mazzoni, E. R., Purves, P. L., Southward, J., Rhodes, R. E., & Temple, V. A. (2009). Effect of indoor wall climbing on self-efficacy and self-perceptions of children with special needs. *Adapted Physical Activity Quarterly, 26*(3), 259–273.

O'Sullivan, M. (2007). Research quality in physical education and sport pedagogy. *Sport, Education and Society, 12*(3), 245–260. doi:10.1080/13573320701463962

Odom, S. L., Brantlinger, E., Gersten, R., Horner, R. H., Thompson, B., & Harris, K. R. (2005). Research in special education: Scientific methods and evidence-based practices. *Exceptional Children, 71*(2), 137–148.

Ogu, O. C., Umunnah, J. O., Nwosu, K. C., & Gloria, I. C. (2017). Perception of physical educators toward teaching students with disabilities in an inclusive class setting in Nigeria. *Palaestra, 31*(1), 23–31.

Park, S. S., Koh, Y., & Block, M. E. (2014). Contributing factors for successful inclusive physical education. *Palaestra, 28*(1), 42–49.

Petty, N. J., Thomson, O. P., & Stew, G. (2012). Ready for a paradigm shift? Part 2: Introducing qualitative research methodologies and methods. *Manual Therapy, 17*, 378–384.

Pringle, R. (2000). Physical education, positivism, and optimistic claims from achievement goal theorists. *Quest, 52*(1), 18–31.

Pritchard Orr, A. B., Keiver, K., Bertram, C. P., & Clarren, S. (2018). FAST Club: The impact of a physical activity intervention on executive function in children with fetal alcohol spectrum disorder. *Adapted Physical Activity Quarterly, 35*, 403–423. doi:10.1123/apaq.2017-0137

Reina, R., Hutzler, Y., Iniguez-Santiago, M. C., & Moreno-Murcia, J. A. (2019). Student attitudes toward inclusion in physical education: The impact of ability beliefs, gender, previous experiences. *Adapted Physical Activity Quarterly, 36*, 132–149. doi:10.1123/apaq.2017-0146

Richardson, H. (2018, June 28). *Characteristics of a comparative research design.* Leaf Group Ltd. Retrieved from https://classroom.synonym.com/characteristics-comparative-research-design-8274567.html

Rizzo, T. L. (1984). Attitudes of physical educators toward teaching handicapped pupils. *Adapted Physical Activity Quarterly, 1*, 263–274.

Rizzo, T. L. (1985). Attributes related to teachers' attitudes. *Perceptual and Motor Skills, 60*, 739–742.

Rizzo, T. L. (1988). Validation of the Physical Educators' Attitudes Toward Teaching Handicapped Students survey. *Abstracts of Research Papers of the Research Consortium of the American Alliance of Health, Physical Education, Recreation and Dance,* Kansas City, MO.

Rizzo, T. L., & Vispoel, W. P. (1992). Changing attitudes about teaching students with handicaps. *Adapted Physical Activity Quarterly*, *9*, 54–63.

Robinson, L. E., Palmer, K. K., & Meehan, S. K. (2017). Dose–Response relationship: The effect of motor skill intervention duration on motor performance. *Journal of Motor Learning and Development*, *5*, 280–290. doi:10.1123/jmld.2016-0004

Sherrill, C., & O'Conner, J. (1999). Guidelines for improving adapted physical activity research. *Adapted Physical Activity Quarterly*, *16*, 1–8.

Slininger, D., Sherrill, C., & Jankowski, C. M. (2000). Children's attitudes toward peers with severe disabilities: Revisiting contact theory. *Adapted Physical Activity Quarterly*, *17*, 176–196.

Táboas-Pais, M. I., & Rey-Cao, A. (2012). Disability in physical education textbooks: An analysis of image content. *Adapted Physical Activity Quarterly*, *29*, 310–328.

Thomas, J. R., Nelson, J. K., & Silverman, S. J. (2015). *Research methods in physical activity* (7th ed.). Champaign, IL: Human Kinetics.

Thompson, B., Diamond, K., McWilliam, R., Snyder, P., & Snyder, S. (2005). Evaluating the quality of evidence from correlational research for evidence-based practice. *Exceptional Children*, *71*(2), 181–194.

Trochim, W., & Donnelly, J. (2006). *The research methods knowledge base* (3rd ed.). Mason, OH: Atomic Dog Publishing.

Tzanetakos, N., Papastergiou, M., Vernadakis, N., & Antoniou, P. (2017). Utilizing physically interactive videogames for the balance training of adolescents with deafness within a physical education course. *Journal of Physical Education and Sport*, *17*(2), 614–623.

United States Department of Education, Office of Special Education and Rehabilitative Services, Office of Special Education Programs. (2018). *40th annual report to congress on the implementation of the individuals with disabilities education act, 2018*. Washington, DC: USDE.

Unsal, A., & Ayranci, U. (2008). Prevalence of students with symptoms of depression among high school students in a district of Western Turkey: An epidemiological study. *Journal of School Health*, *78*(5), 287–293.

Vogler, E. W., Koranda, P., & Romance, T. (2000). Including a child with severe cerebral palsy in physical education: A case study. *Adapted Physical Activity Quarterly*, *17*, 161–175.

What Works Clearinghouse. (2003). *Standards*. Washington, DC: Author. Retrieved from www.w-w-c.org/

Yu, J., Sit, C. H. P., Burnett, A., Capio, C. M., Ha, A. S. C., & Huang, W. Y. J. (2016). Effects of fundamental movement skills training on children with developmental coordination disorder. *Adapted Physical Activity Quarterly*, *33*, 134–155. doi:10.1123/APAQ.2015-0008

Zhang, J., deLisle, L., & Chen, S. (2006). Analysis of AAHPERD research abstracts published under special populations from 1968 to 2004. *Adapted Physical Activity Quarterly*, *23*(2), 203–217.

10

Qualitative inquiry in adapted physical education

Donna Goodwin

Introduction

The aim of this chapter is to highlight the contribution of qualitative inquiry to our understanding of the theory, research, and practice in adapted physical education. A brief introduction of qualitative inquiry will be followed by a description of qualitative paradigmatic perspectives and specific methodological approaches or strategies utilized to capture lived experiences and their application to inclusive physical education, where possible.[1] The chapter ends with a discussion of trends and future contributions of qualitative inquiry to adapted physical education.

I write this chapter not as a disabled person, but as a privileged, educated, White, cis female. By my own admission, in presenting a summary of current qualitative scholarship, I am providing a "voice over" to disability experiences and issues of social and educational importance (Titchkosky, 2003, p. 43). The biases I bring are mine alone and I engage with them as a way of addressing the deficient understanding of disability I bring to my research and teaching. It is not my intention to question our knowledge base; however, sitting with the insecurity that reflexive thinking creates may cultivate an expanded understanding of the disability experience and its meaning for those who prepare teachers, teachers, and students (Standal, 2008).

What is qualitative inquiry?

Defining qualitative inquiry is deceptively complex. The researcher as interpreter means that the notion of the objective researcher is rejected by qualitative scholars. "To be human in the world is to interpret" (Bradley, 1993, p. 433). Qualitative researchers seek to make sense of, or interpret, the meaning of social phenomena in their natural settings, filtered through the multiple lenses of race, social class, ethnicity, language, gender, and ability (Denzin & Lincoln, 2011). There are five phases of the qualitative research process. In phase one, the researcher as a multicultural subject negotiates the conflict that confronts the ethics and politics of research, and the relationality of the research act. Researcher positionality is a researcher responsibility whereby we are alerted to the dangers seen, unseen, and unforeseen that can emerge when researchers do not attend to their own racial, ableistic, gendered, and cultural systems when coming to know, knowing, and experiencing the world (Milner, 2007).

In phase two, researchers acknowledge the principles of ontology, epistemology, and methodology of the theoretical paradigms and perspectives they hold. Milner (2007) asserts that researchers need to research themselves by posing questions to bring awareness to ontological, epistemologies, methodological, and axiological positions. Posing inward-turned questions brings researcher voice and reflexivity to the research process and involves being wakeful to their geographic and historical situatedness, personal investments, biases, and influences (Gergen & Gergen, 2000).

Phase three involves identification of the research methodologies (strategies or approaches) that will be used as researchers move from their paradigm to the empirical world. Qualitative researchers undertake diverse projects. They include, among others, the decolonizing work of Indigenous scholars, critical pedagogues, critical race theorists, feminist and queer materialists, disability auto-ethnographers, and performance ethnographers. The diverse and open-ended nature of qualitative work resists a single *correct* way of engaging with understanding the social (Denzin & Lincoln, 2011).

Phase four is the methods of collecting and analyzing empirical materials. Researchers represent lived experiences through such diverse means as life stories, observations, interviews, conversations, artifacts, visual texts, recordings, poetry, performances, and memos to self to describe individuals' lives and bring meaning to the day-to-day. Qualitative inquirers emphasize an understanding of reality viewed by the participant and developed by the researchers through systematic processes of knowledge creation.

Phase five is represented as the art and politics of interpretation and evaluation during which qualitative interpretations are constructed as the researcher writes public text resulting from creating and recreating meaning and making sense of what was learned. Qualitative researchers continue to experiment with how they represent their research findings (literary/performance styling). Detached, (boring) third-person written accounts of interviews that mute the researcher and participants' voices are giving way to social representations of lived experience, such as poetry, collage, performance, and dance (e.g., Eales & Peers, 2016; Peers & Eales, 2017). As research methodologies expand and researchers include themselves in their representation of findings, the materials generated become increasingly interactive processes and co-constructions between the participants and the researcher (Gilgun, 2005).

"The qualitative-researcher-as-*bricoleur* or a maker of quilts uses the aesthetic and material tools of his or her craft, deploying whatever strategies, methods, or empirical materials are at hand" (Denzin & Lincoln, 2011, p. 4). Given the continuing theoretical and methodological sophistication of the contemporary qualitative inquiry, researchers are said to move in multiple directions at the same time, including such journeys as:

(1) the "detour through interpretive theory" and a politics of the local, linked to (2) the analysis of the politics of representation and the textual analyses of literary and cultural forms, including their production, distribution, and consumption; (3) the ethnographic qualitative study and representation of these forms in everyday life; (4) the investigation of new pedagogical and interpretive practices that interactively engage critical cultural analysis in the classroom and the local community; and (5) a utopian politics of possibility that redresses social injustices and imagines a radical democracy that is not yet.

(Denzin & Lincoln, 2011, p. xiii)

Common to all approaches is the researcher as interpreter, researcher positionality, and literary styling (Bradley, 1993; Gergen & Gergen, 2000; Milner, 2007).

Historical perspectives

Qualitative inquiry has evolved across eight historical moments. Denzin and Lincoln (2011) outline in depth the complex historical context upon which qualitative science has evolved and the controversies it has negotiated. Over time, researchers have struggled with how to position themselves and their participants in the generation and interpretation of reflexive texts. I encourage readers to review Denzin and Lincoln's (2011) discussion of the emergence of qualitative inquiry as a rigorous and well-regarded form of knowledge generation.

> In North America, qualitative research operates in a complex historical field that crosscuts a least eight historical moments. These moments overlap and simultaneously operate in the present. We define them as the traditional (1900–1950), the modernist or golden age (1950–1970), blurred genres (1970–1986), the crisis of representation (1986–1990), the postmodern, a period of experimental and new ethnographies (1990–1995), postexperimental inquiry (1995–2000), the methodologically contested present (2000–2010), and the future (2010–), which is now .... The eighth moment asks that the social sciences and the humanities become sites for critical conversations about democracy, race, gender, class, nation-states, globalization, freedom, and community.
>
> *(Denzin & Lincoln, 2011, p. 3)*

The history of qualitative inquiry in adapted physical education (APE) is relatively short, with the first qualitative research paper appearing in the *Adapted Physical Activity Quarterly* in 1994 (Connolly, 1994). Connolly (1994) explored how physical education student teachers came to terms with others and themselves in an adapted teaching–learning journey through journal writing, with recommendations for teacher education. Since that time, numerous scholars have dedicated their lives' scholarship to a qualitative worldview. The work of some of these scholars will be discussed in the coming pages as they sought to capture individuals' points of view, the constraints of everyday life, and provide rich descriptions of social worlds (Denzin & Lincoln, 2005b).

Research paradigms

A paradigm is a worldview that is grounded in a set of propositions that researchers use to determine what is legitimate and important in systematic inquiry (Annells, 1996). It refers to shared beliefs that influence what should be studied, how it should be studied, and how the results of the study should be interpreted (Mackenzie & Knipe, 2006). It provides a conceptual lens to examine research methodologies or approaches, methods, and data analysis. A paradigm "is a set of assumptions, research strategies and criteria for rigor that are shared" (Fossey, Harvey, McDermitt, & Davidson, 2002, p. 718). Cohesion is present when there is a unified relationship across ontological, epistemological, methodological assumptions, methods of date collection, analysis, and interpretation (Chenail, Duffy, St. George, & Wulff, 2011).

Ultimately, researchers must examine and articulate the relevance of paradigmatic assumptions about reality (beliefs, norms, and values) as they apply to their research problems. Doing so lets us see ourselves (our positionality) in relation to knowledge, provides justification for paradigmatic choices, and provides a holistic and coherent view of knowledge generation (Kivunja & Kuyini, 2017).

Qualitative researchers view the world and act on it according to the abstract principles of ontology (what is the nature of reality), epistemology (the relationship between the inquirer and the known, or how we know what we know), methodology (how we go about gaining knowledge of the world), and axiology (understanding values that comprise right and wrong behavior pertaining to research) (Guba & Lincoln, 1994). Lincoln, Lynham, and Guba (2011) presented current research paradigms as positivism, postpositivism, critical theory, constructionism (interpretivism), and participatory. Given space constraints, only critical theory, constructionism (interpretivism), and participatory paradigms are discussed here.

Proponents of a critical/transformative paradigm situate research in terms of political, social, economic, and social justice issues. This approach is defined by a historical realism ontology (situating knowledge socially and historically), a transactional/subjectivist epistemology (examination of social positioning), a dialogic/dialectical methodology (uncovering agency) with the aim of illuminating the structure needed for change to the benefit of those who struggle under power structures, and an axiology that respects the cultural norms of the participant group, especially as it relates to oppression.

Constructionists (interpretivists) adhere to a relativist and co-constructed ontology, a transactional/subjectivist epistemology, a hermeneutical/dialectical methodology, and a balanced axiology to gain understanding by interpreting subjective perceptions to inform praxis.

> The assumption of a relativist ontology means that you believe that the situation studied has multiple realities, and that those realities can be explored and meaning made of them or reconstruction through human interactions between the research and the subjects of the research, and among the research participants.
>
> *(Kivunja & Kuyini, 2017, p. 33)*

A subjectivist epistemology means that meaning-making of data occurs by the researcher through their own thinking and cognitive processes, at times in interactions with the participants. A hermeneutical/dialectical methodology means that information shared by the participants through interviews and reflective exchanges is interpreted by the researcher, as an instrument of the research. A balanced axiology refers to efforts to present a balanced report of the findings through researcher reflection on values held.

Those who research under a participatory paradigm adhere to a participative reality ontology, a critical subjectivity and practical knowing epistemology, and a political collaborative action methodology to bring transformation through democratic participation between participants and the researcher, and a value-laden axiology (Ozanne & Saatcioglu, 2008). A participative reality means that we "inhabit a co-created, context bound, relational, and situated" social world that is historically constructed and drives social practices (Ozanne & Saatcioglu, 2008, p. 425). A practical, knowing epistemology assumes that study participants are collaborators or co-researchers, challenging the traditional division of power in research relationships A collaborative action methodology is guided by a desire to democratize knowledge production whereby all research actors have the capacity to act on boundaries that enable or constrain social action. Participatory axiology is emancipatory, as co-researchers focus on improving human welfare through reflexion and action at the local level and beyond.

Qualitative methodology in APE

Before discussing qualitative methodology, it is important to make a distinction between methodology (or traditions, see Creswell, 2007) and method, which, unfortunately, tend to be used interchangeably. Methodology refers to the philosophical underpinnings and assumptions that underlie research approaches or strategies. It is the lens through which research methods are justified. Research method refers to technical procedures used to go about conducting the research and collecting data, determined by the methodology (McGregor & Murnane, 2010). "All research traditions are frameworks of assumptions, issues, practices, problems, and evaluation criteria" (Bradley, 1993, p. 423). When writing a research study, both methodology and method should be articulated so readers may understand the "why" and the "way" of research processes.

Numerous methodological approaches have been taken up by APE researchers, including grounded theory, ethnography, interpretive phenomenology, action research, narrative inquiry, and arts-based research. Each will be discussed in turn and illustrated with APE research. When research relevant to teachers and children in school contexts is not available, selected studies in adapted physical activity were presented. I acknowledge that some authors will be omitted from the discussion, but only because of space limitations. My sincere apologies.

Grounded theory

Grounded theory refers to both the method and product of the research and analyses relationships between social structures and human agency (Charmaz, 2011). It is positioned under the variants of a relativist ontology as "a reality that cannot actually be known, but is always interpreted" (Strauss & Corbin, 1990, p. 22). It is also considered to be subjective and interpretivist in epistemology, as researchers focus on the meanings constructed from interpretation of the data (Weed, 2017). Researchers move beyond description, anchored in the empirical world, such that dialectical theory is grounded and located in subjective experiences within larger structures, thereby increasing our understanding of how they work and impact the lives of people—setting agendas for future action becomes a meaningful result (Charmaz, 2005). Structural interrogation of power, agency, resources, constraints, disenfranchisement, oppression, and resources has the potential for re-imagining lives and bringing about potential for change.

According to Charmaz (2011), grounded theory contains tools for logically analyzing and situating processes. It has six areas of methodological strength: (1) defining relevant social processes; (2) demonstrating their contexts; (3) specifying the conditions in which the processes occur; (4) conceptualizing their phases; (5) explicating what contributes to their stability and/or change; and (6) outlining their consequences. "Adopting this logic can assist social justice researchers attend to the construction of inequities and how people act toward them .... to reveal concrete experiences of ... social structure, culture, and social practices or policies" (Charmaz, 2011, pp. 361–362).

In their study, Wheeler, Malone, VanVlack, Nelson, and Steadward (1996) used a grounded theory methodology to generate a theory of athlete retirement. Using semi-structured interviews, 18 female and male and athletes whom Mitchell and Snyder (2015) would refer to as able–disabled, who voluntarily or involuntarily retired from sport due to injury or a change in classification system, shared their experiences of overtraining and ignoring medical advice in order to maintain their identities as athletes. The losses endured due to retirement took an emotional toll, as concerns about chronic injury and aging, filling the loss with meaningful activity, and the work of transitioning back to former roles with family and friends were undertaken. The authors developed a model of the social processes involved in sport and concluded by recommending that an athlete-centered approach to disability sport be taken to reduce the emotional trauma involved in transitioning out of sport.

To date, grounded theory has had a somewhat limited uptake in APE and activity, disability sport, and recreation contexts. Examples of areas where it has been utilized are identity development or redefinition, and the imposing influence of social structures and cultural practices (e.g., Lundberg, Taniguchi, McCormick, & Tibbs, 2011); constraints to elite sport development (e.g., Ashton-Schaeffer, Gibson, Holt, & Willming, 2001; Crawford & Stodolska, 2008; Guan, 2015) and the role of physical activity and leisure in quality of life (e.g., Giacobbi, Stancil, Hardin, & Bryant, 2008; Moola, Fusco, & Kirsh, 2011).

Ethnography

Ethnography is the study of socio-cultural contexts, process, and meanings in human cultural systems that had its beginnings in anthropology (Whitehead, 2004). Contemporary (post-colonial) ethnography is used to pose questions of human realities at the boundaries of diversity, inclusion, and exclusion pertaining to systems of class, race, gender, and ability. Results of the research are reported as "tentative certainty" with no claims of absolute knowledge through an ontology of "circular order" or "paradoxical tentativeness" during which researchers develop theories cumulatively and rhythmically under a constructivist or interdependent epistemology and hermeneutic or creation centered methodology (Gonzalez, 2000, pp. 628, 635).

Fieldwork plays an important role in producing descriptively vivid accounts of lived experience, relationships, and situations of inequity. Participatory observation and focus groups are further powerful tools for uncovering memories, practices, issues, experiences, and ideologies. Participant observation involves observation of daily life while the researcher takes part in day-to-day events within a community (Dewalt & Dewalt, 2011). Focus groups can serve as a research tool for opening topics for further interrogation, resisting the tendency to close down cultural issues too quickly. Further, the dynamics and synergies generated in groups may reveal unarticulated normative assumptions that are unexamined within individual contexts (Kamberilis & Dimtiriadis, 2011).

Within the realm of disability and sport, Howe (2004), using an ethnographic approach, investigated "the relationship between commercialism, medicine and the body, in order to establish the importance of pain, injury and risk in the contemporary world" while centering social, economic, and political sporting practice shifts of sport medicine in elite sport (p. 1). He assumed participatory observation roles while undertaking his research. In a later study, Howe (2008) interrogated Paralympic sport by combining an anthropological and (auto) ethnographic approach to critically examine the political, social, and economic processes impacting sport, the body, and disability culture. Case studies of injury and risk from Paralympic athletes and how they related to pain and injury and the social implications of being an injured athlete were also presented.

Eales (2016) crafted a mad text through autoethnographic performative writing that approximated the embodied experiences and psychiatrized culture of mental illness. The author invites the reader to notice and disrupt the normative embodied reading by printing off, shuffling, and reading the now non-linear piece to facilitate sensory, theoretical, affective, epistemic, and ethical engagements with madness. For further examples of others who have engaged ethnography and its methods to examine the life worlds of those whose participation in active lifestyles has been marginalized by social, cultural, and political values, beliefs, and acts, see Frey, Buchanan, and Rosser Sandt (2005), and Levins, Redenbach, and Dyck (2004).

Interpretive phenomenology[2]

Interpretive phenomenological researchers are interested in understanding the meaning of the everyday flow of people's lived experiences of being in the world (Larkin, Watts, & Clifton, 2006; Smith, Flowers, & Larkin, 2009; Standal & Engelsrud, 2013). It is conducted under an interpretive paradigm with the assumptions of a relativist ontology, subjective epistemology, and hermeneutic and dialectical methodology. Scully (2009, p. 59) asserted that a disability phenomenological ontology renders an

> understanding [of] the experience of disability from the inside, is an essential part of making ethical and ontological judgements about impairment ... [and], in some circumstances, disabled people have rather different takes on ethical questions relevant to disability than do nondisabled people.

Phenomenological perspectives, then, can awaken and transform taken-for-granted understandings and practices aimed at intervening in the lives of others. It can cultivate new and expanded understanding of "unexamined conceptions of bodies and social space" (Titchkosky, 2011, p. xiii). Phenomenology is not used to problem solve, as phenomenological questions ask for the meaning of the significance of a specific phenomenon. It provides a structure for pursuing meaning in a dynamic interplay of six research activities: (a) identifying a phenomenon that commits us to the world; (b) investigating experience as we live it and not how we conceptualize it (e.g., interviews, observations, artifacts); (c) reflecting on essential themes which characterize the phenomenon; (d) applying the art of writing and rewriting to bring the phenomenon to light; (e) maintaining a pedagogical interest in the phenomenon; and (f) balancing the research context by considering the parts and the whole of the experience and context (van Manen, 1997).

Kincheloe and McLaren (2000) point out that critical researchers who engage with hermeneutic interpretation often hold to Dewey's (1916) observation that people adopt the values of their social group as they shape their views of the world, while being conscious of their interpretative frames for bringing meaning to lived experience. "The hermeneutic act of interpretation involves, in its most elemental articulation, making sense of what have been observed in a way that communicates understanding" (Kincheloe & McLaren, 2000, p. 285).

Disability is a relational phenomenon that exists between natural properties and the surrounding physical and social world that demands understanding (Vehmas & Mäkelä, 2009). The body and its actions constitute a form of knowledge in and of itself due to sensation, perceptions, and motion. Embodiment "means all the ways we have to sense, feel, and move in the world as these are mediated by the interests of social environment" (Titchkosky, 2011, p. 3). Of importance to some in APE is the need to understand the embodied meaning of professional practices, such as helping, peer instructing, adapting, correcting, and rehabilitating by those for whom these practices are enacted. Without reflexion, "best practices" become mechanical and sacred with little regard for the harm they may be imposing (Goodwin & Rossow-Kimball, 2012). Standal (2008) investigated the meanings and experiences of disability peer instruction in the learning of wheelchair skills using a hermeneutic phenomenological approach. Using semi-structured interviews, observations, and field notes to gather information, the author concluded that the peer consultants can act as models for imitation, critical discussion partners for broader shared experiences, and a measuring stick against which to judge performance. His work confronted the expert assumption of rehabilitation contexts from a social justice point of view. Hierarchical power relations between those with and without disability were diminished when peers assumed the role of instructors and technical experts to the acquisition of wheelchair skills.

Goodwin and Ebert (2018) were interested in the hidden labor parents assume, educating and employing people to support their children in community physical activity programs (e.g., fitness buddies). They undertook an interpretative phenomenology analysis study to understand how parental hidden labor continues the "systemic, pervasive and public nature of ableism" (Hodge & Runswick-Cole, 2013, p. 316). Focus groups were used to gather stories from nine participants. The authors found that the structure of community physical activity led to an assumption that parents, rather than the professionals and service providers, would provide the support needed to create and sustain inclusivity. Further examples of studies that utilized phenomenological methodology include An and Hodge (2013), Coates (2011), Fitzpatrick and Watkinson (2003), Goodwin (2001), Goodwin, Lieberman, Johnston, and Leo (2011), Goodwin and Watkinson (2000), Haegele, Zhu, and Davis (2017), Hodge, Tannehill, and Kluge (2003), Leo and Goodwin (2014), and Standal and Jespersen (2008).

Action research

Researchers undertaking action research do so with the aim of implementing change by using practice-based knowledge generated in a socially responsible way to solve the immediate and day-to-day problems of practitioners (Elliott, 1991). Action research is ontologically relativist (anti-realism), reflects a constructionist epistemology that supports socially just endeavors as it rejects researcher oversight, and an ideographic methodology (Iivari & Venable, 2009). Through a collaborative relationship of "cogenerative inquiry," members of otherwise marginalized communities come together in a complex situation of change to jointly determine research questions are generated *with*, rather than *for*, community members (Levin & Greenwood, 2011, p. 27). Co-researchers progress through the action research spiral of planning, acting, observing, reflecting on changes, and returning to planning (Greenwood & Levin, 2007).

Taking a reflective stance on practice and social structures fits well with resistance to existing political functions toward social justice and improved quality of life in social settings (Gergen & Gergen, 2000). "Social justice research, particularly participatory action research … proceeds from researchers' and participants' joint efforts and commitments to change practices" (Charmaz, 2005, p. 512). Action researchers utilize practices that "involve collaborative dialogue, participatory decision-making, inclusive democratic deliberating and the maximal participation and representation of all relevant parties" (Denzin & Lincoln, 2011, p. 21). Participatory action researchers "engage[s] research design, methods, analyses, and products through a lens of democratic participation" (Torre, Fine, Stoudt, & Fox, 2012, p. 171). There are multiple action research approaches, including classroom action research, participatory action research, and critical participator action research with the respective aims of improving control over outcomes, enlightening practitioners, and emancipating people and groups from irrationality, unsustainability, and injustice (Kemmis, McTaggart, & Nixon, 2014). Multiple participant and non-participant methods are used in action research, including observation, action research reports, diaries, field notes, personal action logs, analytic memos, photography, and audiotapes (McKernan, 1996).

An example of classroom action research, aimed at empowering students to be leaders, is a unique study by Fitzgerald, Jobling, and Kirk (2003). The researchers embraced a student-centered research approach to study the physical education and sporting experiences of young disabled people at two schools. The student co-researchers at each school planned their research activities, carried out the research, generated the results, and supported the dissemination of the findings specific to their contexts. The research activities included student-led interviews, surveys, posters, and photographs. The research outputs included sheets, displays of the research process, and reports. The researchers rejected the hierarchical nature of other interpretive methodologies, and, in doing so, brought a social justice lens to their study. As such, through the research process, the participants were valued for the embodied knowledge, their leadership skills, the ability to act autonomously, actions to create space to reflect on their experiences and those of their classmates, and their broadening of teachers' understanding of student potential. Ultimately, there was a new awareness of how adult "advocacy" may be thwarting autonomy and student creativity.

An action research study was also undertaken by Standal and Rugseth (2014), aimed at learning what adapted physical activity university students learn from practicum experiences. They utilized observations, reflective journals, and focus groups. The authors worked closely with the students to examine and maximize their practicum experiences to find ways to facilitate student learning. They argued that action research was a dynamic and ongoing process where theory and practice are connected. Action research has the potential to facilitate change in APE and activity contexts by assessing the adequacy of pedagogical theories we reflect *with* as well as the values we reflect *from*.

Narrative inquiry

Narrative inquiry researchers explore how physical, social, and cultural environments impact and shape experiences (Haydon, Browne, & van der Reit, 2018). They assume an ontology of experience and interpretivist relational epistemology to bring both personal and social meaning to lived experience. "Narrative researchers begin with an ontology of experience grounded in Dewey's theory of experience, conceptualizing reality as relational, temporal, and continuous" (Clandinin & Murphy, 2009, p. 599). According to Clandinin and Connelly (2000), we live our lives through stories in a three-dimensional space that is influenced by the three key constructs of temporality, sociality, and place. Narrative researchers seek possibilities through relational living, telling, retelling, and reliving. Field texts, or memory signposts, are created in the field and validated by the participants. Information may also be gathered through observations, interviews, artifacts, and notations. Research texts are created by balancing the tensions of the field texts within the three-dimensional space "that narratively capture[s] the field experiences" (p. 154).

> … temporality [is] along one dimension, the personal and the social along a second dimension, and place along a third … any particular inquiry is defined by this three-dimensional space: studies have temporal dimensions and address temporal matters; they focus on the personal and the social in a balance appropriate to the inquiry; and they occur in specific places or sequences of places.
>
> *(Clandinin & Connelly, 2000, p. 50)*

A narrative inquirer explores a time (past, present, and future) influenced by societal conditions (the external environment); interactions with self and others (one's feelings, hopes, and moral disposition) within a particular place (Clandinin & Connelly, 2000). Because of its focus on inquiry into what matters from an individual's perspective and experiences, "narrative as a means of inquiry is potentially valuable and useful for disability researchers" (Smith & Sparkes, 2008, p. 19).

People shape their daily lives by stories of who they and others are and as they interpret their past in terms of these stories. Story, in the current idiom, is a portal
through which a person enters the world and by which their experience of the
world is interpreted and made personally meaningful. Narrative inquiry, the study of
experience as story, then, is first and foremost a way of thinking about experience.
Narrative inquiry as a methodology entails a view of the phenomenon. To use narrative inquiry methodology is to adopt a particular view of experience as phenomenon
under study.

(Connelly & Clandinin, 2006, p. 375)

Smith and Sparkes (2009) further suggested that narratives possess

tellability, consequences, sequences of speech act, structures, thematic/categorical content, rhetorical tropus, and/or temporality, which comprise particular stories. … Indeed,
whatever form a narrative might take its strength partly lies in the memorable, often
provocative way in which the reader is drawn into the experience, narrative knowing is
shared, and space is opened for multiple ways of knowing.

(Smith & Sparkes, 2009, pp. 2–3)

They outlined seven principles that justify narrative inquiry, which are: (a) meaning and
construing meaning is basic to being human; (b) meaning is creative through narrative; (c)
narratives and meanings are achieved within relationships; (d) narratives are both personal
and social; (e) selves and identities are constituted through narratives; (f) narrative is
a primary way of organizing our experiences of temporality; and (g) the body is a storyteller
and, as such, narratives are embodied (Smith & Sparkes, 2009).

Rossow-Kimball and Goodwin (2018) used a narrative inquiry methodology to know the
inward and personal experiences of leisure and the social and physical places that supported
autonomous retirement of three men labelled as intellectually disabled. To share their retirement experiences, the retirees and first author connected at least twice per week for almost
one year, either face to face, and/or via telephone when they were unable to meet in person.
In addition, and with the retirees' ongoing verbal permission, the first author participated in
daily happenings and special events in their lives. Through writing and audio-recordings of
thoughts, impressions, feelings, and reflections of personal experience, detailed field texts of
the conversations and shared occurrences became research text. Participant narratives disrupted
the belief that professionally crafted programs were necessary for a satisfying, active, and
engaging retirement. The men rejected the professional landscape of expert-driven leisure programs by composing self-directed leisure activities interconnected with their interests, preferred social networks, and skills. An alternate paradigmatic lens of personal coherence
emerged, reflecting self-driven expressions of leisure based upon autonomy and choice.

Smith and colleagues also used narrative inquiry and narrative analysis extensively to
study such topics as disabled men's narrative of health, hope, embodied masculinities, and
athlete activism (Smith, 2013; Smith, Bundon, & Best, 2016; Smith & Sparkes, 2004,
2005; Sparkes & Smith, 2002). Space does not permit an overview of this body of
research, but readers are encouraged to refer to the articles to see how narrative inquiry
and analysis revealed, and provided insight into, the storied self and socio-cultural influence on the embodiment of people's lives in constraining and enabling ways (Smith &
Sparkes, 2008).

Arts-based research

Arts-based research captures qualities of life and how we live through diverse arts practices, methods, and the aesthetics of literary, performance, and visual arts (dance, video, photography, film, theater, music, and drama). Arts-based researchers explore the boundaries of place and space through the human body as a tool for exploring meaning through affective experience, senses, and emotions (Finley, 2011). "… it is an approach to research that exploits the capacities of expressive form to capture qualities of life that impact what we know and how we live" (Barone & Eisner, 2012, p. 5). It has been suggested that arts-based research cannot be integrated into existing paradigms, but requires a new paradigm to be put in place (Finley, 2011; Rolling, 2010). Arts-based research methodologies are "enacted along a spectrum between both scientific *and* artistic ways of comprehending the human experience and doing cultural work" (Rolling, 2010, p. 103). It extends inquiry beyond the constraints of discursive communication to express meanings otherwise inexpressible (Barone & Eisner, 2012).

Arts-based research can be used to advance social justice and political agendas against social inequality. Performance of texts "can expose oppression, and sites of resistance" when political activism is the goal (Denzin & Lincoln, 2005a, p. 642). Performance ethnography is a recent turn in human science that can be disseminated to audiences in an arts-based forum. It brings the interrelated problems of constructing, performing, and critically analyzing performance texts (Denzin, 2003). It is a space that blends research, pedagogy, performance, and activism, while also promoting thinking about emergent methodologies (Kamberilis & Dimtiriadis, 2011). Performance ethnographers use field notes, (auto)ethnographic observations, and narratives to highlight the politics of performative cultural studies. They build collaborative, trusting, and friendly relations with those studied as they reflexively interpret and perform the local, the historical, the political, and the cultural. The resulting performance can serve as an act of intervention, an embodied experience, an act of resistance, public pedagogy through aesthetics, and a form of political criticism (Denzin, 2003).

Eales and Goodwin (2015) highlighted the complexity of the major elements of performance ethnography as process and product. Twelve dancers with diverse embodiments created a research-based integrated dance that regarded disability not as a bodily problem, but a matter of social injustice. To navigate social injustices, care-sharing evolved that involved "life-sustaining, communal acts of radical interdependence; practices of consensus-building and the sharing of discomfort; and a commitment to negotiating complex power relations" (p. 277).

The dancers, whose identities were framed in politicized terms such as physical disability, mental illness, and intellectual impairment, engaged in focus groups, conversational sharing of life experiences, improvisation, and choreography. Through these activities, the performance content for a public, integrated dance performance was gathered and danced for public audiences (the product). Through dancing, the everyday interrelational practices of support for each other emerged as an important way to sustain their dance community, strengthen connections, and negotiate expressions of social injustice (the process). The dancers performed daily what they termed care-sharing—the life-sustaining communal acts of radical interdependence, practices of consensus-building, the sharing of discomfort, and a commitment to negotiating complex power relations. A transformational understanding of the social justice of care was evident, as the injustice of traditional professional, unidirectional, and hierarchical care relationships were rejected and replaced with care-sharing.

> Care-sharing is different than caregiving … [it] is meaningfully shared across and within multiple axes of oppressions in this [dance] community, often to life-enhancing ends. Dancers find joy and meaning in the practice of sometimes reciprocal, non-hierarchical, and communal care-sharing. This practice strengthens their connections to each other, sustains their dance community, and is central to their transformative social justice experiences in this community.
>
> *(Eales & Goodwin, 2015, p. 285)*

Through the embodied experiences of integrated dancers, disability was enacted and understood not as a bodily problem, but, rather, a matter of social (in)justice.

Peers and Eales (2016) used arts-based research and autoethnographic video to engage viewers in disability politics and theory, and anthropological writing: dancer-participants co-creating an alternative reality in which the dancers questioned dominant disability stories. In a further example of dance related arts-based research by these authors, Peers and Eales (2017) presented an arts-based work that embodied a body wheelchair-bound and a wheelchair body-bound. They explored practices, discourses, and materialities of the wheelchair by their "living, playing, moving, and thinking with, and in and through various wheelchairs and other technologies of (im)mobility" (p. 102). The essay weaved performativity, narrative writing, dance, theory, and images into an aesthetic and engaging work that critically explored material culture, tool use, ablebodied/disability divide, contexts, and relationships. In summary, "artistic epistemologies can enrich and expand our inquiry, understanding, and engagement in adapted physical activity" (Peers & Eales, 2016 p. 55).

Future trends: social justice and critical qualitative inquiry

The future of qualitative inquiry is exciting and one that may bring a critical and social justice lens to educational research and professional practice. Kincheloe and McLaren (2000, p. 291) wrote:

> Traditional researchers see their task as the description, interpretation, or reanimation of a slice of reality, whereas critical researchers often regard their work as a first step toward forms of political action that can redress the injustices found in the field site or constructed in the very act of research itself.

Fine (1994) went on to state, "Much of qualitative research has reproduced, if contradiction filled, a colonizing discourse of the 'Other'" (p. 70). Social justice provides a reflexive lens to question the way researchers have spoken "about" and "for" the others. Conversely, sensitivities to social justice issues through qualitative research provide opportunities for change by illuminating social structures, contexts, and ideologies that promote and sustain inequality. The tension between these two views of qualitative research brings wakefulness to researchers' roles in creating disability, while promoting social justice through qualitative research as a way of thinking differently about disability.

When social structures hinder ability, opportunities, choice, or freedom, social (in)justice research issues arise. Denzin (2009) suggested that social justice is ever present in critical interpretive methodologies, or inquiry that makes sense of life. He further stated that critical qualitative inquiry moves in four directions at the same time, including (a) discourses of personal and biological frames that produce and reproduce injustice; (b) ideological discourses pertaining to human rights and non-violence; (c) critical conversations across political and cultural spectra; and (d) methodologies that are free of racial, class, and gender stereotyping toward enhanced moral discernment and social transformation. Interestingly, he omits disability from his list of stereotyping influences, even considering his call for "critical, humane discourse that creates sacred and spiritual spaces for persons and their oral communities— spaces where people can express and give meaning to the tragedies in their lives" (p. 29). Through critical qualitative inquiry, researchers and participants alike perceive social injustices as personal and social reality as something to be critically reflected upon.

Critical perspectives of practice in adapted physical education, adapted physical activity, and sport is emerging (e.g., Connolly & Harvey, 2018; Eales, 2016; Goodwin & Rossow-Kimball, 2012; Peers, 2009, 2012a, b). Not all qualitative researchers align themselves with explicit social justice aims; however, it is embedded to some degree as researchers are increasingly asked to justify the social relevance of their work and translate their findings for non-researchers (Grimshaw, Eccles, Lavis, Hill, & Squires, 2012; Smith, Tomasone, Latimer-Cheung, & Martin Ginis, 2015). Further researcher focus is needed to unveil enlightened ableistic beliefs and disablistic practices of symbolic violence expressed through and on the body in adapted physical education and activity, disability sport comportment, and recreation (Howe, 2008). Slee (2008) suggested that the rhetoric of inclusion has been applied to such levels of saturation that it clouds the path needed to seek real change.

Although the social model of disability is purported to underpin our understanding of disability in adapted physical activity, "enlightened ableism" may be masking the potential impact of the social model as a mechanism for shedding light on the experiences of disabled people and how cultural value systems work to impede or advance one's ability to function in the world (Lyons, 2013, p. 237). Enlightened ableism describes the teacher-speak surrounding inclusive practices in school contexts. Lyons argues that although teachers were supportive of inclusion and could articulate its benefits, sadly, it was not evident in practice. Enlightened ableism "presents a rational, modern, well-informed view of the world, yet allows the continuation of practices that marginalize people" (Lyons, 2013, p. 240). Mitchell and Snyder (2015), in a similar vein, coined the term inclusionism. "Inclusionism requires that disability be tolerated as long as it does not demand an excess degree of change from relatively inflexible institutions, environments, and norms of belonging" (p. 14).

Given notions of compulsory able-bodiedness, symbolic violence, enlightened ableism, and inclusionism, Goodley and Runswick-Cole's (2011) challenge to provide political and social justice readings of bodies is very timely. They revoke disability as cultural lack, and embrace bodies as possibility, not to be relegated as private troubles (Oliver, 1990). This challenge is one in which qualitative researchers can engage and advance knowing about social structures, political agendas, and organizational rigidity. In doing so, however, Withers (2012) encourages the use of relational and collaborative research methodologies that center disabled people, as "social justice can never be achieved without working with disabled people and on disability issues" (p. 11).

Angrosino and Rosenberg (2011) identified three ways in which researchers can contribute to social justice pursuits by interrogating disability representation. The first is for the researcher to be directly connected with the people who are socially marginalized to reject knowing people as simply target populations of research. Second, ask questions and seek answers by embedding discussions in the community under study and not just of academic or theoretical interest. Third, social justice research involves becoming an advocate for the issues defined and uncovered by working with the community to ultimately achieve shared goals. A fourth way is to place marginalization in the middle of inquiry (as opposed to the person), so that one group does not have a monopoly on insight, knowing, and power over another (Henwood, 2008).

Donna Goodwin

Where does it leave us? Implications for qualitative research and practice

With reflexion on professional practice, research, and roles in preparing professionals, cultural discourses of labeling, prescription, and interventions for change may give rise to disability being a valued way of being-in-the-world (Scully, 2009). Can non-disabled qualitative researchers, who are unaware of, or complicit in, the constitution of disability given their privilege, bring change to the wrongs of social injustice (Fine, 1994)? There is always distance of privilege between qualitative researchers and participants. This distance may be lessened when researchers reflexively situate themselves within the social struggles of interest and how they are in (or not in) relationship to the people and contexts being studied. Researcher power and positionality is never absent from the text (Smith et al., 2009).

Including the work of qualitative researchers and disability scholars in the preparation of APE professionals will broaden understanding of the disability experience. "As a pedagogical approach, disability studies provide ways of legitimizing the lives of those occupying peripheral embodiments as offering insightful alternative modes of nonnormative being-in-the-world (Mitchell & Snyder, 2015, p. 74). Bringing a relational and ethical lens to our work through qualitative inquiry and reflexivity may prevent the pathologizing of people (Bergum & Dossetor, 2005; DePauw, 2009; Goodley & Runswick-Cole, 2011).

I want to be clear that the positive gains made in the field of APE have been due to a genuine and passionate concern for people. We have done this by modifying, adapting, and accommodating to "meet unique needs and achieve desired outcomes" (Sherrill, 2004, p. 7). The shortcomings that are becoming apparent with the "top-down instructional (or intervention) model based on adaptation theory" and related research questions asked (Sherrill, 2004, p. 84) is that there is little impetus to change disability social and cultural influences. To quote Sherrill (2004), "… education and service delivery are *adapted*, but behavior is *adaptive*" (p. 9). Adaptive professional research and practice, then, is what we do to *ourselves* that fosters flourishing in others (Seligman, 2011). The social justice work (project) of researchers in APE is to uncover ableism, disablism, the normate as the desired state of being. Although the social model of disability may underpin many of our assumptions about the creation, meaning, and perpetuation of disability, non-reflexivity can lead to theorizing about people's lives rather than bringing passion and humility to our work. Understanding disability through qualitative and social justice lenses will assist in "knowing disability differently" (Titchkosky, 2011, p. 16).

Summary of key points

- Qualitative inquiry is an umbrella term that encompasses many methodologies for capturing the social worlds of people.
- Qualitative research has evolved, and continues to evolve, as controversies are negotiated across eight historical moments.
- Qualitative researchers acknowledge the paradigmatic principles of ontology (nature of reality), epistemology (relationship between the inquirer and the known), methodology (how we gain knowledge), and axiology (researcher values).
- A research paradigm, or worldview, provides a conceptual lens for determining and examining the coherence of research methodologies, methods, data analysis, and criteria for rigor.

- APE researchers have employed a wide range of research methodologies, including grounded theory, ethnography, interpretive phenomenology, narrative inquiry, and arts-based research.
- A trend toward critical qualitative inquiry is emerging in the field of adapted physical activity.
- There are four ways qualitative researchers can contribute to social justice pursuits, which are: (a) connecting to communities; (b) embedding discussions in the disability community; (c) developing shared goals,;and (d) researching marginalizing.

Reflexive questions for discussion

1. Why is it important to identify the ontological, epistemological, and methodological assumptions of the research paradigms in which researchers work?
2. What does coherence in qualitative research mean and how is it achieved?
3. What ethical questions are embedded in the relationality required in qualitative inquiry?
4. How might issues of social justice move adapted physical education and activity research and practice forward?
5. Why is researcher positionality central to qualitative inquiry?
6. Ask yourself, "In what ways does my racial, ableistic, cultural, and gendered background influence how I experience the world, what I emphasize in my research, and how I evaluate and interpret others and their experiences?" How do I know? (modified from Milner, 2007, p. 395).

Notes

1 For in-depth overviews of the discipline, processes, and practices of qualitative inquiry, I refer you to such authors as Creswell (2007), Denzin and Lincoln (2005b; 2011), Smith and Sparkes (2016), and Sparkes and Smith (2013b)
2 For discussions of descriptive phenomenology, see Lopez and Willis (2004), Todres (2005), and Wojnar and Swanson (2007).

References

An, J., & Hodge, S. R. (2013). Exploring the meaning of parental involvement in physical education for students with developmental disabilities. *Adapted Physical Activity Quarterly, 30*, 147–163. doi:10.1123/apaq.30.2.147

Angrosino, M., & Rosenberg, J. (2011). Observations on observation. In N. K. Denzin & Y. Lincoln (Eds.), *The Sage handbook of qualitative research* (4th ed., pp. 467–478). Thousand Oaks, CA: Sage.

Annells, M. (1996). Grounded theory method: Philosophical perspectives, paradigm of inquiry, and postmodernism. *Qualitative Health Research, 6*, 379–393. doi:10.1177/104973239600600306

Ashton-Shaeffer, C., Gibson, H., Holt, M., & Willming, C. (2001). Women's resistance and empowerment through wheelchair sport. *World Leisure, 4*, 11–21. doi: 10.1080/04419057.2001.9674245

Barone, T., & Eisner, E. W. (2012). *Arts based research*. Thousand Oaks, CA: Sage.

Bergum, V., & Dossetor, J. (2005). *Relational ethics: The full meaning of respect*. Hagerstown, MD: University Publishing Group.

Bradley, J. (1993). Methodological issues and practices in qualitative research. *The Library Quarterly: Information, Community, Policy, 63*, 431–449. doi:10.1086/602620

Charmaz, K. (2005). Grounded theory in the 21st century: Applications for advancing social justice studies. In N. K. Denzin & Y. S. Lincoln (Eds.), *The Sage handbook of qualitative research* (3rd ed., pp. 507–535). Thousand Oaks, CA: Sage.

Charmaz, K. (2011). Grounded theory methods in social justice research. In N. K. Denzin & Y. S. Lincoln (Eds.), *The Sage handbook of qualitative research* (4th ed., pp. 359–380). Thousand Oaks, CA: Sage.

Chenail, F. J., Duffy, M., St. George, S., & Wulff, D. (2011). Facilitating coherence across qualitative research. *The Qualitative Report, 16*, 263–275. Retrieved from https://nsuworks.nova.edu/tqr/vol16/iss1/17

Clandinin, D. J., & Connelly, F. M. (2000). *Narrative inquiry.* San Francisco, CA: Jossey-Bass.

Clandinin, D. J., & Murphy, M. S. (2009). Relational ontological commitment in narrative research. *Educational Researchers, 38*, 598–602. doi:10.3102/0013189X09353940

Coates, J. (2011). Physically fit or physically literate? How children with special educational needs understand physical education. *European Physical Education Review, 17*, 167–181. doi:10.1177/1356336X11413183

Connolly, M. (1994). Practicum experiences and journal writing in adapted physical education: Implications for teacher education. *Adapted Physical Activity Quarterly, 11*, 306–328. doi.org/10.1123/apaq.11.3.306

Connolly, M., & Harvey, W. (2018). Critical pedagogy and APA: A resonant (and timely) interdisciplinary blend. *Adapted Physical Activity Quarterly, 35*, 293–307. doi:10.1123/apaq.2017-0106

Connelly, F. M., & Clandinin, D. J. (2006). Narrative inquiry. In J. Green, G. Camilli, & P. Elmore (Eds.), *Handbook of complementary methods in education research* (pp. 375–385). Mahwah, NJ: Lawrence Erlbaum.

Creswell, J. W. (2007). *Qualitative inquiry and research design: Choosing among the five traditions.* Thousand Oaks, CA: Sage.

Crawford, J. L., & Stodolska, M. (2008). Constraints experienced by elite athletes with disabilities in Kenya, with implications for the development of a new hierarchical model of constraints at the societal level. *Journal of Leisure Research, 40*, 128–155. doi:10.1080/00222216.2008.11950136

Denzin, N. K. (2003). *Performance ethnography; Critical pedagogy and the politics of culture.* Thousand Oaks, CA: Sage.

Denzin, N. K. (2009). *Qualitative inquiry under fire: Toward a new paradigm dialogue.* Walnut Creek, CA: Left Coast Press.

Denzin, N. K., & Lincoln, Y. S. (2005a). *The SAGE handbook of qualitative research* (3rd ed.). Thousand Oaks, CA: Sage.

Denzin, N. K., & Lincoln, Y. S. (2005b). Introduction: The discipline and practice of qualitative inquiry. In N. K. Denzin & Y. S. Lincoln (Eds.), *The SAGE handbook of qualitative research* (3rd ed., pp. 1–32). Thousand Oaks, CA: Sage.

Denzin, N. K., & Lincoln, Y. S. (2011). *The SAGE handbook of qualitative research* (4th ed.). Thousand Oaks, CA: Sage.

DePauw, K. (2009). Ethics, professional expectations, and graduate education: Advancing research in kinesiology. *Quest, 61*, 52–58. doi:10.1080/00336297.2009.10483600

Dewalt, K., & Dewalt, B. (2011, 2nd ed.). *Participant observation: A guide for field workers.* Lanham, MD: Altamira Press.

Dewey, J. (1916). *Democracy and education.* New York, NY: Free Press.

Eales, L. (2016). Loose leaf. *Canadian Journal of Disabilities Studies, 5*, 58–76. doi: doi:.10.15353/cjds.v5i3.297

Eales, L., & Goodwin, D. L. (2015). "We all carry each other, sometimes": Care-sharing as social justice practice in integrated dance. *Leisure/Loisir, 39*, 277–298. doi: 10.1080/14927713.2015.1086584

Eales, L., & Peers, D. (2016). Moving adapted physical activity: The possibilities of arts-based research. *Quest, 68*, 55–68. doi: 10.1080/00336297.2015.1116999

Elliott, J. (1991). *Action research for educational change* Philadelphia, PA: Open University Press.

Fine, M. (1994). Working the hyphens. In N. K. Denzin & Y. S. Lincoln (Eds.), *Handbook of qualitative research* (pp. 70–82). Thousand Oaks, CA: Sage.

Finley, S. (2011). Critical arts-based inquiry: The pedagogy and performance of a radical ethical aesthetic. In Denzin, N. K., & Lincoln, Y. S. (Eds.). *The Sage handbook of qualitative research* (4th ed.). Thousand Oaks: Sage, pp. 435-450.

Fitzgerald, H., Jobling, A., & Kirk, D. (2003). Valuing the voices of young disabled people: Exploring experience of physical education and sport. *European Journal of Physical Education, 8*, 175–200. doi: 10.1080/1740898030080206

Fitzpatrick, D., & Watkinson, E. (2003). The lived experience of physical awkwardness: Adults' retrospective views. *Adapted Physical Activity Quarterly, 20*, 279–297. doi:10.1123/apaq.20.3.279

Fossey, E., Harvey, C., McDermott, F., & Davidson, L. (2002). Understanding and evaluating qualitative research. *Australian and New Zealand Journal of Psychiatry, 36*, 717–732. doi: 10.1046/j.1440-1614.2002.01100.x

Frey, G. C., Buchanan, A. M., & Rosser Sandt, D. D. (2005). "I'd rather watch TV": An examination of physical activity in adults with mental retardation. *Mental Retardation, 43*, 241–254. doi:10.1352/0047-6765(2005)43[241:IRWTAE]2.0.CO;2

Gergen, M., & Gergen, K. (2000). Qualitative inquiry, tensions and transformations. In N. K. Denzin & Y. S. Lincoln (Eds.), *The Sage handbook of qualitative research* (2nd ed., pp. 1025–1046). Thousand Oaks, CA: Sage.

Giacobbi, P. R., Stancil, M., Hardin, B., & Bryant, L. (2008). Physical activity and quality of life experienced by highly active individuals with physical disabilities. *Adapted Physical Activity Quarterly, 25*, 189–207. doi:10.1123/apaq.25.3.189

Gilgun, J. F. (2005). "Grab" and good science: Writing up the results of qualitative research. *Qualitative Health Research, 15*, 256–262. doi:10.1177/1049732304268796

Gonzalez, M. C. (2000). The four seasons of ethnography: A creation-centered ontology for ethnography. *International Journal of Intercultural Relations, 24*, 623–650. Retrieved from https://nsuworks.nova.edu/tqr/vol17/iss40/1

Goodley, D., & Runswick-Cole, K. (2011). The violence of disablism. *Sociology of Health and Illness, 33*, 602–617. doi:10.1111/j.1467-9566.2010.01302.x

Goodwin, D. L., & Ebert, A. (2018). Physical activity for youth with impairments: Hidden parental labor. *Adapted Physical Activity Quarterly,35*, 342-360. doi:10.1123/apaq.2017-0110

Goodwin, D. L., Lieberman, L. J., Johnston, K., & Leo, J. (2011). Connecting through summer camp: Youth with visual impairments find a sense of community. *Adapted Physical Activity Quarterly, 28*, 40–55. doi:0.1123/apaq.28.1.40

Goodwin, D. L., & Rossow-Kimball, B. (2012). Thinking ethically about professional practice in adapted physical activity. *Adapted Physical Activity Quarterly, 29*, 295–309. doi: 10.1123/apaq.29.4.295

Goodwin, D. L., & Watkinson, J. (2000). Inclusive physical education from the perspective of students with physical disabilities. *Adapted Physical Activity Quarterly, 17*, 144–160. doi: 10.1123/apaq.17.2.144

Goodwin, D. L. (2001). The meaning of help in PE: Perceptions of students with physical disabilities. *Adapted Physical Activity Quarterly, 18*(3), 289–303.

Greenwood, D. J., & Levin, M. (2007). *Introduction to action research: Social research for social change* (2nd ed.). Thousand Oaks, CA: Sage.

Grimshaw, J. M., Eccles, M. P., Lavis, J. N., Hill, S. J., & Squires, J. E. (2012). Knowledge translation of research findings. *Implementation Science, 7*, 1–17. doi:10.1186/1748-5908-7-50

Guan, Z. (2015). Paralympics in China: A social approach versus and elite approach. *International Journal of the History of Sport, 32*, 115–1120. doi:10.1080/09523367.2015.1038522

Guba, E. G., & Lincoln, Y. S. (1994). Competing paradigms in qualitative research. In N. K. Denzin & Y. S. Lincoln (Eds.), *Handbook of qualitative research* (4th ed., pp. 105–117) Thousand Oaks, CA: Sage Publishing.

Haegele, J. A., Zhu, X., & Davis, S. (2017). The meaning of physical education and sport among elite athletes with visual impairments. *European Physical Education Review, 23*, 375–391. doi:10.1177/1356336X16650122

Haydon, G., Browne, G., & van der Riet, P. (2018). Narrative inquiry as a research methodology exploring person centered care in nursing. *Collegian, 25*, 125–129. doi:10.1016/j.colegn.2017.03.001

Henwood, K. (2008). Qualitative research, reflexivity and living with risk: Valuing and practicing epistemic reflexivity and centering marginality. *Qualitative Research in Psychology, 5*, 45–55. doi: 10.1080/14780880701863575

Hodge, N., & Runswick-Cole, K. (2013). 'They never pass me the ball:' Exposing ableism through the leisure experiences of disable children, young people and their families. *Children's Geographies, 11*, 311–325. doi:0.1080/14733285.2013.812275

Hodge, S. R., Tannehill, D., & Kluge, M. A. (2003). Exploring the meaning of practicum experiences for PETE students. *Adapted Physical Activity Quarterly, 20*, 381–399. doi: 10.1123/apaq.20.4.381

Howe, P. D. (2004). *Sport, professionalism and pain.* New York, NY: Routledge.

Howe, P. D. (2008). *The cultural politics of the Paralympic movement through an anthropological lens.* London: Routledge.

Iivari, J., & Venable, J. R. (2009). Actin research and design science research – Seemingly similar but decisively dissimilar. *Proceedings of the European Conference on Information Systems, 73*. Retrieved from https://aisel.aisnet.org/ecis2009

Kamberilis, G., & Dimtiriadis, G. (2011). Focus groups: Contingent articulations of pedagogy, politics and inquiry. In N. K. Denzin & Y. Lincoln (Eds.), *The Sage handbook of qualitative research* (4th ed., pp. 545–561). Thousand Oaks, CA: Sage.

Kemmis, S., McTaggart, R., & Nixon, R. (2014). Introducing critical participatory action research. In *The action research planner* (pp. 1–31). Springer, Singapore.

Kincheloe, J. L., & McLaren, P. (2000). Rethinking critical theory and qualitative research. In N. K. Denzin & Y. Lincoln (Eds.), *The Sage handbook of qualitative research* (2nd ed., pp. 279–313). Thousand Oaks, CA: Sage.

Kivunja, D., & Kuyini, A. B. (2017). Understanding and applying research paradigms in educational contexts. *International Journal of Higher Education, 6*, 26–41. doi: 10.5430/ijhe.v6n5p26

Larkin, M., Watts, S., & Clifton, E. (2006). Giving voice and making sense in interpretative phenomenological analysis. *Qualitative Research in Psychology, 3*, 102–120. doi: 10.1191/1478088706qp062oa

Leo, J., & Goodwin, D. L. (2014). Negotiated meanings of disability simulations in an adapted physical activity course: Learning from student reflections. *Adapted Physical Activity Quarterly, 31*, 144–161. doi:10.1123/apaq.2013-0099

Levin, M., & Greenwood, D. (2011) *Handbook of qualitative inquiry.* Sage: Thousand Oaks, CA (USA).

Levins, S. M., Redenbach, D. M., & Dyck, I. (2004). Individual and societal influences on participation in physical activity following spinal cord injury: A qualitative study. *Physical Therapy, 84*, 496–509. doi:10.1093/ptj/84.6.496

Lincoln, Y. S., Lynhan, S. A., & Guba, E. G. (2011). Paradigmatic controversies, contradictions, and emerging confluences, revised. In N. K. Denzin & Y. S. Lincoln (Eds.), *The Sage handbook of qualitative research* (4th ed., pp. 97–128). Thousand Oaks, CA: Sage.

Lopez, K. A., & Willis, D. G. (2004). Descriptive versus interpretive phenomenology: Their contributions to nursing knowledge. *Qualitative Health Research, 14*, 726–735. doi:10.1177/1049732304263638

Lundberg, N. R., Taniguchi, S., McCormick, B. P., & Tibbs, C. (2011). Identity negotiating: Redefining stigmatized identities through adaptive sports and recreation participation among individuals with a disability. *Journal of Leisure Research, 43*, 205–225. doi:10.1080/00222216.2011.11950233

Lyons, L. (2013). Transformed understanding or enlightened ableism? The gap between policy and practice for children with disabilities in Aotearoa, New Zealand. *International Journal of Early Childhood, 45*, 237–249. doi:10.1007/s13158-013-0086-1

Mackenzie, N., & Knipe, S. (2006). Research dilemmas: Paradigms, methods and methodology. Issues in educational research, 16(2), 193–205.

McGregor, S., & Murnane, J. (2010). Paradigm, methodology and method: Intellectual integrity in consumer scholarship. *International Journal of Consumer Studies, 34*, 419–427. doi:10.1111/j.1470-6431.2010.00883.x

McKernan, J. (1996). *Action research: A handbook of methods and resources for the reflective practitioner.* (2nd ed.). New York, NY: Routledge.

Milner, R. (2007). Race, culture, and researcher positionality: Working through dangers seen, unseen, and unforeseen. *Educational Researcher, 36*, 388–400. doi:0.3102/0013189X07309471

Mitchell, D. T., & Snyder, S. L. (2015). *The biopolitics of disability: Neoliberalism, ablenationalism, & peripheral embodiment.* Ann Arbor, MI: University of Michigan Press.

Moola, F., Fusco, C., & Kirsh, J. A. (2011). 'What I wish you knew': Social barriers toward physical activity in youth with congenital heart disease (CHD). *Adapted Physical Activity Quarterly, 28*, 56–77. doi:10.1123/apaq.28.1.56

Oliver, M. (1990). *The politics of disablement.* Houndsmills, UK: McMillan Press.

Ozanne, J. L., & Saatcioglu, B. (2008). Participatory action research. *Journal of Consumer Research, 35*, 423–439. doi:10.1086/586911

Peers, D. (2009). (Dis)empowering Paralympic histories: Absent athletes and disabling discourses. *Disability and Society, 24*, 653–665. doi:10.1080/09687590903011113

Peers, D. (2012a). Interrogating disability: The (de)composition of a recovering Paralympian. *Qualitative Research in Sport, Exercise, and Health, 4*, 175–188. doi:10.1080/2159676X.2012.685101

Peers, D. (2012b). Patients, athletes, freaks: Paralympism and the reproduction of disability. *Journal of Sport and Social Issues, 36*, 295–316. doi:10.1177/0193723512442201

Peers, D., & Eales, L. (2017). Moving materiality: People, tools, and this thing called disability. *Art/Research International: A Transdisciplinary Journal, 2,* 101–125. doi:10.18432/R2JS8W

Rolling, H. J. (2010). A paradigm analysis of arts-based research and implications for education. *Studies in Art Education: A Journal of Issues and Research, 51,* 102–114. doi:10.1080/00393541.2010.11518795

Rossow-Kimball, B., & Goodwin, D. (2018). Leisure in later life for people with intellectual impairments: Beyond service provision toward personal coherence. *Leisure/Loisir, 43,* 243–258. doi: 10.1080/14927713.2018.1535908

Sparkes, A. C., & Smith, B. (2013). *Qualitative research methods in sport, exercise and health: From process to product.* London, UK: Routledge.

Scully, J. L., (2009). Disability and the thinking body. In K. Kristiansen, S. Vehmas, & T. Shakespeare (Eds.), *Arguing about disability: Philosophical perspectives.* (pp. 57–73). New York: NY: Routledge.

Seligman, M. (2011). *Flourish.* New York, NY: Atria.

Sherrill, C. (2004). *Adapted physical activity, recreation and sport: Crossdisciplinary and lifespan.* (6th ed.). Boston, MA: McGraw-Hill.

Slee, R. (2008). Beyond special and regular schooling? An inclusive education reform agenda. *International Studies in Sociology of Education, 18,* 99–166. doi:10.1080/09620210802351342

Smith, B. (2013). Disability, sport and men's narratives of health: A qualitative study. *Health Psychology, 31* 110-119. doi: 10.1037/a0029187

Smith, B., Bundon, A., & Best, M. (2016). Disability sport and activist identities: A qualitative study of narratives of activism among elite athletes with impairment. *Psychology of Sport and Exercise, 26,* 139–148. doi:10.1016/j.psychsport.2016.07.003

Smith, B., & Sparkes, A. C. (2004). Men, sport, and spinal cord injury: An analysis of metaphors and narrative types. *Disability and Society, 19,* 613–626. doi:10.1080/0968759042000252533

Smith, B., & Sparkes, A. C. (2005). Men, sport, spinal cord injury, and narratives of hope. *Social Science Medicine, 61,* 1095–1105. doi:10.1016/j.socscimed.2005.01.011

Smith, B., & Sparkes, A. C. (2008). Narrative and its potential contribution to disability studies. *Disability and Society, 23,* 17–28. doi:10.1080/09687590701725542

Smith, B., & Sparkes, A. C. (2009). Narrative inquiry in sport and exercise psychology: What can it mean, and why might we do it? *Psychology of Sport and Exercise, 10,* 1–11. doi:10.1016/j.psychsport.2008.01.004

Smith, B., & Sparkes, A. C. (Eds.). (2016). *Routledge handbook of qualitative research in sport and exercise.* New York: NY: Routledge.

Smith, B., Tomasone, J. R., Latimer-Cheung, A. E., & Martin Ginis, K. A. (2015). Narrative as a knowledge translation tool for facilitating impact: Translating physical activity knowledge to disabled people and health professionals. *Health Psychology, 34,* 303–313. doi: 10.1037/hea0000113

Smith, J. A., Flowers, P., & Larkin, M. (2009). *Interpretative phenomenological analysis.* Thousand Oaks, CA: Sage.

Sparkes, A. C., & Smith, B. (2002). Sport, spinal cord injury, embodied masculinities, and the dilemmas of narrative identity. *Men and Masculinities, 4,* 258–285. doi:10.1177/1097184X02004003003

Standal, Ø. F. (2008). Celebrating the insecure practitioner: A critique of evidence-based practice in adapted physical activity. *Sports, Ethics and Philosophy, 2,* 200–215. doi: 10.1080/17511320802223527

Standal, Ø. F., & Engelsrud, G. (2013). Researching embodiment in movement contexts: A phenomenological approach. *Sport, Education and Society, 18,* 154–166. doi:10.1080/13573322.2011.608944

Standal, Ø. F., & Jespersen, E. (2008). Peers as resources for learning: A situated learning approach to adapted physical activity in rehabilitation. *Adapted Physical Activity Quarterly, 25,* 208–227. doi:10.1123/Capaq.25.3.208

Standal, Ø. F., & Rugseth, G. (2014). Practicum in adapted physical activity: A Dewey-inspired action research project. *Adapted Physical Activity Quarterly, 31,* 219–239. doi:10.1123/apaq.2013-0105

Strauss, A., & Corbin, J. (1990). *Basics of qualitative research – Grounded theory procedures and techniques.* Newbury Park, CA: Sage.

Titchkosky, T. (2003). *Disability, self, and society.* Toronto, ON: University of Toronto Press.

Titchkosky, T. (2011). *The question of access: Disability, space, meaning.* Toronto, ON:University of Toronto Press.

Todres, L. (2005). Clarifying the life world: Descriptive phenomenology. In I. Holloway (Ed.). *Qualitative research in health care* (pp. 104–124). Berkshire, England: McGraw-Hill.

Torre, M. E., Fine, M., Stoudt, B. G., & Fox, M. (2012). Critical participatory action research as public science. *Journal of Social Issues, 68*, 178–193. doi:10.1037/13620-011

van Manen, M. (1997). *Researching lived experiences: Human science for an action sensitive pedagogy.* London, ON: The Althouse Press.

Vehmas, S., & Mäkelä, P. (2009). The ontology of disability and impairment: A discussion of the natural and social features. In K. Kristiansen, S. Vehmas, & T. Shakespeare (Eds.), *Arguing about disability: Philosophical perspectives.* (pp. 42–56). New York, NY: Routledge.

Weed, M. (2017). Capturing the essence of grounded theory: The importance of understanding commonalities and variants. *Qualitative Research in Sport, Exercise and Health, 9*, 149–156. doi:10.1080/2159676X.2016.1251701

Wheeler, G. D., Malone, L. A., VanVlack, S., Nelson, E. R., & Steadward, R. D. (1996). Retirement from disability sport: A pilot study. *Adapted Physical Activity Quarterly*, 13(4), 382–399.

Whitehead, T. L. (2004). What is ethnography? Methodological, ontological, and epistemological attributes. In *Ethnographic Informed Community and Cultural Assessment Research Systems (EICCARS) Working Paper Series.* University of Maryland: College Park.

Withers, A. J. (2012). *Disability politics and theory.* Winnipeg, MB: Fernwood Publishing.

Wojnar, D. M., & Swanson, K. M. (2007). Phenomenology: An exploration. *Journal of Holistic Health, 25*, 172–180.

11

Mixed methods research in adapted physical education

William J. Harvey, Mathieu Michaud, and Shawn Wilkinson

Introduction

This chapter is devoted to the description of mixed methods research (MMR) in adapted physical education (APE). This type of research has not been utilized thoroughly in the contexts of APE or adapted physical activity (APA). It is mainly an introduction to the rationale and underlying assumptions related to MMR in APE and, more broadly, APA. Hence, we explore some of the reasons why graduate students and emerging scholars may wish to perform MMR in APE (e.g., why, when, where, how). We demonstrate the challenges of varying terminology and worldviews while also trying to negotiate a shared understanding of differing, and sometimes opposing, methodological stands. For this reason, please note that this chapter is written in both the first- and third-person tenses to acknowledge the nature of our MMR approach. For example, quantitative researchers tend to write their studies from the third person perspective to demonstrate their unbiased position to the participants, data, and findings, as should be expected from the stance of the scientific method and positivism. Qualitative researchers, on the other hand, often write their studies from the first person perspective to demonstrate their own unique and personal relationship to the participants, data, and findings, as should be expected from the stance of holism and postmodernism. Finally, we provide an introduction to the three basic MMR designs and provide other sources for the reader to find more in-depth material for their research purposes. You will find that MMR is pragmatic in nature and will likely resonate with many APE researchers who hold applied perspectives to physical activity and people with disabilities. We discuss our approach to MMR in relation to APE research in the "Future directions" section. Further, we firmly believe that MMR may assist our field of researchers to thrive within inter- or multidisciplinary research paradigms.

The following operational definitions are used for the purposes of this chapter.

- Adapted physical education (APE): "Adapted Physical Education (APE) is a subdiscipline of physical education with an emphasis on physical education for students with disabilities. The term adapted physical education generally refers to school-based programs for students ages 3–21" (Block, 2016, p. 15). APE can also be considered to fall under the umbrella term of APA because the instructional focus is placed upon learning physical activity for students with disabilities (Harvey, 2014a).

- Adapted physical activity (APA) can be broadly described as a cross-disciplinary human science concerned about the physical activity needs, skills, and experiences of persons with disabilities over the course of life span development (Sherrill, 2004)
- Epistemology: the nature of knowledge construction where knowledge may be considered as being socially constructed (Bredo, 2006; Kincheloe, 2008). It answers the question: "What is the relationship between the researcher and that being researched?" (Creswell & Plano-Clark, 2018, p. 38)
- Ontology: "refers to the nature of reality (and what is real) that researchers assume when they conduct their inquiries". It answers the question: "What is the nature of reality?" (Creswell & Plano-Clark, 2018, pp. 37–38).

Overview

Generally, the use of MMR has a long and unique past that may be perceived as being dependent upon the field of study that one refers to (Creswell & Plano-Clark, 2018). This type of research originated in the social and behavioral sciences and started with researchers who believed qualitative and quantitative methods would be useful when addressing their research questions (Johnson, Onwuegbuzie, & Turner, 2007).

Quantitative or qualitative methods may often be considered as two polar opposites, or two distinct paradigms, with MMR construed as the third methodological movement (Tashakkori & Teddlie, 2006). However, we suggest that qualitative and quantitative research methods may be placed on the opposite sides of a continuum. Perhaps quantitative, qualitative, and mixed methods research may represent different, but intersecting, planes of existence or methodological ellipses. Clearly, there are misunderstandings about the theoretical underpinnings and use of MMR. Researchers must understand why they want to use MMR to answer their research questions. For example, I, as the first author, usually ask the following question when teaching about MMR in classrooms or workshops. Why and what do you want to know about MMR? Mathieu and Shawn, as second and third authors, have heard the usual talk about my journey into the qualitative/MMR paradigm(s) that follows. Please use the following narrative to follow my train of thought. Mathieu and Shawn's journeys into MMR are also presented. We suggest that our perspectives may start to drive understanding into the discussion.

I started out my research career in APA about 30 years ago. My graduate supervisor had my best interests at heart when he wanted me to become an expert in quantitative research methods. I took approximately seven courses in statistics and advanced research methods design in order to prepare to become the best possible quantitative researcher that I could be. I learned, over the course of time, that researchers first explore their phenomenon of interest in order to come up with ideas that will drive their overall research question and hypotheses. The process is much like a pilot who is scouting for a place to land a plane or a light bulb being lit. The researcher then chooses a method in order to answer the overarching question and hypotheses. Research methods are often compared to the use of tools to accomplish work tasks, like using a hammer and nails. Like many graduate students before me, I envisioned the research process as a challenge to overcome, much like walking though a rainstorm or participating in a prize fight. There were definite times when I felt the research experience was like walking a tightrope. However, with much persistence, the delicate work of data collection, statistical analysis, results, and discussion is completed and the student is successful in answering her or his research questions at the end. The feeling is like reaching the peak of a mountain top. We may not find a pot of gold at the end of our rainbow, but we certainly get the opportunity to understand our phenomenon of interest better in some way, shape, or form.

After I had finished my first quantitative research study (Harvey & Reid, 1997), I felt that I had not answered my overarching research question very well. I soon started to explore qualitative research methods to see if I could gain more understanding about my own specific phenomenon of interest (e.g., fundamental movement skills performance of children with attention deficit hyperactivity disorder [ADHD]). I became enthralled with qualitative research methods and even started to draw my notes during my doctoral studies.

I started to appreciate that qualitative research methods could provide a different, but highly related, understanding of my research area. Essentially, I had started to contrast quantitative and qualitative research methods in order to choose which one would provide me with the best answers. Without fully knowing it, I entered into the "paradigm war", a term coined by Tashakkori and Teddlie (2006) to identify the issue that arises when a researcher has to decide between using a qualitative or quantitative research approach by gauging the related advantages and disadvantages. My supervisor and I ended up using a MMR approach in my doctoral dissertation. While we published one of the first MMR studies in APA (Harvey et al., 2009), MMR in APE and APA is still in its relative infancy. In fact, MMR studies are quite new in the context of kinesiology (Thomas, Nelson, & Silverman, 2011). For example, my co-authors' journeys in MMR are a bit different than mine.

Mathieu is just about to start his journey into APE research and he will decide if MMR is the appropriate way to proceed.

I, Mathieu, believe the research question plays an important role in deciding the appropriate methods, whether the researcher "specializes" in MMR or not.

Shawn completed his masters and doctoral research in our physical activity lab, where he played an important role in two MMR studies for our research about children with ADHD (Harvey, Wilkinson, Pressé, Joober, & Grizenko, 2012, 2014) as well as his own MMR study about the leisure experiences of adults with schizophrenia and schizo-affective disorders in the community (Wilkinson, 2017).

I, Shawn, am classically trained as a therapeutic recreation practitioner. Thus, I have always looked for pragmatic ways to address both practice and research. I have used MMR throughout my journey because it has allowed me to gain a more complete understanding of my clientele while providing practical solutions to improving individual health and well-being.

We have provided these narratives of our research journeys because we do not ascribe to the notion that there is a typical, or normal, journey to arrive at one's own philosophical and methodological positioning. Much like APE interventions, we suggest that this process is highly individualized. We further suggest that these types of self-reflective processes should be continual, as our philosophical assumptions may change over time.

We surmise that quantitative research methods and related paradigm assumptions governed the way that much research was performed in kinesiology and physical education circles for a very long time (Haegele, Lee, & Porretta, 2015). Qualitative research has recently emerged in these areas and gained considerable attention and acceptance over the past decade or so (Sparkes & Smith, 2014; Thomas et al., 2011). Hence, we suggest that there has been a paradigm shift to include qualitative research methods in kinesiology circles (Sparkes & Smith, 2014). Further, we suggest a similar shift to MMR in the future. This type of shift may be expected, as Tashakkori and Teddlie (2003) described MMR as the third methodological movement after the quantitative and qualitative research method movements. As we explore later on in this chapter, it is important to understand that the choice of your own research method will include respect for all ideas and a deeper understanding of epistemology, ontology, and the subtlety of the specific research language used.

What is MMR?

There are various definitions of MMR but, essentially, it involves the collection and analysis of both quantitative and qualitative data in a rigorous fashion (Creswell & Plano-Clark, 2018). MMR studies are initially guided by the researcher's philosophical assumptions (Creswell & Plano-Clark, 2018). Researchers must explore the philosophical assumptions, or worldviews, that guide their knowledge, conceptualization and "carrying out" of the research study. The exploration of basic beliefs and assumptions around the nature of reality (ontology), knowledge (epistemology), values (axiology), research process (methodology), and research language (rhetoric) set the foundation from which research studies are conducted (Creswell & Plano-Clark, 2018).

There are four prevailing worldviews that help to guide MMR (Creswell & Plano-Clark, 2018). Knowledge of postpositivist (quantitative approaches), constructivist (qualitative approaches), transformative (social justice approaches), and pragmatist (practical approaches) worldviews can best inform how researchers develop and conduct MMR (Creswell & Plano-Clark, 2018). Researchers may choose to adhere to the notion of selecting one "best" worldview, combine multiple worldviews (dialectical), shift worldviews to fit the context of the study, or incorporate the worldview shaped by their community of practice to help guide the design of their research study (Creswell & Plano-Clark, 2018). To the best of our knowledge, there is no "right" way to include the use of worldviews in one's research. However, it is fundamentally important for researchers to explore their philosophical assumptions, determine where those assumptions fit within the identified worldviews, and how the assumptions impact the design and development of research practices (Creswell & Plano-Clark, 2018).

The knowledge about the researchers' worldviews then helps to identify the theoretical lens, or theoretical approach(es), that may be incorporated throughout the study (e.g., self-determination theory, knowledge-based approach to motor development, theory of affordances and constraints). These two very important steps in the research process then lead to the selection of the preferred methodological approaches (e.g., case study designs, correlational designs) and associated data collection/gathering methods (e.g., interviews, survey data).

Hence, research methods would then be selected to align with the researchers' preferred worldview(s) in order to gather/collect the data. For example, our research team explored the physical activity experiences of children with ADHD through a combination of fundamental movement skill tests, physical activity self-reports, and semi-structured interviews (Harvey et al., 2014). The research team's worldview was a combination of pragmatist and constructivist worldviews. The worldview was pragmatist because the research team wished to find clinically relevant answers to applied research questions that could be used in a real-world context. The results of the movement skills tests, self-report data, and interviews led to a tangible understanding of the physical activity needs for each participant. For example, many of the children with ADHD lacked a concrete understanding of the purpose and goals of the various physical activities that they participated in. Not only did this finding shed light on some of the potential physical activity research issues of children with ADHD, but we were also able to make suggestions to the children and their parents about reflecting on the reasons why she or he would select, and participate in, various physical activities. The hope was for the children to adhere to physical activities of their liking.

The worldview was also constructivist because the participants took part in a scrapbook interviewing approach. For example, one of the main theoretical assumptions for this visual research method is based on the idea that participants co-construct physical activity knowledge while being interviewed by a research assistant (Harvey et al., 2012). It is clear that our study followed the same conceptual path from its start to completion. Zitomer & Goodwin (2014) identified this type of consistent research process as coherence. Not only must we be cautious about keeping the research process coherent for our studies, we must also be careful to gather the data well to reach the next step of analysis in the research process.

Next, Creswell and Plano-Clark (2018) suggested analyzing quantitative and qualitative data separately. The researcher should understand these results from each unique perspective first. While the data may be mixed or integrated at any time, this procedure is typically performed afterwards to place the results together to make appropriate meta-inferences and conclusions. The totality of the results may then be displayed in text and/or table forms. Of course, we always refer back to our hypotheses and central research questions to see if we have answered them after all of the analyses have been completed. Again, it is important to note here that, as researchers, it is imperative to try to stay within the boundaries of each particular worldview in order for our studies to be considered as trustworthy and coherent (Zitomer & Goodwin, 2014).

Hence, traditional research methods alone do not drive the research. As we mentioned beforehand, researchers may observe qualitative and quantitative research methods on the opposite sides of a continuum. We suggest that researchers should try to position, or place, themselves somewhere along the continuum. For example, we could envision an epidemiological researcher placing herself/himself on the far right-hand side of the continuum as a firm quantitative methods expert. Perhaps a narrative inquirer may place herself/himself on the far left-hand side of the continuum as a firm qualitative methods aficionado. Furthermore, researchers who utilize either a case study research methods approach or correlational research methods design may place themselves more towards the middle-left or middle-right of the continuum, respectively. Perhaps mixed methods researchers would place themselves in the direct middle of the continuum. Another way of describing relationships between quantitative, qualitative, and mixed methods research is to suggest that they may represent different, but intersecting, planes of existence or methodological ellipses. Clearly, researchers need to perform some self-exploration into their own philosophical and research assumptions before coming to the decision to utilize MMR in order to gain a comprehensive understanding of the underpinnings of their own research.

Strean, (1998) described causal, prescriptive, and paradigmatic assumptions to be aware of in APA research. He suggested "causal, or descriptive, assumptions involve what we take for granted about how the world is; they help us understand how different aspects of the world work and the conditions under which processes can be altered" (p. 279). He suggested that these assumptions are "the easiest to uncover" (p. 280) and they are often presented as if–then conditional statements. For example, "if" we use individualized instruction in our APE research interventions, "then" each student with a disability will improve on her or his performance outcomes and learn how to become physically active. Prescriptive assumptions were described as "… value based: things that we take for granted about what *ought* to be happening in a particular setting or how the world *should* be" (Strean, 1998, p. 279). For example, new researchers "should" be aware of the most up-to-date knowledge in order to create successful APE research interventions.

Paradigmatic assumptions were described as "… the basic organizing ideas that we use to order the world into fundamental categories" (Strean, 1998, p. 279). For example, scientists once considered the world to be flat until, of course, this paradigm assumption was proved false because it was discovered that the world was, indeed, round. Strean (1998) suggested that some researchers may not recognize paradigm assumptions because they are so deeply ingrained within us and our culture. In this chapter, we mainly explore paradigm assumptions that underlie MMR. We have questioned how well APE and APA researchers know and understand their paradigmatic research methods assumptions (Harvey, Michaud, & Wilkinson, 2018).

Quantitative paradigm assumptions

The assumptions related to quantitative research methods are linked to the philosophy and parameters of this specific set of approaches. For example, positivism has been described as being one of the main drivers of quantitative research. It directly shapes the epistemological, ontological, methodological, axiological and rhetorical practices of quantitative researchers. Human knowledge, according to positivism, is developed through the "confirmable observations of empirical events" (Corry, Porter, & McKenna, 2019, p. 3). Researchers focus on uncovering and verifying reality and they use systematic ways to describe their findings. Positivists believe that one true reality exists within the natural world and that reality is governed and shaped by natural laws (Corry et al., 2018). Science is regarded as a value-free endeavor and the positivist researcher is expected to be independent from the subject of study. The scientific method is the main procedure that underlies quantitative research methods (Harvey, 2014b). It ensures a deductive, top-down, reasoning process that enables researchers to find "product" measures to confirm or disconfirm their hypotheses. Of course, quantitative researchers would like their study findings to be reliable and valid. They also assume that they are objective and reliable players in the research process by strictly abiding to the scientific method.

Hence, it is important, as researchers, to be aware of the parameters of your research methods approach. The parameters are the main paradigm assumptions of the specific approach. For example, there are different types of data to be "collected" (e.g., nominal, ordinal, interval, and ratio). While various sampling approaches may be used, generalizability is well sought after. Random sampling is also a mainstay of this approach. There are a variety of variables to be aware of (e.g., independent, dependent), with three assumptions of normality that exist (e.g., variables are normally distributed, homogeneity of variance, independence of observations: Glass & Hopkins, 1984). Normality, in and of itself, is a major paradigm assumption, as numbers are expected to be regularly distributed with samples sizes of 25 participants and greater (e.g., central limit theorem). Descriptive, non-inferential, and inferential statistics may be used to analyze the data. One of the main purposes of statistical analyses is to explain the variance between participant groups on any given dependent variable(s). The statistical analysis allows the researcher to either accept or reject the null hypothesis based on a concrete, objective result. This result, in a way, confirms or disconfirms the researcher's hypothesis. This process should not be confused with a mathematical proof where there is only one answer to solve a problem. Quantitative researchers use confidence intervals and must be aware of Type I and Type II errors, as well as power estimates, so it is our suggestion that the results should be considered as making a plausible case for or against the decision rendered by the researcher.

Qualitative paradigm assumptions

The assumptions related to qualitative research methods are linked to the philosophy and parameters of this specific set of approaches. Postmodernism and holism have been described as being two of the main drivers of qualitative research (Sparkes & Smith, 2014). The idea of holism suggests that we observe an object or study a phenomenon as a whole (Verschuren, 2001). The researcher is drawn to the "collective characteristics" of a phenomenon as opposed to being interested in "separate aggregated characteristics" (Verschuren, 2001, p. 394). Researchers are also interested in framing their understanding of a phenomenon within the larger narrative of the phenomenon they are studying. In other words, the object of study cannot be separated from the context in which it is observed. Hence, the qualitative researcher values being present and involved with the phenomenon of interest. The research participants and the researcher are the main interpreters that underlie qualitative research methods. It ensures an inductive, bottom-up reasoning process that enables researchers to find "process" measures to explore the meanings related to specific contexts that are indicative of the human experience. Of course, qualitative researchers would like their study findings to be genuine and trustworthy (Sparkes & Smith, 2014).

Again, it is important, as researchers, to be aware of the parameters of their research methods approach. The parameters are the main paradigm assumptions of the specific approach. For example, there are different types of data to be "gathered" (e.g., text, art, drama, personal stories, interviews). Purposeful sampling is usually used to gain and understand the perspectives and unique experiences of specific research participants. Generalizability is not sought after, or valued. In fact, researchers must position themselves within the context of the research to demonstrate that they are credible, genuine, and trustworthy people to interpret and tell the stories of the research participants. They address the essence of unique phenomena through a variety of descriptive and highly rigorous research methods. The gathered data are interpreted or analyzed through a variety of ways (e.g., narratives, dramas, thematic analysis, etc.). The findings are told in a story-like fashion in order to capture the participants' experiences and the readers' attention.

Mixed methods paradigm assumptions

Essentially, a mixed methods researcher must understand the assumptions of both quantitative and qualitative research methods. Further, we must try to incorporate methods that will match well. For example, the MMR approach usually involves the integration of all data and their results in a way that justifies the use of dual approaches (Creswell & Plano-Clark, 2018). One set of data should reinforce the understanding of the other set of data in a clear and relevant way. Johnson and colleagues (2007) described MMR as: "the type of research in which a researcher or a team of researchers combines elements of qualitative and quantitative research approaches […] for the broad purpose of breath and depth of understanding and corroboration" (p. 123). Data from both approaches should be integrated and interpretations be drawn based on the combined strengths of both procedures to better understand the research problem (Watkins & Gioia, 2015). Hence, it is vital to know the importance and ordering of the quantitative and qualitative data in relation to the overarching research question.

The three main types of MMR designs are convergent parallel, explanatory sequential, and exploratory sequential (Creswell & Plano-Clark, 2018; Thomas et al., 2011; Watkins & Gioia, 2015). Quantitative and qualitative data are collected concurrently, or at the same time, when using the convergent parallel design. The two sets of data are analyzed separately and then merged during the interpretation phase. This design may be considered as intuitive, efficient, and time-saving, as both sets of data are collected at the same time. The explanatory sequential design involves collecting and analyzing quantitative data first and then collecting and analyzing qualitative data in a second phase. Thus, the qualitative data gathered are guided by the quantitative data collected. The main emphasis of the design is placed on the quantitative results. However, the qualitative data may be used to confirm, complement, or explain the results of the quantitative phase. The exploratory sequential design involves a qualitative data gathering first. It is then analyzed in order to build a subsequent quantitative phase. Thus, quantitative data may be used to complement the qualitative data gathered, or even lead to the development of research instruments and testable theories to explain the phenomenon being studied (Thomas et al., 2011; Watkins & Gioia, 2015). Therefore, researchers must be aware of the assumptions that underlie both the quantitative and qualitative approaches in order to understand how to answer their specific sets of research questions. Creswell and Plano-Clark (2018) clearly suggested that it takes much time and expertise to be able to develop the depth of researcher knowledge and skills necessary in both approaches so as to best utilize the combined knowledge to create solid MMR. The reader is referred to Creswell and Plano-Clark (2018) for a description and explanation of the more advanced and elaborate research designs that may be used in MMR.

Mixed methods research and adapted physical education

Creswell and Plano-Clark (2018) provided a variety of reasons to perform MMR. They suggested that a need should exist to: "obtain more complete and corroborated results" through the use of quantitative and qualitative methods, "explain initial results" by adding a study to increase the depth of knowledge about a phenomenon, explore a research phenomenon before the development or administration of quantitative research instruments, "enhance the results of an experimental study with the use of a qualitative method", "describe and compare different types of cases", "involve participants in a study" and "develop, implement, and evaluate a program" (Creswell & Plano-Clark, 2018, pp. 9–14).

Harvey et al. (2018) suggested the following reasons to perform MMR about people with disabilities in various physical activity contexts. First, MMR would increase the possibility to tell wonderfully rich "ability" stories through qualitatively focused studies that would involve unique individuals and groups sharing their experiences about their physical activities. Next, MMR is pragmatic and applicable to real-world questions that seem to be the essence of APE research. Third, it would help to address the historic issues of small sample sizes in APE research (Watkinson & Wasson, 1984). MMR could be used as a viable strategy to increase the amount of data and related understanding of a research phenomenon. Fewer study participants may be required to create exploratory sequential designs to answer APE researchers' questions and provide deeper understanding of the research phenomenon of interest. Further, MMR could also address the issue of person by treatment interaction effects (Bouffard, 1993). For example, Bouffard suggested that individual research participants may be expected to respond differently than groups of participants to the same treatment intervention. For instance, the experimental group may perform significantly better than a control group on an intervention. However, not all of the experimental group participants may benefit from the intervention. In fact, they could perform worse and not accrue any benefit at all. It would be tremendous to use a qualitative research method and interview those persons to delve into the reason(s) why they did not respond like the majority of the experimental group. Since the use of person by treatment interaction effects is not well understood (Bouffard, 1993; Bouffard & Reid, 2012; Reid, Bouffard, & MacDonald, 2012), MMR would provide a wonderful opportunity to seek a better understanding of it. Finally, MMR in APE would provide an opportunity to build research based on comprehensive research approaches to further our field of study.

The literature on MMR and APA, including APE, seems to be scarce. Haegele et al. (2015) performed a documentary analysis of research publications in the *Adapted Physical Activity Quarterly* (*APAQ*) for the years between 2004 and 2013. They identified seven published articles, only 7.4% of their sample, considered as MMR. Haegele provided us (personal communication, July, 2019) with a list of these studies (De Bressy de Guast; Van Wersch, & d'Arripe-Longueville, 2013; Giacobbi, Dietrich, Larson, & White, 2012; Giacobbi, Stancil, Hardin, & Bryant, 2008; Harvey et al., 2009; Obrusnikova & Dillon, 2011; Obrusnikova & Miccinello, 2012; Tsai & Fung, 2009). Next, we retrieved and screened the publications to ensure that they were MMR studies. We found that Tsai and Fung (2009) had conducted a qualitative study on parents' perceptions about the sports participation of their child with an intellectual disability, so it was excluded from our review. We found four additional MMR studies (Bremer & Lloyd, 2016; Côté-Leclerc et al., 2017; Harvey et al., 2014; Shirazipour, Meehan, & Latimer-Cheung, 2017).

We describe two of these studies that could be considered as APE (Bremer & Lloyd, 2016; Obrusnikova & Dillon, 2011). Descriptions of two studies closely related to APE were also included, about the fundamental movement skill experiences of children with ADHD (Harvey et al., 2009, 2014). These additional studies were provided as further examples of MMR for each reader to consider, since few APE studies had been identified in our searches.

Bremer and Lloyd (2016) studied the impact of a fundamental movement skill intervention on five children with autism spectrum disorder (ASD) who were between three and seven years. Movement skills proficiency was assessed three times, using the Test of Gross Motor Development-2 (TGMD-2) and scores on the Social Skills Improvement System (SSIS) were used to assess social behaviors. All five participants were assessed at the start of the intervention, after the first six-week block of the intervention, and after the second six-week intervention block. A one-on-one interview was also conducted with the special education teacher to gain her perception of the intervention, its outcomes, as well as her ability to teach physical education. The intervention consisted of three sessions of 45 minutes per week over six weeks for both blocks and it focused on object control and locomotor skills. Precise teaching strategies were used, such as skill breakdown, step-by-step instructions, maximum repetitions, visual aids, etc. A descriptive analysis of the assessment tests were performed and a content analysis was conducted with the teacher interview data. All five participants improved their TGMD-2 scores to varying degrees on three to eight different items. Three participants made significant progress on all items of the SSIS and all five participants improved their score in the responsibility subsection of the test. According to the teacher, improvement was observed in the students' ability to recognize the visual tools used during the program. She also witnessed considerable improvement in her students' movement skills, as well as confidence in performing them. She felt more confident teaching physical education to her students and was never trained as a physical educator. She believed such a program could also be used in all physical education programs. The authors concluded that if students with a disability, such as autism, have developed a variety of movement skills and are confident about their abilities, they may be more inclined to participate in spontaneous play, thus increasing their level of physical activity.

Obrusnikova and Dillon (2011) conducted an MMR study with 43 certified physical educators about teaching challenges for students with ASD related to cooperative, competitive, and individual physical education settings. A background questionnaire was used to collect data about age, sex, and teaching experience for the 29 female and 14 male participants. An elicitation questionnaire was then used to gather more in-depth information about the instructional challenges faced by the teachers for students with ASD. The questionnaire was divided into three parts: a written vignette (i.e., the story of Chris, a 12-year-old student with ASD and his experience in his physical education class), elicitation questions (i.e., about instructional, structural, social, support challenges of teaching students with ASD) and elicitation definitions of the following terms: cooperative, competitive, individualistic, instructional tasks, managerial tasks and social tasks. These six terms were used to categorize the answers to the elicitation questions that, in turn, were then further explored in order to extract a list of concepts and codes. Social impairment, inattention and hyperactive behaviors, as well as social exclusion, were the most frequently reported challenges in cooperative settings. Hyperactive behaviors and emotional regulation and social difficulties were perceived as obstacles to the teaching act in competitive settings. Inattention and hyperactive behaviors, social impairments, and challenges in understanding activities were reported as problematic in individual settings. Overall, the teachers suggested that competitive and cooperative situations were reported as more challenging because students were perceived to compare their performance with that of their peers and have to interact with others. The authors suggested that planning was necessary to decrease teaching challenges and address problematic student behaviors across the learning settings. They also recommended that teachers proactively prevent the problematic behaviors from negatively impacting the learning of other classroom students or causing exclusionary behaviors to occur (i.e., being ignored or isolated).

Harvey et al. (2009) explored the fundamental movement skill performance of 12 boys with and without ADHD aged 9–12 years. They used a concurrent mixed methods research design, so quantitative and qualitative data were collected at the same time, with a higher priority placed on the qualitative data gathered. Two theories were used as theoretical lenses to guide the study and interpret the data gathered (e.g., the knowledge-based approach [Wall, McClements, Bouffard, Finlay, & Taylor, 1985] and the inhibitory model of executive functions [Barkley, 1997]). They found that the boys with ADHD were not skillful, when compared to their peers without ADHD, on their performance for the TGMD-2 (Ulrich, 2000). The thematic analysis showed that the boys with ADHD had similar, but fewer, experiences than boys without ADHD. The qualitative and quantitative data combined well to demonstrate that the boys with ADHD possessed superficial knowledge about fundamental movement skills and many negative feelings about physical activity overall.

Harvey and colleagues (2014) explored the physical activity experiences of ten children with ADHD through a concurrent mixed methods design. Fundamental movement skill performance of each child was assessed with the TGMD-2 and the Movement Assessment Battery for Children-2 for the quantitative component of the study. Self-reports of physical activity and a concurrent scrapbook interview method (Harvey et al., 2012) constituted the qualitative study component that was given the higher priority. Qualitized descriptors for individual raw scores were created from the normative test descriptors from each assessment test. The data were interpreted together once all of the assessment tests and interviews had been completed and analyzed separately. The children with ADHD scored poorly on the skill assessment tests and they spoke about their individual physical activity experiences in a variety of settings. Some of the children organized their physical activities while others did not. Many of the children lacked a concrete understanding of the purpose and goals of the various physical activities that they participated in.

In summary, the depth of knowledge and understanding that can be gained from a MMR approach in APE was demonstrated. Teacher knowledge was definitely gained in the two APE studies that were described. Further, the fundamental movement skill performance of children with ASD was assessed with associated teacher perspectives. Additionally, two MMR studies about the fundamental movement skills and associated experiences of children with ADHD were presented, where a more comprehensive picture of fundamental movement skill development and physical activity participation was gained. Based on the findings of these few studies, there is tremendous potential for MMR in APE.

New directions in the field

MMR has much to offer the world of APE. It is pragmatic in nature because mixed methods researchers try to solve real-world questions (Tashakkori & Teddlie, 2003). Many APE and APA researchers hold applied perspectives to physical activity and people with disabilities (Reid, 2000) and, because of this reality, MMR will resonate within our research community. For example, we share the belief that our approach to MMR is pragmatic. We select the research method(s) that will help to best answer and align with our research question(s) and associated epistemology, ontology, axiology, and rhetoric in order to conduct our research studies in a coherent fashion.

There are five new directions to take for MMR in APE. First, it was a big challenge to identify MMR studies in APE or APA. Our literature searches did not produce many MMR studies in the area. We sincerely apologize to any researchers whose MMR studies in APE we may have missed. Hence, a good new direction would be to list "mixed methods" as keywords when publishing in research journals. This action could make it much easier to locate and retrieve MMR studies. Next, it would be very useful to identify any successful literature search strategies in MMR performed by APE and APA researchers. Third, we recommend APE researchers to name the worldview(s) and theoretical lens that guide their consequent thinking, data collection and gathering, analyses, and research findings. Furthermore, we suggest that they name the specific type of research design being used and describe the sequence of data gathering/collection as well as data analyses. It will also prove valuable to provide thorough descriptions of the data collection instruments and data gathering methods in order to demonstrate why a study is being claimed as MMR. This information will prove useful for other researchers, who may be considering the use of MMR, by encouraging them to delve into the challenges of MMR through strong descriptions of the research process. Thus, it is clear that much time and thought must go into MMR study design in order to be successful. We think it is worth the time and investment to conduct MMR, as the results can provide comprehensive answers to our research questions and a more complete understanding about the research phenomenon of interest. We suggest that MMR may assist our field of researchers to thrive within inter- or multidisciplinary research paradigms. Hence, MMR offers a broader and more complete understanding of interventions that, in return, will guide future APE research studies and unveil new areas of inquiry worth investigating. Finally, we suggest that APE researchers start to use MMR to advance the applied research findings in our field.

However, we realize that adopting a different research approach may be challenging for many researchers to do. For example, Haegele et al. (2015) found that quantitative research methods were still the most predominant approach in *APAQ* up until 2013. Hence, it does make sense to us that the third methodological wave has yet to set sail in the APE/APA world. Although the principles and procedures of MMR and their integration in an APE setting seem to be seldom addressed in academic papers, some researchers have used MMR to further advance the field through their research. In closing, we suggest that the third methodological wave, known as MMR, will be beneficial for APE and APA researchers alike. We welcome you to grab a surfboard and ride that wave with us.

Summary of key points

1. There have been few MMR research studies performed to date in APE.
2. It takes a lot of time to develop the necessary research skills to perform MMR.
3. MMR holds much promise for future APE/APA researchers to combine quantitative and qualitative research approaches.
4. Researchers must position themselves in a research approach(es) and try to understand their own worldviews, philosophies, and related research methods in order to produce coherent research studies.
5. It is too early in time to conclude how MMR may be best utilized in the field. However, MMR holds much promise to solve practical, daily issues in APE.

Reflective questions

1. What would be your first MMR study in APE and why?
2. What types of MMR studies could you envision in APE?
3. Where would you position yourself along the quantitative–qualitative continuum? Why are you placed where you are? What research methods and related philosophies and theories lead you to believe that your positioning is accurate?
4. Consider creating a research team to create your MMR study. What types of researchers would you recruit on your team in relation to your expertise and experience? Why?

References

Barkley, R. A. (1997). *ADHD and the nature of self-control*. New York: Guilford Press.

Block, M. E. (2016). *A teacher's guide to adapted physical education: Including students with disabilities in sports and recreation*. Baltimore, MD: Brookes.

Bouffard, M. (1993). The perils of averaging data in adapted physical activity research. *Adapted Physical Activity Quarterly, 10*, 371–379.

Bouffard, M., & Reid, G. (2012). The good, the bad and the ugly of evidence-based practice. *Adapted Physical Activity Quarterly, 29*, 1–24.

Bredo, E. (2006). Philosophies of educational research. In J. Green, G. Camilli, & P. Elmore (Eds.), *Complementary methods in education research* (pp. 3–31). Washington, DC: American Educational Research Association.

Bremer, E., & Lloyd, M. (2016). School-based fundamental-motor-skill intervention for children with autism-like characteristics: An exploratory study. *Adapted Physical Activity Quarterly, 33*, 66–88.

Corry, M., Porter, S., & McKenna, H. (2019). The redundancy of positivism as a paradigm for nursing research. *Nursing Philosophy, 20*(1), e12230.

Côté-Leclerc, F., Boileau Duchesne, G., Bolduc, P., Gélinas-Lafrenière, A., Santerre, C., Desrosiers, J., & Levasseur, M. (2017). How does playing adapted sports affect quality of life of people with mobility limitations? Results from a mixed-method sequential explanatory study. *Health and Quality of Life Outcomes, 15,* 22.

Creswell, J. W., & Plano-Clark, V. L. (2018). *Designing and conducting mixed methods research* (3rd ed.). Thousand Oaks: SAGE.

De Bressy de, G. V., Golby, J., Van Wersch, W., & d'Arripe-Longueville, F. (2013). Psychological skills training of an elite wheelchair water-skiing athlete: A single-case study. *Adapted Physical Activity Quarterly, 30,* 351–372.

Giacobbi, P., Dietrich, F., Larson, R., & White, L. (2012). Exercise and quality of life in women with multiple sclerosis. *Adapted Physical Activity Quarterly, 29,* 224–242.

Giacobbi, P., Stancil, M., Hardin, B., & Bryant, L. (2008). Physical activity and quality of life experienced by highly active individuals with physical disabilities. *Adapted Physical Activity Quarterly, 25,* 189–207.

Glass, G. V., & Hopkins, K. D. (1984). *Statistical methods in education and psychology* (2nd ed.). Needham Heights: Allyn and Bacon.

Haegele, J. A., Lee, J., & Porretta, D. L. (2015). Research trends in *Adapted Physical Activity Quarterly* from 2004 to 2013. *Adapted Physical Activity Quarterly, 32,* 187–205.

Harvey, W. J. (2014a). Adapted and Inclusive Physical Education. In D. Robinson & L. Randall (Eds.), *Teaching Physical Education Today: Canadian Perspectives* (pp. 137–152). Toronto: Thompson Educational Publishing, Inc.

Harvey, W. J. (2014b). Critical thinking and critical pedagogy. In D. Robinson & L. Randall (Eds.), *Teaching physical education today: Canadian perspectives* (pp. 191–206). Toronto: Thompson Educational Publishing, Inc.

Harvey, W. J., Michaud, M., & Wilkinson, S. (2018). Describing the challenges of conducting mixed methods research in adapted physical activity. Building session presentation at the 14th North American Federation of Adapted Physical Activity. University of Alberta, Edmonton, Alberta.

Harvey, W. J., & Reid, G. (1997). Motor performance of children with attention-deficit hyperactivity disorder: A preliminary investigation. *Adapted Physical Activity Quarterly, 14,* 189–202.

Harvey, W. J., Reid, G., Bloom, G., Staples, K., Grizenko, N., Mbekou, V., Ter-Stepanian, M., & Joober, R. (2009). Physical activity experiences of boys with ADHD. *Adapted Physical Activity Quarterly, 26*(2), 131–150.

Harvey, W. J., Wilkinson, S., Pressé, C., Joober, R., & Grizenko, N. (2012). Scrapbook interviewing and children with attention-deficit hyperactivity disorder. *Qualitative Research in Sport, Exercise, and Health, 4,* 62–79.

Harvey, W. J., Wilkinson, S., Pressé, C., Joober, R., & Grizenko, N. (2014). Children say the darndest things: Physical activity and children with attention-deficit hyperactivity disorder. *Physical Education and Sport Pedagogy, 19,* 205–220.

Johnson, R. B., Onwuegbuzie, A. J., & Turner, L. A. (2007). Toward a definition of mixed methods research. *Journal of Mixed Methods Research, 1*(2), 112–133.

Kincheloe, J. L. (2008). Critical pedagogy and knowledge wars of the 21st century. *The International Journal of Critical Pedagogy.* Retrieved from http://freire.education.mcgill.ca/ojs/public/journals/Galleys/IJCP011.pdf

Obrusnikova, I., & Dillon, S. (2011). Challenging situations when teaching children with autism spectrum disorders in general physical education. *Adapted Physical Activity Quarterly, 28,* 113–131.

Obrusnikova, I., & Miccinello, D. (2012). Parent perceptions of factors influencing after-school physical activity of children with autism spectrum disorders. *Adapted Physical Activity Quarterly, 29,* 63–80.

Reid, G. (2000). Future directions of inquiry in adapted physical activity. *Quest, 52,* 369–381.

Reid, G., Bouffard, M., & MacDonald, C. (2012). Creating evidence-based research in adapted physical activity. *Adapted Physical Activity Quarterly, 29*(115), 131.

Sherrill, C. (2004). *Adapted physical activity, recreation and sport: Crossdisciplinary and lifespan* (6th ed.). Boston: McGraw-Hill.

Shirazipour, C., Meehan, M., & Latimer-Cheung, A. (2017). An analysis of BBC television coverage of the 2014 Invictus games. *Adapted Physical Activity Quarterly, 34,* 33–54.

Sparkes, A. C., & Smith, B. (2014). *Qualitative research methods in sport, exercise and health.* New York: Routledge.

Strean, W. B. (1998). Identifying what we take for granted in our research: Suggestions for assumption hunters. *Adapted Physical Activity Quarterly, 15,* 278–284.

Tashakkori, A., & Teddlie, C. (Eds.). (2003). *Handbook of mixed methods in social & behavioral research.* Thousand Oaks: SAGE Publications.

Tashakkori, A., & Teddlie, C. (2006). Introduction to mixed method and mixed model studies in the social and behavioral sciences. In A. Bryman (Ed.), *SAGE benchmarks in social research methods: Mixed methods* (Vol. 2) (7–26). London: SAGE.

Thomas, J. R., Nelson, J. K., & Silverman, S. J. (2011). *Research methods in physical activity* (6th ed.). Champaign, IL: Human Kinetics.

Tsai, E. H. L., & Fung, L. (2009). Parents' experiences and decisions on inclusive sport participation of their children with intellectual disabilities. *Adapted Physical Activity Quarterly, 26*(2), 151–171.

Ulrich, D. A. (2000). *Test of gross motor development* (2nd ed.). Austin, TX: PRO-ED.

Verschuren, P. J. M. (2001). Holism versus reductionism in modern social science research. *Quality & Quantity, 35,* 389–405.

Wall, A. E., McClements, J., Bouffard, M., Findlay, H., & Taylor, M. J. (1985). A knowledge-based approach to motor development: Implications for the physically awkward. *Adapted Physical Activity Quarterly, 2,* 21–42.

Watkins, D., & Gioia, D. (2015). Mixed methods research. In *Pocket guides to social work research methods.* New York: Oxford University Press.

Watkinson, E. J., & Wasson, D. L. (1984). The use of single-subject time-series designs in adapted physical activity. *Adapted Physical Activity Quarterly, 1,* 19–29.

Wilkinson, S. (2017). Exploring complex relationships between leisure and people with complex mental health problems. Unpublished doctoral dissertation. McGill University, Montreal, Canada.

Zitomer, M. R., & Goodwin, D. (2014). Gauging the quality of qualitative research in adapted physical activity. *Adapted Physical Activity Quarterly, 31,* 193–218.

12

Single-subject research designs in adapted physical education

Jihyun Lee and Phillip Ward

Introduction

Research using single-subject designs has its roots in behavior analysis, a science which has both basic and applied fields (Cooper, Heron, & Heward, 2007). The philosophy of that science is called radical behaviorism (Skinner, 1974). In this chapter, we begin with a discussion of radical behaviorism and the fundamental principles of applied behavior analysis. Following this, we describe the characteristics and use of single-subject research designs in answering questions in adapted physical education (APE). We examine trends and issues related to the use of single-subject research designs in APE. We conclude with a summary of the core messages in the chapter and some reflection questions for readers.

Radical behaviorism

Radical behaviorism is a philosophy developed by B. F. Skinner to explain the assumptions underlying the practice of behavior analysis. In his books, Skinner (1953, 1966, 1974, 1975, 1981) described behavior analysis as a "selectionist" science, arguing that biology was its parent science. Selectionist science is defined by the control exerted on biological, behavioral, and cultural phenomena by the environment, which is operationalized as a consequence. At the biological level, selection occurs where some species' characteristics and not others are selected over the course of multiple generations (Glenn, 1988). For example, a species of birds may reproduce some that fly fast and some that fly slower. Over time, predators may catch and eat the slower birds, reducing their ability to reproduce their slow-flying characteristics. The faster-flying birds reproduce and create offspring that fly fast and, thus, become the most common kind of bird. In this way, the species is shaped by the environment; in this case, the ease with which predators can feed on slow-flying birds.

At the behavioral level, some behaviors are selected by the environment and others are not as a result of individual adaptation within the course of a lifetime (Skinner, 1974). For example, a child's behavior may be reinforced if he cries to get attention. Because the child does get the attention of a parent (i.e., the consequence of crying), the child continues to cry to get attention. Alternatively, a parent might ignore crying for the purpose of getting attention (i.e., a new consequence of crying), and the parent instead might teach appropriate ways to gain attention or may teach the child to be comfortable within a particular context. Similarly, a teacher may use a teaching technique that helps students learn effectively and efficiently. Because of this consequence, she may continue to use the teaching technique. In contrast, consider a teaching technique that a teacher uses for the first time and, in her judgment, it is an ineffective strategy, or it may be difficult to implement. She might not use it again. As such, that teaching technique would not survive as a teaching tool because of its consequences. The outcome is that actions that have successful consequences are repeated and those that have unsuccessful consequences may beused less or never.

Similarly, at the cultural level, cultural practices are selected or rejected because of their consequences (Harris, 1979). For example, depending on where you grow up in the world, you will speak a different language and engage in different cultural practices from someone who grew up in another part of the world. This represents an environmental influence on the reproduction of culture. Even within cultures, there is often significant variation, and that variation is itself a function of the sub-cultures that are operating (e.g., religious beliefs and political affiliation). Glenn (1991, p. 64) describes the relationship between biological, behavioral, and cultural selection:

> Behavioral selection and associated behavioral processes (1) emerged as a result of natural selection and (2) account for the content of individual repertoires. Cultural selection and associated cultural processes (1) emerged as a result of behavioral selection and (2) account for the content of cultural practices. Although individual repertoires may differ vastly, the same behavioral processes account for all of them; differences in content are the result of differences in the characteristics of the behavioral environment that account for each repertoire (in the context of individual genetic differences). Although the content of different cultural practices may differ vastly, the same processes account for all of the practices; differences in cultural content are the result of differences in the environment that accounts for the practices.

Radical behaviorism is frequently misunderstood. For example, many psychological textbooks and papers inaccurately represent the philosophy and the practice of behavior analysis (Schlinger, 2015; Todd & Morris, 1983). A common misunderstanding is that radical behaviorism eschews non-observable behavior, such as feelings and thinking, which it does not. Skinner called his philosophy of the science of behavior radical behaviorism in the sense that the term "radical" meant a comprehensive explanation of behavior (Skinner, 1974). Skinner's radical behaviorism:

> does not insist on truth by agreement and can, therefore, consider events taking place within the private world within the skin. It does not call these events unobservable, and it does not dismiss them as subjective. It simply questions the nature of the objects observed and the reliability of the observations. The position can be stated as follows: what is felt or introspectively observed is not some nonphysical world of consciousness, mind, or mental life but the observer's own body. This does not mean, as I shall show later, that introspection is a kind of physiological research, nor does it mean (and this is the heart of the argument) that what is felt or introspectively observed are the causes of behavior.
>
> (Skinner, 1974, pp. 18–19)

Thus, rather than acting as a causal agent of behavior, a private event is:

> At best no more than a link in the causal chain, and it is usually not even that. We may think before we act in the sense that we may behave covertly before we behave overtly, but our action is not an "expression" of the covert response or the consequence of it. The two are simply attributable to the same variables.
>
> *(Skinner, 1953, p. 279)*

To explain practically, consider a teacher observing a student's interaction with an instructional task. The teacher may think about an appropriate strategy to use to help the student learn the task, and then act accordingly. From a radical behaviorist perspective, the thinking and acting were occasioned by the teacher's observation of the student's interaction. In many cases, thinking is a behavior that occurs at the same time as a teacher's actions (e.g., feedback). Both are occasioned by observation, but thinking may not be part of the causal sequence for the resultant teacher behavior. From a radical behaviorist perspective, the skin is not a barrier in the examination of behavior. Skinner (1974) considered behavior that occurred outside of the skin "overt" and behavior inside of the skin "covert." His point was that regardless of where the behavior occurred, it was subject to the same principles. Skinner was most interested in an explanation of the behavior. Thus, relative to a covert behavior such as thinking, the question is not "Does thinking occur?" but, rather, "Why does it occur?" and "What are its distinguishing characteristics?" (Skinner, 1974).

Applied behavior analysis

Behavior analysis includes both basic and applied science. Basic laboratory research is known as the experimental analysis of behavior. Applied research is known as applied behavior analysis or, more commonly, by its acronym, ABA. The subject matter of this science is behavior. Behavior is defined as everything that a person does. This includes covert behavior, such as thinking and feeling, that a person can self-observe, as well as overt behavior, such as speaking, social interactions, and physical activity that others can observe. The purpose of behavior analysis is to seek explanation and description to enable the prediction and control of behavior.

Prediction allows teachers or researchers, for example, to expect what might happen in a student's learning on the basis of what they have observed in the past in similar situations (O'Donohue & Ferguson, 2001). Teachers often behave on the basis of their past experiences with similar situations. For example, a teacher who has had experience teaching children to catch a ball will also have had experience with which cues and prompts work in teaching the skill (this is the pedagogical content knowledge that the teacher "knows"). When teaching catching in the present, the teacher is likely to use the cues that worked in the past. Reflecting on what teaching techniques work is an example of everyday prediction. Such prediction may not work because the situation may have changed, or this particular student's difficulty with the skill may not be at all similar to what the teacher has encountered in the past with other students. The important point here is that while prediction may not always be accurate, it is still determined, though the causes may remain unclear without further examination (Chiesa, 2003).

Behavior analysis also seeks to examine the controlling variables (i.e., conditions) that occasion behavior. Such knowledge allows teachers and researchers to change the controlling variables to improve a situation. For many individuals, hearing the term "control" suggests to them some immoral purpose similar to manipulation. What is important to recognize is that knowing the controlling variables empowers individuals to pursue the change of the conditions in their own lives. For example, we often rely on the prediction of weather reports to control our dress for the next day, and we rely on our experiences in dealing with children or colleagues to allow us to control our actions as parents or peers. If one assumes orderly, rather than capricious, relations among phenomena, then one cannot step outside of the causal stream. As Skinner (1974, p. 209) explains, "We cannot choose a way of life in which there is no control. We can only change the controlling conditions." Thus, a person can, in this sense, control the world around her- or himself by controlling the conditions. For example, setting a schedule for oneself places priority on some events and less on others. A "to-do" list has the same effect. These changes allow individuals to manage how and where they spend their time.

Behavior analysis is an incredibly effective science, particularly in educational settings. To illustrate, consider the following example. Walberg (1984) conducted an analysis of 3000 studies on teacher and instructional effects on student achievement. The effects of behavioral teaching strategies such as cues, corrective feedback, and reinforcement were very large, with a mean effect size ranging from 0.88 to 1.17. In practical terms, this means that, in a normal distribution, students who began at the 50th percentile would have their score raised to the 84th percentile. Most parents, educators, and politicians would consider such an academic gain as substantive and socially significant.

Forness, Kavale, Blum, and Lloyd (1997) in their review of 18 meta-analyses that included more than 1000 research studies in special education, reported that behavioral interventions had a mean effect size of 0.93. As is the case with Walberg (1984), this represents a very large impact on student learning and behavior change. Though this is significant, what is more impressive is that the next most effective treatments in special education settings were pharmaceutical drugs, with an effect size of 0.58, half that reported for behavioral interventions. Using a behavioral intervention was shown to be not just effective, but twice as effective as using pharmaceutical drugs. Most parents, educators, and politicians would consider a choice between the use of pharmaceutical drugs versus the use of an educational intervention that was twice as effective as more ethical, less invasive, substantive, and, thus, socially significant.

Finally, one of the most effective public health and physical activity interventions is the Sports, Play, and Recreation for Kids (SPARK) curriculum (McKenzie & Rosengard, 2000). The SPARK curriculum is a school physical education curriculum that uses behavioral principles explicitly throughout its content to help teachers to teach and students to successfully meet elementary curriculum goals (McKenzie & Rosengard, 2000). Collectively, these analyses and the SPARK curriculum demonstrate that behavior analysis provides teachers with effective pedagogical practices that can educationally empower students across the entire curriculum, and for students with and without special needs.

Behavior analysis has created for teachers procedured and refined guidelines for what have become essential instructional elements, such as feedback, prompts, and cues (Cooper et al., 2007), as well as highly generalizable instructional strategies (e.g., Becker & Carnine, 1981; Forness et al., 1997; McKenzie & Rosengard, 2000; Walberg, 1984). Behavior analysis also has significantly contributed to a vision of an inclusive society with the development of technologies to enable individuals with disabilities to maximize the quality of their lives (Heward, 2003).

ABA, the applied science of behavior analysis and the science of most interest in this chapter, is defined by the following seven core characteristics (Cooper et al., 2007). First, ABA is applied, requiring that the behaviors to be changed must be meaningful behaviors that improve people's lives. Second, ABA is behavioral, requiring that research should be focused on the actual behavior, not a proxy or a construct, a behavior that can be observed and measured, and a behavior that can be verified through reliability measures. Third, ABA is analytic, requiring researchers to ensure methodologically that behavior change is a result of the independent variable. As such, the primary focus in single-subject research designs is on the internal validity of the design. Fourth, ABA is technological, requiring that descriptions of the procedures, including the independent variable, are detailed to allow the study to stand the test of being replicated by other researchers. Fifth, ABA is conceptually systematic, requiring the studies to be derived from the principles of behavior analysis. Sixth, ABA is effective, requiring that the behavior must be changed in clinically or socially significant ways. Seventh, ABA requires generality to be demonstrated to show that the behavior of interest can last over time or generalize to other behaviors or settings.

Why use single-subject research designs?

APE is provided to individuals with disabilities and uses specially designed instructions based on individual needs through assessments. Thus, APE research is likely to focus on an individual's response to the treatment component that purports to change behaviors of the individual. As Bouffard (1993) mentioned, an ultimate goal of adapted physical activity (APA) is to develop the most effective program for individuals, not a generally effective program for most people. A single-subject research design should not be chosen because of the challenge of recruiting a large group of people with similar characteristics. Rather, single-subject research is a robust way to demonstrate how an intervention or systematic manipulation of an intervention component would interact with, and change, the target behavior of a participant. This is an experimental research method that shows the intervention variable's causal effect on the target behavior. Thus, single-subject research is suitable for the purpose of APE.

One of the advantages of the use of single-subject designs in research is its high applicability to real practices. Researchers can focus on the effects of an instructional strategy that may change behaviors that are meaningful for the research participants. Different education goals are applied to different students with disabilities. Different goals include a different amount of changes and different types of behaviors. In this case, a group design study that aims to find a general effect of the instructional strategy on the same dimension of a behavior would not be useful. The instructional strategy may increase one behavior of a student, but may have an opposite effect on the same behavior of another student, or increase a different behavior of another student. APE takes individual differences among people into consideration when developing programs and applying instructional strategies because of the individual's needs and attributes that might interact with the treatment. People who need individualized and specialized programs and instructions are target populations of APE. Based on these purposes of APE, APE researchers may want to focus on different behaviors, depending on the educational goal of individual students. For example, an intervention may increase correct responses, on-task time, and more positive social interaction. Single-subject research allows researchers to see such differential effects of a variable on the same or different behaviors of participants. Single-subject research methods are also flexible in that the design allows researchers to have quick feedback and day-to-day /session-to-session feedback. This is different from other research methods that require researchers to wait for several days, weeks, or months to determine changes (e.g., pre-post designs).

In group designs (e.g., pre-post), the unit of analysis is the group. The assumption is that all individuals are similar. However, there might be some individuals showing varying reactions to the intervention. Bouffard (1997) argued that aggregating data in typical group-based research designs leads to a false conclusion that the treatment used was effective for all participants. In short, the averaging of data that occurs in group designs hides essential information on how individuals reacted to the treatment.

Bouffard (1997) and Rikli (1997) have argued that single-subject research designs are the first choice for researchers who decide to use a robust way to examine individual-level treatment effects and the interaction between the individual and corresponding environment in APE.

The history of single-subject designs in adapted physical education

Unfortunately, to our knowledge, no document has reported APE graduate training in ABA and single-subject research methods in countries other than the United States. In the United States, graduate education in APE has a relatively long history of training researchers to build skills and knowledge for scientific inquiry. According to DePauw and Sherrill (1994), several Master's and Doctorate programs to prepare professionals in APE were established in the United States, such as those at SUNY Brockport, Texas Woman's University (TWU) at Denton, and The Ohio State University (OSU), because of funding from the federal legislation in 1969. Dunn and McCubbin (1991) reported that there were 12 institutions in the United States from which two more doctoral dissertations in APE were produced. Among those programs, the University of Michigan, OSU, Oregon State University, TWU, and the University of Virginia have included some training for single-subject research in their graduate programs. John Dunn (at that time at the University of Utah and later Oregon State University) and Ron French (then at TWU) published a number of articles and books about behavior management and operant conditioning in physical education and APE. Ron French and Barry Lavay (California State University, Long Beach) strengthened their undergraduate (i.e., California State University, Long Beach) and graduate (i.e., TWU) curricula by emphasizing behavior management and ABA components in the coursework (e.g., Dunn & Fredericks, 1985; Dunn & French, 1982; Lavay, Henderson, French, & Guthrie, 2012).

Beginning in the late 1990s, French and Lavay wrote numerous articles and book chapters emphasizing the importance of behavior management in APE and in integrated physical education and applying principles of ABA (e.g., Block, Henderson, & Lavay, 2016; French, Henderson, Lavay, & Silliman-French, 2014; Lavay et al., 2012). Lavay, French, and Henderson (2015) also wrote a textbook titled *Positive Behavior Management in Physical Activity Settings*, and it has been widely used in physical education teacher education undergraduate and graduate courses in the United States.

In special education research, single-subject designs are the most frequently used methodology (Mastropieri et al., 2009). Despite the history of ABA and single-subject research in APE graduate training (Sherrill & DePauw, 1997), increasingly fewer programs are training their graduates in this science and methodology. This has resulted in fewer single-subject designs used in the APE research field. An analysis of 562 APA abstracts published under special populations in American Alliance for Health, Physical Education, and Dance (AAHPERD, now SHAPE America) conventions from 1968 to 2004 showed that approximately 7% of the abstracts ($n = 38$) were identified as studies using "time series" designs (Zhang, deLisle, & Chen, 2006). It is not clear if the term "time series" used in their analysis encompassed all other single-subject designs or multiple baseline designs only, but the portion of the "time series" was very small compared to other research designs. More recently, Haegele,

Lee, and Porretta (2015) conducted an analysis of research designs used in the journal *Adapted Physical Activity Quarterly* (*APAQ*) between 2004 and 2014 and reported 3% ($n = 5$) of the studies used single-subject research designs compared to 70% ($n = 127$) using group designs. Neither of these analyses is a comprehensive review of the literature, but they are a snapshot that reveals to what extent APE studies have used single-subject designs and provided evidence that there are few single-subject designs being used to analyze data in APE.

Basic features of single-subject research designs

Single-subject research designs focus on the following aspects: (a) the individual participant serving as their own control, (b) the intervention effects judged for each individual and, thus, unlike group designs, there is no need for confidence intervals or margins of error because sampling or aggregating of behavior is eschewed in favor of capturing all instances of the behavior occurring in the setting, (c) the internal validity of studies with the goal of demonstrating meaningful and significant effects as a result of rigorous methodological control for testing educational and behavioral interventions, (d) the elucidation of behavioral processes between the dependent and independent variables, and (e) cost-effectiveness of a study that further guides larger-scale research efforts (Cooper et al., 2007; Horner et al., 2005). The goal of single-subject research is to demonstrate changes in behavior that occur only by the systematic, experimental manipulation of variables in the environment. When predicted behavior change occurs due to a variable responsible for the observed change in the target behavior, experimental control is achieved and a functional relation between the behavior and the variable is established (Baer, Wolf, & Risley, 1968; Cooper et al., 2007). In the following sections, we explain the basic structure of single-subject research, including selecting target behaviors and basic design features.

Target behavior

Single-subject designs require the repeated measurement of all instances of a behavior or behaviors *across* a setting over time, such as all the lessons in an instructional unit. As such, data are seldom sampled across sessions. However, as we will show next, the process of data collection *within* a session or lesson is often sampled as a result of the measurement strategy used to collect the data. Interval recording systems require a coder to make a decision about the behavior that occurred most in a short period of observations, usually six or ten seconds. Interval recording and momentary time sampling strategies may overestimate or underestimate behaviors, not only in terms of the coding conventions (e.g., the behavior reported at the sixth second is reported as having occurred for the six seconds and other behaviors are underestimated), but also because the system requires observation of a period of time followed by recording of the behavior for similar amount of time. As such, only 50% of the lesson time is devoted to actually coding (Cooper et al., 2007).

Basic designs

Withdrawal design

A withdrawal design typically entails three phases, including (a) an initial baseline phase (no intervention), (b) a treatment phase (intervention), and (c) a return to baseline phase (no intervention) by withdrawing the independent variable. This is described as an A-B-A design, and this design can be strengthened by adding one more "B (treatment)" condition to become an A-B-A-B design in which the treatment effect is replicated. This design is known as the most powerful within-subject design (Cooper et al., 2007). Variations of the withdrawal designs are common. A multiple-treatment withdrawal design, such as A-B-C-A-C, is a variation of the A-B-A-B design and uses two more experimental conditions to compare their effects to baseline or one another (Cooper et al., 2007). Withdrawal designs are used for reversible behavior. Those behaviors are likely to change immediately based on the context or stimuli. Behaviors that involve learning effects (e.g., skill learning) are hard to reverse and not appropriate to be measured using these designs. If the behavior is not reversible, researchers should use different designs, such as a multiple-baseline design. Another important aspect to consider when applying a withdrawal design is if withdrawing intervention effects (going back to the baseline) would be ethically and educationally appropriate. An example is self-injurious and aggressive behaviors that can be dangerous to the subject and other students as a target behavior. To minimize practical and ethical concerns, a very brief period of withdrawal (returning to baseline) can be applied.

Multiple-baseline design

This design involves a time-lagged application of treatment variables to the same behaviors of two or more participants. Baseline data are obtained from participants, and the intervention is introduced to the first participant while maintaining baseline conditions for the participants. When the target behavior of the first participant has reached the predetermined criterion level, or change in the target behavior is obvious and stable enough, the intervention would be introduced to the second participant while maintaining the treatment conduction for the first participant and the baseline conduction for other participants. This procedure would be repeated until all participants receive the intervention. In a multiple-baseline design, the independent variable's function for the change of the target behavior is inferred by the lack of changes in untreated behaviors. Verification is established by demonstrating a lack of change in a behavior when an independent variable has not been introduced. In a multiple-baseline design across subjects, each subject does not serve as his or her own control. This means that the verification of the prediction in a multiple-baseline design is only possible by looking to see if other behaviors remained unchanged (Cooper et al., 2007). Thus, the verification and replication of the intervention effects are somewhat weaker and less direct than a withdrawal design. In order to compensate for this weakness, a multiple-baseline design shows its experimental control between the intervention and target responses in a series of subjects. Thus, demonstrating replication is essential in this design, and it is achieved by the successful inference of intervention effects obtained from similar changes in the behavior of other subjects when they are under the influence of the intervention.

Sometimes, applying the same starting point of baseline (concurrent data collection across baselines) for all participants may not be practically possible, or may not be ethical, as in the case where self-injurious behaviors might be occurring. However, non-concurrent data collection across baselines or a non-sequential introduction of intervention across participants may severely weaken the internal validity of the study. A better design strategy, for the case where continuous data collections or the same starting point of baseline across participants is impossible, is to sample across days by adding probe measures (Horner & Baer, 1978). Visual analysis is used to determine if changes in the participant's behaviour occur when the independent variable is introduced and there are no changes in the behavior of the participants who have not yet received the independent variable. This is continued for at least two more participants to demonstrate that changes occurred only in the presence of the independent variable. Multiple baseline designs are often used when dealing with behaviors that cannot be unlearned, such as catching, as opposed to moderate to vigorous physical activity (MVPA) that can be influenced by the organization of instruction.

Multi-element/alternating treatments design

The multi-element design (Hains & Baer, 1989), also known as an alternating treatment design, is used to compare the effects of two or more interventions on a target behavior. These variables may be introduced and altered on a daily basis, in separate sessions within the same day, or even within one session. In this design, internal validity is established when different levels of behavior are observed corresponding to different interventions. Hains and Baer (1989) explain that this design is simply a fast-paced withdrawal design and has the ability to compare the effects of the variables "within the context of uncontrolled and controllable background variables" (p. 57). This design is based on the participant's stimulus discrimination focusing on the independent responding to distinct stimulus (intervention). The data are presented independently for each intervention to enable direct comparison between the interventions (Barlow & Hayes, 1979). The differential effects of interventions can be determined by the vertical distance between the data paths from two or more interventions. If there are no overlaps between two data paths, it can be interpreted that the two interventions have differential effects. Researchers who use this design recognize its advantages, in that treatment withdrawal is not needed and it is suitable for behaviors that tend to show high variability. However, this design also has weaknesses. First, experimental control between two treatments does not always indicate socially significant behavior changes (Cooper et al., 2007). Second, this design has several factors that pose internal validity threats due to the application of multiple types of interventions which may result in multiple-treatment interference. Multiple-treatment interference (Barlow & Hersen, 1984) refers to the effects of one treatment on a subject's behavior being confounded by the influence of another treatment. The possible interaction effects include sequence effects and carryover effects due to the order or sequence of the series of treatments (sequence effects) and rapidly alternated multiple treatments affecting the adjacent treatment (carryover effects). Researchers recommend studies using this design randomize the order of the different interventions, counterbalance treatments, and use slower or more discriminable alternations to minimize multiple-treatment interference (Barlow & Hersen, 1984). Researchers who use this design should address potential interaction effects and carefully interpret the results.

Changing criterion design

The changing criterion design is an effective way to evaluate the effects of a treatment on step-wise changes in the rate, frequency, accuracy, duration, or latency of a single target behavior (Cooper et al., 2007). This design begins with an initial baseline observation on a single target behavior. Then, the implementation of a series of treatment phases in each of which a different criterion rate for the target behavior is applied in a step-wise fashion. The repeated production of new rates of the target behavior is followed as a function of manipulation of the independent variable, which is a step-wise change in criterion rate for the target behavior (Hartmann & Hall, 1976). In this design, each phase serves as a baseline for the following phase. Therefore, the experimental control is demonstrated when the rate of the target behavior changes is followed by each step-wise change in the criterion or the levels of responding do not change, regardless of varying the length of phases. Replication is made when each step-wise change in criterion results in systematic behavior change to a new criterion. This design is appropriate to show gradual behavior changes associated with criterion changes. It is important to note that this design can be used only when the target behavior already exists in the participant's repertoire (Cooper et al., 2007). When varying the size of criterion changes, the researchers should use an achievable criterion and consider potential ceiling effects (Cooper et al., 2007).

Single-subject research designs in APE

In this chapter, we discussed only studies written in English and focused on school-aged children in K-12 integrated physical education or APE settings, or their teachers. Thus, studies published in other languages and studies that used intervention programs that were not conducted in integrated physical education or APE settings were not addressed. APE studies have been conducted in preschool physical education, special school classrooms or self-contained classroom settings (e.g., adult day-cares, group homes), and therapeutic programs (e.g., Casey, Quenneville-Himbeault, Normore, Davis, & Martell, 2015). In addition, we did not intend to address studies with non-educational topics such as the use of an exercise intervention to reduce stereotypic behaviors in children with autism.

The majority of APE single-subject research has focused on peers without disabilities as a behavior change agent. Such tendency has been reported in other reviews (Block & Obrusnikova, 2007; Qi & Ha, 2012; Ward & Barrett, 2002). Thus, studies have been conducted to examine the effects of peer-tutoring or peer-tutoring training on the behavior of students with disabilities. The most common form of peer-tutoring is one-on-one peer tutoring in the context of a physical education lesson (e.g., Houston-Wilson, Dunn, van der Mars, & McCubbin, 1997; Lieberman, Dunn, van der Mars, & McCubbin, 2000; Webster, 1987). In these conditions, a typically developing peer is trained to assist a student with disabilities. Ward and Ayvazo's (2006) study used class-wide peer tutoring, an established peer tutoring intervention widely used in education and special education settings. Class-wide peer tutoring in Ward and Ayvazo involved all students in the class, in this case, those with mild to moderate autism or without disabilities peer teaching each other. Social cognitive theory-based interventions (Haegele & Porretta, 2017) were also conducted using a program called "Plan for Exercise, Plan for Health" (Stevens, 2006), which consisted of nine social cognitive theory constructs-infused instructional lessons during physical education.

The descriptions of independent variables and intervention procedures allow researchers to directly or systematically replicate a study in the future. For example, the procedures and components of peer training should be described, including how much time is used to train peer tutors and detailed instructional components such as cueing and modeling (e.g., Houston-Wilson et al., 1997; Lieberman et al., 2000; Webster, 1987), or social components such as friendly behaviors, soft talking, and providing praise (e.g., Klavina & Block, 2008). The internal validity of these studies can be enhanced by ensuring the peer tutors' capability of delivering their tutoring as planned/trained. These include a written exam (Houston-Wilson et al., 1997; Lieberman et al., 2000); peer tutor checklist (Klavina & Block, 2008); practice and rehearsal (Ward & Ayvazo, 2006); and an evaluation of role-playing based on scenarios (Houston-Wilson et al., 1997).

The dependent variables in APE single-subject studies have included proxy and direct measures of learning. Proxy measures of learning are academic learning time in physical education (ALT-PE) variables (Siedentop, Tousignant, & Parker, 1982) or modified ALT-PE (i.e., Basic-Academic Learning Time-Adapted Physical Education [B-ALT-APE]; Wallstrom, Walsh, Jansma, & Porretta, 1993) such as increasing on-task behavior or time devoted to successful performances (Murata & Jansma, 1997; Webster, 1987; Wiskochil, Lieberman, Houston-Wilson, & Petersen, 2007). Direct measures of student learning are the presence or absence of critical elements in the performance of basic skills such as catching, throwing, striking, and jumping (Houston-Wilson et al., 1997; Ward & Ayvazo, 2006). Similar to ALT-PE, increased MVPA has also been measured in APE. Lieberman et al. (2000) examined the effects of peer tutors on increasing MVPA in lessons using the System for Observing Fitness Time (SOFIT) instrument (McKenzie, Sallis, & Nader, 1991). The behaviors of peers in the class, tutors, and teachers were also measured in some studies (Klavina, 2008; Klavina & Block, 2008; Murata & Jansma, 1997). Haegele and Porretta (2017) measured accumulated daily steps through utilizing a pedometer during after-school hours.

Dependent variables in APE single-subject studies have been measured using both time-based or frequency-based methods, depending on the types of behaviors observed. If the behavior can be measured by duration, such as on-task behavior, then the ALT-PE systematic observation system (e.g., Siedentop et al., 1982) that uses a partial interval method (e.g., Klavina, 2008; Klavina & Block, 2008; Murata & Jansma, 1997) or the SOFIT instrument (McKenzie et al., 1991) that uses momentary time sampling technique (Lieberman et al., 2000) would be appropriate. Data are also collected without sampling when all instances of the behavior can be counted with ease. Counting the occurrence of a behavior, such as the number of correct throws or catches, is reported as a frequency per period of time, such as a lesson segment or lesson as a whole (e.g., Houston-Wilson et al., 1997; Ward & Ayvazo, 2006).

Trends and issues

APE single-subject studies have used small sample sizes ranging from two to eight participants aged 8–21 years and in grade levels from kindergarten to high school. The disabilities of the participants have varied and included intellectual disabilities (Houston-Wilson et al., 1997; Klavina & Block, 2008; Murata & Jansma, 1997; Webster, 1987); autism (Ward & Ayvazo, 2006); deafness (Lieberman et al., 2000); visual impairments (Haegele & Porretta, 2017; Wiskochil et al., 2007); cerebral palsy (Klavina & Block, 2008); and Prader-Willi syndrome (Houston-Wilson et al., 1997). The settings of most prior studies were integrated physical education classes, except two studies (i.e., Haegele & Porretta, 2017; Webster, 1987) that were conducted in APE settings. In judging trends from the APE single-subject studies examined in this chapter, we conclude that: (a) integrated physical education settings were mostly used, (b) the majority of these studies focused on the effect of interactions with, or instructions from (trained or untrained) peers, (c) the most commonly used designs were multiple baseline designs, and (d) all of the studies were conducted in the United States and, as such, may not represent international perspectives. A major conclusion is that we are limited in what we can say about trends with only nine studies. There are, however, a number of issues regarding APE single-subject research that we have identified that should guide future studies.

Internal validity

First, the strength of the APE single-subject studies we reviewed is that we are able to discuss a similar goal in each study that is the improvement of learning or behavior as a function of peer tutoring, theory-based physical education lessons, or instructional conditions. However, while the studies did show positive changes from baseline to intervention phases, there were a number of threats to the internal validity of the results. The internal validity of most of the studies should be considered weak. The main error in many of the designs was the use of baselines and intervention phases that were too short to establish stability within each phase or condition. The problem was most evident in the multiple baseline design studies that did not collect data continuously during the baseline phases. The studies used delayed strategies that, in our view, were not warranted. Baseline length with a minimum of five data points is recommended for a study to be considered high quality based on the standards elaborated by the What Works Clearinghouse team (Kratochwill et al., 2010). However, it is a suggested standard and researchers must make a reasonable decision as to when the treatment should be introduced. For example, given ethical and safety concerns with self-injurious behavior, a baseline phase of fewer than five data points may be appropriate and a design that does not require a baseline can be used.

A second challenge to internal validity lies in insufficient demonstrations of experimental control. Horner et al. (2005) suggested a specific criterion to evaluate the quality of the experimental control: "three demonstrations of the experimental effect at three different points in time with a single participant (within-subject replication), or across different participants" (p. 168). In the studies using multiple baseline designs, the intervention phase should be introduced in a staggered fashion to show the experimental control and its replications across behaviors or participants. In some studies, the researchers used the same length of baseline or very few data points to stagger the baseline (e.g., Lieberman et al., 2000; Wiskochil et al., 2007). Without staggering, the third comparison after the second AB comparison is not possible, and this weakens the reassurance for change in the responding as a function of the independent variable.

A third threat to the internal validity are high levels of variability previously reported within each phase or condition that resulted in comparisons across conditions to be confounded because of overlapping data points. This often occurred regardless of the design that was used. Variability is highly related to the number of data points. The more variability, the more data points are needed to determine the pattern of the variability. Some studies (e.g., Murata & Jansma, 1997) showed significantly high variability in both baseline and intervention phases and led us to conclude that there were influences on the behavior not accounted for in the study. Failure to control variables can reduce confidence that changes are caused by the intervention, not by other factors, and becomes a threat to internal validity. For example, use of different activities across sessions and phases (e.g., Murata & Jansma, 1997; Webster, 1987) can cause variability as the literature showing that the dependent variables (i.e., ALT-PE) could be significantly affected by activity type (Metzler, 1979). Cooper et al. (2007) explain that a highly variable pattern of data does not demonstrate enough stability upon which design decisions can be made. The problem is that the data are not able to show the nature of the relationship between the condition and the response (Johnston & Pennypacker, 2009).

A fourth threat is that the effects of the improvement from baselines to intervention phases were, in terms of the magnitude of effect, typically weak to moderate. The evaluation of the magnitude of any changes in dependent variables caused by the treatment should include the meaningfulness of the changes in practice, social validity, and ethical concerns. APE single-subject studies in general tended to not mention these aspects of the results.

A fifth threat identified to internal validity appears to lie in presenting data correctly using visual analysis guidelines. Many studies used an incorrect visual representation of labels and legends for phases, and vertical dashed lines for conditions, data points. In one study, in particular, the researchers reported that a multiple-baseline design was used, but no line graphs were shown, and the data were aggregated and reported using histograms, making a determination of internal validity impossible and violating the procedures of the multiple-baseline design. Our recommendation is that future research using single-subject designs in APE should focus on improving the internal validity of the designs with the goal of demonstrating strong experimental control and improving a visual representation of the data.

External validity

None of the studies we reviewed could be considered systemic replications of other studies. This fact represents a significant limitation in the research because science advances based on the work of previous research, and it is essential for believability that studies are replicated by other investigators to show that they, too, could produce effects following the same procedures. As such, there is little evidence in this body of research to argue for external validity and clearly this ought to be an important goal of future research in APE.

Finally, we noted early in this chapter that research using single-subject designs has its roots in behavior analysis and that ABA is defined by seven core characteristics (Cooper et al., 2007). These studies should be applied, behavioral, analytic, technological, conceptually systematic, effective, and require generality. In judging the APE single-subject studies, we have reported that the majority of studies focused on peer tutoring in integrated settings. The researchers chose observable behaviors, and this meets the criterion of behavior. The researchers also were analytic in the data collection and analysis as well as technological, for the most part, in their descriptions of their procedures. These are clear strengths of the studies. The studies were effective, though, because of threats to internal validity, this judgment is limited. However, most studies were lacking in the criterion of being conceptually systematic that requires studies to be derived from the principles of behavior analysis. There was a black box in studies that failed to report the behavioral principles or processes they were investigating, or even non-behavioral principles. In short, there was an absence of theory. Future studies ought to be clearly grounded in the principles of behavior analysis and theory.

Conclusion

In this chapter, we focused on the basic features of single-subject research and its use in the APE research field. We provided a brief evaluation on single-subject research in the APE field to provide future recommendations. It is clear that very few studies are being conducted in APE using single-subject designs, and this runs counter to the trends in special education. Possible explanations for the limited use of single-subject designs in APE research would be (a) the absence of both the study of behavior analysis and single-subject research methodology in doctoral training, and (b) journals or reviewers who may not be accepting of single-subject research designs and this, in turn, may be a function of the former rationale. Despite these challenges, single-subject research is an ideal research methodology in the field of APE. The purpose of APE is well aligned with the focus and assumption of single-subject research. We hope this chapter might create a fertile base for a very lively discussion on the evaluation of the quality of behavioral research practice in the APE field and what constitutes good scientific practice in the APE field when single-subject research designs are used.

Summary of key points

- Single-subject research designs are grounded in the science of applied behavior analysis.
- Single-subject research designs are particularly useful in APE contexts because the individual serves as his or her own control, allowing individuals rather than groups to be examined.
- The strengths of single-subject research designs include a strong demonstration of the internal validity of the research.
- Visual presentation of the data is used in single-subject research designs to evaluate the effects of the intervention.
- There have been few single-subject research studies conducted in K-12 APE settings compared to statistical group designs.
- The most studied area in APE is the use of peer tutoring.
- Many studies in APE lack systematic replication of the findings and this limits the external validity of effects.

Reflective questions

- What are the criteria for applied behavior analytic studies?
- Why is single-subject research a good strategy to use in APE research?
- What factors within APE research contexts interact with behaviors and cause variability?
- What are socially important behaviors in APE research and how can they be explored using single-subject research? Provide some examples for variables and conditions.

References

Baer, D. M., Wolf, M. M., & Risley, T. R. (1968). Some current dimensions of applied behavior analysis. *Journal of Applied Behavior Analysis, 1,* 91–97.

Barlow, D. H., & Hayes, S. C. (1979). Alternating treatments design: One strategy for comparing the effects of two treatments in a single subject. *Journal of Applied Behavior Analysis, 12*(2), 199–210.

Barlow, D. H., & Hersen, M. (1984). *Single-case experimental designs: Strategies for studying behavior change* (2nd ed.). New York: Pergamon Press.

Becker, W. C., & Carnine, D. W. (1981). Direct instruction: A behavior theory model for comprehensive educational intervention with the disadvantaged. In S. W. Bijou & R. Ruiz (Eds.), *Behavior modification: Contributions to education* (pp. 145–210). Hillsdale, NJ: Lawrence Erlbaum.

Block, M. E., Henderson, H., & Lavay, B. (2016). Positive behavior support of children with challenging behaviors. In M. E. Block (Ed.), *A teacher's guide to including students with disabilities in general physical education* (4th ed.) (305–332). Baltimore, MD: Paul H. Brooke.

Block, M. E., & Obrusnikova, I. (2007). Inclusion in physical education: A review of the literature from 1995–2005. *Adapted Physical Education Quarterly, 24*(2), 103–124.

Bouffard, M. (1993). The perils of averaging data in adapted physical activity research. *Adapted Physical Activity Quarterly, 10,* 371–391.

Bouffard, M. (1997). Using old research ideas to study contemporary problems in adapted physical activity. *Measurement in Physical Education and Exercise Science, 1*(1), 71–87.

Casey, A. F., Quenneville-Himbeault, G., Normore, A., Davis, H., & Martell, S. G. (2015). A therapeutic skating intervention for children with autism spectrum disorder. *Pediatric Physical Therapy, 27,* 170–177.

Chiesa, M. (2003). Implications of determinism: Personal responsibility and the value of science. In K. A. Lattal & P. N. Chase (Eds.), *Behavior theory and philosophy* (pp. 243–258). New York, NY: Kluwer Academic/Plenum Publishers.

Cooper, J. O., Heron, T. E., & Heward, W. L. (2007). *Applied behavior analysis* (2nd ed.). Upper Saddle River, NJ: Pearson.

DePauw, K. P., & Sherrill, C. (1994). Adapted physical activity: Present and future. *Physical Education Review, 17*, 6–13.

Dunn, J. M., & Fredericks, H. D. B. (1985). The utilization of behavior management in mainstreaming in physical education. *Adapted Physical Activity Quarterly, 2*, 338–346.

Dunn, J. M., & French, R. (1982). Operant conditioning: A tool for special physical educators in the 1980s. *Exceptional Education Quarterly, 3*(1), 42–53.

Dunn, J. M., & McCubbin, J. A. (1991). Preparation of leadership personnel in adapted physical education. *Adapted Physical Activity Quarterly, 8*, 128–135.

Forness, S. R., Kavale, K. A., Blum, I., & Lloyd, J. W. (1997). What works in special education and related services: Using meta-analysis to guide practice. *Teaching Exceptional Children, 29*(6), 4–9.

French, R., Henderson, H., Lavay, B., & Silliman-French, L. (2014). Use of intrinsic and extrinsic motivation in adapted physical education. *Palaestra, 28*(3), 32–37.

Glenn, S. S. (1988). Contingencies and metacontingencies: Toward a synthesis of behavior analysis and cultural materialism. *The Behavior Analyst, 11*, 161–179.

Glenn, S. S. (1991). Contingencies and meta-contingencies: Relations among behavioral cultural, and biological evolution. In P. A. Lamal (Ed.), *Behavioral analysis of societies and cultural practice* (pp. 39–73). New York: Hemisphere.

Haegele, J. A., Lee, J., & Porretta, D. L. (2015). Research trends in *Adapted Physical Activity Quarterly* from 2004 to 2013. *Adapted Physical Activity Quarterly, 32*(3), 187–205.

Haegele, J. A., & Porretta, D. L. (2017). A theory-based physical education intervention for adolescents with visual impairments. *Journal of Visual Impairment & Blindness, 112*(1), 77–84.

Hains, A. H., & Baer, D. M. (1989). Interaction effects in multielement designs: Inevitable, desirable, and ignorable. *Journal of Applied Behavior Analysis, 22*(1), 57–69.

Harris, M. (1979). *Cultural materialism.* New York: Random House.

Hartmann, D. P., & Hall, R. V. (1976). The changing criterion design. *Journal of Applied Behavior Analysis, 9*, 527–532.

Heward, W. L. (2003). *Exceptional children: An introduction to special education edition* (7th ed.). Upper Saddle River, NJ: Prentice Hall.

Horner, R. D., & Baer, D. M. (1978). Multiple-probe technique: A variation on the multiple baseline design. *Journal of Applied Behavior Analysis, 11*, 189–196.

Horner, R. H., Carr, E. G., Halle, J., McGee, G., Odom, S., & Wolery, M. (2005). The use of single-subject research to identify evidence-based practice in special education. *Exceptional Children, 71*(2), 165–179.

Houston-Wilson, C., Dunn, J. M., van der Mars, H., & McCubbin, J. (1997). The effect of peer tutors on motor performance in integrated physical education classes. *Adapted Physical Activity Quarterly, 14*, 298–313.

Johnston, J. M., & Pennypacker, H. S., Jr. (2009). *Strategies and tactics of behavioral research* (3rd ed.). New York: Routledge/Taylor & Francis Group.

Klavina, A. (2008). Using peer-mediated instructions for students with severe and multiple disabilities in inclusive physical education: A multiple case study. *European Journal of Adapted Physical Activity, 1*, 7–19.

Klavina, A., & Block, M. (2008). The effect of peer-tutoring on interaction behaviors in inclusive physical education. *Adapted Physical Activity Quarterly, 25*, 132–158.

Kratochwill, T. R., Hitchcock, J., Horner, R. H., Levin, J. R., Odom, S. L., Rindskopf, D. M., & Shadish, W. R. (2010). Single-case designs technical documentation. Retrieved from What Works Clearinghouse website: http://ies.ed.gov/ncee/wwc/pdf/wwc_scd.pdf.

Lavay, B., French, R., & Henderson, H. (2015). *Positive behavior management in physical activity settings* (3rd ed.). Champaign, IL: Human Kinetics.

Lavay, B., Henderson, H., French, R., & Guthrie, S. (2012). Behavior management instructional practices and content of college/university physical education teacher education (PETE) programs. *Physical Education and Sport Pedagogy, 17*(2), 195–210.

Lieberman, L. J., Dunn, J. M., van der Mars, H., & McCubbin, J. (2000). Peer tutors' effects on activity levels of deaf students in inclusive elementary physical education. *Adapted Physical Activity Quarterly, 17*, 20–39.

Mastropieri, M. A., Berkeley, S., McDuffie, K. A., Graff, H., Marshak, L., Conners, N. A., … Cuenca-Sanchez, Y. (2009). What is published in the field of special education? Analysis of 11 prominent journals. *Exceptional Children, 76*, 95–109.

McKenzie, T., & Rosengard, P. (2000). *SPARK physical education program grades 3-6.* San Diego: San Diego State University Foundation.

McKenzie, T. L., Sallis, J. F., & Nader, P. R. (1991). SOFIT: System for observing fitness instruction time. *Journal of Teaching in Physical Education, 11,* 195–205.

Metzler, M. (1979). The measurement of academic learning time in physical education (Doctoral Dissertation, The Ohio State University). *Dissertation Abstracts International, 40,* 536A. (University Microfilm No. 8009314).

Murata, N. M., & Jansma, P. (1997). Influence of support personnel on students with and without disabilities in general physical education. *Clinical Kinesiology, 51,* 37–46.

O'Donohue, W., & Ferguson, K. E. (2001). *The psychology of B. F. Skinner.* Thousand Oaks, CA: Sage.

Qi, J., & Ha, A. (2012). Inclusion in physical education: A review of literature. *International Journal of Disability, Development and Education, 59*(3), 257–281.

Rikli, R. (1997). Measurement challenges in assessing special populations: Implications for behavioral research in adapted physical activity. *Measurement in Physical Education and Exercise Science, 1,* 117–126.

Schlinger, H. D. (2015). Training graduate students to effectively disseminate behavior analysis and to counter misrepresentations. *Behavior Analysis in Practice, 8,* 110–112.

Sherrill, C., & DePauw, K. P. (1997). Adapted physical activity and education. In J. D. Massengale & R. A. Swanson (Eds.), *The history of exercise and sport science* (pp. 39–108). Champaign, IL: Human Kinetics.

Siedentop, D., Tousignant, M., & Parker, M. (1982). *Academic learning time physical education - 1982 revision manual.* Columbus: School of Health, Physical Education, and Recreation, The Ohio State University.

Skinner, B. F. (1953). *Science and human behavior.* New York: Appleton-century-Crofts.

Skinner, B. F. (1966). The phylogeny and ontogency of behavior. *Science, 153,* 1205–1213.

Skinner, B. F. (1974). *About behaviorism.* London: Jonathan Cape.

Skinner, B. F. (1975). The shaping of phylogenic behavior. *Acta Neurobiologiae Experimentalis, 35,* 409–415.

Skinner, B. F. (1981). Selection by consequences. *Science, 213,* 501–504.

Stevens, E. (2006). *Evaluation of a social cognitive theory-based adolescent physical activity intervention: Plan for exercise, plan for health.* Columbus: Ohio State University.

Todd, J. T., & Morris, E. K. (1983). The misrepresentation of behavior analysis in psychology textbooks: Misconception and miseducation. *The Behavior Analyst, 6,* 153–160.

Walberg, H. J. (1984). Improving the productivity of America's schools. *Educational Leadership, 41,* 19–27.

Wallstrom, T., Walsh, M., Jansma, P., & Porretta, D. (1993). Supervision in adapted physical education: The Ohio State University adapted physical education intern evaluation form. *NCPERID Advocate, 21,* 4.

Ward, P., & Ayvazo, S. (2006). Classwide peer tutoring in physical education: Assessing its effects with kindergartners with autism. *Adapted Physical Activity Quarterly, 23,* 233–244.

Ward, P., & Barrett, T. (2002). A review of behavior analysis research in physical education. *Journal of Teaching in Physical Education, 21*(3), 242–266.

Webster, G. E. (1987). influence of peer tutors upon academic learning time–physical education of mentally handicapped children. *Adapted Physical Activity Quarterly, 6,* 393–403.

Wiskochil, B., Lieberman, L. J., Houston-Wilson, C., & Petersen, S. (2007). The effects of trained peer tutors on the physical education of children who are visually impaired. *Journal of Visual Impairment & Blindness, 101*(6), 339–350.

Zhang, J., deLisle, L., & Chen, S. (2006). Analysis of AAHPERD research abstracts published under special populations from 1968 to 2004. *Adapted Physical Activity Quarterly, 23*(2), 203–217.

13

Systematic reviews and meta-analysis

Xihe Zhu

Systematic reviews summarize available evidence pertaining to a research question or phenomenon, while statistical pooling and re-analyzing of findings to reach statistical estimates is called meta-analysis (Gough, Thomas, & Oliver, 2012; Montori, Swiontkowski, & Cook, 2003). Philosophically, both systematic reviews and meta-analyses are positivistic in that (a) both approaches rely on existing empirical articles, and (b) researchers using these methods often use deductive analyses (Comte, 1855). Regardless of the approach used by the existing articles (i.e., qualitative or quantitative), researchers consider the empirical primary studies as recorded observations. In other words, these articles have to exist objectively based on prescribed criteria. Researchers conducting systematic reviews and meta-analyses do not interact with the participants; rather, they review, categorize, analyze, and evaluate the primary studies as objectively as possible using sound logic and deductive approaches.

Systematic reviews and meta-analyses share similar steps, such as formulating research questions, conducting a literature search, and findings extraction, whereas they differ on analytical protocols. In this chapter, I first describe the similar steps for systematic reviews and meta-analysis. I also briefly describe analytics approaches separately where systematic reviews and meta-analysis diverge. I then describe commonly used protocols for quality control and tools and protocols that are available for researchers to conduct systematic reviews and meta-analyses. Finally, I summarize select, recent, systematic reviews and meta-analyses conducted among individuals with disabilities.

Conducting systematic reviews and meta-analyses

Currently, the most commonly used guideline for systematic review and meta-analyses is perhaps the Preferred Reporting Items for Systematic Reviews and Meta-Analyses (PRISMA, Moher, Liberati, Tetzlaff, Altman, & Group, 2009). PRISMA has a dedicated website hosting its statement, protocols, and other practical documents, such as sample flowcharts and checklists: www. prisma-statement.org. Many research journals suggest, or even require, following the PRISMA protocols for submissions of systematic reviews and meta-analyses. For example, the whole literature search, screening, applying inclusion/exclusion criteria, and quality appraisal process can be illustrated through a flowchart, which should be included in the method section of the systematic reviews and meta-analyses. In healthcare-related research, the Cochrane reviews have a well-known guideline to review intervention studies (Higgins & Green, 2008). There are extensive Cochrane handbooks and guidelines on their website as well: https://training. cochrane.org/handbooks. These guidelines are periodically updated and are freely accessible. Additionally, when researchers start a systematic review or meta-analysis, it will be worthwhile to check on the quality appraisal instrument to enhance the quality of the ongoing review. For example, A Measurement Tool to Assess Systematic Reviews (AMSTAR) has been used to assess the quality and systematic reviews and meta-analysis (Shea et al., 2009). While some of earlier studies did not use PRISMA protocols, most recent systematic reviews and meta-analyses in adapted physical education (APE) follow PRISMA or a close variation of the protocols. However, many systematic reviews and meta-analyses did not include quality appraisal.

Formulating the research question

For systematic reviews and meta-analyses, formulating a research question is the first critical step to conducting these types of analyses. Besides having the typical requirement of bearing theoretical/practical significances, research questions for systematic reviews and meta-analyses should (a) have a well-focused area of research, and (b) have an extensive existing primary study pool so that related research articles can be identified and extracted. While there is no specific magic number for conducting systematic reviews, there are guidelines for the number of primary studies needed based on power analyses for conducting meta-analyses (c.f., Valentine, Pigott, & Rothstein, 2010). For example, researchers interested in further examining the effects of exercise/physical activity programs among youth with intellectual disabilities (ID) should peruse the recent systematic reviews and meta-analyses, such as Bartlo and Klein (2011) and Jeng et al.'s (2017) studies. Based on these existing reviews, a new literature search can begin to answer the new research questions, such as: what types of physical activity/exercise programming would be most effective on improving balance among individuals with ID?

Literature search

Once a research question is formulated, the next step is to conduct a thorough literature search using established databases. In the field of APE, typically researchers use ERIC®, Medline®, Web of Sciences®, PsycINFO®, ProQuest® (PEI), and SportDiscus®. To start the literature search process, researchers first have to identify a list of keywords that will be used for the search. Commonly used acronyms such as BMI for body mass index should be included on the keyword list as well. Additionally, commonly recognized synonyms or interchangeable terms should be used for the search, such as visual impairment in place of blindness. To maximize the possibility of retrieving all related research articles, researchers should use all possible unique combinations to conduct the literature search. Importantly, researchers should factually document the search date, terms, databases, and combinations of terms used for the literature. Additionally, researchers should consult the reviews on the specific topic that may have been published recently and use the reference lists included in the articles to further identify possible articles to include.

In addition to factually recording the literature search results, researchers should also have clear criteria for article inclusion and exclusion, as the literature search often results in many articles that may not fit the reviewers' interest. The criteria for inclusion and exclusion commonly include (a) topic of the research (e.g., studies focusing on fitness of individuals with

ID), (b) certain research paradigm or methods (e.g., systematic review of qualitative studies, or meta-analysis on studies using randomized controlled trials), (c) participants' characteristics (e.g., studies limited to school-aged children), (d) publication characteristics such as publication date (e.g., past five or ten years), geographic location (e.g., North America), or language used (e.g., published in English). To apply these prescribed criteria and extract the articles, researchers need to review the abstract, or occasionally review the entire article, to determine if the study meets the inclusion/exclusion criteria. Almost all the systematic reviews and meta-analyses published in the past five years in APE have provided good details on the literature search section (e.g., Augestad & Jiang, 2015; Martin Ginis, Ma, Latimer-Cheung, & Rimmer, 2016).

Review and extract findings

After locating possible articles that meet the inclusion criteria, the next important step is to thoroughly review the articles and extract the data/findings from them. It is important for this step to organize the data/findings from the studies systematically, using an Excel spreadsheet or other computer software. From each study, researchers need to extract the pertinent publication information, such as authors, publication year, and produce a record for the reference list. Extraction should also include the participant information such as sample size, age range, disability and disability severity indicators, sex, and other unique characteristics that could be used for further analysis. Study design, such as sampling method (e.g., convenient or cluster), group assignment (e.g., random or matching), group conditions (for both control and experiment), outcome measures, and data analysis should also be documented during the extraction. Reviewers should factually record the numerical values for quantitative studies and summarize the findings for qualitative studies. At least two reviewers should independently conduct the article review and data extraction to establish interrater reliability through percentage of agreement, Cohen's kappa, or similar measures. Small percentages of disagreement could be resolved through discussion, and, when necessary, involving a third reviewer. When large percentages of disagreement appear, reviewers need to review and revise the extraction protocol to re-extract and resolve the disagreement. At the end of the data/findings extraction, reviewers should tally the number of studies included for analysis. Many of the current systematic reviews and meta-analyses in APE have not provided clear descriptions about extracting processes or types of agreement used. For example, Augestad and Jiang (2015) described their extracting protocol for a systematic review, but it was not clear whether extracting agreement was checked.

Quality appraisal

Studies using different designs tend to produce different levels of evidence (Ho, Peterson, & Masoudi, 2008). For example, multisite randomized clinical trials yield more rigid evidence than a case-controlled study, which has higher-level evidence than case studies. As such, it is important to appraise the quality of evidence/design or reporting consistency so that evidence generated from stronger primary study design should outweigh those with lower levels of evidence. The extent to which researchers adhere to the study and reporting protocols would impact the feasibility of other scholars' conducting systematic reviews and meta-analysis, as shown in Chanias, Reid, and Hoover (1998) and Lang et al. (2010). There are many quality appraisal tools available, and researchers need to choose based upon the nature of the primary studies that will be used in the systematic review or meta-analysis. For example, the Oxford Centre for Evidence-Based Medicine has a list of appraisal worksheets on their website: https://www.cebm.net/2014/06/critical-appraisal/. In meta-analysis of clinical trials, the PEDro scale is often used to appraise the methodological quality of the included trials or interventions (Maher, Sherrington, Herbert, Moseley, & Elkins, 2003). Similarly, there are existing tools to appraise the primary qualitative studies used in systematic reviews (Flemming, Booth, Hannes, Cargo, & Noyes, 2018; Noyes et al., 2018). Researchers should review the type of the primary studies and select an appraisal tool that fits their research purpose and primary studies. For studies conducted in APE, many systematic reviews and meta-analyses do not include clear quality appraisal (e.g., Shin & Park, 2012). As such, reviews conducted on similar topics sometimes can yield different results (e.g., balance performance among individuals with ID), which would cast doubt on the existing findings.

Finding analysis for systematic review

After applying the inclusion/exclusion criteria and conducting the quality appraisal, the final sample of included studies are determined. Occasionally, the quality appraisal process will determine that a certain included study may not be a good fit for the systematic review or meta-analysis as researchers scrutinize the research designs used in the primary studies. Researchers can proceed with data/findings analysis. For systematic reviews, that often starts with quality appraisal results, then a descriptive analysis of the characteristics of the included studies, including purposes of the study, sample/population, study design, and brief findings. In many cases, these characteristics are typically summarized in long tables, while the researchers summarize each of the characteristics as the results of the systematic reviews. For example, Bartlo and Klein (2011) first presented the quality appraisal for both qualitative and quantitative studies on the effects of exercise and physical activity programs on adults with ID. After listing the synopsis of the included studies in a large table, Bartlo and Klein (2011) subsequently summarized the findings in the areas of cardiovascular fitness, muscular strength, balance, and quality of life. To ensure that a quality review is conducted, researchers should not only read the primary studies in detail, but also use a quality appraisal instrument for systematic review (e.g., AMSTAR) to enhance its quality.

Meta-analyses

A unique aspect of meta-analysis is that it quantifies the magnitude and direction of findings through the computation of effect size, in medical research referred to as treatment effect. Depending on the study design and nature of the data collected, the effect size computed from a single study could take a variety of forms, using a number of statistical estimates (e.g., d, g). Borenstein, Hedges, Higgins, and Rothstein (2009) recommended considering four areas when selecting an effect size statistic for meta-analysis: (a) the effect sizes reported/computed from different studies should be comparable to one another in the sense that they are measuring approximately similar variables; (b) an estimated effect size can be extracted or computed from the reported data in published articles without re-analyzing the raw data which typically are not available; (c) the effect size should have good technical properties estimated from known sampling distributions, such that the variances and confidence intervals can be computed; and (d) the effect size should be a meaningful interpretation in a pool of the primary studies.

Typically, based on the type of data collected in the primary studies, researchers could identify the types of effect size to be used. In general, three groups of the effect sizes are reported and commonly used in primary research studies: (a) effect sizes based on mean differences, (b) effect sizes based on binary or categorical data, and (c) effect sizes based on correlational data or amount of variances explained (Borenstein et al., 2009). In primary research studies, the effect size may be unstandardized for meaningful interpretation; however, in meta-analysis, it is a common practice to compute the standardized effect size to accommodate for variation in measures, units, and study designs. Based on the type of effect size and their standardized statistics, researchers can do *a priori* power analysis for the meta-analysis to determine the number of the primary studies needed for the desired level of power (Valentine et al., 2010). Unfortunately, this step is often overlooked in most of the meta-analysis studies in APE. In other words, meta-analysis studies often proceeded without specifying the level of power desired and types of effect size statistics, then presented outcome from the software or template. As such, understanding the type of effect size statistics is essential. I briefly describe the standardized computation for the commonly used statistics of each of the three effect size types below. Interested readers seeking for more in-depth readings should consult with more extensive texts (e.g., Borenstein et al., 2009; Cohen, 1988; Lipsey & Wilson, 2001).

The effect sizes based on mean differences typically apply in the contexts of pre/post study designs and controlled experiments, where the mean difference or change in dependent variables is the interest of the study. Cohen's *d* is often used in this scenario. While the criteria for small, medium, and large effect size are relative, depending on the subject area, in social sciences, Cohen (1988) suggested the criteria for this effect size include: trivial $d < 0.20$, small $0.50 > d \geq 0.20$, medium $0.80 > d \geq 0.50$, and large $d \geq 0.80$. Cohen's *d* is computed as follows:

$$d = \frac{\overline{x}_1 - \overline{x}_2}{s} \tag{1}$$

where the numerator is the mean difference between the groups, as noted by $\overline{x}_1$ and $\overline{x}_2$, and s is the pooled standard deviation of both groups. There are several derivatives of Cohen's *d* such as Hedge's *g* and Glass's *Δ*. As noted above, there are variations of Cohen's *d* which either use a different denominator of Equation (1, e.g., using the standard deviation of the second group or posttest), or have a different scalar included in Equation (1).

The effect sizes based on binary or categorical data are often used in studies examining the association between the binary or categorical variables, such as whether ethnicity is associated with obesity classification or whether sex is associated with experiment outcome for an intervention. For binary outcomes, the most commonly used effect size is odds ratio (OR) which determines whether the probability of an outcome is the same or different across two groups. When OR = 1, that means the outcome is equally likely in both groups. In a two-group context, as shown in Table 13.1, the OR for outcome success can be computed as:

$$OR = n_1 * n_4 / n_2 * n_3 \tag{2}$$

where n_1, n_2, n_3, n_4 are occurrence count in each respective cell. When there are more than two categories in columns and rows of Table 13.1, Cramer's *V* is often computed:

Table 13.1 An example scenario for odds ratio

Group	Outcome	
	Success	Failure
Low risk group	n_1	n_2
High risk group	n_3	n_4

$$V = \sqrt{\frac{\chi^2}{N(k-1)}} \tag{3}$$

where χ^2 is the chi-square statistic, N is the sample size, and k is the smaller value of the number of categories within the columns and rows in the contingency table, similar to Table 13.1. There are other variations for effect size statistics, such as relative risk for OR, φ or Cohen's ω for V. Cohen's (1988) recommended cut-offs for small, medium, and large effect sizes are 0.10, 0.30, 0.50 for V or φ, and 1.49, 3.45, and 9.00 for OR, respectively. Recently, Chen and colleagues (2010) showed that using the original Cohen's (1988) cut-off d values for small (0.20), medium (0.50), and large (0.80) effects, the effect size criteria as expressed in OR change depending on the disease rate of the non-exposed group. For example, the cut-offs for small, medium, and large associations are 1.68, 3.47, 6.71, respectively, for a disease rate of 1%, while these OR cut-offs become 1.52, 2.74, and 4.72, respectively, for a disease rate of 5%.

The effect sizes based on correlational data or the amount of variances explained often apply to correlational studies of continuous variables, and studies using correlational or factorial designs to predict a continuous variable. For correlational studies of continuous variables, the commonly used effect size statistic is the Pearson correlation coefficient, r, which gives a direction and magnitude of the correlation. There are comparable statistical coefficients used studies of other types of variables or using different design such as standardized β, and ρ. Cohen (1988) recommended the following cut-offs for $|r|$ values of 0.10, 0.30, and 0.50 for small, medium, and large effect sizes, respectively. For studies using a factorial or correlational design to determine the amount of variances explained in the dependent variable, the commonly used statistics include r^2 reported in regression analyses, η^2 and ω^2 in analysis of variance. The effect size for these statistics can be computed as:

$$f^2 = \frac{\eta^2}{1 - \eta^2} \tag{4}$$

where the effect size statistic Cohen's f^2 is expressed as a rational of η^2 and $1 - \eta^2$. The effect sizes for r^2 and ω^2 can be computed in the same way as shown in Equation (4). For social sciences, the recommended cut-offs for small, medium, and large effect sizes are 0.02, 0.15, and 0.35, respectively (Cohen, 1988).

As shown in Equations (1) and (3), effect size statistics are susceptible to sample size change in the primary studies. That is, the computed effect size tends to be negatively related to the sample size of the study. As sample size (n) increases, the estimated effect size tends to be smaller, holding other factors constant. As such, a weighted approach for effect size computation is recommended to take into consideration of the various sample sizes employed in the primary studies. In APE primary research, sample sizes sometimes are small, as such proper weighting should be used for meta-analysis, otherwise, the computed effect size will be improperly inflated. Additionally, effect size estimates may not be directly comparable without taking into consideration the sample information. The estimated different effect sizes can be converted to other effect size statistics for meta-analysis based on their calculation. For example, there are guidelines to convert OR to other effect sizes for meta-analysis (Chinn, 2000).

Analytic tools and software

Systematic reviews and meta-analyses used to require a significant amount of literature management time and statistical competence, as there were not many analytic tools and software available for researchers. Currently, there are multiple analytic tools that a researcher can choose for conducting systematic reviews and meta-analyses. The software can range from a simple set of Microsoft Excel macros to dedicated, stand-alone software packages. Some software packages are commercialized for sale; others are offered free of charge. For example, a widely used software, Review Manager (Cochrane Reviews, 2014) is offered free of charge for purely academic use. There are articles reviewing these analytic tools and software based on their usability and features (e.g., Wallace, Schmid, Lau, & Trikalinos, 2009) that should interest researchers and graduate students intending to conduct systematic reviews and meta-analyses.

Recent systematic reviews and meta-analyses of studies in APE

The usage of review methods in APE, as well as in the larger field of adapted physical activity, has flourished in the recent decades. A variety of review methods have been applied to disability-specific studies on populations with autism spectrum disorders (ASD; Lang et al., 2010), developmental coordination disorder (DCD; Hillier, 2007; Pless & Carlsson, 2000; Smits-Engelsman et al., 2013), Down syndrome (Bolt, 2017), intellectual disabilities (ID; Bartlo & Klein, 2011; Chanias et al., 1998; Hutzler & Korsensky, 2010; Jeng et al., 2017; Shin & Park, 2012), physical disabilities (Bloemen et al., 2015; Martin Ginis, Ma, Latimer-Cheung, & Rimmer, 2016), and visual impairments (VI) (Augestad & Jiang, 2015; Haegele & Porretta, 2015). Review methods have also been used in APE research areas that cross multiple disabilities, such as inclusion in physical education (Block & Obrusnikova, 2007), student perspectives (Haegele & Sutherland, 2015), barriers and facilitators of physical activity participation (Martin Ginis et al., 2016; Shields, Synnot, & Barr, 2011), benefits of physical activity (Bartlo & Klein, 2011; Johnson, 2009), and interventions (Hillier, 2007; Smits-Engelsman et al., 2013). Among these review studies, systematic reviews and meta-analyses are the most commonly used methodologies.

ASD. Lang and colleagues (2010) conducted a systematic review on exercise and its effects among youth with ASD. Since a majority of the included studies (13 out of 18) used a single-subject design, the magnitude of the effects was not analyzed. The systematic review focused on teaching procedures, mode of exercise used in the primary studies, as well as research methods and findings. The most commonly used exercise was running or jogging on a track or in an open space, and, typically, modelling and guidance were used where a teacher or a therapist would run along with the participants. In general, the exercise interventions reported increases in academic responding, on-task behaviors, appropriate motor behaviors, and reported decrease in stereotypy, aggression, and off-task behaviors for individuals with ASD. Lang et al. (2010) pointed out the need for experimental studies and clearer reporting for exercise intervention studies among youth with ASD.

DCD. For youth with DCD, Pless and Carlsson (2000) conducted a meta-analysis on studies published from 1970 to 1996 on motor skill interventions. While results were generally positive among the 13 studies included for the meta-analysis, Pless and Carlsson (2000) reported that motor skill interventions yielded higher positive effect size when they targeted children over five years old, used specific theoretical approach (versus general and sensory integration approaches), provided sessions at least three times a week, and conducted interventions in a group setting. Hillier (2007) conducted a systematic review on intervention studies among youth with DCD (from 1970 to 2004), and reported a high heterogeneity of intervention approaches and outcome measures, with over 40 different outcomes reported. Among the 47 studies included in the review, only two were rated with strong evidence using randomized controlled trials. The most frequently assessed outcome measures included Movement Assessment Battery for Children (M-ABC), Bruininks-Oseretsky Test of Motor Proficiency (BOMP), and the Developmental Test of Visual Motor Integration (VMI). While over 30 different intervention programs were reported in the studies, Hillier (2007) categorized them into perceptual-motor therapy ($n = 9$), sensory-integration therapy ($n = 7$), and kinesthetic training ($n = 4$) approaches. Smits-Engelsman and colleagues (2013) conducted a systematic review and meta-analysis of literature from 1995 to 2011 on the efficacy of interventions to improve motor performance in youth with DCD. In general, the intervention produced a moderate positive effect on improved motor performance with $d = 0.56$. Task-oriented and physical/occupational therapies had higher effect size than process-oriented interventions. Treatment with chemical supplements such as methylphenidate had a positive moderate effect based on three studies included in the review. Hence, Smits-Engelsman et al. (2013) suggested that there is insufficient evidence to support higher efficacy of the chemical supplement on motor skill performance than traditional intervention.

ID. Researchers have conducted several systematic and meta-analyses on the effects of exercise or physical activity programs on the physical fitness of persons with ID. Many, however, focus more on adult populations rather than youth. For example, Bartlo and Klein (2011) reviewed studies of physical activity interventions of adults with ID and found moderate-to-strong evidence that physical activity has positive effects on balance, muscle strength, and quality of life. Similarly, Chanias and colleagues (1998) found that exercise programs yielded large positive effects on muscular and cardiovascular endurance, moderate effects for muscular strength, and trivial or no effects on flexibility and body composition. Hutzler and Korsensky (2010) conducted a systematic review on the motivational correlates of physical activity in persons with ID and noted that the improved physical fitness and skills through physical activity participation appear to serve as mediators for increased self-efficacy and social competence. Peer modelling, video/audio reinforcement can help maintain exercise program compliance for persons with ID (Hutzler & Korsensky, 2010). Most recently, Jeng et al. (2017) conducted a systematic review and meta-analysis on the effects of exercise programs on skill-related fitness among adolescents with ID. The meta-analysis showed that exercise programs seemed to have positive effects on agility, power, reaction time, and speed, but not on balance performance, which conflicts with Bartlo and Klein (2011) and Shin and Park (2012)'s findings.

Shin and Park (2012) conducted a meta-analysis examining the effects of exercise programs on biometric/body composition, physiological variable, fitness performance, and psychological perception, such as self-esteem. Unlike the other discussed analyses, while most of the studies analyzed in Shin and Park (2012) focused on adults with ID, a few focused on youth or older adults. Although a moderate positive effect was reported, Shin and Park (2012) found that the exercise programs produced high positive effects on self-esteem, limited effects on body composition, and moderate effects on physical performance such as balance and strength. Additionally, Shin and Park (2012) conducted a subgroup analysis and found that the effect size was greater for adults (mostly 20–40 years old) than younger people with more frequent program (e.g., four times a week) producing a greater effect size than less frequent programs (three or less times a week). Even though there are several systematic reviews and meta-analyses in the existing literature, researchers have noted that there were inconsistencies in reporting, and not reporting critical statistical, sample, and exercise program information that hindered their ability to conduct further analysis (Chanias et al., 1998; Jeng et al., 2017; Leung, Siebert, & Yun, 2017).

Physical disability

There are a few recent review pieces focusing on physical activity participation among individuals with physical disabilities, and almost all the reviews were on barriers and facilitators (e.g., Bloemen et al., 2015; Martin Ginis et al., 2016). Bloemen and colleagues (2015) reviewed 18 studies including six qualitative and 12 quantitative publications that examined a wide range of positive and negative factors associated with physical activity participation among children and adolescents with physical disabilities. They broadly categorized the factors into environmental and personal factors; within each category there were barriers and facilitators ranging from family, school, sport experiences, and transportation dimensions. Bloemen and colleagues (2015) noted lack of fitness, motivation, time, and support from others as barriers, while having proper fitness, motivation, time, and positive support from others were facilitators for children and adolescents with physical disabilities. Using a social-ecological model as an organizational theoretical framework, Martin Ginis and colleagues (2016) conducted a systematic review on review articles ($n=22$) pertaining to factors associated with leisure time physical activity participation among children and adults with physical disabilities. They placed the barriers and facilitators into five hierarchical levels according to the social-ecological framework: intrapersonal (e.g., personal psychological factors), interpersonal (e.g., family/social supports), institutional (e.g., capacity/knowledge of the organization), community (e.g., infrastructure/climate of the community), and policy levels (e.g., health policies). They urged researchers to conduct studies developing and/or delivering strategies that could potentially improve leisure-time physical activity participation among individuals with physical disabilities.

Visual impairments

For individuals with VI, two recent systematic reviews summarized findings on physical activity and physical fitness among children and young adults with VI (Augestad & Jiang, 2015; Haegele & Porretta, 2015). Specifically, Augestad and Jiang (2015) reviewed 29 studies published between 1984 and 2014. In general, the findings showed that individuals with VI tend to have lower levels of physical activity participation, lower levels of physical fitness, and higher prevalence of obesity/overweight than their sighted counterparts. Similarly, Haegele and Porretta (2015) reviewed 18 studies among school-aged children with VI, with 11 being descriptive/correlational and seven using interventions to examine physical activity participation. The findings are generally consistent, in that lower physical activity participation was reported for children with VI than those who are sighted. Several preliminary studies show that interventions can increase levels of physical activity participation among children with VI. Haegele and Porretta (2015) reported that while studies show children with VI enjoyed physical activity, parent and self-reported barriers could be an important factor for the low physical activity participation. Both reviews (Augestad & Jiang, 2015; Haegele & Porretta, 2015) recognized the need for more intervention and longitudinal studies among individuals with VI.

Summary

While no scientific breakthrough was made through systematic reviews and/or meta-analyses (Sohn, 1995), they are valuable methodologies to summarize the extant research literatures in a relatively well-defined research area. In this chapter, I have briefly summarized systematic reviews and meta-analyses and provided the essential steps and analytic methods needed to conduct these kinds of studies. Systematic reviews and meta-analyses have been used in APE research in the past decade, although there is need for consistency in reporting and analyses. Understanding the protocols and standardized statistics is crucial to conducting systematic reviews and meta-analysis studies. Once studies accumulate in one line of scientific inquiry, researchers and graduate students are encouraged to conduct systematic reviews and/or meta-analyses based on the nature of the studies and using the existing guidelines.

Summary of key points

- Systematic reviews and meta-analyses have been used in the APE research with some inconsistencies.
- Proper literature search, screening, inclusion/exclusion, and coding are important data collection steps for systematic reviews and meta-analyses.
- There are essential steps, statistical concepts, and report protocols that should be carefully followed for systematic reviews and meta-analyses.
- Identifying a theoretical thread/conceptual framework and empirical chains of primary studies is critical for conducting systematic review.
- Power analysis is needed to determine the number of primary studies necessary for conducting a meta-analysis.
- For systematic reviews and meta-analyses, researchers should recognize that different types of study designs yield different levels of empirical evidence.
- Researchers need to have an essential understanding of the different effect sizes that can be used in meta-analyses.
- Similar to quality appraisals for the primary studies, there are appraisal protocols for systematic reviews and meta-analyses.
- Based on the results of prior systematic reviews and meta-analyses, there appears to be a great need for intervention, experimental, and longitudinal studies on persons with disabilities.
- There is need for reporting consistency among the studies, as inconsistencies in reporting statistical, study sample, and intervention information hinders researchers' ability to conduct further analyses.

Reflective questions

- Considering the content in the chapter, please develop a research question appropriate for a systematic review. How might that change when using a meta-analysis?

- What are critical differences between the implementation of and results derived from systematic reviews and meta-analyses?
- When the primary studies in a research area are mostly qualitative, considering the systematic review and meta-analysis approaches, what approach is appropriate? Why?
- If the existing qualitative and single-subject studies show very favorable results for an instructional method in adapted physical education while the latest controlled trials show minimal effects, how will you reconcile these conflicting findings in a systematic review?
- If there are many existing intervention studies on promotion of physical activity participation in adapted physical education, considering the systematic review and meta-analysis approaches described in the chapter, what approach is appropriate? Why?

References

Augestad, L. B., & Jiang, L. (2015). Physical activity, physical fitness, and body composition among children and young adults with visual impairments: A systematic review. *British Journal of Visual Impairment*, *33*(3), 167–182.

Bartlo, P., & Klein, P. J. (2011). Physical activity benefits and needs in adults with intellectual disabilities: Systematic review of the literature. *American Journal on Intellectual and Developmental Disabilities*, *116*(3), 220–232.

Block, M. E., & Obrusnikova, I. (2007). Inclusion in physical education: A review of the literature from 1995-2005. *Adapted Physical Activity Quarterly*, *24*(2), 103–124.

Bloemen, M. A., Backx, F. J., Takken, T., Wittink, H., Benner, J., Mollema, J., & De Groot, J. F. (2015). Factors associated with physical activity in children and adolescents with a physical disability: A systematic review. *Developmental Medicine & Child Neurology*, *57*(2), 137–148.

Bolt, C. I. (2017). The effects of adapted physical education on students with Down syndrome: A meta-analysis (mater's thesis). Retrieved from https://digitalcommons.humboldt.edu/etd/52/

Borenstein, M., Hedges, L. V., Higgins, J. P., & Rothstein, H. R. (2009). *Introduction to meta-analysis*. Hoboken, NJ: John Wiley & Sons.

Chanias, A. K., Reid, G., & Hoover, M. L. (1998). Exercise effects on health-related physical fitness of individuals with an intellectual disability: A meta-analysis. *Adapted Physical Activity Quarterly*, *15*(2), 119–140.

Chen, H., Cohen, P., & Chen, S. (2010). How big is a big odds ratio? Interpreting the magnitudes of odds ratios in epidemiological studies. *Communications in Statistics—Simulation and Computation*, *39*(4), 860–864.

Chinn, S. (2000). A simple method for converting an odds ratio to effect size for use in meta-analysis. *Statistics in Medicine*, *19*(22), 3127–3131.

Cohen, J. (1988). *Statistical power analysis for the behavioral sciences* (2nd ed.). Hillsdale, NJ: Erlbaum.

Comte, A. (1855). *The positive philosophy of Auguste Comte*. (H. Martineau, Trans.). New York: Calvin Blanchard.

Flemming, K., Booth, A., Hannes, K., Cargo, M., & Noyes, J. (2018). Cochrane Qualitative and Implementation Methods Group guidance series—Paper 6: Reporting guidelines for qualitative, implementation, and process evaluation evidence syntheses. *Journal of Clinical Epidemiology*, *97*, 79–85.

Gough, D., Thomas, J., & Oliver, S. (2012). Clarifying differences between review designs and methods. *Systematic Reviews*, *1*, 28. doi:10.1186/2046-4053-1-28

Haegele, J. A., & Porretta, D. (2015). Physical activity and school-age individuals with visual impairments: A literature review. *Adapted Physical Activity Quarterly*, *32*(1), 68–82.

Haegele, J. A., & Sutherland, S. (2015). Perspectives of students with disabilities toward physical education: A qualitative inquiry review. *Quest*, *67*(3), 255–273.

Higgins, J., & Green, S. (2008). *Cochrane handbook for systematic reviews of interventions*. Hoboken, NJ: John Wiley & Sons.

Hillier, S. (2007). Intervention for children with developmental coordination disorder: A systematic review. *Internet Journal of Allied Health Sciences and Practice*, *5*(3), 7.

Ho, P. M., Peterson, P. N., & Masoudi, F. A. (2008). Evaluating the evidence: Is there a rigid hierarchy? *Circulation, 118*, 1675–1684.

Hutzler, Y., & Korsensky, O. (2010). Motivational correlates of physical activity in persons with an intellectual disability: A systematic literature review. *Journal of Intellectual Disability Research, 54*(9), 767–786.

Jeng, S. C., Chang, C. W., Liu, W. Y., Hou, Y. J., & Lin, Y. H. (2017). Exercise training on skill-related physical fitness in adolescents with intellectual disability: A systematic review and meta-analysis. *Disability and Health Journal, 10*(2), 198–206.

Johnson, C. C. (2009). The benefits of physical activity for youth with developmental disabilities: A systematic review. *American Journal of Health Promotion, 23*(3), 157–167.

Lang, R., Koegel, L. K., Ashbaugh, K., Regester, A., Ence, W., & Smith, W. (2010). Physical exercise and individuals with autism spectrum disorders: A systematic review. *Research in Autism Spectrum Disorders, 4*(4), 565–576.

Leung, W., Siebert, E. A., & Yun, J. (2017). Measuring physical activity with accelerometers for individuals with intellectual disability: A systematic review. *Research in Developmental Disabilities, 67*, 60–70.

Lipsey, M. W., & Wilson, D. B. (2001). *Practical meta-analysis.* Thousand Oaks, CA: Sage Publications.

Maher, C. G., Sherrington, C., Herbert, R. D., Moseley, A. M., & Elkins, M. (2003). Reliability of the PEDro scale for rating quality of randomized controlled trials. *Physical Therapy, 83*(8), 713–721.

Martin Ginis, K. A., Ma, J. K., Latimer-Cheung, A. E., & Rimmer, J. H. (2016). A systematic review of review articles addressing factors related to physical activity participation among children and adults with physical disabilities. *Health Psychology Review, 10*(4), 478–494.

Moher, D., Liberati, A., Tetzlaff, J., Altman, D. G., & Group, T. P. R. I. S. M. A. (2009). Preferred reporting items for systematic reviews and meta-analyses: The PRISMA statement. *PLoS Medicine, 6*(7), e1000097. doi:10.1371/journal.pmed1000097

Montori, V. M., Swiontkowski, M. F., & Cook, D. J. (2003). Methodologic issues in systematic reviews and meta-analyses. *Clinical Orthopaedics and Related Research, 413*, 43–54.

Morgan, P. J., Barnett, L. M., Cliff, D. P., Okely, A. D., Scott, H. A., Cohen, K. E., & Lubans, D. R. (2013). Fundamental movement skill interventions in youth: A systematic review and meta-analysis. *Pediatrics, 132*(5), e1361–e1383 peds-2013.

Noyes, J., Booth, A., Flemming, K., Garside, R., Harden, A., Lewin, S., … Thomas, J. (2018). Cochrane qualitative and implementation methods group guidance series—Paper 3: Methods for assessing methodological limitations, data extraction and synthesis, and confidence in synthesized qualitative findings. *Journal of Clinical Epidemiology, 97*, 49–58.

Pless, M., & Carlsson, M. (2000). Effects of motor skill intervention on developmental coordination disorder: A meta-analysis. *Adapted Physical Activity Quarterly, 17*(4), 381–401.

Reviews, C. (2014). *Review manager (revman) [computer program].* Version 5.3. Copenhagen: The Nordic Cochrane Centre, The Cochrane Collaboration.

Shea, B. J., Hamel, C., Wells, G. A., Bouter, L. M., Kristjansson, E., Grimshaw, J., & Boers, M. (2009). AMSTAR is a reliable and valid measurement tool to assess the methodological quality of systematic reviews. *Journal of Clinical Epidemiology, 62*(10), 1013–1020.

Shields, N., Synnot, A. J., & Barr, M. (2011). Perceived barriers and facilitators to physical activity for children with disability: A systematic review. *British Journal Sports Medicine, 46*(14), 989–997 bjsports-2011.

Shin, I. S., & Park, E. Y. (2012). Meta-analysis of the effect of exercise programs for individuals with intellectual disabilities. *Research in Developmental Disabilities, 33*(6), 1937–1947.

Smits-Engelsman, B. C., Blank, R., Van der Kaay, A. C., Mosterd-van der Meijs, R., Vlugt-van den Brand, E., Polatajko, H. J., & Wilson, P. H. (2013). Efficacy of interventions to improve motor performance in children with developmental coordination disorder: A combined systematic review and meta-analysis. *Developmental Medicine & Child Neurology, 55*(3), 229–237.

Sohn, D. (1995). Meta-analysis as a means of scientific discovery. *American Psychologist, 50*, 108–110.

Valentine, J. C., Pigott, T. D., & Rothstein, H. R. (2010). How many studies do you need? A primer on statistical power for meta-analysis. *Journal of Educational and Behavioral Statistics, 35*(2), 215–247.

Wallace, B. C., Schmid, C. H., Lau, J., & Trikalinos, T. A. (2009). Meta-analyst: Software for meta-analysis of binary, continuous and diagnostic data. *BMC Medical Research Methodology, 9*(1), 80.

Part III

Conceptual and theoretical frameworks

14

Embodiment

Philosophical considerations of the body in adaptive physical education

Øyvind F. Standal

Introduction

In this chapter, I introduce the concept of embodiment. This will be done by taking the perspective of phenomenological philosophy. This philosophical school of thought emphasizes lived experience and theorizes the body as something more than a biological object. Embodiment, in this perspective, helps us see how the body is intimately connected with things in the world and with other people. By drawing on relevant research in the area of adaptive physical education,[1] the practical consequences of this theoretical perspective are described.

In the German language, the body can be spoken about using two different words: *Körper* and *Leib*. The founder of phenomenology, an important philosophical school of thought in Continental philosophy, Edmund Husserl (1859–1938), used this distinction to ground his philosophy of the body. Roughly speaking, *Körper* refers to the body as a thing or object and *Leib* refers to the lived-through body. While the word *Leib* has the same root as the word *Leben* which means living and life, *Körper* can be translated to corpse (i.e., the dead body). It is, however, a crucial point that these two words do not imply a separation between living and lifeless matter (Slatman, 2016). *Körper* can also refer to the living, physical body. The two words are, in that sense, referring to different aspects of the same body:

> The experience of one's *own* body necessarily assumes the difference between *Leib* and *Körper*. If this difference would not be there, it would imply that my body is either purely a *Leib* or purely a *Körper*. In the first case, the body is robbed of all its corporeality because a pure *Leib* is nothing else but a pure spirit, and one may wonder whether such situations occur in the real world. In the second case the body is robbed of its dignity. This experience, whereby one's own body is reduced to a pure being-*Körper*, does occur indeed. Mostly it involves extreme situations such as rape, humiliation, excessive violence, and traumas. In these cases one will want to dissociate oneself from one's own body.

> *(Slatman, 2016, pp. 75–76)*

Originating from philosophical insights about the body, the concept of embodiment has become a key term in many disciplines over the past couple of decades (Cheville, 2005). Embodiment provides a way of describing, analyzing, and explaining the body, which is richer and different from what has been called the Cartesian understanding of the body. Cartesianism implies that it is our thinking, or our mind, that makes us human. The body, on the other hand, is a mere thing, an object governed by the same causal forces as other things in nature (i.e., it is a *Körper*-body). In this picture, it is our thinking mind, or the soul, that makes us human, while the body is denigrated. The Cartesian image of the human body is a disembodied image, where "the body is felt more as one object among other objects in the world than as the core of the individual's own being" (Laing, 1965, p. 69, quoted by Sheets-Johnstone, 2018, p. 9).

In this chapter, the body is viewed as not merely *connected* to our subjective experiences, but, indeed, the very ground of our subjective experiences. Embodiment highlights how the body and the world are intertwined in our experience. A quote from the French phenomenologist, Maurice Merleau-Ponty, highlights this: "Inside and outside are inseparable. The world is wholly inside and I am wholly outside of myself" (Merleau-Ponty, 2002). By introducing a number of analytical distinctions, the aim of this chapter is to explicate the concept of embodiment, lay out its philosophical background, and show how the concept has been utilized within the area of sports and physical education for people with disabilities/impaired bodies.

Embodiment: initial considerations

Phenomenology has been applied to physical education in general (Arnold, 1979; Connolly, 1997; Standal, 2015; Stolz, 2014) and to adaptive physical education in particular (Connolly, 2008). Embodiment is connected to a host of other concepts from phenomenological philosophy. In this chapter, only embodiment will be covered, but I have to make explicit that other concepts, such as the first-person perspective, intentionality, and the phenomenological method are all interrelated. To fully appreciate these concepts, I would refer readers to Dan Zahavi's (2018) introductory book as one of many useful introductions written by qualified philosophers. However, a short explanation is provided.

The first-person perspective (i.e., I or we) is important, because it underscores the crucial difference between the phenomenological approach and the traditional third-person scientific approach to understanding human beings. Physical activity can serve as an example. The common definition of physical activity is: "any bodily movement produced by skeletal muscles that results in energy expenditure" (Caspersen, Powell, & Christenson, 1985, p. 126). While this definition is useful for physiologists, it is meaningless for a phenomenologist (Standal, 2015). For the physiologists, this way of understanding physical activity is useful because it allows them to study the physical activity of *anybody* in a third person perspective. For the phenomenologist, it is meaningless because, under that definition, it does not matter if the person engaging in physical activity is running on a treadmill with a gun to her head, or enjoying a run in the beautiful sunset. That is, the definition overlooks what it is like for *somebody* to be physically active (the first-person perspective).

Intentionality is not to be confused with having intentions; for instance, a student's intention to read this chapter. Rather, intentionality is a fundamental characteristic of the directedness of consciousness. When we are conscious, our consciousness is always directed at some object. Analyzing the structures of intentionality is at the heart of the philosophical project of phenomenology, because it helps clarify the relation between the mind and the world (Zahavi, 2018). Here, it is important to note that Zahavi (2018) refers to the embodied, and not a disembodied, mind.

The phenomenological method is a description of the way phenomenological philosophers proceed when they study phenomena. This is not to be confused with various qualitative research methods that use the term phenomenological. Central to the phenomenological method is the concept of bracketing, which involves suspending one's theoretical or common-sense assumptions about the phenomenon under study. This allows the phenomenologist to attain a so-called phenomenological attitude, which allows her to describe the phenomenon as it appears to her, in order to give an account of experience without theorizing or explaining the experience.

In terms of embodiment, Dreyfus and Dreyfus (1996) distinguish between three dimensions. The first is the *facts of our embodiment*, by which they mean the simple and seemingly universal facts that human beings have the bodies we have. We have hands that can grip things, heads that can turn (but not eyes in the neck), knees that can bend, and so on. Another important fact of our embodiment is that human bodies are vulnerable. The always open possibility of not having two hands is also a fact of our embodiment. These facts of embodiment both enable and constrain our interaction with our environment: our knees can bend, so certain objects afford sitting down. The position of our eyes gives us a specific perspective on our world, which is different from if we also had eyes in our neck. Because we have the bodies we have, mountains appear to be large and flying is impossible. The world shows up for us in the way it does due to our bodily constitution. This also means that changes in our vulnerable, bodily constitution can result in changes in our world (Leder, 1990; Toombs, 1992).

The second dimension of embodiment is that human beings can develop skills, habits, and dispositions (Dreyfus & Dreyfus, 1996). This is a central point, because it suggests that the body is not only a thing (*Körper*), but it is also performative, something we do. Thus, embodiment implies that we are both *having* and *being* our bodies. A common misconception is that since phenomenologists are critical of Cartesian dualism (i.e., the body as something one has, *Körper*), they tend to focus only on the subjective part of the body (i.e., the body as something one is, *Leib*). This, however, is not correct: one of the main insights of phenomenology is the duality of both having and being a body. The subjective and the objective sides of our bodies are always intertwined. Embodiment also suggests that the body extends beyond the surface of our skin and into the surrounding world. We can make use of things, such as a hockey stick or a wheelchair, and these objects can become experienced as a part of our body (Standal, 2011). Through socialization and learning, we therefore refine our embodiment and, in so doing, we come to experience the world differently.

The third dimension of embodiment described by Dreyfus and Dreyfus (1996) is its cultural dimension. Our bodies become cultivated, for instance, in that some gestures are meaningful in one culture, but rude or meaningless in other cultures. For example, in the 1970s and 1980s in Norway, hardly anyone except sailors had tattoos. Today, this practice of ornamenting the body is common, a way of cultivating the body, making it an expression of one's own individuality (Crossley, 2006).

In relation to disability, the cultural dimension means the impaired body has a history and is as much a cultural phenomenon as it is a biological entity. One aspect of this cultural history is the idea of what constitutes a normal body and what is considered an abnormal or deviant body. We could, for instance, object to the statement made regarding the first dimension of embodiment (i.e., that it is a fact of our embodiment that we have two hands). Such a statement might be considered as an unwarranted normative consideration about what counts as a proper human body. As Scully (2008) states, "beliefs about normal embodiment become normative" (p. 58). In other words, what we perceive as a normal body is influenced and shaped by our cultural context and the often implicit norms we hold. The cultural dimension of embodiment thus takes into account how our bodies are always shaped by cultural influences. This is not only a matter of lived experiences of the body, but also a matter that enables and disables what bodies are allowed to do.

The body and the world: a phenomenological perspective

As already mentioned, phenomenology is a branch of philosophy developed in Europe in the early part of the 1900s. Phenomenology has developed into different directions (e.g., realistic, constitutive, existential, and hermeneutical phenomenology (Embree, 1997) and has had an impact in other disciplines such as sociology, psychology, and the cognitive sciences. While Husserl clearly paid attention to the body in his development of phenomenology (Zahavi, 2003), it is generally agreed that it was his successor, Maurice Merleau-Ponty, who first developed a full-blown account of the body from a phenomenological perspective. So, what does a phenomenology of the body mean?

Phenomenologists investigate experiences as these are presented to the subjects who are having the experiences (Romdenh-Romluc, 2011). Merleau-Ponty held that phenomenology:

> ... offers an account of space, time and the world as we "live" them. It tries to give a direct description of our experience as it is, without taking account of its psychological origin and the causal explanations which the scientist, the historian or the sociologist may be able to provide.
>
> *(Merleau-Ponty, 2002, p. vii)*

As this quote implies, phenomenologists are trying to describe the *what it is like* qualities of experiences rather than trying to explain the origin or cause of the subject's experience. This is an example of the difference between a first-person and a third person perspective, respectively. For instance, if we want to understand the experience of breathlessness while exercising, phenomenologists would try to describe how it is experienced for the subjects to be out of breath, rather than trying to find a cause for the breathlessness (pulmonary infection?; vigorous activity?). This aspect of embodiment is oftentimes referred to as the lived body: how the body appears in experience.

The body and things

By focusing on the lived body, phenomenologists find that a strict separation between the body and the world cannot be upheld. Normally—in what phenomenologists refer to as the natural attitude we believe that the body ends at the surface of our skin. The skin is the boundary between an individual and the surrounding world and other people. By adopting a phenomenological attitude, however, we come to see that the skin is not the boundary between the body and the world. Merleau-Ponty discusses this in relation to blind people's use of a cane:

> The blind man's stick has ceased to be an object for him, and is no longer perceived for itself; its point has become *an area of sensitivity, extending the scope and active radius of touch*, and providing a parallel to sight ....
>
> *(Merleau-Ponty, 2002, p. 165, italics added)*

In the same passage, he also notes how—when we are proficient at driving—one can drive through a narrow opening "without comparing the width of the opening with that of the wings, just as I go through a doorway without checking the width of the doorway against that of my body" (ibid.). Thus, in the phenomenological perspective, this means that "to get used to a hat, a car or a stick is to be transplanted into them, or conversely, to incorporate them into the bulk of our own body" (ibid.).

These quotes might need some unpacking: Through use, tools and objects become incorporated, taken up in the body. Standal (2009) has analyzed how the wheelchair becomes incorporated—experienced as a part of one's own body—through the dual process of both learning how to use it and learning how to become a wheelchair user. However, Merleau-Ponty also points out that we become "transplanted" into these objects. One way of interpreting such a sentiment is to say that objects are not neutral things. Things become the objects that they are by us using them. A ball, for instance, could be a joyful piece of PE equipment or a lethal object (Quennerstedt, Almqvist, & Öhman, 2011). Objects intended to be played with can appear as strange and meaningless, while objects that are not intended for that purpose can be enthralling instruments of play (Evensen, Standal, & Ytterhus, 2017). The point here is that our intentions are transplanted into the objects, thus making them what they are.

The body and movement

The original phenomenological analysis of things as use-objects can be found in the German phenomenologist Martin Heidegger's (1996) *Being and Time*, where he elaborated on a carpenter's relation to the hammer. According to Heidegger, the hammer is understood through hammering, not by looking at, or observing, its different parts. It is through using the hammer that it is given its meaning: it is used in order to strike a nail, in order to build a house, in order to get shelter from the rain. As Dreyfus (1991) says, the hammer is "defined by its function (in-order-to) in a referential whole. ... to actually function, equipment must fit into a context of meaningful activity" (p. 91, italics in original).

This way of thinking about things as primarily use-objects highlights two issues that are captured by Merleau-Ponty's (2002) notion of bodily space. First of all, our engagement with the world is primarily practical rather than theoretical. In other words, it is a matter of knowing how before knowing that (Ryle, 1949). Second, bodily space is not only revealed, but also structured by bodily movement. Two examples will be used to explain the idea that bodily space is revealed and structured by movement. The first is Merleau-Ponty's (1963) analysis of a football player (that is, a soccer player in American parlance—however, the general point is the same), and the second is taken from Kay S. Toombs (1992) analysis of the lived experience of disability. The football field, says Merleau-Ponty:

> ... is pervaded by lines of force (the 'yard lines'; those which demarcate the 'penalty area') and articulated in sectors (for example, the 'openings' between the adversaries) which calls for a certain mode of action and which initiate and guide the action as if the player were unaware of it. The field itself is not given to him, but present as the immanent term of his practical intentions. The player becomes one with it and feels the direction of the 'goal', for example, just as immediately as the vertical and horizontal planes of his body.
>
> *(Merleau-Ponty, 1963, pp. 168–169)*

As an example of bodily space, the football field is partly constrained by objective structures, such as the penalty area, the sidelines and so on. They are objectively given in the sense that they are measured geometrically. However, through engagement on the field, the player also creates space, sectors in which runs can be made (or where runs are not feasible) or where passes can be made. This is what is meant by the expression that the field is "not given", but is present to the players due to their "practical intentions". Through engagement on the field, a dialectic between the actions of the players and the field is established, so that movements, passes, dribbles, and so on, modifies the character of the field, establishing "in it new lines of forces which in turn unfold and are accomplished, again altering the phenomenal field" (Merleau-Ponty, 1963, p. 169). The more skilled the footballers are, the more nuanced and detailed the bodily space becomes. This is why Mohammed Salah and Lionel Messi are able to see openings and act upon them in ways that the average hobby footballers cannot.

A second example of movement and bodily space is from the philosopher Kay S. Toombs' (1995) article on the lived experience of disability. She outlines how acquiring a disability through a progressive illness influences her experience of space. Similarly to Merleau-Ponty, she takes movement as opening up space "allowing one freely to change position and move towards objects in the world" (p. 11). However, she goes on to explain that the loss of mobility that she experiences "anchors one in the Here, engendering a heightened sense of distance between oneself and surrounding things" (ibid.). Again, there is a relationship between the practical intentions and the experience of bodily space. When getting from A to B becomes problematic, or even impossible, this influences the experience of bodily space: for Toombs it is about being stuck in a Here, rather than getting to There.

These two examples illustrate how embodiment is intertwined with the surrounding world. Van Manen (1990) refers to four existentials, that is, heuristic guides that help us in reflecting on lived experience: these are lived space, lived body, lived time, and lived relationships. While the term embodiment foregrounds the lived body, the two examples just given help us see that embodiment can only be foregrounded with the other existentials in the background. The foreground–background relationship is to be thought of as a gestalt relationship, such as those we see in gestalt figures like the duck/rabbit picture: you can only see either the duck or the rabbit at one time, but seeing either the duck or the rabbit is premised on the other figure being in the background. Embodiment is, likewise, foregrounded on the lived experience of space, time, and other people.

The *lived* dimension is also important. As the two examples highlight, geometrical distances, that is, the distances that are measured in meters and that are the same for everybody, lose their importance. Toombs (1995) describes how what used to be an "unremarkable" walk from her office to the classroom completely changed its character as her illness developed into a loss of mobility. The geometrical distance had not changed, but the lived space constituted by her movement from the office to the classroom shows "how the subjective experience of space is intimately related both to one's bodily capacities and to the design of the surrounding world" (p. 12). While the example of the football field suggests that developing skills and playing these skills out in relation to space and other people (teammates and opponents) changes how the world shows up for the player, Toombs points out how loss of mobility constricts space. Together, these two examples have implications for adaptive physical education in the sense that they show the centrality of embodiment for understanding space, time, and relations with other people in movement activities.

Embodiment and disability

In the field of adaptive physical education there is some literature that deals with different understandings of disability, and the consequences these have for adaptive physical education (Grenier, 2007; Haegele & Hodge, 2016). Drawing on work in disability studies, this literature refers to the difference between medical and social models of disability. In both models, the difference between impairment and disability is essential. While impairment refers to changes in body functions and structures that deviate from the statistical norm, disability is about limitations in activities and participation. The medical model sees the relationship between impairment and disability as a causal one: the impairment is what causes the disability. This leads to the idea of rehabilitation and medical interventions on the individual (Grue & Heiberg, 2006): by fixing or reducing the impairment, the disability will consequently be reduced. The medical model has historically been the traditional way of thinking about disability, but during the latter decades of the 20th century, scholars and activists endorsing the social model of disability criticized the medical model for being a form of oppression (Oliver, 1996; Shakespeare, 2006). Their key move was to sever the causal relationship between impairment and disability: disability is not caused by deviations in body functions or structures. It is, rather, the result of an unaccommodating society. Impairment is a normal human variation and disability then becomes a political issue: why are societies not accommodating these variations?

More detailed explications of the conflicting relationship between the medical and social model of disability can be found elsewhere (Shakespeare, 2006). The point here, and which is also taken up by Haegele and Hodge (2016), as well as within this handbook in the chapter by Haslett and Smith, is how embodiment can be an alternative way of understanding disability, which addresses weaknesses found in both the medical and the social model. More specifically, these weaknesses are that both models ignore the lived experiences of the individual living with a disability. The medical model, as Toombs (1992) has shown, emphasizes the medical profession's third-person perspective on impairment and disability. According to Toombs, the third-person, medical perspective represents "abstractions from lived experience" (p. 42) that are "distinct from and not identical with" (ibid.) the experiences of the person with a disability. Similarly, the social model has also been criticized for ignoring the lived experiences of people with disabilities. In order to focus on the political side—how social arrangement produces dis-abling conditions— social model activists explicitly rejected the importance of attending to lived bodily experiences. According to Hughes and Paterson (1997), "there is a powerful convergence between biomedicine and the social model of disability with respect to the body. Both treat it as a pre-social, inert, physical object, as discrete, palpable and separate from the self" (p. 329). In other words, both models promote a third-person perspective with Cartesian dualism.

The concept of embodiment helps us further to realize the intersection between body and world in disability. In simultaneously criticizing the medical and the social models, critics point out that disability cannot be attributed to the body or the environment, respectively (Weiss, 2015). It is more appropriately understood as located in the relationship between body and environment. By locating disability there, we can see why the concept of embodiment has been employed in theorizing the dual critique of the medical and social models (Paterson & Hughes, 1999; Weiss, 2015).

Exemplary studies of adaptive physical education

So far, embodiment has been theorized from a phenomenological perspective, emphasizing the intertwined relationship between body and space (or environment/world) and the importance of lived experience. Through our active engagement in the world, the world becomes embodied and the body's active engagement is simultaneously enabled or disabled by the design of the surrounding world. As Inahara (2009) reminds us, this design is not solely a physical, architectural matter—it is also psycho-social. Attitudes and responses from other people in the world are also important. Embodiment represents a fruitful approach to disability in the sense that it represents an alternative way between the medical and the social model (Hughes & Paterson, 1997; Paterson & Hughes, 1999). In the following section, I show how this way of thinking about the body and disability can be applied to adaptive physical education. This is done by examining the work of Maureen Connolly as exemplary studies of embodiment.

The work of Maureen Connolly is of particular relevance for adaptive physical education since she has been pioneering phenomenologically inspired research in the field for more than two decades (Connolly, 1995, 2008; Connolly & Craig, 2002; Connolly & Harvey, 2018). Connolly (1995) holds that the primary responsibility of physical educators is the "responsibility to the body" (p. 26), because the body is "the origin of knowing and being in the world" (ibid.). One of the key features of Connolly's work is her attention to insiders' experiences, that is, the lived experience of the students and others taking part in physical education. Listening to the stories of insiders and examining what these experiences can reveal as significant can be used heuristically to inform "teaching–learning dialogue, feedback, description, progression, and more" (p. 37).

In two subsequent articles, Connolly goes on to show how these ideas can be applied (Connolly, 2008; Connolly & Craig, 2002). First, Connolly and Craig (2002) consider the lived experiences of autism and the auto-immune disease myalgic encephalomyelitis (ME). In the first case, Connolly and Craig examine how some people with autism might engage in "inappropriate nudity … going outside in cold weather wearing only underwear or nothing at all, or removing clothing and pressing the naked body against a hard or definitive surface, such as a wall or floor" (p. 454). In the latter case, the authors take up how some people who experience ME can feel overpowered by scents from the surroundings, leading to headache, nausea, dizziness, and so on. Both cases can, according to Connolly and Craig (2002), be described as *stressed embodiment*. The point from a phenomenological point of view is not to explain what causes the stressed experiences, but, rather, to devise strategies that emerge from an understanding of these lived, embodied experiences.

As the authors note, the typical strategy in working with behaviors which, normally—and, thus, normatively—are referred to as deviant, is to manage them. But, Connolly and Craig (2002) offer an alternative to behavior management, which is that educators should ground their work in the lived experience of those persons they are set to serve. This viewpoint also provides an avenue into understanding how educators may use the eidetic feature of embodied experiences of others in the work. Connolly (1995) argued that eidetic features can be used in the construction of "individualized education plans (IEPs)" (p. 37). She points out that a limiting factor in the design and implementation of such plans is the *able-bodiedness* of the persons making and practicing them. Being able-bodied means that those persons have different frames of reference in terms of embodiment as compared to the students they are working with. The advantage in grounding the design process in the lived experiences of the students is that—given that it is properly carried out—it can bracket the assumptions and habits of the adaptive physical education specialists.

Later, Connolly (2008) presented an embedded movement curriculum developed for persons with autism. The content of the curriculum and the pedagogical processes embedded in it are grounded on "the premise that the lived body is the site of meaning-making" (p. 243) and that the behaviors displayed by persons with autism are solutions to stressed embodiment, rather than displays of deliberate deviance. Connolly describes the environmental requirements of the curriculum (e.g., surfaces, obstacles, lighting, objects, and equipment), content and process (e.g., attunement for body signs, dignified interventions for calming), instructional strategies (e.g., attention to the person's "developmental repertoire" [p. 248]), and gymnasium space and pedagogic intentionality (e.g., how mats soften noise). A more detailed presentation of the embedded curriculum is beyond the scope of this chapter. The main point here is to highlight the possibilities of work from a phenomenological perspective to ensure that the embodiment of the participants are respected and honored.

While the work of Maureen Connolly highlights how embodiment can be a fruitful perspective to parallel, supplement, or even replace medically oriented work, it has also inspired others to use embodiment as a theoretical perspective of relevance for adaptive physical education. For example, Evensen et al. (2017) studied the intersection of the lived body and lived things in a special needs education unit. Lived things are, in this case, objects that are put to practical–pedagogical use in the special needs education unit and, thus, structure the experiences of the students. By way of close observations based on a phenomenological methodology (van Manen, 2014), Evensen et al. (2017) investigated the meaning of things used in the unit. They found that traditional toys were not favored by the students and the educators, because these toys carry with them specific intentions; for instance, by demanding motor skills that were beyond the reach of the children or requiring the imaging of a world that these children had little or no experience of. This meant that the relations between the participants' ways of being in the world and those ways suggested by pre-defined things broke down. On the other hand, things that one might not think of as traditional toys, such as a golden chain or an IKEA bag, provided open, multi-sensory possibilities allowing the participants to play with them in their own way. Much like the work of Connolly, this study highlights pedagogical work grounded in professionals' attunement to students' lived experiences. By seeking confirmation of their pedagogical decisions in the embodied expressions of their students, the professionals let students without symbolic language seek out and play with things that correspond to their subjective way of being.

Closing comments

In this chapter, I have presented embodiment mainly from a phenomenological perspective. This perspective allows us to understand the intertwining of the body and the world, thus overcoming body–mind and body–world dualisms. There is, therefore, also a strong affinity between this perspective on embodiment and understandings of disability that seek to be alternatives to the medical and the social models of disability.

One challenge with the phenomenological perspective is that it emphasizes individual experiences. Although phenomenology clearly is not subjectivist or introspective, it is regularly criticized by contemporary scholars for not being able to take up structural issues, such as politics or oppression. As an example, Weiss (2015, p. 80) has formulated this critique as the "male philosopher's tendency to presume that his descriptions of lived experience hold true for all human beings, regardless of gender, race, class, ethnicity, age, ability, etc." Similarly, proponents of the social model of disability would argue in the same way: attending to individual experiences of pain and suffering would derail the political work needed to tear down unjust and disabling political structures.

However, as Standal (2015) has pointed out, the work of phenomenological, feminist philosophers, such as Gail Weiss or Iris Marion Young, shows how conceptual and theoretical resources from phenomenology can be employed precisely to show how embodied experiences are never exclusively a result of universal bodily structures, but also of gender, race, class, ability, and so on. Despite this, there is still an aspect of embodiment that is not covered properly from a phenomenological perspective. This is the discursive aspect of embodiment. As Weiss (2015) points out, experiences and perceptions are shaped by norms that themselves are not explicitly thematicized in experience and perception. How we perceive and experience our own and others' embodiment is formed by perceptual norms about, for instance, what an appropriate body looks like or what abilities a normal body should be able to display.

In an endnote to this chapter, I referred to researchers who prefer the term adap*tive* over adap*ted* physical education. As Connolly and Harvey (2018) point out, the term is used to highlight the "organic and responsive character [of professional practice] and to emphasize that the context and individual sensitive responses required are indeed ongoing and autopoetic, arising from the conditions and contingencies of mundane and intense engagements" (p. 295). Indeed, if the field of adaptive physical education moves from a medical model of disability, the term adaptive can be seen as a response to this move. The concept of embodiment as it is presented in this chapter helps explain this, because when the body is taken seriously as a site of experience and when it is realized that the body is not just something we have—it is also something we are—then we can begin to see the need for a context-sensitive, persons-centered approach to professional practice.

Summary of key points

- Phenomenology is an important school of thought in Continental philosophy. It was founded by Edmund Husserl at the beginning of the 20th century.
- Phenomenology, as a philosophical discipline, has been highly influential for other disciplines, such as sociology, psychology, and the cognitive sciences. It has also been important for the development of qualitative research methods. However, it is important to keep in mind the differences between phenomenology as philosophy and as methodology. There are currently ongoing debates as to what the term phenomenology means when it is used in relation to qualitative research. This is a topic which is not dealt with in this chapter.
- A central point of relevance from phenomenology to adaptive physical education (as well as physical education more generally) is the non-dualistic understanding of the body.
- Phenomenologists such as Husserl, Heidegger, and Merleau-Ponty have shown that human beings are embodied subjects, which means that the body is not just something we *have*, it is, at the same time, also something we *are*.
- The concept of embodiment reflects the idea that a subject experiences the world through the body. Therefore, changes in the bodily capacities change one's perceptions and experiences of the surrounding world. Likewise, how the world is structured, architecturally as well as attitudinally, enables and disables what bodies can do.
- Embodiment further means that the subject can come to embody objects in the world, such as a hockey stick or a wheelchair. We can also come to embody other people's attitudes towards us.
- In disability studies, embodiment has been a helpful concept because it has represented a "third way" between the medical and social models of disability. Embodiment has drawn attention to the lived experiences of impairment.

Reflective questions for discussion

- What does it mean to *have* a body and to *be* a body?
- What are the most important differences between, on the one hand, understanding the body only as a biological entity and, on the other hand, taking a non-dualistic approach to the body?
- Researchers in the area of adaptive physical education who have worked from a phenomenological perspective and have used the term embodiment seem to come to similar conclusions regarding the professional practice of, for example, adaptive physical educators. What are the most important consequences for practitioners?

Note

1 Traditionally, the field of study that this handbook covers has been named adapted physical education. However, there have been recent suggestions for a shift in terminology towards adap*tive*, rather than adap*ted* (e.g., Connolly & Harvey, 2018; Goodwin & Howe, 2016; Standal & Rugseth, 2016). The difference in terminology is intended to capture the difference between flexible, person-centered approaches to teaching and professional practice (adaptive) as opposed to pre-determined, expert-driven programs (adapted). In this chapter, I use the term adaptive. This reflects my conviction about the nature of professional practice in our field, and—as is clear in this chapter—it also reflects the theoretical position I draw on in presenting the role of the body in adaptive physical education (and adaptive physical activity, more broadly).

References

Arnold, P. J. (1979). *Meaning in movement, sport and physical education.* London, UK: Heinemann.

Caspersen, C. J., Powell, K. E., & Christenson, G. M. (1985). Physical activity, exercise, and physical fitness: Definitions and distinctions for health-related research. *Public Health Reports.*, *100*(2), 126.

Cheville, J. (2005). Confronting the problem of embodiment. *International Journal of Qualitative Studies in Education.*, *18*(1), 85–107. doi:10.1080/09518390412331318405

Connolly, M. (1995). Phenomenology, physical ducation, and special populations. *Human Studies.*, *18*, 25–40. doi:10.1007/BF01322838

Connolly, M. (1997). *Physical education Encyclopedia of phenomenology.* L. Embree. 535–537. Dordrecht, The Netherlands: Kluwer.

Connolly, M. (2008). The remarkable logic of autism: Developing and describing an embedded curriculum based in semiotic phenomenology. *Sport, Ethics & Philosophy Sport, Ethics and Philosophy.*, *2*, 234–256. doi:10.1080/17511320802223824

Connolly, M., & Craig, T. (2002). Stressed embodiment: Doing phenomenology in the wild. *Human Studies.*, *25*, 451–462. doi:10.1023/A:1021226510898

Connolly, M., & Harvey, W. J. (2018). Critical pedagogy and APA: A resonant (and timely) interdisciplinary blend. *Adapted Physical Activity Quarterly.*, *35*(3), 293–307. doi:10.1123/apaq.2017-0106

Crossley, N. (2006). *Reflexive embodiment in contemporary society.* New York: Open University Press.

Dreyfus, H. L. (1991). *Being-in-the-world. A commentary on Heidegger's Being and Time, Division I.* London, UK: The MIT Press.

Dreyfus, H. L., & Dreyfus, S. E. (1996). The challenge of Merleau-Ponty's phenomenology of embodiment for cognitive science: Perspectives on embodiment. In G. Weiss & H. Haber (Eds.), *Perspectives on embodiment: The intersections of nature and culture* (pp. 103–120). London, UK: Routledge.

Embree, L. (1997). *Introduction Encyclopedia of phenomenology.* L. Embree. 1–5. Dordrecht, The Netherlands: Kluwer.

Evensen, K. V., Standal, Ø. F., & Ytterhus, B. (2017). Golden paper, a chain and a bag: A phenomenology of queer things in a special needs education unit. *Phenomenology & Practice.*, *11*(2), 60–69.

Goodwin, D., & Howe, P. D. (2016). Framing cross-cultural ethical practice in adapt[ive] physical activity. *Quest*, *68*(1), 43–54. doi:10.1080/00336297.2015.1117501

Grenier, M. (2007). Inclusion in physical education: From the medical model to social constructionism. *Quest.*, *59*(3), 298–310. doi:10.1080/00336297.2007.10483554

Grue, L., & Heiberg, A. (2006). Notes on the history of normality: Reflections on the work of Quetelet and Galton. *Scandinavian Journal of Disability Research.*, *8*(4), 232–246. doi:10.1080/15017410600608491

Haegele, J. A., & Hodge, S. (2016). Disability discourse: Overview and critiques of the medical and social models. *Quest.*, *68*(2), 193–206. doi:10.1080/00336297.2016.1143849

Heidegger, M. (1996). *Being and time.* Albany, NY: SUNY press.

Hughes, B., & Paterson, K. (1997). The social model of disability and the disappearing body: Towards a sociology of impairment. *Disability & Society.*, *12*(3), 325–340. doi:10.1080/09687599727209

Inahara, M. (2009). The body which is not one: The body, femininity and disability. *Body & Society.*, *15*, 47–62. doi:10.1177/1357034X08100146

Leder, D. (1990). *The Absent body.* Chicago, Ill.: The University of Chicago Press.

Merleau-Ponty, M. (1963). *The structure of behavior.* Pittsburg, PN: Duquesne University Press.

Merleau-Ponty, M. (2002). *Phenomenology of perception.* London: Routledge.

Oliver, M. (1996). *Understanding disability. From theory to practice.* New York, NY: St. Martin's Press.

Paterson, K., & Hughes, B. (1999). Disability Studies and phenomenology: The carnal politics of everday life. *Disability & Society.*, *14*(5), 597–610. doi:10.1080/09687599925966

Quennerstedt, M., Almqvist, J., & Öhman, M. (2011). Keep your eye on the ball: Investigating artifacts-in-use in physical education. *Interchange.*, *42*(3), 287–305. doi:10.1007/s10780-012-9160-0

Romdenh-Romluc, K. (2011). *Merleau-Ponty and phenomenology of perception.* Oxon, UK: Routledge.

Ryle, G. (1949). *The concept of mind.* London, UK: Penguin books.

Scully, J. L. (2008). Disability and the thinking body. In K. Kristiansen, S. Vehmas, & T. Shakespeare (Eds.), *Arguing about disability: Philosophical perspectives* (pp. 57–73). London, UK: Routledge.

Shakespeare, T. (2006). *Disability rights and wrongs.* London, UK: Routledge.

Sheets-Johnstone, M. (2018). Why kinesthesia, tactility and affectivity matter. *Body & Society.*, 1357034X1878098. doi:10.1177/1357034x18780982

Slatman, J. (2016). *Our strange body: Philosophical reflections on identity and medical interventions.* Amsterdam, Netherlands: Amsterdam University Press.

Standal, Ø. F. (2009). *Relation of meaning. A phenomenologically oriented case study of learning bodies in a rehabilitation context.* Oslo, Norway: Norwegian School of Sport Sciences.

Standal, Ø. F. (2011). Re-embodiment: Incorporation through embodied learning of wheelchair skills. *Medicine, Health Care and Philosophy.*, *14*(2), 177–184. doi:10.1007/s11019-010-9286-8

Standal, Ø. F. (2015). *Phenomenology and pedagogy in physical education.* Oxon, UK: Routledge.

Standal, Ø. F., & Rugseth, G. (2016). Experience, intersubjectivity, and reflection: A human science perspective on preparation of future professionals in adaptive physical activity. *Quest.*, *68*(1), 29–42. doi:10.1080/00336297.2015.1117000

Stolz, S. (2014). *The philosophy of physical education. A new perspective.* London, UK: Routledge.

Toombs, S. K. (1992). *The meaning of illness. A phenomenological account of the different perspectives of physician and patient.* Dordrecht, The Netherlands: Kluwer Academic Publishers.

Toombs, S. K. (1995). The lived experience of disability. *Human Studies.*, *18*, 9–23. doi:10.1007/BF01322837

van Manen, M. (1990). *Researching lived experience. Human science for an action sensitive pedagogy.* Ontario, Canada: SUNY Press.

van Manen, M. (2014). *Phenomenology of practice. Meaning-giving methods in phenomenological research and writing.* Walnut Creek, CA: Left Coast Press.

Weiss, G. (2015). The normal, the natural, and the normative: A Merleau-Pontian legacy to feminist theory, critical race theory, and disability studies. *Continental Philosophy Review.*, *48*(1), 77–93. doi:10.1007/s11007-014-9316-y

Zahavi, D. (2003). *Husserl's phenomenology.* Stanford, CA: Stanford University Press.

Zahavi, D. (2018). *Phenomenology: The basics.* London, UK: Routledge.

15

Constructivism and social constructionism in physical education and adapted physical education

Michelle Grenier

In this chapter, I investigate the theoretical and operational understanding of, and the distinction between, social constructivism and social constructionism. Both theories have ontological and epistemological foundations similarly used in research to investigate institutional or social phenomenon. Constructivism and constructionist theories are not unitary positions; rather, they comprise a continuum of arrangements resulting in multiple applications. Typically, this continuum is divided into three broad categories that include: radical constructivism, cognitive constructivism, and social constructionism.

Historical overview

Constructivism espouses the idea that the world we live in is not necessarily evident and that individuals actively construct the way they view their everyday life. A constructivist epistemology emphasizes the importance of culture and context in constructing knowledge based on the understanding that there is no objective truth (Fosnot, 2013). Constructivism was influenced by a number of philosophical writers, including Judith Butler, John Dewey, Karl Marx, Maurice Merleau-Ponty and Ludwig Wittgenstein (Weinberg, 2008). Psychological theorists closely associated with the theory include Lev Vygotsky, Jerome Bruner, and Albert Bandura. Within constructivist orientations, learners actively construct their own knowledge and meaning from their experiences (Fosnot, 2013; Steffe & Gale, 1995).

The primary premise of constructivism is that the world, as it is understood, is a multifaceted series of socially built realities. It is based on specific assumptions about reality, knowledge, and learning, constructed through human activity. Members of a society together invent the properties of the world (Kukla, 2000). For the constructivist, reality cannot be discovered, as it does not exist prior to its social invention. The language and the communicative discourses upheld by a particular culture have a central role in the processes by which the world is understood. Within a constructivist orientation, it is important to reflect on the historical and cultural backgrounds of personal assumptions to maintain the possibility that there are other realities (Sandu, 2016).

Constructivism, sometimes referred to as cognitive constructivism in education, is a philosophy that advocates the construction of knowledge through experiences that foster learning. In contrast to individual or passive functions, learning is a social process created through social interactions and activities (Fosnot, 2013). The role of the teacher is not to transmit or to impose knowledge, but to guide the learner through his or her experience of socially constructed learning (Gredler, 1997; Prawat & Floden, 1994; von Glasersfeld, 1995a). Early examples of constructivism in education were proposed by John Dewey (1930), who described thinking as a natural act that should be supported by a rich environment rather than classroom uniformity or the rigidity imposed by texts. Another significant contributor to constructivism was Jean Piaget (1957), who saw learning as a continuous process where a student assimilates knowledge entities into meaningful knowledge constructs.

Constructed knowledge as a theoretical framework

Constructivism assumes a relativist ontology of multiple realities and a subjectivist epistemology whereby the knower and respondent co-create reality (Schwandt, 2003). Different views on methods for use investigating social phenomena and those central to education arise out of the particular assumptions made on issues of ontology and epistemology (Guba & Lincoln, 1989). Epistemological assumptions guide the researcher's judgment of the appropriateness of different methodological choices.

Four essential epistemological tenets form the foundation of constructivism (von Glasersfeld, 1984).

1. Knowledge is not passively accumulated, but, rather, is the result of active cognition by the individual.
2. Cognition is an adaptive process that functions to make an individual's behavior more viable given a particular environment.
3. Cognition organizes and makes sense of one's experience, which may not be an accurate representation of reality.
4. Knowledge has roots in both biological/neurological construction, with social, cultural, and language based interactions (Dewey,1917; Gergen, 1995; Maturana, 1978).

Thus, constructivism acknowledges the learner's active role in the personal creation of knowledge, the importance of experience (both individual and social) and the realization that the knowledge created will vary in the degree to which it may accurately represent reality. The range of constructivist thought is contingent on the relevance of the principles and the formation of knowledge within constructivism As will be seen, these tenets may be emphasized differently, resulting in various "degrees" or "types" of constructivism.

Types of constructivism

Cognitive constructivism

Cognitive constructivism represents one end of the constructivist continuum, associated with psychology, information processing, and the component processes of cognition (Larochelle &

Garrison, 1998). As indicated in the first two tenets, knowledge acquisition is an adaptive process that results from active cognizing by the individual learner. This stance emphasizes the external nature of knowledge through an independent reality knowable to the individual. From the cognitive constructivist position, knowledge is the result of internalization and (re) construction of external reality (Prawat & Floden, 1994). These structures correspond to processes that exist in the real world. The claim that reality is knowable to the individual differentiates cognitive constructivism from radical constructivism and social constructionism.

The internalization and (re)construction of external reality is considered learning. That is, learning is the process of building accurate internal models or representations that mirror or reflect external structures that exist in the *real* world. This perspective on learning focuses on (a) the procedures or processes of learning, and (b) how what is learned is represented or symbolized in the mind (Lave & Wenger, 1991). Cognitive constructivism is considered a weak form of constructivism, as it embraces only two of the four epistemological tenets. The construction of knowledge involves creating mental structures and has led to significant empirical findings regarding learning, memory, and cognition (Fosnot, 2013).

Radical constructivism

Radical constructivism represents the far end of the constructivist paradigm, exemplifying the four tenets, in particular the fourth, that social interactions are a source of knowledge (Larochelle et al., 1998). This epistemological emphasis leads to defining principles that maintain the internal nature of knowledge and the idea that while an external reality may exist, it is unknowable to the individual (von Glasersfeld, 1984). Because external forms are mediated by the senses, one is not adept at rendering an accurate representation of objects and social interactions. Therefore, while knowledge is constructed from experience, that which is constructed is not in any discernible way an accurate representation of the external world (von Glasersfeld, 1995b).

Von Glasersfeld (1995b) provides two basic premises as a starting point for understanding constructivism: (a) knowledge is actively rather than passively received; and (b) knowledge is adaptive and individuals actively participate in developing knowledge (Raskin & Debany, 2018). A constructivist approach stresses the viability of knowledge, or how well it works (von Glasersfeld, 1995b). In this regard, constructivism has much in common with philosophical pragmatism, which evaluates knowledge not so much in terms of its correspondence with things in themselves, but in terms of its ability to help us achieve desired ends (Butt, 2005).

Similar to a general understanding of constructivism, radical constructivism also maintains that people never know the world directly (von Glasersfeld, 1995b; LaRochelle & Desautels, 2007). Rather, a presumed external world triggers internal processes within people, who then respond based on their physical and psychological structures (Maturana, 1978). According to Ernst von Glasersfeld (1995b), the purpose of knowledge is not to replicate the world as it is, but to help people survive in whatever circumstances they find themselves. The *radical* element of radical constructivism views human constructions as personal and private, with minimal ethical balance for recognizing that one's understanding of reality actually reflects a social reality (von Glasersfeld, 1995b). Social reality is subjective and multi-faceted, created by the individual actors, who, in the process of creating reality, actually establish their own meaning and representation of reality (Creswell, 2003).

One criticism of constructivists is that they are "antirealist" because they reject the possibility of an external, independent reality and that such realities can be judged to be true or false (Burr, 1998). Placing constructivism at the far end of the reality continuum implies that it misrepresents the "real" world as a simple construction. As a result, constructivists have been characterized as "deniers of reality" (Burr, 2018, p. 370). Burr (2018) argues that material reality is often a battleground for contested versions of reality, but reminds us that these distinctions are products of our own human condition within the material world.

Situating constructivism and constructionism

In previous sections, I described two forms of constructivism—cognitive and radical. However confusing these terms may be, they are often used interchangeably with the term *constructionism*. Grounded in Émile Durkheim's (1964) framework, constructionism examines the distinction between established knowledge and the actions that contribute to the justification of a particular type of knowledge. Research utilizing a constructionist framework considers questions on the nature of social reality and how social reality is assembled, at times alternating between the two questions (Crotty, 2003).

Contrary to the emphasis in radical constructivism, the focus here is not on the meaning-making activity of the individual mind, but the collective generation of meaning as shaped by conventions of language and other social processes. Kenneth Gergen (2015) challenges the idea of an objective basis for knowledge claims and the process of knowledge construction. In lieu of focusing on the matter of individual minds and cognitive processes, he turns his attention outward to the world of intersubjectively shared, social constructions of meaning and knowledge. Acknowledging a debt to the phenomenology of Schutz and Luckmann (1973), Gergen (1985) labels his approach "social constructionism."

Within a social constructionist framework, human constructions are a collection of shared meanings through relationship and the ensuing discourses (Burr, 2018; Gergen, 1994, 2015). The idea of truth-as-socially-constructed is rooted in the assumption that what people take to be true is inevitably a relationally, culturally derived product (Burr, 2018; Gergen, 1994). Burr (2018) argues otherwise, stating that knowledge constructed within the individual should be understood as emerging from the social and psychological realm of the individual "filling the subjectivity gap" (p. 369).

Social constructionism differs from constructivism in that the former focuses on collective generation of meaning while the latter suggests that the individual mind is active exclusively in meaning-making activity. Crotty (2003) distinguishes "accounts of constructionism where this social dimension of meaning is at center stage from [constructivism] where it is not" (p. 57). Both constructivism and constructionism are alike in their position of anti-essentialism and the possibility of unmediated knowledge. Social constructionists, such as Kenneth Gergen (1991, 1995) dispute their identification as constructivists due to the fundamental premise that meaning is personal and private. In this way, social constructionism is treated as a variant of constructivism, as it emphasizes the social conditions and referential possibilities.

Foundation of constructionist research

Constructionist research refutes the idea of permanency and views the production of knowledge as the result of historical and social processes. Because social constructionists examine assumptions and the cultural processes that inform the object of study, they are critical of mainstream institutional disciplines. For the social constructionist, reality, as is commonly understood, could be alternatively understood.

Constructionism is similar to constructivism in that it contains nuanced subsets. There are, for example, social and psychological forms of constructionism (see Gergen, 1994; Phillips, 1995), and within social constructionism a weak version is further distinguished from a strong one, depending on the stance they take on "the role that social factors play in what constitutes legitimate knowledge" (Schwandt, 2003, p. 308). Specifically, both the weak and strong forms of constructionism share the assumption that knowledge is not disinterested and apolitical. However, the weak form attempts to preserve some way of distinguishing levels of interpretations while the strong form advocates a more skeptical stance towards our collectively understood realities.

A challenge to using and applying a constructivist or constructionist pedagogy is that the strategies are not clear and, as a result, scholarship suffers from a scope of theoretical underpinnings which can result in clouded or disordered outcomes (Brooks & Brooks, 1993; Johassen, 1991). Both constructivism and constructionism are typically aligned with qualitative inquiry that may include multiple epistemological, methodological, and ethical criticisms of social scientific research (Schwandt, 2003, p. 293). Clarification between the forms of constructivism is necessary because radical constructivism and social constructionism each have a distinct epistemological agenda, which will have an impact on methodological practices.

As I discuss later, the literature pertaining to inclusion, general physical education, and adapted physical education (APE) for students with disabilities can reflect a tradition grounded in the medical model of disability (Haegele & Hodge, 2016). As a result, a constructivist or constructionist interpretation raises questions on the assertion of objectivity and the potentially undesirable consequences for the individuals it is intended to serve (Gallagher, 2007). Similar to the tensions that exist between constructivism and constructionism, research associated with the two perspectives makes it difficult to synthesize the two approaches (Weinberg, 2008).

Methods associated within a constructivist or constructionist framework can be transferred into a number of methodologies, focused mainly on how the question is conceptualized and the data analyzed. Procedural and analytical practices are interwoven throughout qualitative inquiry and it is useful to consider the type of data collected to sort out the research process. Typical procedures within the social constructionist process include naturalist ethnography, grounded theory method, emancipatory research, and discourse analysis (Charmaz, 2008; Crotty, 2003).

Within ethnographic practices, data collection focuses on details of the setting of interest (Holstein & Gubrium, 2008). Capturing as much detail as possible is prioritized with constructionist ethnographers through field notes that transform events through the use of words and language. A constructionist analysis looks for what participants are "doing with words" (p. 389) shifting the focus from "the what" to "the how" through bracketing that captures emergent relations between action and context.

Grounded theory is a second approach that allows researchers to answer the why of questions as a method for understanding participants' social constructions (Charmaz, 2008). Depending on their epistemological stance, grounded theory is attractive to those who endorse social constructionism, particularly for those who do not subscribe to traditional grounded theory techniques. Discourse analysis is a third form of analytic analysis, with a strong social constructionist epistemology that espouses the belief that language is of central importance in constructing ideas that make up our social world (Potter & Wetherwell, 1994). This epistemological stance leads towards a specific kind of analysis and interpretation. While there is no particular technique, practice and example are the primary means for using this method.

Applications to research

The view adopted in this chapter is consistent with constructionist research, which challenges a fixed and universal conception through a socio-cultural narrative. Because constructionists question objective truth and challenge the notion that objective truth should be the goal of inquiry, the application of scholarship will provide evidence of truth-challenging while also revealing the unintended consequences of a field grounded in a medical tradition (Goodwin & Dunn, 2018). Labels and the educational context of practice can be problematic, particularly given that most students with identified disabilities (approximately 96%) are educated in general education schools (An & Meaney, 2015). In fact, most (63.1%) students aged 6–21 served under *IDEA*, Part B, are educated inside general education classrooms 80% or more of the day (United States Department of Education, 2018). Studying the ways in which discourses construct socio-cultural identities can reveal culturally reinforced constructions of disability, which oftentimes present obstacles to student learning and achievement.

In the following section, I identify the dilemma of interpretation when classifying students and the cultural values, societal beliefs, and social arrangements that constitute disability (Gallagher, 2007). I utilize a constructionist framework to dispute the authority of knowledge by challenging the construction of ability and the research on teacher attitudes and practices towards students with disabilities. In this section, I consider the limitations of current understandings of disability and disability identity and explore the social construction of disability through a constructionist lens in order to expand discourses of disability. In the process, I pose critical questions that challenge the biomedical phenomena of disability as a key aspect of research on individuals with disabilities (Grenier, 2007).

The construction of ability

Rethinking the concept of normalcy through a constructionist lens can shift the burden of proof from the child to the disability and the contextual factors that may discredit the student. The valued truths associated with disability frame epistemological questions and research methodologies, particularly when addressing issues of difference and the acceptance of differences in the American educational system (Bouffard, Strean, & Davis, 1998; Goodwin & Dunn, 2018). Shogan (1998) further challenges constructions of disability that influence research and practice by posing the question, "How much do research and professional practice in adapted physical activity depend upon notions of the norm while giving experts license to intervene to make bodies or abilities more normal?" (p. 275).

Research within APE and physical education more generally suggests that professionals tend to (a) assume student bodies are homogeneous, (b) insufficiently describe characteristics of samples, and (c) utilize instruments that may not be appropriate across socio-demographic groups (Grenier, Horrell, & Genovese, 2014; Hodge, Kozub, Robinson, & Hersman, 2007). The disability is essentialized as a trait, enhanced through social structures that promote categorical superiority of intellectual and physical functioning (Jones, 1996). Individuals with disabilities are viewed as deviations from the norm, with the person's disability standing at the forefront of who she or he is and who that individual may become (Davis, 1995).

Because labels hinge on individual deficits in the person, choice and opportunity are limited. This is the dis/ability conundrum, as many physical education teachers continue to value particular kinds of activities and abilities (Petrie, Devcich, & Fitzgerald, 2018). Evans (2004) problematizes the concept of ability and the privileged status that "physical ability" has in the relationship between physical education teachers and learners. The teachers are required to embody the curriculum. They must perform the physical education curriculum, and their ability to teach is enmeshed with the knowledge/content of the subject and the performative act of pedagogy (Grenier et al., 2014). The valued sports practices in physical education classes where performance and ability is prioritized results in a lack of participation Alves, Grenier, Haegele, & Duarte, 2018.

Individuals with non-conforming bodies, those that do not achieve the type of makeup typically desired in physical education contexts, such as those with disabilities, may experience instances of being restricted in participation in performance-based pedagogies (Fitzgerald, 2012; Fitzgerald & Hay, 2015; Haegele & Sutherland, 2015; Petrie et al., 2018). Students with disabilities are identified for their disabling conditions rather than their potential contributions. Davis (1995) reinforces this notion in stating that, "the idea of the norm pushes a variation of the body through a stricter template, guiding the way the body should be. The social construction of normalcy is what creates the disabled person's problem" (p. 24). To some extent the evaluative process for placement within the least restrictive environment within physical education entails a similar codifying process (Grenier, 2007).

The social construction of ability in physical education, which inscribes bodies with meaning, may well create a hegemonic reinforcement of ability that works to exclude teachers with disabilities (Tischler & McCaughtry, 2011). Evans (2004) indicates that ability in physical education is characterized and informed by White masculine notions of skill that privilege organized sport. Because physical education has long been charged with producing a sporting and political field in terms of ordering of bodies in social space, health practices, and athletic performance, disabled bodies may be stigmatized because they do not conform to normal conceptions of ability (Brown, 2005; Evans, Bright, & Brown, 2013; Howson, 2004). In effect, the dominant discourse of a pedagogy that relies on a narrowly defined conception of ability may act to constrain the freedoms of those with disabilities to become teachers through the curriculum and evaluation processes (Evans, 2004; Grenier, 2007). More so, physical education teachers may undermine inclusive practices because of training typically grounded in a medicalized deficit perspective that maintains static assumptions on ability (Brittain, 2004; Evans, 2004). Students who are not deemed able are marginalized and treated differently (Fitzgerald & Hay, 2015; Haegele & Sutherland, 2015).

Within schools, discourses of disability impact on the pedagogical decisions of teachers that can hinder the scope for students with disabilities to be included, feel valued as learners, and have their learning needs meet (Kemmis et al., 2014; Wilhelmsen & Sorensen, 2017). Oftentimes, the social interaction experiences of students with disabilities are negative because of placement, organizational practices, or lack of peer support (Benia, Fletcher, & Chróinínb, 2017: Block & Obrusnikova, 2007; Li & Rukavina, 2012; Spencer-Cavaliere & Watkinson, 2010). For example, when physical education is competitively institutionalized with little adaptation, students are excluded (Fitzgerald, 2012; Fitzgerald & Kirk, 2009; Tant & Watelain, 2016). Activities such as team game activities reflect curricular choices and teacher values (Alves et al., 2018). The literature on children's experiences raises questions on the social arrangements established by the teacher and how this shapes an understanding of performative skills (Alves et al., 2018; Block & Obrusnikova, 2007; Grenier, 2007).

Teacher attitudes

The manner in which students with disabilities are conceptualized in schools requires an analysis of power structures, the processes of identity construction, group identification, and the discriminatory effects of social structures that contribute to a disabling environment (Jones,

1996). Historically, society has viewed people with disabilities from a medical model perspective, in which individuals were labeled as ill, dysfunctional, and in need of medical treatment (Haegele & Hodge, 2016). As a legitimized doctrine, science's authoritative stance is premised on a neutral method of control as researchers construct knowledge of objects within the materials and values of a culture. Rational thoughts are embedded in value orientations aligned with power allegiances that maintain an ordered social hierarchy of all that is considered real and good (Gergen, 2015). For persons with disabilities whose physical and psychological dispositions fall outside established codes, differences translate into deficits (Linton, 1998). These handicaps act as social, physical, and intellectual barriers that hinder the person's ability to lead a productive life within his or her local community. Similarly, the minoritized group paradigm treats disability as an issue of oppression, diversity, and difference (Haegele & Hodge, 2016). A short review of the literature on teacher attitudes illustrates a pattern within the profession whereby teachers are challenged on how best to instruct students with disabilities (Block & Obrusnikova, 2007; Combs, Elliott, & Whipple, 2010; Hodge, Ammah, Casebolt, LaMaster, & O'Sullivan, 2004; Lytle & Collier, 2002; Morley, Bailey, Tan, & Cooke, 2005; Qi & Ha, 2012; Wilhelmsen & Sorensen, 2017).

In an in-depth systematic review, Tant and Watelain (2016) examined teacher representations, defining them as "the product of processes of mental activity through which an individual or group reconstitutes the reality with which it is confronted and to which it attributes a specific meaning" (Abric, 1994, p. 13). Their findings suggest that the attitudes of teachers depended on the type of disability, the student's age (class level), and the severity of the disability. The teacher-specific factor that most influenced their positive attitude towards the inclusion of students with disabilities was perceived teaching competence (Tant & Watelain, 2016). For instance, teachers in Brazil were confident and expressed feeling more effective teaching students with mild disabilities compared to those with severe disabilities, particularly when resources were limited (e.g., no ramps for wheelchair access to playing surfaces) (Hodge, Haegele, Gutierres Filho, & Rizzi Lopes, 2018). Researchers also report that disability label and type of disability is associated with negative social attitudes towards students with behavioral disorders (Hodge et al., 2018; Meegan & MacPhail, 2006; Obrusnikova, 2008).

In many cases, schools and the educators working in the schools are not adequately prepared to create educational programs that address the academic needs of students with disabilities, nor do they have a critical understanding of the socially constructed nature of disability (Hodge et al., 2018). Kirk (2010) suggests that physical education teachers are resistant to change, in part due to a lack of preparedness to teach within inclusive settings (e.g., Hardin, 2005; Hersman & Hodge, 2010; Jerlinder, Danermark, & Gill, 2010; Obrusnikova, 2008).

Educational practices should be viewed as a social construction closely related to power relations that reflect societal values (Alves et al., 2018). A number of scholars, including McDermott and Varenne (1995) offer complex accounts of how the interactions between teachers and students can both marginalize and stratify students with disabilities. Routine school practices, such as separating children by ability, produces categories that focus on disability as an attribute and social category. What is clear is that more support is needed in training teachers to be effective practitioners for their students with disabilities (Block & Obrusnikova, 2007; Combs et al., 2010; Tant & Watelain, 2016). Critical pedagogies should focus on complex profiles of disability with emphasis on pedagogic practices and communication systems for expression (Connelly & Harvey, 2018), as well as environmental supports that support access and participation (Wilhelmsen & Sorensen, 2017).

Conclusion

Utilizing a constructivist framework encourages debate on epistemological and ontological assumptions underlying the construction of disability. Concerns regarding the process of labeling and identifying students with disabilities and their experiences are not new conversations to the field of physical education, including APE. This issue has caught the attention of researchers and scholars, who argue for closer examinations of what it means to be disabled and how disability is constructed and acted upon in the schools (Grenier, Wright, Collins, & Kearns, 2014; Haegele & Hodge, 2016). Complicating the process of identifying children in need of special education services are the diverse ways in which ability is defined, interpreted, and situated (Evans, 2004). The challenge for the social constructionist is to move away from the individualizing discourses of disability to an understanding of culturally derived modes of thought, words, and actions that specify constructions of disability.

A constructivist or constructionist lens in general physical education and APE has the potential to help educators make the gymnasium a more hospitable place for students to participate with their peers. By working against a fixed idea of what it means to be disabled, practitioners can create conditions that are less restrictive for their students. Avoiding the stigma associated with a label and opting for an approach that considers factors that will support students will make their work more liberating.

Constructionist research can assist us in appreciating the value of difference and how we can optimize student performance through learning outcomes aligned with students' needs, rather than normed values. These practices can inform the way knowledge is viewed and can lead to greater pedagogical innovation and "democracy in negotiating what counts in educational practice ... and a shift from subject and child centered modes of education to a focus on relationship" (Gergen & Wortham, 2001, p. 136).

If teachers are to be prepared to meet the needs of teaching diverse populations in the 21st century, a view of disability grounded in the social factors as influenced by teacher and student behaviors should be undertaken. In turn, an appreciation of the context that reflects a relational analysis can provide a view of the inclusive classroom that allows for "differentiating characteristics of groups to be discovered rather than presumed" (Holliday, 2002, p. 12). The need to consider serious dialogue exchanges across lines of considerable differences of interest, perspective, and intellectual style that attends to social differences that may prevent educators from understanding the phenomena of disability holistically (Weinberg, 2008) is paramount. Why we engage in dialogue and who we engage in it with should not be governed by our fixed philosophical stance, but by our interest and desire to improve the conditions of those we study, and, more progressively and inclusively, co-research with.

Summary of key points

- Constructivism and constructionism highlight the dynamic contours of social reality and the way it is understood.
- Constructivism and constructionism are composed of many articulations that offer a useful empirical perspective.
- Although constructivism and constructionism are diverse, there are shared theoretical groundings and significances.
- A primary difference between constructivism and constructionism is that the former focuses on meaning-making activity of the individual mind and the latter on the

collective generation of meaning as shaped by conventions of language and other social processes.

- A constructionist lens can challenge the nature of reality within the socio-political system of the schools.
- Understanding how labels create social barriers requires a reimagining of the complex relationship we have with labels and the special education system.
- Utilizing a constructivist or constructionist lens can shed light on the cultural values, beliefs, and social arrangements that shape disability.
- Educators should examine the intersection of curriculum, pedagogy, and practice as a shared value system to avoid positioning students with disabilities in negative terms and to insure all learners achieve success.

Reflective questions for discussion

- Distinguish between a constructivist and constructionist orientation to research.
- What types of epistemological stances would position researchers to use a constructionist framework?
- What are the types of research questions that could be supported with a constructionist framework?
- Are there alternatives to the construction of ability through competency and skilled-based performance?
- How can educators contend with the need to provide support and resources while challenging the nature of schooling and the dominant ideologies of the school culture?

References

Abric, J. C. (1994). *Pratiques sociales et representations*. Paris: Presses Universitaires de France.

Alves, M., Grenier, M., Haegele, J., & Duarte, E. (2018). "I didn't do anything, I just watched:" Perspectives of Brazilian students with physical disabilities toward physical education. *International Journal of Inclusive Education*. Published on- line 17, August, 2018.

An, J., & Meaney, K. (2015). Inclusion practices in elementary physical education: A social cognitive perspective. *International Journal of Disability, Development and Education, 62*(2), 143–157. doi:10.1080/1034912X.2014.998176

Benia, S., Fletcher, T., & Chróinínb, D. (2017). Meaningful experiences in physical education and youth sport: A review of sthe literature. *Quest, 69*(3), 291–312. doi:10.1080/00336297.2016.1224192

Block, M. E., & Obrusnikova, I. (2007). Inclusion in physical education: A review of the literature from 1995-2005. *Adapted Physical Activity Quarterly, 24*(2), 103–124. doi:10.1123/apaq.24.2.103

Bouffard, M., Strean, W. B., & Davis, W. E. (1998). Questioning our philosophical and methodological research assumptions: Psychological perspectives. *Adapted Physical Activity Quarterly, 15*(3), 250–268.

Brittain, I. (2004). Perceptions of disability and their impact upon the involvement in sport for people with disabilities at all levels. *Journal of Sport and Social Issues, 28*(4), 429–452.

Brooks, J. G., & Brooks, M. G. (1993). *In search of understanding: The case for constructivist classrooms*. Alexandria, VA: Association for Supervision and Curriculum Development.

Brown, D. (2005). An economy of gendered practices? Learning to teach physical education from the perspective of Pierre Bourdieu's embodied sociology. *Sport Education and Society, 10*(1), 3–23.

Burr, V. (1998). Realism, relativism, social constructionism, and discourse. In I. Parker (Ed.), *Social constructionism, discourse and realism* (pp. 13–25). London: Sage.

Burr, V. (2018). Constructivism and the inescapability of moral choices: A response to Raskin and Debany. *Journal of Constructivist Psychology, 31*(4), 369–375. doi:10.1080/10720537.2017.1384339

Butt, T. (2005). Personal construct theory, phenomenology, and pragmatism. *History & Philosophy of Psychology, 7*(1), 23–35.

Charmaz, K. (2008). Constructionism and the grounded theory method. In J. Holstein & J. Gubrium (Eds.), *Handbook of constructionist research* (pp. 397–412). New York: Guilford Press.

Combs, S., Elliott, S., & Whipple, K. (2010). Elementary physical education teachers' attitudes toward the inclusion of children with special needs: A qualitative investigation. *International Journal of Special Education, 25*(1), 114–125.

Connelly, M., & Harvey, W. (2018). Critical pedagogy and APA: A resonant (and timely) interdisciplinary blend. *Adapted Physical Activity Quarterly, 35*(3), 293–307. doi:10.1123/apaq.2017-0106

Creswell, J. W. (2003). *Research design: Qualitative, quantitative and mixed methods.* London: Sage.

Crotty, M. (2003). *The foundations of social research: Meaning and perspective in the research process.* Thousand Oaks, CA: Sage.

Davis, L. J. (1995). *Disability, deafness and the body. Enforcing normalcy.* New York: Routledge.

Dewey, J. (1930). *The quest for certainty: A study of the relation of knowledge and action.* London: Allyn & Unwin.

Durkheim, E. (1964). *The division of labor in society. Translated by.* New York:Free Press.

Evans, A., Bright, J., & Brown, L. (2013). Non-disabled secondary school children's lived experiences of a wheelchair basketball programme delivered in the east of England. *Sport Education and Society, 20*(6), 741–761. doi:10.1080/13573322.2013.808620

Evans, J. (2004). Making a difference? Education and 'ability' in physical education. *European Physical Education Review, 10*(1), 95–108.

Fitzgerald, H. (2012). Drawing' on disabled students' experiences of physical education and stakeholder responses. *Sport, Education and Society, 17*(4), 443–462. doi:10.1080/13573322.2011.609290

Fitzgerald, H., & Hay, P. (2015). Understanding dis/ability in physical education through the lens of Bourdieu. In S. Lisahunter & E. Emerald (Eds.), *Pierre Bourdieu and physical culture* (pp. 117–125). London: Routledge.

Fitzgerald, H., & Kirk, D. (2009). Physical education as a normalizing practice: Is there space for disability sport?. In H. Fitzgerald (Ed.), *Disability and youth sport* (pp. 91–105). Oxon: Routledge.

Fosnot, C. T. (2013). *Constructivism: Theory, perspective, and practice.* New York: Teachers College Press.

Gallagher, D. (2007). Challenging orthodoxy in special education: On longstanding debates and philosophical divides. In L. Florian (Ed.), *The sage handbook of special education.* (pp. 515–527). London: Sage.

Gergen, K. (2015). *An invitation to social constructionism.* (3rd ed.). London: Sage.

Gergen, K., & Wortham, S. (2001). Social construction and pedagogical practice. In K. Gergen (Ed.), *Social construction in practice.* (pp. 115–136). London: Sage.

Gergen, K. J. (1991). *The saturated self: Dilemmas of identity in contemporary life.* New York: Basic Books.

Gergen, K. J. (1994). *Realities and relationships: Soundings in social construction.* Cambridge, MA: Harvard University Press.

Gergen, K. J. (1995). Social construction and the education process. In L. P. Steffe & J. Gale (Eds.), *Constructivism in education* (pp. 17–39). Hillsdale, NJ: Erlbaum.

Gergen, K. J. (1985). Social constructionist inquiry: Context and implications. In KJ Gergen and KE Davis *The social construction of the person* (pp. 3–18). Springer, New York.

Goodwin, D., & Dunn, J. (2018). Revisiting our research assumptions 20 years on: The role of interdisciplinarity. *Adapted Physical Activity Quarterly, 35*, 249–253. doi:10.1123/apaq.2017-0192

Gredler, M. (1997). *Learning and instruction: Theory into practice.* Merrill: Prentice Hall.

Grenier, M. (2007). Inclusion in physical education: From the medical model to social constructionism. *Quest, 59*(3), 298–310.

Grenier, M., Horrell, A., & Genovese, B. (2014). Doing things my way: Teaching physical education with a disability. *Adapted Physical Activity Quarterly, 31*(4) PubMed, 325–342. 10.1123/apaq.2013-0089.

Grenier, M., Wright, S., Collins, K., & Kearns, C. (2014). "I thought it was going to be lame:" Perceptions of a disability sport unit in general physical education. *Adapted Physical Activity Quarterly, 31*(1), 49–66. doi:10.1123/apaq.2013-0006

Guba, E. G., & Lincoln, Y. S. (1989). *Fourth generation evaluation.* Newbury Park, CA: Sage.

Haegele, J., & Hodge, S. (2016). Disability discourse: Overview and critiques of the medical and social models. *Quest, 68*(2), 193–206. doi:10.1080/00336297.2016.1143849

Haegele, J. A., & Sutherland, S. (2015). Perspectives of students with disabilities toward physical education: A qualitative inquiry review. *Quest, 67*(3), 255–273. doi:org/10.1080/00336297.2015.1050118

Hardin, B. (2005). Physical education teachers' reflections on preparation for inclusion. *Physical Educator*, *62*(1), 44–56.

Hersman, B. L., & Hodge, S. R. (2010). High school physical educators' beliefs about teaching differently abled students in an urban school district. *Education and Urban Society*, *42*(6), 730–757.

Hodge, S. R., Ammah, J. O., Casebolt, K., LaMaster, K., & O'Sullivan, M. (2004). High school general physical education teachers' behaviors and beliefs associated with inclusion. *Sport, Education and Society*, *9*, 395–419. doi:10.1080/13573320412331302458

Hodge, S. R., Haegele, J. A., Gutierres Filho, P. J., & Rizzi Lopes, G. (2018). Brazilian physical education teachers' beliefs about teaching students with disabilities. *International Journal of Disability, Development and Education*, *65*(4), 408–427. doi:10.1080/1034912X.2017.1408896

Hodge, S. R., Kozub, F. M., Robinson, L. E., & Hersman, B. L. (2007). Reporting gender, race, ethnicity, and sociometric status: Guidelines for research and professional practice. *Adapted Physical Activity Quarterly*, *24*(1), 21–37.

Holliday, A. (2002). *Doing and writing qualitative research*. London: Sage.

Holstein, J., & Gubrium, J. (2008). Constructionist impulses in ethnographic fieldwork. In J. Holstein & J. Gubrium (Eds.), *Handbook of constructionist research* (pp. 373–392). New York: Guilford Press.

Howson, A. (2004). *The body in society: An introduction*. Oxford, UK: Polity. doi:10.1080/13573320 41233130248

Jerlinder, K., Danermark, B., & Gill, P. (2010). Swedish primary-school teachers' attitudes to inclusion—The case of PE and pupils with physical disabilities. *European Journal of Special Needs Education*, *25*, 45–57. doi:10.1080/08856250903450830

Johassen, D. H. (1991). Objectivism versus constructivism: Do we need a new philosophical paradigm?. *Educational Technology Research and Development*, *39*(3), 11–12.

Jones, S. (1996). Toward inclusive theory: Disability as social construction. *NASPA Journal*, *33*(4), 347–355.

Kemmis, S., Wilkinson, J., Edwards-Groves, C., Hardy, I., Peter Grootenboer, P., & Bristol, L. (2014). *Changing practices, changing education*. Singapore: Springer.

Kirk, D. (2010). *Physical education futures*. London: Routledge.

Kukla, A. (2000). *Social constructivism and the philosophy of science*. New York: Routledge.

LaRochelle, M., & Desautels, J. (2007). On Ernst von Glasersfeld's contribution to education: One interpretation, one example. *Constructivist Foundations*, *2*(2-3), 90–97.

Larochelle, N. B., & Garrison, J. (Eds.). (1998). *Constructivism and education*. Cambridge: Cambridge Press.

Lave, J., & Wenger, E. (1991). *Situated learning: Legitimate peripheral participation*. Cambridge, UK: Cambridge University Press.

Li, W., & Rukavina, P. (2012). The nature, occurring contexts, and psychological implications of weight-related teasing in urban physical education programs. *Research Quarterly for Exercise and Sport*, *83*, 308–317.

Linton, S. (1998). *Claiming disability*. New York: New York University Press.

Lytle, R., & Collier, D. (2002). The consultative process: Adapted physical education specialists' perceptions. *Adapted Physical Activity Quarterly*, *19*, 261–279.

Maturana, H. R. (1978). Biology of language: The epistemology of reality. In G. A. Miller & E. Lenneberg (Eds.), *Psychology and biology of language and thought* (pp. 27–63). New York: Academic Press.

McDermott, R., & Varenne, H. (1995). Culture as disability. *Anthropology & Culture Quarterly*, *26*, 324–348.

Meegan, S., & MacPhail, A. (2006). Irish physical educators' attitude toward teaching students with special educational needs. *European Physical Education Review*, *12*(1), 75–97. doi:org/10.1177/1356336X 06060213

Morley, D., Bailey, R., Tan, J., & Cooke, B. (2005). Inclusive physical education: Teachers' views of including pupils with special educational needs and/or disabilities in physical education. *European Physical Education Review*, *11*(1), 84–107. doi:10.1177/1356336X05049826

Obrusnikova, I. (2008). Physical educators' beliefs about teaching children with disabilities. *Perceptual and Motor Skills*, *106*, 637–644.

Petrie, K., Devcich, J., & Fitzgerald, H. (2018). Working towards inclusive physical education in a primary school: 'some days I just don't get it. *Right.*' *Physical Education and Sport Pedagogy*, *23*(4), 345–357. doi:10.1080/17408989.2018.1441391

Phillips, D. C. (1995). The good, the bad, and the ugly: The many faces of constructivism. *Educational Researcher*, *24*(7), 5–12.

Piaget, J. (1957). *Construction of reality in the child*. London: Routledge.

Potter, J., & Wetherwell, M. (1994). Analyzing discourse. In A. Bryman & R. G. Burgess (Eds.), *Analyzing qualitative data* (pp. 41–66). London: Routledge.

Prawat, R. S., & Floden, R. E. (1994). Philosophical perspectives on constructivist views of learning. *Educational Psychologist, 29*(1), 37–48.

Qi, J., & Ha, A. S. (2012). Inclusion in physical education: A review of literature. *International Journal of Disability, Development and Education, 59*, 257–281. doi:10.1080/1034912X.2012.697737

Raskin, J., & Debany, A. (2018). The inescapability of ethics and the impossibility of "anything goes:" A constructivist model of ethical meaning making. *Journal of Constructivist Psychology, 31*(4), 343–360. doi:10.1080/10720537.2017.1383954

Sandu, A. (2016). *Social construction of reality as communicative action.* Cambridge, UK: Scholars Publishing.

Schutz, A., & Luckmann, T. (1973). *The Structures of the life-world.* Evanston: Northwestern University Press.

Schwandt, T. A. (2003). Three epistemological stances for qualitative inquiry: Interpretivism, hermeneutics, and social constructionism. In N. K. Denzin & Y. S. Lincoln (Eds.), *The landscape of qualitative research: Theories and issues* (2nd ed., pp. 292–331). Thousand Oaks, CA: Sage.

Shogan, D. (1998). The social construction of disability: The impact of statistics and technology. *Adapted Physical Activity Quarterly, 15*, 269–277.

Shotter, J. (2000). Concepts and transformation. *International Journal of Action Research and Organizational Renewal, 5*(3), 349–362.

Steffe, L. P., & Gale, J. (1995). *Constructivism in education.* Hillsdale, NJ: Lawrence Erlbaum.

Tant, M., & Watelain, E. (2016). Forty years later, a systematic literature review on inclusion in physical education (1975–2015): A teacher perspective. *Educational Research Review, 19*, 1–17.

Tischler, A., & McCaughtry, N. (2011). PE is not for me: When boys' masculinities are threatened. *Research Quarterly for Exercise and Sport, 82*(1), 37–48.

United States Department of Education, Office of Special Education and Rehabilitative Services, Office of Special Education Programs (2018). *40th Annual Report to Congress on the implementation of the Individuals with Disabilities Education Act, 2018.* Washington, DC: USDE.

von Glasersfeld, E. (1984). An introduction to radical constructivism. In P. Watzlawick (Ed.), *The invented reality* (pp. 17–40). New York: Norton.

von Glasersfeld, E. (1995a). A constructivist approach to teaching. In L. P. Steffe & J. Gale, *Constructivism in education* (pp. 3–16). Hillsdale, NJ: Erlbaum.

von Glasersfeld, E. (1995b). *Radical constructivism: A way of knowing and learning.* London, UK: Falmer.

Weinberg, D. (2008). The philosophical foundations of constructionist research. In J. Holstein & J. Gubrium (Eds.), *Handbook of constructionist research* (pp. (pp.13–40).). New York: Guilford Press.

Wilhelmsen, T., & Sorensen, M. (2017). Inclusion of children with disabilities in physical education: A systematic review of literature from 2009 to 2015. *Adapted Physical Activity Quarterly, 34*(3), 311–337. doi:org/10.1123/apaq.2016-0017

16

Re-thinking disability and adapted physical education

An intersectionality perspective

Laura Azzarito

Introduction

In recent years, several scholars have claimed that the overrepresentation of learning disabilities among ethnic minorities might be the result of various forms of discrimination, such as racism, classism, and ableism (Blanchett, Klinger, & Harry, 2009; Codrington & Fairchild, 2012; O'Connor & Deluca Fernandez, 2006; Reid & Knight, 2006). From a disability studies (DS) perspective, numerous critical scholars have questioned how the public school system might be associated with the disproportionate representation of ethnic minorities identified with disabilities being placed in special education and/or special programs and how it is linked to negative perceptions of Blackness and poverty and, thus, related to the inequitable treatment (Biklen & Burke, 2006; Blanchett, 2006; Morgan et al., 2017; O'Hara, 2003). In the context of North America, Blackness, constructed in opposition to "White America," is a racialized category through which negative images of Blacks are constructed, circulated, and naturalized in society (Coates, 2015, p. 42). Blanchett (2006), for example, has suggested that the disproportionate representation of ethnic minoritized young people being identified as having disabilities and, thus, being placed in special programs, is a complex sociocultural, political, and economic problem that calls for critical research that questions the role of schooling in the social reproduction of inequalities. In this vein, O'Hara (2003) has suggested that the intersectionality of issues of disability, culture, race/ ethnicity, disability, and language might offer a useful frame to theorize the overwhelming representation of learning disabilities among ethnic minoritized young people in urban public schools. "Learning disabilities" is the largest disability category of students served under the *Individuals with Disabilities Education Improvement Act* (*IDEA*), according to the United States Department of Education (2018) (i.e., 2,336,960, or 38.6%, of the 6,048,882 students ages 6–21 served under *IDEA*, Part B). Issues of disability at the intersection of other social categories, if not addressed from a critical perspective, might have a negative impact on groups of students who have been historically marginalized, in terms of their self-perceptions, self-concepts, and learning experiences.

Many ethnic minoritized young people do not enter high-quality public schools equipped with all kinds of educational resources and opportunities available to other students. Blanchett et al. (2009) stressed that "schools that serve a majority of students of color population are quantitatively and qualitatively different in terms of their resources and the quality of schooling afforded their children from those attended by predominantly White middle class students" (p. 390). Ethnic minoritized students who live in poverty in metropolitan urban areas are more at risk of being identified as having disabilities compared to White middle-class students due to their limited access to educational resources and to early intervention services, which leads them often to receive culturally unresponsive and inappropriate services (O'Connor & Deluca Fernandez, 2006; Reid & Knight, 2006; Skiba, Simmons, Ritter, Gibb, Rausch, Cuadrado, & Chung, 2008). As well, when those students are labeled as having disabilities, the special education system might not always work as a supportive system that helps them progress toward integrating into the mainstream educational system; instead, it may function as a system of segregated classrooms. In particular, Blanchett (2006) has characterized special education as a "form of segregation from the mainstream" (p. 25) that keeps many ethnic minoritized young people from being placed in general education classroom settings. Special education might include, as examples, children who have intellectual disabilities; who are identified with autism; who have orthopedic impairments; who are deaf and/or blind; and who are diagnosed with emotional disturbance (ED) or learning disabilities (LD). Although special education was initially conceptualized as a "service delivery structure" (Blanchett, 2006, p. 25) that aimed to provide more individualized and appropriate educational support for students identified as having disabilities compared to students placed into general education classrooms, special education has failed to achieve its original educational aims. Some scholars have referred to special education as a form of "institutionalized racism" (Codrington & Fairchild, 2012, p. 6), while others have identified it as "discriminatory" (Skiba, Polony-Staudinger, Simmons, Feggins-Azzis, & Chung, 2005, p. 142). Likewise, Blanchett (2006) has characterized special education as a "new legalized form of structural segregation and racism" (p. 25).

The overrepresentation of ethnic minoritized students identified with a disability in urban diverse school contexts located in poor neighborhoods is also likely to be reflected in self-contained adapted physical education (APE) classes. While education scholars have critically problematized the issues of overrepresentation of ethnic minoritized young people in special education programs (O'Connor & Deluca Fernandez, 2006; O'Hara, 2003; Reid & Knight, 2006), to date, there is a dearth of research that examines how issues of disability intersect with race, gender/sex, and social class in special education classrooms and are carried over to the gym, specifically in self-contained APE classes. Since the 1950s, "specialists" were the teachers of self-contained APE classes in school (segregated classes), and their pedagogies were informed by a medical model that positioned the disabled body as abnormal, framed by deficit (Fitzgerald, 2006). Whether placed in special education classes or special education programs or categories with "specialists" (i.e., APE teachers), many ethnic minoritized students identified with disabilities who are placed in segregated school learning environments might face multiple forms of oppression and prejudices, such as ableism, racism, sexism, and classism.

When placed in special education or self-contained APE classes, in the current context of urban schooling framed by deficit thinking (Baldridge, 2014; Ishimaru et al., 2016; Yosso, 2005), disability issues at the intersection of race, ableism, social class, and gender/sex, play a substantial role in the social construction of different, non-normative, or other students in school. As long as school curricula in special programs (i.e., special education classrooms, self-contained APE classes) are segregated and narrowly constructed upon the Western notion of normalcy, social inequalities institutionalized in schools will continue to persist. In the next sections of this chapter, first, I problematize the link between ideals of normalcy, disability, and difference, suggesting that the current "normative culture of school" works as a system of discrimination against ethnic minoritized young people identified as having disability. Second, contesting the notion of remediating unhealthy minds in unhealthy bodies, I advocate for re-positioning the unitary, static notion of disability to acknowledge the multiple forms of oppression ethnic minoritized students with disability might face in their daily lives. Third, I attempt to re-think disability from an intersectionality perspective to account for the individual's social reality of disability based on intersecting social categories, such as race, gender/sex, and social class. With a commitment to social justice and acknowledging the multi-faceted aspects of identity of ethnic minoritized young people who self-identify as having disability, I conclude the chapter by interrogating the possibility of moving theoretically and pedagogically toward genuine inclusion through the lenses of intersectionality. In this chapter, I use the term *ethnic minorities* with disabilities not to minoritize, universalize, or fix a cohort of population, but, rather, in the attempt to articulate "difference" from an intersectionality perspective to recognize multiple axes of identity, and, thus, challenging the unified category of disability.

Problematizing the "normative culture of school"

The high incidence of learning disabilities among ethnic minorities and their placement in k-12 special education programs (i.e., self-contained APE, special education classes) implicitly produce a categorization of those cohorts of young people as different or non-normal. When placed into special education programs, students often do not develop the knowledge and skills needed to move into general education classrooms but instead become defined by the system as different from mainstream students, often remaining in those segregated classes throughout their educational careers. For instance, self-contained APE classes are segregated learning environments historically informed by the medical community and conceptualized as pedagogical remedies for abnormal or different students (Fitzgerald, 2006). In self-contained APE, the idea of the disabled person as a defective person is grounded in the ideology of normalcy rooted in eugenics and social Darwinism, and it still functions in contemporary Western society as a powerful regime of truth, naturalizing the notion of difference constructed as a negative term (McPhail & Freeman, 2005). The ideology of normalcy functions as a powerful means of representation of the image of the normal/abnormal category, which, in turn, when pedagogically taken for granted in school, produces binary constructions that position non-normative students as disabled and thus, different from the normative student. As a result, according to McPhail and Freeman (2005), the ideology of normalcy colonizes young people with disabilities, enacting the "othering" process through which students placed in disability groups and/or special programs are marked as different, the other, or abnormal. Through the othering process, normalizing difference in school contexts might contribute, either implicitly or explicitly, to the problem of overrepresenting learning disabilities among ethnic minority students in urban public schools (Reid & Knight, 2006).

At the very center of the source of all otherness is the concept of a norm, which according to Garland Thompson (2002), is a normative type against which all intellectual, behavioral, and physical characteristics that appear as differences and/or variations are constructed as deviant or inferior. Further, O'Connor and Deluca Fernandez (2006) maintained that the notion of "norm" in the context of schooling "situates middle-class [White] children as the unmarked norm against which the development of 'other' children is evaluated" (p. 6). In

Western society, the norm is assumed to possess natural physical, behavioral, and intellectual superiority. The notion of normalcy displayed by the male, White, heteronormative, able-bodied superiority is constructed in opposition to physical, intellectual, or behavioral variations represented by female, Black, disabled, or homosexual statuses. Norms circulate in society as cultural imperatives and impact individuals' experiences and identities in powerful ways, maintaining the rigidity of the social order while obscuring the ambiguity and complexity of all social identities. In Western modern society, the unmarked norm, such as Whiteness, is the reference point and indicates privilege and power. Whiteness, unlike the social category of disability, which is marked as "different" and often visible, is invisible, neutral, and normative. Through the racialization process sustained by Whiteness and White privilege, Whiteness remains invisible and unmarked, while ethnic minorities become marked as the "other," carrying the burden of race.

When the notion of normalcy permeates school contexts, and ethnic minoritized young people identified as having disabilities are classified as different, Black and disabled doubly mark their identity as the other and, thus, they become perceived as even more deficient, inferior, and deviant from the normative cultural standard. As O'Hara (2003) stated, the notion of White supremacy has dominated the Western historical and sociocultural landscape since the 19th century, and it has fuelled issues of exploitation, racism, ableism, and sexism. In this vein, Mitchell and Snyder (2003) pointed out that the ideology of normalcy considers the White, middle-upper social class, abled body as the normal standard and still circulates in today's society. Multiple negative social meanings attributed to Black disabled individuals cast them as deviant or inferior, producing marginalization and exclusion from full participation in society. When societal ideals that conform to White European standards are established and infuse the public sphere, Eurocentric, White, sexist, and ableist conceptions and ideals become cultural belief systems that permeate the institution of school in powerful ways. O'Connor and DeLuca Fernandez (2006, p. 9) further clarified:

> It is *the normative culture of school* [emphasis added] that places poor children at risk by privileging the developmental expression more likely to be nurtured among White middle-class children. In the process, the developmental expressions that are more likely to be nurtured among poor minority youth are marginalized and are positioned to produce low achievement.

Dangerously, through the use of categorization and human binaries, ideals of normalcy historically constructed upon the intersectionality of ableism, race, social class, and gender/sex are systematically imposed on students. Systems of discrimination become institutionalized in schools, functioning, implicitly or explicitly, as a means to pedagogically normalize issues of difference, especially in school contexts constructed upon White middle-class norms as the dominant culture. This might then result in a systematic exclusion of traditionally marginalized ethnic minority groups and poor young people from mainstream education curricula, which tend to privilege White middle-class standards (Reid & Knight, 2006). In this vein, as O'Hara (2003) pointed out, in addition to the social prejudice ethnic minorities identified with disabilities might face, more dangerous and damaging is the "issue of institutionalized generated inequality" (p. 167) produced by the current schooling system.

Deficit thinking is an example of institutionally generated inequality, and, moreover, as Yosso (2005) maintained, the current "deficit thinking" is the most widespread form of discrimination and inequality that permeates US society, including US schools. In addition, Blanchett et al. (2009) noted that deficit thinking "had become a well-established part of the educational belief system and would become the driving force behind decisions about how to educate those who appear different from mainstream" (p. 395). Through institutionalized deficit thinking in schools, issues of disability, race, gender/sex, and social class are often coded as a cultural difference in negative terms, which means different from White normative cultural knowledge and skills (Yosso, 2005). Personal investment in a social justice agenda of education, as well as pedagogical efforts toward social justice in education, need to be seriously considered to challenge the social construction of difference in negative terms and institutionally generated inequality. Yosso (2005) recommended that the struggle against deficit thinking "necessitates a challenge of personal and individual race, gender and class prejudices expressed by educators, as well as a critical examination of systematic factors that perpetuate deficit thinking and reproduce educational inequalities for students from nondominant sociocultural and linguistic backgrounds" (p. 75).

Against the deficit thinking paradigm, drawing on DS, Reid and Knight (2006) claimed that the social construction of difference in negative terms positions ethnic minoritized groups with disability as the other, in opposition to normative students, the reproducing positions of marginality in society. DS, thus, critically interrogates how issues of disability intersect with issues of race, social class, gender/sex and structure ongoing educational inequalities, bearing upon historically oppressed ethnic minority groups disproportionately (O'Connor & DeLuca Fernandez, 2006). Further, DS questions the higher incidence of ethnic minority students who are designated as disabled and problematizes how the label of having disabilities might impact their identity development and progress toward integration into general education. In addition, DS challenges the Western historical construction of difference informed by an ableistic perspective, which, in turn, considers disability as a personal tragedy or as an individual condition to cure, fix, or correct (Garland Thompson, 2002). Finally, DS problematizes the deficit paradigm framed by the medical post-positivist paradigm that constructs and positions the disabled person as the other, and at the same time, pathologizes the disabled person as being deficient, thus constructing and circulating a negative imagery of the individual with disability as being defective.

From special education classes to APE: remediating "unhealthy minds" in "unhealthy bodies"

Similar to special education classes, in APE, how the normative culture of society informing schooling (i.e., White male, abled, middle class) constructs and positions ethnic minoritized students identified as having physical, emotional, and intellectual disabilities, is an urgent issue. For instance, because medical treatment models are viewed as colonizing strategies of the deficient body, Connolly and Craig (2002) challenged taken-for-granted ideologies that privilege *normal* subjects, stressing the notion of embodiment to reconceptualize disability. Further, Connolly and Harvey (2018) proposed engaging in an interdisciplinary dialogue between adapted physical activity and critical pedagogy to advance issues of social justice, inclusion, and cultural expression. To account for culture, context, and individual needs, they suggested making a conceptual shift from the conventional notion of adapted physical activity to the concept of adaptive physical activity. Connolly (2008) thus called for considering alternative theoretical frameworks that use inclusion-based and cultural perspectives approaches, accounting for, legitimating, and shedding light on students' embodiment in the context of adaptive physical activity. The impact of the socially constructed disabled body at the intersection of race, gender/sex, and social class on the learning experiences of ethnic minoritized young people placed in self-contained APE remains under-theorized. Critical scholars have problematized how the ideology of normalcy embraces the idea of the healthy mind in a healthy body view—a Western historical body–mind construction that has historically served to exclude, ostracize, and marginalize people with disabilities in society (DePauw, 1997; Goodwin & Peers, 2012; McPhail & Freeman, 2005). The body–mind dichotomy still informs the learning environment constructed in general education classes (Reid & Knight, 2006), as well as mainstream physical education (PE) classes (McPhail & Freeman, 2005). When the Western racialized construction of the body–mind dichotomy permeates the school system, this dichotomy is reproduced pedagogically through the othering process in special education, as well as self-contained APE classes. While in school classrooms, based on perceived intellectual underachievement compared to the norm—*unhealthy minds*—are referred and placed in special education programs, in the context of PE, based on physical underachievement or impairment compared to the normative body—*unhealthy bodies* —are placed in self-contained APE (Fitzgerald, 2006; McPhail & Freeman, 2005).

The term *disability* originally was informed by the Judeo-Christian view as "an act of higher being and … as an opportunity for miracles to occur" (Haegele & Hodge, 2016, p. 193). Historically, in the West, the disabled body was been rooted in the Cartesian body–mind dichotomy, which, in turn, regards the body as a separate, yet inferior, entity to the mind (Huge & Paterson, 1997). Later, the notion of disability was heavily influenced by the medical community, producing definitions of disability as impairment, deficiency, dysfunctionality, or abnormality—a medical phenomenon to be fixed. In self-contained APE classes, the impairment of the individual identified as having disability can be sensory, affective, cognitive, or physical. This dualistic thinking also was embraced by Enlightenment discourses associated with eugenics and functioned as a colonization process through which disabled, as well as indigenous, people were colonized, classified and/or othered as primitive, abnormal, and other (McPhail & Freeman, 2005). As Haegele and Hodge (2016) further explained, such "deficit-based definitions and perceptions" (p. 196) of the notion of disability have a substantial impact on the societal perceptions of disability. Through the othering process, those people who deviated from the average man were ranked below this norm, justifying remedial activities, such as schooling practices, in an attempt to help the disabled and/or different to become normal (McPhail & Freeman, 2005). This medicalized view has implicitly produced a social perception of disability in negative terms, fixing the notion of disability to an individual's impairment and constructing the impairment as the individual's defining characteristic. As Huge and Paterson (1997) stressed, "[T]his dualistic approach produces a theoretical rigidity which involves the medicalization of disabled people and the politicization of their social lives" (p. 331).

In the past decade, several scholars have adopted the social model to re-position the disabled body, historically constructed as a medicalized body, as a socially produced entity, shifting the debate about disability and impairment from a medical problem to a social issue (Goodwin & Peers, 2012; Grenier, 2007; Haegele & Hodge, 2016; Huge & Paterson, 1997). While the medical model conceptualizes the disabled body as a personal tragedy, or as physical or intellectual dysfunctions (in other words, the result of a pathology), disability framed by the social model is "socially produced by systematic patterns of exclusion that were–quite literally–built into the social fabric" (Huge & Paterson, 1997, p. 328). In this vein, Haegele and Hodge (2016, p. 197) contended that the social model "contests that it is society that imposes disability on individuals with impairments" (p. 197). Similarly, Grenier (2007) called for new forms of pedagogy to address issues of difference and diversity when working with students who identify as having disability. Moving beyond the medical model, reconceptualizing disability from a social model perspective enables scholars to re-position the notion of disability as being the result of social oppression, marginality, and exclusion, putting forward the struggle for emancipation and social justice (Biklen, 2000; Biklen & Burke, 2006; Peters, Babel, & Symeonidou, 2009). The social model challenges the Cartesian construction of the body–mind dichotomy and the medicalization of the disabled body, positioning the body as a social entity—a sociocultural text that, in complicated ways, expresses the multi-faceted aspects of identity.

While the Cartesian dichotomy circulates a dualistic thinking of the body–mind dichotomy that justifies the need to remediate and, thus, normalize individuals with non-mainstream characteristics who deviate from the norm, in contrast, the social model advances an educational orientation for individuals' human rights. While the social model has been useful for challenging the dominant medicalized discourse of disability, even with the integration of the social model, for diverse students whose race, gender/sex, ability, and/or socioeconomic levels are different from those of the mainstream, their experiences, views, struggles, and multi-faceted aspects of their identities remain under-theorized. While the social model resists a static and unitary understanding of disability, rejecting stereotypes and prejudices (Biklen, 2000), the social model "does not account for differences between individuals with disabilities" (Haegele & Hodge, 2016, p. 198). The social model resists narratives that simply aim to normalize or mainstream the other, but it fails to account for the system of multiple oppressions ethnic minoritized young people with disability have to face and negotiate in their daily lives. Within a social model perspective, ableism remains a homogeneous social category rather than being recognized as a socially produced category intersecting with race, gender/sex, and social class.

Rethinking disability from an intersectionality perspective

Ableism and the prejudice it fosters against individuals with disabilities do not take shape in society independent from other forms of oppression, such as racism, sexism, and classism. Grenier (2007) maintained that "like gender and race, disability has been linked to potential challenging interpretation of the body and mind, especially when social traditions equate disability with deficiency or lack of ability" (p. 299). Critical race theory (CRT) and intersectionality provide useful theoretical lenses through which scholars can interrogate the persistent construction of disability informed by deficit thinking, and as a socially constructed, fluid category intersecting with race/ethnicity, social class, and gender/sex. Intersectionality calls attention to how the current schooling system is poorly equipped to identify how issues of race, gender/sex, disability, and social class play a role in students' learning, self-concept, and identity development; and how to redress discrimination and social inequalities, supporting historically oppressed and marginalized young people who "sit" at the intersection of multiple social categories. As an integral aspect of social justice, intersectionality is a concept associated with CRT (Bowleg, 2012; Brown & Jackson, 2013; Solorzano, 2013). Crenshaw (1991) originally conceptualized the concept of intersectionality to demonstrate how race/ethnicity, social class, race, disability, gender/sex are not mutually exclusive, independent, and unitary social categories, instead, they are fluid, inconsistent, and intersecting, impacting individuals with multiple, overlapping forms of oppression. Crenshaw (1991) specifically aimed to reveal and politicize how the experiences and identities of women of color—who belong to historically marginalized groups—were not informed solely by racism but also by institutionalized inequalities that resulted from the intersectionality of sexism, racism, and classism.

Drawing on Crenshaw's (1991) perspective, intersectionality offers a useful framework to account for differences among young people with disabilities, revealing how ableism is not a unitary and homogeneous social category that discriminates against a disabled individual, but, rather, a category that fluidly intersects with race, gender/sex, and social class, taking a shape in the lives of historically marginalized groups in contextualized and complicated ways. This means taking into account and shedding light on the multiple identities ethnic minorities with disability embody and express in the local context of their schools in an effort to support positive identity development, to enhance their quality of life, and to advance a social justice agenda. Notably, ethnic minoritized students identified as having disabilities might not face only ableism as a unitary form of oppression; instead, they may occupy various sites of oppression in school and, thus, must face and negotiate multiple disadvantaging factors. Working toward an intersectionality perspective on disability thus poses important questions: how does a young lesbian Latina identified with disability see herself in her own cultural terms and experience disability at the intersection of gender/sex in her adapted PE class? How does she negotiate multiple forms of oppression in a school context constructed upon a White, middle-class, heteronormative dominant culture? What multiple disadvantage factors might she face in her daily life?

Such intersectionality allows scholars to interrogate the link between identity and social inequalities, destabilizing and dismantling Western socially constructed dichotomies, such as disabled/abled, Black/White, and straight/gay, by attempting to understand the individual's social reality as not only based on a unitary categorical understanding of disability, but also as a reality based on the full dimensions of multiple, intersecting forms of oppression, such as ableism, racism, sexism, and classism. Social categories are neither homogeneous nor unified or essentialist. Moving beyond the ways in which the social world is organized along binaries, Delgrado and Stefancic (2001) explained: "Intersectionality means the examination of race, sex, class, national origin, and sexual orientation and how their combinations play out in various settings" (p. 15). Intersectionality recognizes multiple axes of identity, paying particular attention to the complex ways in which disability, race, gender/sex, and social class fluidly and inconsistently intersect and play a role in the lives and identities of traditionally marginalized groups, highlighting the importance of exploring and shedding light on multiple identities. Thus, challenging a stable, single notion of disability, intersectionality can offer a useful frame to explain, for instance, what it means to be a young Latina, self-identified lesbian having disability, enabling her to locate her identity construction and expression meaningfully in the specific context of her daily life. Exploring identity meanings according to the specificity of the context in which they are shaped and produced can generate personal stories that diverge from mainstream White, able-bodied accounts, challenging the idea of fixating "disability" in negative terms to a narrow, normative categorization and homogeneous experience of disability. Personal stories, understandings, and self-representations grounded in the experiences of historically marginalized groups of young people self-identified as having disabilities—with less privilege and advantage—create counter-narratives that work to dismantle normative ways of being. Bringing to light such counter-narratives is crucial to redress social inequalities institutionalized in schools: when those counter-narratives are public and centered in school contexts, they become transformative for the young people themselves, as well as for educators and scholars in the struggle for social justice and equality.

The Western socially constructed binaries of abled/disabled, Black/White, women/men are not additive and cannot be ranked, but contextualized as fluid, inconsistent, and intersecting and, thus, experienced and negotiated by young people in complicated and different ways (Bowleg, 2012). In addition to the struggle against the process of racialization as a process of subjectification through which the Black exists only as the other trapped within power relations established by the White dominant culture, ethnic minorities with disabilities have to face another set of challenges and social barriers. Ethnic minorities who are identified, categorized, and labeled as having disabilities often face double discrimination (O'Hara, 2003) or experience "double jeopardy" (Blanchett et al., 2009, p. 391). While the stigma of disability (intellectual disability or physical impairment) creates significant emotional difficulty for students and their families, as a result of racism and ableism, ethnic minorities identified as having disabilities also have to negotiate double discrimination. Racism combined with the stigma of disability has a significant negative impact on students' learning experiences in school, in addition to the double disadvantage they have to face in their daily lives.

The forms of oppression experienced by ethnic minoritized women is multiple, when, besides racism and ableism, they have to face sexism as well, being forced to deal with triple discrimination. For instance, in the Western construction of normalcy, the notion of disability was historically associated with femaleness. In Western patriarchal culture, the notion of disability is intertwined with the normative notions of femininity and womanhood (Garland Thompson, 2002). Just like the disabled body, in Western society, the female body has been historically con-figured as deviant from, and in opposition to, the ideal White male. The unfeminine, unbeautiful female body represented by the disabled, fat, Black, and lesbian is defined in opposition to the ideal feminine body. Disabled women are often discouraged from enacting their reproductive role as well as their role of motherhood, because they are considered defective or deviant from appropriate feminine norms. The sexuality of a disabled woman is often invisible or erased, con-structed as inappropriate to a heteronormative, ableistic eye.

In Western society, the different, non-conforming femininity that the disabled woman represents was historically associated with asexual and unfeminine behavior, contributing to the cancellation of ideals of femininity, as well as to rolelessness (Garland Thompson, 2002). For instance, O'Hara (2003) draws attention to how Asian women, in the context of their historical cultural beliefs, might often face a triple jeopardy: a triple discrimination in which issues of racial difference intersect with disability and, moreover, with gender/sexuality, espe-cially when impairment is associated with abnormality regarding the role of motherhood. In other cases, ethnic minoritized young women might experience a triple jeopardy with issues of disability when those traditionally oppressed individuals who also identify as gay, intersex, transgender, pansexual, or lesbian transgress—in addition to the racialized and ableistic binar-ies—the system of compulsory heterosexuality. The racialized representation of the disabled body is, thus, complicated by an interrogation of gender/sex framed by the heteronormative matrix (Butler, 1998) and recognition of multiple axes of identity.

In summary, adopting an intersectionality frame to investigate the overrepresentation of learning disabilities among ethnic minorities receiving APE services can be beneficial in a number of ways. First, intersectionality requires an understanding of the body as a cultural text inscribed with multiple meanings, rather than a medicalized entity, an impairment to be fixed. Cultural work on the body identified with disability is crucial to destigmatize the medicalized view of disability as lacking or deficient. Schools have an educational responsi-bility to destigmatize difference constructed upon multiple axes of identity in deficit terms, re-presenting the notion of difference through positive lenses. Second, rather than emphasiz ing deficits differently from normalcy, school curricula that recognize strengths of students with disabilities can foster positive identity development in school. This means strategically using intersectionality to invoke, shed light on, and represent multiple identities in positive ways, challenging the so-called static notion of normalcy. In other words, through the lenses of the intersectionality, special education programs set up as segregated learning environ-ments implicitly construct the notion of normalcy, where the overrepresentation of ethnic minorities with disabilities position and mark them as the other, forcing them to face mul-tiple disadvantaging factors.

There are some pedagogical situations, however, when the self-imposed segregation of marginalized groups can foster a positive identity and a sense of solidarity, belonging, and community. While segregation informed by the notions of normalcy and deficit thinking is detrimental to student learning and reproduces social inequalities, Garland Thompson (2002, p. 245) recognized that that "the highly politicized deaf community, for example, arose from segregated schools for the deaf," and its political commitment to segregated institutionalized education raised a critical consciousness and struggle for social justice, bringing people together with a strong sense of community. Third, because intersectionality emphasizes the multiplicity of identities of ethnic minorities with disability, acknowledging the role of subjectivity from which young people with disability can speak up about who they are, how they see themselves, and express themselves in their own terms, can produce counter-narratives, opening up different ways of being, beyond the normative way (Azzarito, 2019). Such counter-narratives might challenge the stable, rigid social categories of cultural otherness that permeate the school context, from special education to APE to general educational classes, creating new ways of seeing a "person experiencing disability" or "young people who have claimed a disability-related identity" (Goodwin & Peers, 2012, p. 187).

Moving beyond "cultural otherness" in school: toward "genuine inclusion"

Students with disability who are viewed, categorized, and positioned in school according to the social perception that they are deficient are likely to learn to see themselves from normative ways of being. Just like everyone else in society, ethnic minorities identified with disability themselves absorb cultural stereotypes, act upon the cultural stereotypes, and often become the cultural stereotypes. While schools should offer equitable education and positive, supportive, and high-quality learning experiences to *all* students, because of the powerful impact of cultural stereotypes on identities, ethnic minoritized young people might eventually invest themselves in externally imposed societal views, which, in turn, position them in categorical ways as disabled/abled, Blacks/Whites, girls/boys, or straight/gay. As Garland Thompson (2002, p. 244) asserted, "[C]ategories of cultural otherness thus reduce individuals to particular identifying traits, rendering a multifaceted individual a 'Black,' a 'gay,' or one of the 'disabled.'"

When tracked in special programs, not only might ethnic minoritized students with disabilities be impacted in detrimental ways, but also, White students placed in mainstream classes might not benefit from opportunities to learn from culturally diverse experiences, and, thus, they might not learn how to see the world beyond the narrow lenses of Whiteness. As Blanchett et al. (2009, p. 390) asserted:

> In addition to robbing students of color of an equitable education, having students of color concentrated in schools with other students of color (many who also live in poverty) also robs them as well as their White peers of an opportunity to attend and benefit from racially, culturally, and linguistically diverse schools.

As long as schools continue to fail to place issues of race, social class, disability, gender/sex, and language and the intersectionality of these social categories at the very center of the public school system, ethnic minoritized students with disabilities will continue to face, and struggle with, educational inequalities, while White middle-upper-class students will continue to be privileged, yet have their learning experiences confined by normative Whiteness.

Unless prejudice, ableism, racism, sexism are challenged, and normative White privilege and its sense of entitlement are revealed and destabilized in school, negative perceptions of ethnic minoritized students with disabilities are likely to take shape and become visible in schools through categorization, labeling, and, thus, placement decisions. As Blanchett (2006) stressed, "[E]ducators tend to see Whiteness as the norm and consequently the academic skills, behavior, and social skills of African American and other students of color are constantly compared to White peers" (p. 27). It is, thus, crucial to carefully examine the experiences of ethnic minoritized students identified with disabilities in their own cultural terms while, at the same time, working to develop school curricula that are responsive to their cultures, language, experiences, and interests to better address their needs. This also means challenging the widespread concept of deficit still rooted in today's public school system, which, implicitly and/or explicitly, operates as the driving force behind the social construction of disability and cultural otherness.

In the context of APE, for instance, the educational dimension of the learning environment is often lost in pedagogies that implement "therapeutic remedies" (Fitzgerald, 2006, p. 753). To challenge the deficit paradigm of schooling, scholars have proposed the notion of genuine inclusion to envision inclusive classes constructed upon ideals of tolerance, equity, and pluralism (McPhail & Freeman, 2005). Genuine inclusion means creating school learning environments that foster full participation and access to rich learning environments for *all* students. With the emergence of the social model, there has been a recent shift from the segregated education of young people with disability in self-contained APE classes toward the inclusion of young people with disability in mainstream educational settings. As Fitzgerald (2006) has pointed out, however, the mainstreaming of disabled groups can only result in simple integration unless genuine inclusion becomes a process committed to reveal and root out the notion of normalcy institutionalized in schools, and to shed light on the voices, experiences, and views of students with disability (Goodwin, 2009; Goodwin & Watkinson, 2000).

Considering "inclusion as a process" (Fitzgerald, 2006, p. 754) demands that schools re-position APE services as "inclusive" classes by engaging in thinking, problematizing, challenging, and reconceptualizing the pervasive dualistic thinking to move toward an understanding of students as human beings. In an attempt to progress pedagogically and theoretically toward reconceptualizing disability in inclusive PE from an intersectionality perspective, and in an effort to sustain a social justice agenda (Azzarito, Macdonald, Dagkas, & Fisette, 2017), I conclude the chapter by questioning what counter-narratives might emerge from the voices, experiences, and views of ethnic minoritized young people who claim a disability-related identity (Goodwin & Peers, 2012, p. 187) in inclusive classes, thus opening up new ways of seeing, perceiving, and thinking about disability. New insights through the lens of intersectionality might help educators and scholars debunk the myth of normalcy that positions disability in a negative frame, thus shedding light on multiple forms of oppression, as well as opening a window to a view of disability as articulated through multiple axes of identity.

Summary of key points

1) When the notion of normalcy permeates school contexts and ethnic minoritized young people identified as having disabilities are classified as different, Black and disabled students doubly mark their identity as the other and, thus, deficient, inferior, and deviant from the normative cultural standard.

2) Issues of disability, if not addressed from a critical perspective, might have a negative impact on groups of students who have been historically marginalized in terms of their self-perceptions and embodied identity.

3) Disability issues at the intersection of race, ableism, social class, and gender/sex play a substantial role in the social construction of different, non-normative, or other students in school.

4) The idea of the disabled person as a defective person is grounded in the ideology of normalcy and still functions in contemporary Western society as a dominant discourse, naturalizing the notion of difference constructed as a negative term.

5) In Western society, the notion of normalcy displayed by male, White, heteronormative, able-bodied superiority is constructed in opposition to physical, intellectual, or behavioral variations represented by female, Black, disabled, or homosexual statuses.

6) The notion of disability was heavily influenced by the medical community, producing definitions of disability as indicating impairment, deficiency, dysfunctionality, or abnormality—a medical problem to be fixed.

7) The ideology of normalcy functions as a powerful means of representation of the image of the normal/abnormal category, which, in turn, when pedagogically taken for granted in school, produces binary constructions that position non-normative students as disabled and, thus, different from normative students.

8) Norms circulate in society as cultural imperatives and impact individuals' experiences and identities in powerful ways, maintaining the rigidity of the social order, while obscuring the ambiguity and complexity of all social identities.

9) The social model resists narratives that simply aim to normalize or mainstream the other, but it fails to account for the system of multiple oppressions that ethnic minoritized young people with disability have to face and negotiate in their daily lives.

10) Intersectionality offers a useful framework to account for differences among young people with disabilities, revealing how ableism is not a unitary and homogeneous social category that discriminates against a disabled individual but, rather, a category that fluidly intersects with race, gender/sex, and social class, taking shape in the lives of historically marginalized groups in contextualized and complicated ways.

11) Reconceptualizing disability from an intersectionality perspective enables scholars to re-position the notion of disability as being the result of social oppression, marginality, and exclusion, putting forward the struggle for emancipation and social justice.

Reflective questions

- How does Whiteness play a role in teachers' perspectives of ethnic minoritized young people who are identified as having disability, as well as teachers' pedagogical practices in APE?

- How does the intersectionality of disability, gender/sex, race, and social class inform the overrepresentation of learning disabilities among ethnic minoritized groups in APE classes?

- How can APE be reconceptualized as "inclusive PE" (Fitzgerald, 2006, p. 754) to account for the multiple forms of oppression that traditionally marginalized groups of students face in their daily lives and to create learning experiences built upon their "strengths"?

References

Azzarito, L. (2019). *Social justice in globalized fitness and health: Bodies out of sight.* London: Routledge.

Azzarito, L., Macdonald, D., L. Dagkas, S., & Fisette, J. (2017). Revitalizing the PE social-justice agenda in the global era: Where do we go from here?. *Quest, 69*(2), 205–219.

Baldridge, B. J. (2014). Relocating the deficit: Reimagining Black youth in neoliberal times. *American Educational Research Journal, 51*(3), 440–472.

Biklen, D. (2000). Constructing inclusion: Lessons from critical, disability narratives. *International Journal of Inclusive Education, 4*(4), 337–353.

Biklen, D., & Burke, J. (2006). Presuming competence. *Equity & Excellence in Education, 39*, 166–175.

Blanchett, W. J. (2006). Disproportionate representation of African American students in special education: Acknowledging the role of White privilege and racism. *Educational Researcher, 35*(6), 24–47.

Blanchett, W. J., Klinger, J. K., & Harry, B. (2009). The intersection of race, culture, language, and disability. Implication for urban education. *Urban Education, 44*(4), 189–409.

Bowleg, L. (2012). The problem with the phrase women and minorities: Intersectionality – an important theoretical framework for public health. *American Journal of Public Health, 102*(7), 1267–1273.

Brown, K., & Jackson, D. D. (2013). The history and conceptual elements of critical race theory. In M. Lynn & A. D. Dixon (Eds.), *Handbook of critical race in education* (pp. 9–22). New York, NY: Routledge.

Butler, J. (1998). Performative acts and gender constitution: An essay in phenomenology and feminist theory. *Theatre Journal, 40*(4), 519–531.

Coates, T. N. (2015). *Between the world and me.* New York, NY: Penguin Random House LLS.

Codrington, M. J., & Fairchild, H. H. (2012). *Special education and mis-education of African American children: A call for action.* Washington, DC: The Association of Black Psychologists.

Connolly, M. (2008). The remarkable logic of autism: Developing and describing an embedded curriculum based in semiotic phenomenology. *Sport, Ethics and Philosophy, 2*, 234–256. doi:10.1080/17511320802223824

Connolly, M., & Craig, T. (2002). Stressed embodiment: Doing phenomenology in the wild. *Human Studies, 25*, 451–462. doi:10.1023/A:1021226510898

Connolly, M., & Harvey, W. J. (2018). Critical pedagogy and APA: A resonant (and timely) interdisciplinary blend. *Adapted Physical Activity Quarterly., 35*(3), 293–307. doi:10.1123/apaq.2017-0106

Crenshaw, K. (1991). Mapping the margins: Intersectionality, identity politics, and violence against women of color. *Stanford Law Review, 43*(6), 1241–1299.

Delgrado, R., & Stefancic, J. (2001). *Critical race theory: An introduction.* New York: NYU Press.

DePauw, K. (1997). The (in)visibility of disability: Cultural contexts and sporting bodies. *Quest, 49*(4), 416–430.

Fitzgerald, H. (2006). Disability and physical education. In D. Kirk, D. Macdonald, & M. O'Sullivan (Eds.), *Handbook of physical education* (pp. 752–766). London: Sage publications.

Garland Thompson, R. (2002). *Extraordinary bodies: Figuring physical disability in American culture and literature.* New York: Columbia University press.

Goodwin, D. (2009). The voices of students with disabilities: Are they informing inclusive physical education practice?. In H. Fitzgerald (Ed.), *Disability and Youth sport* (pp. 53–75). London: Routledge.

Goodwin, D., & Peers, D. (2012). Disability, sport and inclusion. In S. Dagkas & K. Armour (Eds.), *Inclusion and exclusion through youth sports* (pp. 186–203). London: Routledge.

Goodwin, D., & Watkinson, J. (2000). Inclusive physical education from the perspective of students with disabilities. *Adapted Physical Activity Quarterly, 17*(2), 144–160.

Grenier, M. (2007). Inclusion in physical education: From the medical model to social constructionism. *Quest., 59*(3), 298–310. doi:10.1080/00336297.2007.10483554

Haegele, J. A., & Hodge, S. R. (2016). Disability discourse: Overview and critiques of the medical and social models. *Quest, 68*(2), 193–206.

Huge, B., & Paterson, K. (1997). The social model of disability and the disappearing body: Towards a sociology of impairment. *Disability & Society, 12*(3), 325–340.

Ishimaru, A., Torres, K. E., Salvador, J. E., Lott, J., II, Cameron Williams, D. M., & Tran, C. (2016). Reinforcing deficit, journeying toward equity: Cultural brokering in family engagement initiatives. *American Educational Research Journal, 53*(4), 850–882.

McPhail, J. C., & Freeman, J. G. (2005). Beyond prejudice: Thinking toward genuine inclusion. *Learning Disabilities Practice, 20*(4), 254–267.

Mitchell, D. T., & Snyder, S. L. (2003). *Narrative prosthesis: Disability and the dependencies of discourse*. Ann Arbor, MI: University of Michingan press.

Morgan, P. L., Farkas, G., Cook, M., Strassfeld, N. M., Hillemeier, M. M., Hung Pung, W., & Schussler, D. L. (2017). Are Black children disproportionately overrepresented in special education? A best-evidence synthesis. *Exceptional Children, 83*(2), 181–198.

O'Connor, C., & Deluca Fernandez, S. (2006). Race, class, and disproportionality: Reevaluating the relationship between poverty and special education placement. *Educational Researcher, 35*(6), 6–11.

O'Hara, J. (2003). Learning disabilities and ethnicity: Achieving cultural competence. *Advances in Psychiatric Treatment, 9*, 166–174.

Peters, S., Babel, S., & Symeonidou, S. (2009). Resistance, transformation and the politics of hope: Imagining a way forward for the disabled people's movement. *Disability & Society, 24*(5), 543–556.

Reid, D. K., & Knight, M. G. (2006). Disability justifies exclusion of minority students: A critical history grounded in disability studies. *Educational Researcher, 35*(6), 17–23.

Skiba, R. J., Polony-Staudinger, L., Simmons, A. B., Feggins-Azzis, L. R., & Chung, C. (2005). Unproven links: Can poverty explain ethnic disproportionality in special education?. *The Journal of Special Education, 39*, 130–144.

Skiba, R. J., Simmons, A. B., Ritter, S., Gibb, A. C., Rausch, M. K., Cuadrado, J., & Chung, C. (2008). Achieving equity in special education: History, status, and current challenges. *Exceptional Children, 74*, 264–288.

Solorzano, D. G. (2013). Critical race theory's intellectual roots. In M. Lynn & A. D. Dixon (Eds.), *Handbook of critical race in education* (pp. 48–68). New York, NY: Routledge.

United States Department of Education, Office of Special Education and Rehabilitative Services, Office of Special Education Programs. (2018). *40th Annual Report to Congress on the implementation of the Individuals with Disabilities Education Act, 2018* (pp. 38–74 and 132–159). Washington, DC: USDE.

Yosso, T. J. (2005). Whose culture has capital? A critical race theory discussion of community cultural wealth. *Race Ethnicity and Education, 8*(1), 69–91.

17

Bioecological theory

Jihoun An and Sheresa Boone Blanchard

Introduction

Studying the development and learning of children with disabilities in physical education is one of the core areas in adapted physical education (APE) research, including understanding the impact of physical education programs, as well as instructional strategies, peer interaction, and relations among educators, administrators, and parents, on the child's developmental changes (An & Hodge, 2013; An & Meaney, 2015; Klavina & Block, 2008). A child's learning and development can be affected by many interrelated sociocultural contexts, such as the child's attributes, family functioning, community setting (i.e., rural, urban), policies, and social and cultural values. For example, if the child's condition requires full-time medical support, it may limit his or her participation in physical activity due to safety concerns. He or she may function better when receiving individualized instruction in a specially designed program (i.e., APE). If parents have little interest in, or have insufficient knowledge about, physical activity, the chance for their child with a disability to participate in physical activity may be low, leading to potentially unhealthy behaviors for both parents and child.

Over the past four decades, many leaders, such as educational professionals, administrators, politicians, and activists in the world have advocated for the full participation of persons with disabilities in society by improving the quality of education and reducing inequity (United Nations Department for Economic and Social Affairs, 2018; United Nations Educational, Scientific and Cultural Organization [UNESCO], 2009). Inclusion in education became a global social movement since the UNESCO's Salamanca Agreement (1994); as a result, many governments and international organizations agreed on promoting policies and advocating policy changes to support inclusive education (Hardy & Woodcock, 2015). The global advocacy in inclusive education has led researchers in the field of APE to explore the issues of inclusion in a broader context, encompassing societal attitudes toward persons with disabilities, institutional value (e.g., teacher preparation, school policies), and personal factors (e.g., students' grade level, disability type, the severity of disabling conditions) (Block & Obrusnikova, 2007; Qi & Ha, 2012; Tant & Watelain, 2016; Wilhelmsen & Sørensen, 2017).

Bronfenbrenner's bioecological theory is a well-known theoretical model in the field of child development. Bronfenbrenner constructed his model from a contextualist paradigm, which emphasizes the significance of contextual influences on human development (Tudge, 2008). That is, the development of a person is an outcome produced by the interaction between person and environment throughout the lifespan (Griffore & Phenice, 2016). He further distinguished the context into four different systems; the immediate setting in which the child interacts and engages in the majority of time (microsystem), the interrelations between microsystems (mesosystem), the environments in which the child whose development is considered is not a member (exosystem), and the most distant settings that regard social value or culture (macrosystem) (Bronfenbrenner, 1979, 1992). Bronfenbrenner's model is also a dynamic relational view between an active person and context in the process of human development (Bronfenbrenner & Morris, 1998, 2006). His formulation later evolved to constitute four interrelated elements: (a) the dynamic relation of the person and the context, (b) the attributes and functioning of the person, (c) the influences of multilayered environmental systems surrounding the person, and (d) the dimension of time, which is also known as a paradigm of process-person-context-time (PPCT) (Lerner, 2005; Rosa & Tudge, 2013).

In this chapter, we provide an overview of Bronfenbrenner's theory and how it has evolved and been applied as a theoretical lens for research concerning child development. Second, we describe the critical concepts and characteristics constituting four elements of PPCT model. Then, the PPCT model is situated within the APE literature to elucidate the theoretical accounts on the issues of, and pedagogical practices regarding, the learning and development of children with disabilities in physical education. Finally, we suggest ways to incorporate these elements appropriately in APE research.

A historical overview

Bioecological theory is a sociocultural perspective, proposed by developmental psychologist Urie Bronfenbrenner (1917–2005), theorizing that human development occurs through interaction between person and environment (or context) (Rosa & Tudge, 2013). In the earlier version of Bronfenbrenner's theory, it primarily focused on describing the influences of different environmental settings and characteristics of the context on a child's development (Rosa & Tudge, 2013). Bioecological theory has gone through many changes and reformulation of Bronfenbrenner's theory by underscoring other aspects, such as roles played by the characteristics of a person, the mechanism of interaction (later termed proximal process), and the dimension of time (Rosa & Tudge, 2013).

Bronfenbrenner initially termed his theory the "ecological model of human development" (1970–1979), which is considered to be the first phase in the evolution of this theory (Rosa & Tudge, 2013). Bronfenbrenner's theory, in this first phase, focused on the person–context interrelatedness (Tudge, Mokrova, Hatfield, & Karnik, 2009). Bronfenbrenner proposed that human development did not occur in isolation, but was shaped in relation to the environments by which a developing person is surrounded (e.g., home, school, community, and society) (Adamsons, O'Brien, & Pasley, 2007). He envisioned the environment as an arrangement of four interrelated structures, conceptualized as four ecological environments, called systems (i.e., microsystem, mesosystem, exosystem, and macrosystem) (Rosa & Tudge, 2013).

During the second phase (1980–1993), Bronfenbrenner revised and extended his initial conceptualization. He called his model ecological systems theory, emphasizing the roles and characteristics of five environmental systems, adding the passage of time. The dimension of time was identified as another layer of environmental systems (i.e., chronosystem) affecting the development of a person and considered a significant force. He further modified the concepts of development, defining it as "the set of processes through which properties of the person and environment interact to produce constancy and change in the characteristics of the person over the life course" (Bronfenbrenner, 1992, p. 191). Bronfenbrenner specifically attended to the characteristics of processes that affect, or are affected by, a developing person in the context in which s/he interacts (Bronfenbrenner, 1992; Rosa & Tudge, 2013). In this period, his views extended and shifted to include "process" as a research paradigm, termed "process-person-context" (PPC).

The third and last version of Bronfenbrenner's theory (1993–2006), called the "bioecological theory of human development", is "an evolving theoretical system for the scientific study of human development over time" (Bronfenbrenner & Morris, 2006, p. 793). Bronfenbrenner noted that the roles of a person's characteristics were consistently neglected when examining his or her development; thereby, the goal of the final version of his theory was to redefine the key propositions underlying the classical model (Rosa & Tudge, 2013). The bioecological theory incorporates "a four-element model, involving the synergistic interconnection among proximal processes, person characteristics, context, and time (the PPCT model)" (Tudge et al., 2016, p. 428). These four components became the essence of the bioecological theory.

To summarize, Bronfenbrenner's bioecological theory is a model that constitutes four components of the proximal process, person, context, and time (or PPCT model) to conceptualize the course of human development. In particular, later versions of his theory stress the impact of characteristics of the developing individual on development in association with the settings. Most importantly, it signifies the effects of proximal process (i.e., reciprocal interaction) on human development because both the developing individual and the context influence the proximal process simultaneously and synergistically (Tudge et al., 2016). The literature indicates that Bronfenbrenner's theory is used inaccurately in many studies by using the older version or not providing a comprehensive analysis of the PPCT model (Tudge et al., 2009, 2016). Therefore, it is essential for researchers to recognize the concepts of Bronfenbrenner's theory comprehensively in studies and how it has been reformulated to understand human development. This chapter outlines the revised model of his work.

PPCT model

Proximal process

The term proximal process implies a reciprocal interaction between an individual and environment, including the person, objects, and symbols, operating over time (Bronfenbrenner & Morris, 2006). Explicitly, it exemplifies the relationship between two individuals (e.g., parent–child, child–child interaction) and the relation among objects and symbols with which the developing individual comes into contact in its immediate context (e.g., reading, writing, motor skill, sports activities) (Bronfenbrenner & Morris, 2006; Rosa & Tudge, 2013). A proximal process also comprises an exchange of energy between the person and environment in either direction—from a developing person to characteristics of the environment or from characteristics of the environment to the developing person—or both directions separately or simultaneously (Bronfenbrenner & Evans, 2000). As the core of the theory, it functions as the engine of development, so it is distinguished to produce significant developmental outcomes, such as promoting competence and diminishing the possibility of dysfunctional outcomes (Rosa & Tudge, 2013).

The operation of the proximal processes shaping the development of an active individual is varied systematically. An individual's developmental outcome is a product constructed by the joint function of a person's characteristics, the environmental context, either immediate or remote, in which the process takes place, and the length and the frequency of the time when the individual has been exposed to the particular process and the contextual settings (Bronfenbrenner & Evans, 2000; Bronfenbrenner & Morris, 2006).

Person

Person, representing the second P of the PPCT model, implies the significance of biological, genetic, emotional, cognitive, and behavioral aspects to subsequent development (Lerner, 2005; Tudge et al., 2009). In Bronfenbrenner's later works, he paid more attention to explaining the characteristics of an individual that are brought into his or her social situations. Bronfenbrenner distinguished these characteristics into three types, which are termed demands, resources, and forces, and viewed them as most influential in shaping human development (Tudge et al., 2009). *Demand* characteristics refer to the qualities of the developing person, such as age, gender, skin color, and physical appearance. They were originally called personal stimulus characteristics in Bronfenbrenner's earlier writings, stipulating that demand characteristics work as an immediate reaction to another person (Tudge, 2008).

Resources are another type of personal characteristics that represent biopsychological liabilities and assets to influence a person's ability to disrupt, or engage in, proximal processes (Bronfenbrenner & Morris, 2006). It is not an apparent or noticeable characteristic, compared to demand characteristics (visible), because it relates to emotional and mental resources (e.g., experiences, skills, and intelligence) and social and material resources (e.g., caring parents, educational opportunities pertinent to the needs of the particular society) (Tudge et al., 2009).

Last, *forces* embody differences of temperament, motivation, and persistence. For instance, two individuals may exhibit the same characteristics of resource (e.g., skills and intelligence). However, their developmental outcomes or trajectories may occur differently—influenced by one's forces that are either generative (e.g., curiosity, readiness, persistence) or disruptive (e.g., inability to defer gratification, distractibility, impulsiveness) (Bronfenbrenner & Morris, 2006; Tudge et al., 2009).

Context

Context (or environment) is conceptualized as a series of nested structures influencing a person's development, as portrayed in Russian dolls (Berk, 2013). That is, it is a set of four interrelated systems of micro-, meso-, exo-, and macro-. These four environmental systems represent from the most proximal level (e.g., parent–child, teacher–student, child–child) to the most distal level (e.g., sociocultural beliefs) (Bronfenbrenner, 2005, 1995).

Microsystem

The *microsystem* is the innermost structure where a person's development is directly affected by the surrounding environment (i.e., home, school, or peer group), in which the developing person uses the majority of their time engaging in activities and interaction with others (Tudge et al., 2009). Bronfenbrenner (Bronfenbrenner, 1995) defined microsystem as:

> a pattern of activities, social roles, and interpersonal relations experienced by the developing person in a given face-to-face setting with particular physical, social, and symbolic features that invite, permit, or inhibit, engagement in sustained, progressively more complex interaction with, and activity in, the immediate environment.
>
> *(cited in Bronfenbrenner & Morris, 2006, p. 814)*

Mesosystem

The *mesosystem* refers to "the relationships existing between two or more settings … .a system of two or more microsystems" (Bronfenbrenner & Morris, 2006, p. 817). Particularly, it denotes "the linkages and processes taking place between two or more settings containing the developing person (e.g., the relations between home and school, school and workplace)" (Bronfenbrenner, 2005, p. 148). For instance, a child's development is influenced by the relations between parents and teachers.

Exosystem

The *exosystem* is a social setting in which "the developing person of interest is not situated, and thus does not participate actively within it, but nonetheless experiences its influence, and, at times, can also influence it, whether formally or informally" (Rosa & Tudge, 2013, pp. 246–247). A child's development is influenced by his or her parents' employment or experiences in the workplace in which the developing individual does not belong. That is, a parent's behavior toward his or her child can be more irritable than usual if the parent has been stressed at work (Rosa & Tudge, 2013). Other examples include a teacher's experiences and training, curriculum policies, and educational support from a school or school district (McLinden, Ravenscroft, Douglas, Hewett, & Cobb, 2017; Ruppar, Allcock, & Gonsier-Gerdin, 2017).

Macrosystem

The *macrosystem*, an outermost layer of context, signifies the cultural and social structure whose members share value or belief systems, or where the child is raised. It includes the institutional systems of a culture or subculture, such as laws, economic and political systems, and cultural and social expectation (Tudge, 2008). It also involves the relationship among policies, cultural beliefs, and organization for opportunities that influences the inner levels of systems and persons within the systems (Rosa & Tudge, 2013; Ruppar et al., 2017). It means that teachers, parents, and administrators are influenced by those variables to determine educational programs and instructional placement (i.e., APE service) for children with disabilities.

Time

The last component of the PPCT model is *time*. The dimension of time was originally termed as chronosystem in Bronfenbrenner's earlier writing. According to Bronfenbrenner (1986), chronosystem was a proposed term for designating a research model that permits one to examine "the influence on the person's development of changes (and continuities) over time in the environments in which the person is living" (p. 724). In regard to chronosystem, an individual's developmental changes are caused by life experiences or events that are classified as internal (e.g., puberty, severe illness, disability) and external transition (entering school, the birth of a sibling, divorce, death, moving) over a social-historical period of a person's life (Bronfenbrenner, 1992).

In Bronfenbrenner's later publications, the dimension of time was reconceptualized to constitute three successive levels of microtime, mesotime, and macrotime (Bronfenbrenner & Morris, 2006). *Microtime* refers to "continuity versus discontinuity in ongoing episodes of proximal process" (p. 796) (i.e., things occur during the course of interactions). Second, *mesotime* is "the periodicity of these episodes across broader time intervals, such as days and weeks" (p. 796) (i.e., how often interactions occur over days and weeks). Finally, *macrotime* "focuses on the changing expectations and events in the larger society, both within and across generations, as they affect and are affected by, processes and outcomes of human development over the life course." (p. 796)

Development of children with disabilities and physical education

For the past two decades, there has been a plea for a more comprehensive perspective in research and practices focused on whole child development and education of children in school (Institute of Medicine, 2013; World Health Organization, 2018). Also, there has been a global movement promoting inclusive education in school and community for children with disabilities. Inclusive learning opportunities themselves are still challenged by many interrelated variables, such as child's attributes, family functioning, community setting (i.e., rural, urban, socioeconomic status), policies, and cultural values (Duerden & Witt, 2010). In this section, we synthesize the roles of four elements of bioecological theory applied in the APE literature. The issues and pedagogical practices concerning the learning and development of children with disabilities are identified and explained within the PPCT model (see Table 17.1).

Table 17.1 Synthesis of school-based proximal process found in APE research

Category/topic	Description	Level of system
Agents of change	• Child–teacher interaction • Child–child interaction • Child–parent interaction	Microsystem
Communication and collaboration	• Parent–teacher partnership • Relationships among educational professionals • Special educator • General physical educator • Adapted physical educator • Paraeducator	Mesosystem
Professional development	• Initial teacher preparation • Continuing education	Exosystem
Sociocultural influences	• Families who hold different cultural values and beliefs • Families who live in rural, urban or suburban areas • Families who are challenged economically	Macrosystem
Transition process	• IEP planning through the level of schooling • Pedagogical practices – Segregation vs. inclusion • Socio-historical time – Longitudinal study	Chronosystem (or Time)

Child attributes and behaviors in proximal process

Children with disabilities are more likely to be physically inactive than their peers without disabilities, due to the lack of knowledge and awareness of physical activity and healthy behaviors, low level of skill performance, and social–environmental barriers (Grumstrup & Demchak, 2017; Jones et al., 2017). Personal factors, such as cognitive, physical, and social impairment, influence the development of children with disabilities significantly when interacting with people (e.g., parents, teachers, and peers) or contacting objects (e.g., equipment) in the context (e.g., general physical education). For example, if a child has a diagnosis of spina bifida and uses a wheelchair, the child's participation in physical education would be inhibited by his or her limited physical function (An & Goodwin, 2007). If a child with autism spectrum disorder (ASD) participates in physical education, the child's interaction with people or objects in the process can be limited or absent because of the deficits in communication, restricted interests, stereotypical behaviors, and motor delays (Bremer & Lloyd, 2016; Jones et al., 2017; MacDonald, Hatfield, & Twardzik, 2017).

While the characteristics of a person have been included in research focused on physical activity, variability in how disability is addressed limits our understanding of how specific disability traits impact physical activity and inclusion in general physical education (GPE). Through contemplation of a person's ecological niches or personal characteristics over time, we can refine our understanding of how a person is related to bidirectional physical outcomes and activities. Moreover, it is necessary for individual qualities—demand, resource, and forces—to be clearly defined in the research to understand child development systematically, and further exploration is needed for the mechanism of the proximal process; how the interaction between person and context promotes personal attributes of competence and diminishes the possibility of dysfunctional outcomes.

Agents of change in microsystem

Bronfenbrenner described that child development is influenced by multiple environmental systems in which a child belongs and the ways s/he interacts between and within the interrelated contexts over time. In the level of microsystem, the child interacts with various people (teachers, peers, and parents), objects (equipment, tasks), and symbols (pictures, words) when participating in physical education across the different settings, such as home, school, and community. However, this chapter mainly focuses on the school context.

Within the microsystem, one of the significant agents interacting with a child with a disability is a teacher (McLinden et al., 2017; Ruppar et al., 2017). A large body of research has explored physical education teachers' beliefs and attitudes toward the inclusion of students with disabilities. Tant and Watelain (2016) reviewed studies published from 1975 to 2015 regarding inclusion in physical education from a teacher perspective. They found that physical education teachers' attitudes toward the inclusion of students with disabilities were influenced by their characteristics, such as experiences in teaching GPE and students with disabilities, training in APE, and perceived competence in teaching, and some of the child-related factors (i.e., age and class level, disability type and severity). Teachers' attitudes toward the inclusion of students with disabilities impacted their practices. In other words, those who favored inclusion adapted the practices to include students with disabilities in the program and aimed to develop the performance of students with disabilities in the program along with their participation.

Second, the peer relationship may be an integral part of socialization for children, along with skill development (Ruppar et al., 2017; Seymour, Reid, & Bloom, 2009; Qi & Ha, 2012). In some instances, children with disabilities may have personal attributes inhibiting peer interaction and relationships. However, with the appropriate supports, social relationship with their peers without disabilities can be developed in physical education. Klavina and Block (2008) found that peers with disabilities, after training, could support students with severe and multiple disabilities to increase their engagement in, and interactions during, GPE. Nurturing and supporting peer relationships for students with disability is a microsystem promotion for inclusion and can be useful in physical education settings.

Last, parents are an active agent to promote or inhibit their children's development in physical education by playing various roles, such as an advocate, instructor, mediator, and collaborator (An & Goodwin, 2007; An & Hodge, 2013; Kuo, Magill-Evans, & Zwaigenbaum, 2015; Wilhelmsen & Sørensen, 2018). For example, Kuo and her colleagues (2015) considered how parent mediation related to the child's use of screens correlated to physical activity. When parents are aware of the physical activity benefits, they may be better able to advocate for the physical activity needs of their child and more likely to intentionally provide physical activity opportunities, despite time being a potential barrier. They can also engage in strategies for reducing their children's screen time at home. These factors may influence their children to be physically active and reduce the prevalence of sedentary behavior.

Communication and collaboration as mesosystem

The development of children with disabilities in physical education is also affected by the relationship between agents who interact with the child in the immediate environment: for example, parent–teacher dyad, APE–GPE teacher relationship or with a special education teacher. If each agent in the setting (home and school) keeps communication open and shares the goals for the children, the child's development can be promoted (An & Hodge, 2013; Columna, Pyfer, Velez, Bridenthrall, & Canabal, 2008; Wilhelmsen & Sørensen, 2018). According to An and Hodge (2013), the parents of children with developmental disabilities perceived the importance of collaboration with educational professionals. They recognized that increasing the frequency of communication with APE and GPE teachers could facilitate parents' understanding of the physical education program and how they might incorporate similar activities at home (An & Hodge, 2013; Chaapel, Columna, Lytle, & Bailey, 2013). Also, parents continuously communicate with the teachers or other specialists in the decision-making process (i.e., individualized education program [IEP]) to represent the strengths and needs regarding their children's learning (An & Hodge, 2013; Wilhelmsen & Sørensen, 2018). Although parents claimed that they actively engaged in school by assisting programs and communicating with teachers, their relationships with physical educators tend to be weak due to personal or social barriers (e.g., lack of interest, limited opportunity to interact) (An & Hodge, 2013; Columna et al., 2008; Wilhelmsen & Sørensen, 2018).

Within the framework of inclusive education, a collaboration among educational professionals is critical in planning, service delivery, and evaluation because it can impact the extent and quality of services provided to children with disabilities (Hernandez, 2013). There is a large body of research exploring collaboration or collaborative practices (e.g., multidisciplinary, interdisciplinary, and transdisciplinary approach and co-teaching) in education for children with disabilities (Hernandez, 2013; Mulholland & O'Connor, 2016; Pancsofar & Petroff, 2016). Concerning physical education, the relationship between teachers, such as GPE–APE, GPE–Special Educator, GPE–paraeducators, was investigated in the literature (An & Meaney, 2015; Pedersen, Cooley, & Rottier, 2014). Studies showed that the GPE teachers had limited communication and collaboration with the APE teachers, due in part to the high caseload for the APE teacher and limited training or background of paraeducators in APE (An & Meaney, 2015; Tant & Watelain, 2016).

Professional development as exosystem

Exosystems include the social structures and processes in two or more settings that affect the developing person in the immediate setting indirectly (Ruppar et al., 2017). A range of exosystems, such as parents' workplace, teachers' training, or school district requirement, also influences the learning and development of children with disabilities in physical education. According to Tant and Watelain (2016), teachers' experiences and training in APE, including initial preparation and continuing education, was one of the contributing factors on their decision to include children with disabilities in GPE. Teachers often identified their insufficient training in APE and inclusive practices as a barrier to serving children with disabilities in GPE successfully (Block & Obrusnikova, 2007; Wilhelmsen & Sørensen, 2017). Additionally, at primary school level, physical education is often taught by general education teachers (or special education teachers), so their insufficient training in physical activity may delay the learning and development of children with disabilities (Nobre, Coutinho, & Valentini, 2014).

Cultural influences as macrosystem

Culture is one of the variables representing the outermost level of environmental systems in the bioecological theory and is a particular group whose members share their beliefs or values about who should or should not be allowed (Tudge, 2008). For instance, Columna and colleagues (2008) explored the perspectives of Hispanic parents of children with disabilities on their expectation of APE regarding their children's purposeful play and transition to school programming. In this study, not all Hispanic parents understood the APE services provided to their children in school, so they desired to learn more about APE services. Parents' lack of knowledge of APE negatively affected their support for their children's physical activity engagement at home, in the community, or in school. Although Hispanic parents desired to share the responsibility of their children's education with the teachers, their participation was interfered with by cultural and language barriers, their educational backgrounds, and socioeconomic status.

According to Vélez-Agosto, Soto-Crespo, Vizcarrondo-Oppenheimer, Vega-Molina, and García Coll (2017), culture is crucial to consider from the microsystem level, possibly affecting how one develops interventions and evaluates their effectiveness. Although we discuss the culture at the level of macrosystem as Bronfenbrenner theorized, consideration at the microsystem level will also enable one to address how culture is intertwined with proximal development processes and how it may define the microsystem and social communities, such as families. When researchers focused on physical education and children with disabilities do not consider culture within the bioecological model, it may limit the impact of results, implications, and interventions.

Transition process as time

Bronfenbrenner's concept of temporal dimension, time or chronosystem, explains changes and continuity occurring in a person's development over the life course. One aspect of changes take place in the person over time. Transition plans between schools and levels of programs (i.e., preschool to primary, primary to secondary, secondary to postsecondary) may facilitate the positive development of children with disabilities to live independent, healthy lives (Ruppar et al., 2017). As the developing child grows older, s/he is challenged to learn and access the GPE curriculum, another aspect of time affecting the change in the environment. When engaging with the GPE curriculum, the learning environment (e.g., one-on-one setting, paraprofessional support, general setting) in physical education may need to be determined carefully according to the needs and interests of children with disabilities (Ruppar et al., 2017).

Implications for research

Bronfenbrenner's bioecological theory is a renowned perspective to comprehend child development, used in other disciplines such as family science, developmental science, and child development; however, the model is quite unusual in the field of APE. We reviewed Bronfenbrenner's works that have been published to date and traced the studies conducted in APE research. Very few studies used bioecological theory as a theoretical foundation for their work (An & Hodge, 2013; Columna et al., 2008), with none of the currently identified research correctly presenting the model. In this section, we will explain how this model can be used as a theoretical framework for research and what to consider when designing research to test the model or explore the issues regarding the learning and development of children with disabilities in APE or GPE.

The bioecological theory is very complex and challenging to apply when designing research because of the philosophical underpinning of the theory (Tudge, 2008). Those who use the bioecological theory in their research as a theoretical foundation should recognize that this theory is constructed from a contextualist paradigm, meaning that people's views of realities are varied, even if it is one reality, according to the power, time, situation, or culture-specific pressures (Tudge, 2008; Tudge et al., 2016). Thus, the bioecological theory should not be treated in a view of mechanist paradigm, understanding the context as one of various factors influencing the individual's development. What Bronfenbrenner proposed in his model is that "development occurs because of the synergistic relation between individual and context in the course of proximal processes" (Tudge et al., 2016, p. 430).

The central element of Bronfenbrenner's theory to focus on for research is a proximal process because it provides a means to show the synergistic influences of both the person's characteristics and the context (Tudge et al., 2016). For example, the development of socialization between students with and without disabilities in GPE can be affected by the characteristics of a child with disabilities and the environmental settings in which they participate for physical activities during the process. In this case, socialization—an interaction between students with and without disabilities—is a proximal process, and the process can be promoted or inhibited by the person's characteristics (e.g., type and severity of disability, skill level, level of social behaviors) and the context (e.g., task, learning environment). Also, the socialization between students can be improved or undeveloped in the process, depending on the length of a program offered (time).

Last, we recommend using the last version of Bronfenbrenner's model, bioecological theory of human development, when designing a study. Researchers should incorporate all four elements of PPCT in their research, and all these elements should be evaluated with the data obtained or that emerged. In studies, researchers provide a description of the theory in the introduction as guiding their research, but, occasionally, the findings of the research have not tested the model or situated it with the data. Theory plays an essential role in research that explains phenomena implicitly and rationally (Collins & Stockton, 2018). Without the evaluation of the theory with the data, there may be a chance for the researchers to make critical errors, misrepresent the theory, or provide no support for the data from the theory. Thus, researchers should employ the theory with caution to avoid such flaws.

Chapter summary

- Bronfenbrenner's bioecological theory is a sociocultural perspective that explains the complex nature of human development. Bronfenbrenner posited that development is influenced by the synergistic relations between a developing individual and context in the course of proximal processes over time.
- Bronfenbrenner's bioecological theory forms a four-element framework of the process, person, context, and time (PPCT) that influences the developmental change of human beings.
- A proximal process is a particular form of dynamic interactions between an active agent (i.e., person) and environment (i.e., context) driving throughout the life course. It is the central force shaping the development of a person in the areas of ability, motivation, knowledge, and skills (Bronfenbrenner & Morris, 2006).
- Person, a driving force to shape subsequent development, is classified into three characteristics of demand, resource, and force. Demand characteristics are the qualities of a developing person (e.g., age, gender, race, and physical appearance) that invite or discourage reactions from the context. The resource characterstics are the biopsychological liabilities (e.g., genetic defects, severe illness) and assets (knowledge, skills) facilitating or disrupting a person's engagement in the proximal processes (reciprocal interaction). The force characteristics are behavioral dispositions that sustain their operation (curiosity, motivation) or interfere with their occurrence (impulsiveness, distractibility).
- The context, or environment, is theorized as a set of four nested, interrelated systems (i.e., micro-, meso-, exo-, and macro-) that a developing individual is in constant interaction with. The systems signify an environmental setting that is either closed (direct influence, i.e., home or school) or distant (indirect influence, i.e., family's or society's values/expectation) to a developing individual.
- The concept of time refers to changes and continuities that occur in the life course of the person. An individual's development is affected by the internal (changes in the person) and external (changes in the environment) transition over a socio-historical period.
- When conducting research using Bronfenbrenner's theory, the research should focus on examining the proximal process to understand the complex human development, because it is the way of presenting the synergistic influences caused by both the person's characteristics and the environment.
- Currently, APE research incorporating the PPCT model is minimal, but future research, including those elements, is possible and necessary in APE and inclusive physical education.

Reflective questions for discussion

1. How has the bioecological theory been applied to research analyzing the development of children with disabilities in physical education?
2. Bronfenbrenner introduced the framework of the PPCT model as a means to design research. How are these elements applied to APE research?

3. How might a child's characteristics—demand, resource, and force—influence their development in physical education?
4. How can physical activity-related proximal process occurring in home, school, and community microsystems be adjusted to meet the needs of children with disabilities?
5. What influences do agents, such as parents, teacher, and peers, contribute to the development of the children with disabilities in APE and inclusive physical education?
6. How might culture be considered as an influence at the macrosystem or microsystem levels?
7. What cultural and social issues might be influencing the learning and development of children with disabilities in school-based or community-based physical activity or sports programs?
8. How can we interpret the impact and nature of the proximal process within and between microsystems (e.g., home, school, and community) in different ethnic groups and socioeconomic status from the bioecological theory?
9. Which level of environmental systems is the most significant for children with disabilities and why?

References

Adamsons, K., O'Brien, M., & Pasley, K. (2007). An ecological approach to father involvement in biological and stepfather families. *Fathering, 5*, 129–147. doi:10.3149/fth.0502.129

An, J., & Goodwin, D. L. (2007). Physical education for students with spina bifida: Mothers' perspectives. *Adapted Physical Activity Quarterly, 24*, 38–58. doi:10.1123/apaq.24.1.38

An, J., & Hodge, S. R. (2013). Exploring the meaning of parental involvement in physical education students with developmental disabilities. *Adapted Physical Activity Quarterly, 29*, 147–163. doi:10.1123/apaq.30.2.147

An, J., & Meaney, K. S. (2015). Inclusion practices in elementary physical education: A social-cognitive perspective. *International Journal of Disability, Development and Education, 62*, 143–157. doi:10.1080/1034912X.2014.998176

Berk, L. E. (2013). *Child development* (9th ed.). Boston, MA: Allyn and Bacon.

Block, M. E., & Obrusnikova, I. (2007). Inclusion in physical education: A review of the literature from 1995-2005. *Adapted Physical Activity Quarterly, 24*, 103–124. doi:10.1123/apaq.24.2.103

Bremer, E., & Lloyd, M. (2016). School-based fundamental-motor skill intervention for children with autism-like characteristics: An exploratory study. *Adapted Physical Activity Quarterly, 33*, 66–88. doi:10.1123/APAQ.2015-0009

Bronfenbrenner, U. (1979). *The ecology of human development.* Cambride: MA: Harvad University Press.

Bronfenbrenner, U. (1986). Ecology of the family as a context for human development: Research perspectives. *Developmental Psychology, 22*, 723–742. doi:10.1037/0012-1649.22.6.723

Bronfenbrenner, U. (1992). Ecological systems theory. In R. Vasta (Ed.), *Six theories of child development: Revised formulations and current issues* (pp. 187–249). London, PA: Jessica Kingsley Publishers.

Bronfenbrenner, U. (1995). Developmental ecology through space and time: A future perspective. In P. Moen, G. H. Elder, Jr., & K. Lüscher (Eds.), *Examining lives in context: Perspectives on the ecology of human development* (pp. 619–647). Washington, DC: American Psychological Association.

Bronfenbrenner, U. (2005). On the nature of bioecological theory and research. In U. Bronfenbrenner (Ed.), *Making human beings human: Bioecological perspectives on human development* (pp. 1–15). Thousand Oaks, CA: Sage Publications.

Bronfenbrenner, U., & Evans, G. W. (2000). Developmental science in the 21st century: Emerging questions, theoretical models, research designs and empirical findings. *Social Development, 9*, 115–125. doi:10.1111/1467-9507.00114

Bronfenbrenner, U., & Morris, P. A. (1998). The ecology of developmental processes. In W. Damon & R. M. Lerner (Eds.), *Handbook of child psychology: Volume 1 Theoretical models of human development* (5th ed., pp. 993–1028). New York: John Wiley & Sons.

Bronfenbrenner, U., & Morris, P. A. (2006). The bioecological model of human development. In R. M. Lerner (Ed.), *Handbook of child psychology: Volume 1 Theoretical models of human development* (6th ed., pp. 793–828). Hoboken, NJ: John Wiley & Sons.

Chaapel, H., Columna, L., Lytle, R., & Bailey, J. (2013). Parental expectations about adapted physical education services. *The Journal of Special Education, 47*, 186–196. doi:10.1177/0022466912447661

Collins, C. S., & Stockton, C. M. (2018). The central role of theory in qualitative research. *International Journal of Qualitative Methods, 17*, 1–10. doi:10.1177/1609406918797475

Columna, L., Pyfer, J., Velez, L., Bridenthrall, N., & Canabal, M. Y. (2008). Parental expectations of adapted physical educators: A Hispanic perspective. *Adapted Physical Activity Quarterly, 25*, 228–246. doi:10.1123/apaq.25.3.228

Duerden, M. D., & Witt, P. A. (2010). An ecological systems theory perspective on youth programming. *Journal of Park and Recreation Administration, 28*(2), 108–120.

Griffore, R. J., & Phenice, L. A. (2016). Proximal processes and causality in human development. *European Journal of Educational and Development Psychology, 4*(1), 10–16. Retrieved from: https://eajournals.org

Grumstrup, B., & Demchak, M. (2017). Obesity, nutrition, and physical activity for people with significant disabilities. *Physical Disabilities: Education and Related Services, 36*, 13–28. doi:10.14434/pders. v36i1.23144

Hardy, I., & Woodcock, S. (2015). Inclusive education policies: Discourses of difference, diversity and deficit. *International Journal of Inclusive Education, 19*, 141–164. doi:10.1080/13603116.2014.908965

Hernandez, S. J. (2013). Collaboration in special education: Its history, evolution, and critical factors necessary for successful implementation. *US-China Education Review B, 3*, 480–498. doi:10.17265/2161-6248/ 2013.06B.007

Institute of Medicine. (2013). *Educating the student body: Taking physical activity and physical education to school*. Washington, DC: The National Academic Press.

Jones, R. A., Downing, K., Rinehart, N. J., Barnett, L. M., May, T., McGillivray, J. A., & Hinkley, T. (2017). Physical activity, sedentary behavior and their correlates in children with Autism Spectrum Disorder: A systematic review. *PLoS ONE, 12*(1-23). doi:10.1371/journal.pone.0172482

Klavina, A., & Block, M. E. (2008). The effect of peer tutoring on interaction behaviors in inclusive physical education. *Adapted Physical Activity Quarterly, 25*, 132–158. doi:10.1123/apaq.25.2.132

Kuo, M. H., Magill-Evans, J., & Zwaigenbaum, L. (2015). Parental mediation of television viewing and videogaming of adolescents with autism spectrum disorder and their siblings. *Autism, 19*, 724–735. doi:10.1177/1362361314552199

Lerner, R. M. (2005). Urie Bronfenbrenner: Career contributions of the consummate developmental scientist. In U. Bronfenbrenner (Ed.), *Making human beings human: Bioecological perspectives on human development* (pp. ix–xxvi). Thousand Oaks, CA: Sage.

MacDonald, M., Hatfield, B., & Twardzik, E. (2017). Child behaviors of young children with autism spectrum disorder across play settings. *Adapted Physical Activity Quarterly, 34*, 19–32. doi:10.1123/ APAQ.2016-0028

McLinden, M., Ravenscroft, J., Douglas, G., Hewett, R., & Cobb, R. (2017). The significance of specialist teachers of learners with visual impairments as agents of change: Examining personnel preparation in the United Kingdom through a bioecological systems theory. *Journal of Visual Impairment & Blindness, 111*, 569–584. doi:10.1177/0145482X1711100607

Mulholland, M., & O'Connor, U. (2016). Collaborative classroom practice for inclusion: Perspectives of classroom teachers and learning support/resource teachers. *International Journal of Inclusive Education, 20*, 1070–1083. doi:10.1080/13603116.2016.1145266

Nobre, F. S. S., Coutinho, M. T. C., & Valentini, N. C. (2014). The ecology of motor development in coastal school children of Brazil Northeast. *Journal of Human Growth and Development, 24*, 263–273. doi:10.7322/jhdg.88910

Pancsofar, N., & Petroff, J. G. (2016). Teachers' experiences with co-teaching as a model for inclusive education. *International Journal of Inclusive Education, 20*, 1043–1053. doi:10.1080/13603116.2016.1145264

Pedersen, S. J., Cooley, P. D., & Rottier, C. R. (2014). Physical educators' efficacy in utilizing paraprofessionals in an inclusive setting. *Australian Journal of Teacher Education, 39*(10), 1–5. doi:10.14221/ ajte.2014v39n10.1

Qi, J., & Ha, A. S. (2012). Inclusion in physical education: A review of literature. *International Journal of Disability, Development, and Education, 59*, 257–281. doi:10.1080/1034912X.2012.697737

Rosa, E. M., & Tudge, J. (2013). Urie Bronfenbrenner's theory of human development: Its evolution from ecology to bioecology. *Journal of Family Theory & Review, 5*, 243–258. doi:10.1111/jftr.12022

Ruppar, A. L., Allcock, H., & Gonsier-Gerdin, J. (2017). Ecological factors affecting access to general education content and contexts for students with significant disabilities. *Remedial and Special Education, 38*, 53–63. doi:10.1177/0741932516646856

Seymour, H., Reid, G., & Bloom, G. A. (2009). Friendship in inclusive PE. *Adapted Physical Activity Quarterly*, 26, 201–219.

Tant, M., & Watelain, E. (2016). Forty years later, a systematic literature review on inclusion in physical education (1975-2015): A teacher perspective. *Educational Research Review, 19*, 1–17. doi:10.1016/j.edurev.2016.04.002

Tudge, J. (2008). *The everyday lives of young children: Culture, class, and child rearing in diverse societies.* Cambridge: Cambridge University Press.

Tudge, J. R. H., Mokrova, I., Hatfield, B. E., & Karnik, R. B. (2009). Uses and misuses of Bronfenbrenner's bioecological theory of human development. *Journal of Family Theory & Review, 1*, 198–210. doi:10.1111/j.1756-2589.2009.00026.x

Tudge, J. R. H., Payir, A., Merçon-Vargas, E., Cao, H., Liang, Y., Li, J., & O'Brien, L. (2016). Still misused after all these years? A reevaluation of the uses of Bronfenbrenner's bioecological theory of human development. *Journal of Family Theory & Review, 8*, 427–445. doi:10.1111/jftr.12165

United Nations Department for Economic and Social Affairs (2018). *UN flagship report on disability and development 2018.* Paris, France. Retrieved from www.un.org/development/desa/disabilities/publication-disability-sdgs.html

United Nations Educational, Scientific and Cultural Organization. (1994). *The Salamanca statement and framework for action on special needs education.* Paris: UNESCO Special Education, Division of Basic Education.

Vélez-Agosto, N. M., Soto-Crespo, J. G., Vizcarrondo-Oppenheimer, M., Vega-Molina, S., & García Coll, C. (2017). Bronfenbrenner's bioecological theory revision: Moving culture from the macro into the micro. *Perspectives on Psychological Science, 12*, 900–910. doi:10.1177/1745691617704397

Wilhelmsen, T., & Sørensen, M. (2017). Inclusion of children with disabilities in physical education: A systematic review of literature from 2009 to 2015. *Adapted Physical Activity Quarterly, 34*, 311–337. doi:10.1123/apaq.2016-0017

Wilhelmsen, T., & Sørensen, M. (2018). Physical education-related home–School collaboration: The experiences of parents of children with disabilities. *European Physical Education Review*, 1–17. doi:10.1177/1356336X18777263

World Health Organization. (2018). *Global action plan on physical activity 2018-2030: More active people for a healthier world.* Geneva: WHO. www.who.int/ncds/prevention/physical-activity/en/

18

Social cognitive theory

Jeffrey J. Martin and Michelle D. Guerrero

Introduction

The purpose of this chapter is to provide an overview and criticism of social cognitive theory (SCT) and to provide future research directions for using SCT within adapted physical education (APE). Authors of other chapters in this handbook explain and review research done with specific theories (i.e., self-determination, self-efficacy, theory of planned behavior [TPB] and various motivational theories) and the research findings generated by them in APE. In the current chapter, we take a different approach, as illustrated by our four broad goals. First, we view SCT as a meta-theory and, therefore, spend some time discussing what that means and the implications of it for research in APE. Second, as the name suggests, SCT highlights the role of critical cognitive constructs and important social influences. Unfortunately, SCT minimizes the role of other influences on human behavior (e.g., environment, biology, affect). Therefore, we provide critical analyses of specific SCTs and their shortcomings.

Third, we use our critique of various SCTs as a springboard to provide future research directions that address SCT weaknesses so that researchers in APE have a direction and path to help them extend, and go beyond, traditional SCT's formulations. Finally, we specifically highlight a new theory, affective-reflective theory (ART), which was recently introduced, in part, to address some of the shortcomings of SCTs (Brand & Ekkekakis, 2017). The value of the ART is that it acknowledges the influence of both cognition and affect and the role they play in not only physical activity (PA) but also sedentary behavior. Sedentary behavior is increasingly being viewed as a health risk factor independent of PA (Biswas et al., 2015). Individuals with disabilities have very high rates of sedentary behavior (Dunlop et al., 2015) so a theory such as ART, that can explain both PA and sedentary behavior, is particularly appealing. While researchers in adapted physical activity (APA) and APE have examined PA in PE settings, we are not aware of any research that specifically targets sedentary behavior in PE settings.

SCT as a meta-theory

SCT describes a large, multi-dimensional, casual structure reflecting how people learn and develop competencies and, in turn, regulate those competencies (Bandura, 1977). Examples of SCT explanations of human behavior are far ranging and include how we learn (e.g., modelling), develop self-efficacy, disengage from thought for routine behaviors (e.g., well learned sport skills), use forethought to set goals, anticipate expected outcomes and associated affective states, create supportive environments to facilitate our goals, and engage in moral behavior (Bandura, 1977). SCT is best thought of as a meta-theory because it does not highlight specific hypothetical constructs that influence behavior and a variety of theories can be subsumed under the SCT umbrella. For instance, the TPB is considered an SCT because of its emphasis on social cognitive constructs, and Ajzen (1991) is quite explicit in hypothesizing that perceived behavioral control, attitudes, subjective norms, and intent are the four major cognitions that influence behavior. Additionally, various theories under the SCT umbrella make competing claims about the most critical cognitions that drive behavior. For example, self-efficacy theory indicates the most proximal cause of behavior, such as trying a new motor skill, is self-efficacy whereas the TPB argues it is intention. While SCT has helped us understand PA behavior, Ekkekakis and Zenko (2016) argue that only a limited number of theories subsumed under the SCT umbrella are typically used in PA research and are often redundant as they employ constructs that share variance and overlap (e.g., self-efficacy and physical self-concept; see Bong & Skaalvik, 2003). Ekkekakis and Zenko (2016) argue that scholars in the field have neglected discussions of meta-theory and one result of this failure is an emphasis on a SCT perspective of human functioning. The social cognitive perspective, as noted earlier, highlights the rational thinking capabilities of people, such as our ability to set goals, self-evaluate, employ forethought, examine the pros and cons of various decisions, and effectively employ our cognitive abilities.

Other important influences, such as how people feel and the role of affect in PA behavior are minimized or missing from SCT and the specific theories under it (TPB; Conner, Gaston, Sheeran, & Germain, 2013). The meta-theoretical philosophical stance implicitly endorsed by SCT is that social cognitive constructs are the most critical influences on behavior. As noted by Ekkekakis and Zenko (2016) it is this unquestioned assumption (until recently) that a meta-theoretical discussion can dissect. A goal of the current chapter is to encourage researchers in APE to critically think about the shortcomings of SCTs in general and how they can design strong research studies that incorporate affect. In the following section, we support our contention that SCT has done a modest job of explaining PA behavior with some empirical evidence on PA.

SCT shortcomings

A number of specific theories (e.g., TPB, self-efficacy theory, self-determination theory [SDT]) have been used extensively in APA settings such as PE. In recent years, scholars have pointed out that PA psychologists using SCTs have done a poor job of understanding and changing exercise behavior. For instance, a recent meta-analysis of 206 research papers using the TPB to examine PA accounted for approximately 24% of the variance (McEachan, Conner, Taylor, & Lawton, 2011). Other criticisms are grounded in the high rates of sedentary behavior and low rates of PA found in most developed nations (Ekkekakis & Zenko, 2016). Ekkekakis and Zenko (2016) claim that an over-reliance on SCT in PA research has led to an inability to understand why more people are not physically active. While their criticism appears to be leveled at mostly able-bodied individuals, it can be equally applied to understanding PA behavior with people with disabilities. Using the low levels of PA engaged in by people with and without disabilities is an indirect condemnation of researchers using SCT and likely a somewhat unfair one, given the plethora of reasons why people do and do not engage in PA. Nonetheless, similar to Ekkekakis and Zenko (2016), we take this approach to highlight that if a major goal of APE and APA researchers is to change PA behavior, we have been far from successful.

When PA is measured objectively (e.g., accelerometers) abled-bodied Americans, Canadians, and the British all have quite low and dismal levels of PA. For example, only 3.5% of Americans between the ages of 20 and 59 meet the national recommendation of 150 minutes of moderate to vigorous PA in a week (Tudor-Locke, Brashear, Johnson, & Katzmarzyk, 2010). Individuals with disabilities, in general, obtain even less PA and are more sedentary than able-bodied individuals (Martin, 2018). We next provide a snapshot of four diverse studies that vary across sample, setting, and disability to illustrate the low PA levels of children with disabilities.

First, in an observational study examining PA levels among children with mild intellectual disabilities in PE, students only accrued 9.1 and 4.6 minutes of moderate to vigorous PA in PE and recess, respectively (Sit, McKenzie, Lian, & McManus, 2008). In a second study, using a more diverse sample of children with disabilities (i.e., hearing, vision, intellectual, and physical disabilities), similar results were found as children only obtained 7.8 and 8.9 minutes of moderate to vigorous PA in PE and recess, respectively (Sit, McManus, McKenzie, & Lian, 2007). Third, a meta-analysis of five studies found that even when researchers designed PA interventions to increase PA levels of children with disabilities, they were generally ineffective (McGarty, Downs, Melville, & Harris, 2018). Finally, in one observational study, the authors reported that children with mild disabilities engaged in significantly less successful and appropriate motor activity related to PE lesson goals when compared to peers without disabilities (Temple & Walkley, 1999).

One reason that SCT may be limited in its ability to predict and explain PA in people with disabilities is its failure to consider environmental (e.g., no ramps, lack of curb cuts), physiological (e.g., high obesity levels, the impairment) and affective (e.g., pain) influences. The above examples represent barriers to PA and while identical and similar barriers exist for people without disabilities, a strong case can be made that the barriers faced by individuals with disabilities are even greater. For instance, obesity levels and chronic pain are much higher in people with disabilities compared to individuals without disabilities. Additionally, while cold temperatures and snow can make running in the winter challenging for people without impairments, clearly such factors make pushing a wheelchair extremely difficult for even the most physically fit (e.g., Paralympian rugby player) person with a disability. In PE settings, where obtaining PA is often a direct goal, or a byproduct, of motor skill and sport skill development, children with disabilities also face many difficulties that reflect environmental factors. For instance, children with disabilities have difficulty participating in sports (e.g., a basketball hoop that is too high) or games that teachers do not adapt to their disability. Sport fields (e.g., soccer, baseball) made of grass are not conducive to wheelchair use like a basketball court is for wheelchair rugby. Affective responses such as anxiety or shame as a function of being stared at, teased, or bullied, are not uncommon among children with disabilities in PE (Haegele & Sutherland, 2015; Martin, 2018. Anger is also another strong emotion experienced by children with disabilities in reaction to bullying (Danes-Staples, Lieberman, Ratcliff, & Rounds, 2013).

Ekkekakis and colleagues (e.g., Decker & Ekkekakis, 2017; Ekkekakis & Lind, 2006; Ekkekakis & Zenko, 2016) believe that exercise psychology researchers examining able-bodied individuals have, for the most part, ignored the role of affect. We believe researchers in APA and APE have also relied too heavily on various SCTs. Ekkekakis and Lind (2006) argue that while affect is important to all people, it is particularly salient for individuals that are overweight or obese. This is due to unpleasant feelings associated with high levels of uncomfortable perceived exertion, which may result in less pleasure. Because people with disabilities have higher rates of overweight and obesity, we find their argument extends well into the disabled population. Additionally, people with disabilities also experience chronic pain at much higher levels than able-bodied individuals, making the feeling of pain particularly relevant for individuals with disabilities. Finally, feelings of tiredness and fatigue are particularly relevant to individuals with disabilities, given qualitative research highlighting the prominent role that pain, fatigue, and energy (or lack of it) seems to play in PA engagement decisions (Henderson & Bedini, 1995). Given this brief generic overview of the shortcomings of SCT in general, we next briefly highlight very specific shortcomings of four SCT theories used in APE and APA research and provide suggestions for future research. We should note that we use a very broad definition of SCT, as the authors of some theories (e.g., SDT) we discuss would likely refute being classified as an SCT. However, our rationale for examining the following four theories is that they all highlight and prioritize cognitions and rational thinking.

Self-efficacy theory

Self-efficacy is defined as the extent to which individuals feel capable of engaging in behaviors that will lead to desired outcomes, and is a primary focus of self-efficacy theory (Bandura, 1977). Much of the earlier dialogue/debate surrounding self-efficacy focused on how it differs from self-concept (e.g., Marsh, Roche, Pajares, & Miller, 1997)—which is defined as a person's self-perceptions shaped through experience and interpretations of his/her environment (Shavelson, Hubner, & Stanton, 1976)—and still remains a frequently discussed topic (see Marsh et al., 2018). Unfortunately, a lack of discrepancy between constructs can lead to the jingle–jangle fallacies (Marsh et al., 2018), a term coined by Kelley (1927). The jingle fallacy occurs when scales with similar names might measure different constructs, whereas the jangle fallacy occurs when scale names are seemingly different, yet might measure similar constructs. Self-efficacy was traditionally developed as a domain- and task-specific construct, whereas self-concept was historically viewed as a global construct (Bandura, 1986). What makes self-efficacy and self-concept vulnerable to the jangle-fallacy is the relatively recent shift in how these constructs have been used within the literature; researchers have begun to examine general levels of self-efficacy and domain-specific self-concept. Marsh et al. (2018) conducted a comprehensive investigation into the murky distinction between generalized self-efficacy and self-concept (as well as outcome expectations) and found that these constructs measured very similar constructs (correlations mostly greater than 0.9), despite their distinct construct names, providing evidence of the jingle-jangle fallacy.

Although seemingly obvious, one way APE researchers can avoid the jingle-jangle fallacy is to use "pure" self-efficacy inventories to assess self-efficacy (i.e., domain-specific beliefs). As noted by Marsh et al. (2018), pure measures of self-efficacy include items that are domain-specific, solely descriptive, future oriented (what can I do), free of frame-of-reference effects (i.e., external and internal comparison), and should not include an evaluative component. When these criteria are not met, one can reasonably argue that the test items more closely assess self-concept than self-efficacy (Pajares, 2009; Pintrich, 2003). In fact, some would argue that test items that fail to meet these criteria are antithetical to the foundations of self-efficacy research and theory. We adopt Marsh et al.'s position regarding generalized self-efficacy measures, whereby the contention is not that these measures are necessarily inappropriate or bad, but, rather, they are not true measures of self-efficacy. If researchers insist on using generalized self-efficacy measures yet continue to term these measures as self-efficacy, the responsibility falls on their shoulders to conceptually and theoretically defend their selected "self-efficacy" inventory, though we imagine that this will be a difficult battle to fight, given Marsh et al.'s recent work. An example of the jingle–jangle fallacies in APE can be found in the work of (Cairney, Hay, Faught, Mandigo, & Flouris, 2005) and their research on children with developmental coordination disorder and PA. In their work, they suggest in the title and the measures section that they are examining self-efficacy. However, an examination of the scale they label self-efficacy indicates that the 20-item scale is composed of three factors: confidence, preference for PA, and enjoyment of PA. Clearly, the latter two factors (example items: "like to take it easy at recess" and "have fun in physical education class") are not self-efficacy. Furthermore, items on the scale such as, "Like to relax and watch TV" appear to have little to do with self-efficacy or PA. Disregard for the theoretical and conceptual bases of theories like self-efficacy when conducting research are also responsible for the jingle–jangle fallacies.

Theory of planned behavior

A prominent SCT used in APE research is the TPB. The TPB stipulates that subjective norms (i.e., social pressure to perform a behavior), attitudes (i.e., an evaluation of the behavior), and perceived behavior control (PbC; the perception that a behavior is under one's control) all influence a person's intention (i.e., a goal/desire to perform a behavior) to engage in a behavior. Additionally, PbC is also thought to directly influence behavior, as well as have its influence mediated by intentions. Out of the four theories discussed in this chapter, the TPB has faced the most criticism, with some researchers suggesting that it should be retired (Sniehotta, Presseau, & Araujo-Soares, 2014). See Ajzen (2015) for a refutation of Sniehotta et al. (2014). While the argument for retiring the TPB is multi-faceted, a major rationale is that it lacks predictive validity. Like other SCTs discussed in this chapter, it has been criticized for ignoring the role of emotion in people's decision-making processes, as well as the role of unconsciousness processes (Sheeran, Gollwitzer, & Bargh, 2013). In particular, Sheeran et al. (2013) note that implicit affect, or automatic affective reactions (missing from the TPB) are important determinants of health behaviors.

Another criticism of the TPB focuses on subjective norm (SN), which reflects people's perceptions of (and their willingness to comply with) pressure from significant others to perform various behaviors. A criticism of SN is that it reflects a very narrow (and negative) conceptualization of the role of social influence and, within the PA and exercise domain, social support may better capture the role of social influence (Rhodes, Jones, & Courneya, 2002). Social support reflects people's perceptions that others want to help them perform a behavior. Clearly, subjective norm and social support are two very different forms of social influence. A plethora of studies has supported a link between positive social support and PA (Carron, Hausenblas, & Mack, 1996; Laird, Fawkner, Kelly, McNamee, & Niven, 2016). In APE settings, we know that positive peer support is critical to PA engagement, whereas negative peer interactions can be barriers to PA (Martin, 20187). Other researchers have not been so adamant that the TPB should be retired and have argued that it should be augmented with additional measures such as self-efficacy, self-identity, and moral norms (Conner & Armitage, 1998).

One additional measure to the TPB that has received empirical support is anticipated regret (AR). AR is forethought of a negative emotional state that can be avoided pre-behaviorally by acting differently and, thus, avoiding the anticipated negative affect. For instance, despite a lack of self-efficacy and feelings of anxiety, a student with cerebral palsy

(CP) may play basketball in PE in order to avoid feelings of self-recrimination in the antici-pated future (e.g., at the end of the school day) that he has previously experienced when choosing not to play. A meta-analysis of AR within the TPB has supported its link with intention and its distinctiveness from attitude (Sandberg & Conner, 2008).

For APE researchers who want to use the TPB, despite the criticisms of it, we recom-mend augmenting it in the following three ways. First, consider using multi-dimensional measures of social support (e.g., emotional, shared social reality support, instrumental, informational, etc.) in addition to SN. Second, incorporate measures of affect such as AR. Of course, other measures of affect with a sound rationale for their employment should not be dismissed. Third, employ longitudinal designs (versus cross-sectional) that allow an assessment of the cause (i.e., an intention) to precede a measure of the effect (e.g., PA behavior). Ajzen (2015) notes the time period between an assessment of inten-tions and the behavior also allows for barriers to PA to emerge (e.g., an unanticipated snowfall that negates a prior intention to engage in a wheelchair workout on the track). In addition, intentions can change between their time of their assessment and the meas-urement of the behavior. For instance, children with CP may note an increase in muscle spasticity and muscle tightness over the course of a day, leading them to reconsider their intention to swim in an after school program. Finally, it is not entirely clear from various commentaries when a theory, like the TPB, stops being the TPB with the addition of various constructs. For example, adding a SCT construct, such as self-efficacy, to the TPB seems somewhat routine and doesn't appear to come under intensive criticism. However, it likely becomes more and more difficult to argue that the TPB is being tested as researchers add an increasing number of constructs. Theoretical, conceptual, logical, and empirical arguments are all likely to play a role in the degree to which adding additional constructs to the TPB are defensible.

Self-determination theory

SDT is made up of five smaller "mini-theories" (Vansteenkiste, Niemiec, & Soenens, 2010), which, in varying degrees, fit under a SCT umbrella. We include SDT under the SCT umbrella because of its heavy reliance on the cognitive processes people employ when evalu-ating if their basic needs are met, what motivates their behavior, or whether environments support or thwart their basic needs. It should be acknowledged that the developers of SDT, Richard Ryan and Edward Deci, refer to SDT as an organismic dialectical theory (Ryan & Deci, 2000) and do not classify SDT as an SCT. A core tenet of SDT is the notion that all humans—regardless of individual characteristics (e.g., age, sex, social class, race, and ethni-city)—have three basic psychological needs (Deci & Ryan, 1985, 2000). These three basic needs represent basic needs theory (BNT) and reflect an organismic (as opposed to an SCT) viewpoint in that these needs are thought to be innate psychological needs similar to our biological needs for food and water. These psychological needs include autonomy (i.e., the need to experience choice and psychological freedom), competence (i.e., the need to experi-ence mastery through effective interaction with the environment), and relatedness (i.e., the need to feel a connection with significant others). According to SDT, these basic psycho-logical needs are "innate psychological nutriments that are essential for on-going psycho-logical growth, integrity, and well-being" (Deci & Ryan, 2000, p. 229). Ironically, much of the criticism toward SDT stems from this core tenet—the basic psychological needs. Several scholars, for example, have questioned whether there are, indeed, only three fundamental needs, what exactly constitutes a basic human need, the evidence supporting the three specific needs, and the structure equivalence of the basic needs (e.g., Buunk & Nauta, 2000; Van den Broeck, Ferris, Chang, & Rosen, 2016).

One particular criticism of SDT that has received a substantial amount of attention within recent years is the notion that the three needs are universal and, thus, have universal need-satisfaction effects. In other words, SDT postulates that all individuals will reap similar benefits from need-satisfying experiences. Several authors have questioned this universality principle of the basic psychological needs (Hardy, 2015; Schüler, Brandstätter, & Sheldon, 2013; Schüler, Sheldon, & Frohlich, 2010; Schüler, Sheldon, Prentice, & Halusic, 2016). Specifically, Hardy (2015) questioned why autonomy, competence, and relatedness are the only personal characteristics in all of psychology that are not susceptible to individual differences. Recent research by Schüler and colleagues (Schüler et al., 2013, 2010, 2016) provides some evidence illustrating that the degree to which people experience need-satisfying benefits depends on personality variables. Their research has shown that the individuals with a high implicit achievement and affiliation motive experienced greater positive effects of competence and related need satisfaction on well-being outcomes than did individuals with a weak corresponding motive (Schüler & Brandstätter, 2013; Schüler et al., 2013, 2010). These findings, as noted by Schüler and colleagues, do not necessarily contradict SDT's universality assumption, but, rather, complements and extends it.

A second point of criticism concerns how the basic psychological needs have been conceptualized. Researchers have typically used two different approaches when assessing basic psychological needs (see Brunet, Gunnel, Teixeira, Sabiston, & Bélanger, 2016): the specific-factor approach (i.e., "trees") and the general-factor approach (i.e., "forest"). Whereas the former approach focuses on the satisfaction/frustration of each psychological need, the latter approach focuses on overall psychological need satisfaction/frustration (i.e., aggregating scores of competence, relatedness, and autonomy). Several scholars have acknowledged that both approaches can lead to conceptual ambiguity (see Chen, Hayes, Carver, Laurenceau, & Zhang, 2012). On the one hand, some authors (e.g., Van den Broeck et al., 2016) have argued that combining the needs into one score contradicts SDT's tenets. Van den Broeck et al.'s (2016) meta-analytic review on the multi-dimensionality of basic psychological needs provides evidence against combining the needs into one need satisfaction/ frustration score. On the other hand, Ryan and Deci (2017) have more recently adopted the terms need satisfaction and need frustration, recognizing that each need is independent yet interdependent and, therefore, it may be reasonable to create an overall need satisfaction/frustration score. Evidently, there is confusion within the literature regarding the conceptualization of basic needs.

On a similar note, the assessment of the needs, and particularly the need for competence, has also been criticized. In their seminal *American Psychologist* article, Deci and Ryan (2000, p. 74) stated that a psychological need "is an energizing state that, if satisfied, conduces toward health and well-being but, if not satisfied, contributes to pathology and ill-being." In contrast, within the exercise and sport psychology literature, perceived competence is viewed as "the sense that one has the ability to master a task ..." (Feltz, 1988, p. 450). Clearly, a need for competence is not the same thing as viewing oneself as competent. Despite the clear conceptual differences in these two constructs and their definitions, sport psychology researchers often assess a need for competence with scales and questions that look an awful lot like perceived competence. For instance, Curran, Hill, Ntoumanis, Hall, and Jowett (2016) used a scale with the following item, "I have the ability to perform well in soccer", to measure a need for competence.

A third criticism involves the conceptualization and operationalization of motivation, as found in another SDT mini-theory, the orgasmic integration theory (OIT). OIT suggests that there are different types of motivation that fall along a continuum, ranging from a-motivation to extrinsic motivation to intrinsic motivation. Consequently, the argument that the motivation types align along a continuum has led researchers to describe the different regulations as varying in terms of their *level* of self-determination (e.g., introjected regulation is less self-determined than identified regulation) rather than varying in *kind* (see Chemolli & Gagné, 2014). This interpretation is problematic because it has directly affected how researchers compute motivational scores. For example, researchers have used the relative autonomy index approach (RAI) to compute a general (or global) score of motivation. This approach involves weighting each type of motivation according to its place on the continuum, whereby controlled forms of motivation are subtracted from autonomous forms of motivation. Chemolli and Gagné (2014) outline several problems associated with the RAI, such that it assumes that an individual's motivation score is neatly positioned on one location of the continuum even though this score was generated from various motivation types (Chemolli & Gagné, 2014). Chemolli and Gagnè provide some preliminary evidence against the continuum structure underlying motivation, showing that motivation is best conceptualized as multi-dimensional rather than uni-dimensional.

Fortunately, the criticisms outlined above can be addressed in future studies. First, researchers should carefully consider how individual differences moderate the degree to which they experience need satisfaction/frustration. This line of research is especially pertinent for researchers seeking to design and implement SDT-based interventions, considering that the effects of the intervention may be stronger (or weaker) for some individuals than others. Second, using bifactor modeling, either within a confirmatory factor analytical framework or an exploratory structural equation modeling framework, will allow researchers to simultaneously examine basic psychological needs as distinct dimensions and as a global factor, and, thereby, eliminates having to choose between the general-factor approach or the specific-factor approach (Myers, Martin, Ntoumanis, Celimli, & Bartholomew, 2014). Third, researchers are encouraged to describe the different types of motivation as varying in kind rather than in degree. Doing so acknowledges that individuals engage in behaviors for various reasons (e.g., for money as well as enjoyment) and are not positioned along the continuum at one location. Fourth, when examining SDT basic needs, researchers should be sure that they are actually measuring a need for competence versus perceived competence.

Achievement goal theory

Achievement goal theory focuses on individuals' adaptive and maladaptive responses to achievement challenges (Dweck, 1986). Two goals have been extensively discussed and examined: mastery goals and performance goals. Mastery goals focus on acquiring and developing skills and expertise, whereas performance goals focus on demonstrating and validating one's skills by outperforming others. Initially, mastery goals were believed (and shown) to promote greater educational outcomes than performance goals (Dweck, 1986). However, just as the achievement goal literature began to grow, so, too, did the evidence revealing occasional benefits of performance goals (Harackiewicz, Barron, & Elliot, 1998), prompting some theorists to propose a revision of achievement goal theory (Elliot, 1999; Harackiewicz et al., 1998). This revision included dividing both performance and mastery goals into approach and avoidance forms, thereby adopting the "multiple goal perspective"

(Elliot, 1999; Harackiewicz, Barron, Pintrich, Elliot, & Thrash, 2002). Performance goals were divided into performance-approach (the desire to outperform others) and performance-avoidance (the desire to avoid doing worse than others). Moreover, mastery goals were divided into mastery-approach (the desire to learn and improve skills) and mastery-avoidance (the desire to avoid discovering failures). The debate in perspective—original "mastery goal perspective" versus newer "multiple goal perspective"—has been controversial. Consequently, one of the biggest theoretical weaknesses of achievement goal theory pertains to how goal constructs are defined.

Some theorists advocate for more narrow definitions of goal constructs, suggesting that goals should be strictly competence oriented. This approach is evident in some goal measures. For example, mastery-approach goal items include, "One of my goals in class is to learn as much as I can" (Midgley et al., 2000) and "My goal in this class is to perform better than the other students" (Elliot & Murayama, 2008). Both of these items clearly include goal language and competence-related outcomes. Other theorists believe goal constructs should encompass the various elements of one's experience. Such elements might include affect, attributions, and interest and have been included in some goal measures, such as "I like to learn something interesting" (Skaalvik, 1997) and "I feel really successful when I am the smartest" (Duda & Nicholls, 1992).

Scholars in APE seeking to ground their research questions in achievement goal theory can help improve the field in two distinct ways. First, researchers need to foster conceptual–operational alignment within their studies (Hulleman & Senko, 2010), regardless of which goal perspective (mastery versus multiple) is adopted. In other words, the way in which researchers conceptualize goals must align with the inventories they use to measure it. It is, therefore, the responsibility of the researcher to understand the conceptual framework implied by how the items are written. Second, and similar to the first point, researchers should consider supplementing achievement goal self-report data with qualitative, observational, or experimental methods. Brophy (2005) argued that relying solely on self-report data to understand people's achievement goals may provide an inaccurate portrayal of why people actually pursue goals. Researchers interested in how coaches create motivational climates that are thought to influence the development of achievement goals can use a new observational system created by Smith and colleagues (2015).

Affective–reflective theory (ART)

As noted earlier, the role of affect and its influence on PA behavior in most theories falling under the SCT label is missing or minimized. In the current chapter, we recognize there is a long history of research into emotion, affect, and mood, and such terms are not synonymous. For the purposes of this chapter, however, we use the term "affect" as an overarching umbrella term that captures mood and emotion and is conceptually distinct from cognition. To recognize the important role that cognition plays and simultaneously recognize the role of affect, Brand and Ekkekakis (2017) developed the ART of physical inactivity and exercise. In the following section, we have three goals related to the ART. We first describe, in broad strokes, how the ART is different from most SCTs. We then explain the dynamics, from an ART perspective, of PA behavior. Finally, we provide some guidance as to how the ART might be used for APE research.

In contrast to most SCTs, the ART acknowledges the role of thinking and feeling and of conscious and unconscious processes. The ART also highlights both sedentary behavior and PA and the notion that a decision to engage in PA also involves a decision to discontinue inactivity. Hence, the ART accounts for the complexity inherent in stopping a behavior (e.g., reading a good book) that is often pleasurable and valued to engage in a behavior (e.g., go running) that is often viewed with mixed or negative feelings. Stated differently, when people are inactive it is often because the feelings (i.e., positivity) associated with their current sedentary behavior (e.g., watching a good movie) are greater than the potential positive feelings linked to PA. Importantly, the ART goes beyond the typical meta-theoretical perspective of focusing solely on the behavior of interest, such as PA. The ART also recognizes that understanding why we engage in a behavior such as PA is also occurring simultaneously with the motivational dynamics entailed in leaving a currently engaged in sedentary behavior.

The ART is a dual-process theory and we next explain the processes of the ART that are responsible for PA engagement. Initially, an affective evaluation occurs, and that reflects a type1 process. The first step in this chain occurs when an internal stimulus (e.g., "I think I should play wheelchair basketball") or an external one (e.g., "the PE teacher starts describing a basketball shooting drill") triggers an automatic affective evaluation or response. The automatic affective evaluation is grounded in the student's history of emotional experiences that can be cognitively mediated, or simply core affective reactions. The automatic affective evaluations can be positive or negative. For instance, a child with a disability may react negatively to learning that the day's PE lesson involves a non-adapted (e.g., basketball hoop is too high) activity of free throw basketball shooting. Her negative reaction occurs because of a cognitively mediated automatic feeling of shame grounded in many experiences of past failure. Additionally, an automatic affective evaluation that is not cognitively mediated but simply arises from the body might be generated. For instance, prior feelings of muscular discomfort and pain associated with trying to reach the basketball hoop height may also cause an automatic negative affective evaluation. Stated differently, the stimulus, such as a teacher directive to engage in a particular PA game or skill or drill, activates automatic affective associations grounded in history. Positive affective evaluations lead to a PA approach impulse, whereas negative affective evaluations lead to a PA avoidance impulse. It is important to recognize that this type 1 process usually occurs below conscious awareness and that it occurs swiftly, effortlessly, and automatically (Brand & Ekkekakis, 2017) and produces an "action impulse".

The second step in the ART relies on type 2 processes, hence the "dual" process moniker. The type 2 process is a slower but higher level cognitive operation where reflective evaluation (versus automatic evaluations) occurs and results in an "action plan". The ART doesn't stipulate specific higher-level cognitive operations, but Brand and Ekkekakis (2017) offer a multitude of possibilities, all derived from various SCTs. For instance, a student with a disability might consider her level of self-efficacy for basketball shooting, decide it is low, and find ways to avoid the drill (e.g., the competent bystander) without the teacher noticing. Consideration of a need for relatedness from SDT might provide impetus for an action plan to complete the drill in order to develop peer relationships. Finally, from the TPB, perceptions of social pressure (i.e., subjective norm) may also contribute to an action plan to participate. Resolution of conflicting action impulses and action plans is a function of self-regulation resources such as self-control. Action impulses are thought to rule when self-regulation resources are limited. In contrast, action plans dominate when self-control resources are high. The ART also describes how both driving and restraining forces operate simultaneously. For example, during the type 2 process, a student may decide she should engage in the basketball shooting drill in order to get a good grade in PE (a "pro" in the transtheoretical model, another SCT). However, despite this driving force behind an action plan, the type 1 process affective evaluation (e.g., feelings of embarrassment from failing) acts as a restraining force. The ART acknowledges how we feel in a given moment about our current behavior and the affective-laden memories about an anticipated behavior's (type 1 processes) equal status and how we reconcile them with thoughts during the type 2 process. In brief, it considers both thoughts and feelings about current and future behavior.

The development of the ART of physical inactivity and exercise is in its initial stages and appears to be developed for, and geared towards, situations where individuals have control over their choices. Hence, its applicability to research involving people with disabilities is relatively straightforward when considering adults and PA broadly, despite environmental constraints (e.g., lack of transportation to fitness facilities) that might limit PA and factors unique to individuals with disabilities that should not be overlooked (e.g., shoulder pain in wheelchair users, phantom limbs in amputees). Within APE, researchers need to be cognizant that students have limited control of their own behavior and teachers are in charge. Hence, researchers using the ART will need to be sure to consider SCT constructs, during the type 2 processing, that get at the social dynamics children in APE face that might drive their PA action plans. Examples of such influences include peer relationships, teacher, peer tutor, and teacher's aids (e.g., subjective norm and positive social support), children's perceptions of control (i.e., perceived behavioral control), as well as context-specific considerations (Haegele & Sutherland, 2015; Lieberman, Dunn, Van der Mars, & McCubbin, 2000; Martin, 2018). When assessing type 1 processes, researchers typically use the implicit association test (IAT) to get at the automatic evaluation of PA (Greenwald, McGhee, & Schwartz, 1998). Preliminary evidence for the ART in exercise psychology research shows promise (Antoniewicz & Brand, 2014; Brand & Antoniewicz, 2016). Finally, a key construct in the ART is self-control. Self-control determines if type 1 affective evaluations leading to action impulse are dominant, or if type 2 cognitive reflective evaluations leading to an action plan dominate. Researchers interested in the ART should be aware that the research on self-control and ego-depletion (i.e., when self-control resources are diminished) has garnered some mild controversy (see: Carter, Kofler, Forster, & McCullough, 2015; Englert, 2016).

Conclusion

In conclusion, we hope that our commentary on common SCTs used in APA and APE research provides an impetus for researchers to consider how they employ various theories and measures in their own work. We also hope our brief overview of ART may intrigue readers enough that they delve further into how they might employ it in their APA and APE research to further our understanding of the psychological mechanisms undergirding PA behavior in individuals with disabilities.

Summary of key points

- Social cognitive theory (SCT) is a meta-theory and, therefore, comprises a variety of theories that are subsumed under the SCT umbrella. As outlined in this chapter, some of these sub-theories include self-efficacy theory, theory of planned behavior, self-determination theory, and achievement goal theory.
- While SCT underscores the role of critical cognitive constructs and important social influences, it pays little to no attention to the role of other influences on human behavior (e.g., environment, biology, affect).

- People with disabilities are consistently less physically active than people without disabilities (Martin, 2018). Thus, strong theoretical frameworks are needed in order to understand, predict, and change behavior among people with disabilities. However, physical activity psychology researchers using SCT have been far from successful in understanding and changing physical activity behavior.

- Some scholars (Ekkekakis & Zenko, 2016) believe that we have relied too heavily on SCT to understand physical activity and not enough time spent understanding why people are physically inactive. Other reasons for the lack of success may be due to SCT's failure to consider environmental, physiological, and affective influences.

- People with disabilities often experience negative affective responses (e.g., anxiety, shame, anger) as a function of being stared at, teased, or bullied in APA settings (Haegele & Sutherland, 2015; Martin, 2018). Although these affective responses are important to consider when attempting to understand physical (in)activity, the role of emotions has been largely ignored in most SCTs (e.g., Ekkekais & Zenko, 2016).

- A main topic of debate regarding self-efficacy theory is how it differs from self-concept (e.g., Marsh et al., 2018), leading to the occurrence of the jingle–jangle fallacies. What makes self-efficacy and self-concept vulnerable to the jangle fallacy is the relatively recent shift in how these constructs have been used within the literature; researchers have begun to examine general levels of self-efficacy and domain-specific self-concept.

- The theory of planned behavior has received the most criticism out of the four theories discussed in this chapter. Some scholars believe that this theory should be retired (Sniehotta et al., 2014), while others believe it should be augmented with additional measures (e.g., self-efficacy). Criticisms of theory of planned behavior include its lack of predictive validity and lack of consideration for the role of emotion in people's decision-making processes.

- Much of the criticism toward self-determination theory stems from how the basic psychological needs are conceptualized, the tenets of the basic needs (e.g., whether they are truly universal, what constitutes a basic need), and how the types of motivation are described and measured (e.g., Hardy, 2015; Schüler et al., 2013; Schüler, Sheldon, & Frohlich, 2010; Schüler et al., 2016).

- One theoretical weakness of achievement goal theory pertains to how goal constructs are defined (mastery goal perspective versus multiple goal perspective).

- Affective–reflective theory (Brand & Ekkekakis, 2017) is a new theory, and was recently introduced in part to address some of the shortcomings of SCT. It aims to explain and predict people's decision to either remain in a sedentary behavior or engage in exercise.

- The affective–reflective theory is a dual-process theory, whereby a type 1 process occurs when an affective evaluation occurs ("action impulse") and a type 2 process occurs when a reflective evaluation occurs ("action plan").

Reflective questions

1 Using one of the social cognitive theories discussed in this chapter, design a 60-minute APE class. How would you address the shortcomings of this selected theory? How would you measure effectiveness? How might your design depend on whether the class was inclusive or integrated?

2   Given that affective–reflective theory is new, what empirical research is deemed most important in order to prove its effectiveness?
3   Using affective–reflective theory as the theoretical framework, design a physical activity intervention for sixth grade children with disabilities. How might your design depend on whether the class was inclusive or integrated?
4   What are some shortcomings of the affective–reflective theory, and how should these shortcomings be addressed?

References

Ajzen, I. (1991). The theory of planned behavior. *Organizational Behavior and Human Decision Processes, 50*, 179–211.

Ajzen, I. (2015). The theory of planned behaviour is alive and well, and not ready to retire: A commentary on Sniehotta, Presseau, and Araújo-Soares. *Health Psychology Review, 9*, 131–137.

Antoniewicz, F., & Brand, R. (2014). Automatic evaluations and exercise setting preference in frequent exercisers. *Journal of Sport and Exercise Psychology, 36*, 631–636.

Bandura, A. (1977). Self-efficacy: Toward a unifying theory of behavioral change. *Psychological Review, 84*, 191–215. doi:10.1037/0033-295X.84.2.191

Bandura, A. (1986). *Social foundations of thought and action: A social cognitive theory.* Englewood Cliffs, NJ: Prentice Hall.

Biswas, A., Oh, P. I., Faulkner, G. E., Bajaj, R. R., Silver, M. A., Mitchell, M. S., & Alter, D. A. (2015). Sedentary time and its association with risk for disease incidence, mortality, and hospitalization in adults: A systematic review and meta-analysis. *Annals of Internal Medicine, 162*, 123–132.

Bong, M., & Skaalvik, E. M. (2003). Academic self-concept and self-efficacy: How different are they really?. *Educational Psychology Review, 15*, 1–40.

Brand, R., & Antoniewicz, F. (2016). Affective evaluations of exercising: The role of automatic–Reflective evaluation discrepancy. *Journal of Sport and Exercise Psychology, 38*, 631–638.

Brand, R., & Ekkekakis, P., (2017). Affective-reflective theory of physical inactivity and exercise. *German Journal of Exercise and Sport Research, 48*, 48–58.

Brophy, J. (2005). Goal theorists should move on from performance goals. *Educational Psychologist, 40*, 167–176.

Brunet, J., Gunnel, K. E., Teixeira, P., Sabiston, C. M., & Bélanger, M. (2016). Should we be looking at the forest or the trees? Overall psychological need satisfaction and individual needs as predictors of physical activity. *Journal of Sport & Exercise Psychology, 38*, 317–330.

Buunk, B. P., & Nauta, A. (2000). Why intraindividual needs are not enough: Human motivation is primarily social. *Psychological Inquiry, 11*, 279–283.

Cairney, J., Hay, J., Faught, B., Mandigo, J., & Flouris, A. (2005). Developmental coordination disorder, self-efficacy toward physical activity, and play: Does gender matter? *Adapted Physical Activity Quarterly, 22*, 67–82.

Carron, A. V., Hausenblas, H. A., & Mack, D. (1996). Social influence and exercise: A meta-analysis. *Journal of Sport and Exercise Psychology, 18*, 1–16.

Carter, E., Kofler, L., Forster, D., & McCullough, M. (2015). A series of meta-analytic tests of the depletion effect: Self-control does not seem to rely on a limited resource. *Journal of Experimental Psychology: General, 144*, 796–815. doi: 10.1037/xge0000083

Chemolli, E., & Gagné, M. (2014). Evidence against the continuum structure underlying motivation measures derived from self-determination theory. *Psychological Assessment, 26*, 575.

Chen, F. F., Hayes, A., Carver, C. S., Laurenceau, J. P., & Zhang, Z. (2012). Modeling general and specific variance in multifaceted constructs: A comparison of the bifactor model to other approaches. *Journal of Personality, 80*, 219–251.

Conner, M., & Armitage, C. J. (1998). Extending the theory of planned behavior: A review and avenues for further research. *Journal of Applied Social Psychology, 28*, 1429–1464.

Conner, M., Gaston, G., Sheeran, P., & Germain, M. (2013). Some feelings are more important: Cognitive attitudes, affective attitudes, anticipated affect, and blood donation. *Health Psychology, 32*, 264–272. doi:10.1037/a0028500.

Curran, T., Hill, A. P., Ntoumanis, N., Hall, H. K., & Jowett, G. E. (2016). A three-wave longitudinal test of self-determination theory's mediation model of engagement and disaffection in youth sport. *Journal of Sport and Exercise Psychology*, *38*, 15–29.

Danes-Staples, E., Lieberman, L. J., Ratcliff, J., & Rounds, K. (2013). Bullying experiences of individuals with visual impairment: The mitigating role of sport participation. *Journal of Sport Behavior*, *36*, 365–386.

Deci, E. L., & Ryan, R. M. (1985). *Intrinsic motivation and self-determination in human behavior.* New York: Plenum.

Deci, E. L., & Ryan, R. M. (2000). The "what" and "why" of goal pursuits: Human needs and the self-determination of behavior. *Psychological Inquiry*, *11*, 227–268.

Decker, E. S., & Ekkekakis, P. (2017). More efficient, perhaps, but at what price? Pleasure and enjoyment responses to high-intensity interval exercise in low-active women with obesity. *Psychology of Sport and Exercise*, 28, 1–10. https://doi.org/10.1016/j.psychsport.2016.09.005

Duda, J. L., & Nicholls, J. G. (1992). Dimensions of achievement motivation in schoolwork and sport. *Journal of Educational Psychology*, *84*, 290.

Dunlop, D. D., Song, J., Arntson, E. K., Semanik, P. A., Lee, J., Chang, R. W., & Hootman, J. M. (2015). Sedentary time in US older adults associated with disability in activities of daily living independent of physical activity. *Journal of Physical Activity and Health*, *12*, 93–101.

Dweck, C. S. (1986). Motivational processes affect learning. *American Psychologist*, *41*, 1040–1048.

Ekkekakis, P., & Lind, E. (2006). Exercise does not feel the same when you are overweight: The impact of self-selected and imposed intensity on affect and exertion. *International Journal of Obesity*, 30(4), 652–660. http://doi.org/10.1038/sj.ijo.0803052

Ekkekakis, P., & Zenko, Z. (2016). Escape from cognitivism: exercise as hedonic experience. In M. Raab, P. Wyllemann, R. Seiler, A.M. Elbe, & A. Hatzigeorgiadis (Eds.), *Sport and exercise psychology research. From theory to practice* (pp. 389–414). Amsterdam: Elsevier. https://doi.org/10.1016/B978-0-12-803634.

Elliot, A. J. (1999). Approach and avoidance motivation and achievement goals. *Educational Psychologist*, *34*, 169–189.

Elliot, A. J., & Murayama, K. (2008). On the measurement of achievement goals: Critique, illustration, and application. *Journal of Educational Psychology*, *100*, 613–628.

Englert, C. (2016). The strength model of self-control in sport and exercise psychology. *Frontiers in Psychology*, 7, 314–323. doi:10.3389/fpsyg.2016.00314

Feltz, D. L. (1988). Self-confidence and sports performance. *Exercise and Sport Science Reviews*, *16*, 423–457.

Greenwald, A. G., McGhee, D. E., & Schwartz, J. L. (1998). Measuring individual differences in implicit cognition: The implicit association test. *Journal of Personality and Social Psychology*, *74*, 1464–1480.

Haegele, J. A., & Sutherland, S. (2015). Perspectives of students with disabilities toward physical education: A qualitative inquiry review. *Quest*, *67*, 255–273.

Harackiewicz, J. M., Barron, K. E., & Elliot, A. J. (1998). Rethinking achievement goals: When are they adaptive for college students and why? *Educational Psychologist*, *33*, 1–21.

Harackiewicz, J. M., Barron, K. E., Pintrich, P. R., Elliot, A. J., & Thrash, T. M. (2002). Revision of achievement goal theory: Necessary and illuminating. *Journal of Educational Psychology*, *94*, 638–645.

Hardy, L. (2015). Epilogue. In S. D. Mellalieu & S. Hanton (Eds.), *Contemporary advances in sport psychology: A review* (pp. 258–269). New York, NY: Routledge.

Henderson, K. A., & Bedini, L. A. (1995). "I have a soul that dances like Tina Turner, but my body can't": Physical activity and women with mobility impairments. *Research Quarterly for Exercise and Sport*, *66*(2), 151–161.

Hulleman, C. S., & Senko, C. (2010). Up around the bend: Forecasts for achievement goal theory and research in 2020. Invited chapter in T. C. Urdan & S. A. Karabenick (Eds.), *Advances in motivation and achievement* (pp. 71–104), Emerald: Bingley, UK.

Kelley, T. L. (1927). *Interpretation of educational measurements.* Oxford, England: World Book Co.

Laird, Y., Fawkner, S., Kelly, P., McNamee, L., & Niven, A. (2016). The role of social support on physical activity behaviour in adolescent girls: A systematic review and meta-analysis. *International Journal of Behavioral Nutrition and Physical Activity*, *13*, 79–93.

Lieberman, L. J., Dunn, J. M., Van der Mars, H., & McCubbin, J. (2000). Peer tutors' effects on activity levels of deaf students in inclusive elementary physical education. *Adapted Physical Activity Quarterly*, *17*, 20–39.

Marsh, H. W., Pekrun, R., Parker, P. D., Murayama, K., Guo, J., Dicke, T., & Arens, A. K. (2018). The murky distinction between self-concept and self-efficacy: Beware of lurking jingle-jangle fallacies. *Journal of Educational Psychology*. Advance online publication. doi:10.1037/edu0000281.supp

Marsh, H. W., Roche, L. A., Pajares, F., & Miller, D. (1997). Item-specific efficacy judgments in mathematical problem solving: The downside of standing too close to trees in a forest. *Contemporary Educational Psychology, 22*, 363–377. doi:10.1006/ceps.1997.0942

Martin, J.J. (2018). *Handbook of disability sport & exercise psychology*. Oxford University Press: Oxford.

McEachan, R. R. C., Conner, M., Taylor, N., & Lawton, R. J. (2011). Prospective prediction of health-related behaviors with the theory of planned behavior: A meta-analysis. *Health Psychology Review, 5*, 97–144. 10.1080/17437199.2010.521684.

McGarty, A. M., Downs, S. J., Melville, C. A., & Harris, L. (2018). A systematic review and meta-analysis of interventions to increase physical activity in children and adolescents with intellectual disabilities. *Journal of Intellectual Disability Research, 62*, 312–329.

Midgley, C., Maehr, M. L., Hruda, L. Z., Anderman, E., Anderman, L., Freeman, K. E., & Urdan, T. (2000). *Manual for the patterns of adaptive learning scales*. Ann Arbor, MI: University of Michigan Press.

Myers, N. D., Martin, J. J., Ntoumanis, N., Celimli, S., & Bartholomew, K. J. (2014). Exploratory bifactor analysis in sport, exercise, and performance psychology: A substantive-methodological synergy. *Sport, Exercise, and Performance Psychology, 3*, 258–272.

Pajares, F. (2009). Toward a positive psychology of academic motivation: The role of self-efficacy beliefs. In R. Gilman, E. S. Huebner, & M. J. Furlong (Eds.), *Handbook of positive psychology in schools* (pp. 149–160). New York, NY: Routledge.

Pintrich, P. R. (2003). Motivation and classroom learning. In W. M. Reynolds & G. E. Miller (Eds.), *Handbook of psychology: Educational psychology* (pp. 103–122). Hoboken, NJ: Wiley.

Rhodes, R. E., Jones, L. W., & Courneya, K. S. (2002). Extending the theory of planned behavior in the exercise domain: A comparison of social support and subjective norm. *Research Quarterly for Exercise and Sport, 73*, 193–199.

Ryan, R. M., & Deci, E. L. (2000). Self-determination theory and the facilitation of intrinsic motivation, social development, and well-being. *American Psychologist, 55*, 68–78.

Ryan, R. M., & Deci, E. L. (2017). *Self-determination theory: Basic psychological needs in motivation, development, and wellness*. New York, NY: Guilford.

Sandberg, T., & Conner, M. (2008). Anticipated regret as an additional predictor in the theory of planned behaviour: A meta-analysis. *British Journal of Social Psychology, 47*, 589–606.

Schiiler, J., & Brandstiitter, V. (2013). How basic need satisfaction and dispositional motives interact in predicting flow experience in sport. *Journal of Applied Social Psychology, 43*, 687–705.

Schüler, J., Brandstätter, V., & Sheldon, K. M. (2013). Do implicit motives and basic psychological needs interact to predict well-being and flow? Testing a universal hypothesis and a matching hypothesis. *Motivation and Emotion, 37*, 480–495.

Schüler, J., Sheldon, K. M., & Frohlich, S. M. (2010). Implicit need for achievement moderates the relationship between felt competence and subsequent motivation. *Journal of Research in Personality, 44*, 1–12.

Schüler, J., Sheldon, K. M., Prentice, M., & Halusic, M. (2016). Do some people need autonomy more than others? Implicit dispositions toward autonomy moderate the effects of felt autonomy on well-being. *Journal of Personality, 84*, 5–20.

Shavelson, R. J., Hubner, J. J., & Stanton, G. C. (1976). Self-concept: Validation of construct interpretations. *Review of Educational Research, 46*, 407–441.

Sheeran, P., Gollwitzer, P. M., & Bargh, J. A. (2013). Nonconscious processes and health. *Health Psychology, 32*(5), 460.

Sit, C. H., McKenzie, T. L., Lian, J. M., & McManus, A. (2008). Activity levels during physical education and recess in two special schools for children with mild intellectual disabilities. *Adapted Physical Activity Quarterly, 25*, 247–259.

Sit, C. H., McManus, A., McKenzie, T. L., & Lian, J. (2007). Physical activity levels of children in special schools. *Preventive Medicine, 45*, 424–431.

Skaalvik, E. M. (1997). Self-enhancing and self-defeating ego orientation: Relations with task and avoidance orientation, achievement, self-perceptions, and anxiety. *Journal of Educational Psychology, 89*, 71–81

Smith, N., Tessier, D., Tzioumakis, Y., Quested, E., Appleton, P., Sarrazin, P., … Duda, J. L. (2015). Development and validation of the multidimensional motivational climate observation system. *Journal of Sport and Exercise Psychology, 37*, 4–22.

Sniehotta, F. F., Presseau, J., & Araujo-Soares, V. (2014). Time to retire the theory of planned behaviour. *Health Psychology Review, 8*, 1–7.

Temple, V. A., & Walkley, J. W. (1999). Academic learning time – Physical education (Alt-PE) of students with mild intellectual disabilities in regular Victorian schools. *Adapted Physical Activity Quarterly, 16,* 64–74.

Tudor-Locke, C., Brashear, M. M., Johnson, W. D., & Katzmarzyk, P. T. (2010). Accelerometer profiles of physical activity and inactivity in normal weight, overweight, and obese US men and women. *International Journal of Behavioral Nutrition and Physical Activity,* 7:60 www.ijbnpa.org/content/7/1/60

Van den Broeck, A., Ferris, D. L., Chang, C. H., & Rosen, C. C. (2016). A review of self-determination theory's basic psychological needs at work. *Journal of Management, 42*(5), 1195–1229.

Vansteenkiste, M., Niemiec, C. P., & Soenens, B. (2010). The development of the five mini- theories of self-determination theory: An historical overview, emerging trends, and future directions. In T. C. Urdan, & S. A. Karabenick (Eds.), *The decade ahead: Theoretical perspectives on motivation and achievement* (pp. 105–165). Bradford, UK: Emerald Group Publishing Limited.

19

Self-determination theory

Janice Causgrove Dunn and Chantelle Zimmer

Introduction

Physical education is intended to contribute to the development of the whole child by fostering the knowledge, skills, and attitudes necessary to lead an active and healthy lifestyle (Physical and Health Education Canada, 2018; Ryan & Deci, 2017). As a physical activity setting experienced by all (or almost all) school-aged children, it is positioned to play a prominent role in this regard. Children can achieve this overarching goal if provided with quality experiences that motivate them to actively engage with the curriculum. One theoretical framework that contributes to the understanding and prediction of individual and social factors that influence motivated learning behavior, and can guide interventions to increase student engagement and enjoyment in physical education, is self-determination theory (SDT; Deci & Ryan, 1985; Ryan & Deci, 2017). The current chapter includes an overview of the theory as well as a review of current relevant research in adapted physical education (APE) and implications for practice.

Overview of self-determination theory

SDT is an organismic–dialectic approach to human motivation, psychological development, and wellness. It assumes that humans have a natural tendency to actively seek out challenges and experiences to master and integrate into a coherent sense of self, a process that is nurtured or impeded by the social environment (Deci & Ryan, 1985; Ryan & Deci, 2002, 2017). The theory has gradually developed over the past 45 years through theoretical and applied research within fields such as education, healthcare, psychology, work and organizations, and sport and physical activity (Ryan & Deci, 2019). SDT has evolved to its current form as a meta-theory organized into six mini-theories, each of which focuses on a distinct but interrelated aspect of the overall SDT framework: cognitive evaluation theory (CET), organismic integration theory (OIT), causality orientations theory (COT), basic psychological needs theory (BPNT), goal contents theory (GCT), and relationship motivation theory (RMT) (see Table 19.1).

According to SDT, humans are motivated to engage in experiences and contexts that fulfill innate psychological needs for autonomy, competence, and relatedness. These three basic needs are seen as essential nutrients for psychological growth, resilience, vitality, self-congruence, and optimal well-being, whereas frustration or thwarting of psychological need satisfaction can lead to serious psychological harm (Ryan & Deci, 2017, 2019). *Autonomy* refers to the need to self-regulate, or be the origin of, your own experiences and actions. However autonomy is not the

Table 19.1 The six SDT mini-theories in brief (Ryan & Deci, 2017)

Cognitive evaluation theory	Describes processes through which basic psychological needs and intrinsic motivation are supported or thwarted by the social environment, in turn impacting the quality of learning, performance, and well-being.
Organismic integration theory	Focuses on extrinsic motivation, how it becomes more autonomous through the internalization and integration of values and regulations, and the impact of the social context on this process.
Causality orientations theory	Describes individual differences in how people tend to motivate themselves through tendencies to orient themselves toward specific features in the social environment and adopt corresponding motives.
Basic psychological needs theory	Identifies the three universal psychological needs of autonomy, competence, and relatedness, and examines the impact of need support on well-being and vitality, and of need thwarting on ill-health.
Goal contents theory	Explains the relationships between aspirations and attainment of intrinsic goals (e.g., personal growth, meaningful relationships, community involvement) and extrinsic goals (e.g., wealth, fame, and image) to psychological need satisfaction, and, in turn, to learning, performance, and well-being.
Relationship motivation theory	Examines the qualities of relationships in satisfying the innate need for relatedness, as well as the consequences. Highlights the interconnections between relatedness and autonomy needs satisfaction; relatedness satisfaction requires perception that self and other are willingly (i.e., autonomously) engaged.

same as independence or contingent upon the ability to act independently in the environment (Deci & Ryan, 2000; Ryan & Deci, 2017). Rather, "the hallmark of autonomy is instead that one's behaviors are self-endorsed, or congruent with one's authentic interests and values" (Ryan & Deci, 2017, p. 10). Therefore, individuals can act autonomously through independent, interdependent, or dependent action. As stated by Reeve (2012), "students experience autonomy in accordance with how much they personally endorse the value and significance of the way of thinking or behaving" (p. 154). *Competence* is the need to feel effectance and mastery while interacting with the environment (White, 1959), and *relatedness* is the need to feel a meaningful sense of belonging or connectedness to others (Baumeister & Leary, 1995). The SDT mini-theory, basic psychological needs theory, focuses on the relationship of the innate universal needs for autonomy, competence, and relatedness to intrinsic motivation, effective functioning, and psychological health and well-being (Ryan & Deci, 2002, 2017).

Unlike other theories that view motivation as a unitary concept varying in strength or intensity (e.g., Bandura, 1986; Eccles & Wigfield, 1983), SDT posits that there are different types and sources of motivation that vary in the degree to which they are autonomous versus controlled. Autonomous motivation is more self-determined than controlled motivation, and is associated with more adaptive outcomes. For example, research in physical education has revealed that more autonomous motivation patterns are associated with higher levels of effort, concentration, and enjoyment, and higher quality of learning and performance (Boiché, Sarrazin, Grouzet, Pelletier, & Chanal, 2008; Ntoumanis, 2002; Standage, Duda, & Ntoumanis, 2005). As shown in Figure 19.1, SDT proposes intrinsic motivation, extrinsic motivation, or amotivation regulate individuals' behavior (Ryan & Deci, 2017).

Behavior:	Non-self-determined					Self-determined
Motivation:	Amotivation	Extrinsic motivation				Intrinsic motivation
Regulatory styles:	Non-regulation	External regulation	Introjected regulation	Identified regulation	Integrated regulation	Intrinsic regulation
Perceived locus of causality:	Impersonal	External	Somewhat external	Somewhat internal	Internal	Internal
Relevant regulatory processes:	Nonintentional, non-valuing incompetence, lack of control	Compliance, external rewards and punishments	Self-control, ego-involvement internal rewards and punishments	Personal importance, conscious valuing	Congruence, awareness, synthesis with self	Interest, enjoyment, inherent satisfaction

Figure 19.1 The self-determination continuum of motivation with corresponding regulatory styles, loci of causality and regulatory processes. Adapted from Ryan and Deci (2000, p. 72)

Intrinsic motivation

Intrinsic motivation is the motivation to engage in activities for their own sake—for feelings of enjoyment, interest, and satisfaction experienced while performing the activity (Deci & Ryan, 1985; Ryan & Deci, 2017). An intrinsically motivated student in physical education actively participates to experience the feelings of interest and enjoyment inherent in the activities themselves. This is the most self-determined form of motivation, in which individuals engage in behaviors that reflect their interests and values of their own volition, without the need for external persuasion, pressure, or rewards. Intrinsic motivation is enhanced when the social environment supports satisfaction of autonomy and competence needs in particular, though satisfaction of the need for relatedness may also affect intrinsic motivation (Ryan & Deci, 2017). Social–contextual factors or events that enhance or undermine intrinsic motivation, behavior, and well-being are the focus of the first formally identified SDT mini-theory, CET (Ryan & Deci, 2002). Early research in this mini-theory revealed that the imposition of contingent rewards for intrinsically motivated behaviors actually undermines intrinsic motivation (Deci, 1971, 1972). Extensive research has examined the influence of extrinsic rewards, punishment, surveillance, competition, imposed goals, choice, and feedback on intrinsic motivation (Ryan & Deci, 2017). Based on this work, CET posits that events such as rewards and feedback are experienced as controlling or informational, depending on the context in which they are presented. Events experienced as controlling undermine satisfaction of the need for autonomy, while events experienced as informational facilitate satisfaction of the need for competence, both of which affect intrinsic motivation (Ryan & Deci, 2002, 2017). The degree to which the interpersonal climate in physical education is perceived as supportive of basic needs is important for students' intrinsic motivation and well-being.

Researchers such as Vallerand and Losier (1999) propose that intrinsic motivation can be differentiated into three related but distinct types. Intrinsic motivation toward knowledge involves engaging in an activity for the enjoyment and pleasure of learning something new or learning more about it. For example, a child who enjoys physical education for the pleasure of learning new skills and how to play new games and sports is displaying this type of intrinsic motivation.

Intrinsic motivation toward accomplishment involves engaging in an activity for the pleasure of trying to out-do oneself to reach new personal goals. In this case, a child may enjoy physical education for the pleasure of mastering challenging skills and improving physical fitness. Last, intrinsic motivation toward experiencing stimulation involves engaging in an activity for the pleasant sensations associated with it, such as a child who enjoys participating in physical education for the pleasure of doing exciting things.

Extrinsic motivation

Extrinsic motivation is instrumental motivation, or the motivation to engage in activities that are not intrinsically interesting or enjoyable in order to bring about contingent benefits that are not inherent in the activity itself (Ryan & Deci, 2019). It is the focus of the SDT mini-theory of OIT (Ryan & Deci, 2017). Deci and Ryan (1985, 2000, Ryan & Deci, 2017) proposed that there are four types of extrinsic motivation, differing from each other to the extent that they are internalized and self-determined (see Figure 19.1). Internalization is an important concept in SDT, defined as "the process of taking in values, beliefs, or behavioral regulations from external sources and transforming them into one's own" (Ryan & Deci, 2017, p. 182). OIT is concerned with how autonomous forms of extrinsic motivation develop through internalization and integration, and on the causes and consequences of the different types of extrinsic motivation (Ryan & Deci, 2002, 2017). Within OIT, internalization and integration of social values and regulations (i.e., norms, rules, shared attitudes, and values) are seen as natural active processes, and the basic psychological needs are important energizers for this process. The need for relatedness prompts individuals to engage in uninteresting activities endorsed by significant others, and satisfaction of all three basic needs leads to greater internalization and self-determination (Ryan & Deci, 2002, 2017).

External regulation

External regulation is the least self-determined form of extrinsic motivation because it involves behaviors that are clearly motivated or controlled by external contingencies, such as the promise of a reward or the threat of a punishment. For example, a student who engages in activities in physical education in order to avoid being disciplined or punished by the teacher is externally regulated. Because of the dependency on the expectation of a contingent reward or punishment, external regulation undermines satisfaction of the need for autonomy and so maintenance and stability of these behaviors is poor (Ryan & Deci, 2019). As well, because the behaviors are seen as instrumental and not personally valued, externally regulated behaviors are often associated with low effort and little concern for performance quality.

Introjected regulation

Introjected regulation refers to behaviors that are driven by internal pressure about what a person feels he or she should or must do, with self-administered contingent affective and self-esteem contingencies. For example, students who participate in physical education because they fear disapproval from the teacher or parents if they do not, are operating under introjected regulation. Behaviors are beginning to become internalized because the pressure to act is internal to the person; however, the motivational source of the behaviors, such as the "shoulds" of teachers or parents, is external to the person (Walker, Kleiber, & Mannell, 2019). Introjected behaviors are more likely to be maintained than externally regulated behaviors, but are not self-determined, so are still relatively unstable (Deci & Ryan, 2000). Both external regulation and introjected regulation are referred to as controlled motivations.

Identified regulation

Identified regulation is a more internalized and self-determined type of extrinsic motivation than either external or introjected regulations, and is categorized as an autonomous form of motivation. Identified regulation refers to behaviors that are done because they produce outcomes that are valued as important and worthwhile. Essentially, the person identifies and accepts the value of the behavior. An example is a student who participates in physical education because he understands and accepts that this will enhance or improve his fitness and health. The behavior entails a sense of choice and personal commitment; however, it is extrinsically motivated because it is instrumental in producing a separate outcome from the behavior itself (i.e., in the example above, it is done to improve or maintain fitness and health) (Deci & Ryan, 2000).

Integrated regulation

Integrated regulation is the most autonomous type of extrinsic motivation. It refers to behaviors that are not only identified as important and worthwhile, but are also integrated to the extent that they are congruent with the person's beliefs and values. Students who actively engage in physical education because being physically active is part of their identity illustrate integrated regulation. Integrated regulation is similar to intrinsic motivation in terms of the degree to which it is self-determined but as was the case with identified regulation, the behavior is done for its instrumental value in producing an outcome separate from the behavior, even though it is volitional and valued by the self (Ryan & Deci, 2000).

Though the different types of extrinsic motivation are ordered along the autonomous–controlled continuum in Figure 19.1, this should not be interpreted to imply that the continuum is developmental or that individuals must progress through each form of extrinsic motivation during the internalization process. As discussed by Ryan and Deci (2017), an individual's engagement in a behavior (e.g., exercise) may be externally regulated at the outset, but move fairly quickly to identified regulation as the increased fitness and vitality leads to recognition and acceptance of the benefits of exercise for health and well-being.

Amotivation

Amotivation is what regulates behavior in situations where both intrinsic motivation and extrinsic motivation are absent. It is described as "a state in which one either is not motivated to behave, or one behaves in a way that is not mediated by intentionality" (Ryan & Deci, 2017, p. 190). According to SDT, amotivation may result from two different sources. First, amotivation may be due to a perceived lack of competence. This occurs when individuals are unmotivated to act because they either believe that the behavior will not produce the desired outcome, or feel they are unable to perform the activities or behaviors required to effectively attain the desired outcome. Second, amotivation may be due to a lack of interest, relevance, or value in the activities or behaviors, possibly because the individual does not believe engagement in them will satisfy his or her needs for competence, autonomy, and relatedness. In some cases, individuals may feel autonomous if they choose to not engage in a behavior, possibly because they feel that engaging would thwart their basic need for autonomy or relatedness (Ryan & Deci, 2017).

According to SDT, individuals likely hold multiple motivations for any given behavior (Ryan & Deci, 2017; Sun, Li, & Shen, 2017). By considering all of the motivational regulations simultaneously, researchers have identified groups of participants with similar motivational profiles that reflect patterns observed in the "real world". For example, Ntoumanis (2002) used cluster analysis to identify three motivational profiles in 14 −16-year-old physical education students: a "self-determined" profile (i.e., students with high intrinsic motivation and identified regulation, moderate introjected regulation, and low external regulation and amotivation); a "moderate motivation" profile (i.e., students with moderate levels across all types of motivation), and a "controlling motivation/amotivation" profile (i.e., students with high amotivation and external regulation, and low introjected and identified regulation, and low intrinsic motivation). More recently, Bechter, Dimmock, Howard, Whipp, and Jackson (2018) identified five profiles in high school physical education students using latent profile analysis: amotivated, moderately autonomous, mixed motivation, moderately controlled, and high autonomous. Moreover, basic need satisfaction was found to predict profile membership, which was associated with effort in physical education in accord with SDT. Consistent with research in other domains, research in physical education indicates that autonomy-supportive environments promote need satisfaction and autonomous motivation (Parish & Treasure, 2003; Standage, Gillison, Ntoumanis, & Treasure, 2012; Ulstad, Halvari, Sørebø, & Deci, 2016). Instructional styles that facilitate perceptions of an autonomy-supportive climate are discussed in the next section of this chapter.

To date, the majority of research examining the context of physical activity from an SDT perspective has used BPNT, CET, and OIT, though GCT is an emerging research focus (Ryan & Deci, 2017). GCT focuses on the contents of the goals people strive to accomplish and highlights that the contents of goals are important for basic psychological need satisfaction and wellness (Reeve, 2012; Ryan & Deci, 2017). Greater emphasis on extrinsic goals, such as the accumulation of wealth, fame, and image, is associated with lower psychological need satisfaction that negatively impacts well-being. In contrast, individuals who place greater importance on intrinsic goals (e.g., personal growth, meaningful relationships, and contributions to the community) report greater psychological need satisfaction and enhanced well-being (Ryan & Deci, 2019). Though less prevalent in the physical education research so far, causality orientations theory (COT) focuses on personality-level individual differences in causality orientations that regulate behavior, where causality orientations are seen as "propensities to focus on specific features and affordances within social contexts, and to express corresponding motives" (Ryan & Deci, 2019, p. 126). Three causality orientations have been identified: (1) an *autonomy orientation* is a focus on interests, opportunities for growth, and self-endorsed values in the regulation of behavior; (2) a *controlled orientation* involves a focus on external controls and directives regarding what one should do, and; (3) an *impersonal orientation* is a focus on the fear of failure or need for safety (Ryan & Deci, 2002, 2019). The most recent mini-theory to emerge in the SDT framework is relationship motivation theory (RMT), which examines factors related to satisfaction of the need for relatedness and the consequences for wellness. RMT highlights the intertwined nature of relatedness and autonomy, indicating that "people need to feel volitional about being in a relationship, and to see the other as volitional, for the connection to be high in quality" (Ryan & Deci, 2019, p. 131).

Summary of current research

SDT is one of the most commonly used theories in research that aims to understand children's motivation in physical education because its major components—the basic psychological needs for autonomy, competence, and relatedness—are highly relevant in this context (Sun et al., 2017). BPNT, in particular, proposes that "satisfaction of each of the three psychological needs is facilitated by autonomy support, whereas controlling contexts and events can disrupt not only autonomy satisfactions, but relatedness and competence need fulfilments as well" (Ryan & Deci, 2017, p. 247). This is not to say that autonomy is more important than the other two needs, as all three are essential for wellness. However, autonomy support is critical in most contexts, particularly physical education, where the teacher controls the environment, because it enables children to actively satisfy all their needs. As is evident in the review of research that follows, social contextual factors that support or thwart children's need for autonomy also impact their needs for competence and relatedness. This research has been grouped based on the basic psychological need it aligns with most, although it should be noted that study findings have implications beyond a single need.

Autonomy

Teachers play an integral role in fostering children's motivation in physical education, since they control the environment through planning and delivering lessons, cultivating the social climate, and monitoring learning and achievement (Sun & Chen, 2010). Children are perceived to be engaged when they are listening to instructions, responding to physical requests, and participating with interest and enthusiasm. Unfortunately, children with impairments often struggle to perform physical tasks or activities and tend to demonstrate low autonomous motivation towards physical activity. Due to the nature of physical education, Sun et al. (2017) state that understanding children's perceptions of controlling teacher behaviors and the controlling environment is critical.

Depending on the type and severity of a child's impairment, he or she may be assigned an aide or educational assistant to increase engagement. Egilson and Traustadottir (2009) and Asbjørnslett, Engelsrud, and Helseth (2015) explored the school experiences of children with physical impairments who received such support. The children recognized the importance of aides in providing them with the necessary help to participate more fully. However, the type and extent of help received was a point of contention. The children valued physical education and perceived it as fun, but felt they were unable to participate to the degree desired (Asbjørnslett et al., 2015). Children expressed wanting to determine when and how assistance was provided, since aides sometimes interfered with their ability to perform activities on their own and in their own way. This finding was echoed in the study by Egilson and Traustadottir (2009), where one participant said, "I would like to get less support and I would like to decide who supports me … and in which parts of my schedule" (p. 27). Parents and teachers even thought that some assistants helped more than needed, although this may occur more in the classroom than the gymnasium. Haycock and Smith (2011) interviewed teachers about their perspectives of the roles of learning support assistants in physical education. While some assistants were viewed favorably for helping integrate children with impairments into activities, other assistants held negative attitudes towards the subject and left the responsibility of meeting children's needs and offering support to the teachers.

Children with physical impairments appear to be satisfied with the support they receive from paraprofessionals as long as it does not undermine their need for autonomy. Too much assistance

Table 19.2 Instructional styles that predict children's perceptions of autonomy supports and thwarts

Supportive teacher behaviors	Controlling teacher behaviors
• Taking time to attentively listen to the child. • Allowing time for the child to work independently in his or her own way. • Giving the child time to talk. • Praising the child when he or she demonstrates improvement or mastery. • Offering words of encouragement to sustain the child's engagement. • Providing suggestions when the child is not making progress on a task. • Being responsive to child-generated questions. • Acknowledging the child's perspective or experience.	• Monopolizing learning materials. • Showing the solution to a problem before the child has time to discover it. • Telling the child the answer before he or she is able to independently solve the problem. • Making demands about how a task is to be completed. • Using controlling language such as *should, must,* or *have to.* • Using directed questions as a way to control the child's actions

Note: Based on empirical research conducted by Reeve and Jang (2006) that investigated supportive and controlling teacher behaviors that promoted autonomous versus controlled motivation among children without impairments.

or control exercised in physical education will hamper the autonomous motivation of children, particularly those who already value the subject. Research conducted with children without impairments supports this notion. Specific teacher behaviors have been shown to predict autonomous versus controlled motivation among children for learning activities (see Table 19.2). Children with physical and intellectual impairments may experience negative consequences of controlling behaviors most, compared to other children. These impairments are typically considered more "severe" and adults often believe these children are incapable of performing tasks on their own. Similar to children without impairments, children with impairments are more likely to thrive when social contextual factors support their innate psychological needs (Wehmeyer & Little, 2013). Ryan and Deci (2017) indicate that educators generally respond to activity limitations children experience as a result of their impairment as if they were motivational deficits. More external control is then exerted to change their outcomes, but what children really need is more structure provided in an autonomy-supportive way.

Competence

The purpose of physical education is to effectively prepare children to be active for life by learning *of* and *through* the physical body (Ennis, 2010). This makes developing competence a primary goal not only for participation in daily physical activity, but for fostering a healthy lifestyle. Pan, Tsai, Chu, and Hsieh (2011) investigated physical activity and motivation in physical education and found that adolescents diagnosed with autism spectrum disorders were significantly less active than peers without the diagnosis. Adolescents diagnosed with autism spectrum disorders had significantly lower perceived competence, intrinsic motivation, identified regulation, introjected regulation, and higher amotivation than their peers. Consequently, their effort, enjoyment of physical education, and intention to be physically active were significantly lower. Children with impairments exposed to autonomy supportive climates may be more likely to experience positive outcomes, including changes in their physical activity levels, motor performance, perceived competence, and attitudes toward participation (Hastie, Rudisill, & Wadsworth, 2013). In the literature, high autonomy and low autonomy climates are commonly referred to as task-goal and ego-goal perspectives (Nicholls, 1984), or mastery motivational and performance-oriented climates (Ames, 1992). Briefly stated, a high autonomy climate encourages children to focus on self-referenced evaluation criteria, with children receiving rewards for individual effort, learning, and improvements. In contrast, a low autonomy climate is characterized by the use of normative evaluation criteria, interpersonal competition, and desire to demonstrate superiority over others.

Johnson et al. (2018) examined differences in the physical activity levels of children with and without impairments in a high versus low autonomy-supportive climate. Children both with and without neurodevelopmental impairments spent significantly more time in moderate-to-vigorous physical activity (MVPA) in a high autonomy climate compared to a low autonomy climate, although time spent in MVPA was significantly greater among children without neurodevelopmental impairments in both conditions. Research conducted with children without impairments shows climates that provide free choice are associated with greater MVPA among children with high and low self-determined motivation for physical education (Lonsdale, Sabiston, Raedeke, Ha, & Sum, 2009). As expected, though, children with high self-determined motivation engage in more MVPA than those with low self-determined motivation. Lonsdale and colleagues (2009) believe a free choice environment may satisfy autonomy and competence needs because children are able to choose activities they are good at. However, an unstructured high autonomy climate consisting of complete free choice may not increase children's motor performance or knowledge of health (Sun et al., 2017). It is recommended that teachers provide children with choices as part of their structured lessons to improve children's overall development.

Robinson and Goodway (2009) examined the effects of instructional climates on object control skill performance of children at risk for developmental disorders. Children were randomly assigned to a high autonomy, low autonomy, or comparison group. Children in the high and low autonomy sessions demonstrated increased object control skill scores from pretest to posttest, but decreased performance from posttest to retention, which was attributed to a lack of opportunity to practice (Robinson & Goodway, 2009). Interestingly, the comparison group of children who had complete free choice showed no significant changes in their performance over time. The authors concluded that well designed and developmentally appropriate motor skill instruction might lead to developmental gains for children regardless of the climate. Hastie, Rudisill, and Boyd (2016) decided to take a different approach by intensively looking at the engagement of children at risk for developmental disorders in a high autonomy physical education program over a six-month period. Children received motor skill instruction for 30 minutes, twice per week. Most children initially were not engaged and demonstrated off-task or inappropriate behavior. As the program progressed, though, children increasingly engaged in the program, displaying more appropriate behavior and mastering motor skills. The results of this study illustrate the significance of time in increasing children's engagement within lessons and in physical education more broadly.

Autonomy supportive climates have great promise for children with impairments, but require knowledgeable and competent teachers. In their review, Coates and Vickerman (2008) indicate that teachers do not feel equipped to teach children with impairments in physical education because of a lack of training and professional development. Haegele, Zhu, and Davis (2018) investigated barriers and facilitators of physical education participation for children with impairments from the views of in-service physical educators. The most common teacher-related barrier reported was a lack of knowledge in teaching children with impairments. Other barriers included their abilities to plan quality lessons and adapt activities. On the other hand, instructional quality, which encompassed providing appropriate cues, clear directions, and assisting with skills was the most common teacher-related facilitator. Children with visual impairments express feeling excluded in physical education when no adaptations are provided for them to participate in activities with other children (Alves, Haegele, & Duarte, 2018). Several adults with visual impairments also recalled being left out of activities in public schools, but having access to adaptations at residential schools (Haegele, Sato, Zhu, & Avery, 2017). How teachers provide structure can influence whether children feel included or excluded, and either support or thwart their needs for autonomy, competence, and relatedness.

Relatedness

The attitudes of teachers toward impairment and inclusion affect children's experiences in physical education. Inclusion is a subjective experience associated with a sense of belonging, acceptance, and value in a group (Stainback & Stainback, 1990). Adults too often assume that children with impairments are not competent enough to participate fully (Coates & Vickerman, 2008) or in the same kinds of activities as other children (Alves et al., 2018). These negative views held by teachers have been shown to influence children's acceptance of those who are different, reproducing the same negative attitudes in children without impairments (Qi & Ha, 2012).

Obrusnikova (2008) examined variables that contributed to physical educators' beliefs about teaching children with different impairments. On average, teachers held positive beliefs toward teaching children with learning, sensory, intellectual, and physical impairments. The least positive beliefs were toward children with emotional and behavioral impairments who demonstrated aggressive or impulsive behaviors, general pervasive unhappiness, depression, hyperactivity, and social maladjustment. The teachers' perceived competence, quality of experience, and APE coursework significantly predicted their overall attitudes toward instructing children with intellectual and sensory impairments. However, only their perceived competence in general physical education was significantly associated with their attitudes about teaching children with learning, physical, and emotional and behavioral impairments. Children with autism spectrum disorders discussed times when they were excluded in physical education because their teachers sent them from activities (Healy, Msetfi, & Gallagher, 2013). Similarly, those with visual impairments spoke of experiences of exclusion, integration, and segregation, which often stemmed from teachers' lack of understanding about their needs and interests (Alves et al., 2018).

If children with impairments are not included in physical education lessons, they will have limited opportunities to interact and develop relationships with their peers. Children with neurodevelopmental impairments in Spencer-Cavaliere and Watkinson's (2010) study voiced that having friends was significant to gaining entry to play and feeling like a legitimate participant in games and sports. Encouragement, support, and having fun were associated with feelings of inclusion, whereas being teased, bullied, and made fun of were critical in not feeling included. These findings complement those of Healy and colleagues (2013) in which children with autism spectrum disorders contrasted positive and negative experiences with their peers in physical education. On the one hand, physical education was viewed as a catalyst for friendships where children could socially benefit. One participant stated, "… everybody can be your friend and you can make loads of friends …" (p. 224). On the other hand, bullying and social comparisons resulted in difficult experiences. One child shared that the worst day in physical education for him was when the other children started teasing him.

Positive attitudes toward teaching children with impairments in physical education seem to be salient to children experiencing meaningful learning opportunities (Haegele & Sutherland, 2015). It appears that teachers require more awareness about the experiences of children with various impairments in physical education to challenge their views (Coates & Vickerman, 2008). Teachers should demonstrate sensitivity to the needs of children by being attuned to their own assumptions and biases, and to cues from the children themselves. More training and professional development might increase teachers' reflexivity, as well as their knowledge and competence. Collectively, these changes would enable teachers to provide more autonomy support for children with impairments, ultimately fulfilling their three basic psychological needs.

Current trends

SDT has been extensively applied in physical education research with children without impairments. However, this is not the case in research on the experiences of children with impairments at school, in physical education, or physical activity. The studies presented in our summary of current research focused on at least one of the major components of SDT, but only two were intentionally guided by the theory (Johnson et al., 2018; Pan et al., 2011). Most of the remaining studies did not mention SDT in the introduction or discussion, and a couple were informed by other motivational theories, such as achievement goal theory (Robinson & Goodway, 2009) and the theory of reasoned action (Obrusnikova, 2008). When reviewing these studies through an SDT lens, the majority of researchers examined different facets of physical education that supported or thwarted children's need for autonomy, followed by their need for competence and relatedness, respectively.

The participants in the reviewed studies were largely elementary and middle school aged children with impairments. This is not surprising, since, in recent decades, APE scholars have called for more research on the experiences of children with impairments from their own perspectives (Fitzgerald, 2006; Fitzgerald, Jobling, & Kirk, 2003). However, there were a handful of studies conducted with teachers. The primary purpose of these studies was to understand how the structure and support provided by teachers and paraprofessionals affected children's participation and outcomes in physical education. Research seems to be moving away from teachers' perspectives of how children with impairments experience physical education and towards their pedagogical practices. This shift is important, given that teachers' competence in supporting children with impairments is continually noted as a barrier to their engagement, potentially hindering the fulfillment of their three basic psychological needs.

Researchers are also beginning to explore the experiences of children with a variety of impairments. Children with neurodevelopmental impairments, including autism spectrum disorders, specific learning disorder, and cerebral palsy, as well as children with physical (e.g., neuromuscular, musculoskeletal disorders) and sensory impairments (e.g., visual) made up the participants of most studies. Unfortunately, the experiences of children with hearing and intellectual impairments are underresearched. In their review of qualitative studies on the perspectives of children with impairments towards physical education, Haegele and Sutherland (2015) suggest children with different impairments may experience physical education in a similar fashion. Greater research with diverse children is needed to determine common themes across children with different types of impairment, while understanding their unique perspectives.

Qualitative methods were typically used to obtain in-depth understandings of children's experiences in physical education, with semi-structured interviews being the most common data collection method. Observational methods were used to examine support children received from teachers and aides and to code teacher behaviors. Quantitative methods consisted of a motivational scale to measure major components of SDT, accelerometers to quantify physical activity, a motor assessment to examine object control skill performance, and questionnaires to determine teachers' attitudes towards teaching children with impairments. Interestingly, researchers who implemented different instructional climates (Hastie et al., 2016; Johnson et al., 2018; Robinson & Goodway, 2009) to investigate their effects had qualified instructors carry out the interventions. Given that structured high autonomy-supportive climates have been shown to positively impact physical activity levels, motor skill performance, and engagement among children with impairments, more research should be conducted in natural settings with regular teachers.

Implications for practice

Based on our review of research, it seems that children with impairments are at risk of experiencing thwarting of their basic psychological needs in physical education. This is most apparent in the research that focuses on children's perspectives of physical education in which instances of overt exclusion and segregation by teachers were discussed. One child mentioned that her teacher "just says 'sit down and stay there because you can't do PE'" (Alves et al., 2018, p. 157) and another recalled the teacher sent him from a game because he was not ready (Healy et al., 2013). One girl explained, "[the other children] do something else, they play ball and other things that the teacher invents to be able to move ... .I usually play checkers, dominos, and these things" (Alves et al., 2018, p. 158). However, some children request to be excluded. "They all play football but I just watch; it's ok with my teacher if I just watch. He thinks I'm the best student in the whole class; he's great friends with me" (Healy et al., 2013, p. 225). While it appears some teachers support children with impairments very little, if at all, paraprofessionals may provide more help than is necessary. The behaviors exhibited by both teachers and paraprofessionals would be considered need-thwarting and may lead to more controlled forms of extrinsic motivation or amotivation among children.

Teacher and paraprofessional behaviors may be implicitly driven by their beliefs toward instructing children with impairments (Azjen & Fishbein, 1980). From an SDT perspective, even when individuals have good intentions, as illustrated in the quote above from a participant in Healy et al.'s (2013) study which indicated the teacher allowed the child to be excluded, the need for autonomy can be undermined. Professionals should be adaptive, or continually engaging with their beliefs, attitudes, and pedagogical practices (Sherrill, 2004). In adapted physical activity, the attitude is to embrace individual differences in order to promote self-determined physical activity participation among children with impairments (Reid, 2003). Being aware of one's own assumptions and biases is important in acknowledging children's perspectives and actively engaging them in lessons. Teachers, in particular, should model positive attitudes through the structure and support they provide students in physical education, as their behaviors may influence those of aides and children without impairments. Keep in mind, however, that teachers can only create opportunities for children to experience autonomy and not directly give it (Reeve, Deci, & Ryan, 2004). Children may not experience autonomy when choice and options are provided. Reeve and colleagues (2004) recommend that teachers use the following strategies to support children's perceived autonomy and self-determined motivation: (a) nurture inner motivational resources by developing learning activities based on children's preferences, competencies, choices, or sense of challenge and fun, (b) communicate expectations using informational and flexible messages that consist of non-controlling language free of pressure and coercion, (c) help children internalize non-intrinsically motivated activities and behaviors by explaining and identifying the values, importance, personal benefit, and application of activities and behaviors, and (d) understand children's negative feelings by acknowledging their perspectives and accepting their feelings as a valid reaction to the demands, structures, and learning activities of the lesson (as cited in Sun et al., 2017, p. 280).

Aside from providing an autonomy-supportive environment, it may be just as important for teachers to develop close relationships with children with impairments to increase their engagement in physical education. Positive interactions between teachers and children are fundamental for holistic development (Pianta, Hamre, & Allen, 2012). This is because engagement can be viewed as a relational process that facilitates the internalization of extrinsically motivated activities and behaviors. Children often accept as their own the values and practices of individuals to whom they feel connected and from contexts in which they feel a sense of belonging (Katartzi & Vlachopoulos, 2011). Sparks, Dimmock, Whipp, Lonsdale, and Jackson (2015) conducted a qualitative study to identify teacher behaviors perceived to be relatedness-supportive by adolescents without impairments in physical education. The three themes that emerged from the focus groups were: (a) teacher communication, characterized by individualized, enthusiastic, energetic, and friendly conversation, (b) in-class social support, where the teacher encouraged and facilitated interaction and cooperation among adolescents, and (c) teacher attentiveness, demonstrated by a level of caring and concern for adolescents' well-being. Teachers who form positive relationships with children with impairments can obtain a better understanding of their perceived needs, and, with appropriate training, be more equipped to address their needs in physical education.

To summarize, teachers who foster autonomy-supportive environments, provide clear structure, and are involved will fulfill children's needs for autonomy, competence, and relatedness (refer to Table 19.3), leading to positive psychomotor, cognitive, and affective outcomes (Sun et al., 2017). Future research might begin to explore associations among teachers' and paraprofessionals' attitudes toward impairment and inclusion, their

Table 19.3 Social contextual factors that support or thwart children's basic psychological needs (Ryan and Deci, 2017)

	Need-supporting	Need-thwarting
Autonomy	• Voice and choice. • Minimum constraints. • Freedom of expression.	• Control and coercion. • Pressured by rewards. • Social comparison.
Competence	• Provision of clear expectations. • Contingent responses. • Consistent and predictable. • Developmentally appropriate activities.	• Lack of information to guide behavior. • Non-contingent responses. • Inconsistent and chaotic. • Activities are too complex and challenging.
Relatedness	• Dedicate energy and resources. • Warm and dependable. • Express interest and care	• Physically and emotionally unavailable. • Cold and distant. • Actively reject or hate

instructional styles, and children's perceived autonomy. This will help to distinguish pedagogical practices experienced as need-supporting versus need-thwarting. Whether these practices increase or decrease self-determined motivation and how they affect children's overall development could be further examined (Katartzi & Vlachopoulos, 2011). An investigation into how well regular teachers are able to create autonomy-supportive climates is also warranted, given that they often do not feel confident or competent in teaching children with impairments.

Summary of key points

- Research on SDT in adapted physical education is sparse, but findings from other studies interpreted through a SDT lens show promise for its application to the field.
- Studies that drew on SDT focused primarily on children's need for competence (Johnson et al., 2018; Pan et al., 2011).
- Researchers who used SDT to investigate physical activity and motivation in physical education found that children with autism spectrum disorders had significantly lower perceived competence, self-determined motivation, and physical activity levels than their peers without the disorders. Behavioral consequences such as effort, enjoyment of physical education, and intention to be physically active was significantly lower as well (Pan et al., 2011).
- When SDT was used to examine differences in physical activity levels in a high versus low autonomy-supportive climate, children with neurodevelopmental disorders spent significantly more time in MVPA in a high compared to low autonomy climate. Not surprisingly, children without neurodevelopmental disorders spent more time in that intensity of physical activity under both climates (Johnson et al., 2018).
- Structured high autonomy-supportive climates seem to increase both physical activity levels and motor skill performance among children with impairments, while unstructured high autonomy-supportive climates only result in greater physical activity.
- Implementing a structured high autonomy-supportive climate in physical education necessitates knowledgeable and competent teachers, which is problematic, as findings from studies indicate that teachers are not equipped to support children with impairments (Alves et al., 2018; Haegele et al., 2017, 2018).
- The support children with physical impairments receive from paraprofessionals at school is perceived as both a help and hindrance. These children require assistance with daily living activities, but want to be involved in decisions about additional support provided throughout the school day (Asbjørnslett et al., 2015; Egilson & Traustadottir, 2009). Aides or assistants undermine their need for autonomy at times.
- Teachers' attitudes toward impairment and inclusion play a critical role in children feeling a sense of belonging in physical education and being accepted by their peers without impairments (Healy et al., 2013; Spencer-Cavaliere & Watkinson, 2010). Poor inclusion practices appear to thwart children's need for relatedness.
- The relationships children have with teachers and paraprofessionals will affect the fulfillment of their three basic psychological needs, since teachers, and sometimes aides, control all aspects of the learning environment in physical education. Their beliefs toward teaching children with impairments seem to contribute to the instructional style they utilize, mainly hampering children's satisfaction of their need for autonomy, but competence and relatedness too.

Reflective questions for discussion

1 Given the research describing the experiences of students with impairment in this chapter, what motivational profile might be predicted for these students in physical education?
2 Research based on SDT has focused on teacher behaviors associated with autonomy-supportive and controlling environments. How might teachers' attitudes toward impairment and inclusion influence the satisfaction of students' basic psychological needs?
3 To what extent does teacher reflexivity facilitate students' need satisfaction?
4 How do the concepts of dependence and interdependence relate to autonomy? What guidelines should be given to paraprofessionals who provide support for students with impairment to facilitate students' need satisfaction?
5 How might teachers facilitate cooperative activities for children with and without impairments to satisfy their need for relatedness, without perpetuating the belief that children with impairments are dependent on others for help?

References

Alves, M. L. T., Haegele, J. A., & Duarte, E. (2018). "We can't do anything": The experiences of students with visual impairments in physical education classes in Brazil. *British Journal of Visual Impairment, 36*, 152–162. doi:10.1177/0264619617752761

Ames, C. (1992). Achievement goals, motivational climate, and motivational processes. In G. C. Roberts (Ed.), *Motivation in sport and exercise* (pp. 161–176). Champaign, IL: Human Kinetics.

Asbjørnslett, M., Engelsrud, G. H., & Helseth, S. (2015). Inclusion and participation in everyday school life: Experiences of children with physical (dis)abilities. *International Journal of Inclusive Education, 19*, 199–212. doi:10.1080/13603116.2014.916353

Azjen, I., & Fishbein, M. (1980). *Understanding attitudes and predicting social behavior*. Englewood Cliffs, NJ: Prentice Hall.

Bandura, A. (1986). *Social foundations of thought and action: A social cognitive theory*. Englewood Cliffs, N.J.: Prentice-Hall.

Baumeister, R. F., & Leary, M. R. (1995). The need to belong: desire for interpersonal attachments as a fundamental human motivation. *Psychological Bulletin, 117*(3), 497.

Bechter, B. E., Dimmock, J. A., Howard, J. L., Whipp, P. R., & Jackson, B. (2018). Student motivation in high school physical education: A latent profile analysis approach. *Journal of Sport & Exercise Psychology, 40*, 206–216. doi:10.1123/jsepp.2018-0028

Boiché, J., Sarrazin, P. G., Grouzet, F. M., Pelletier, L. G., & Chanal, J. P. (2008). Students' motivational profiles and achievement outcomes in physical education: A self determination perspective. *Journal of Educational Psychology, 100*, 688–701. doi:10.1037/0022-0663.100.3.688

Coates, J., & Vickerman, P. (2008). Let the children have their say: Children with special educational needs and their experiences of physical education - A review. *Support for Learning, 23*, 168–175. doi:10.1111/sufl.2008.23.issue-4

Deci, E. L. (1971). Effects of externally mediated rewards on intrinsic motivation. *Journal of Personality and Social Psychology, 18*, 105–115. doi:http://dx.doi.org/10.1037/h0030644

Deci, E. L. (1972). Effects of contingent and non-contingent rewards and controls on intrinsic motivation. *Organizational Behavior and Human Performance, 8*, 217–229. doi:https://doi.org/10.1016/0030-5073(72)90047-5

Deci, E. L., & Ryan, R. M. (1985). *Intrinsic motivation and self-determination in human behavior*. New York, NY: Plenum.

Deci, E. L., & Ryan, R. M. (2000). The "what" and "why" of goal pursuits: Human needs and the self-determination of behavior. *Psychological Inquiry, 11*, 227–268. https://psycnet.apa.org/doi/10.1207/S15327965PLI1104_01

Eccles, J. S., Wigfield, A. (1983). Expectancies, values, and academic behaviours. *Theoretical perspective. Educational Psychology Review, 1*: 23–29.

Egilson, S. T., & Traustadottir, R. (2009). Assistance to pupils with physical disabilities in regular schools: Promoting inclusion or creating dependency?. *European Journal of Special Needs Education*, *24*, 21–36. doi:10.1080/08856250802596766

Ennis, C. D. (2010). On their own: Preparing students for a lifetime. *Journal of Physical Education, Recreation & Dance*, *81*, 17–22.

Fitzgerald, H. (2006). Disability in physical education. In D. Kirk, D. Macdonald, & M. O'Sullivan (Eds.), *Handbook of physical education* (pp. 752–766). London: SAGE Publications Ltd.

Fitzgerald, H., Jobling, A., & Kirk, D. (2003). Valuing the voices of young disabled people: Exploring experience of physical education and sport. *European Journal of Physical Education*, *8*, 175–200. doi:10.1080/1740898030080206

Haegele, J. A., Sato, T., Zhu, X., & Avery, T. (2017). Physical education experiences at residential schools for students who are blind: A phenomenological inquiry. *Journal of Visual Impairment & Blindness*, *111*, 135–147.

Haegele, J. A., & Sutherland, S. (2015). Perspectives of students with disabilities toward physical education: A qualitative inquiry review. *Quest*, *67*, 255–273. doi:10.1080/00336297.2015.1050118

Haegele, J., Zhu, X., & Davis, S. (2018). Barriers and facilitators of physical education participation for students with disabilities: An exploratory study. *International Journal of Inclusive Education*, *22*, 130–141. doi:10.1080/13603116.2017.1362046

Hastie, P. A., Rudisill, M. E., & Wadsworth, D. D. (2013). Providing students with voice and choice: Lessons from intervention research on autonomy-supportive climates in physical education. *Sport, Education and Society*, *18*, 38–56. doi:10.1080/13573322.2012.701203

Hastie, P. A., Rudisill, M. E., & Boyd, K. (2016). An ecological analysis of a preschool mastery climate physical education programme. *Physical Education and Sport Pedagogy*, *21*, 217–232. doi:https://doi.org/10.1080/17408989.2015.1017454

Haycock, D., & Smith, A. (2011). To assist or not to assist? A study of teachers' views of the roles of learning support assistants in the provision of inclusive physical education in England. *International Journal of Inclusive Education*, *15*, 835–849. doi:10.1080/13603110903452325

Healy, S., Msetfi, R., & Gallagher, S. (2013). "Happy and a bit nervous": The experiences of children with autism in physical education. *British Journal of Learning Disabilities*, *41*, 222–228. doi:10.1111/bld.12053

Johnson, J. L., Miedema, B., Converse, B., Hill, D., Buchanan, A. M., Bridges, C., & Pangelinan, M. (2018). Influence of high and low autonomy-supportive climates on physical activity in children with and without developmental disability. *Journal of Developmental and Physical Disabilities*, *30*, 427–437. doi:https://doi.org/10.1007/s10882-018-9594-0

Katartzi, E. S., & Vlachopoulos, S. P. (2011). Motivating children with developmental coordination disorder in school physical education: The self-determination theory approach. *Research in Developmental Disabilities*, *32*, 2674–2682. doi:10.1016/j.ridd.2011.06.005

Lonsdale, C., Sabiston, C. M., Raedeke, T. D., Ha, A. S., & Sum, R. K. (2009). Self- determined motivation and students' physical activity during structured physical education lessons and free choice periods. *Preventive Medicine*, *48*, 69–73. doi:10.1016/j.ypmed.2008.09.013

Nicholls, J. G. (1984). Achievement motivation: Conceptions of ability, subjective experience, task choice, and performance. *Psychological Review*, *91*, 328–346. doi:10.1037/0033-295X.91.3.328

Ntoumanis, N. (2002). Motivational clusters in a sample of British physical education classes. *Psychology of Sport and Exercise*, *3*(177-194). doi:10.1016/S1469-0292(01)00020-6

Obrusnikova, I. (2008). Physical educators' beliefs about teaching children with disabilities. *Perceptual and Motor Skills*, *106*, 637–644. doi:10.2466/PMS.106.2.637-644

Pan, C.-Y., Tsai, C.-L., Chu, C.-H., & Hsieh, K.-W. (2011). Physical activity and self- determined motivation of adolescents with and without autism spectrum disorders in inclusive physical education. *Research in Autism Spectrum Disorders*, *5*, 733–741. doi:10.1016/j.rasd.2010.08.007

Parish, L. E., & Treasure, D. C. (2003). Physical activity and situational motivation in physical education: Influence of the motivational climate and perceived ability. *Research Quarterly for Exercise and Sport*, *74*, 173–182. doi:10.1080/02701367.2003.10609079

Physical and Health Education Canada. (2018). *Quality daily physical education*. Retrieved from https://phecanada.ca/activate/qdpe

Pianta, R. C., Hamre, B. K., & Allen, J. P. (2012). Teacher-student relationships and engagement: Conceptualizing, measuring, and improving capacity of classroom interactions. In S. L. Christenson,

A. L. Reschly, & C. Wylie (Eds.), *Handbook of research on student engagement* (pp. 365–386). New York, NY: Springer.

Qi, J., & Ha, A. S. (2012). Inclusion in physical education: A review of literature. *International Journal of Disability Development and Education, 59,* 257–281. doi:10.1080/1034912X.2012.697737

Reeve, J. (2012). A self-determination theory perspective on student engagement. In S. L. Christensen, A. L. Reschly, & C. Wylie (Eds.), *Handbook of research on student engagement* (pp. 149–172). New York, NY: Springer.

Reeve, J., Deci, E. L., & Ryan, R. M. (2004). Self-determination theory: A dialectical framework for understanding sociocultural influences on student motivation. In D. M. McInerney & S. Van Etten (Eds.), *Big theories revisited* (pp. 31–60). Greenwich, CT: Information Age Press.

Reeve, J., & Jang, H. (2006). What teachers say and do to support students' autonomy during a learning activity. *Journal of Educational Psychology, 98,* 209–218. doi:10.1037/0022-0663.98.1.209

Reid, G. (2003). Defining adapted physical activity. In R. D. Steadward, G. Wheeler, & E. J. Watkinson (Eds.), *Adapted physical activity* (pp. 11–25). Edmonton: University of Alberta Press.

Robinson, L. E., & Goodway, J. D. (2009). Instructional climates in preschool children who are at-risk: Part I. *Research Quarterly for Exercise and Sport, 80,* 533–542. doi:10.1080/02701367.2009.10599591

Ryan, R. M., & Deci, E. L. (2000). Intrinsic and extrinsic motivations: Classic definitions and new directions. *Contemporary Educational Psychology, 25,* 54–67. doi:https://doi.org/10.1006/ceps.1999.1020

Ryan, R. M., & Deci, E. L. (2002). Overview of self-determination theory: An organismic dialectical perspective. In E. L. Deci & R. M. Ryan (Eds.), *Handbook of self- determination* (pp. 3–33). Rochester, NY: University of Rochester.

Ryan, R. M., & Deci, E. L. (2017). *Self-determination theory: Basic psychological needs in motivation, development, and wellness.* New York, NY: The Guilford Press.

Ryan, R. M., & Deci, E. L. (2019). Brick by brick: The origin, development, and future of self-determination theory. In A. J. Elliot (Ed.), *Advances in motivation science* (Vol. 6, pp. 111–156). Rochester, NY: University of Rochester.

Sherrill, C. (2004). *Adapted physical activity, recreation, and sport: Crossdisciplinary and lifespan* (6th ed.). Boston, MA: McGraw-Hill.

Sparks, C., Dimmock, J., Whipp, P., Lonsdale, C., & Jackson, B. (2015). "Getting connected": High school physical education teacher behaviors that facilitate students' relatedness support perceptions. *Sport, Exercise, and Performance Psychology, 4,* 219–236. doi:10.1037/spy0000039

Spencer-Cavaliere, N., & Watkinson, E. J. (2010). Inclusion understood from the perspectives of children with disability. *Adapted Physical Activity Quarterly, 27,* 275–293.

Stainback, W., & Stainback, S. (1990). *Support networks for inclusive schooling: Interdependent integrated education.* Baltimore, MD: P.H. Brookes Publishing Company.

Standage, M., Duda, J. L., & Ntoumanis, N. (2005). A test of self-determination theory in school physical education. *British Journal of Educational Psychology, 75,* 411–433. doi:10.1348/000709904X22359

Standage, M., Gillison, F. B., Ntoumanis, N., & Treasure, G. C. (2012). Predicting students' physical activity and health-related well-being: A prospective cross-domain investigation of motivation across school physical education and exercise settings. *Journal of Sport & Exercise Psychology, 34,* 37–60.

Sun, H., & Chen, A. (2010). A pedagogical understanding of the self-determination theory in physical education. *Quest, 62,* 364–384. doi:10.1080/00336297.2010.10483655

Sun, H., Li, W., & Shen, B. (2017). Learning in physical education: A self-determination theory perspective. *Journal of Teaching in Physical Education, 36,* 277–291. doi:10.1123/jtpe.2017-0067

Ulstad, S. O., Halvari, H., Sørebø, Ø., & Deci, E. L. (2016). Motivation, learning strategies, and performance in physical education at secondary school. *Advances in Physical Education, 6,* 27–41. doi:10.4236/ape.2016.61004

Vallerand, R. J., & Losier, G. F. (1999). An integrative analysis of intrinsic and extrinsic motivation in sport. *Journal of Applied Sport Psychology, 11,* 142–169. doi:10.1080/10413209908402956

Walker, G. J., Kleiber, D. A., & Mannell, R. C. (2019). *A social psychology of leisure* (3rd ed.). Urbana, IL: Sagamore-Venture Publishing.

Wehmeyer, M. L., & Little, T. D. (2013). Self-determination. In M. L. Wehmeyer (Ed.), *The oxford handbook of positive psychology and disability* (pp. 116–136). New York, NY: Oxford University Press.

White, R. W. (1959). Motivation reconsidered: The concept of competence. *Psychological Review, 66,* 297–333. ble 3.

20

Self-efficacy theory

Chunxiao Li

Introduction

Distinguished from other concepts, such as self-concept and self-esteem, Bandura (1997) defined self-efficacy as "beliefs in one's capabilities to organize and execute the courses of action required to produce given attainments" (p. 3). Since the introduction of the concept of self-efficacy (also known as perceived capacity) to the psychological literature, researchers and practitioners have applied and tested its role in different fields, such as adapted physical education (APE), business, exercise, health, sport, and therapy. In the context of APE, self-efficacy is expected to influence important outcomes such as teachers' and learners' motivation, self-regulation, and achievement (Beamer & Yun, 2014; Block, Hutzler, Barak, & Klavina, 2013; Li, Wang, Block, Sum, & Wu, 2018). This chapter focuses on the role of self-efficacy in the teaching and learning of APE. A brief historical overview of self-efficacy theory is provided, followed by its theoretical framework. Recent empirical research using this theoretical framework in APE is then summarized and discussed to identify gaps for future research. The chapter closes with practical suggestions based on the existing empirical evidence.

A brief historical overview

In 1977, Albert Bandura outlined a theoretical framework, self-efficacy theory, for analyzing behavioral changes in psychotherapy in his seminal article titled "Self-efficacy: Toward a unifying theory of behavioral change" (Bandura, 1977a). Although the term "self-efficacy" (originally labelled "efficacy expectancy") was only formalized in Bandura's 1977 article, there has been a long history in philosophy and psychology exploring the relationships between beliefs about personal competence and human behavior. For example, scholars such as Avid Hume, John Locke, and William James tried to understand the importance of self-efficacy in human behavior (Maddux, 1995).

Indeed, self-efficacy theory lies at the center of social cognitive theory. According to social cognitive theory (Bandura, 1986), people are recognized as empowered agents, who can actively exert control over environmental events through the regulation of their actions, cognitions, emotions, and motivations, rather than as passive reactors to their environment. People's behaviors are acquired and regulated through cognitive processes (e.g., observing the outcomes of actions and evaluating sports performance from others) in a social context where there are

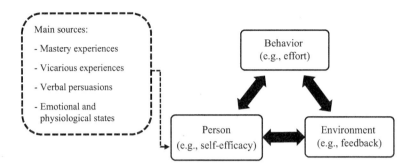

Figure 20.1 Conceptual framework of social cognitive theory and sources of self-efficacy

dynamic and reciprocal interactions among persons (e.g., belief), behaviors (e.g., effort), and environments (e.g., feedback; see Figure 20.1). As self-efficacy represents one's personal perception of a social factor or context, it is an integral part of social cognitive theory.

In addition to social cognitive theory, other theories, such as social learning (Bandura, 1977b) and self-concept (Snyder, 1965), have contributed to the development of self-efficacy theory. Nowadays, it is almost impossible not to consider the role self-efficacy plays when explaining human functioning (e.g., learning, motivation, and achievement) given the significance and utility of self-efficacy theory in different fields (Van Dinther, Dochy, & Segers, 2011). Compared with other fields, such as health psychology and education, the history of using self-efficacy theory in APE is relatively short. To our best knowledge, Hutzler, Zach, and Gafni (2005) were the first group of researchers who applied this theory in this field. The theoretical framework of self-efficacy is reviewed in the next section before summarizing relevant studies in APE.

Theoretical framework

Self-efficacy theory

Self-efficacy representing an internal cognitive process that can affect people's behaviors (Bandura, 1997). Self-efficacy theory assumes that people tend to choose tasks or activities that they perceive themselves capable of performing and avoid tasks that they are not confident in. Self-efficacy determines to what extent people will put effort into a task, persist when facing adversity, and recover after experiencing setbacks. Higher efficacious people are inclined to have greater effort, persistence, and resilience. In addition to affecting human behavior, self-efficacy can also affect how people think and feel (Bandura, 1997). For example, Zimmerman (2000) found that students with higher self-efficacy are more likely to work harder, persist longer, and participate more readily than those with lower self-efficacy. Likewise, research by Martínez-López and colleagues (2017) found that high efficacious physical education teachers tended to have positive attitudes toward teaching obese or overweight students.

Dimensionality and measures

It is worth noting that self-efficacy is a domain-specific construct rather than a global one (Bandura, 1997). For example, physical educators may feel capable of carrying out a task in a general physical education lesson but still lack the efficacy to organize an activity in which a student with autism spectrum disorder is included. This example implies that there are different types of self-efficacy, such as barrier self-efficacy (i.e., perceived capacity to overcome barriers), learner self-efficacy (i.e., perceived capacity to learn new skills, strategies, and behaviors), and teacher self-efficacy (i.e., perceived capacity to promote student learning). Thus, a specific domain of functioning should be assessed through self-efficacy measures. Furthermore, a level of specificity that is aligned with the target outcomes should be chosen to optimize the measuring precision (Wyatt, 2014). Self-efficacy measures should also be designed to assess one's efficacy to perform a given task (e.g., I think I can manage students' behavioral problems in my class) rather than to ask whether one has a certain skill to carry out a task (e.g., I have excellent class management skills) (Bandura, 1997). Finally, one's degree of self-efficacy about carrying out a given task is usually captured through a response scale (e.g., from 0 to 10 or 0 to 100% in ten-unit intervals).

Sources of self-efficacy

According to Bandura (1997), efficacy beliefs are products of processing diverse sources of information. Four major sources are believed to influence self-efficacy formation, including mastery experiences, vicarious experiences, verbal persuasions, and emotional and physiological states (see Figure 20.1).

Mastery experiences

The mastery experience is the most reliable and powerful source for people to gauge their capacities (Bandura, 1997). Successful past experiences, or mastery experiences, will enhance people's self-efficacy, whereas failure experiences will diminish it. Mastery experiences help people believe that they are able to succeed at a specific task (e.g., hit a tennis ball) and successfully perform it again later on. The interpretation of these mastery experiences creates a sense of self-efficacy. Bandura (1997) added that past successes on tough tasks, tasks successfully accomplished without others' help, and tasks attempted with occasional failures have greater positive effects on heightening self-efficacy than those tasks that are easily performed, tasks completed with external assistance, and tasks accomplished with many more numbers of failures than successes.

Vicarious experiences

Vicarious experiences (e.g., observational learning, social comparison, and self-modelling) can also be an important source of self-efficacy information. People observe others' behavior and its outcomes, then use this information to judge their own performance (Bandura, 1997). Observing a successful experience of similar others can elevate observers' self-efficacy, as they are inclined to believe that if others can make it, they can, too. On the other hand, observing similar others fail in performing a task reduces observers' self-efficacy with that given task. In fact, people tend to find comparable others or models who can provide them salient information for judging their own performance. It was found that models who have similar or slightly higher performance provide the most salient information for making judgements on one's own efficacy (Bandura, 1997). In general, vicarious experiences have a weaker influence on self-efficacy than mastery experiences (Byars-Winston, Diestelmann, Savoy, & Hoyt, 2017). Furthermore, people who have little successful experience, or are uncertain about their capacities, are expected to be more sensitive to the vicarious source (Bandura, 1997).

Verbal persuasion

A third source of self-efficacy information that people draw from is verbal persuasion, feed-back, and expectations of significant others (e.g., teacher's encouragement). Compared with the two previously mentioned sources, verbal persuasion is a less potent source of self-efficacy and alone has limited power to create a strong sense of self-efficacy. However, verbal persuasions play a significant role in motivating people (Bandura, 1997). The effects of verbal persuasion depend on factors such as the attractiveness, expertise, and trustworthi-ness of the persuader. Persuasive messages are more effective when they are conveyed by people who are viewed by receivers as knowledgeable and reliable (Bong & Skaalvik, 2003).

Emotional and physiological states

A final source of self-efficacy information comes from emotional and physiological states, such as anxiety, excitement, and vigor (Bandura, 1997). Emotional and physiological reac-tions to a given task provide people with cues for interpreting their efficacy. People may interpret negative feelings or emotional states as a sign of failure, leading them to doubt their self-efficacy beliefs. For example, students who often fail in a multi-stage fitness test will feel anxious and stressed because they think they are likely to fail again in the future. These negative reactions undermine their self-efficacy to pass the exam. Therefore, physiological and emotional cues influence self-efficacy (Maddux, 1995). In general, physiological and emotional states are not as powerful an influence on self-efficacy relative to the other three major sources (Bandura, 1997).

The four main sources of efficacy beliefs described above provide people with relevant information to judge their own capacity for performing a specific task. Although some sources are more influential than others, they are not independent of each other (Bandura, 1997). In addition, the relationships between these sources and self-efficacy may be moder-ated by other factors. For example, a recent meta-analysis demonstrated that subject area (STEM vs. non-STEM) and grade level moderated the associations between sources and learning self-efficacy (Byars-Winston et al., 2017).

Criticisms of self-efficacy theory

Several criticisms of self-efficacy theory have appeared in the recent literature. First, the processes about how self-efficacy affects human motivation or behavior seem ambiguous. Theorists have criticized that the role of self-efficacy in affecting human behavior is not clearly explained in self-efficacy theory (Vancouver, 2012). For example, it is unclear how the four main sources of self-efficacy interact to yield personal judgements on a given task. Second, it is important to note that self-efficacy is not the only positive influence of human behavior. People should have prerequisite skills, positive values, and outcome expectations to enable self-efficacy to act on desirable behaviors (Schunk & DiBenedetto, 2016). Third, Schmidt and DeShon (2010) demonstrated that self-efficacy may have negative effects on behaviors. Bandura (2012) endorsed this finding and explained that ambiguous feedback (unclear progress made on the task) and task requirements (what to do and where to achieve) may contribute to the negative effects of self-efficacy on behavior. Seemingly, Bandura's explanations to the ambiguous feed-back and task requirements are still unclear (e.g., what is unambiguous feedback?). Given the equivocal explanations, empirical research has been conducted to delineate the possible pro-cesses of the effects of self-efficacy on behavior (see Vancouver & Purl, 2017). Finally, researchers have criticized traditional measures of self-efficacy that typically ask people whether they *can do* a target task (see Williams & Rhodes, 2016). By providing some preliminary evidence, Williams and Rhodes (2016) argued that traditional self-efficacy measures may also measure motivation, reflecting a confounded self-efficacy construct. These researchers suggested conducting more research to confirm the issue of "confounded self-efficacy construct". In the meantime, while some researchers are criticizing and further developing self-efficacy theory, others are applying it in its current form to a wide range of fields.

Current scholarships and future research directions

A large number of researchers have examined the utility of self-efficacy theory in fields such as education (for a review, see Schunk & DiBenedetto, 2016). In this section, empirical findings in APE research from the past decade (2008–2018) are summarized and future research directions are proposed. These recent empirical studies are classified into four major domains: scale development and validation, self-efficacy correlates, interventions to improve teacher self-efficacy, and interventions to promote student self-efficacy.

Scale development and validation

A number of studies examined psychometric properties of self-efficacy based scales. The five-item Difficult Behavior Self-Efficacy Scale was initially developed for measuring staff, caregivers, and special education teachers' self-efficacy toward behavioral problems of individuals with disabilities (Hastings & Brown, 2002). Oh and Kozub (2010) adopted the scale for assessing physical educators' self-efficacy to deal with challenging behaviors of students with autism spectrum disorder. The adopted scale was administered to 139 American and 229 Korean in-service physical educators. The scale showed good internal consistency and its one-factor structure was also supported based on the findings of a confirmatory factor analysis. However, the results of invariance testing across the two samples supported metric invariance, but not scalar invariance. These results indicate that comparing sample mean differences is biased and suggests possible cultural differences in interpreting item contents.

Instead of adopting an existing scale, Taliafero (2010) designed the ten-item Physical Educators' Self-Efficacy Toward Including Students with Disabilities-Autism (PESEISD-A) to assess physical educators' self-efficacy toward including students with autism spectrum disorders. In her study, the internal reliability, test–retest reliability with a two-week interval, and one-factor measurement model were supported with 236 in-service physical educators in the US. These psychometric properties were also supported among preservice physical education teachers in Hong Kong (n = 227) and mainland China (n = 205) in a more recent validation study (Li et al., 2018). This later validation research also provided initial evidence of external validity that the scale scores were associated with theoretically relevant constructs, including burnout and life satisfaction in both samples. However, the results of invariance tests across the two samples of teachers from Hong Kong and mainland China supported metric invariance, but not scalar invariance. Thus, comparing mean scores between these two samples is inaccurate.

Block et al. (2013) created the Self-Efficacy Scale for Physical Education Teacher Education Majors toward Children with Disabilities (SE-PETE-D) with three scales to measure pre-service physical education teachers' self-efficacy toward the inclusion of students with intellectual disabilities, physical disabilities, and visual impairment, respectively. The internal reliability and content/factorial validity of the three scales with six to ten items were supported among 486 pre-service physical educators. Each of the three scales measures two to three of the following factors: peer instruction, safety, staying on task, and specific adaptations. The three scales were translated to Czech, and their internal reliability and factorial validity were supported among 200 pre-service physical education teachers (Kudláček, Baloun, & Ješina, 2018). It is important to note that several error terms across different factors were correlated in these two validation studies, which suggests there is an issue of content overlap across items. Thus, further validation research is necessary to revise some of the items to solve this issue.

Building upon the PESEISD-A and SE-PETE-D, Hutzler and Barak (2017) developed a ten-item scale to assess in-service physical educators' self-efficacy towards teaching students with cerebral palsy in each of three mobility categories (independent, using an assistive device, and using a wheelchair). The scale was administered to 121 in-service physical education teachers in Israel. The scale showed good internal reliability and its factor structure was supported based on the result of exploratory factor analysis. The external validity was also evident, as teachers who had more previous experiences (e.g., having school practicum and specializing in APE) demonstrated a higher level of self-efficacy than those who had fewer experiences (Hutzler & Barak, 2017).

Compared with measures of teacher self-efficacy, very few scales have been developed to measure self-efficacy beliefs towards physical activity of students with disabilities. Cervantes and Porretta (2013) designed a ten-item Self-efficacy for Overcoming Barriers to Physical Activity Scale for Adolescents with Visual Impairment. Its content validity was reviewed and supported by a panel of six professional experts. However, other psychometric properties of this scale have not been examined to date. Similarly, Todd, Reid, and Butler-Kisber (2010) designed only two questions to assess self-efficacy for cycling in students with autism spectrum disorder, without going through a systematic scale development process (e.g., item generation and factor analysis). In general, a minimum of three questions are recommended to assess a construct such as self-efficacy.

In sum, it is encouraging to see that several self-efficacy based scales have been adapted or designed for use in the APE field. As scale development is an ongoing process, comprehensive validation studies are needed to further examine the psychometric properties (e.g., test–retest reliability, concurrent validity, and predictive validity) of the existing scales using different statistical approaches (e.g., confirmatory factor analysis, exploratory structural equation modeling, and item response analysis). In addition, the existing scales of teacher self-efficacy cover only a few types of disabilities (e.g., autism spectrum disorder and intellectual disability) and are dominated by teaching self-efficacy. New scales are needed for measuring physical educators' teaching self-efficacy toward other groups of students with disabilities (e.g., attention deficit and hyperactivity disorder, developmental coordination disorder, and hearing impairment) and other types of self-efficacy such as collaborative self-efficacy (i.e., perceived capacity to work with other people) and collective self-efficacy (i.e., perceived capacity of the group as a whole to achieve a common goal). New scales for measuring self-efficacy of students with disabilities, such as exercise self-efficacy (i.e., perceived capacity to successfully exercise), should also to be developed to proliferate self-efficacy research in this area. Finally, developing valid measures of potential sources of self-efficacy is warranted, as research on the sources of teacher/student self-efficacy has direct implications for identifying salient correlates of self-efficacy.

Self-efficacy correlates

Limited research has been conducted to examine the correlates of teacher self-efficacy. Beamer and Yun (2014) employed a cross-sectional approach with a national stratified random sample in the US (n = 142) to understand selected antecedents and consequences of in-service physical education teachers' self-efficacy. Theory of planned behavior-based constructs (attitude, intention, and behavior), teaching experience, support from special education teacher, and in-service training on autism spectrum disorder were positively associated with self-efficacy toward including students with autism spectrum disorders. However, Beamer and Yun also found that coursework in APE, which is commonly associated with teacher self-efficacy (e.g., Kwon & Block, 2017), was not related to self-efficacy. The findings may question the effectiveness of current physical education teacher education programs on improving teacher self-efficacy. Given that self-efficacy is a domain-specific construct (Bandura, 1997), the lack of a specific training program to prepare physical educators on how to include students with autism spectrum disorder may explain this counterintuitive finding. Furthermore, the authors cautioned that, although a random sampling approach was used, the final response rate was lower than 10%, suggesting the study results may not be representative of all in-service physical educators' preparation to teach students with autism spectrum disorder in the US. In other words, sampling error may also contribute to this conflicting finding.

Qualitative evidence is available regarding the sources of teacher self-efficacy. Casebolt and Hodge (2010) interviewed six high school physical educators and showed that American teachers' self-efficacy in including students with mild to severe disabilities was contingent on their formal training, informal learning (self-help preparation), teaching experiences, availability of resources and space, and students' disability type and severity. In a more recent study, similar results were found after interviewing six Brazilian in-service physical educators (Hodge, Haegele, Gutierres Filho, & Rizzi Lopes, 2018).

There is little empirical evidence regarding self-efficacy correlates in students with disabilities. Martin, Shapiro, and Prokesova (2013)'s cross-sectional comparison study is one exception, in which they found that barrier self-efficacy toward physical activity participation (i.e., perceived capacity to overcome exercise barriers) was associated with social support among 64 children with hearing impairment. However, barrier self-efficacy was not related to levels of enjoyment and physical activity, which is contradictory to self-efficacy theory. The small sample size may contribute to this conflicting result. In line with self-efficacy theory, social support was found to predict self-efficacy for physical activity, which subsequently influenced physical activity participation among 152 adults with intellectual disabilities in the US (Peterson et al., 2008).

The aforementioned findings identified some salient factors that may be important determinants or sources of teaching (i.e., coursework and teaching experience) and physical activity self-efficacy (i.e., social support). In addition, these self-efficacy beliefs may influence teaching behaviors and physical activity participation and its outcomes. However, more research needs to be conducted to understand additional correlates of self-efficacy (e.g., academic performance, learning motivation, and teaching behavior), as related empirical evidence is very limited. The limited research evidence may be attributed to the lack of context-specific self-efficacy measures. For example, Martin et al. (2013) employed generic scales that may not be sensitive enough for the deaf group for measuring related outcomes (e.g., barrier self-efficacy). Using a non-context-specific measure may also confound study findings. Moreover, most of the existing studies were conducted in the Western context, suggesting more research needs to be conducted in other contexts. Even though self-efficacy is a universal construct, there are cross-cultural differences that merit future investigation (Scholz, Doña, Sud, & Schwarzer, 2002). Finally, all of the included survey studies used a cross-sectional design, which has limited power for causal inference. To document the change of self-efficacy and its correlates, longitudinal studies with the experience sampling method or ecological momentary assessment, asking participants to give responses to survey instruments on multiple occasions over time, can be useful (for details about this approach, see Csikszentmihalyi & Larson, 2014).

Interventions to improve teacher self-efficacy

Several studies have examined the effects of pre-service or in-service training on physical educators' self-efficacy toward inclusion of students with disabilities. For example, Taliaferro, Hammond, and Wyant (2015) designed a pre-service training program that consisted of a 15-week APE course (130–160 min/week) plus nine-week supervised practicum experience (60 min/week). The training program was found to significantly improve self-efficacy toward inclusion of students with autism spectrum disorders, intellectual disabilities, physical disabilities, and visual impairments among 98 pre-service physical education teachers. Tindall, Culhane, and Foley (2016) examined the effects of a ten-week adapted physical activity program on pre-service teachers' self-efficacy toward inclusion of students with different types of disabilities. Each of the participants ($n = 64$) was paired with a student with a disability and was required to engage the student in physical activity during a weekly one-hour adapted physical activity program. The participants' self-efficacy level improved immediately after the program (Tindall et al., 2016). However, it is unclear whether the positive training effects of these two studies were sustained after the participants became in-service physical educators. Moreover, the positive findings should be cautiously interpreted, as a control group was not included in these two studies.

Innovatively, Kwon and Block (2017) investigated the impact of an e-learning supplement of introductory APE on pre-service physical educators' self-efficacy toward including students with intellectual disabilities. The participants ($n = 75$) were randomly assigned into e-learning groups with online supplements, traditional group with printed supplements, and control group without course materials. The online and printed supplements consisted of the same information related to instructional strategies, environment/equipment/rule modification, and basic information and characteristics of intellectual disability. The results showed that both the e-learning and traditional groups improved their self-efficacy and had higher self-efficacy than the control at posttest. The authors recommended that a moderator who can create more engagement in e-learning activities is required to bring more positive effects on self-efficacy (Kwon & Block, 2017).

Regarding in-service training, Taliaferro and Harris's (2014) controlled trial showed that a one-day workshop that offered educational information for including students with autism spectrum disorders (e.g., individualized education plan, communication, and safety) did not improve in-service physical educators' self-efficacy toward the inclusion of this population of students. The authors asserted that the short duration of intervention and small sample size ($n = 65$) may contribute to the non-significant finding. More recently, Umhoefer, Vargas, and Beyer (2015) conducted a retrospective survey to examine the effects of different APE service approaches on self-efficacy beliefs toward working with students with disabilities among 102 in-service physical educators. These service approaches included consultation (i.e., APE specialists provided consultation to teachers and parents), itinerant (i.e., APE specialists directly worked with students with disabilities), and collaborative (i.e., APE specialists and general physical education teachers worked together in a collaborative setting). Compared with the consultation and itinerant approaches, the collaborative method produced the strongest effect (Umhoefer et al., 2015).

The outlined findings provide some initial evidence on developing programs and strategies (e.g., coursework plus on-campus practicum and e-learning supplement) to improve pre-service and in-service physical educators' self-efficacy toward inclusion of students with disabilities. More longitudinal studies and well-designed controlled trials are needed to provide further evidence regarding the effects of different types of training programs (e.g., a two-day workshop and virtual learning experiences) on teachers' self-efficacy toward inclusion of students with a specific type of disability. As some of the programs integrated different sources of self-efficacy information, it might be useful to conduct in-depth interviews to understand which aspects and elements of the training program are most effective in enhancing teacher self-efficacy (Koh, 2018).

Interventions to promote student self-efficacy

Few intervention studies have examined the effects of training programs on students' self-efficacy beliefs. For instance, Mazzoni, Purves, Southward, Rhodes, and Temple (2009) investigated the effect of a six-week (once per week and 60 min/session) climbing program on self-efficacy toward climbing among children with different types of disabilities, such as Angelman syndrome, Down syndrome, and spina bifida. Compared with the waitlist control (n = 23), children in the intervention group (n = 23) significantly increased their self-efficacy after completing the climbing program (Mazzoni et al., 2009). It should be noted that the sample was heterogeneous, as a wide range of disability type was involved, confounding the study findings and limiting the generalizability of the results to a specific disability group.

Cervantes and Porretta (2013) conducted a single-subject experiment to understand the impact of a five-week afterschool activity program on barrier self-efficacy toward physical activity participation among four adolescents with visual impairments. The participants received nine lesson units of instruction across five weeks that were intended to increase social cognitive-based outcomes such as self-efficacy. They found that two of the participants increased their self-efficacy beliefs. However, they did not observe the maintenance effect 1–3 weeks after the intervention (Cervantes & Porretta, 2013). Similarly, a 16-week cycling program was administered to three adolescents with severe autism spectrum disorders to see whether it improved self-efficacy toward cycling (Todd et al., 2010). In addition to participating in the regular cycling activity (three times/week, 30 min/session), the participants were also required to learn self-monitoring, goal setting, and self-reinforcement skills. The results of this single-subject experiment suggested a significant improvement of self-efficacy (Todd et al., 2010). As different components were included in the intervention programs, it is difficult to ascertain whether the increased physical activity participation can be attributed to the change in self-efficacy.

The above intervention studies suggested that a short duration of intervention of five weeks may be effective in improving students' self-efficacy levels. In line with self-efficacy theory (Bandura, 1997), the positive change of self-efficacy may be attributed to the successful experiences of performing specific tasks (e.g., climbing and cycling) and the environment where social persuasions are available to the participants (e.g., informative feedback and social support). Despite the positive findings, it is worthy to note that little is known on how to use a training program to enhance students' learning self-efficacy. In addition, because of the lack of longitudinal research, it is unknown if the impact of these interventions is short or long term. Finally, future work may be beneficial in identifying the most salient sources of exercise self-efficacy.

Possible implications for practice

Some possible practical implications for teacher training and teaching can be derived based on the emerging empirical evidence. First, teacher training and professional development programs should be carefully designed to enhance teacher self-efficacy. Seemingly, a short-term training program (e.g., one-day workshop) may not be effective for self-efficacy improvement (Taliaferro & Harris, 2014). It is highly plausible that effective training programs will last for weeks. In addition, as people should have prerequisite skills to enable self-efficacy beliefs to act on desirable behaviors, an effective teacher training program should not neglect to prepare the prerequisite skills (e.g., mastery of passing skills) in order to allow self-efficacy to act on teachers' behaviors (e.g., demonstration of a passing skill; Schunk & DiBenedetto, 2016).

Second, although it is still unclear what specific component is needed in terms of training (Beamer & Yun, 2014), training programs providing continuous successful experiences of including students with disabilities are essential for enhancing teachers' self-efficacy (Bandura, 1997; Block, Taliaferro, Harris, & Krause, 2010). To help teachers attain mastery experiences, an optimally challenging teaching task should be offered during practicum. In general and if possible, beginner teachers should start with teaching students with mild disabilities and then gradually increase the difficulty level to build their self-efficacy. Repeated exposure to a difficult task that is far beyond novice teachers' capacity will result in failure and undermine their self-efficacy (Bandura, 1997). In cases where novice teachers have exposure only to students with moderate to severe disabilities, more intensive professional supports from APE specialists and special education teachers should be provided to help teachers gain successful teaching experiences (Umhoefer et al., 2015).

Third, it is suggested that beginner teachers should observe skillful mentors or role models' successful practices, such as behavior management, instruction planning, and modifications in inclusive physical education settings (Hodge et al., 2018). If opportunities for direct observations are limited, symbolic models, such as filmed case studies, can be used (Kwon & Block, 2017). Meanwhile, it is recommended to provide verbal or social persuasions for helping teachers gain vicarious experiences. To secure authentic or effective vicarious experiences, sincere and specific feedback from credible and knowledgeable observers or significant others will be important (Bong & Skaalvik, 2003).

Finally, it is important to help students achieve desirable outcomes (e.g., exercise motivation and behavior) through promoting individual self-efficacy (Bandura, 1997). Mastery experiences, the most important source of self-efficacy, can be attained by increasing students' time on task through effective teaching strategies. An effective teaching strategy enables students to experience less waiting time (e.g., transition from task to task) and to spend more time on practice, which increases their chances of accomplishing a specific task. Teachers can use the inclusive physical education environment, in which there are ample opportunities for peer-based modelling (e.g., students with disabilities can observe good motor behaviors from students without disabilities) to facilitate mastery learning experiences through which students can increase self-efficacy. Teachers should design physical education or activity programs that focus on mastery and collaboration, rather than competition and peer comparison. In addition to peer support, the social support network can extend to significant others, such as family members, to convey a coherent and positive message (e.g., active lifestyle) to students.

Summary of key points

- Recent self-efficacy research in the APE field mainly focuses on developing self-efficacy measures, understanding self-efficacy correlates, and interventions to increase teacher/student self-efficacy.
- Several scales are available to measure physical education teachers' self-efficacy toward including students with different types of disabilities. However, few scales with strong psychometric properties are specifically developed for assessing learning and physical activity self-efficacy for students with disabilities. Advanced statistical approaches can be considered in future scale development and refinement studies.
- There is some initial evidence supporting the sources and antecedents of teacher self-efficacy. However, limited studies have investigated the correlates of student self-efficacy. Future research needs to use more rigorous study design to examine key sources and outcomes of self-efficacy and consider cultural differences.
- Several training approaches are found to increase physical education teachers' self-efficacy toward including students with disabilities. Exercise self-efficacy of students with disabilities is enhanced through different kinds of physical activity-based programs. More randomized controlled trials are necessary to support the intervention findings.

Reflective questions for discussion

- What is self-efficacy, and why is it important to consider in the field of adapted physical education?
- What are some shortcomings of self-efficacy theory, and who should these shortcomings be addressed?
- How are correlates of student self-efficacy distinguishable from correlates of teacher self-efficacy?
- Using the content about self-efficacy discussed in this chapter, design an intervention program to improve teacher/student self-efficacy in physical education. How would you measure effectiveness? What improvements would you focus on?

References

Bandura, A. (1977a). Self-efficacy: Toward a unifying theory of behavioral change. *Psychological Review*, *84*(2), 191–215. doi:10.1037/0033-295X.84.2.191

Bandura, A. (1977b). *Social learning theory*. Englewood Cliffs, NJ: Prentice Hall.

Bandura, A. (1986). *Social foundation of thought and action: A social-cognitive view*. Englewood Cliffs, NJ: Prentice-Hall.

Bandura, A. (1997). *Self-efficacy: The exercise of control*. New York, NY: W.H. Freeman.

Bandura, A. (2012). On the functional properties of perceived self-efficacy revisited. *Journal of Management*, *38*(1), 9–44. doi:10.1177/0149206311410606

Beamer, J. A., & Yun, J. (2014). Physical educators' beliefs and self-reported behaviors toward including students with autism spectrum disorder. *Adapted Physical Activity Quarterly*, *31*(4), 362–376. doi:10.1123/apaq.2014-0134

Block, M. E., Hutzler, Y., Barak, S., & Klavina, A. (2013). Creation and validation of the self-efficacy instrument for physical education teacher education majors toward inclusion. *Adapted Physical Activity Quarterly*, *30*(2), 184–205. doi:10.1123/apaq.30.2.184

Block, M. E., Taliaferro, A., Harris, N., & Krause, J. (2010). Using self-efficacy theory to facilitate inclusion in general physical education. *Journal of Physical Education, Recreation & Dance*, *81*(3), 43–46.

Chunxiao Li

Bong, M., & Skaalvik, E. M. (2003). Academic self-concept and self-efficacy: How different are they really?. *Educational Psychology Review, 15*(1), 1–40. doi:10.1023/A:102130240

Byars-Winston, A., Diestelmann, J., Savoy, J. N., & Hoyt, W. T. (2017). Unique effects and moderators of effects of sources on self-efficacy: A model-based meta-analysis. *Journal of Counseling Psychology, 64*(6), 645. doi:10.1037/cou0000219

Casebolt, K. M., & Hodge, S. R. (2010). High school physical education teachers' beliefs about teaching students with mild to severe disabilities. *Physical Educator, 67*(3), 140–155.

Cervantes, C. M., & Porretta, D. L. (2013). Impact of after school programming on physical activity among adolescents with visual impairments. *Adapted Physical Activity Quarterly, 30*(2), 127–146. doi:10.1123/apaq.30.2.127

Csikszentmihalyi, M., & Larson, R. (2014). Validity and reliability of the experience-sampling method. In M. Csikszentmihalyi (Ed.), *Flow and the foundations of positive psychology* (pp. 35–54). Dordrecht: Springer.

Hastings, R. P., & Brown, T. (2002). Behavior problems of children with autism, parental self-efficacy, and mental health. *American Journal on Mental Retardation, 107*(3), 222–232.

Hodge, S. R., Haegele, J., Gutierres Filho, P., & Rizzi Lopes, G. (2018). Brazilian physical education teachers' beliefs about teaching students with disabilities. *International Journal of Disability, Development and Education, 65*(4), 408–427. doi:10.1080/1034912X.2017.1408896

Hutzler, Y., & Barak, S. (2017). Self-efficacy of physical education teachers in including students with cerebral palsy in their classes. *Research in Developmental Disabilities, 68*, 52–65. doi:10.1016/j.ridd.2017.07.005

Hutzler, Y., Zach, S., & Gafni, O. (2005). Physical education students' attitudes and self-efficacy towards the participation of children with special needs in regular classes. *European Journal of Special Needs Education, 20*(3), 309–327. doi:10.1080/08856250500156038

Koh, Y. (2018). A strategy to improve pre-service teachers' self-efficacy towards inclusive physical education for students with intellectual disability and autism. *International Journal of Inclusive Education, 22*(8), 839–855. doi:10.1080/13603116.2017.1412511

Kudláček, M., Baloun, L., & Ješina, O. (2018). The development and validation of revised inclusive physical education self-efficacy questionnaire for Czech physical education majors. *International Journal of Inclusive Education*, doi:10.1080/13603116.2018.1451562

Kwon, E. H., & Block, M. E. (2017). Implementing the adapted physical education E-learning program into physical education teacher education program. *Research in Developmental Disabilities, 69*, 18–29. doi:10.1016/j.ridd.2017.07.001

Li, C., Wang, L., Block, M. E., Sum, R. K. W., & Wu, Y. (2018). Psychometric properties of the Physical Educators' Self-efficacy Toward Including Students With Disabilities-autism among Chinese pre-service physical education teachers. *Adapted Physical Activity Quarterly, 35*(2), 159–174. doi:10.1123/apaq.2017-0086

Maddux, J. E. (Ed.). (1995). *Self-efficacy, adaptation, and adjustment: Theory, research, and application.* New York, NY: Plenum Press.

Martin, J. J., Shapiro, D. R., & Prokesova, E. (2013). Predictors of physical activity among European and American hearing impaired children. *European Journal of Adapted Physical Activity, 6*(2), 38–47.

Martínez-López, E. J., Zamora-Aguilera, N., Grao-Cruces, A., & De la Torre-Cruz, M. J. (2017). The association between spanish physical education teachers' self-efficacy expectations and their attitudes toward overweight and obese students. *Journal of Teaching in Physical Education, 36*(2), 220–231. doi:10.1123/jtpe.2014-0125

Mazzoni, E. R., Purves, P. L., Southward, J., Rhodes, R. E., & Temple, V. A. (2009). Effect of indoor wall climbing on self-efficacy and self-perceptions of children with special needs. *Adapted Physical Activity Quarterly, 26*(3), 259–273. doi:10.1123/apaq.26.3.259

Oh, H.-K., & Kozub, F. M. (2010). The psychometric properties of the Difficult Behavior Self-efficacy Scale. *Adapted Physical Activity Quarterly, 27*(3), 191–207. doi:10.1123/apaq.27.3.191

Peterson, J. J., Lowe, J. B., Peterson, N. A., Nothwehr, F. K., Janz, K. F., & Lobas, J. G. (2008). Paths to leisure physical activity among adults with intellectual disabilities: Self-efficacy and social support. *American Journal of Health Promotion, 23*(1), 35–42.

Schmidt, A. M., & DeShon, R. P. (2010). The moderating effects of performance ambiguity on the relationship between self-efficacy and performance. *Journal of Applied Psychology, 95*(3), 572–581.

Scholz, U., Doña, B. G., Sud, S., & Schwarzer, R. (2002). Is general self-efficacy a universal construct? Psychometric findings from 25 countries. *European Journal of Psychological Assessment, 18*(3), 242–251. doi:10.1027//1015-5759.18.3.242

Schunk, D. H., & DiBenedetto, M. K. (2016). Self-efficacy theory in education. In K. R. Wentzel & D. B. Miele (Eds.), *Handbook of motivation at school* (Vol. 2, pp. 34–54). New York: Routledge.

Snyder, E. E. (1965). Self-concept theory: An approach to understanding the behavior of disadvantaged pupils. *The Clearing House: A Journal of Educational Strategies, Issues and Ideas, 40*(4), 242–246. doi:10.1080/00098655.1965.11476955

Taliafero, A. R. (2010). Validation of an instrument to explore physical educators' beliefs toward inclusion: Application of self-efficacy theory [doctoral dissertation]. University of Virginia, Charlottesville.

Taliaferro, A. R., Hammond, L., & Wyant, K. (2015). Preservice physical educators' self-efficacy beliefs toward inclusion: The impact of coursework and practicum. *Adapted Physical Activity Quarterly, 32*(1), 49–67. doi:10.1123/apaq.2013-0112

Taliaferro, A. R., & Harris, N. P. (2014). The effects of a one-day workshop on physical educators' self-efficacy toward inclusion of students with autism. *Palaestra, 28*(3), 38–43.

Tindall, D., Culhane, M., & Foley, J. (2016). Pre-service teachers' self-efficacy towards children with disabilities: An Irish perspective. *European Journal of Adapted Physical Activity, 9*(1), 27–39.

Todd, T., Reid, G., & Butler-Kisber, L. (2010). Cycling for students with ASD: Self-regulation promotes sustained physical activity. *Adapted Physical Activity Quarterly, 27*(3), 226–241. doi:10.1123/apaq.27.3.226

Umhoefer, D. L., Vargas, T. M., & Beyer, R. (2015). Adapted physical education service approaches and the effects on the perceived efficacy beliefs of general physical education teachers. *Physical Educator, 72*(3), 361–381.

Van Dinther, M., Dochy, F., & Segers, M. (2011). Factors affecting students' self-efficacy in higher education. *Educational Research Review, 6*(2), 95–108. doi:10.1016/j.edurev.2010.10.003

Vancouver, J. B. (2012). Rhetorical reckoning: A response to Bandura. *Journal of Management, 38*(2), 465–474. doi:10.1177/0149206311435951

Vancouver, J. B., & Purl, J. D. (2017). A computational model of self-efficacy's various effects on performance: Moving the debate forward. *Journal of Applied Psychology, 102*(4), 599–616. doi:10.1037/apl0000177

Williams, D. M., & Rhodes, R. E. (2016). The confounded self-efficacy construct: Conceptual analysis and recommendations for future research. *Health Psychology Review, 10*(2), 113–128. doi:10.1037/apl0000177

Wyatt, M. (2014). Towards a re-conceptualization of teachers' self-efficacy beliefs: Tackling enduring problems with the quantitative research and moving on. *International Journal of Research & Method in Education, 37*(2), 166–189.

Zimmerman, B. J. (2000). Self-efficacy: An essential motive to learn. *Contemporary Educational Psychology, 25*(1), 82–91. doi:10.1006/ceps.1999.1016

21

Theory of planned behavior

Terry L. Rizzo and Luis Columna

Introduction

Attitude theory is the groundwork by which we assess beliefs and attitudes that, we hope, will predict intentions and behaviors about teaching students with disabilities in general physical education (GPE). Theory provides an organized structure to enable us to ask questions about the attitudinal conditions best suited for teaching students with disabilities. It is theory that allows us to understand how and why physical educators feel the way they do about teaching students with disabilities. Theory uses specific language to define constructs (i.e., beliefs, attitudes, social normative components, and perceived behavior control) associated with predicting intention and behavior about teaching students with disabilities. It represents critical thinking with specific language/terms universally accepted and understood by people about behaviors we expect of physical educators.

In this chapter, we present a brief overview of the theory of planned behavior (TPB) (Ajzen, 1991, 2002, 2017) and its relevance and application to adapted physical education (APE). However, to appreciate the utility of the TPB, it is helpful to have a general conceptual understanding of the evolution of attitude and its measurement, particularly, the theory of reasoned action (TRA) (Ajzen & Fishbein, 1980), the precursor to the TPB. Throughout the chapter, the two theories are described in relation to teaching students with disabilities in GPE classes. In addition, in this chapter reference is made to the focus of this handbook; working with individuals with disabilities in physical education contexts. Therefore, we focus on physical educators' attitude and behavior associated with teaching students with disabilities in GPE classes. In addition, we present results from research associated with individuals with disabilities, peers, parents/guardians to illustrate the application and relevance of the TPB in other APE settings.

Our interest in studying physical educators' attitudes toward working with students with disabilities is because of our passion and commitment to enhance the lives of individuals with disabilities. The salient issue is for us to understand how teachers feel about teaching students with disabilities. The issue is what will teachers do, how will they behave if, and when, they teach these students? After all, it is one thing to include students with disabilities in classes, but we know physical educators can also functionally exclude them from class activities.

Overview of attitude theory

Attitude derives its meaning from the Latin word *habitus*, meaning a disposition or condition that translates a person's capacity to do something. Leading authorities (Ajzen & Fishbein, 1980) attribute one of the first records of the concept of attitude to Spencer (1862) who suggested attitude is what gives us "correct judgements on disputed questions" (Spencer, 1862, p. 13). The etymology of attitude shows a time-worn systematic pattern of describing a person's mental thoughts as a readiness for action, a capacity to do something, or simply a behavior (Baldwin, 1901–1905). Similar to any theory, the TPB evolved over time since one of the first attitude scientific papers by Thomas and Znaniecki (1918) appeared in the literature.

There was a time when attitude was thought to symbolize social psychology and the psychology of personality (Allport, 1935). From the onset of scholarly work on attitudes, the assumption was that attitudes are related to behavior. The common themes among early researchers defined attitude, like the Latin expression suggests, as a general preparation or readiness to behave or a capacity to do something (e.g., teaching students with disabilities; Fishbein & Ajzen, 1975).

Along with the scholarly evolution of attitudes as a psychological construct, psychometric methods evolved from the exceptional work of Thurstone (1929, 1931), Likert (1932), Guttman (1944), Osgood, Suci, and Tannennbaum (1957), and others. These researchers placed emotive end marks on statements to measure the likelihood of doing something (or not). As attitude research evolved, issues about the efficacy of the attitude–behavior link troubled social psychologists since the publication of LaPiere's (1934) landmark paper. It is important to recognize the classic attitude–behavior consistency issue, which has a long history. For more than 100 years, researchers have tried to predict the relationship between attitude and behavior, and to better understand what individuals say and what they may actually do and how they do it. Attitude theorists attempted to resolve a potential lack of association between attitude and the actual behavior by refining theory with measurement models and data analysis. Beginning in the late 1950s, attitude theorists (Fishbein, 1963; Rosenberg, 1956; Triandis, 1964) developed models to improve the attitude–behavior prediction by having evaluation of objects, intentions, and behaviors.

Attitude theory, in the context of APE, can help explain collective beliefs toward teaching students with disabilities in GPE classes and ecological constructs associated with peers, perceived behavioral control variables, and families. The TPB is one such attitude theory that expands on historical models by including beliefs associated with attitudes, subjective normative groups, and perceived behavior control in its prediction about intention to teach students with disabilities in GPE classes. Clearly, the TPB has application and relevance to identify factors that influence behaviors related to individuals with disabilities. The TPB suggests the measures of the model are strongly associated with behavior toward individuals with disabilities. The TPB mode is a useful, rigorous, scientific theoretical approach that can help individuals construct a survey to predict the overall pattern of beliefs, attitudes, intentions, and behavior related to teaching students (Ajzen, 2017).

Theory of reasoned action: the precursor to theory of planned behavior

In this section, we outline how the TRA (Ajzen & Fishbein, 1980) served as a model designed to understand only persons' beliefs associated with subjective norms and attitudes to measure the strength of intentions to predict behavior, as well as its application to APE. In addition, TRA theoretical constructs are explained and applied to survey construction.

An overview of the TRA

The TRA is a linear model designed to understand and predict behavior from behavioral intention (Figure 21.1). The TRA views behavioral intentions as the precursor to behaviors.

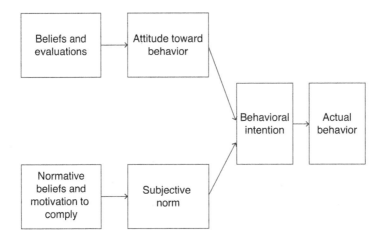

Figure 21.1 The theory of reasoned action. Adapted from Ajzen and Fishbein (1980)

In this theory (Ajzen & Fishbein, 1980), behavioral intentions are a collective result of specific behavioral beliefs assessed and then associated with attitudes and subjective norms of physical educators toward teaching students with disabilities. Such attitudes and subjective norms toward teaching students with disabilities are based on a weighted sum of behavior beliefs and normative beliefs, respectively. According to the TRA, attitudes and subjective norms are determinants of intention, but beliefs underlie these components so we can understand the basis for teaching students with disabilities in GPE classes.

Historically, the TRA had a category identified as external variables, now identified as background variables. These variables were used by researchers to identify characteristics of people and their affect. With regard to teaching individuals with disabilities, these variables include, but are not limited to, experience in teaching students with disabilities, highest degree earned, gender, and perceived competence in teaching students with disabilities. These factors may provide insight into influences that determine beliefs and help us understand what occurs when physical educators teach students with disabilities or when families are interested in physical activity programs for their children with disabilities. In short, there is an association between beliefs about students with disabilities and teachers' and parents'/guardians' behavior about physical activity (PA) programs. Experiences, education, gender, and other salient variables notwithstanding, beliefs determine attitudes and subjective norms about intentions to teach students with disabilities and, ultimately, behavior in GPE or PA programs. It behoves researchers to review Ajzen and Fishbein's (1980) work to understand the conceptual and operational approach of this model.

Components of the TRA

Behavioral beliefs

The fundamental elements of both attitudes and subjective norms are behavioral beliefs. In order for us to know what the source of physical educators' attitudes and subjective norms are, we must identify and assess behavioral and normative beliefs. Behavioral beliefs link physical educators' responses to questions about teaching students with disabilities in GPE classes with expected outcomes. The strength of each belief is weighted by an evaluation associated with teaching students. Behavioral beliefs indicate the likelihood that teaching students will result in outcomes anchored by endpoints such as "likely–unlikely", "agree–disagree" and other appropriate markers. Physical educators may have numerous behavioral beliefs about teaching students with disabilities; however, the TRA and the TPB recommend that we will typically discover about five to seven salient beliefs when we survey people about their beliefs. In summary, both theories (TRA and TPB) suggest that beliefs, along with subjective values of the expected outcomes associated with teaching students with disabilities, are associated with attitude toward teaching students in GPE.

A sample behavioral belief item might read like this:

I will need more education before I can teach a student with level 1 autism spectrum disorders (ASD) *in my general physical education class in the next three weeks.*

    *strongly agree*_____:_____:_____:_____:_____:_____:_____*strongly disagree*

An evaluative belief statement might read like this:

It is not worth my effort to teach a student with level 1 ASD in my general physical education class in the next three weeks.

    *strongly agree*_____:_____:_____:_____:_____:_____:_____*strongly disagree*

Normative beliefs

The expectations of important people (e.g., principals, parents of students with disabilities) are normative beliefs. Both theories (TRA and TPB) state that normative beliefs, when taken collectively with the physical educator's motivation to comply with their specific referents, define the main subjective norms of teachers. The motivation to comply with the physical educators' social referents contributes to the subjective norm. The construct is measured by its proportion to the physical educators' subjective probability with what they believe the referent thinks about their teaching students with disabilities.

Here is an example of a normative belief statement:

My school principal thinks that I should teach a student with level 1 ASD in my GPE class in the next three weeks:

    *strongly agree*_____:_____:_____:_____:_____:_____:_____*strongly disagree*

Listed below is a sample of a subjective normative evaluative statement:

Generally speaking, I would do what my principal thinks I should do when teaching a student with level 1 ASD in my GPE class in the next three weeks.

    *strongly agree*_____:_____:_____:_____:_____:_____:_____*strongly disagree*

Physical educators' beliefs about how people in general feel about them teaching a student with ASD in their GPE should also be assessed. For instance, the survey could have a statement requesting a response to an item like this:

Most people who are important to me think that I should teach a student with level 1 ASD *in my GPE class in the next three weeks.*

    *strongly agree*_____:_____:_____:_____:_____:_____:_____*strongly disagree*

Physical educators' attitudes toward teaching students with disabilities in GPE are assessed with specific statements with end points such as "good or bad", "pleasant or unpleasant", "favorable or unfavorable", "positive or negative", and other reasonably acceptable end points. It is essential that attitude items are specific, written in precise language originating from physical educators to allow us to understand how they feel about teaching students with disabilities in GPE. In this theoretical model, attitude should relate with behavioral beliefs.

By knowing what components of the model may have an effect on teachers' intentions or behaviors, we can employ strategies during professional development to help implement effective practices related to teaching students with disabilities. Again, for details associated with the equations used to measure attitudes and the other components of the models, the interested reader should read the work of Ajzen (1991, 2017), and Ajzen and Fishbein (1980).

Here is a sample item to assess attitude:

For me, to teach a student with level 1 ASD in my GPE class in the next three weeks is:
$$good\_\_\_\_\_:\_\_\_\_\_:\_\_\_\_\_:\_\_\_\_\_:\_\_\_\_\_:\_\_\_\_\_:\_\_\_\_\_bad$$

Subjective norms

Another necessary element of the TRA is the concept of subjective norms. This concept is associated with beliefs that physical educators have about significant others (e.g., peers, principals, parents) and teaching students with disabilities. The subjective norm component is estimated by normative beliefs of people who physical educators value and associate with teaching students with disabilities. Physical educators' normative beliefs are determined by multiplying and then summing a scaled (weighted value) of the teachers' willingness to comply with subjective norms when thinking about teaching students with disabilities.

Intentions

We must also measure physical educators' intentions to teach students with disabilities. Intention tells us about physical educators' willingness to teach students with disabilities in their GPE classes. It is linked with the behavior associated with teaching students with disabilities. In the TRA and the TPB, intention is grounded in beliefs, attitude, and subjective norms weighted for their relative importance associated with teaching students with disabilities in GPE. Just because students with disabilities appear in GPE classes does not mean they are treated fairly and accepted by teachers and peers as valued class members.

Here is an example of an item to assess intention:

If a student with level 1 ASD appears in my general PE class in the next three weeks I will teach her/him.
$$strongly\ agree\_\_\_\_\_:\_\_\_\_\_:\_\_\_\_\_:\_\_\_\_\_:\_\_\_\_\_:\_\_\_\_\_:\_\_\_\_\_strongly\ disagree$$

Theory of planned behavior (TPB)

The main difference between the TRA and TBP models is that the TPB includes beliefs about PbC as an additional factor to measure the strength of intentions and understanding

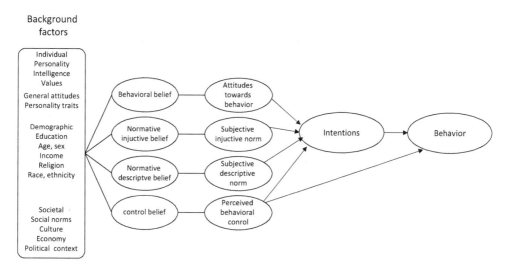

Figure 21.2 The theory of planned behavior with background factors. Adapted from Ajzen (2017)

behavior (Figure 21.2). The PbC component of the model asks physical educators to rate the extent to which they can teach students with disabilities in GPE classes. PbC will ask physical educators what factors would hinder or make it easier to teach students with disabilities in GPE. Alternatively, it is possible to ask physical educators what would prevent them from teaching students with disabilities. For instance, some factors that may impede physical educators' PbC to teach students with disabilities in GPE may include: large class sizes, a lack of academic preparation about modifying activities, a lack of knowledge about individualizing instruction within the context of group activities, and lack of paraprofessional teacher assistants.

Here is an example of a PbC item:

If I wanted to, I am confident I have the physical resources to teach a student with level 1 ASD in my general PE class in the next three weeks.

strongly agree_____:_____:_____:_____:_____:_____:_____strongly disagree

A word of caution

Oftentimes, researchers will adopt and modify existing instruments that appear in the literature for their use. While this is an expedient approach to conducting research, it is not acceptable or recommended unless the survey is theoretically driven and addresses the exact population of interest, target behavior, and context. For instance, it is acceptable to use a survey that assesses attitude toward teaching students with disabilities if the survey is an exact match with the researchers' intent. However, for example, using a survey designed for middle and high school classroom teachers is not acceptable for elementary school physical educators. Likewise, using a survey that was designed to assess attitudes toward teaching a student with an attention deficit disorder to assess attitudes toward teaching a student with ASD is not advisable.

Survey construction

Notwithstanding the population you wish to survey, you should follow the TPB protocol. In the TRA and its successor, the TPB, researchers must specify essential behavioral elements (e.g., behavior, target, context, and time) at the beginning stages of survey construction. For purpose of this chapter, those specific elements are teaching (behavior), students with disabilities (target), in GPE (context) at a specified period of time (e.g., in the next three weeks). The TPB survey construction begins with nine specific elicitation questions from which researchers develop the survey. The nine elicitation questions survey should match the population you want to investigate, the target (specific disabilities), context (GPE class or APE class) and time (in the next three weeks). At the first stage of constructing a TPB survey, these elements are identified by preparing nine questions to ask a small group of physical educators ($n = \sim25$) to enable you to construct a survey. A small sample of physical educators representative of the research population (e.g., elementary, middle or high school physical educators) is used to elicit readily accessible behavioral outcomes and normative referents. It is recommended that this sample represent the intended sample you will survey with your research. Although the physical educators can be assembled in groups to begin this process of survey construction, the elicitation should occur individually in a free response format with physical educators' responses recorded.

Eliciting salient beliefs

The basis for developing the TPB survey lies in the responses to nine questions to ask physical educators (Figure 21.3). For instance, start by asking the physical educator to take a few

---

Behavioral beliefs

1. What do you see as advantages of teaching students with level 1 ASD in your GPE classes in the next three weeks?
2. What do you see as disadvantages of teaching students with level 1 ASD in your GPE classes in the next three weeks?
3. What else comes to mind when you think about teaching students with level 1 ASD in your GPE classes in the next three weeks?

Subjective norms

4. When it comes to teaching students with level 1ASD in the next three weeks, what individuals or groups think you should teach these students in your GPE classes?
5. When it comes to your teaching students with level 1ASD in your GPE classes in the next three weeks, what individuals or groups think you should not teach these students in your classes?
6. Who else comes to mind when you think about teaching students with level 1 ASD in your GPE classes in the next three weeks?

Perceived behavioral control

7. What factors or circumstances would make it easy or enable you to teach students with level 1 ASD in your GPE classes in the next three weeks?
8. What factors or circumstances would make it difficult to teach students with level 1 ASD in your GPE classes in the next three weeks?
9. What other factors come to mind when you think about teaching students with level 1 ASD in your GPE classes in the next three weeks?

Figure 21.3 Nine elicitation beliefs for the TPB

minutes to tell you what s/he thinks about the possibility of teaching students with level 1 ASD in their GPE classes in the next three weeks. Tell the physical educator that there is no correct answer. Assure the teacher that you are simply interested in her/his personal opinions about teaching students with level 1 ASD in the GPE classes. On average, each interview will take about 15 minutes, with a range of 10–25 minutes per interview. This qualitative aspect of survey construction is essential to develop the ultimate survey. Participant responses serve as the basis for a thematic analysis.

Constructing sets of modal salient beliefs.

Thematic analysis

You and a colleague familiar with the TPB and thematic analysis should individually review the participant responses. Categorize responses to find patterns of salient beliefs and outcomes, salient referents, and control beliefs associated with teaching students with disabilities. Categorizing the response frequency for the nine elicitation questions will occur by summing the total number of salient responses from the interviews. You and your colleague should have about five to seven salient responses per question. To reach consensus, the two of you should come together to decide a level of agreement of physical educators' responses. Set an *a priori* level of 80% agreement to identify salient beliefs to serve as the basis for survey items (Neuman, 1997). The results from the thematic analysis are used to construct TPB items to be included in the final questionnaire.

Survey development

Survey items are developed according to the protocol of the TPB (Ajzen, 1991) with anchors (i.e., five-point Likert Scale—strongly agree to strongly disagree) to measure responses to statements. For example, an attitude item may be *"My teaching a student with level 1 ASD in my GPE class in the next three weeks is good idea"*. An intention item could read as: *"I intend to teach a student with level 1 ASD in my GPE class in the next three weeks"*. Your survey should clearly define the target. Try to keep the survey short, but not at the expense of compromising the TPB model.

Pilot test-survey

Plan on a pilot test of the survey to assess the clarity of survey items, estimate the amount of time necessary to complete the survey, identify any adverse issues, provide evidence to estimate an appropriate sample size, and improve upon the study design prior to the full-scale study. For your pilot test, consider surveying about 20–30 physical educators who did not take part in the interview phase of the survey development. Use participant feedback to gather comments or suggestions about survey items from the responses to the beliefs, attitude, and intention to teach a student with level 1 ASD. Ask for feedback to shore up your survey, especially suggestions to the nomenclature of your items. Use the data from the pilot study to revise your survey and provide data to establish sample size for the actual study.

The final survey

Establish content relevance for your survey using a model, such as Messick's (1989, 1995) theoretical framework to evaluate content relevance (i.e., validity). The framework

(Messick, 1989, 1995) uses six criteria (i.e., content, substantive, structural, generalizability, external, and consequential) to judge the content relevance. Following the Messick (1995) model, have experts review the survey for face and content validity and theoretical appropriateness (attributes associated with validity). Using the TPB for survey construction should meet the criteria for construct or substantive relevance. Establishing the structural aspect or representativeness of the survey takes place by judging the fidelity of the scoring structure to the structure of the content by using the correlation coefficients among theoretical components. Taken collectively, these suggested content relevance procedures are consistent with theoretical modeling recommended by Ajzen (1991) for survey development, Messick (1995) for establishing aspects of validity, Allen and Yen (1979) for sampling validity, and Kerlinger (1986) for content validity.

You can easily establish reliability of your survey by computing an alpha coefficient (Cronbach, 1951), an index of overall internal consistency (Allen & Yen, 1979). The alpha coefficient is used to account for any change that may occur as a result of the administration of your survey. Our surveys tend to have many items and place high demands on our respondents. Coefficient alpha helps us assess error variance due to fatigue, fluctuating attention, familiarity with the items, and even practice across your survey.

An overview of research on attitude toward teaching students with disabilities

In 2010, the United States Government Accounting Office (GAO) estimated that 92% of students with disabilities in grades 1–7 participated in GPE, while 88% of students with disabilities in grades 7–12 participated in GPE. Yet, the GAO report (2010) indicated that many teachers did not feel prepared to teach students with disabilities. The movement toward education of students with disabilities in GPE classes has changed the responsibilities of physical educators internationally in providing direct service to students with disabilities (Block & Obrusnikova, 2007; Cyran, Kudláček, Block, Malinowska-Lipień, & Zyznawska, 2017; Ozer et al., 2013). With the trend to teach students with disabilities in GPE classes, teacher education programs must modify their curricula in order to address the changing role of the physical educator (Block & Obrusnikova, 2007). As more students with disabilities appear in GPE classes, it is important that physical educators are prepared to teach students with disabilities using instructional strategies that promote learning and lead to a healthy, physically active lifestyle for students.

Many variables contribute to quality GPE experiences for students. As we have discussed, one important prerequisite for effective teaching and student learning are physical education teachers' favorable beliefs, attitudes, and intentions toward teaching students with disabilities in GPE classes (Beamer & Yun, 2014; Block & Obrusnikova, 2007; Hodge & Elliott, 2013; Obrusníková, 2008). Beliefs, attitudes, and related psychological constructs about teaching students with disabilities in GPE classes are part of a hidden curriculum, yet are a "starting point" (Petrie, Devcich, & Fitzgerald, 2018; Sherrill, 2004; Tanure Alves, Grenier, Haegele, & Duarte, 2018) toward successful educational experiences of students with disabilities. Consequently, physical education teacher education (PETE) programs must prepare future professionals to work in different contexts (e.g., school physical education, sport and PA environments) and with students with diverse abilities (Block & Obrusnikova, 2007; Casebolt & Hodge, 2010; Combs, Elliott, & Whipple, 2010; Hersman & Hodge, 2010). A few leaders have even called for a change in the culture of physical education (Tripp, Rizzo, & Webber, 2007) moving away from simply making activity modifications to making philosophical program changes in the physical education instructional processes and curriculum.

Studies have shown that several student- and teacher-related variables are associated with pre-service teachers' beliefs and attitudes towards teaching students with disabilities (Beamer & Yun, 2014; Hodge & Elliott, 2013; Obrusníková, 2008). However, it is difficult to draw definitive conclusions from this body of literature because of differences in research designs, limitations in the quality of the science (i.e., a lack of theoretically driven studies), individuals sampled, and survey instruments used. Nonetheless, several student- and teacher-related variables have been associated with beliefs and attitudes toward teaching students with disabilities.

The student-related variables, such as grade level and disability types, affect attitudes of physical education teachers. For instance, students in lower grade levels that have disabilities have been viewed more favorably than those in higher grade levels (Minner & Knutson, 1982; Rizzo, 1984). In addition, students with mild disabilities tend to be viewed more favorably than students with more severe disabilities (Casebolt & Hodge, 2010; Hodge, Ammah, Casebolt, LaMaster, & O'Sullivan, 2004; Hodge, Haegele, Gutierres, & Rizzi, 2018).

Teacher-related variables found to affect attitudes toward teaching students with disabilities include perceived competence, experience of teaching students with disabilities, and academic preparation in special education or APE. Attitudes of physical educators are more likely to be favorable in teachers who have higher perceived teaching competence (Beamer & Yun, 2014; Hodge et al., 2018; Ozer et al., 2013), more academic preparation in APE (Haegele, Hodge, Gutierres, & Gonçalves de Rezende, 2018; Hodge & Elliott, 2013; Hodge, Gutierres, Haegele, & Kozub, 2015; Oh et al., 2010; Pedersen, Cooley, & Hernandez, 2014) and experience associated with perceived competence about teaching individuals with disabilities (Beamer & Yun, 2014; Hodge et al., 2009; Obrusníková, 2008). Significantly, Tripp and Rizzo (2006) found that teacher beliefs and attitudes were less favorable about teaching a student with a disability label (i.e., ADHD) than a student with an identical description but without the label.

Other characteristics of physical educators, such as gender and age, have shown less consistent relationships with attitudes. Folsom-Meek and Rizzo (2002) found that women have more favorable attitudes toward teaching students with disabilities than men, but other studies (Petkova, Kudlácek, & Nikolova, 2012) revealed no significant gender differences. Of note, Hodge and Jansma (1999) reported that when initial gender differences were controlled by use of statistical procedures with the variable experience level as a covariate (ANCOVA), males and females were not significantly different in their attitudes toward teaching students with disabilities. Significant negative correlations were found between age and attitude (Oh et al., 2010). These results indicate that older physical educators possess less favorable attitudes than do their younger counterparts.

Pre-service teachers have many educational and experiential differences to those of teachers already in the field. That notwithstanding, investigators have consistently and successfully employed similar student- and teacher-related variables to explain favorable attitudes of future teachers. Furthermore, there are unique student-related variables that warrant consideration, such as the grade level of students with disabilities and the type of disability. Outcomes of research indicate that pre-service teachers have expressed mixed emotions about teaching students with disabilities. For example, Hodge, Davis, Woodard, and Sherrill (2002) found that future physical education teachers held favorable attitudes toward individuals with disabilities when participating in practicum experience. Conflictingly, however, Santiago,

Lee, and Roper (2016) examined the effects of a practicum experience on the attitudes of undergraduate kinesiology students toward children with disabilities, and found no difference in attitudes toward teaching children with disabilities between the students who participated in the practicum experience versus those who served as the control group. Other researchers found that physical education majors had less favorable attitudes toward teaching students with disabilities than their counterparts in elementary education, women had more favorable attitudes than men, and hands-on experiences make a positive impact on attitudes (Folsom-Meek & Rizzo, 2002).

It is important to emphasize that many of the aforementioned variables, including students' disability types and teachers' age and gender, can be under the control of teacher education programs in colleges and universities. For example, if a kinesiology or PETE program admits a vast majority of White teacher candidates and very few, if any, students of color, which happens often (Russell, Hodge, Frank, & Vaughn, 2018), the program, in fact, may impact such variables in terms of the teacher workforce. While it is important to understand the relationships between these variables and attitudes, the variables of greater interest to professionals involved in teacher preparation programs are those that educational institutions and programs of instruction can influence (Obrusníková, Válková, & Block, 2003). In this regard, findings from the previously cited studies involving factors that can be influenced suggest that favorable attitudes can be cultivated within educational institutions by providing physical educators with the most appropriate coursework and experience.

Limited research, coupled with differences in the quality of attitude instruments, individuals who participated, and the research design, make it difficult to draw definitive conclusions about how to influence psychological constructs. One reason why it is difficult to draw conclusions with this line of research is because, previously, many surveys used were a-theoretical (Haegele, Lee, & Porreta, 2015), or modified for use without regard to theoretical design or the population originally intended. Other studies used a survey that only addresses a part of the theoretical model (Kozub & Lienert, 2003). These issues underscore the need for technically correct and theoretically driven attitude research. That notwithstanding, it seems clear that teacher-related variables associated with teaching students with disabilities may affect the teaching–learning ecology of the GPE class.

It is essential for researchers to follow an ecological approach to understanding experiences of individuals with disabilities in society or GPE. For instance, assessing beliefs, attitudes, and intentions of physical educators is only one complex dimension of the ecological school milieu individuals with disabilities experience. Included in their life experiences are peers, families, parents/guardians, and students without disabilities. The TPB enables us to understand and explain the beliefs, attitudes, intentions, and behaviors of social normative groups such as peers—including peers without disabilities, teacher candidates, families, and, especially, parents/guardians.

TPB research application and significant others

Peers without disabilities

Researchers have used the TPB to explore the beliefs, intentions, and attitudes of children (Kwan, Cairney, Hay, & Faught, 2013; Obrusnikova, Block, & Dillon, 2010; Obrusnikova & Dillon, 2012). For example, using the TPB, Obrusnikova and Rocco-Dillon (2012) assessed beliefs and physical education goals associated with intentions of students without disabilities to play with a hypothetical peer with a physical disability in GPE. Results indicated that task-involved, social responsibility, and social intimacy significantly contributed to students' positive behavioral, normative, and control beliefs to play with a hypothetical peer with a physical disability in GPE.

Obrusnikova et al. (2010) assessed salient behavioral, normative, and control beliefs of children without disabilities toward playing with a hypothetical peer with a disability in their future physical education classes. Results from this study indicated that:

> Salient beliefs elicited provide the basis for constructing a theoretically sound TPB scale for use in intervention studies examining factors that affect intentions of children without disabilities to play with a peer with a disability in physical education. Development of such a scale can assist researchers and practitioners when designing strategies that facilitate social acceptance and inclusion in physical education settings. The ultimate goal of this line of research is to facilitate inclusive environments where children with disabilities are accepted as equals and foster positive socio-educational experiences for both children with and without disabilities.
>
> *(Obrusnikova et al., 2010, p. 140)*

Similarly, Kwan et al. (2013) assessed how theory-based PA cognitions (e.g., knowing the benefits of PA) influenced PA behaviors for children with and without disabilities. The authors reported deficits in PA motivation, and a greater need to promote positive attitudes among these children. Advocates for PA programs now recommend that when developing interventions to promote PA, one primary focus of attention should be on beliefs.

Parents

The intent of this handbook is to provide evidence-based information regarding the instruction of students with disabilities in school settings. In this chapter, we attempted to stay within those guidelines. However, there is a paucity of published research using the TPB associated with beliefs and attitudes of parents of children with disabilities toward PA, physical education, or physical literacy. In our view, one goal of a high quality, professionally designed APE program is the generalization of skills taught in physical education to PA settings in the community. Generalization of physical education skills requires physical educators to teach activities that are possible in community settings. Teaching parents how to generalize PA from school to the community is a colossal task, but it is a task that parents and their children want and need. Thus, in this section, we provide results from studies that have used the TPB to influence parents' beliefs, attitude, intentions, and behaviors to include their children in PA settings.

Parents are key stakeholders in the promotion of PA for children with disabilities (An & Goodwin, 2007; Pitchford, Siebert, Hamm, & Yun, 2016). Demonstrating positive attitudes toward PA may assist in the promotion of PA participation for their children with disabilities (Columna, Fernández-Vivó, Lieberman, & Arndt, 2015; Pitchford et al., 2016). Using the TPB, researchers have explored parental beliefs and intentions toward PA of parents of children with a variety of disabilities (Mihye, So-Yeun, & Euikyung, 2015)

Mihye et al. (2015), using the TPB as a theoretical framework, examined the validity and reliability evidence of a questionnaire regarding parents' beliefs and intentions toward supporting PA participation of their children with disabilities. Results from their study indicated that intentions to participate in PA were associated with behavior (e.g., supporting PA participation) of Korean parents of children with disabilities. These results indicate that parents with favorable behavioral and normative beliefs had greater intention to encourage their children with disabilities to participate in PA programs.

The implications for professionals who work with families are clear. There is a distinct need for us to teach parents about the benefits of PA and how to assist their children in participating in PA programs across the lifespan. The problem is that, because of the lack of communication, and the lack of experience in collaborating with parents, physical educators do not offer these opportunities to their students' families (Chaapel, Columna, Lytle, & Bailey, 2013; Columna, Cook, Foley, & Bailey, 2014; Mihye et al., 2015). Prerequisite to developing favorable behaviors in families about engaging with PA is understanding the contextual variables affecting the family unit.

For instance, Columna, Rocco-Dillon, Norris, Dolphin, and McCabe (2017), using the TPB as a theoretical framework, conducted a two-fold study with North American parents of children with visual impairments. First, the authors explored why families with children with visual impairments seek out and participate in PA (e.g., their motives to participation in PA). Then, they described the strategies and supports needed by these families to improve PA participation. Results indicated that parents valued PA but lacked skills to teach and advocate for their children to participate in PA programs. Consequently, parents expressed the need for a support system that would help their families become more physically active. Furthermore, parents requested interventions to teach them skills to engage in PA with their children.

To address the desires and PA needs of families of children with visual impairment and utilizing the TPB as a framework, Columna et al. (2018) and Columna et al. (2019) designed PA interventions or protocols in an effort to maximize PA opportunities for families. In Columna et al. (2018) and Columna et al. (2019), perceived behavioral control was operationalized as the perceived amount of control parents believed they have over engaging in PA with their child with a disability. The authors understood that some behaviors (e.g., parent-led PA at home) may be easier to perform, while others (e.g., integrating child into PA within community-based programming) may be considerably more difficult. Columna et al. (2019) found that after participating in the PA interventions, parents demonstrated a higher positive attitude about PA. Further, prior to the intervention, the participating parents indicated they lacked the skills necessary to teach PA to their children (Columna et al., 2017). However, parents perceived this PA intervention provided them with the tools to enhance their teaching skills. Consequently, their intentions and their behavior (engaging in PA) were also evident, as reported by the participating parents.

As previously mentioned, we believe, the goal of a well-designed physical education program should be of promoting PA participation and independent living skills associated with PA and leisure pursuits of children with disabilities and their families in their community. We believe, further, that physical education is the place where children can learn the skills to be physically active. However, for them to learn these skills, physical educators must have the teaching skills, attitudes, and intentions to promote an active engagement in their community.

Critics of the TPB

The TPB is not without its critics (Hagger, 2015; Sniehotta, Presseau, & Araújo-Soares, 2014). Critics have concerns with: (a) predictions of intentions and behaviors, (b) self-reports, (c) the subjective norm construct, (d) PbC versus self-efficacy, and (e) timing of measurements.

Prediction of intentions and behaviors

One criticism is that the TPB is less predictive of behavior when studies used a longitudinal, rather than a short-term, design, when participants were not university students, and when outcome measures were taken objectively rather than as a self-report (Sniehotta et al., 2014). Further, others challenge the validity and reliability of the TPB in which some (Rhodes & Dickau, 2012) indicated that changes in intentions do not necessarily translate to changes in behavior. Armitage and Conner (2001) state that intentions capture motivational factors that influence a behavior and to indicate how much a person is willing to try, or how much effort they are willing to exert, in performing that behavior. Yet, having the intentions or desires to perform a behavior does not mean that the behavior will be enacted. Therefore, researchers recommend that these critiques should be addressed. Most importantly, as previously highlighted, researchers have voiced the need for longitudinal studies.

Self-reports

Even though results from self-report instruments have been proven to predict intentions and behaviors better than objective measures, the use of self-reports is criticized (Sniehotta et al., 2014). Research using the TPB typically relies on self-reports by having participants complete a survey, raising questions about the validity or accuracy of the response set. These researchers offered solutions to this limitation and recommended the use of objective measures of exercise (e.g., actual attendance at a fitness facility) and diverse samples of multiple age groups or clinical populations to strengthen the cross-validation of the findings.

Subjective norm construct

Another criticism is related to the validity of the construct of subjective norm and its relation to intentions (Hagger, 2015). Critics state the construct of subjective norm has not performed well in explaining exercise intentions across studies when controlling for attitude and perceived behavioral control (Rhodes, Courneya, & Jones, 2002). For instance, Downs and Hausenblas (2005) indicated that some of the reasons for inconsistency among TPB subjective normative constructs may occur because: (a) significant others might not play an important role in exercise intentions for individuals who are physically active, and (b) it is not well understood whether people's exercise intentions are influenced by their motivation to comply with the belief that others want them to exercise, or whether it is the actual presence of social support associated with exercising that influences their intentions. As such, it is believed that social support might be a better predictor of intentions than subjective norm. However, data in this regard are inconclusive.

PbC versus self-efficacy

According to Ajzen (2002), PbC is a better predictor of exercise behavior than self-efficacy. Whereas self-efficacy focuses on the cognitive perceptions of control based on internal factors, PbC focuses primarily on external factors (Armitage & Conner, 2001). In other words, PbC is defined as the perceived ease or difficulty of performing a behavior (Rhodes et al., 2002). Self-efficacy, on the other hand, is defined as an individual's personal confidence in his/her own abilities to carry out a behavior.

In this regard, Ajzen (2002) asserted that PbC comprises two components: self-efficacy and controllability. Self-efficacy refers to the ease or difficulty of performing a behavior, whereas controllability refers to the extent to which performing a behavior is up to the individual. As such, when measuring PbC, Ajzen (2002) recommends that survey instruments should include self-efficacy and controllability items.

Timing of the measurement

Scholars assert that when measuring intentions, this should be in close proximity to performing the behavior (Ajzen & Fishbein, 2000). To this end, Downs and Hausenblas (2005) conducted a meta-analysis review to examine the influences of five moderator variables. One of the hypotheses of this study was that a larger intention–behavior association would be evidenced when the time interval between intention and behavior is shorter rather than longer. The results of this study regarding time interval indicated that intention–behavior association was larger in studies that measured intention and behavior within a one-month period compared to the studies with a larger time interval. For this reason, the authors recommend measuring exercise behavior within one month of the assessment of the intentions.

Recommendations to improve constructs of the TPB

A single theory cannot explain all factors relevant to human behaviors. Noar and Head (2014) indicated that behavior involves both motivation and action. They indicated that the TPB focuses primarily on the motivational aspect of behaviors, without accounting for other factors that can influence the actual behavior (e.g., barriers to PA). In response to these critics, Ajzen (2015) clearly states the TPB is a theory that explains intentions and behaviors.

Undoubtedly, the contributions of the TPB are evident in the extraordinary number of scientific papers using the theory to measure the relationship between intentions and behaviors (Hagger, 2015). However, concerns have been raised because the theory has not been revised (Noar & Head, 2014), even when some constructs have been weak in predicting intentions or the actual behaviors. On this subject, for example, Rhodes et al. (2002) proposed the addition of a social support construct. It is worth noting that Ajzen (2015) states that there is nothing in the TPB to prevent the expansion of new indicators based on scientific evidence. Therefore, he welcomed additions that are well justified and make intuitive sense. This was the case of the TRA, resulting in Ajzen (1991) adding the construct of perceived behavioral control, giving origin to the TPB.

However, if new constructs are added, this will alter the nature of the relationships expressed (Sniehotta et al., 2014). Sniehotta et al. (2014) indicated if new constructs are added, then these new constructs need to be validated. These authors stated (p. 13),

> For a viable extension of a theory, authors should first formalize the extended theory, or a version or a variant of a theory and then test it. Once an extended or modified theory is shown to be superior, its predecessor can be retired.

Hagger (2015) identified several suggestions to enhance the theory. For example, Hagger indicated that most of the research using the TPB has been short-term follow-ups, using mainly correlational designs, direct measures, and self-report behavioral assessments. Hagger (2015, pp. 127–128) asserted,

The current debate does much to highlight how theory and thinking of health behavior has moved on from the static, short-term, correlational tests of the theory and has provided some thoughtful suggestions as to how social and health psychologists can continue to advance knowledge and thinking of the processes and mechanisms that underpin health behavior forward.

For this reason, Hagger (2015) and others (Sniehotta et al., 2014) proposed the use of experimental research to test health behaviors. One of the limitations of cross-sectional designs, according to Noar and Head (2014), is that this type of research tends to inflate evidence for theory. These are only few of the plethora of recommendations to enhance the TPB found in the literature.

Recommendation for interventions

Ajzen (2015) provides a detailed response to the challenges presented by Sniehotta et al. (2014) and Rhodes et al. (2002) to the TPB. Ajzen (2015) asserts that the TPB can be used as a framework for designing interventions. However, certain considerations must be in place. For example, Ajzen (2015) indicated that the TPB is less effective in interventions with individuals who are already motivated (e.g., positive attitudes toward PA). To address this issue, Sniehotta et al. (2014) recommend a needs assessment to identify attitudes prior to an intervention.

With this in mind, Rhodes et al. (2002) indicated that when using the TPB as a framework and when working with unmotivated individuals, the focus of these interventions should be on beliefs and attitudes. Attitudes influence intention and, ultimately, behavior. Downs and Hausenblas (2005) indicated that individuals' attitudes (how people feel about themselves) is associated with an individual's intention to exercise. In other words, if you feel good about yourself, most likely you will perform an activity. If an intervention helps an individual's self-concept, he or she will feel good about their "self", they will feel more comfortable and competent, and, in turn, their beliefs, attitudes, and intentions about engaging in PA improve. Theoretically speaking, as intentions to participate in PA improve, the likelihood of engaging in PA increases (Ajzen, 2002).

In addition to assessing individuals' beliefs and attitudes toward a behavior, it is also important to assess their past experiences with the behavior. Favorable or unfavorable past experiences will impact beliefs, attitudes, and intentions to pursue PA. Even though it is known that there are certain variables that tend to predict behaviors, Sniehotta et al. (2014) asserted that it is more important to know how we can promote change. One of the variables that seems to be effective in promoting behavior change is goal setting (Rhodes et al., 2002). As such, Rhodes et al. (2002) stated that interventions must be in place that teach participants about time management and setting achievable goals.

Downs and Hausenblas (2005) indicated that the association between self-efficacy and intention was greater than for perceived behavioral control–intention and perceived barriers–intention. However, contrary to their expectations, the association for self-efficacy–behavior was larger than perceived barriers–behavior but not compared to perceived behavioral control–behavior. According to the authors, these findings are fundamental when trying to implement intervention research because they suggest that self-efficacy (e.g., one's beliefs about one's ability to be active) could be more important than perceived behavioral control (e.g., resources and skills to be active) for influencing a person's exercise intention.

Summary

- In this chapter, the authors' emphasized the importance for using theory when one is interested in assessing beliefs and attitudes associated with teaching students with disabilities, as well as peers', families', and parents/guardians' attitudes and intentions toward engaging in PA programs.
- Included in the presentation was a brief overview about attitude theory and the TPB and the TRA. The theory presentation is followed by an overview of research on physical educators' attitudes toward teaching students with disabilities. It concludes with an application of the TPB associated with peers, families, and parents/guardians.
- The implications of this chapter indicate that attitude research must follow a rigorous scientific approach as we advance our knowledge about individuals with disabilities and physical education/activity.
- Much work is needed to address the issues that appear in the research, including the need to use a theoretical model to advance our knowledge base.
- Identification and development of favorable attitudes and the factors associated with positive behaviors toward teaching students with disabilities in GPE is essential.

Reflective questions

1. Can a physical education curriculum in a public school affect teacher beliefs and attitudes toward teaching students with disabilities in GPE classes?
2. Using the theory of planned behavior as a framework, how would you design an intervention targeting teachers and the parents of children with disabilities in regard to the teaching of physical education concepts, especially physical literacy, at school and at home?
3. How do today's teachers' beliefs and attitudes compare with those of 35 years ago?
4. What external variables influence physical educators' beliefs and attitudes?
5. Who influences teachers' beliefs and attitudes toward teaching students with disabilities in physical education?
6. Does the type of disability associated with a student influence physical educators' willingness to teach children with a disability?
7. Does a label associated with a disability affect physical educators' beliefs and attitudes?
8. What factors influence parents' beliefs, attitudes and intentions to engage their families in physical activity across the lifespan?
9. Can physical activity interventions support the physical education curriculum by providing parents with the strategies to promote physical activities with their children, especially those with disabilities?
10. Taking into consideration the critics of the TPB, how would you revise the theory to be more applicable to adapted physical education?

References

Ajzen, I. (1991). The theory of planned behavior. *Organizational Behavior and Human Decision Processes, 50,* 179–211.
Ajzen, I. (2002). *Constructing a TPB questionnaire: Conceptual and methodological considerations.* Retrieved from www.people.umass.edu/aizen/TPB.html.

Ajzen, I. (2015). The theory of planned behaviour is alive and well, and not ready to retire: A commentary on Sniehotta, Presseau, and Araújo-Soares. *Health Psychology Review, 9*(2), 131–137.

Ajzen, I. (2017). The theory of planned behavior with background factors. Retrieved from http://people. umass.edu/aizen/TPB.background.html.

Ajzen, I., & Fishbein, M. (1980). *Understanding attitudes and predicting social behavior.* New Jersey: Englewood Cliffs.

Ajzen, I., & Fishbein, M. (2000). Attitudes and the attitude-behavior relation: Reasoned and automatic processes. In W. Stroebe & M. Hewstone (Eds.), *European Review of Social Psychology* (pp. 1–33). Hoboken, NJ: John Wiley & Sons.

Allen, M. J., & Yen, W. M. (1979). *Introduction to measurement theory.* Belmont, CA: Wadsworth.

Allport, G. W. (1935). Attitudes. In C. Murchison (Ed.), *A handbook of social Psychology* (pp. 798–844). Worcester, MA.: Clark University Press.

An, J., & Goodwin, D. L. (2007). Physical education for students with spina bifida: Mothers' perspectives. *Adapted Physical Activity Quarterly, 24*(1), 38–58.

Armitage, C. J., & Conner, M. (2001). Efficacy of the theory of planned behaviour: A meta-analytic review. *British Journal of Social Psychology, 40*(4), 471. doi:10.1348/014466601164939

Baldwin, J. M. (1901-1905). *Dictionary of philosophy and psychology (3 vols.).* New York: MacMillian.

Beamer, J. A., & Yun, J. (2014). Physical educators' beliefs and self-reported behaviors towards including students with autism spectrum disorder. *Adapted Physical Activity Quarterly, 31*, 362–376. doi:10.1123/apaq.2014-0134

Block, M. E., & Obrusnikova, I. (2007). Inclusion in physical education: A review of the Literature from 1995-2005. *Adapted Physical Activity Quarterly, 24*, 103–124.

Casebolt, K. M., & Hodge, S. R. (2010). High school physical education teachers' beliefs about teaching students with mild to severe disabilities. *Physical Educator, 67*(3), 140–155.

Chaapel, H., Columna, L., Lytle, R., & Bailey, J. (2013). Parental expectations about adapted physical education services. *The Journal of Special Education, 47*(3), 186–196. doi:10.1177/0022466912447661

Columna, L., Cook, A., Foley, J. T., & Bailey, J. (2014). Survey development to assess parental satisfaction with adapted physical education teachers' abilities working with children with autism. *Physical Education and Sport Pedagogy, 19*(5), 481–493.

Columna, L., Dillon, S. R., Dolphin, M., Streete, D. A., Hodge, S. R., Myers, B., … Heffernan, K. S. (2019). Physical activity participation among families of children with visual impairments and blindness. *Disability and Rehabilitation, 41*(3), 357–365. doi:10.1080/09638288.2017.1390698.

Columna, L., Fernández-Vivó, M., Lieberman, L. J., & Arndt, K. (2015). Recreational physical activity experiences among Guatemalan families with children with visual impairments. *Journal of Physical Activity and Health, 12*(8), 1119–1127. doi:10.1123/jpah.2014-0257

Columna, L., Rocco-Dillon, S., Norris, M. L., Dolphin, M., & McCabe, L. (2017). Parents' perceptions of physical activity experiences for their families and children with visual impairments. *British Journal of Visual Impairments, 35*(2), 88–102. doi:10.1177/0264619617691081

Columna, L., Streete, D. A., Hodge, S. R., Dillon, S. R., Myers, B., Norris, M. L., … Heffernan, K. S. (2018). Parents' beliefs about physical activity for their children with visual impairments. *Adapted Physical Activity Quarterly, 35*(4), 361–380.

Combs, S., Elliott, S., & Whipple, K. (2010). Elementary physical education teachers' attitudes towards the inclusion of children with special needs: A qualitative investigation. *International Journal of Special Education, 25*, 114–125.

Cronbach, L. J. (1951). Coefficient alpha and the internal structure of tests. *Psychometrika, 16*(3), 297–334.

Cyran, M., Kudláček, M., Block, M., Malinowska-Lipień, I., & Zyznawska, J. (2017). Attitudes of teachers towards inclusion of students with disabilities in physical education: Validity of the ATIPDPE-R instrument in Polish cultural context. *Acta Gymnica, 47*(4), 171–179.

Downs, D., & Hausenblas, H. A. (2005). The theories of reasoned action and planned behavior applied to exercise: A meta-analytic update. *Journal of Physical Activity and Health, 2*(1), 76–97. doi:10.1123/jpah.2.1.76

Fishbein, M. (1963). An investigation of the relationships between beliefs about an object and the attitude toward that object. *Human Relations, 16*, 233–240.

Fishbein, M., & Ajzen, I. (1975). *Belief, attitude, intention, and behavior: An introduction to theory and research.* Reading, MS.: Addison-Wesley.

Folsom-Meek, S., & Rizzo, T. L. (2002). Validating the physical educators' attitudes toward teaching individuals with disabilities (PEATID III) survey for future professionals. *Adapted Physical Activity Quarterly, 19*(2), 141–154. doi:http://dx.doi.org/10.1123/apaq.19.2.141.

Government Accountability Office (2010). Students with disabilities: More information and guidance could improve opportunities in physical education and athletics. Report to Congressional Requestors. Retrieved from: www.gao.gov/products/GAO-10-519.

Guttman, L. (1944). A basis for scaling qualitative data. *American Sociological Review, 9*, 139–150.

Haegele, J. A., Hodge, S. R., Gutierres Filho, P. J. B., & Gonçalves de Rezende, A. L. (2018). Brazilian physical education teachers' attitudes before and after participation in a professional development workshop. *European Physical Education Review, 24*(1), 21–38. doi:10.1177/1356336X16662898.

Haegele, J. A., Lee, J., & Porreta, D. L. (2015). Research trends in adapted physical activity quarterly from 2004 to 2013. *Adapted Physical Activity Quarterly, 32*(3), 187–206. doi:http://dx.doi.org/10.1123/APAQ.2014-0232.

Hagger, M. S. (2015). Retired or not, the theory of planned behaviour will always be with us. *Health Psychology Review, 9*(2), 125–130. doi:10.1080/17437199.2015.1034470.

Hersman, B. L., & Hodge, S. R. (2010). High school physical educators' beliefs about teaching differently abled students in an urban school district. *Education and Urban Society, 42*(6), 730–757.

Hodge, S., Ammah, J. O. A., Casebolt, K. M., LaMaster, K., Hersman, B., Samalot-Rivera, A., & Sato, T. (2009). A diversity of voices: Physical education teachers' beliefs about inclusion and teaching students with disabilities. *International Journal of Disability Development and Education, 56*(4), 401–419. doi:10.1080/10349120903306756.

Hodge, S. R., Ammah, J. O., Casebolt, K., LaMaster, K., & O'Sullivan, M. (2004). High school general physical education teachers' behaviors and beliefs associated with inclusion. *Sport, Education, & Society, 9*(3), 395–419.

Hodge, S. R., Davis, R., Woodard, R., & Sherrill, C. (2002). Comparison of practicum types in changing preservice teachers' attitudes and perceived competence. *Adapted Physical Activity Quarterly, 19*, 155–171.

Hodge, S. R., & Elliott, G. (2013). Physical education majors' judgments about inclusion and teaching students with disabilities. *Journal of Education and Training Studies, 1*, 151–157. doi:10.11114/jets.v1i1.88.

Hodge, S. R., Gutierres Filho, P. J. B., Haegele, J. A., & Kozub, F. M. (2015). Underlying dimensions of the *Physical Educators' Judgments about Inclusion* instrument: Brazilian-version. *Journal of Curriculum and Teaching, 4*(2), 96–103. doi:10.5430/jct.v4n2p.

Hodge, S. R., Haegele, J. A., Gutierres Filho, P. J. B., & Rizzi Lopes, G. (2018). Brazilian physical education teachers' beliefs about teaching students with disabilities. *International Journal of Disability, Development and Education, 65*(4), 408–427. doi:10.1080/1034912X.2017.1408896.

Hodge, S. R., & Jansma, P. (1999). Effects of contact time and location of practicum experiences on attitudes of physical education majors. *Adapted Physical Activity Quarterly, 16*, 48–63.

Kerlinger, F. N. (1986). *Foundations of behavioral research*. Chicago: Holt, Rinehart, & Winston.

Kozub, F. M., & Lienert, C. (2003). Attitudes toward teaching children with disabilities: Review of literature and research paradigm. *Adapted Physical Activity Quarterly, 20*, 323–346.

Kwan, M. Y., Cairney, J., Hay, J. A., & Faught, B. E. (2013). Understanding physical activity and motivations for children with developmental coordination disorder: An investigation using the theory of planned behavior. *Research in Developmental Disabilities, 34*(11), 3691–3698.

LaPiere, R. T. (1934). Attitudes versus. actions. *Social Forces, 13*, 230–237.

Likert, R. A. (1932). *A technique for the measurement of attitudes*. New York: Archives of Psychology.

Messick, S. (1989). Validity. In R. L. Linn (Ed.), *Educational measurement* (3rd ed., pp. 13–103). New York: Macmillan.

Messick, S. (1995). Validity of psychological assessment: Validation of inferences from persons' responses and performances as scientific inquiry into score meaning. *American Psychologist, 50*, 741–749.

Mihye, J., So-Yeun, K., & Euikyung, L. (2015). Parents' beliefs and intentions toward supporting physical activity participation for their children with disabilities. *Adapted Physical Activity Quarterly, 32*(2), 93–105.

Minner, S. H., & Knutson, R. (1982). Mainstreaming handicapped students into physical education: Initial considerations. *The Physical Educator, 39*, 13–15.

Neuman, W. L. (1997). *Social research methods: Qualitative and quantitative approaches* (3rd ed., pp. 138–139). Boston: Allyn and Bacon.

Noar, S. M., & Head, K. J. (2014). Mind the gap: Bringing our theories in line with the empirical data – A response to commentaries. *Health Psychology Review*, *8*(1), 65–69. doi:10.1080/17437199.2013.855593

Obrusníková, I. (2008). Physical educators' beliefs about teaching children with disabilities. *Perceptual and Motor Skills*, *106*, 637–644.

Obrusnikova, I., Block, M., & Dillon, S. (2010). Children's beliefs toward cooperative playing with peers with disabilities in physical education. *Adapted Physical Activity Quarterly*, *27*(2), 127–142. doi:10.1123/apaq.27.2.127.

Obrusnikova, I., & Dillon, S. R. (2012). Students' beliefs and intentions to play with peers with disabilities in physical education: Relationships with achievement and social goals. *Journal of Teaching in Physical Education*, *31*(4), 311–328. doi:10.1123/jtpe.31.4.311

Obrusníková, I., Válková, H., & Block, M. (2003). Impact of inclusion in general physical education on students without disabilities. *Adapted Physical Activity Quarterly*, *20*, 230–245.

Oh, H. K., Rizzo, T. L., So, H. S., Chung, D. H., Park, S. J., & Lei, Q. (2010). Preservice physical education teachers' attributes related to teaching a student labeled ADHD. *Teaching and Teacher Education*, *26*, 885–890. doi:10.1016/j.tate.2009.10.027.

Osgood, C. E., Suci, G. J., & Tannennbaum, R. H. (1957). *The measurement of meaning*. Urbana, Ill.: The University of Illinois Press.

Ozer, D., Nablant, S., Aglamis, E., Baran, F., Kaya Samut, P., Aktop, A., & Hutzler, Y. (2013). The impact of time in service, gender, and previous acquaintance. *Journal of Intellectual Disability Research*, *57*(11), 1001–1013. doi:10.1111/j.1365-2788.2012.01596.x.

Pedersen, S. J., Cooley, P. D., & Hernandez, K. (2014). Are Australian pre-service physical education teachers prepared to teach inclusive physical education?. *Australian Journal of Teaching Education*, *39*(4), 53–62.

Petkova, A., Kudlácek, M., & Nikolova, E. (2012). Attitudes of physical education students (last university year) and physical education teachers toward teaching children with physical disabilities in general physical education classes in Bulgaria. *European Journal of Adapted Physical Activity*, *5*(2), 82–98.

Petrie, K., Devcich, J., & Fitzgerald, H. (2018). Working toward inclusive physical education in primary school: 'Some days I just don't get it right'. *Physical Education & Sport Pedagogy*, *23*(4), 345–357.

Pitchford, E. A., Siebert, E., Hamm, J., & Yun, J. (2016). Parental perceptions of physical activity benefits for youth with developmental disabilities. *American Journal of Intellectual and Developmental Disabilities*, *121*(1), 25–32. doi:10.1352/1944-7558-121.1.25.

Rhodes, R. E., & Dickau, L. (2012). Experimental evidence for the intention-behavior relationship in the physical activity domain: A meta-analysis. *Health Psychology*, *31*(6), 724–727.

Rhodes, R. E., Courneya, K. S., & Jones, L. W. (2002). Personality, the theory of planned Behavior, and exercise: A unique role for extroversion's activity face. *Journal of Applied Social Psychology*, *32*(8), 1721–1736.

Rizzo, T. L. (1984). Attitudes of physical educators toward teaching handicapped pupils. *Adapted Physical Activity Quarterly*, *1*, 263–274.

Rosenberg, M. J. (1956). Cognitive structure and attitudinal affect. *Journal of Abnormal and Social Psychology*, *53*, 367–372.

Russell, J. A., Hodge, S. R., Frank, A. M., & Vaughn, M. (2018). Academic administrators' beliefs about diversity. *Quest*, *71*(1), 66–89. doi:10.1080/00336297.2018.1525569.

Santiago, J. A., Lee, J., & Roper, E. A. (2016). The influence of a service-learning on kinesiology students' attitudes toward teaching children with disabilities. *Journal of Higher Education Outreach and Engagement*, *20*(2), 109–126.

Sherrill, C. (2004). *Adapted physical activity, recreation, and sport: Crossdisciplinary and lifespan* (6th ed.). Dubuque, IA: WCB/McGraw–Hill.

Sniehotta, F. F., Presseau, J., & Araújo-Soares, V. (2014). Time to retire the theory of planned behaviour. *Health Psychology Review*, *8*(1), 1–7. doi:10.1080/17437199.2013.869710.

Spencer, H. (1862). *First Principles*. New York: Burt.

Tanure Alves, M. L., Grenier, M., Haegele, J. A., & Duarte, E. (2018). 'I didn't do anything, I just watched': Perspectives of Brazilian students with physical disabilities toward physical education. *International Journal of Inclusive Education*. doi:10.1080/13603116.2018.1511760.

Thomas, W. I., & Znaniecki, F. (1918). *The Polish peasant in Europe and America*. Boston: Badger.

Thurstone, L. L. (1929). The theory of attitude measurement. *Psychological Bulletin, 36,* 222–241.

Thurstone, L. L. (1931). The measurement of attitudes. *Journal of Abnormal and Social Psychology, 26,* 222–241.

Triandis, H. C. (1964). Exploratory factor analysis of the behavioral component of social attitudes. *Journal of Abnormal and Social Psychology, 68,* 420–430.

Tripp, A., & Rizzo, T. L. (2006). Disability labels affect physical educators. *Adapted Physical Activity Quarterly, 23,* 310–326.

Tripp, A., Rizzo, T. L., & Webber, L. (2007). Inclusion in physical education: Changing the culture; Creating truly inclusive environment requires a change in culture. *Journal of Physical Education, Recreation, and Dance, 78*(2), 32–36.

22

Motivational theories

Jeffrey J. Martin, Erin Snapp, and Leah Ketcheson

Introduction

The purpose of this chapter is to introduce the reader to motivational theories that are applicable to adapted physical education (APE) as well as adapted physical activity (APA) settings for children and youth and influential adults in these settings, such as teachers. More specifically, we examine identity theory, expectancy value theory (EVT), competence motivation theory, self-worth theory, the transtheoretical (TTM), and health action process approach (HAPA) models. After describing each theory, we also review the limited research done with them. Few APE researchers have used the motivational theories we discuss, making our review of the knowledge base short. Hence, we spend considerable time discussing future research directions and how each theory can be implemented in applied settings, such as after-school APA programs for children in addition to APE. Some of the above theories are developmental in nature and have been used to guide youth sport and physical activity (PA) research with children without disabilities for the past 40 years. In contrast, other theories have been used in health and exercise psychology examining adults. We examine the lessons learned and insights gained in both able-bodied youth research and adult disability research to provide future research directions. Our goal here is to help APE researchers avoid repeating mistakes noted in prior research in order to craft meaningful research projects in APE and APA settings.

Before discussing each theory, associated research, and future research, we emphasize four important points that come from years of research with youth without disabilities (Gould, 1982; Weiss & Bredemeier, 1983) and youth with disabilities (Martin, 2018). First, researchers in APE should ask important research questions that will eventually lead to enhancing the sport and PA experiences of children with disabilities. Furthermore, researchers are urged to test and refine existing theory (Gould, 1982). Relative to youth in able-bodied sport, the experiences of an impairment (e.g., chronic pain), peer relationship challenges (e.g., bullying and teasing), and parental influence (e.g., heightened worry) may all necessitate theory refinement and/or building to account for the uniqueness of disability sport and PA. Second, given the age range of participants in APE, researchers should strive to employ theory that has a cognitive–developmental perspective (Weiss & Bredemeier, 1983). For example, APE researchers have often studied perceived competence and self-esteem in children with disabilities, yet have rarely considered developmental processes. Thelma Horn has written extensively on how sources of perceived competence change over time and how the multi-dimensionality of self-esteem also varies developmentally (e.g.,

Horn & Butt, 2014). Researchers in APE are encouraged to consult developmental-based youth sport research for insights on how similar research might be conducted in APE. For example, researchers have shown that, in general physical education, children's intrinsic motivation and enjoyment declines over time, but we do not know if that is the case in APE (Barkoukis, Ntoumanis, & Thøgersen-Ntoumani, 2010; Digelidis & Papaioannou, 1999).

Third, some theories are likely very applicable to guiding research with students with disabilities because of their development focus (i.e., EVT, competence motivation theory, self-worth theory), whereas other theories (i.e., TTM, HAPA) are inherently more applicable to research with adults (e.g., teachers, paraeducators) in APE settings. Finally, some theories (such as identity theory) can be used to understand both youth and adults in APE and APA. Readers will note that a host of self-perceptions are discussed in this chapter with important and subtle distinctions among them. However, most (self-efficacy, self-worth, competence, perceived competence) involve self-judgements about one's worth and capabilities. In physical education (PE) many children with disabilities have limited or no opportunities to develop skills, enjoy PA games, and develop expectations of success (hallmarks of EVT) as they often sit on the sidelines, are assigned sedentary roles (e.g., team manager) or receive medical excuses to not participate.

In other cases, games and sports are not adapted and, as a result, the ability to learn and experience success and enjoy the positive feelings associated with mastery are rare. For instance, Kalyvas and Reid (2003) compared adapted to general physical education activities and found a discouraging pattern. In the games (with no adaptations), compared to adapted games, children had less active time on task, more inactive time on task, fewer successful passes (about one) and more unsuccessful passes. Effect sizes for the differences were typically moderate to large (-.6–0.8). As might be anticipated, the children with disabilities enjoyed the game with adaptations more than the game void of adaptations. We next discuss the following six theories: identity theory, EVT, competence motivation theory, self-worth theory, and the TTM and HAPA models.

Identity theory

We use identity theory as an umbrella term to designate a wide range of research that falls under different "identity" theoretical orientations. For instance, social identity theory focuses on highly valued group membership that becomes part of a person's identity (Tajfel, 2010). Many researchers studying identity theory hold a psychological perspective that highlights how psychological processes influence group membership (Tajfel, 2010). For example, in disability sport, Martin (2018) speculated on whether a strong military identity held by injured veterans might motivate them to join adapted sport organizations such as the wounded warriors. Other researchers have examined how group membership might influence cognition and behavior. For instance, does being a member of a Paralympic team increase motivated behavior and enhance self-esteem?

Much of the research done in disability sport has focused on adults and how an athletic identity results in adaptive as well as maladaptive behaviors (e.g., Guerrero & Martin, 2018; Martin, 2013, 2015, 2018; Martin, Mushett-Adams, & Smith, 1995; Martin & Vitali, 2011). However, a small body of work with schoolchildren has been conducted. In one study, 21 boys and girls discussed the role of PA and sport (Taub & Greer, 2000). One unique finding highlighted how sport and peer interactions helped children with disabilities claim an identity as a "child", feel similar to their peers, and feel accepted (Taub & Greer, 2000). Other researchers have found that sporting opportunities designed specifically for individuals with disabilities were of value (Groff & Kleiber, 2001). Such opportunities contributed to a feeling that participants could express themselves fully and claim a "self" identity that felt genuine and that they could "be themselves" (Groff & Kleiber, 2001, p. 329). In a third study examining the influence of sport participation, the researchers also found that participants reported an identity that included feeling "normal" as a major benefit to participating in sport with individuals without disabilities (Lundberg, Taniguchi, McCormick, & Tibbs, 2011). According to Lundberg et al. (2011), feeling "normal" is represented by the following: doing things other people can do, enjoying hanging out with friends, and not feeling different. Sport and PA experiences allows children with disabilities to interact with peers, demonstrate ability, have similarities (e.g., the joy of playing sport) highlighted, and differences accepted.

Participation in Special Olympic programming has also been established to improve physical, psychological/emotional, social, and identity related outcomes in individuals with developmental disabilities (Tint, Thomson, & Weiss, 2017). In fact, competition in Special Olympic World Games has been shown to contribute to an athlete's self-identity, where factors such as recognition of athletic ability and pride in athletic accomplishments led to the development of an enhanced athletic self-identity (Werner, 2015). Further, several researchers have identified enhanced views of self following participation in Special Olympic programming (Weiss & Bebko, 2008; Weiss, Diamond, Demark, & Lovald, 2003). Specifically, longitudinal participation in Special Olympic activities (Weiss & Bebko, 2008) and the opportunity for competition (Weiss et al., 2003) were cited as contributing factors that positively enhance an athlete's identity.

While Special Olympic is most commonly associated with sport and game competitions for individuals with intellectual disabilities, initiatives to promote a more inclusive school and community culture have recently surfaced as a national priority. Special Olympics Unified Champion Schools© extends the concepts from Special Olympic to promote social inclusion through sport. Schools who adopt this framework host inclusive sports, leadership opportunities, and whole school programs. Emerging research from the Unified Sport program suggests there are positive psycho-social benefits in athletes with and without disabilities who participate in such programming. In one study that measured the outcomes of an eight-week long Unified Sports soccer program, high school athletes with disabilities significantly increased their social competency and positive self-perceptions (Özer et al., 2012). In this same study, participating athletes without disabilities improved their attitudes and positive impressions of their peers with disabilities (Özer et al., 2012). In a separate study examining the self-image in athletes with disabilities who had participated in a Unified Sports program, a positive correlation between perceived athletic competence and positive self-image was discovered (Bota, Teodorescu, & Şerbănoiu, 2014).

In a qualitative study examining the parental perspectives on their child's participation in community sport activities, a high value was placed on the importance of feeling "accepted, included and equal" (Renker, Helmer, Panetta, Pimentel, & Sawanec, 2017), meaning that for children with disabilities who had engaged in community sport programs, parents believed that their participation contributed to their overall sense of self. Collectively, these findings support that participation in a community-based sport program such as Special Olympic Unified Sports, can promote a positive self-identity in individuals both with and without disabilities. However, larger scaled studies examining the nature of social inclusion are needed.

While integrated adapted sport programming has been shown to positively contribute towards the identity of self, it is equally important to explore the impact of adapted sport settings for students with disabilities. There is evidence to suggest that adapted sport settings where all participating children have impairments can be particularly uplifting. The mutual understanding of living with a disability and the reciprocated shared social reality support found in adapted sport settings is something often not experienced to the same degree in integrated (both able-bodied and disabled youth participate) sport (Goodwin & Staples, 2005; Groff & Kleiber, 2001). Hence, adapted sport experiences can be particularly empowering and contribute to identity development. All of the above findings suggest that APE has similar potential.

In summary, sport and games in APE can help youth with disabilities develop an identity as a "regular" child. While many able-bodied children and adolescents without disabilities struggle with developmentally related (e.g., puberty) identity issues and feeling accepted by peers, able-bodied sport is not typically reported as a setting where claiming an identity as a "regular" child is critical. Sport and PA as a vehicle facilitating the development of a strong identity is a very important finding and should not be minimized. Prominent authors dating back to Erikson (1968) and Marcia (1966) have all discussed the negative ramifications that result from an inadequately defined self. In a review of identity crisis research, twelve different affective and cognitive struggles were identified that ranged from value confusion, feelings of emptiness, malaise, anxiety, and confusion to hostility to parents and authority (Baumeister, Shapiro, & Tice, 1985).

Future researchers may also consider if older adolescents in high school APE settings use sport and PA to develop athletic, exercise, and disability identities or, conversely, how non-supportive APE climates created by teachers, support staff, and peers prevent adolescents from developing identities in these areas.

Expectancy value theory

EVT was first proposed by Martin Fishbein and Icek Ajzen (1975) and suggests that an individual's behavior is manifested as a combination between the value of the end goal and the extent to which the individual expects to succeed. As such, utilizing EVT as a framework to elicit a desired behavioral response is best understood through student motivation. The premise behind EVT is that individuals are motivated to strive for achievement when they expect to be successful and when they value the behavior or task (Eccles, 1983). Hence, youth who are confident in their abilities and expect to be successful in PA and value PA are typically physically active. In contrast, children who lack confidence and do not value PA will rarely seek out PA opportunities of their own volition. Additionally, confident adolescents who value PA are far more likely to put forth effort and persistence compared to less confident adolescents who do not think PA is important.

Although task or activity value can be broadly thought of as how much importance children place on PA, it is a much more nuanced construct made up of four related components. An adolescent places importance on how valuable it is to be good (i.e., attainment value) in a particular activity like sport or PA. In general, disability sport is often seen by the general public as a "second class" sport without the status of normalized sport, and even Paralympians experience feelings of being marginalized (Martin, 2017). Hence, children with disabilities may be socialized into developing a less than ideal attainment value for disability sport. Second, intrinsic value refers to how much someone enjoys an activity. Third is utility value, and this refers to how the activity relates to future goals and behaviors. For example, the utility value of PA might be quite high for an adolescent who views PA in PE as training that contributes to a goal of becoming a Paralympian. Finally, the fourth value element is cost. The cost of PA in PE might be the exacerbation of impairment-related pain or the psychological stress of being teased by peers in PE settings. Both of these latter two elements may be particularly salient issues that are relevant for youth with impairments. To our knowledge, researchers in APE have not examined the relevancy of, or provided, descriptive data (e.g., means) of the four elements that compose value. The importance of Eccles' (1983) theory is that she also postulates a series of mediational hypotheses about the socialization processes that influence the development of children's expectations of success and how much they value PA. For example, gender stereotypes held by significant others and their beliefs and behaviors (e.g., role modeling) all influence children's perceptions, goals, affect, and identity. However, children are not passive recipients of these influences, as their own achievement experiences (e.g., success versus failure) also influence their goals.

The EVT framework has been used extensively in pediatric PA research for children without disabilities. In one study that examined elementary student motivation in PE through the lens of the expectancy value model, future participation in PE was positively associated with children's subjective task value (i.e., attainment or usefulness) and expectancy related beliefs (i.e., ability and expectancy to succeed) (Xiang, McBride, Guan, & Solmon, 2003). This finding suggests that if students found the activity attainable or useful, they were more likely to succeed. Further, lower elementary students had higher motivation for PE than upper elementary students, suggesting that younger children are more likely to feel competent and see value in PE than older children (Xiang et al., 2003). Examining PA participation through the lens of an EVT framework may assist future researchers in more appropriately tailoring interventions for students with disabilities.

Researchers from APE and APA have long employed techniques derived from EVT; however, there is very little consistency in the reporting of strategies used from this framework. A popular early intervention program which employs concepts from EVT is called pivotal response teaching (PRT) (Stahmer, Suhrheinrich, Reed, Bolduc, & Schreibman, 2011). While the two frameworks vary in their naming of outcome expectancies, they both place a value on the outcome following the attainment of a skill. Briefly, PRT is a naturalistic behavioral intervention which employs an operant model of conditioning that consists of three primary components. In this framework, there are three phases of interaction between the instructor and student that include an antecedent (an experience which occurs prior to the behavior), a behavior (a response by the student), and a consequence (shared with student in order to promote behavioral changes). The key to PRT is that motivating activities or objects (selected by the student) are implemented to promote and sustain positive behavioral changes. In this way, PRT and EVT are similar, as they both employ a structure of reinforcement which is desired following an expected behavior. The PRT framework has been adopted successfully in a motor skill intervention for young children with autism spectrum disorder (ASD) (Ketcheson, Hauck, & Ulrich, 2017). Results from the eight-week long early and intensive PRT intervention suggest that a significant gain in both locomotor and ball skills were experienced by children in the experimental group. Due to the variability and presentation of symptoms in children with disabilities, future researchers should begin by examining the impact of specific motivational theories on a well-defined sub-population of children with disabilities.

Due to the positive behavior outcomes that manifest as a result of the EVT and PRT frameworks, there is preliminary support to embed these strategies in PA research for children with disabilities. However, another consideration is the consistency of strategies presented within a student's academic domains. To maximize the opportunity to generalize positive behavioral outcomes, the APE and APA researcher should work in combination with the student's individualized education team. One motivational strategy easily adopted between academic domains is a positive behavior reward chart. For example, if all members of a student's educational team believe "time on task" is an important skill, for every increment of "on task" time that is achieved, the student could earn points towards a specified reward. Key to maintaining saliency for the learning task is individualizing the reward chart to match the student's preferences. As a researcher, you may notice during baseline testing that a child really enjoys dribbling, so this skill can be used as the reward for achieving the desired "time on task" behavior in the APE or APA environment. In this way, components from the EVT framework are adopted as the task is attainable, predictable, and based on student preference.

In summary, while the EVT and PRT frameworks have been operationalized in research examining PA in neurotypical youth, the adoption of these strategies in APE and APA are emerging. To maximize learning outcomes, future researchers should adopt strategies congruent with a student's individualized education plan (IEP). By doing so, the student may have a greater chance of generalizing positive behavioral changes between academic outcomes.

Competence motivation theory

Harter's (1978) competence motivation theory has been used extensively to guide research in youth sport. According to Harter (1978), people are inherently motivated to master their environment and, in doing so, often experience enhanced perceptions of competence and increased motivation. Youth are motivated by a number of internal desires, such as being curious and seeking out challenges to their abilities. According to Weiss and Williams (2004), competence motivation theory is well suited for the study of youth sport because of its developmental focus and its acknowledgement of the role of peers, enjoyment, and competence. Two specific sport developmental considerations are offered by Weiss and Williams (2004) and are discussed next. First, young children (typically 8–13 years) recognize that their competence varies across five areas: school, athletics, social, appearance, and behavior (e.g., following adults' rules). Children in this age group also start to understand that they might be really good at soccer and average in basketball. Stated differently, they understand that their competence within a specific domain can vary. Second, with cognitive maturity, adolescents around ages 14–18 start to recognize more domains. For instance, new and changing social relationships and responsibilities contribute to youth expanding their competence domains to include work competence, intimate relationships, and friendships.

Harter's multi-dimensional model was built from White's (1959) initial work on effectance motivation. The major premise behind the model is that perceptions of competence and control lead to competence motivation. In turn, an adequate sense of competence motivation leads children to engage in mastery attempts and successful mastery attempts lead to a preference for optimal challenges. Success at optimal challenges will lead to positive affective experiences, such as feelings of pride and joy, which, in turn, enhance competence motivation. Another important element of the model is the role of important socializers such as the APE teacher, classmates, paraeducators, and parents. Adequate feedback by parents that is specific and contingent will contribute to the building of perceptions of competence and control. Harter's model recognizes that socialization is bi-directional, such that while parents and teachers influence may be critical, children can also influence significant adults such as APE teachers. Children are not passive recipients of socialization influences. When APE teachers and parents provide feedback on controllable mastery attempts (versus uncontrollable outcomes such as winning or losing) they help children develop self-regulation skills such as the ability to self-reinforce (e.g., feel pride absent of any external feedback) when judging competence on controllable personally relevant goals such as improvement, exerting effort, and learning (despite objective failure).

Ninot, Bilard, Delignières, and Sokolowski (2000) found that, over time, children with mental retardation (now called intellectual disabilities) experienced drops in perceived competence (greatest for integrated versus segregated settings) that the authors suggested may have been a reflection of more accurate perceptions. At the same time, it is plausible that the children based their perceived competence on social comparison processes (i.e., the children without disabilities in the segregated groups) and uncontrollable standards (e.g., winning versus losing) instead of the standards advocated above for self-regulation development that are personally more relevant and controllable (i.e., skill improvement). Most children in the study objectively improved their sport skills, so the decrease in perceived competence is disconcerting. In a second study by Ninot and colleagues, they found similar results and reasoned that participants' comparisons with the children who did not have intellectual disabilities encouraged a more realistic evaluation of their perceived competence (Ninot, Bilard, & Delignières, 2005).

It is our opinion that such conclusions are ill-conceived and misleading for three reasons. First, participants objectively assessed skills improved, so reduced perceptions of competence are, in fact, not realistic or accurate, but erroneous. Second, reduced perceptions of competence over a season are not likely to "instill a greater opportunity of undertaking athletic projects" (Ninot et al., 2005, p. 7) as the authors assert, but lead to reduced motivation and sport drop-out. Third, a large body of research examining motivational orientations and the motivational climate all conclude that mastery orientations and climates produce superior outcomes (i.e., efficacy, competence, motivation, reduced drop-out)—in general, relative to ego orientations and climates (see Martin 2018 for a more elaborate discussion). Finally, we do not discount, as Weiss and Williams (2004), and Ninot et al. (2005) assert, that children can have inaccurate perceptions of their competence and typically become more accurate with age. However, we believe it is almost always critical to understand the sources of information athletes use to make competence assessments and a sole reliance on social comparison, especially in youth sports, is unsupported.

In a third study, using Harter's (1978) model the researchers substantiated many of the paths described above. For instance, Hurley and Burt (2015, p. 9) concluded that:

> The pattern that emerged from this research is as follows: successful experience (not just outcome but also the daily riding process), positive affect (excitement, enjoyment), increased self-esteem and motivation as children expressed desire to continue the camp experience and future aspirations for engagement in other physical activities. This mirrors Harter's (1990) motivation model for self-perceptions in achievement domains.

In summary, APE researchers are urged to read Harter (1978) and related youth sport work (e.g., Weiss & Williams, 2004) in order to design studies in APE that examine many of the untested hypotheses generated from Harter's model of competence motivation. It should be noted that APE researchers seeking to test the full model, which we advocate, will likely need to employ structural equation modeling techniques. Hence, researchers will be challenged to find an adequate sample size that is sufficiently powered to test the many parameters and constructs.

Global self-worth model

Harter (1978) also developed a model of self-worth describing both the antecedents and consequences of self-worth perceptions. Two major classes of antecedents are articulated: perceptions of competence in valued domains (e.g., sport) and feedback from important others (e.g., coaches, teammates). When children perceive they are successful in mastering skills, such as defending in wheelchair basketball, and they receive positive feedback on their abilities, then they should experience strong self-worth. Of course, children are also simultaneously receiving feedback and experiencing success or failure in other domains (e.g., academics, peer relationships) that also influence their global self-worth. In particular, research with children without disabilities indicates that the appearance domain has the strongest link to self-worth. Researchers in APE should be particularly cognizant of this finding and if similar results are found in APE settings with children with impairments. Because a disability may be salient (e.g., missing a leg), its influence on self-worth may be particularly strong because the disability may limit perceptions of competence and other children may provide negative feedback about the competence and appearance of children with disabilities. There are also two major classes of consequences of self-worth. First are the affective states children experience when feeling they are valuable or, conversely, marginalized and devalued. Consequences include both positive (e.g., joy) and negative affective states (e.g., anger) and the motivational consequences of self-worth.

Self-esteem has been a popular research topic in disability, partly because of the mistaken assumption that children with disabilities lack self-worth. This assumption is partly the result of the implicit (and, at times, explicit) erroneous belief held by individuals without disabilities that having a disability is synonymous with a poor quality of life, feeling depressed, and lacking self-esteem (i.e., the tragedy model of disability). Researchers examining self-esteem in children with disabilities tend to report mixed findings and that individuals with disabilities, like most people, express a range of scores on global self-esteem scales. There is some evidence that when multi-dimensional self-esteem is examined, some individuals with disabilities may report lower self-concept in areas that correspond with their impairment. For instance, children with cerebral palsy report lower coordination self-concept (Martin, 2018). Given the often a-theoretical nature of self-esteem research with children with disabilities, researchers in APE are urged to examine self-esteem within a theoretical framework such as Harter's (1978) global self-worth model. Such research efforts would extend the knowledge base by shedding light on the important antecedents and consequences of global self-worth. Within the affective consequences of the self-worth model, researchers are also urged to examine the full gamut (with appropriate theoretical and practical rationales) of positive and negative affective states. Researchers are also encouraged to be clear on whether they are assessing affect, mood, or emotion (Ekkekakis, 2013). Recent research examining retrospective memories of PE experiences among individuals without disabilities reveals many emotionally salient themes (i.e., anxiety, embarrassment, enjoyment, etc.) that were linked to present day attitudes and intentions toward physical activity (Ladwig, Vazou, & Ekkekakis, 2018). Similar work has not been done in APE but might prove illuminating, as we currently do not know if the many negative experiences reported by children in APE become potential barriers of their current and future PA engagement.

Transtheoretical model (TTM)

The TTM was developed to integrate various theory components into a temporal stage model of behavior change (Prochaska & DiClemente, 1982; Prochaska & Velicer, 1997). The temporal model implies that changes in behavior happen over time, a concept that is overlooked in many theories. The five stages include: (a) precontemplation, (b) contemplation, (c) preparation, (d) action, and (e) maintenance. A person in the precontemplation stage appears uninterested or unmotivated and has no intention to make any changes in the foreseeable future. Most behavior change theories do not acknowledge someone at this stage. In the contemplation stage, a person has become more informed about the pros and cons of behavior change and plans to make a change within the next six months. The preparation stage is when the person intends to take action in the immediate future; they often have a plan of action and are ideal recruits for action-oriented programs. In the action stage, people make specific changes in their lifestyle within the past six months, causing observable change, typically meeting a specifically identified threshold continuously. Once people reach the goal in the action stage continuously, they move to the maintenance stage and work to prevent relapse. As time goes by, people are less tempted to relapse and develop confidence in their ability to continue with their changes. Maintenance is estimated to last from six months to five years. Early forms of the TTM included additional stages of relapse, a form of regression to an earlier stage, and termination, when an individual has no temptation and complete self-efficacy in their ability to continue the changes under all circumstances (Prochaska & DiClemente, 2005).

Though the stages are the framework of the TTM, there are several other important concepts that formulate behavior change within this model. Processes of change are the activities individuals use to progress through the stages, providing guides for intervention. Throughout the literature, ten different processes have received the most support, including consciousness raising, dramatic relief, self-reevaluation, environmental reevaluation, self-liberation, social liberation, counterconditioning, stimulus control, contingency management, and helping relationships. Individuals rely on these processes in order to progress through the model (Prochaska et al., 2005). Decision balance often happens in the contemplation stage and is the weighing of pros and cons of changing behavior. This concept may resurface in later stages as barriers to behavior change arise. Additionally, self-efficacy and confidence in one's ability to change behavior and overcome barriers is important within this model (Prochaska & Velicer, 1997).

The TTM has been widely used in promoting PA for children and adolescents without disabilities, determining different levels of PA and exercise participation throughout different stages of the model (Annesi, Faigenbaum, & Westcott, 2010; Haas & Nigg, 2009; Nigg & Courneya, 1998). The results suggest that the TTM is an effective tool for predicting and intervening on PA. Despite this knowledge, only minimal research has been done examining PA of individuals with disabilities using the TTM. For example, Kosma, Cardinal, and McCubbin (2004) used the TTM to examine the stages of change to determine the most influential predictors of PA for adults with physical disabilities. Findings revealed that processes of change and self-efficacy predicted PA stage of change. Additionally, research examining the psycho-social aspects of importance within this model found that processes of change were most important for physically active individuals with disabilities, while self-efficacy was most influential for inactive individuals with disabilities (Kosma, Gardner, Cardinal, Bauer, & McCubbin, 2006). In their work, Korologou, Barkoukis, Lazuras, and Tsorbatzoudis (2015) used the TTM in examining the model with deaf individuals and they found that PA participation was stronger and self-efficacy was higher in the preparation stage. The processes of change were higher in preparation, action, and maintenance stages compared to the other stages. Findings provided evidence that processes of change in the TTM are relevant for individuals with disabilities.

Jin, Yun, and Wegis (2013) proposed including the TTM to improve inclusivity within physical education teacher education (PETE). The researchers suggested a three-stage model: (a) changing intentions, (b) changing intentions and behavior, and (c) changing behavior. These would be incorporated into a curriculum approach through a sequence: (a) lecture-focused course, (b) lectures with teaching practicum course, and (c) internship-focused course. The different processes of change would be used throughout the curriculum sequence. Using the TTM framework to increase inclusion training during PETE could create achievable change across all training environments and increase ability to meet standards related to inclusion (Jin et al., 2013). The TTM provides a temporal framework for progression of behavior change over time. Using the model, one can determine what stage an individual is at, then determine the process for how to change behavior from their current state. Existing research suggests that the various processes of change are the most influential component of change within this model.

Health action process approach (HAPA)

Many theories aimed at impacting a health behavior are built on either a continuum model or a stage model. The HAPA appproach combines these two models in order to bridge the intention–behavior gap (Schwarzer, 2008). The HAPA model is broken down into two phases. The pre-intentional motivation phase creates behavior intention and the post-intentional volition process leads to actual behavior change (Schwarzer, Lippke, & Luszczynska, 2011).

The motivational phase consists of three main components that, when considered together, result in creating intention for behavior change: (a) risk perception, (b) outcome expectancies, and (c) perceived self-efficacy. Risk perception is the initial stimulus that brings attention to the potential consequences of not changing behavior. Positive outcome expectations develop when an individual weighs the pros and cons of changing behavior. Self-efficacy is necessary for people to believe in their ability to change behavior. Once the individual starts moving toward engaging in a health behavior change, an intention is developed, and an action plan is created. This is the transition into the volition phase. The volition phase consists of planning and self-efficacy, but these constructs must be further broken down to understand and intervene on health behaviors.

Intentions are more often turned into actions when a plan is created. Within the volition phase of HAPA, planning is further broken down into action planning and coping planning (Schwarzer, 2008). An action plan includes specific situation parameters, such as when and where PA will occur. These details make it more likely that a plan will become an action. Coping planning is anticipating barriers to PA and ways to overcome them. This is done after the action plan is created by imagining what challenges may arise within the action plan.

In this model, perceived self-efficacy shifts through three different phases specific to the individual's process of behavior change (Schwarzer, 2008). Action self-efficacy refers to creating the motivation to act by imagining success, anticipating potential positive outcomes, and developing confidence in their ability to initiate a new behavior. This form of self-efficacy is important when formulating an intention in order to move forward to PA planning. Maintenance self-efficacy refers to the belief in one's ability to overcome PA barriers that arise while trying to maintain the changed behavior. This form of self-efficacy is import-ant in the planning stages for belief in one's ability to execute the plan and to overcome barriers. Recovery self-efficacy refers to people's confidence in their ability to regain control following a failure or setback. This form of self-efficacy is important for a continuous engagement in the behavior change and continuation of the new healthy behavior. The dif-ferent stages of perceived self-efficacy may be happening at the same time or at different times, but the concept is that they operate differently and are all important for creating behavior change.

Though HAPA has been used to change various health behaviors and has been effectively used with adults with chronic illnesses, little research has been done examining how to use the model to change PA for individuals with disabilities (Schwarzer et al., 2011). However, HAPA appears to be an appropriate framework for PA research with people with disabilities. Perrier, Sweet, Strachan, and Latimer-Cheung (2012) sought to predict sport participation among individuals with acquired physical disabilities and they found the HAPA model to be a good tool. Overall, results suggest that the model has some utility for predicting sport par-ticipation for this population, but with some suggestions. The researchers found that plan-ning may be more influential in predicting maintenance self-efficacy, which is contrary to the original model. In the original model, maintenance self-efficacy was posited to predict planning. Additionally, specific sport-related outcome expectancies were predictive of sport participation. This is an important finding for future research, as outcome expectations vary for different disability populations. Additionally, Latimer-Cheung et al. (2013) employed an intervention study to examine PA in adults with spinal cord injury found similar results and suggested that future interventions should focus on building self-efficacy, intention, and action planning to increase the potential success of behavior change.

The HAPA focuses on self-efficacy and planning in order to create behavior change. Though minimal, the current research suggests that the model is an effective framework of PA participation for individuals with disabilities. More research is needed to better under-stand how this approach works for children with disabilities in APE. Cognitions such as bar-rier self-efficacy are predictive of typically developing children's PA participation (Martin, McCaughtry, Flory, Murphy, & Wisdom, 2011). APE researchers should also consider if barrier self-efficacy scales predict children's PA in APE and after-school PA. However, researchers should also consider if additional barriers to PA are relevant (e.g., chronic pain, equipment, negative social interactions).

Conclusion

The motivational theories included in this chapter represent decades of research in PA, including adapted sport, school-based APE, and APA intervention work. While the breadth of motivational theory research used with schoolaged children with disabilities is limited, the opportunity for the initiation of research is suggested within each of the highlighted theories.

The motivational theories summarized below offer valuable insight into the direction of future research in APE. First, identity theory was defined in this chapter as an umbrella term to understand how participation in sport or PA influences the development of identity. While the scope of this theory in disability sport is broad, many of the findings in children with disabilities stem from sport participation. Regardless of education or competition envir-onment, a common theme emerged from children with disabilities. Following participation in inclusive PE or Special Olympic competition, the development of self was enhanced (Bota et al., 2014; Özer et al., 2012).

Next, the EVT (Fischbein, 1975) purports that children who are confident in their skills both value PA and expect to be successful in PA. As such, the EVT framework is very much in line with the Society of Health and Physical Educators (SHAPE) of America's National Physical Education Standard 5, which states "the physically literate individual recognizes the value of PA for health, enjoyment, self-expression and/or social interaction" (SHAPE, 2013, p. 1). Therefore, the inclusion of the EVT framework when building an APE curriculum, or planning for APA intervention research, should include the opportunity to build skill competency in order to help children value participation in PA.

Competence motivation theory (Harter, 1978) suggests individuals are intrinsically motivated to master their environment, and, as a result, a strong perception of competency is linked to motivation to participate in PA. It is recommended that future researchers in APE and APA test the theory in its entirety. This has the potential to discover all the factors associated with competence assessment beyond merely social comparisons with peers.

Next, within the context of sport, global self-worth (Harter, 1987) suggests that both the perception of competence and the feedback from others can influence an individual's self-worth. It is important to recognize that the availability of research examining this theory suggests that children with and without disabilities can experience a range of beliefs about their self-esteem. Too often, it can be assumed that children with disabilities experience a lower self-worth simply because they have a disability.

The TTM includes five stages and suggests that change in behavior occurs over time (Prochaska & DiClemente, 1982; Prochaska & Velicer, 1997). Findings from this research suggest the importance of examining the processes of change, meaning the activities individuals use to progress through the five stages are the most critical components of research in APE, as it has the potential to provide critical information which can guide intervention research.

The HAPA (Schwarzer et al., 2011) model comprises two phases, the pre-intentional motivation phase and the post-intentional volition phase. The limited but encouraging results examining HAPA in APA research suggests that it can be used as an effective tool in predicting sport participation (Perrier et al., 2012). However, further recommendations, including self-efficacy, intention, and action planning, are important to consider when building PA interventions for children with disabilities.

When taken together, the motivational theories presented in this chapter are by no means an exhaustive list but, rather, a review of a number of popular theories that have been embedded within physical activity research for many years. Given the limited scope of available research examining PA participation in children with disabilities, the importance of grounding intervention research in sound motivational theoretical frameworks is needed. This chapter provides concrete suggestions for the way in which the fields of APE and APA can expand their current knowledge base and build upon a repertoire of meaningful intervention research.

Summary of key points

1. There is limited research within the APE field using the previously discussed motivational theories, so utilizing research from other normalized sport settings may be helpful in providing the foundation for continued APE research.
2. Sport and PA can be used as vehicles for facilitating the development of an identity and inclusion.
3. EVT and pivotal response teaching both place value on attainment of a skill, while adopting student preferences and personal evaluation of the task at hand.

4. More research is needed to investigate the construct of competence within APE settings and how this can be measured across areas and developmental levels.
5. It is currently unknown how negative experiences in APE may be determinants of future PA engagement.
6. The TTM can be used to determine where students in APE are in regard to their desire for behavior change and how to effectively create change for the individual.
7. Barrier self-efficacy should be examined within the APE field to determine what specific obstacles are most common for these students and how that may impact their overall motivation for PA engagement.
8. Implementing motivational strategies that a student believes are meaningful will be key to elicit a change in their motor behavior.
9. The unique challenges posed by children with various disabilities provides justification for creating methodology grounded in motivational theory to encourage positive behavior change.

Reflective questions

1. How can motivational theories be used within an APE setting to encourage behavior change?
2. Which theory or theories do you think you could use in your APE classes to better understand your students' motivation and barriers to engaging in PA?
3. How does research from APA and disability sport translate to the APE setting?
4. How can you use motivation to meet the diverse learning needs of students in your respective teaching environments?
5. Can we train support staff (such as paraprofessionals) in motivational techniques to further build child engagement in APE?
6. When using motivational theories in APE settings, think carefully about how students' impairments might require the adaptation of some questions (e.g., questions about running are not relevant to children in wheelchairs).
7. Consider the pros and cons of doing research using two theories and pitting them against each other to determine which one provides a better explanation of sport and PA behavior.
8. The theories described in this chapter are inherently cognitive in nature, so consider how you might also account for the role of affect, emotion, and mood in your research.
9. Self-worth theory implies that, broadly speaking, social influences affect behavior through self-perceptions. To accurately test such hypotheses, researchers will frequently need to use sophisticated statistical analyses (e.g., multiple mediation models) to examine if self-perceptions mediate the relationship between social influences and behavior.

References

Annesi, J. J., Faigenbaum, A. D., & Westcott, W. L. (2010). Relations of transtheoretical model stage, self-efficacy, and voluntary physical activity in African American preadolescents. *Research Quarterly for Exercise and Sport, 81*, 239–244.

Baran, F., Aktop, A., Ozer, D., Nalbant, S., Aglamis, E., Barak, S., & Hutzler, Y. (2013). The effects of a special olympics unified sports soccer training program on anthropometry, physical fitness and skilled performance in special olympics soccer athletes and non-disabled partners. *Research in Developmental Disabilities, 34*, 695–709.

Barkoukis, V., Ntoumanis, N., & Thøgersen-Ntoumani, C. (2010). Developmental changes in achievement motivation and affect in physical education: Growth trajectories and demographic differences. *Psychology of Sport and Exercise, 11*, 83–90.

Baumeister, R. F., Shapiro, J. P., & Tice, D. M. (1985). Two kinds of identity crisis. *Journal of Personality, 53*, 407–424.

Bota, A., Teodorescu, S., & Şerbănoiu, S. (2014). Unified Sports–A social inclusion factor in school communities for young people with intellectual disabilities. *Procedia-Social and Behavioral Sciences, 117*, 21–26.

Digelidis, N., & Papaioannou, A. (1999). Age-group differences in intrinsic motivation, goal orientations and perceptions of athletic competence, physical appearance and motivational climate in Greek physical education. *Scandinavian Journal of Medicine & Science in Sports, 9*, 375–380.

Eccles, J. S. (1983). Expectancies, values, and academic behavior. In T. Spencer (Ed.), *Achievement and achievement motivation* (pp. 75-146). San Francisco, CA: W. H. Freeman.

Ekkekakis, P. (2013). *The measurement of affect, mood, and emotion: A guide for health-behavioral research*. Cambridge, UK: Cambridge University Press.

Erikson, E. H. (1968). *Identity youth and crisis*. New York: Norton.

Fishbein, M., & Ajzen, I. (1975). *Belief, attitude, intention, and behavior: An introduction to theory and research*. Reading, MA: Addison-Wesley.

Goodwin, D. L., & Staples, K. (2005). The meaning of summer camp experiences to youths with disabilities. *Adapted Physical Activity Quarterly, 22*(2), 160-178.

Gould, D. (1982). Sport psychology in the 1980s:Current status and future directions in youth sportsresearch. *Journal of Sport Psychology, 4*, 203–218.

Groff, D. G., & Kleiber, D. A. (2001). Exploring the identity formation of youth involved in an adapted sports program. *Therapeutic Recreation Journal, 35*(4), 318.

Guerrero, M., & Martin, J. (2018). Para sport athletic identity from competition to retirement: A brief review and future research directions. *Physical Medicine and Rehabilitation Clinics of North America, 29*, 387–396. doi:10.1016/j.pmr.2018.01.007.

Haas, S., & Nigg, C. R. (2009). Construct validation of the stages of change with strenuous, moderate, and mild physical activity and sedentary behaviour among children. *Journal of Science and Medicine in Sport, 12*, 586–591.

Harter, S. (1978). Effectance motivation reconsidered. Toward a developmental model. *Human Development, 21*(1), 34–64.

Horn, T. S., & Butt, J. (2014). Developmental perspectives on sport and physical activity participation. *Routledge Companion to Sport and Exercise Psychology: Global Perspectives and Fundamental Concepts, 3*, 3–23.

Hurley, K. S., & Burt, T. L. (2015). Development of physical competence through motor skill acquisition for children and youth with disabilities: Parental perceptions. *Health Psychology Report, 3*, 1–12.

Jin, J., Yun, J., & Wegis, H. (2013). Changing physical education teacher education curriculum to promote inclusion. *Quest, 65*, 372–383.

Kalyvas, V., & Reid, G. (2003). Sport adaptation, participation, and enjoyment of students with and without physical disabilities. *Adapted Physical Activity Quarterly, 20*, 182–199.

Ketcheson, L., Hauck, J., & Ulrich, D. (2017). The effects of an early motor skill intervention on motor skills, levels of physical activity, and socialization in young children with autism spectrum disorder: A pilot study. *Autism, 21*, 481–492.

Korologou, S., Barkoukis, V., Lazuras, L., & Tsorbatzoudis, H. (2015). Application of the transtheoretical model to physical activity in deaf individuals. *Adapted Physical Activity Quarterly, 32*, 223–240.

Kosma, M., Cardinal, B. J., & McCubbin, J. A. (2004). Recruitment techniques among understudied populations and their implications for physical activity promotion. *Quest, 56*, 413–420.

Kosma, M., Gardner, R. E., Cardinal, B. J., Bauer, J. J., & McCubbin, J. A. (2006). Psychosocial determinants of stages of change and physical activity among adults with physical disabilities. *Adapted Physical Activity Quarterly, 23*, 49–64.

Ladwig, M. A., Vazou, S., & Ekkekakis, P. (2018). "My best memory is when I was done with it": PE memories are associated with adult sedentary behavior. *Translational Journal of the American College of Sports Medicine, 3*, 119–129.

Latimer-Cheung, A. E., Arbour-Nicitopoulos, K. P., Brawley, L. R., Gray, C., Justine Wilson, A., Prapavessis, H., … Martin Ginis, K. A. (2013). Developing physical activity interventions for adults with spinal cord injury. Part 2: Motivational counseling and peer-mediated interventions for people intending to be active. *Rehabilitation Psychology, 58*, 307–315.

Lundberg, N. R., Taniguchi, S., McCormick, B. P., & Tibbs, C. (2011). Identity negotiating: Redefining stigmatized identities through adaptive sports and recreation participation among individuals with a disability. *Journal of Leisure Research, 43*, 205–225.

Marcia, J. E. (1966). Development and validation of ego-identity status. *Personality and Social Psychology, 3*, 551–558.

Martin, J. J. (2013). Identity and disability sport. In C. Mohiyeddini (Ed.), *Advances in the psychology of sport and exercise* (pp. 15–24). New York, NY: Nova Science.

Martin, J. J. (2015). The dynamics of disability sport identity development. In J. Jaworsky (Ed.), *Advances in sociology research* (pp. 111–124). New York, NY: Nova Science.

Martin, J. J. (2018). *Handbook of disability sport and exercise psychology*. Oxford, UK: Oxford University Press.

Martin, J. J., McCaughtry, N., Flory, S., Murphy, A., & Wisdom, K. (2011). Using social cognitive theory to predict physical activity and fitness in underserved middle school children. *Research Quarterly for Exercise and Sport, 82*, 247–255.

Martin, J. J., Mushett-Adams, C., & Smith, K. L. (1995). Athletic identity and sport orientation of adolescent swimmers with disabilities. *Adapted Physical Activity Quarterly, 12*, 113–123.

Martin, J. J., & Vitali, F. (2011). Social identity implications for active individuals with physical disabilities. In M. Wearing (Ed.), *Social Identity* (pp. 163–174). London, England: Nova Science.

Nigg, C. R., & Courneya, K. S. (1998). Transtheoretical model: Examining adolescent exercise behavior. *Journal of Adolescent Health, 22*, 214–224.

Ninot, G., Bilard, J., & Delignières, D. (2005). Effects of integrated or segregated sport participation on the physical self for adolescents with intellectual disabilities. *Journal of Intellectual Disability Research, 49*, 682–689.

Ninot, G., Bilard, J., Delignières, D., & Sokolowski, M. (2000). Effects of integrated sport participation on perceived competence for adolescents with mental retardation. *Adapted Physical Activity Quarterly, 17*, 208–221.

Özer, D., Baran, F., Aktop, A., Nalbant, S., Ağlamış, E., & Hutzler, Y. (2012). Effects of a special olympics unified sports soccer program on psycho-social attributes of youth with and without intellectual disability. *Research in Developmental Disabilities, 33*, 229–239.

Perrier, M. J., Sweet, S. N., Strachan, S. M., & Latimer-Cheung, A. E. (2012). I act, therefore I am: Athletic identity and the health action process approach predict sport participation among individuals with acquired physical disabilities. *Psychology of Sport and Exercise, 13*, 713–720.

Prochaska, J. M., Paiva, A. L., Padula, J. A., Prochaska, J. O., Montgomery, J. E., Hageman, L., & Bergart, A. M. (2005). Assessing emotional readiness for adoption using the transtheoretical model. *Children and Youth Services Review, 27*, 135–152.

Prochaska, J. O., & DiClemente, C. C. (1982). Transtheoretical therapy: Toward a more integrative model of change. *Psychotherapy: Theory, Research & Practice, 19*, 276–288.

Prochaska, J. O., & DiClemente, C. C. (2005). The transtheoretical approach. *Handbook of Psychotherapy Integration, 2*, 147–171.

Prochaska, J. O., & Velicer, W. F. (1997). The transtheoretical model of health behavior change. *American Journal of Health Promotion, 12*, 38–48.

Renker, J., Helmer, K., Panetta, V., Pimentel, J., & Sawanec, C. (2017). Parents' perspectives on the participation of children with disabilities in community-based youth sports. (Order No. 10269549, Utica College). *ProQuest Dissertations and Theses*, 41. Retrieved from http://search.proquest.com. proxy.lib.wayne.edu/docview/1891348481?accountid=14925

Schwarzer, R. (2008). Some burning issues in research on health behavior change. *Applied Psychology, 57*(1), 84–93.

Schwarzer, R., Lippke, S., & Luszczynska, A. (2011). Mechanisms of health behavior change in persons with chronic illness or disability: The Health Action Process Approach (HAPA). *Rehabilitation Psychology, 56*, 161–170.

SHAPE America. (2013). *Grade-level outcomes for K-12 physical education*. Reston, VA: SHAPE America.

Stahmer, A., Suhrheinrich, J., Reed, S., Bolduc, C., & Schreibman, L. (2011). *Classroom pivotal response teaching: A guide to effective implementation*. New York: Guilford Press.

Tajfel, H. (Ed.). (2010). *Social identity and intergroup relations*. Cambridge, UK: Cambridge University Press.

Taub, D. E., & Greer, K. R. (2000). Physical activity as a normalizing experience for school-age children with physical disabilities: Implications for legitimation of social identity and enhancement of social ties. *Journal of Sport and Social Issues*, 24(4), 395-414.

Tint, A., Thomson, K., & Weiss, J. A. (2017). A systematic literature review of the physical and psychosocial correlates of special olympics participation among individuals with intellectual disability. *Journal of Intellectual Disability Research*, *61*, 301–324.

Weiss, J., Diamond, T., Demark, J., & Lovald, B. (2003). Involvement in special olympics and its relations to self-concept and actual competency in participants with developmental disabilities. *Research in Developmental Disabilities*, *24*, 281–305.

Weiss, J. A., & Bebko, J. M. (2008). Participation in special olympics and change in athlete self-concept over 42 months. *Journal on Developmental Disabilities*, *14*, 1–8.

Weiss, M. R., & Bredemeier, B. L. (1983). Developmental sport psychology: A theoretical perspective for studying children in sport. Journal of Sport Psychology, 5, 216–230.

Weiss, M. R., & Williams, L. (2004). The Why of Youth Sport Involvement: A Developmental Perspective on Motivational Processes. In M. R. Weiss (Ed.), *Developmental sport and exercise psychology: A lifespan perspective* (pp. 223-268). Morgantown, WV: Fitness Information Technology.

Werner, S. (2015). Athletes', parents', and siblings' experiences from the special olympics world games. *Journal of Intellectual & Developmental Disability*, *40*, 167–178. doi:10.3109/13668250.2015.1010148

White, R. (1959). Motivation reconsidered: The concept of competence. *Psychological Review*, *66*, 297-323.

Xiang, P., McBride, R., Guan, J., & Solmon, M. (2003). Children's motivation in elementary physical education: An expectancy-value model of achievement choice. *Research Quarterly for Exercise and Sport*, 74(1), 25-35.

23

Occupational socialization theory and the lived experiences of adapted physical educators

Wesley J. Wilson and K. Andrew R. Richards

Over the past four decades, occupational socialization theory has been used to study the recruitment, education, and ongoing career socialization of physical education teachers (Lawson, 1983a, 1983b). What started as a largely US-based approach to understanding the lived experiences of teachers has now taken on an international focus, with scholars in countries across the world studying teacher socialization (Richards & Gaudreault, 2017b). The theory has also recently been used to examine the experiences of APE teachers (Wilson, Richards, & Kelly, 2017). This growing area of research has explored the unique socialization processes that lead future teachers to enroll in APE teacher education programs (APETE), the formal training of APE teachers, and how physical education and APE teachers experience teaching students with disabilities throughout their careers (O'Leary, Longmore, & Medcalf, 2015; Park & Curtner-Smith, 2018; Richards & Wilson, 2019; Sato & Haegele, 2017). Further, APE scholarship in occupational socialization theory is becoming more salient in the field as APETE programs are not immune to the decline in number (Newell, 1990, 2007) and size (Solmon & Garn, 2014) of physical education teacher education programs. Thus, a better understanding of APE teachers' experiences is critical to both sustaining and advancing the field of APE (Wilson et al., 2017).

This chapter is organized so that the reader is first presented with an introduction to occupational socialization theory, which expands on the three phases of socialization that physical education teachers experience: acculturation, professional socialization, and organizational socialization. With the stage set, the discussion shifts toward teachers' socialization into the APE field, where a review of extant empirical research and current trends are provided. While priority is given to the discussion of articles published in peer reviewed journals, conference presentations and doctoral dissertations are discussed as well, due to the paucity of published research. Next, implications for practice and directions for future research that have emerged through this theoretical perspective are discussed. A concise conclusion and key summary points then synthesize the chapter's major themes. Finally, a series of reflective questions are posited to engage graduate students and researchers with the chapter's content. It is acknowledged at the onset that the content of this chapter focuses primarily on the US context, which is reflective of the available scholarship related to APE teacher socialization. While some of the research discussed has international application and relevance, it is important for future scholars to extend this emerging body of research across geographical and cultural contexts.

Introduction to occupational socialization theory

Socialization refers to a broad process through which individuals learn the norms, values, cultures, and ideologies of social groups or institutions in which they are seeking member-ship (Billingham, 2007; Clausen, 1968). Related to the study of workplace socialization in a broader sense (e.g., Bauer & Erdogan, 2011), teacher socialization research traces its roots to the seminal work of education scholars, including Waller (1932), Jackson (1968), Lortie (1975), Lacey (1977), and Zeichner & Gore (1990). Lacey (1977) defined teacher socializa-tion as "the process of change by which individuals become members of the teaching profes-sion" (p. 61). Scholars studying teacher socialization have, therefore, been concerned with the ways in which individuals are recruited into, prepared for, and socialized through, careers as educators (Richards & Gaudreault, 2017b). This field of research has led to greater under-standing of (a) the influence of teaching recruits' biographies on teaching beliefs and prac-tices, (b) the effectiveness of teacher education programming, (c) formal and informal tactics used by school organizations to socialize new teachers, and (d) the outcomes or effects of socialization both in terms of teacher effectiveness and subjective well-being (Achinstein, Ogawa, & Speiglman, 2004; Feiman-Nemser, 2001; Richards, Templin, & Graber, 2014).

With notable exceptions (e.g., Achinstein et al., 2004; Pogodzinski, 2012; Tahir & Qadir, 2012), the study of teacher socialization within the general education literature has slowed over the years, but it remains a vibrant focus in physical education (Templin & Richards, 2014). The most common framework for studying physical education teacher socialization is occupational socialization theory, which was initially articulated by Lawson (1983a, 1983b) in a two-part article published in the *Journal of Teaching in Physical Education*. Lawson (1986) later explained that occupational socialization includes "all the kinds of socialization that ini-tially influence persons to enter the field of physical education and that later are responsible for their perceptions and actions as teacher educators and teachers" (p. 107). Since the publi-cation of these seminal works, nearly 300 empirical, theoretical, and practical articles and book chapters have been framed through the lens of occupational socialization theory across more than 15 different countries (Richards & Gaudreault, 2017b).

Early theories of socialization operated from a structural–functionalist perspective in which it was assumed that individuals were passively socialized into the groups in which they sought membership (Merton, Reader, & Kendall, 1957). Scholars using occupational socialization theory, however, adopt a dialectical approach in which individuals are viewed as active agents of their own socialization and capable of overtly and covertly resisting the influence of those who seek to socialize them (Richards et al., 2014). The dialectics of socialization becomes particularly important when considering how individuals interact with one another and social institutions. In teacher education programs, for example, it cannot be assumed that pre-service teachers will automatically accept and follow the guidelines and expectations set by teacher educators. Some whose past socialization experiences conflict with these expectations may exercise their sense of agency and resist (Graber, 1991). Social-ization agents and institutions often hold an imbalance of power in the dialectical relationship (e.g., teacher educators serve as gatekeepers to program completion). Nevertheless, socialization remains a process whereby both parties can learn from one another, adapt, and change through the socialization process (Schempp & Graber, 1992).

Another distinguishing element of occupational socialization theory is recognition that socialization begins prior to formal career training in a teacher education program. Scholars recognize the potent influence of early exposure to, and experiences in, physical education on potential recruits' beliefs about the discipline (Curtner-Smith, 2017). Further, socialization is not viewed as a linear process because individuals do not experience all forms of socialization at the same time or in the same way (Lortie, 1975). The non-linear nature of socialization led Lawson (1983b) to characterize the process as problematic rather than automatic. Nevertheless, scholars using occupational socialization typically divide the types of socialization experienced by physical educators using a temporal continuum that includes the three phases of acculturation, professional socialization, and organizational socialization (Richards et al., 2014).

Acculturation

Acculturation refers to pre-training socialization that occurs during formative education and prior to the time when individuals make a formal commitment to pursue teaching careers (Lawson, 1983b). During this time, potential recruits engage in an apprenticeship of observation (Lortie, 1975) through interacting with, and observing, their own physical education teachers and coaches, and interacting with other socializing agents such as parents and counselors (Curtner-Smith, 2017). These experiences lead recruits to develop subjective theories related to what it means to be a physical education teacher (Betourne & Richards, 2015). Grotjahn (1991) defined subjective theories as "complex cognitive structures that are highly individual, relatively stable, and relatively enduring, and that fulfill the task of explaining and predicting such human phenomena as action, reaction, thinking, emotion and perception" (p. 188). Potential recruits' subjective theories are often flawed or incomplete because they do not have complete insight into the technical and sociopolitical nature of teaching (Curtner-Smith, Hastie, & Kinchin, 2008).

While flawed, recruits' initial conceptions of what it means to teach physical education are well developed prior to training, are difficult to change, and reflect the type of physical education recruits experienced during their own formative education. In many schools, this tends to be a curriculum that focuses on team sport (Ferry & McCaughtry, 2013; Flory, 2016) and that is delivered using a multi-activity model or non-teaching approach (Crum, 1993; Curtner-Smith, 1998). As a result, many physical education recruits are resistant to more progressive pedagogical approaches and the use of evidence-based practices, including assessment (Starck, Richards, & O'Neil, 2018). Many potential recruits, who are influenced by sport coaches, pursue physical education as a career contingency for their true passion of coaching (Curtner-Smith, 2017). Collectively, these experiences have implications both for which recruits are socialized into the field, as well as which are socialized out of it. Typically, only those recruits whose subjective theories replicate the practices they experience in physical education will enroll in teacher education programs (O'Neil & Richards, 2018). This is one way the physical education profession reproduces itself through socialization.

Professional socialization

When recruits formalize their commitment to pursue a career in physical education by enrolling in a teacher education program, they enter professional socialization (Lawson,

1983b). Through this phase of socialization, pre-service teachers learn the knowledge and skills deemed to be most important to teaching physical education by the faculty members at their particular institution (Richards et al., 2014). While some examples of effective teacher education programs have been highlighted in the literature (e.g., McMahon & MacPhail, 2007), evidence also indicates that many programs struggle to challenge the subjective theories recruits developed through acculturation (Curtner-Smith et al., 2008; Stran & Curtner-Smith, 2009). Reinforcing that all socialization is dialectical, Graber (1991), for example, found that recruits exercised their sense of agency to resist the influence of teacher education when they encountered practices with which they did not agree. These students utilized a version of strategic compliance (Lacey, 1977) whereby they feigned compliance with expectations without allowing their core beliefs to be challenged or changed.

The socialization challenges faced by teacher education programs have led some scholars to argue that teacher educators should be intentional about helping future educators question and reformulate their subjective theories and prepare for the socio-political realities of teaching in schools (Mansfield, Beltman, Broadley, & Weatherby-Fell, 2016; Richards, Housner, & Templin, 2018). Accordingly, teacher education faculty members should develop a shared technical culture in which they communicate agreement relative to key aspects of the program (Curtner-Smith, 1997, 2001). Teacher educators should also provide pre-service teachers with extensive time learning in school environments through field experiences that are closely supervised by both university supervisors and cooperating teachers (Christensen & Barney, 2011; Young & MacPhail, 2015). These field experiences should be supported with on-campus learning experiences that promote reflection through learning activities that are grounded in constructivist principles of teaching and learning (Richards, Templin, & Gaudreault, 2013). Examples of such activities include case-based learning (Timken & van der Mars, 2009), group discussions (Gore, 1990), critical incident reflections (Curtner-Smith & Sofo, 2004), and autobiographical essays (Betourne & Richards, 2015).

Organizational socialization

Upon completion of initial teacher education and entrance into the workforce, physical educators enter organization socialization (Lawson, 1983a), which is "the process by which one is taught and learns the ropes of a particular organizational role" (Van Maanen & Schein, 1979, p. 211). This process is guided largely by unwritten norms or rules that guide teachers' social interactions and provide status based primarily on experience (Curtner-Smith et al., 2008). Some physical educators begin their careers working in environments that value progressive approaches to teaching and promote collegiality and community (e.g., Pennington, Prusak, & Wilkinson, 2014; Prusak, Pennington, Graser, Beighle, & Morgan, 2010). On the other hand, schools have been referred to as custodial bureaucracies (Lawson, 1983a, 2018) in which preservation of the status quo is prioritized over innovative and new ideas. This emphasis on continuity has been referred to as the institutional press (Zeichner & Tabachnick, 1983).

When faced with custodial working conditions, some beginning teachers overtly exercise their sense of agency by seeking to redefine the status quo. Given that senior members of the school community hold the balance of power, however, taking an active approach to redefinition can result in social sanctions (Richards, 2015). A gradualist approach in which innovations are introduced slowly and over time is more likely to achieve success (Skelton, 1990). Other teachers, however, adopt a stance of strategic compliance whereby they feign compliance with practices they know to be inappropriate to avoid social sanctions (Lacey, 1977). Finally, a third group of teachers internally adjusts to the expectations of the custodial environment by abandoning their previously held beliefs in favor of the status quo at the school. This process has been referred to as the washout effect (Blankenship & Coleman, 2009) and is another way in which the physical education profession reproduces itself through socialization.

In addition to the social challenges and stressors faced by all teachers, physical educators also teach a subject that is often socially constructed as marginal or peripheral to the primary mission of schooling (Kougioumtzis, Patriksson, & Stråhlman, 2011; Laureano et al., 2014). Marginalization results from the belief that schools are primarily responsible for white collar (i.e., cognitive) education and that blue collar (i.e., physical) learning is of less relevance (Sparkes, Templin, & Schempp, 1993). Over time, physical educators may internalize feelings of marginalization and begin to believe that their subject is not as important as, or is only there to support learning in, traditional academic subjects such as mathematics, science, and language arts (Richards, Gaudreault, Starck, & Woods, 2018). Physical educators can also experience physical and intellectual isolation from their teaching colleagues, particularly in schools that only employ one physical educator and in environments where the gymnasium is distal to, or separate from, the main school building (Richards et al., 2014). Nevertheless, some evidence indicates that physical educators can increase their status and the extent to which they and their subject matter to others by building positive relationships with students, colleagues, and administrators, and advocating for the discipline (Gaudreault, Richards, & Woods, 2018; Lux & McCullick, 2011).

Socialization into adapted physical education (APE)

While occupational socialization theory has been used to understand the experiences of physical educators for nearly 40 years, less is known about the ways in which APE teachers are recruited, educated, and socialized into their work roles. While some generalizations can be extrapolated from the physical education socialization literature, Wilson, Richards, and colleagues (2017) posited that the unique experiences of APE teachers influence the socialization process differently than that of their physical education counterparts. For example, APE teachers tend to work more individually with students with disabilities and can have caseloads ranging from 51 to 76 students who all have unique and specific needs related to their disabilities (Dillon & Sherrill, 2003; Obrusnikova & Kelly, 2009). They must rely on their understanding of their students' disabilities as they modify content, equipment, rules, and participation requirements to meet individual needs (Hodge, Lieberman, & Murata, 2012). Further, many APE teachers' job duties are often itinerant in nature, as they split their teaching and consulting responsibilities across multiple schools or districts (Wilson et al., 2017).

In the US, federally enforced special education laws, such as the *Individuals with Disabilities Education Improvement Act* (2004), also create different working conditions for APE teachers, as they are held accountable for implementing individualized education programs and working toward the least restrictive environment (Lavay, Sakai, Ortiz, & Roth, 2015; Wilson, 2018). Such experiences with special education laws are not unique to APE teachers in the US. Similar legislation exists in other countries, such as the UK's *Children and Families Act* (2014), which, in part, guides the types of services students with disabilities receive. Additional discussion of international special education legislation can be found in Chapter 2 of this handbook.

Further, there is growing evidence of challenges regarding communication between APE teachers and their colleagues (Bryan, McCubbin, & van der Mars, 2013; Wilson, 2018), as well as experiences of greater marginalization (Wilson, 2018), that differ from those reported in the physical education literature. Ultimately, the distinctiveness of APE teachers' lived experiences has compelled recent scientific inquiry using occupational socialization theory as a guiding lens. In the following sections, the available research that has used occupational socialization theory to study the experiences of APE teachers is reviewed along the phases of acculturation, professional socialization, and organizational socialization.

Acculturation of APE teachers

Research into the socialization experiences of APE recruits during their formative years has been explored in recent years. One area of scholarship has focused on the influence of the apprenticeship of observation (Lortie, 1975), which has been found to be instrumental in forming emerging physical education recruits' perceptions of their future profession (Betourne & Richards, 2015). Borrowing from the special education teacher socialization literature (see Pugach, 1992), APE scholars have posited that, since direct exposure to APE during recruits' formative years is limited, APE recruits may not develop as rich a vision, or subjective theory, for what it means to be an APE teacher (Wilson et al., 2017). Recent evidence has supported this notion of an incomplete apprenticeship of observation (Park & Curtner-Smith, 2018; Richards & Wilson, 2019), suggesting formative socialization experiences with APE teachers is not as powerful in the recruitment process for APE recruits as it is for PE recruits (Wilson et al., 2017). As a result, APE recruits may be more receptive toward pedagogical practices and values espoused by APETE faculty because their subjective theories are not as well formed as those of physical education recruits (Park & Curtner-Smith, 2018; Wilson et al., 2017). Wilson, Richards, and colleagues (2017) have also suggested the presence of a "false apprenticeship", which may occur when APE recruits develop subjective theories based on their physical education experiences and apply them to APE. Regardless, a lack of exposure to APE teachers during recruits' formative years likely contributes to delayed recruitment into APETE programming, especially since some individuals are unaware that careers in APE are a possibility (Park & Curtner-Smith, 2018; Richards & Wilson, 2019). In contrast to APE recruits, acculturation appears to more powerfully influence the experiences of general physical educators who are teaching children with disabilities in an integrated environment (O'Leary et al., 2015). While the experiences of these individuals goes beyond the specific purpose of this chapter, physical educators still represent an important population for consideration, as many children with disabilities spend at least part of their time in general education classes in the US (U.S. Department of Education, 2018) and abroad (Qi & Ha, 2012).

Similar to general physical educators (Lee & Curtner-Smith, 2011), participation in physical education and physical activity has generally facilitated APE teacher recruitment, as APE recruits have expressed a combination of enjoyment in physical education as well as a desire to teach more effectively than they were taught during their own class experiences (Park & Curtner-Smith, 2018; Richards & Wilson, 2019). Nevertheless, participation in such activities is not as essential to APE recruits' identity, as is frequently cited among their PE counterparts (Curtner-Smith, 2017; Richards et al., 2014). Some APE recruits, for example, report a preference for non-competitive, community sports programming rather than participation in interscholastic leagues (Richards & Wilson, 2019). While traditional socializing agents, such as parents, teachers, and coaches have some influence on APE recruitment, interactions with individuals with disabilities appears to be even more powerful (Park & Curtner-Smith, 2018). These interactions may come during formative education, or after recruits have already begun post-secondary degree programs, such as in an adapted physical activity class with a field experience, which can contribute to delayed recruitment (Richards & Wilson, 2019).

Perhaps as a function of their delayed recruitment, APE recruits come from a variety of different backgrounds and with multiple different career goals. Work by Richards and Wilson (2019) demonstrates that, while some APE recruits have background training in physical education, others come from general kinesiology studies and pre-physical therapy/pre-occupational therapy tracks. While some APE recruits eliminate alternative career paths prior to entry into APETE (Park & Curtner-Smith, 2018), other recruits view APETE as a stepping stone to other professional schooling (e.g., physical therapy school; Richards & Wilson, 2019). Interestingly, and in contrast to general physical education recruits (Curtner-Smith, 2017), APE recruits are more likely to be teaching oriented and to hold more "progressive" views of physical education and APE (Park & Curtner-Smith, 2018; Richards & Wilson, 2019).

Professional socialization of APE teachers

Recent research into the professional socialization of APE teachers has yielded insights into how APE teachers experience teacher education and has revealed that high quality APETE serves as a powerful influencer on how APE teachers understand what it means to be an APE teacher (Park & Curtner-Smith, 2018; Wilson et al., 2017). The powerful influence of APETE is in contrast to the physical education socialization literature, which has indicated that teacher education is not a strong enough intervention to overcome recruits' initial subjective theories developed through acculturation (Richards et al., 2014). As noted earlier, Wilson and colleagues (2017) have posited that increased receptivity to APETE may be a function of recruits' incomplete apprenticeship of observation, which can result in more permeable subjective theories. Importantly, and similar to recommendations in the physical education literature (Richards et al., 2013), high-quality APETE includes clinical and practicum experiences as the foundation of the training (Nichols, Block, & Wilson, 2018). Thus, some evidence suggests that APETE programs that do not provide sufficient clinical practice create challenges for APE teachers, who feel more unprepared for the realities of the profession as they transition into schools (Park & Curtner-Smith, 2018). Moreover, APE teachers' ability to overcome the reality shock (Stokking, Leenders, Jong, & Tartwijk, 2003) of working with students with severe disabilities has been linked to collaborating with cooperating teachers in field experiences (Sato & Haegele, 2017).

While field experiences are important to APE teacher development, challenges can arise when these experiences create role ambiguity driven by vague or under-articulated job responsibilities for APE teachers (Sato & Haegele, 2017). Further, pre-service APE teachers likely must navigate issues of liminality during their field training (Richards et al., 2014), as they can be "stuck" between the role of a student and that of a licensed expert (Sato & Haegele, 2017). Liminality can, for example, manifest during individualized education program meetings when APE recruits are expected to make recommendations similar to those made by licensed practitioners, and when making important decisions related to assessment, program planning, and program implementation, where they may be seen as "just a student."

Additionally, the ways in which pre-service physical education and APE teachers are taught to implement special education law during their training has recently been examined. Some research has demonstrated that teacher education programs place a relatively low emphasis on the importance of federal special education laws that influence APE (Piletic & Davis, 2010; Wilson, 2018). Further, in the eyes of pre-service APE teachers, understanding special education law that guides the practice of physical education for students with disabilities may not be seen to be as useful as learning about assessments, disabilities, and how to adapt content (Park & Curtner-Smith, 2018). In the same vein, while learning about laws is often a focus in many degree programs, pre-service APE courses do not receive adequate opportunities to actually practice making important decisions in response to federal mandates, such as APE eligibility and least restrictive environment placement, during their teacher training (Wilson, 2018).

Organizational socialization of APE teachers

Limited research exists as it pertains to the organizational socialization of in-service APE teachers (Wilson et al., 2017). Available evidence suggests that school culture plays an important role in either supporting, or creating barriers for, APE teachers seeking to implement innovative practices (Park & Curtner-Smith, 2018), which is in concert with the experiences of physical education teachers (Curtner-Smith et al., 2008). Specific to APE teachers, research suggests that school cultures that perpetuate value and support for APE yield better working environments. In fact, APE teachers who have access to the mentorship of more experienced and "progressively oriented" APE colleagues tend to be more shielded from these custodial school cultures (Park & Curtner-Smith, 2018). Such mentorship, combined with support from students' parents, may help shift the APE teachers who begin their careers with custodial orientations focused on traditional values and approaches to more of a "progressive" teaching orientation.

In contrast to innovative school cultures, more custodial working conditions that are characterized by a lack of equipment, inappropriate facilities, and inopportune interruptions have negative implications for APE teachers and the instruction they provide (Park & Curtner-Smith, 2018). Moreover, inadequate support staff has been reported as a major barrier when considering the most appropriate placement for students to receive APE services (Wilson, 2018). Importantly, when cultures are characterized by custodianship rather than innovation, APE teachers are more likely to feel isolation and marginalization (Park & Curtner-Smith, 2018).

While marginalization is a well-documented trend in physical education (Kougioumtzis et al., 2011; Laureano et al., 2014), some scholars argue that APE is even more marginalized as a discipline (Lieberman & Houston-Wilson, 2011), which is reflective of current societal values (Chan, Livneh, Pruett, Wang, & Zheng, 2009). Particularly troubling is that many APE teachers report feeling marginalized by their physical education counterparts (Park & Curtner-Smith, 2018), which often manifests through limited support and the use of custodial or inappropriate teaching practice in integrated physical education (Wilson, 2018). For example, APE teachers trying to integrate a student from their caseload into a general physical education class that is disorganized and inappropriate may struggle to make the experience meaningful and safe, and, ultimately, be forced to remove that child from that setting. APE teachers may be further marginalized by physical education teachers who are unreceptive to educating students with disabilities in their classes (Bredahl, 2013; Haegele & Zhu, 2017), which can perpetuate exclusionary practices (Wilkinson, Harvey, Bloom, Joober, &

Grizenko, 2013). This exclusion is often the result of physical educators feeling underprepared for instructing students with disabilities (Morley, Bailey, Tan, & Cooke, 2005).

Given the innovative or custodial nature of the school culture, Park and Curtner-Smith (2018) provide four coping strategies that APE teachers may adopt. First, in an innovative culture that presents a supportive environment, a teacher may fully comply due to the favorable situation. Second, teachers who work in custodial environments characterized by a lack of support may eventually leave the position to find another in the field. Under this scenario, the likelihood of teacher burnout, which has been found to be positively related to physical education teachers who work with a large number of students with disabilities in integrated settings (Fejgin, Talmor, & Erlich, 2005), may become increasingly probable for APE teachers (Wilson et al., 2017). Third, teachers facing a custodial culture may also strategically comply (Lacey, 1977) and passively wait, hoping that the situation improves. Fourth, some teachers working in custodial environments may attempt to strategically redefine and improve the working conditions through collaboration with other school personnel (Richards et al., 2014). At times, these attempts at redefinition can also be combative and forceful (Park & Curtner-Smith, 2018), which may result in problems for newer APE teachers who do not have the social and political capital to make changes to the culture of their school (Richards, 2015).

Current trends and directions for future research

Current trends related to APE teacher socialization have continued to build knowledge of teachers' lived experiences in the three phases of socialization; this emerging line of scholarship has been disseminated at national and international conferences. While not inclusive, research using occupational socialization theory is investigating topics such as the effects of professional socialization on graduate-level pre-service APE teachers who student teach in both regular and special schools (Richards, Wilson, & Richards, 2017) and undergraduate pre-service physical educators learning to differentiate instruction for students with disabilities (Breithoff, Taliaferro, Bulger, & Jones, 2017). Occupational socialization theory is also being used to explore the impact of sports camp for youth with visual impairments on a diverse group of pre-service professionals that includes pre-service physical educators and optometry students (Wilson, Haegele, Richards, & Kelly, 2017). More globally, these ongoing investigations are reflective of Wilson and colleagues' (2017) call for additional scholarship of teacher socialization in APE, and will continue to enhance this particular body of literature.

Building from the current body of literature, there are several directions for future research that scholars may consider following. First, in-depth case studies focusing on each of the three phases of occupational socialization should be conducted to further understand differences between APE teacher and general physical education teacher socialization. These studies help to further isolate the unique socialization experiences of APE pre-service and in-service teachers when compared to their generalist colleagues. Since available evidence suggests that interactions with individuals with disabilities prior to formal teacher education are a powerful influence for APE recruits, for example, researchers may find investigation into the effects of volunteering in disability sports programs, such as Special Olympics, a worthwhile endeavor. Moreover, the incomplete and false apprenticeships of observation (Wilson et al., 2017), and how these experiences influence APE recruits' value orientations, are not yet well understood. It is possible, for example, that having an underdeveloped understanding of APE may make pre-service teachers more open to professional socialization. On the other hand, pre-service teachers may try to apply what they learned about physical education during acculturation to APETE, which could create additional challenges for teacher educators.

Relatedly, pre-service teachers' experiences during APETE are not well understood. Future researchers should seek to understand the extent to which pre-service teachers are open to learning about best practices in APETE, and the teaching strategies that are most successful. This work could extend research in physical education teacher socialization that suggests the development of teacher education programs that are field-based and provoke pre-service teachers to more deeply reflect on their experiences through the inclusion of constructivist-oriented teaching strategies (Richards et al., 2013). Given evidence suggesting that pre-service APE teachers take on more responsibilities than what might be typical among their physical education counterparts (Sato & Haegele, 2017), researchers should examine the issues related to liminality, as APE preservice teachers find themselves teetering between the roles of student and expert.

With regard to organizational socialization, researchers could more fully examine the ways in-service APE teachers experience marginalization and grow to develop perceptions of mattering (Laureano et al., 2014; Lux & McCullick, 2011). Based on the limited available literature (Lieberman & Houston-Wilson, 2011; Park & Curtner-Smith, 2018), this work should take a particular emphasis on how in-service physical educators can sometimes exacerbate feelings of marginalization among their APE colleagues and how these challenges can be mitigated. Given that many APE teachers are itinerant, they may also feel more isolated and have a more difficult time making connections to others in their working environments (Richards, Hemphill, & Templin, 2018). Further, this work should seek to understand the role that school culture and working conditions play in the development of APE teachers' lives and careers, as well as how they are able to balance and manage large caseloads and the need to be involved in IEP meetings about their students.

While beyond the immediate purpose of this chapter, this research could also be extended to include the experiences of APETE faculty members and teacher educators. This would align with the shift that has recently occurred in the physical education teacher socialization literature, whereby occupational socialization theory has been extended to include a focus on doctoral education and faculty socialization (Casey & Fletcher, 2012; Russell, Gaudreault, & Richards, 2016). This work represents an important direction forward for the study of teacher socialization, as faculty members are increasingly being viewed as disciplinary stewards (Lawson, 2016) due to their involvement in both educating the next generation of teachers and conducting research to advance their disciplines. Relative to APE, faculty socialization research could help to understand the ways in which APETE faculty members are recruited into the field, the ways in which they are prepared for their teaching and research responsibilities, and the challenges and opportunities they face as a field that straddles both physical education and special education in college and university environments. While also beyond the purview of this chapter, advancing earlier research (O'Leary et al., 2015) related to how physical education generalists experience socialization regarding the instruction of students with disabilities would be fruitful. This is particularly the case given that more students with disabilities are being integrated in general physical education settings internationally (Qi & Ha, 2012).

Future research related to APE teacher socialization should also heed recommendations forwarded by Richards & Gaudreault (2017a) to adopt a wide variety of methodological approaches so as to more completely understand socialization. Quantitative research can examine the association among variables, such as perceived mattering, marginalization, stress, and burnout and investigate group differences based on characteristics such as gender, school location (e.g., urban, suburban, rural), and race/ethnicity. On the other hand, qualitative research can provide deeper understanding into participants' lived experiences as they navigate the socio-political cultures of their schools. Regardless of the methods adopted, it is incumbent upon scholars to investigate the socialization experience from multiple perspectives, which includes capturing the voices of potential APE recruits, pre-service teachers, and practicing APE professionals. The perspectives of key stakeholders, such as school administrators, colleagues, parents, and children can also aid in understanding the socialization process and should be included. Ultimately, socialization research should also include the perspectives of, and be targeted toward, policymakers in order to more fully influence the relevance of research in impacting public policies related to APE.

Finally, given that occupational socialization theory has historically focused more on the US context, and that nearly all the current APE teacher socialization research has been situated in the US, it is imperative that scholars make an intentional effort to examine how socialization differs across geographic and cultural boundaries. This is especially important given that policies and expectations for teachers differ around the world. For example, while APE teachers in some countries, such as the US, are required to follow certain procedures in compliance with special education law, those in other countries that do not have developed legislation may experience the phases of socialization differently. It is likely that other differences specific to teaching APE will arise as research proliferates.

Conclusion

The purpose of this chapter was to provide an overview of occupational socialization theory as a framework for studying the recruitment, education, and ongoing socialization of APE teachers. Toward this end, the phases of acculturation, professional socialization, and organizational socialization have been described generally, and with specific reference to APE recruits and pre-service and in-service teachers. Current research trends and future directions were also explored. Similarly to how it has been positioned within the physical education literature (Richards & Gaudreault, 2017b), occupational socialization theory reflects both a theoretical perspective for conducting research in APE settings, as well as a conceptual framework for structuring both pre-service and in-service teacher professional learning opportunities. This latter purpose allows APETE and continuing professional development opportunities to be developed around, and guided by, evidence-based principles of practice.

While occupational socialization could serve as a framework for teacher education and learning, the field of socialization research in APE is still underdeveloped. Some lessons learned through physical education teacher education and continuing professional development research can be used to guide practices in APE. Nevertheless, the review of the available research has indicated that the socialization experiences of APE teachers is different in many ways than that which has been conducted with their physical education counterparts. We hope this chapter serves as inspiration for APE doctoral students and faculty members to become involved in APE teacher socialization research to develop a larger evidence base and improve the extent to which the theory can be used for teacher education and development.

Key summary points

- Socialization is dialectical in nature, suggesting that individuals may resist the influence of those who seek to socialize them.
- Occupational socialization is described in three phases, which include acculturation, professional socialization, and organizational socialization.

- Acculturation refers to pre-training socialization, which occurs during formative education and captures the process through which individuals are recruited into APETE.
- APE recruits may experience an incomplete apprenticeship of observation due to limited exposure to APE teachers during their formative years.
- Early research suggests that APE recruits are more teaching oriented than general physical education teachers.
- Recruits enter professional socialization once they formally enroll in APETE. During this experience, they are taught the knowledge and skills required to teach APE.
- Given that they are more teaching oriented and have less well-formed beliefs as a result of an incomplete apprenticeship of observation, pre-service APE teachers may be more receptive to APETE than their generalist counterparts.
- Organizational socialization begins as individuals begin their jobs as APE teachers and continues throughout their careers. During this time, key socializing agents include other teachers, administrators, parents, and students.
- APE teachers may experience greater degrees of marginalization and isolation than generalists due to their varied caseloads and inconsistent working environments. General physical education teachers may contribute to this marginalization.

Reflective questions for further consideration

1. How do the three phases of socialization contribute to individuals' socialization into and through careers in APE?
2. What are the implications of occupational socialization taking a dialectical approach to understanding socialization into APE?
3. How might a false or incomplete apprenticeship of observation during formative education influence APE recruits' perception of APETE?
4. Based on the available research, what are the similarities and the differences between the socializing experiences between APE teachers and physical education generalists?
5. To what extent might the marginalization and isolation of APE teachers contribute to teacher burnout and early career exit?
6. How can occupational socialization theory be used as a framework for developing APETE programs and continuing professional development opportunities?

References

Achinstein, B., Ogawa, R. T., & Speiglman, A. (2004). Are we creating seperate and unequal tracks of teachers? The effects of state policy, local conditions, and teacher characteristics on new teacher socialization. *American Educational Research Journal, 41*, 557–603.

Bauer, T. N., & Erdogan, B. (2011). Organizational socialization: The effective onboarding of new employees. In S. Zedeck (Ed.), *APA handbook of industrial and organizational psychology: Maintaining, expanding, and contracting the organization* (Vol. 3, pp. 51–64). Washington, DC: American Psychological Association.

Betourne, J., & Richards, K. A. R. (2015). Using autobiographical essays to encourage student reflection on socialization experiences. *Journal of Physical Education, Recreation and Dance, 86*(2), 34–40.

Billingham, M. (2007). Sociological perspectives. In B. Stretch & M. Whitehouse (Eds.), *Health and social care* (pp. 301–334). Oxford, UK: Heinemann.

Blankenship, B. T., & Coleman, M. M. (2009). An examination of "wash out" and workplace conditions of beginning physical education teachers. *Physical Educator, 66*, 97–111.

Bredahl, A. M. (2013). Sitting and watching the others being active: The experienced difficulties in physical education when having a disability. *Adapted Physical Activity Quarterly*, *30*, 40–58.

Breithoff, C., Taliaferro, A., Bulger, S., & Jones, E. (2017, July). Learning to differentiate instruction in student teaching: The need for greater intentionality. Paper presented at the National Consortium for Physical Education for Individuals with Disabilities (NCPEID), Arlington, VA.

Bryan, R. R., McCubbin, J., & van der Mars, H. (2013). The ambiguous role of the paraeducator in the general physical education environment. *Adapted Physical Activity Quarterly*, *29*, 164–183.

Casey, A., & Fletcher, T. (2012). Trading places: From physical education teachers to teacher educators. *Journal of Teaching in Physical Education*, *31*, 362–380.

Chan, F., Livneh, H., Pruett, S. R., Wang, C., & Zheng, L. (2009). Societal attitudes toward disability: Concepts, measurements, and interventions. In F. Chan, E. Da Sillva Cardoso, & J. Chronister (Eds.), *Understanding psychosocial adjustment to chronic illness and disability* (pp. 333–367). New York, NY: Springer.

Children and Families Act. (2014). London, UK: Queen's Printer of Acts of Parliament.

Christensen, R., & Barney, D. C. (2011). Cooperating teachers' expectations for student teachers during the student teaching experience in physical education. *Asian Journal of Physical Education and Recreation*, *17*(2), 6–15.

Clausen, J. A. (Ed.). (1968). *Socialization and society*. Boston, MA: Little Brown and Company.

Crum, B. J. (1993). Conventional thought and practice in physical education: Problems of teaching and implications for change. *Quest*, *45*, 339–356.

Curtner-Smith, M. (1997). The impact of biography, teacher education, and organizational socialization on the perspectives and practices of first-year physical education teachers: Case studies of recruits with coaching orientations. *Sport, Education and Society*, *2*, 73–94.

Curtner-Smith, M. (1998). Influence of biography, teacher education, and entry into the workforce on the perspectives and practices of first-year elementary school physical education teachers. *European Journal of Physical Education*, *3*, 75–98.

Curtner-Smith, M. (2001). The occupational socialization of a first-year physical education teacher with a teaching orientation. *Sport, Education and Society*, *6*, 81–105.

Curtner-Smith, M. (2017). Acculturation, recruitment, and the development of orientations. In K. A. R. Richards & K. L. Gaudreault (Eds.), *Teacher socialization in physical education: New perspectives* (pp. 33–46). New York, NY: Routledge.

Curtner-Smith, M., Hastie, P., & Kinchin, G. D. (2008). Influence of occupational socialization on beginning teachers' interpretation and delivery of sport education. *Sport, Education and Society*, *13*, 97–117.

Curtner-Smith, M., & Sofo, S. (2004). Preservice teachers' conceptions of teaching within sport education and multi-activity units. *Sport, Education and Society*, *9*, 347–377.

Dillon, S. R., & Sherrill, C. (2003). Self-reported job responsibilities of public school adapted physical educators. *Perceptual & Motor Skills*, *96*, 305–310.

Feiman-Nemser, S. (2001). From preparation to practice: Designing a continuum to strengthen and sustain teaching. *Teachers College Record*, *103*, 1013–1055.

Fejgin, N., Talmor, R., & Erlich, I. (2005). Inclusion and burnout in physical education. *European Physical Education Review*, *11*, 29–49.

Ferry, M., & McCaughtry, N. (2013). Secondary physical edudcators and sport content: A love affair. *Journal of Teaching in Physical Education*, *32*, 375–393.

Flory, S. B. (2016). Professional socialization experiences of early career urban physical educators. *European Physical Education Review*, *22*, 430–449.

Gaudreault, K. L., Richards, K. A. R., & Woods, A. M. (2018). Understanding the perceived mattering of physical education teachers. *Sport, Education and Society*, *23*, 578–590.

Gore, J. (1990). Pedagogy as text in physical education teacher education: Beyond the preferred reading. In D. Kirk & R. Tinning (Eds.), *Physical education, curriculum and culture: Critical issues in the contemporary crisis* (pp. 101–138). London, UK: Falmer Press.

Graber, K. C. (1991). Studentship in preservice teacher education: A qualitative study of undergraduates in physical education. *Research Quarterly for Exercise and Sport*, *62*, 41–51.

Grotjahn, R. (1991). The research programme subjective theories: A new approach in second language research. *Studies in Second Language Acquisition*, *13*, 187–214.

Haegele, J. A., & Zhu, X. (2017). Experiences of individuals with visual impairments in integrated physical education: A retrospective study. *Research Quarterly for Exercise & Sport*, *88*, 425–435.

Hodge, S. R., Lieberman, L. J., & Murata, N. M. (2012). *Essentials of teaching adapted physical education.* Scottsdale, AZ: Holcomb-Hathaway.

Individuals with Disabilities Education Act. (2004). *P.L. 108-446.*

Jackson, P. (1968). *Life in classrooms.* New York, NY: Holt, Rinehart, and Winston.

Kougioumtzis, K., Patriksson, G., & Stråhlman, O. (2011). Physical education teachers' professionalization: A review of occupational power and professional control. *European Physical Education Review, 17,* 111–129.

Lacey, C. (1977). *The socialization of teachers.* London, UK: Methuen.

Laureano, J., Konukman, F., Gümüşdağ, H., Erdoğan, S., Yu, J., & Çekin, R. (2014). Effects of marginalization on school physical education programs: A literature review. *Physical Culture and Sport: Studies and Research, 64,* 29–40.

Lavay, B., Sakai, J., Ortiz, C., & Roth, K. (2015). Tablet technology to monitor physical education IEP goals and benchmarks. *Journal of Physical Education, Recreation and Dance, 86*(6), 16–23.

Lawson, H. A. (1983a). Toward a model of teacher socialization in physical education: Entry into schools, teachers' role orientations, and longevity in teaching (part 2). *Journal of Teaching in Physical Education, 3*(1), 3–15.

Lawson, H. A. (1983b). Toward a model of teacher socialization in physical education: The subjective warrant, recruitment, and teacher education (part 1). *Journal of Teaching in Physical Education, 2*(3), 3–16.

Lawson, H. A. (1986). Occupational socialization and the design of teacher education programs. *Journal of Teaching in Physical Education, 5,* 107–116.

Lawson, H. A. (2016). Stewarding the discipline with cross-boundary leadership. *Quest, 68,* 91–115.

Lawson, H. A. (Ed.). (2018). *Redesigning physical education: An equity agenda in which every child matters.* New York, NY: Routledge.

Lee, H. M., & Curtner-Smith, M. (2011). Impact of occupational socialization on the perspectives and practices of sport pedagogy doctoral students. *Journal of Teaching in Physical Education, 30,* 296–313.

Lieberman, L. J., & Houston-Wilson, C. (2011). Strategies for increasing the status and value of adapted physical education in schools. *Journal of Physical Education, Recreation and Dance, 82*(6), 25–28.

Lortie, D. C. (1975). *Schoolteacher: A sociological study.* Chicago: University of Chicago Press.

Lux, K., & McCullick, B. A. (2011). How one exceptional teacher navigated her working environment as the teacher of a marginal subject. *Journal of Teaching in Physical Education, 30,* 358–374.

Mansfield, C., Beltman, S., Broadley, T., & Weatherby-Fell, N. (2016). Building resilience in teacher education: An evidenced informed framework. *Teaching and Teacher Education, 54,* 77–87.

McMahon, E., & MacPhail, A. (2007). Learning to teach sport education. *The Experiences of Pre-service Teachers European Physical Education Review, 13,* 229–246.

Merton, R. K., Reader, G., & Kendall, P. (1957). *The student-physician: Introductory studies in the sociology of medical education.* Cambridge, MA: Harvard University Press.

Morley, D., Bailey, R., Tan, J., & Cooke, B. (2005). Inclusive physical education: Teachers views of including pupils with special education needs and/or disabilities in physical education. *European Physical Education Review, 11,* 84–106.

Newell, K. M. (1990). Kinesiology: The label for the study of physical activity in higher education. *Quest, 42,* 269–278.

Newell, K. M. (2007). Kinesiology: Challenges of multiple agendas. *Quest, 59,* 5–24.

Nichols, C., Block, M. E., & Wilson, W. J. (2018). Analysis of graduate programs in adapted physical education in the United States. *International Journal of Kinesiology in Higher Education.* doi:10.1080/24711616.2018.1535262

O'Leary, N., Longmore, C., & Medcalf, R. (2015). The influence of occupational socialisation upon the teaching of pupils experiencing social and emotional behavioural difficulties (SEBD) in physical education. *Journal of Research in Special Needs Education, 15,* 247–256.

O'Neil, K., & Richards, K. A. R. (2018). Breaking from traditionalism: Strategies for the recruitment of physical education teachers. *Journal of Physical Education, Recreation and Dance, 89*(2), 34–41.

Obrusnikova, I., & Kelly, L. E. (2009). Caseloads and job demographics of adapted physical educators in the United States. *Perceptual & Motor Skills, 109,* 737–746.

Park, C. W., & Curtner-Smith, M. (2018). Influence of occupational socialization on the perspectives and practices of adapted physical education teachers. *Adapted Physical Activity Quarterly, 35,* 214–232.

Pennington, T., Prusak, K. A., & Wilkinson, C. (2014). Succeeding together of failing alone: Going from good to great in physical education. *Journal of Teaching in Physical Education, 33,* 28–52.

Piletic, C. K., & Davis, R. (2010). A profile of the introduction to adapted physical education course within undergraduate physical education teacher education programs. *ICHPER-SD Journal of Research*, *5*(2), 26–32.

Pogodzinski, B. (2012). The socialization of new teachers into teacher unions. *Labor Studies Journal*, *37*, 183–202.

Prusak, K. A., Pennington, T., Graser, S. V., Beighle, A., & Morgan, C. F. (2010). Systematic success in physical education: The East Valley phenomenon. *Journal of Teaching in Physical Education*, *29*, 85–106.

Pugach, M. (1992). Uncharted territory: Research on the socialization of special education teachers. *Teacher Education and Special Education*, *15*, 133–147.

Qi, J., & Ha, A. S. (2012). Inclusion in physical education: A review of literature. *International Journal of Disability, Development and Education*, *59*(3), 257–281. doi:https://doi.org/10.1080/1034912X.2012.697737

Richards, K. A. R. (2015). Role socialization theory: The sociopolitical realities of teaching physical education. *European Physical Education Review*, *21*, 379–393.

Richards, K. A. R., & Gaudreault, K. L. (2017a). Future directions for the study of teacher socialization in physical education. In K. A. R. Richards & K. L. Gaudreault (Eds.), *Teacher socialization in physical education: New perspectives* (pp. 262–273). New York, NY: Routledge.

Richards, K. A. R., & Gaudreault, K. L. (Eds.). (2017b). *Teacher socialization in physical education: New perspectives*. New York, NY: Taylor & Francis.

Richards, K. A. R., Gaudreault, K. L., Starck, J. R., & Woods, A. M. (2018). Physical education teachers' perceptions of perceived mattering and marginalization. *Physical Education and Sport Pedagogy*, *23*, 445–459.

Richards, K. A. R., Hemphill, M. A., & Templin, T. J. (2018). Personal and contextual factors related to teachers' experiences with stress and burnout. *Teachers and Teaching: Theory and Practice*, *24*, 768–787.

Richards, K. A. R., Housner, L. D., & Templin, T. J. (2018). Addressing physical education teacher socialization through standards-based reform of physical education teacher education. *Quest*, *70*, 334–353.

Richards, K. A. R., Templin, T. J., & Gaudreault, K. L. (2013). Understanding the realities of school life: Recommendations for the preparation of physical education teachers. *Quest*, *65*, 442–457.

Richards, K. A. R., Templin, T. J., & Graber, K. C. (2014). The socialization of teachers in physical education: Review and recommendations for future works. *Kinesiology Review*, *3*, 113–134.

Richards, K. A. R., & Wilson, W. J. (2019). Recruitment and initial socialization into adapted physical education teacher education. *European Physical Education Review*. doi:https://doi.org/10.1177/1356336X18825278

Richards, K. A. R., Wilson, W. J., & Richards, A. L. (2017, November). *The professional socialization of adapted physical education teachers*. Paper presented at the Association Internationale des Écoles Supérieures d'Éducation Physique (AIESEP), Gosier, Guadeloupe.

Russell, J., Gaudreault, K. L., & Richards, K. A. R. (2016). Doctoral student socialization: Developing stewards of the physical education profession. *Quest*, *68*, 439–456.

Sato, T., & Haegele, J. A. (2017). Graduate students' practicum experiences instructing students with severe and profound disabilities in physical education. *European Physical Education Review*, *23*, 196–211.

Schempp, P. G., & Graber, K. C. (1992). Teacher socialization from a dialectical perspective: Pretraining through induction. *Journal of Teaching in Physical Education*, *11*, 329–348.

Skelton, A. (1990). Development sites: A gradualist approach to strategic redefinition. *British Journal of Sociology of Education*, *11*, 387–395.

Solmon, M. A., & Garn, A. C. (2014). Effective teaching in physical education: Using transportation metaphors to assess our status and drive our future. *Research Quarterly for Exercise and Sport*, *85*, 20–26.

Sparkes, A., Templin, T. J., & Schempp, P. G. (1993). Exploring dimensions in marginality: Reflecting on the life histories of physical education teachers. *Journal of Teaching in Physical Education*, *12*, 386–398.

Starck, J. R., Richards, K. A. R., & O'Neil, K. (2018). A conceptual framework for assessment literacy: Opportunities for physical education teacher education. *Quest*. doi:10.1080/00336297.2018.1465830

Stokking, K., Leenders, F., Jong, J. D., & Tartwijk, J. V. (2003). From student to teacher: Reducing practice shock and early dropout in the teaching profession. *European Journal of Teacher Education*, *26*, 329–350.

Stran, M., & Curtner-Smith, M. (2009). Influence of occupational socialization on two preservice teachers' interpretation and delivery of the sport education model. *Journal of Teaching in Physical Education*, *28*, 38–53.

Tahir, A., & Qadir, S. A. (2012). Challenges of classroom management to effective teacher socialization: A study of beginning English teachers. *Pakistan Journal of Social Sciences*, *32*, 21–37.

Templin, T. J., & Richards, K. A. R. (2014). C. H. McCloy lecture: Reflections on socialization into physical education: An intergenerational perspective. *Research Quarterly for Exercise and Sport*, *85*, 431–445.

Timken, G., & van der Mars, H. (2009). The effect of case methods on preservice physical education teachers' value orientations. *Physical Education and Sport Pedagogy*, *14*, 169–187.

US Department of Education. (2018). *The condition of education 2018: Children and youth with disabilities.* Washington, DC: Author.

Van Maanen, J., & Schein, E. (1979). Toward a theory of organizational socialization. In B. Staw (Ed.), *Research in organizational behavior* (Vol. 1, pp. 209–261). Greenwich, CT: JAI Press.

Waller, W. (1932). *The sociology of teaching.* New York: Russell & Russell.

Wilkinson, S., Harvey, W. J., Bloom, G. A., Joober, R., & Grizenko, N. (2013). Student teacher experiences in a service-learning project for children with attention-deficit hyperactivity disorder. *Physical Education and Sport Pedagogy*, *18*, 475–491.

Wilson, W. J. (2018). Teachers' knowledge and implementation of least restrictive environment in physical education. (Doctor of Philosophy Doctoral Dissertation), University of Virginia, Charlottesville, VA.

Wilson, W. J., Haegele, J., Richards, K. A. R., & Kelly, L. E. (2017, July). The influence of sports camps for youth with disabilities on the socialization of preservice teachers. Paper presented at the National Consortium for Physical Education for Individuals with Disabilities (NCPEID), Arlington, VA.

Wilson, W. J., Richards, K. A. R., & Kelly, L. E. (2017). The socialization of adapted physical educators: What is known and future directions. *Palaestra*, *31*(4), 26–31.

Young, A., & MacPhail, A. (2015). "Standing in the periphery:" Cooperating teachers' perspectives and responses to the role of supervision. *European Physical Education Review*, *21*, 222–237.

Zeichner, K. M., & Gore, J. M. (1990). Teacher socialization. In W. R. Houston, M. Haberman, & J. Sikula (Eds.), *Handbook of research on teacher education* (pp. 329–348). New York: Macmillan Publishing Company.

Zeichner, K. M., & Tabachnick, B. (1983, April). Teacher perspectives in the face of the institutional press. Paper presented at the Annual Meeting of American Educational Research Association, Montreal, Canada.

Part IV
Research trends in adapted physical education

24

Pre-service teacher training in adapted physical education

E. William Vogler

Introduction

The purpose of this chapter is to provide an overview of pre-service teacher education in adapted physical education (APE). For this chapter, pre-service teacher education in APE refers to any or all training experiences related to the preparation of physical education teachers in working with children with disabilities. This includes the training of APE specialists with significant coursework and practicum experiences in their preparation programs, as well as general physical educators with much less APE-related coursework or experience. Throughout the chapter, the phrase pre-service teacher training is used interchangeably with the terms professional preparation and physical education teacher education (PETE). Pre-service students may also be referred to as teacher candidates.

Historical overview

APE, arguably, became most prominent internationally in the 1950s and 1960s (for an overview of the history of APE, please see Chapter 1). Importantly, legislation and laws have mandated that educational services, including APE, must be provided by trained teachers rather than therapists or psychologists. This meant that physical educators seeking to teach APE must have specific training in this area. Early on, APE was largely implemented in either one-to-one or self-contained small group settings separate from peers without disabilities. In the United States, the solution of the question of how best to train new teachers to work with children with disabilities became the provision of a number of federally funded Master's degree level training grants, which would help prepare teachers at the graduate level (Winnick, 1986). These newly trained specialists were to be provided a body of specialized training in areas such as assessment, writing individualized education programs (IEPs) and behavior management (Kelly, 2006). These "APE specialists" had knowledge and skills that were distinct and separate from traditionally trained undergraduate physical education teachers who may have had only a singularly required APE course and minimal practical pre-service experience. An unintended consequence of this training approach, however, was the development of a dichotomous educational system, with general education on the one hand and special education on the other (Stainback & Stainback, 1990). This divergence in training has become a challenge, as students with disabilities are increasingly educated in general physical education contexts with their peers without disabilities.

As a result of the movement toward inclusive education (see Chapter 4), the schooling of children with and without disabilities together became commonplace in the early to mid-1990s (Hossain, 2012). Overall, reviews regarding the efficacy of students with disabilities receiving APE in general physical education suggest the knowledge base has insufficient depth and specificity to be conclusive (Block & Obrusnikova, 2007; Makopoulou & Thomas, 2016; Wilhelmsen & Sorensen, 2017). One consistent finding across reviews, however, was that pre-service teaching exposure to children with disabilities can lead to more favorable attitudes by future teachers, reinforcing Dewey's (1938) notion that experiential education should be based on real life interactive experiences (Dewey, 1938) and Allport's (1954) contact theory.

Regarding the professional preparation needed for inclusive education, Hardman (2009) stated that pre-service training programs were often mismatched with the practice of teaching (Hardman, 2009). Teacher education programs still tended to be distinct among themselves in the form of early childhood, primary, secondary, special, and physical education (Hardman, 2009). However, the move towards inclusion called for a more integrated or collaborative pre-service training model in which professors from the distinct educational perspectives crossed curricular lines and worked together on the best inclusive professional preparation program. One example in physical education was a collaborative model presented by Kowalski (1995) and Rizzo, Broadhead, and Kowalski (1997), in which "infusion" of information about individuals with disabilities was to be placed systematically into an entire professional preparation curriculum. This meant, in addition to an APE course, information about disability would be infused into all professional preparation coursework (e.g., elementary and secondary physical education [PE]), activity courses (e.g., tennis, badminton, volleyball, basketball, swimming, etc.), and sub-disciplinary courses (e.g., motor behavior, biomechanics, exercise physiology, sport psychology). Despite the promising ideology of a collaborative/integrative professional preparation model, it is not yet an evidence-based practice due to the lack of empirical examinations (Nevin, Thousand, & Villa, 2009) in the area.

Critical features of pre-service training

The history of pre-service training in APE leads to several important features about how to properly structure and implement training programs. Examples include considerations regarding the type of skills and knowledge that are needed in pre-service training, the types of coursework and practicum experiences that are necessary, and what pedagogical models can be successful. The following sections provide overviews of each of these features when discussing pre-service APE training.

Skills and knowledge

The skills and knowledge valued for professional preparation in physical education, specific to the US, are outlined in the National Standards for Initial Physical Education Teacher Education [Society of Health and Physical Educators (SHAPE) of America, 2017]. The standards are: (a) Content and Foundational Knowledge (Standard 1), (b) Skillfulness and Health Related Fitness (Standard 2), (c) Planning and Implementation (Standard 3), (d) Instructional Delivery and Management (Standard 4), Assessment of Student Learning (Standard 5), and Professional Responsibility (Standard 6). While these are generally accepted standards for physical educators in the US, there is no specific mention of any unique set of skills and knowledge required to teach children with disabilities in these initial standards.

Prompted by leadership in the National Consortium for Individuals with Disability in Physical Education (NCPEID), a set of national standards with implications for teacher education in APE were established in 1995 (Kelly, 2006). These standards are referred to as the Adapted Physical Education National Standards (APENS) and are considered to be logical extensions of the previously referred to SHAPE standards. The APENS teacher standards stress knowledge and skills unique to students with disabilities in movement-based programs. These include knowledge of the following standards: (a) Human Development (Standard 1), Motor Behavior (Standard 2), Exercise Science (Standard 3), Measurement and Evaluation (Standard 4), History and Philosophy (Standard 5), Unique Attributes of Learners (Standard 6), Curriculum Theory and Development (Standard 7), Assessment (Standard 8), Instructional Design and Planning (Standard 9), Teaching (Standard 10), Consultation and Staff Development (Standard 11), Student and Program Evaluation (Standard 12), Continuing Education (Standard 13), Ethics (Standard 14), and Communication (Standard 15) (Kelly, 2006).

Accompanying the move by the NCPEID to produce APE standards was implementation of a written examination testing knowledge of standards needed to successfully engage children with disability in PE, also known as the Adapted Physical Education National Standards (APENS) exam. The assumption behind both SHAPE and APENS standards is that teacher candidates who have met them would have the skills and knowledge to be competent teachers of students with disabilities.

Coursework

When considering coursework needed to be a competent APE teacher, it is logical to extend assertions from Tinning (2006) about physical educators to APE teachers. Tinning wrote that the discussion must address various curricular approaches which could be used to deliver: (a) content skills and knowledge necessary to teach children, (b) opportunities for personal development as a responsible teacher, and (c) the understanding of teacher responsibilities for improving the sociocultural environment.

When considering the necessary content of skills and knowledge, this could include disciplinary content related to the foundations of kinesiology (e.g., biomechanics and motor learning), PE content in movement related content such as skills and games, generic pedagogical knowledge important to all teaching, such as lesson plan writing, content related to behavior management, and knowledge of students with disabilities. Content may also relate to pedagogical content knowledge (PCK) (Shulman, 1987), or the bridging of disciplinary and pedagogical knowledge. While a host of studies have examined PCK in PE teacher education contexts (e.g., Iserbyt, Ward, & Li, 2017), no research on this concept has emerged in APE to date. Regarding the personal development of an individual teacher candidate, coursework such as psychology of sport could be tailored towards understanding the psychology of personal attributes, dispositions, motivation, and behavior of responsible and mature teachers. Coursework pertaining to sociocultural development may include the history or sociology of sport to provide the teacher candidate knowledge about how different cultures exist within the greater society and preparation to facilitate fairness and social justice in the teaching environment (Tinning, 2006). Again, however, research is currently lacking with regard to personal development and understanding teacher responsibilities for improving sociocultural environments specific to APE.

Practicum experiences

The discussion surrounding practicum experiences must address the value of various delivery models in teacher education. For example, some programs may emphasize models where pre-service teacher candidates are sent to practicum sites which are singular and more controlled, such as a professional development school (PDS). A PDS site can be characterized as one where a partnership between a university program and a school in the community exists and where energies and resources are highly focused on professional preparation (National Association for Professional Development Schools [NAPDS], 2019). This contrasts with many practicum experiences where pre-service teacher candidates are sent out to multiple sites where there is little control over training experiences (NAPDS, 2019).

Models may also focus more on learning the proper technical aspects of teaching in artificial university gym settings, where there can be pauses and restarts in a lesson for discussion and reflection. When certain skills are mastered, subsequent practicum experiences can include off-campus observation of real teaching in the field, teaching smaller before larger parts of a class in the field, teaching full classes on occasion, and, finally, performing student teaching in full immersion for a semester of classes. For an example of this model of practicum in a PETE context, please see Dervant, Ward, Devrilmez, and Tsuda (2018). Other models may focus on implementing disability sport experiences with a focus on improving pre-service teachers' attitudes and views toward teaching students with disabilities (Alves, Santos, & Duarte, 2018).

Reflective teaching

The role of "reflective teaching", where teacher candidates think and muse over their practicum teaching experiences, is central to the mission of pre-service teacher preparation in all of education (Rink, 2014). Reflective teaching is thought to be more cognitive or introspective, rather than technical or correct in nature. In this case, pre-service teachers try out different ways of teaching, reflect on what has occurred, then change how they subsequently teach (Rink, 2014). Specifically, Standard 5c (under Assessment of Student Learning) in the 2017 National Standards for Initial PE Teacher Education (implied for APE) state that PE teacher candidates will implement a reflective cycle to guide decision making specific to candidate performance, student learning, and short- and long-term plan objectives (SHAPE, 2017). Thus, there is an expectation that a reflective teaching component is built into any pre-service model where practicum experiences contain multiple journal writings, group discussions, and other reflective assignments as part of their experiences. While some would argue that reflective teaching is a stand-alone model for teacher education (Tinning, 2006), others would say it is more of a personal disposition that could perhaps be studied within the context of the personal development of a teacher candidate (Feiman-Nemser, 1990).

Review of pre-service training research

In 2003, Vogler reported that, at the end of the 20th century, scholarly literature in APE could be characterized as "a mile wide and an inch deep" (p. 83). At this time, it was concluded that scholarship in pedagogical APE was largely in a very early stage of development, as described by Rosenshine and Furst (1973). Clearly, this includes research about pre-service teacher training. Since then, there has been a substantial amount of research conducted, but with very little depth, as evidenced in documentary analyses in the *Adapted Physical Activity Quarterly* and other reviews (e.g., Block & Vogler, 1994; Haegele, Lee, & Porretta, 2015; Kozub & Lienert, 2003; Porretta & Sherrill, 2005; Reid & Broadhead, 1995; Vogler, Kudlacek, O'Connor, & Wiseman, 2000; Wilhelmsen & Sorensen, 2017). These subsequent reviews of APE research have revealed a shift in scholarship, resulting in more theoretical, empirical, mixed method, and/or qualitative work with a greater interest in social constructionism, indicating signs of a more mature field (Block & Obrusnikova, 2007; Wilhelmsen & Sorensen, 2017). However, a review of research trends in *Adapted Physical Activity Quarterly* by Haegele and colleagues (2015) determined that there was a "gap between current research trends in APAQ and directions for research suggested by scholars" (p. 202) and that there was little change in over a ten-year period which suggests, perhaps, still a rather slowly developing field of study.

While slowly developing, research examining pre-service training has been a central focus of APE research. The purpose of the following section is to review published research examining pre-service teacher training in APE. Borrowed from teacher education (Feiman-Nemser, 1990) and PE teacher education (Rink, 1993; Tinning, 2006), research pertaining to pre-service training in APE can be organized into five distinct, yet often overlapping, orientations: (a) academic, (b) practical, (c) behavioral or technological, (d) personalistic, and (e) critical/social.

Academic orientation

Tinning (2006) commented that academic orientation could refer to the disciplinary or professionally related curricular and other course content, including kinesiology (e.g., biomechanics, motor behavior, exercise physiology) and/or methods (e.g., elementary, secondary, and adapted), or skill-related coursework used for the development of teachers. While there is a significant area of research in PE teacher education (Rink, 1993; Tinning, 2006), to date few studies in APE (e.g., Davis, Kotecki, Harvey, & Oliver, 2007; Gutierres Filho, Ferreira Monteiro, Silva, & Hodge, 2013; Jarrett, Eloi, & Harvey, 2014; Maher & Macbeth, 2013; Piletic & Davis, 2010) have specifically targeted academically oriented research, leading this impactful area of inquiry to be significantly underdeveloped. For example, Jarrett and colleagues (2014) performed a small-scale action research project which exposed pre-service PE majors to the Teaching Games for Understanding (TGFU) curricular model in learning how to teach wheelchair rugby, and participants came away with a greater appreciation for the possibilities of the model for a host of reasons, including games modification and the value of providing participants with a "voice" to reflect upon the content of their PETE curriculum. In addition, Gutierres Filho and colleagues (2013) examined how course instructors felt about infusing concepts of the theory of planned behavior into their undergraduate coursework in order to enhance their attitudes towards individuals with disability. The study used qualitative measures in which interviews were the primary method for data collection and constant comparison for data analysis. A primary theme noted in the analysis revealed that instructors held beliefs ranging from skepticism to encouragement for the practice. A final example, Maher and Macbeth (2013) used an online survey to examine the training culture of special education needs coordinators (SENCOs) who facilitate APE in Europe, and found that neither SENCOs or learning assistants had specific training in PE or APE, making them insensitive to the needs of those with disabilities.

Overall, it appears that APE researchers are beginning to engage in academically oriented research, including those that examine how curricular variables (e.g., infusing theory into coursework; Gutierres Filho et al., 2013) influence training. However, there appears to still be a dearth of studies looking at various other academic issues that should be important in the preparation of pre-service APE teachers. For example, research examining the right balance and combination of pre-service coursework between disciplinary, PE pedagogy, and special education can help enhance program construction. Further, the encroachment of disciplinary or other coursework (e.g., teacher education), leaving little room to meet national teaching standards, has been of concern to PE teacher education programs (Tinning, 2006) and perhaps should warrant attention in the field of APE as well.

Practical orientation

Practical research is that which stresses field experiences and practice (Feiman-Nemser, 1990; Rink, 1993). According to Tinning (2006) there has been a rise in the number of field-based studies internationally since the turn of the century, many of which involve service-learning programs. The basic premise of service learning is that one learns to teach and accomplishes societal needs by practicing teaching in real-life community venues (Conway, Amel, & Gerwien, 2009). As such, since the year 2000, service-learning centers and programs have become widely popular on college campuses, so it only makes sense to see an increase in studies focusing on field experiences from this perspective (USC Dornsife, 2019).

A number of examples are available of APE research examining the effectiveness of service-learning programs (Lee, Santiago, Chang, & Haegele, 2017). For examples, Miller (2017) studied service learning using reflective journal logs with pre-service APE teachers to determine its influence on vocational interest in teaching children with and without disability, and themes drawn from qualitative study revealed, among other things, a greater "tolerance" for diversity. Similarly, Woodruff and Sinelnikov (2015) found that three distinct stages of teaching and personal development occurred when pre-service students worked with young adults with disabilities in biweekly service-learning fitness training. First came an "anticipation" associated with meeting their pupils, then a "familiarization" set in which everyone got used to each other and finally there was a "commitment" after acceptance of their role in teaching.

While studies in the practical orientation differ with respect to length of practicum program (e.g., days or weeks), disability types (e.g., attention deficit hyperactivity disorder [ADHD], intellectual disabilities), age of participants (e.g., children, adults), setting (e.g., school or community), or teaching style (e.g., team teaching, small group teaching), similar positive outcomes are common across studies. These outcomes include (a) improved attitudes, (b) clarity of vocational purpose, (c) greater understanding of diversity, and (d) greater feelings of confidence (Lee et al., 2017; Miller, 2017; Wilkinson, Harvey, Bloom, Joober, & Grizenko, 2013; Woodruff & Sinelnikov, 2015).

Behavioral or technical orientation

Behavioral or technological work is that which focuses on teacher effectiveness skills. While there are a host of studies in general PE demonstrating the role of learning managerial and technical teaching skills important to the development of effective teacher candidates (Rink, 2013, 2014), little research has been done in this area in APE. As such, just one study (LaMaster, Kinchin, Gall, & Siedentop, 1998) was found that may be considered behavioral or technological orientation research in APE. This study dealt with inclusion practices of already highly effective veteran teachers who had little previous experience with children with disability. The results of the qualitative study found that highly effective elementary level teachers, without the support of an APE teacher, expressed frustration at the time management conflicts that existed when constantly attending to children with severe disability. These otherwise highly effective teachers became relatively ineffective, despite the experimentation with many different teaching styles such as: (a) individualized instruction, (b) peer teaching, (c) direct instruction, and (d) modification of lesson plans and equipment. They expressed guilt, described a sense of inadequacy, and cited a lack of human resource support and incomplete pre-service training for inclusion. An interesting point of the study was that simply being highly effective teachers alone could not overcome a lack of pre-service preparation that is required in more modern-day programs in working with children with disability in inclusion settings. In addition, the study pointed to the importance of having someone in the classroom to "help" the otherwise effective teachers.

Personalistic orientation

Research with a personalistic orientation relates to personal meaning in development as a teacher candidate (Rink, 1993). This orientation connects the value of the development of the self, which is thought to be the key concept, to the development of competent teaching (Feiman-Nemser, 1990). Research in this area before the year 2000 has been reviewed extensively elsewhere (e.g., Kozub & Lienert, 2003), and has demonstrated that attitudes toward children with disability are largely linked to pre-service teacher coursework and experience.

When examining this line of inquiry since 2000, studies using a personalistic orientation often employ surveys using the theory of planned behavior (Ajzen, 2001) as the theoretical basis for research. Supporting this notion, a host of instruments to measure pre-service teachers' beliefs about teaching students with disabilities have emerged in the literature, including: Physical educators' attitudes toward teaching individuals with disabilities (Rizzo, 1993), "Physical educators' judgments about inclusion" (Hodge, Murata, & Kozub, 2002), the Attitudes towards individuals with physical disabilities in physical education (Kudlacek, Valkova, Sherrill, Myers, & French, 2002), and the Attitudes towards individuals with physical disabilities in physical education – revised (Martin & Kudlacek, 2010). Using the aforementioned survey instruments and others, it has been collectively determined that the following variables mostly positively influenced the attitudes of pre-service teachers in their professional development: (a) APE coursework (Di Nardo, Kudlacek, Tafuri, & Sklenarikova, 2014; Taliaferro, Hammond, & Wyant, 2015), (b) practicum sites (Hodge, Davis, Woodard, & Sherrill, 2002; Nolan, Duncan, & Hatton, 2000), (c) prior experience with persons with disabilities (Hodge & Elliott, 2013; Hodge & Jansma, 2000), (d) being a novice pre-service PE teacher education candidate (Martin & Kudlacek, 2010), (f) special education coursework, (Oh et al., 2010), (g) longer practicum experiences (Pederson, Cooley, & Hernandez, 2014), and (h) pre-service training (Petkova, Kudlacek, & Nikolova, 2012). In addition, working with students with severe disability was not viewed as a positive experience (Sato, Hodge, Casebolt, & Samalot-Rivera, 2015).

Other studies not using the theory of planned behavior as a premise but investigating personalistic variables have also noted positive outcomes associated with variables of study, such as gender (Jovanovic, Kudlacek, Block, & Djordjevic, 2014), and behavioral training and field experiences (Kozub, 2002). Further, a number of qualitative studies have been conducted, which, summarized, have found that (a) disability simulation exercises helped PSTE appreciate individuals with disability (Baghurst, 2014), (b) coursework and training positively affects perceived readiness and confidence in one's teaching (Coates, 2012), (c) pre-service APE instructors were skeptical about infusing the theory of planned behavior into undergraduate coursework (Gutierres Filho et al., 2013), (d) disability simulation course requirements change the perspective pre-service teachers have of disability (Leo & Goodwin, 2013), (e) a sense of "dread" prior to teaching children with disability was diminished as a function of a service learning experience (Roper & Santiago, 2014), (f) proper undergraduate training and practicum experiences lead to adequate preparation to teach (Rust & Sinelnikov, 2010), (g) attitude and perception of pre-service physical educators of children with disability became more positive after taking an APE course combined with a practical experience (Tindall, MacDonald, Carroll, & Moody, 2015), and (h) pre-service physical educators and newly qualified teachers did not perceive readiness (Vickerman & Coates, 2009).

Critical/social orientation

The final orientation involves studies which view the social construction of culture and society in the educational climate of APE (Tinning, 2006). Unfortunately, while research using a critical/social orientation may be found in other APE-related areas (e.g., Alves, Grenier, Haegele, & Edison, 2018), research with such aspirations for social change seem lacking from the pre-service APE literature. As such, while critical orientation pedagogy intuitively appears to indicate a promising practice, there is little empirical data to support it.

Summary of key points

1. There is a shift in APE scholarship between prior to 2000 and the present, resulting in more theoretical, empirical, mixed method, and/or qualitative work with a greater interest in social constructionism, indicating signs of a more mature field.
2. The most prominent area for recent research has been in the personalistic (teacher development) category, studying the impact of changing pre-service teacher attitudes through the lens of the theory of planned behavior.
3. Proper academic coursework, previous experience, APE and special education coursework, and practical fieldwork experiences positively influence pre-service teachers' attitudes towards students with disability.
4. The length of practicum, disability types found in the practicum, age of practicum students, practicum setting (school or community), and teaching styles used in practicum sites broad in scope are impactful in APE training.
5. Behavioral research could be useful for measurement and evaluation of pre-service teacher effectiveness. The quantitative aspect of behavioral research lends itself to determining accountability in pre-service teacher training, according to Rink (1993).
6. Research orientations other than the personalistic appear to be lacking (academic and practical) or devoid (behavioral and critical) of research evidence.
7. Service learning research is becoming more popular, whereby field experiences in the form of student teaching are conducted with service learning premises that match teaching to community goals.

Reflective questions for discussion.

1. What empirically based research will best lend itself to helping the field of APE achieve a state of maturity and why?
2. Why has the personalistic (teacher development) area of research received so much attention in the scholarly literature while other areas have languished?
3. What might be some good practical outcomes by producing more behavioral and/or critical pedagogy research in APE?
4. What would be a proper blend of PE and disciplinary course content for a model pre-service APE program?
5. What are some practical examples of infusing critical pedagogy into pre-service training?
6. Why is service learning such a valuable experience in pre-service education?
7. How can national SHAPE and APENS standards best be met in an effective pre-service teacher candidate program?

References

Ajzen, I. (2001). Nature and operation of attitudes. *Annual Review of Psychology, 52*, 27–58.

Allport, G. W. (1954) *The nature of prejudice*. Reading, MA: Addison-Wesley.

Alves, M., Grenier, M., Haegele, J., & Duarte, E. (2018). "I didn't do anything, I just watched:" Perspectives of Brazilian students with physical disabilities toward physical education. *International Journal of Inclusive Education*. Published on-line 17, August, 2018.

Alves, M., Santos, L., & Duarte, E. (2018). Improving practicum experience for undergraduates using Paralympic sports event for children. *Journal of Physical Education & Sport, Suppl, 2*(18), 1118–1122.

Baghurst, T. (2014). Encouraging disability appreciation among physical education, teacher education students through practical simulation. *Palaestra, 28*(4), 44–47.

Block, M. E., & Obrusnikova, I. (2007). Inclusion in physical education: A review of the literature from 1995-2005. *Adapted Physical Activity Quarterly, 24*, 103–124.

Block, M. E., & Vogler, E. W. (1994). Inclusion in regular physical education: The research base. *Journal of Physical Education, Recreation and Dance, 65*(1), 40–44.

Coates, J. K. (2012). Teaching inclusively: Are secondary physical education student teachers sufficiently prepared to teach in inclusive environments?. *Physical Education and Sport Pedagogy, 17*(4), 349–365.

Conway, J. M., Amel, E. L., & Gerwien, D. P. (2009). Teaching and learning in the social context: A meta-analysis of service learning's effects on academic, personal, social, and citizenship outcomes. *Teaching of Psychology, 36*(4), 233–245.

Davis, R., Kotecki, J., Harvey, M., & Oliver, A. (2007). Responsibilities and training needs of Paraeducators in physical education. *Adapted Physical Education Quarterly, 24*, 70–83.

Dervant, F., Ward, P., Devrilmez, E., & Tsuda, E. (2018). Transfer of content development across practica in physical education teacher education. *Journal of Teaching in Physical Education, 37*, 330–339.

Dewey, J. (1938). *Experience and education. The Kappa Delta Pi Lecture Series. Republished in 1997 as a Touchstone Book*. New York: Simon & Schuster.

Di Nardo, M., Kudlacek, M., Tafuri, D., & Sklenarikova,. (2014). Attitudes of preservice physical educators toward individuals with disabilities at University Parthenope of Napoli. *Acta Gymnica, 44*(4), 211–221.

Feiman-Nemser, S. (1990). Teacher preparation: Structural and conceptual alternatives. In W. R. Houston, M. Haberman, & J. Sikula, *Handbook of Research on Teacher Education* (pp. 212–233). New York: Macmillan.

Gutierres Filho, P. J. B., Ferreira Monteiro, M. D. A., Silva, R., & Hodge, S. R. (2013). Instructors' application of the theory of planned behavior in teaching undergraduate physical education courses. *Educational Research and Reviews, 8*(10), 589–595.

Haegele, J. A., Lee, J., & Porretta, D. L. (2015). Research trends in *Adapted Physical Activity Quarterly* from 2004 to 2013. *Adapted Physical Activity Quarterly, 32*, 187–206.

Hardman, M. L. (2009). Redesigning the preparation of all teachers within the framework of an integrated program model. *Teaching and Teacher Education, 25*, 583–587.

Hodge, S. R., Davis, R., Woodard, R., & Sherrill, C. (2002). Comparison of practicum types in changing preservice teachers' attitudes and perceived competence. *Adapted Physical Activity Quarterly, 19*, 155–171.

Hodge, S. R., & Elliott, G. (2013). Physical education majors' judgments about inclusion and teaching students with disabilities. *Journal of Education and Training Studies, 1*(1), 151–157.

Hodge, S. R., & Jansma, P. (2000). Physical education majors' attitudes toward teaching students with disabilities. *Teacher Education and Special Education, 23*(3), 211–224.

Hodge, S. R., Murata, N. M., & Kozub, F. M. (2002). Physical educators' judgments about inclusion: A new instrument for preservice teachers. *Adapted Physical Activity Quarterly, 19*, 435–452.

Hossain, M. (2012). *An overview of inclusive education in the United States. Communication technology for students in special education or gift ed programs.* (J. K. Carlson, ed). Hershey, PA.: IGI Global.

Iserbyt, P., Ward, P., & Li, W. (2017). Effects of improved content knowledge on pedagogical content knowledge and student performance in physical education. *Physical Education and Sport Pedagogy, 22*(1), 71–78.

Jarrett, K., Eloi, S., & Harvey, S. (2014). Teaching games for understanding (TGFU) as a positive and versatile approach to teaching adapted games. *European Journal of Adapted Physical Activity, 7*(1), 6–20.

Jovanovic, L., Kudlacek, M., Block, M. E., & Djordjevic, I. (2014). Self-efficacy of pre-service education teacher toward teaching students with disabilities in general physical education classes. *European Journal of Adapted Physical Activity, 7*(2), 32–46.

Kelly, L. E.. (2006). *Adapted physical education national standards.*Champaign, IL: Human Kinetics.

Kowalski, E. (1995). The infusion approach to teacher development. *Journal of Physical Education, Recreation, and Dance, 66*, 49–54.

Kozub, F. M. (2002). Perceptions of challenging behavior by pre-service physical educators: A preliminary study. *Physical Educator, 59*, 104-112.

Kozub, F. M., & Lienert, C. (2003). Attitudes toward teaching children with disabilities: Review of Literature and research paradigm. *Adapted Physical Activity Quarterly, 20*, 323–346.

Kudlacek, M., Valkova, H., Sherrill, C., Myers, B., & French, R. (2002). An inclusion instrument based on planned behavior theory for prospective physical educators. *Adapted Physical Activity Quarterly, 19*, 280–299.

LaMaster, K., Kinchin, G., Gall, K., & Siedentop, D. (1998). Inclusion practices of effective elementary specialists. *Adapted Physical Activity Quarterly, 15*, 64–81.

Lee, J., Santiago, J., Chang, S., & Haegele, J. A. (2017). Academic community engagement research in kinesiology: Undergraduate students' attitudes toward individuals with disabilities. In H. K. Evans (Ed.), *Community engagement findings across the disciplines: Applying course content to community needs* (pp. 119–129). Lanham, MD: Rowman & Littlefield.

Leo, J., & Goodwin, D. (2013). Pedagogical reflections on the use of disability simulations in higher education. *Journal of Teaching in Physical Education, 32*, 460–472.

Maher, A., & Macbeth, J. (2013). Physical education, resources, and training: The perspective of special educational needs coordinators working in secondary schools in north-west England. *European Physical Education Review, 20*(1), 90–103.

Makopoulou, K., & Thomas, G. (2016). Educating teachers for effective inclusive pedagogies. In C. D. Ennis (Ed.), *Routledge Handbook of Physical Education Pedagogies* (pp. 473–484). London: Routledge.

Martin, K., & Kudlacek, M. (2010). Attitudes of pre-service teachers in an Australian university towards inclusion of students with physical disabilities in general physical education programs. *European Journal of Adapted Physical Activity, 3*(1), 30–48.

Miller, M. (2017). The role of service-learning to promote early childhood physical education while examining its influence upon the vocational call to teach. *Physical Education and Sport Pedagogy, 17*(1), 61–77.

National Association for Professional Development Schools (2019). Retrieved from https://napds.org/visionpurposehistory/

Nevin, A. I., Thousand, J. S., & Villa, R. A. (2009). Collaborative teaching for teach educators – what does the research say?. *Teaching and Teacher Education, 25*, 569–574.

Nolan, J., Duncan, C., & Hatton, V. (Feb., 2000). Comparison of pre-service physical educators' attitudes toward individuals with disabilities before and after adapted physical course work. Paper presented at the Annual Meeting of the Association of Teacher Educators. Orlando, FL.

Oh, H. K., Rizzo, T. L., So, H., Chung, D. H., Park, S. J., & Lei, Q. (2010). Preservice physical education teachers' attributes related to teaching a student labeled ADHD. *Teaching and Teacher Education*, *26*, 885–890.

Pederson, S. J., Cooley, P. D., & Hernandez, K. (2014). Are Australian pre-service physical education teachers prepared to teach inclusive physical education. *Australian Journal of Teacher Education*, *39*(8), 53–62.

Petkova, A., Kudlacek, M., & Nikolova, E. (2012). Attitudes of physical education students (last university year) and physical education teachers toward teaching children with physical disabilities in general physical education classes in Bulgaria. *European Journal of Adapted Physical Activity*, *5*(2), 82–98.

Piletic, C. K., & Davis, R. (2010). A profile of the introduction to adapted physical education course within undergraduate physical education programs. *ICHPER-SD Journal of Research*, *5*(2), 26–32.

Porretta, D. L., & Sherrill, C. (2005). APAQ at twenty: A documentary analysis. *Adapted Physical Activity Quarterly*, *22*, 119–135.

Reid, G., & Broadhead, G. (1995). APAQ at ten: A documentary analysis. *Adapted Physical Activity Quarterly*, *12*(2), 103–112.

Rink, J. E. (1993). Teacher education: A focus on action. *Quest*, *45*, 308–320.

Rink, J. E. (2013). Measuring teacher effectiveness in physical education. *Research Quarterly for Exercise and Sport*, *84*(4), 407–418.

Rink, J. E. (2014). Teacher effectiveness in physical education – Consensus?. *Research Quarterly for Exercise and Sport*, *85*(3), 282–286.

Rizzo, T. L. (1993). The physical educators' attitude toward teaching individuals with disabilities-III survey. Unpublished survey. San Bernardino, CA: California State University.

Rizzo, T. L., Broadhead, G. D., & Kowalski, E. (1997). Changing kinesiology and physical education by infusing information about individuals with disabilities. *Quest*, *49*, 229–237.

Roper, E. A., & Santiago, J. A. (2014). Influence of service-learning on kinesiology students' attitudes toward P-12 students with disabilities. *Adapted Physical Activity Quarterly*, *31*, 162–180.

Rosenshine, B., & Furst, N. (1973). Research on teacher performance criteria. In B. O. Smith (Ed.), Research in teacher education: A symposium. Englewood Cliffs, NJ: Prentice- Hall.

Rust, R., & Sinelnikov, O. (2010). Practicum in a self-contained environment: Pre-service teacher perceptions of teaching students with disabilities. *Physical Educator*, *67*(1), 33–45.

Sato, T., Hodge, S. R., Casebolt, K., & Samalot-Rivera, A. (2015). Physical education teacher candidates' beliefs about instructing students with disabilities in adapted aquatics. *International Journal of Aquatic Research and Education*, *9*(3), 1–21.

Shulman, L. (1987). Knowledge and teaching: Foundations of the new reform. *Harvard Educational Review*, *57*(1), 1–22.

Society of Health and Physical Educators (SHAPE) of America. (2017). 2017 *National standards for initial physical education teacher education*. Retrieved from www.shapeamerica.org/accreditation/upload/2017-SHAPE-America-Initial-PETE-Standards-and-Components.pdf

Stainback, W., & Stainback, S. (1990). *Support networks for inclusive schooling*. Baltimore: Brookes.

Taliaferro, A. R., Hammond, L., & Wyant, K. (2015). Preservice physical educators' self-efficacy beliefs toward inclusion: The impact of coursework and practicum. *Adapted Physical Activity Quarterly*, *32*, 49–67.

Tindall, D., MacDonald, W., Carroll, E., & Moody, B. (2015). Pre-service teachers' attitudes towards children with disabilities: An Irish perspective. *European Physical Education Review*, *21*, 206–221.

Tinning, R. (2006). Theoretical orientations in physical education teacher education. In D. Kirk, D. Macdonald, & M. O' Sullivan (Eds.), *Handbook of Physical Education* (pp. 369–385). Thousand Oaks, CA: Sage Publishing.

USC Dornsife (2019). A brief history of service learning. Retrieved from https://dornsife.usc.edu/joint-educational-project/service-learning-theory/

Vickerman, P., & Coates, J. K. (2009). Trainee and recently qualified physical education teachers' perspectives on including children with special educational needs. *Physical Education and Sport Pedagogy*, *14*(2), 137–153.

Vogler, E. W. (2003). Students with disabilities in physical education. In S. Silverman & C. D. Innes (Eds.), *Student learning in physical education: Applying research to enhance instruction* (2nd ed.) (pp. 83–105). Champaign, IL: Human Kinetics.

Vogler, E. W., Kudlacek, M., O'Connor, J., & Wiseman, R. (November, 2000). Synthesis review of pedagogical research in physical education for students with disability. North American Federation of Adapted Physical Activity Symposium. New Orleans, LA.

Wilhelmsen, T., & Sorensen, M. (2017). Inclusion of children with disabilities in physical education: A systematic review of literature from 2009 to 2015. *Adapted Physical Activity Quarterly*, *34*, 311–337.

Wilkinson, S., Harvey, W. J., Bloom, G. A., Joober, R., & Grizenko, N. (2013). Student teacher experiences in a service-learning project for children with attention-deficit hyperactivity disorder. *Physical Education and Sport Pedagogy*, *18*(5), 475–491.

Winnick, J. P. (1986). History of Adapted Physical Education: Priorities in Professional Preparation. *Adapted Physical Activity Quarterly*, *3*, 112–117.

Woodruff, E. A., & Sinelnikov, O. A. (2015). Teaching young adults with disabilities through service learning. *European Physical Education Review*, *21*, 292–308.

25

Technology-based professional development in adapted physical education

Seán Healy

Introduction

Technology-based professional development (PD) is an umbrella term encompassing the variety of ways technology (e.g., eLearning technologies, social media networks [SMNs], augmented/virtual reality, video, mobile applications) can be utilized to improve the professional knowledge, competence, skill, and effectiveness of teachers. The purpose of this chapter is to explore technology-based PD as an emerging research topic in the field of adapted physical education (APE). But, before I delve into the current research on technology-based PD, and contemplate future trends, it is worthwhile to consider the factors that led to its emergence as a critical and fertile research area in the field of APE.

Necessity is the mother of invention. A substantial body of work reports on the challenges faced by physical educators to instruct students with disabilities in their classes. A US Governmental Accountability Office (2010) report specifically linked the challenge of successfully educating students with disabilities in general physical education classes to the inadequate preparation of physical educators to do so. Research involving physical education teachers attests to this lack of training and feelings of unpreparedness (Anunah & Hodge, 2005; Chandler & Greene, 1995; Hardin, 2005; Hodge, 1998; Kowalski & Rizzo, 1996; Lienert, Sherrill, & Myers, 2001; Rekaa, Hanisch, & Ytterhus, 2018). This situation is unsurprising when one considers that pre-service physical education teachers are typically receiving just one course devoted to APE (Piletic & Davis, 2008). Overall, there exists a consensus that many physical education teachers lack the competencies necessary to effectively teach students with disabilities. Furthermore, the competencies necessary to teach students with disabilities are constantly evolving; physical educators are expected to remain current on the newest knowledge, including topics such as technology-integration and evidence-based instructional strategies. The lack of adequate pre-service education in the field of APE, and the need for continuous professional development to allow teachers to remain abreast of emerging knowledge in the field, results in a need for educational reform.

PD—an experience that improves teachers' knowledge, informs pedagogy, and contributes to personal and professional growth (Cohen, McLaughlin, & Talbert, 1993)—has been identified as a link between the implementation of educational reform and its ultimate success (DeMonte, 2013). Researchers in the field of APE have long understood the need for a focus on PD. This has generally focused on traditional PD; typically, this PD consists of face-to-face, expert-led PD delivered via workshops, conferences, and classroom-based coursework (Feiman-Nemser, 2001). APE research on traditional PD has generally focused on improving self-efficacy and has demonstrated limited success (Haegele, Hodge, Gutierres Filho, & Gonçalves de Rezende, 2018; Taliaferro & Harris, 2014). In addition to the inconclusive impact of traditional PD, researchers are also increasingly aware of its limitations, including constraints related to cost, time, location and availability (Armour & Yelling, 2007; Elliott, 2017).

It was from this milieu—one of unprepared teachers, ever-evolving competency requirements, and inadequate methods of PD—that teacher educators and researchers have turned to technology-based PD solutions. The aim of this chapter is to provide a broad overview of technology-based PD in APE. With research on this topic currently in its infancy in the field of APE, I will also delve into the topic of technology-based PD in other disciplines so as to inform future research related to APE. Four major areas related to research in technology-based PD in APE will be discussed, including (a) theoretical frameworks underpinning technology-based PD research, (b) research related to formal online PD (OPD) in APE, (c) research on informal online communities and networks as a source of teacher PD, and (d) current trends and issues pertaining to technology-based PD.

Theoretical/conceptual frameworks underpinning technology-based PD research

"There is nothing so practical as a good theory" (Lewin, 1951, p. 169).

Researchers have long worked to understand and improve the competencies of physical educators to teach students with disabilities. Theories of learning have often guided this research and practice; researchers are aware that as well as knowing *what* works, it is essential that we also know *why* it works (Chibucos, Leite, & Weis, 2005). The utilization of a detailed theoretical underpinning allows research results to be better understood and replicated in research and in practice. With the shift in PD delivery from offline to online, we are required to revisit and review prominent theories of learning and question their conceptual relevance and applicability to technology-based PD. Researchers of technology-based PD have not always adhered to this recommendation, however; the absence of theoretical frameworks underpinning PD programs remains a critical weakness of existing research on the topic.

Researchers seeking to evaluate and refine the use of technology-based PD to advance the field of APE should be aware of the lack of theoretically sound research on PD in general, and seek to address this void in their work. To assist in this endeavor, the purpose of this section is to examine theoretical frameworks that may guide the use of technology-based PD related to APE. With a dearth of research on the topic in the field of APE, I delve into the wider body of work on theories of learning, and examine examples of theoretically sound technology-based PD research. Specifically, in this chapter, I will examine three prominent theories that may guide the implementation and evaluation of PD in APE; constructivism, andragogy, and theories of multimedia learning. Wenger's model of Communities of Practice (CoP) is also discussed, as it is a popular and highly relevant theory for informal PD, and highlights how models of instruction derived from multiple theories are often required to underpin complex instruction and teaching processes. Other theories with implications for technology-based PD, not discussed in this chapter, include the traditional learning theories of behaviorism (Skinner, 1976) and cognitivism (Ertmer & Newby, 2008), and newer theories based on networked contexts, such as heutagogy (Phelps, Hase, & Ellis, 2005) and connectivism (Siemens, 2005).

Constructivism

Constructivists believe in the philosophy and scientific position that "knowledge arises through a process of active construction" (Mascolo & Fischer, 2005, p. 49), or that learners *build* knowledge rather than *receive* knowledge (Berg-Sorensen, Holtuh, & Lippert-Rasmussen, 2010). Instructors guided by this theory strive to provide learners with opportunities to construct meaning through active mental effort and social interaction; it is then that learning and development occurs (Altman, 2009). Constructivist approaches to learning have long shaped instruction, and research on instruction, including the development and research of PD for physical educators (Patton, Parker, & Pratt, 2013). Traditional PD built upon constructivist principles employs strategies such as mentoring, engagement in communities of practice, or self-directed learning (Little & Curry, 2008). With a shift now towards OPD, the challenge is to adapt the constructivist principles for a new environment. One popular means of doing so is by the establishment of authentic learning environments, in which learners collaboratively engage in challenging experiences based on realistic settings and contexts (Keengwe, 2019). To aid researchers of OPD in APE, readers may contemplate how they can integrate eight design principles put forth by Salmon (2002) that provide a framework for the development of constructivist OPD.

1. Provide authentic contexts that reflect the way knowledge will be used in real life.
2. Provide opportunities for social negotiation and mediation.
3. Focus on content and skills that are relevant for the learner.
4. Present content and skills within the framework of the learner's previous knowledge.
5. Make assessment informative, serving to enhance future learning.
6. Learners should be self-regulatory and self-mediated.
7. Serve as guides and facilitators of learning.
8. Provide for, and encourage, multiple perspectives and representations of content.

For a more in-depth explanation of the above principles, see Keengwe (2019). A constructivist framework has yet to be applied to OPD in the area of APE. However, researchers may look to the literature base on OPD and online instruction in general for several examples of how the principles, outlined above, can be reflected in the pedagogy and content of online courses (Chitanana, 2012; Gold, 2001; Huang, 2002; Salter, Richards, & Carey, 2004). For example, Chitanana (2012) examined how constructivist theory shaped the design and implementation of an OPD course focused on information, communication, and technology skills, as reflected by the interactions of 28 educators. Data showed the constructivist framework to be reflected throughout the OPD program, and noted the opportunities for collaborative knowledge building, reflection, and authentic tasks and experiences to be key elements contributing to the success of the program. Noteworthy in this study, and of relevance to future researchers of technology-based PD in APE, is the thorough description of how constructivism underpinned the OPD's design. This strength is a rarity in research on this topic.

Andragogy

Andragogy is the art and science of helping adults to learn (Knowles, 1980). The popularity of andragogy in PD creation and implementation warrants its examination for underpinning OPD also. Andragogy does not meet the criteria to be classified as a theory, but, rather, is a model rooted in the theory of humanism (Elias & Merriam, 1995). Andragogy was suggested as a "system of concepts" by Knowles (Knowles, 1980, p. 8) but has also been referred to as a "theory, method, technique and set of assumptions" (Davenport & Davenport, 1985, p. 152). Andragogy proposes five assumptions for the adult learner, including that adults (a) have a preference for self-direction, (b) bring experience to the learning process, (c) have a readiness to learn based on a need to know basis, (d) exhibit a problem-centered approach to learning, and (e) have a high degree of internal motivation. Based on these assumptions, Knowles posits four principles that should be applied to adult learning experiences (Knowles, 1980). Although a substantial body of literature exists detailing how the andragogy principles can be applied to various fields of adult education, including teacher PD (Terehoff, 2002), there remains a scarcity of studies on the effect of andragogy-based instructional design programs. In one of few studies examining OPD related to APE for in-service physical educators, Healy, Block, and Kelly (2019) demonstrated how an asynchronous OPD course, built upon the tenets of andragogy, could result in significant learning for participants on the topic of peer tutoring. Table 25.1 outlines the four principles of andragogy, and how they were reflected in the OPD course "Peer tutoring in physical education" (Healy et al., 2019).

Further demonstrating the utility of andragogy as a theoretical framework for OPD in the field of APE, Sato and colleagues (Sato & Haegele, 2018; Sato, Haegele, & Foot, 2017b) examined the perspective of in-service physical educators who participated in two OPD courses, "Introduction to APE" and "Practicum in APE"; each course consisted of 45 contact hours. Overall, data, collected from journal reflections, assignments, and face-to-face interviews, revealed that the physical educationphysical education teachers believed the OPD course to be beneficial, and served to help them develop their lessons and teaching strategies, and make academic adjustments to different teaching settings. Importantly, similar to Healy et al. (2019) Sato, Haegele, and Foot (2017a) provide in-depth information on how the andragogical principles were reflected in the course design.

In addition to the andragogical principles being applied to APE courses for in-service physical educators (Healy et al., 2019; Sato & Haegele, 2018; Sato et al., 2017a, 2017b), researchers may also turn to research on adult education in other fields to inform future technology-based PD in APE. For example, andragogy has underpinned research focusing on the development of library staff competencies related to technology (Quinney, Smith, & Galbraith, 2013); teachers' technological integration (Glazer, Hannafin, Polly, & Rich, 2009); and nursing education (Norrie & Dalby, 2007). Although andragogy has been recommended for underpinning teacher development, and there is emerging evidence to support this claim, common methodological weaknesses permeate the literature on the topic, including a lack of experimental designed studies and a failure to adequately detail how andragogy underpinned the program under study. Future researchers of technology-based PD in APE would do well to overcome these limitations.

Theories of multimedia learning

Whereas theories and philosophies such as constructivism and andragogy are useful for providing a structure to learning activities within OPD, creating technology-based OPD often

Table 25.1 Knowles' principles and their application to online professional development

Knowles Principles	Example of an application to the OPD program "Peer tutoring in physical education"
1. Adults need to be involved in the planning and evaluation of their instruction.	• When beginning the course, learners were encouraged to choose a student in one of their classes that they felt would benefit from a peer tutor.
2. Adults require experience to learn.	• Throughout the course, teachers were directed to design and implement a peer tutoring program for the chosen student.
	• After watching each course podcast, learners were prompted to reflect and report on how the course lessons related to their class.
	• In each of the four sections of the course, participants completed an application activity; this involved the learners taking the course lessons and applying it to their classroom.
3. Adults are most interested in learning content that has immediate relevance and impact to their job or personal life.	• Teachers were provided with an evidence-based strategy to overcome a challenge that they identified in their physical education class.
	• The course was designed so that each section had a practical lesson that could be applied directly to the teacher's class. This allowed teachers to see the immediate relevance of the course to their teaching.
4. Adult learning should be problem-centered rather than content-oriented.	• At the beginning of the course, teachers identified a student who presents a challenge to teach in physical education; a student who may benefit from peer tutoring.
	• Throughout the course, teachers were reminded that they should choose from the array of strategies offered depending on their unique situation.

Note: OPD = Online professional development

also requires a method of transferring information, and this, too, should be theoretically sound. Most often, this requires the presentation of information in an asynchronous manner that often involves the learner receiving information via text, audio, images, and/or videos. Mayer's (2009) cognitive theory of multimedia learning (CTML) is a popular theory for guiding research in this area. CTML suggests three elements that must be considered in the design of technology-based instructional material. First, instructors must seek to reduce extraneous processing, or cognitive processing that does not support the instructional goal and is attributable to confusing instructional design. Second, instructors must manage essential processing, or cognitive processing needed to mentally represent the incoming material and that is attributable to the complexity of the material. Finally, Mayer suggests that instruction should foster generative processing, or cognitive processing, aimed at making sense of the incoming material, including organizing it and integrating it with prior knowledge (Mayer, 2009). Mayer provides ten principles outlining how the above requirements can be achieved in the design process (see Table 25.2). Kennedy and colleagues (2011, 2012, 2014) demonstrate how these principles can provide the basis for the creation of "enhanced podcasts" that can transfer knowledge to pre-service and in-service teachers in the field of special education. Furthermore, Healy and colleagues (Healy et al., 2019) have replicated the use of enhanced podcasts based on Mayer's principles with in-service physical education teachers. Overall, CTML and its associated design principles offer researchers of technology-based PD in APE a theoretically sound design process. The growing body of research demonstrating its success within OPD is encouraging, and it is recommended as a basis for asynchronous information delivery.

Table 25.2 Mayer's principles (Mayer, 2011)

1. *Coherence principle.* People learn better when extraneous words, pictures, and sounds are excluded rather than included.
2. *Redundancy principle.* People learn better from animation and narration than from animation, narration, and on-screen text.
3. *Signaling principle.* People learn better when the words include cues about the organization of the presentation.
4. *Spatial contiguity principle.* People learn better when corresponding words and pictures are presented near rather than far from each other on the page or screen.
5. *Temporal contiguity principle.* Learners must have the corresponding words and pictures in working memory simultaneously so as they can make connections between them.
6. *Segmenting principle.* People learn better when a multimedia lesson is presented in learner-paced segments rather than as a continuous unit.
7. *Pre-training principle.* People learn better from a multimedia lesson when they know the names and characteristics of the main concepts.
8. *Modality principle.* People learn better from pictures and narration than from pictures and on-screen text.
9. *Personalization principle.* People learn better when the words are in conversational style rather than formal style.
10. *Multimedia principle.* Learners learn better when they receive a verbal and visual representation of the same material; a cognitive process of integration of the material can then occur.

Communities of practice

Wenger's Communities of Practice (CoP) (Wenger, 1999) model is one of the most common frameworks through which to understand and evaluate OPD. Most commonly, this has involved informal OPD (Macià & García, 2016). Wenger, Trayner, and de Laat (2011) define CoP as a "learning partnership among people who find it useful to learn from, and with, each other about a particular domain. They use each other's experience of practice as a learning resource" (p. 9). Characteristics of a CoP include (a) a domain, the knowledge that brings the community together; (b) the community, the people for whom the domain is relevant and the nature of the interaction among the people; and (c) the practice, the knowledge, methods, tools, stories, cases, and documents, which members share and develop together within their community to solve challenges facing the community (Wenger, 1999).

Researchers of informal OPD have previously used this framework to examine concepts such as the nature of online communities, and how knowledge sharing occurs in online environments (Booth, 2012; Cranefield & Yoong, 2009; Duncan-Howell, 2010). For example, Booth (2012) examined the common practices that support and encourage knowledge sharing within online learning communities for K-12 educators. Using a multiple-case study design, two online communities for teachers were examined. Based on interviews with moderators, community members, and community documentations, the authors reported that knowledge sharing and trust were cultivated and sustained within the community. This was ascribed to the community having a clear purpose and common identity, multiple opportunities for social learning, the active involvement of an experienced and credible moderator, and modeling and enforcement of appropriate online behavior. In the field of APE, various online communities exist where practitioners and researchers meet, interact, and share knowledge, experiences, and frustrations; however, research remains to be conducted on their impact on physical educators. As Booth (2012) notes, we cannot expect productive interactions to occur *spontaneously*. In APE, researchers should examine what communities are effective, and what characteristics make them so. Wenger's CoP theory may provide the framework necessary to guide this examination.

In summary, sound education relies on sound learning theory (Haythornthwaite & Andrews, 2011). The above theories are examples that may be used to guide technology-based PD in APE. Applying a theoretical lens to the design and evaluation of technology-based PD will allow us to conceptualize how learning and teaching interactions, facilitated by technology, will affect outcomes. Researchers interested in technology-based PD should seek to not merely state the theoretical construct that underlies the PD, but clearly detail how an underlying theory guides the design, implementation, and evaluation of the PD.

A review of current scholarship: formal OPD and informal OPD

Formal OPD

Online PD has been touted as having the potential to address shortcomings in teacher competence related to the learning of students with disabilities in physical education (Healy et al., 2017). This is unsurprising, as the literature suggests OPD provides a plethora of benefits for the teacher and the teacher-educator, including allowing the learning experience to be made available to teachers at their convenience, the ability for learners to access experts and resources otherwise unavailable, and for the learning experience to be scalable to more people and places than in-person PD (Dede, Ketelhut, Whitehouse, Breit, & McCloskey,

2009). Prior to exploring the research on the topic of OPD, it is worthwhile to remind the reader of the vastness of this topic. Foremost, OPD is *professional development,* and therefore may vary in its pedagogical design, participants, duration, and purpose. The addition of *online* further confounds this topic: OPD can vary widely. It can be synchronous (online learning that occurs in real time) or asynchronous (online learning that occurs at different times for different participants). It can also be online or hybrid (a combination of in-person, face-to-face instruction coupled with online learning) and can employ an array of online tools. Extrapolating from the research, therefore, requires close consideration of the OPD design under study. For the purpose of this section, I will maintain a broad definition of OPD, only stipulating that this is a discussion of *formal* OPD—that is, PD that occurs online that may be mandated, and generally has a fixed duration, curriculum, instructional strategy, and anticipated outcomes (Dede, Eisenkraft, Frumin, & Hartley, 2016).

From the onset, it appears OPD as a means to improve the skills of physical educators in the field of APE is an avenue of research and practice with much promise. However, research examining OPD's utility, in the field of APE, is in its infancy. The previously mentioned study by Healy and colleagues (2019) involved 44 physical educators in a randomized control trial that sought to determine the effectiveness of an asynchronous OPD course, built upon andragogy theory and Mayer's principles, to provide physical educators with increased knowledge about, and motivation to implement, a peer-tutoring program. Results revealed that participation in the OPD course contributed to a significant increase in knowledge related to peer tutoring for physical educators who participated in the OPD course compared to the waitlist control group. Furthermore, participation in the OPD course resulted in over 70% ($n = 15$) of teachers reporting that they applied lessons learned from the course to their classes. Although the results suggest OPD has potential for addressing the lack of knowledge among physical education teachers about evidence-based APE practices, the lack of an objective assessment of the teachers' application of the strategies learned to their classroom, and the absence of a measure of the impact on students, limits the inferences that can be made about OPD's ultimate goal: student learning. Such limitations were also evident in research by Sato and colleagues (2017b), who examined the perspective of in-service physical educators who participated in two OPD courses. A descriptive–qualitative methodology using an explanatory case study design, utilizing data collected from journal reflections, assignments, and face-to-face interviews, revealed teachers to have an overall positive and meaningful experience of the OPD courses. Several findings emerged which led to recommendations for future OPD development in the field of APE. These included the need for OPD instructors to provide thorough, regular, and timely feedback and for them to be sensitive and responsive to learners' needs (e.g., flexibility to time schedules and interests) (Sato et al., 2017b). The limited research on formal OPD in APE suggests OPD has potential for bridging the APE knowledge gap for physical educators in an environment with the flexibility, versatility, and scalability that they require. This area remains fertile ground for future research, with a particular emphasis on OPD's effect on student learning being especially warranted.

With a paucity of research on OPD in the field of APE, we may turn to the literature on OPD for teacher development in other subject areas to guide and inform research on the topic. First, we should look to a number of studies that exemplify quality research designs in this area. For example, researchers should seek to employ experimental designs to examine OPD, as was done by Masters and colleagues (2010) in their study of an OPD program's effect on the knowledge and instructional practices of fourth grade English language teachers. Research on the effect of OPD in APE should also consider study designs that compare

OPD versus more traditional methods of PD, such as that by Powell and colleagues (2010) who present us with an example where they compared the effect of on-site, face-to-face PD versus remote-coaching OPD on teachers' use of evidence-based literacy instruction and student learning. Future research on OPD in APE should also contemplate the contentious issues of OPD evaluation. The literature on OPD reveals a variety of methodologies employed to assess the effect of OPD, including teacher knowledge tests (Masters et al., 2010); teacher observation, including video recordings (Powell et al., 2010); teacher and student satisfaction assessment (Fisher et al., 2010); self-reported frequency of desirable instructional practices (Masters, 2010); and student learning tests (Fisher et al., 2010).

Second, the research base provides several characteristics of effective OPD that should inform future research on OPD in APE. Desimone and Garet's (2015) discussion of evidence-based practices in OPD summarizes five key features that make PD effective. They propose that OPD should include: (1) content focus, learning activities that are focused on subject matter content and how students learn; (2) active learning opportunities, in which learners engage in active learning activities, such as observations of fellow teachers, interaction with other learners, and interaction with student work; (3) coherence, the OPD's aims, content, and learning activities should be coherent with the teachers' school curriculum, prior knowledge and beliefs, school and district policies, and their teaching needs; (4) sustained duration, OPD should involve at least 20 hours of contact time, and be provided ongoing throughout the school year; and (5) collective participation, where programs involve groups of teachers with common grades, subject-areas, and PD needs. To conclude, despite a scarcity of research on OPD in APE, the evidence is mounting for the effect of OPD on teachers of other subject areas. This should be encouraging to researchers in APE, and prompt them to replicate exemplary features of study and OPD design, and overcome the shortcomings, as are highlighted above.

Informal online communities and networks

In contrast to *formal* PD, *informal* teacher learning (or informal PD) is typically teacher-driven and voluntary, with the duration, content, and desired outcomes dependent upon the teachers' preferences (Dede et al., 2016). Similar to formal PD, informal PD is also shifting to an online environment. Informal idea sharing between teachers, which previously occurred in school corridors, staff rooms, and during downtime at formal conferences, is now occurring within online SMNs; SMNs are web-based platforms that facilitate the sharing of information, ideas, interests, and other forms of expression via virtual communities and networks. Informal learning through SMNs is now part of daily life for teachers (Haythornwaite, 2009). This offers teachers, including those providing physical education services to students with disabilities, a new avenue through which to improve their teaching effectiveness. To harness the full potential of SMNs to contribute to the ability of physical educators to teach students with disabilities, we must first understand teachers' current use of these networks and the impact that participation within these communities and networks have on teaching.

Thus far, research on this topic in the field of APE is absent. Research in the field of general physical education teacher development does, however, suggest that SMNs have great promise as a setting for informal OPD. The extant literature suggests physical educators view SMNs favorably, and believe SMNs provide convenient opportunities to connect, collaborate, and exchange information with others in similar professional circumstances (Goodyear, Casey, & Kirk, 2014; Krause, Franks, & Lynch, 2017). For example, Goodyear and colleagues (2014) examined the communication between physical educators on Twitter and reported SMNs to be effective platforms to refine teachers' practice by allowing them to receive critical feedback, collaborate with others, and innovate within a virtual group. We can also look outside the field of physical education to the broader field of teacher education. Macià and García's (2016) review of informal online communities and networks as a source of teacher development provides us with a synthesis of the current body of work that may guide future research related to APE. The review of literature presents the main characteristics of online communities and networks used by teachers for informal PD; the communities and networks studied varied to a great degree including heterogeneity in sample size (from fewer than ten to thousands); topic (ranging from singular thematic focus to generic foci); practice/purposes (from sharing experiences, knowledge, and skills, to peer support); and platforms (ranging from forums to private messaging). The review also provides us with an overview of the research on the processes that foster participation in the communities and networks. Trust is identified as a key construct that influences community participation. Trust can be fostered when participation is based around work-related problems, when peers in the community are perceived as competent, and a sufficient level of digital literacy (Macià & García, 2016).

Other research foci within the literature on the topic of informal PD include the nature of the dialogue that occurs within the online communities and barriers to participation. Despite the frequent assertion that informal OPD has a positive impact on the development of teachers, research has yet to establish this link. As Macià and García (2016) explain, studying the impact of informal online interactions on teaching practices and student learning would require costly and time-consuming approaches. Nevertheless, research must extend beyond understanding the nature of informal OPD participation, to an examination of how such participation affects practice. Future researchers with an interest in informal OPD in APE would be well served to keep this in mind.

Current trends and issues

Technology may have the potential to revolutionize PD in the field of APE. Coupled with effective pedagogical design, and relevant content and goals—factors of PD that will always remain fundamental to effective PD—technology may offer the chance to make PD more scalable, cost-effective, flexible, and tailored than ever before. However, in this nascent field, the true scope of technology for APE-based PD has yet to be understood. To inform researchers with an interest in the area, an understanding of emerging technologies and trends in the use of technology for PD is needed. For further reading on the topic, I direct the reader to the New Media Consortiums Horizons reports (Johnson et al., 2016) and textbooks dedicated to this topic (Dede et al., 2016). These resources provide excellent overviews of current trends in technology within education, including PD. Three topics receiving increased attention within the literature and believed to be central to the future of technology for PD are (a) a move towards hybrid learning environments, (b) gamification for teacher development, and (c) technology-based individualized learning experiences.

A move towards hybrid learning environments

The sweeping wave of enthusiasm for online learning has left few sectors unaffected. Most commonly, this online learning comes in the form of massive open online courses (MOOCs), or similar style instructivist online courses. The instructor has simply moved from lecture podium to online; the pedagogical style remains largely teacher centered. Numerous OPD courses for teachers now exist, yet the success of these efforts remains unclear. While the MOOC-style course is beneficial in its scalability and cost-effectiveness, it is largely constrained as a medium for knowledge delivery for the teacher. Many of the core features of effective PD—including active learning, applicability to other school initiatives, and collective participation of teachers from the same school or district (Desimone & Garet, 2015)—are often absent in instructivist, MOOC-like, OPD courses.

The limitations of MOOC-style courses is leading teacher-educators to experiment with hybrid learning environments; these courses involve a combination of in-person, face-to-face instruction coupled with online learning. These environments capitalize on the strengths of both the online and face-to-face environments. Implementation of hybrid teacher development courses are ongoing and emerging research suggests they can hold great value (Curtis & Swenson, 2003; Motteram, 2006; Oliver, Herrington, & Reeves, 2006). For example, Owston, Sinclair, and Wideman (2008) reported on the effectiveness of two one-year hybrid OPD programs for middle school mathematics and science/technology teachers. Teachers engaged in four face-to-face sessions and three eight-week online sessions over the course of a year. Positive effects were reported for teacher attitudes, content knowledge, and their motivation to transform their classroom practice. The effects on students were mixed: whereas students viewed science/technology more favorably after the program, their attitudes towards mathematics became less favorable. The authors noted that the hybrid nature of the OPD reduced the number of face-to-face sessions, and the online portion of the OPD allowed for the teachers to receive ongoing feedback from their peers and expert program facilitators as the teachers applied the OPD's lesson to their classrooms. Based on the amassing evidence demonstrating the potential of hybrid methods of OPD, those responsibility for the provision of PD to physical educators in the field of APE, and researchers of the topic, should seek to experiment with this emerging trend in PD delivery.

Gamification for teacher development

The New Media Consortiums Horizons reports (Johnson et al., 2016) also cites the use of gamification, including virtual simulations, as an emerging trend in education, and its merits for teacher education are receiving increased attention in the literature (Dede et al., 2016). The use of virtual simulations overcomes a challenge that faces providers of PD: the need to engage teachers to actively participate in a task that is often mandated. Furthermore, simulations may help overcome the challenge of making PD relevant and practical. For example, simulated teaching environments, such as SimSchool, Quest2teach, and TeachLivE, allow teachers (pre-service and in-service) to rehearse teaching strategies in a virtual, simulated classroom (Dede et al., 2016). For example, Garland and colleagues (2012) examined how individualized clinical coaching within a virtual reality learning modality (TLE TeachLivE virtual classroom laboratory) affected pre-service teachers' fidelity of implementation of discrete trial (DDT) teaching when working with a student with autism spectrum disorder. Using a multiple baseline cross participants design, six 15-minute intervention sessions were shown to improve participants' ($n = 4$) DDT accuracy on average from 37% to 87%. Such results should inspire researchers in APE to refine and test virtual environments for overcoming challenges in the area of teacher education and development. For example, one challenge teacher educators' face in APE is how to prepare physical educators with the knowledge and skills to educate students who have unique and rare disabilities. Online simulations may hold promise for providing them with the opportunity to observe and practice the necessary pedagogical strategies to appropriately educate these students.

Technology-based individualized learning experiences

The ability for teachers to self-direct and individualize their learning experiences for their professional needs echoes the principles of accepted learning theories. Traditional PD is limited in its ability to achieve this individualization. Now, with the emergence of technology, learners can enjoy highly tailored learning experiences; technology provides teachers with endless opportunities regarding what, how, with whom, and from whom learning occurs. Mobile and personal technologies, in particular, are driving this individualization of learning revolution (Dede et al., 2016), with teachers having instant access to learning via Skype, YouTube, podcasts, and online communities.

One challenge grappled with by providers of PD is how this learning can be tracked and rewarded; what will be the *currency* of technology-based PD (Bowen & Thomas, 2014)? Jovanovic and Devedzic (2015) suggest the use of digital badges may bear utility for overcoming this challenge. Digital badges are web-enabled "tokens of accomplishment" that document learning and achievement (O'Byrne, Schenke, Willis, & Hickey, 2015), a feature commonly used for tracking progress in video games. Although yet unproven in research, this technology could offer a novel method of motivating, scaffolding, recognizing, and credentialing learning. For example, teachers could gain digital badges for completing PD courses, attending education workshops, or engaging in online communities of practice. Perhaps researchers of PD in APE can be among the first to demonstrate the utility of this emerging technology.

Possible implications for research and practice

As previously stated, technology-based PD is already commonplace in teacher education, including APE teacher education. Universities and physical education-related organizations and webpages offer courses to in-service physical education teachers focused on teaching students with disabilities. However, the impact of these courses on teacher behavior and student learning remains understudied. This section briefly summarizes the implications that can be drawn from the extant literature on the topic, specifically related to (a) OPD design for practitioners and researchers, (b) research design, and (c) the application of *new* technologies to overcome unique challenges in the field of APE.

First, providers and researchers of OPD alike should look to the literature to ensure that the OPD program is evidence-based and theoretically sound. For example, several characteristics of OPD have been tested in rigorous randomized control trials (Desimone & Garet, 2015). Providers and researchers of OPD for APE should consider whether these evidence-based factors are reflected in their OPD courses. For example, it should be ensured that OPDs (a) have a clear content focus, (b) provide active learning opportunities, (c) are relatable to the learners' context and work, (d) is of a suitable duration, and (e) involve collective participation (Desimone & Garet, 2015). Both researchers and practitioners should be aware of these elements of effective OPD that have empirical evidence supporting their usefulness. Similarly, both practitioners and researchers of OPD in APE should consider the theoretical frameworks that have demonstrated utility for OPD creation, including theories related to the OPD structure (e.g., constructivism) and multimedia being used (e.g., CTML).

Second, there are implications, from the extant literature, related to study design for technology-based PD research in APE. A number of shortcomings of previous research should challenge researchers to advance their research agenda with increasing rigor. For example, research on technology-based PD must have clear research questions that go beyond program evaluation (e.g., teacher perceptions of the program). A specific research aim —deally focused on student learning—should remain the focal point of research on technology-based PD. Furthermore, theoretical constructs with demonstrated utility for underpinning OPD should be used in the design, delivery, and study of OPD. These include traditional learning theories such as social constructivism and andragogy, and more digital-age theories, such as connectivism and heutagogy. For us in the field of APE to capitalize on technology-based PD, and utilize it to its full capacity, we must build and extend upon what the literature and theories tell us about learning in the digital age.

Finally, researchers and practitioners in the field of APE should not shy away from embracing the emerging technologies that have yet to be proven for teacher development, and research their merit for overcoming challenges related to PD for APE. Emerging technologies, such as virtual environments and augmented realities, may have untold applications for the field of APE. Similarly, there has been a call for the use of a variety of mobile applications in APE (Cummiskey, 2011; Krause & Taliaferro, 2015); the use of a variety of mobile applications for the support and development of physical educators in APE is an area ripe for research.

A summary of key points

1. Technology-based PD solutions in APE are warranted due to the lack of APE knowledge and skills among physical educators and the inadequacies of traditional PD modalities.
2. A range of theories and models exist that may (and should) underpin OPD in APE, including constructivism, andragogy, theories of multimedia learning, and Wenger's model of Communities of Practice.
3. Formal OPD shows great promise for bridging the knowledge gap among physical educators related to APE; its benefits include allowing the learning experience to be made available to teachers at their convenience, the ability for learners to access experts and resources otherwise unavailable, and for the learning experience to be scalable to more people and places than traditional, in-person PD.
4. Informal teacher learning (or informal PD) is typically teacher driven and voluntary, with the duration, content, and desired outcomes dependent upon the teacher's preferences; this type of PD is increasingly occurring in an online environment, including on SMNs.
5. Despite the popularity and pervasiveness of informal online communities related to APE, their effect on physical educators remains unstudied. Future research is this area can be guided by research on informal OPD in the broader field of physical education and general teacher development.
6. Hybrid courses are increasingly favored in teacher education and involve a combination of in-person, face-to-face instruction coupled with online learning. The impact of this modality of teacher education in the field of APE remains to be studied.
7. Providers and researchers of OPD for APE should ensure their courses are evidence-based and theoretically sound; for example, OPDs should: (a) have a clear content focus, (b) provide active learning opportunities, (c) be relatable to the learners' context and work, (d) be of a suitable duration, and (e) involve collective participation.
8. Several weakness permeate the literature on OPD including a lack of focus on student learning, and a lack of a theoretically sound underpinning; research of technology-based PD in APE should work to overcome these limitations

9. Researchers and practitioners in the field of APE should embrace the emerging technologies (e.g., virtual and augmented realities, digital badges, mobile applications) that have yet to be proven for teacher development, and research their merit for overcoming challenges related to PD in APE.

Reflective questions

1. What factors have led to the need for technology-based PD solution in the field of APE?
2. Contrast formal and informal PD, and explain how both can be fostered in an online environment.
3. Discuss the importance of applying a theoretical framework to the design and study of an OPD course in the field of APE.
4. Compare the advantages and disadvantages of the following PD modalities: traditional (face-to-face), online PD, and hybrid PD.
5. The lack of focus on student learning is a common weakness in the study of OPD; what are some ways in which this limitation can be overcome?
6. Various emergent technologies (e.g., virtual and augmented reality technologies) have yet to be studied in the field of technology-based PD in APE. Suggest one way you would envision one of these technologies being used to provide PD to physical educators in the field of APE.

References

Altman, B. A. (2009). Determining US workers' training: History and constructivist paradigm. *Journal of European Industrial Training, 33*(6), 480–491. doi:https://doi.org/10.1108/03090590910974383

Anunah, J., & Hodge, S. R. (2005). Secondary physical education teachers' beliefs and practices in teaching students with severe disabilities: A descriptive analysis on JSTOR. *The High School Journal, 89*(2), 40–54.

Armour, K. M., & Yelling, M. (2007). Effective professional development for physical education teachers: The role of informal, collaborative learning. *Journal of Teaching in Physical Education, 26*(2), 177–200. doi:https://doi.org/10.1123/jtpe.26.2.177

Berg-Sorensen, A., Holtuh, N., & Lippert-Rasmussen, K. (2010). Essentialism vs. constructivism: Introduction. *Distinktion: Journal of Social Theory, 11*(1), 39–45. doi:https://doi.org/10.1080/1600910X.2010.9672754

Booth, S. E. (2012). Cultivating knowledge sharing and trust in online communities for educators. *Journal of Educational Computing Research, 47*(1), 1–31. doi:https://doi.org/10.2190/EC.47.1.a

Bowen, K., & Thomas, A. (2014). Badges: A common currency for learning. *Change: the Magazine of Higher Learning, 46*(1), 21–25. doi:https://doi.org/10.1080/00091383.2014.867206

Cohen, D. K., McLaughlin, M. L. W., & Talbert, J. E. (1993). *Teaching for understanding: Challenges for policy and practice.* San Francisco, CA: Jossey-Bass.

Chandler, J. P., & Greene, J. L. (1995). A statewide survey of adapted physical education service delivery and teacher in-service training. *Adapted Physical Activity Quarterly, 12*(3), 262–274. doi:https://doi.org/10.1123/apaq.12.3.262

Chibucos, T. R., Leite, R. W., & Weis, D. L. (2005). *Readings in family theory.* Thousand Oaks, CA: Sage Publications.

Chitanana, L. (2012). A constructivist approach to the design and delievery of an online professional development course: A case of the iEarn online course. *International Journal of Instruction, 5*(1), 23–48.

Cranefield, J., & Yoong, P. (2009). Crossings: Embedding personal professional knowledge in a complex online community environment. *Online Information Review, 33*(2), 257–275. doi:https://doi.org/10.1108/14684520910951203

Cummiskey, M. (2011). There's an app for that: Smartphone use in health and physical education. *Journal of Physical Education, Recreation & Dance, 82*(8), 24–30. doi:https://doi.org/10.1080/07303084.2011.10598672

Curtis, L., & Swenson, P. (2003). Hybrid courses plus: Blending F2F, online and handheld computer for effective learning. In *Society for Information Technology & Teacher Education International Conference* (pp. 520–523). Association for the Advancement of Computing in Education (AACE).

Davenport, J., & Davenport, J.A. (1985). A chronology and analysis of the andragogy debate. *Adult Education Quarterly, 35*(3), 152-159.

Dede, C., Eisenkraft, A., Frumin, K., & Hartley, A. (2016). *Teacher learning in the digital age: Online professional development in STEM education.* Cambridge, MA: Harvard Education Press.

Dede, C., Ketelhut, D. J., Whitehouse, P., Breit, L., & McCloskey, E. M. (2009). A research agenda for online teacher professional development. *Journal of Teacher Education, 60*(1), 8–19. doi:https://doi.org/10.1177/0022487108327554

DeMonte, J. (2013). High-quality professional development for teachers. Washington, DC. Retrieved from www.americanprogress.org/issues/education-k-12/reports/2013/07/15/69592/high-quality-professional-development-for-teachers/.

Desimone, L. M., & Garet, M. S. (2015). Best practices in teachers' professional development in the United States. *Psychology, Society, & Education, 7*(3), 252–263. doi:https://doi.org/10.25115/psye.v7i3.515

Duncan-Howell, J. (2010). Teachers making connections: Online communities as a source of professional learning. *British Journal of Educational Technology, 41*(2), 324–340. doi:https://doi.org/10.1111/j.1467-8535.2009.00953.x

Elias, J. L., & Merriam, S. B. (1995). *Philosophical foundations of adult education.* Melbourne, FL: Krieger Publishing Company.

Elliott, J. C. (2017). The evolution from traditional to online professional development: A review. *Journal of Digital Learning in Teacher Education, 33*(3), 114–125. doi:https://doi.org/10.1080/21532974.2017.1305304

Ertmer, P. A., & Newby, T. J. (2008). Behaviorism, cognitivism, constructivism: Comparing critical features from an instructional design perspective. *Performance Improvement Quarterly, 6*(4), 50–72. doi:https://doi.org/10.1111/j.1937-8327.1993.tb00605.x

Feiman-Nemser, S. (2001). From preparation to practice: Designing a continuum to strengthen and sustain teaching. *Teachers College Record, 103*(6), 1013–1055.

Fisher, J. B., Schumaker, J. B., Culbertson, J., & Deshler, D. D. (2010). Effects of a Computerized Professional Development Program on Teacher and Student Outcomes. *Journal of Teacher Education, 61*(4), 302–312.

Garland, K. V., Vasquez III, E., & Pearl, C. (2012). Efficacy of individualized clinical coaching in a virtual reality classroom for increasing teachers' fidelity of implementation of discrete trial teaching. *Education and Training in Autism and Developmental Disabilities,* 502–515.

Glazer, E. M., Hannafin, M.J., Polly, D., & Rich, P. (2009). Factors and interactions influencing technology integration during situated professional development in an elementary school. *Computers in the Schools, 26*(1), 21–39.

Gold, S. (2001). A constructivist approach to online training for online teachers. *Journal of Asynchronous Learning Networks, 5*(1), 35–57.

Goodyear, V. A., Casey, A., & Kirk, D. (2014). Tweet me, message me, like me: Using social media to facilitate pedagogical change within an emerging community of practice. *Sport, Education and Society, 19*(7), 927–943. doi:https://doi.org/10.1080/13573322.2013.858624

Haegele, J. A., Hodge, S. R., Gutierres Filho, P. J. B., & Gonçalves de Rezende, A. L. (2018). Brazilian physical education teachers' attitudes before and after participation in a professional development workshop. *European Physical Education Review, 24*(1), 21–38. doi:10.1177/1356336X16662898

Hardin, B. (2005). Physical education teachers' reflections on preparation for inclusion. *Physical Educator, 62*(1), 44–53.

Haythornthwaite, C. A., & Andrews, R. (2011). *E-learning theory and practice.* Thousand Oaks, CA: Sage Publications.

Haythornwaite, C. (2009). Participatory transformations. In W. Cope & M. Kalantzis (Eds.), *Ubiquitous learning* (pp. 31–48). Urbana: University of Illinois Press.

407

Healy, S., Block, M. E., & Kelly, L. (2019). The impact of online professional development on physical educators' knowledge and implementation of peer tutoring. *International Journal of Disability, Development and Education*, 1–13. https://www.tandfonline.com/doi/full/10.1080/1034912X.2019.1599099.

Healy, S., Colombo-Dougovito, A., Judge, J., Eunhye, K., Strehli, I., & Block, M. E. (2017). A practical guide to the development of an online course in adapted physical education. *Palaestra*, *31*(2), 48–54.

Hodge, S. R. (1998). Prospective physical education teachers' attitudes toward teaching students with disabilities. *Physical Educator*, *55*(2), 68–81.

Huang, H. M. (2002). Toward constructivism for adult learners in online learning environments. *British Journal of Educational Technology*, *33*(1), 27–37. doi:https://doi.org/10.1111/1467-8535.00236

Johnson, L., Adams Becker, S., Cummins, M., Cummins, M., Estrada, V., Freeman, A., & Hall, C. (2016). The NMC horizon report: 2016 higher education edition. Retrieved from www.learntechlib.org/p/171478/.

Jovanovic, J., & Devedzic, V. (2015). Developing open badges: A comprehensive approach. *Technology, Knowledge and Learning*, *20*(1), 115–122.

Keengwe, J. (2019). *Handbook of research on virtual training and mentoring of online instructors*. Hershey, PA: IGI Global.

Kennedy, M.J., Hart, J.E., & Kellems, R.O. (2011). Using enhanced podcasts to augment limited instructional time in teacher preparation. *Teacher Education and Special Education*, *34*(2), 87-105.

Kennedy, M. J. & Thomas, C.N. (2012). Effects of Content Acquisition Podcasts to Develop Preservice Teacher's Knowledge of Positive Behavioral Interventions and Supports. *Exceptionality*, *20*(1), 1–19.

Kennedy, M. J., Thomas, C. N., Aronin, S., Newton, J. R., & Lloyd, J. W. (2014). Improving teacher candidate knowledge using content acquisition podcasts. *Computers & Education*, *70*(1), 116–127.

Knowles, M. (1980). What is andragogy?. In M. S. Knowles (Ed.), *The modern practice of adult education: From pedagogy to andragogy* (pp. 40–62). Chicago, IL: Association Press.

Kowalski, E. M., & Rizzo, T. L. (1996). Factors influencing preservice student attitudes toward individuals with disabilities. *Adapted Physical Activity Quarterly*, *13*(2), 180–196. doi:https://doi.org/10.1123/apaq.13.2.180

Krause, J., Franks, H., & Lynch, B. (2017). Current technology trends and issues among health and physical education professionals. *The Physical Educator*, *74*(1), 164–180. doi:https://doi.org/10.18666/TPE-2017-V74-I1-6648

Krause, J., & Taliaferro, A. (2015). Supporting students with autism spectrum disorders in physical education: There's an app for that!. *Palaestra*, *29*(2), 45–51.

Lewin, K. (1951). *Field theory in social science: Selected theoretical papers*. Oxford, England: Harpers.

Lienert, C., Sherrill, C., & Myers, B. (2001). Physical educators' concerns about integrating children with disabilities: A cross-cultural comparison. *Adapted Physical Activity Quarterly*, *18*(1), 1–17. doi:https://doi.org/10.1123/apaq.18.1.1

Little, J. W., & Curry, M. (2008). Structuring talk about teaching and learning: The use of evidence in protocol-based conversation. In L.M. Earl & H. Timperly (Eds.), *Professional learning conversation: challenges in using evidence for improvement* (pp. 29-42). New York: Springer.

Macià, M., & García, I. (2016). Informal online communities and networks as a source of teacher professional development: A review. *Teaching and Teacher Education*, *55*(1), 291–307. doi:https://doi.org/10.1016/j.tate.2016.01.021

Mascolo, M.F., & Fischer, K.W. (2005). Constructivist theories. *Cambridge encyclopedia of child development*, 49-63.

Masters, J., De Kramer, R. M., O'Dwyer, L. M., Dash, S., & Russell, M. (2010). The effects of online professional development on fourth grade English language arts teachers' knowledge and instructional practices. *Journal of Educational Computing Research*, *43*(3), 355-375.

Mayer, R. E. (2009). Cognitive theory of multimedia learning. In R. E. Mayer (Ed.), *The Cambridge handbook of multimedia learning* (2nd ed.). New York: Cambridge University Press.

Mayer, R. E. (2011). *Applying the science of learning*. Boston, MA: Pearson/Allyn & Bacon.

Motteram, G. (2006). "Blended" education and the transformation of teachers: A long-term case study in postgraduate UK Higher Education. *British Journal of Educational Technology*, *37*(1), 17–30. doi:https://doi.org/10.1111/j.1467-8535.2005.00511.x

Norrie, P., & Dalby, D. (2007). How adult are our learners? A cross-sectional exploration of the learning characteristics of nursing students in a United Kingdom University. *Journal of Research in Nursing*, *12*(4), 319–328.

O'Byrne, I., Schenke, W., Willis, J., & Hickey, D. (2015). Digital badges: Recognizing, assessing, and motivating learners in and out of school contexts. *Journal of Adolescent & Adult Literacy, 58*(6), 451–454.

Oliver, R., Herrington, J., & Reeves, T. (2006). Creating authentic learning environments through blended learning approaches. In C. Bonk & C. Graham (Eds.), *The handbook of blended learning: Global perspectives, local designs* (pp. 502–514). San Francisco: Pfeiffer.

Owston, R., Sinclair, M., & Wideman, H. (2008). Blended learning for professional development: An evaluation of a program for middle school mathematics and science teachers. *The Teachers College Record, 110*(5), 1033–1064.

Patton, K., Parker, M., & Pratt, E. (2013). Meaningful learning in professional development: Teaching without telling. *Journal of Teaching in Physical Education, 32*(1), 441–459. doi:https://doi.org/10.1123/jtpe.32.4.441

Phelps, R., Hase, S., & Ellis, A. (2005). Competency, capability, complexity and computers: Exploring a new model for conceptualising end-user computer education. *British Journal of Educational Technology, 36*(1), 67–84. doi:https://doi.org/10.1111/j.1467-8535.2005.00439.x

Piletic, C. K., & Davis, R. (2008). A profile of the introduction to adapted physical education course within undergraduate physical education teacher education programs. *ICHPER-SD Journal of Research, 5*(2), 26–32.

Powell, D. R., Diamond, K. E., Burchinal, M. R., & Koehler, M. J. (2010). Effects of an early literacy professional development intervention on Head Start teachers and children. *Journal of Educational Psychology, 102*, 299–312.

Quinney, K. L., Smith, S.D., & Galbraith, Q. (2013). Bridging the gap: self-directed staff technology training. *Information Technologies and Libraries, 29*(1), 205-213.

Rekaa, H., Hanisch, H., & Ytterhus, B. (2018). Inclusion in physical education: Teacher attitudes and student experiences. A systematic review. *International Journal of Disability, Development and Education, 66*(1), 36–55. doi:https://doi.org/10.1080/1034912X.2018.1435852

Salmon, G. (2002). *E-moderating: The key to teaching and learning online*. London, UK: London Page.

Salter, D., Richards, L., & Carey, T. (2004). The 'T5' design model: An instructional model and learning environment to support the integration of online and campus-based courses. *Educational Media International, 41*(3), 207–218. doi:https://doi.org/10.1080/09523980410001680824

Sato, T., & Haegele, J. A. (2018). Physical educators' engagement in online adapted physical education graduate professional development. *Professional Development in Education, 44*(2), 272–286. doi:https://doi.org/10.1080/19415257.2017.1288651

Sato, T., Haegele, J. A., & Foot, R. (2017a). Developing online graduate coursework in adapted physical education utilizing andragogy theory. *Quest, 69*(4), 453–466. doi:https://doi.org/10.1080/00336297.2017.1284679

Sato, T., Haegele, J. A., & Foot, R. (2017b). In-service physical educators' experiences of online adapted physical education endorsement courses. *Adapted Physical Activity Quarterly, 34*(2), 162–178. doi: https://doi.org/10.1123/apaq.2016-0002

Siemens, G. (2005). Connectivism: A learning theory for the digital age. *Instructional Technology and Distance Education, 2*(1), 3–10.

Skinner, B. F. (1976). *About behaviorism*. New York: Alfred A. Knopf.

Taliaferro, A., & Harris, N. (2014). The effects of a one-day workshop on physical educators' self-efficacy towards inclusion of students with autism. *Palaestra, 28*(3), 38–43.

Terehoff, I. I. (2002). Elements of adult learning in teacher professional development. *NASSP Bulletin, 86* (632), 65-77.

U.S. Governmental Accountability Office. (2010). *Students with disabilities: More information and guidance could improve opportunities in physical education and athletics (GAO-10-519)*. Retrieved from http://www.gao.gov/assets/310/305770.pdf.

Wenger, E. (1999). *Communities of practice: Learning, meaning, and identity*. Cambridge, MA: Cambridge University Press.

Wenger, E., Trayner, B., & de Laat, M. (2011). *Promoting and assessing value creation in communities and networks: A conceptual framework*. Netherlands: Ruud de Moor Centrum.

26

Adapted physical education research from the perspectives of teachers, peers, and parents

Francis M. Kozub, Cathy McKay, and Luis Columna

Introduction

A major premise of this chapter is that perspectives of teachers, peers, and parents of children with disabilities are important to the field of adapted physical education (APE). Traditionally, researchers have studied these groups in isolation without measuring the influence between groups. The purpose of this chapter is to encourage more study of variables related to examining how teachers, peers, and parents interact, as well as how their perspectives affect learning for children with disabilities in physical education (PE). Further, to ensure the promotion of evidence-based practices, researchers have to understand the dynamic nature of school and community-based relationships within different school, home, and community environments. With respect to PE settings, teachers, peers, and parents interact dynamically and influence one another. By studying children with disabilities, their parents, peers, and teachers from a more systematic perspective, the mediating effects of the different influences in the learning setting are better understood.

The current chapter encourages future researchers to consider both interventions (inputs) and outcomes, with an eye towards improved levels of independent functioning in key areas. Figure 26.1 identifies these areas in relation to motor behavior, social interactions, levels of independent functioning, and individual functional constraints as output variables which are the result of well-studied interventions which become the evidence-based practices for teachers and parents. Individual functional constraints are highlighted in this chapter because these are the factors within children that many researchers have focused on when studying teachers, peers, and parents in APE research. These attitudes, beliefs, perceptions, and self-efficacy can change quickly within individuals and potentially impact how a person interacts with individuals with disabilities.

The inputs found in Figure 26.1 represent types of interventions that are used in conjunction with the perspectives of acting agents, which is a major focus of the current chapter. Future research should focus on isolating important variables that influence the target outcomes using a more dynamic and systematic perspectives approach, which can include individual functional constraints such as attitudes, beliefs, perceptions, self-efficacy, and judgements. These variables have been studied in the past in relation to the perspectives of acting agents found in Figure 26.1 and researchers are now ready to examine how training for teachers, grouping patterns for

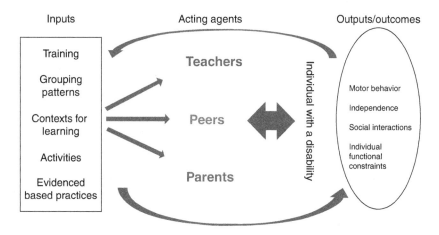

Figure 26.1 Study in adapted physical education should consider the interaction of variables to produce successful outcomes

learners, home- versus school-based contexts, learning activities, and other evidence-based practices from the broader special education field potentially improve learning outcomes in APE for children with disabilities.

The knowledge base in APE has resulted in numerous measures, theories, and paradigms that support the study of how teachers, peers, and parents impact students with disabilities in PE and physical activity (PA) settings. This chapter aims to provide researchers with information necessary to learn about the existing knowledge base in APE related to teachers, peers, and parents. The following sections include a historical overview, content overview, theoretical and conceptual frameworks, and review/summary of current scholarship as they pertain to teachers, peers, and parents. This is followed by a section on current trends and implications for practice.

Historical overview of research on teachers, peers, and parents

Historically, research trends related to teacher, peer, and parent perspectives in APE have been centered around the concepts of inclusion, equitable access, and opportunities for individuals with disabilities. Researchers have examined teacher and teacher candidate attitudes, beliefs, and judgements as well as other individual variables such as perceived competence in teaching children with disabilities, experiences during their teacher preparation program, and experiences at school (Beamer & Yun, 2014; Taliaferro, Hammond, & Wyant, 2015). Peers have been studied in both inclusive and segregated contexts using observational systems to examine interactions (Klavina, 2008; Reichow & Volkmar, 2010). Peer attitudes and perceptions toward inclusion and disability sport have also been explored (Grenier, Collins, Wright, & Kearns, 2014; McKay, Block, & Park, 2015; McKay, Haegele, & Block, 2018a; Obrusnikova, Block, & Dillon, 2010). Research in APE has shown a preference for studying parents' perceptions toward both PE and PA programming (An & Hodge, 2013; Ayvazoglu, Kozub, Butera, & Murray, 2015; Buchanan, Miedema, & Frey, 2017) and studies exploring the benefits and barriers to PA among families of children with disabilities (Cartwright, Reid, & Hammersley, 2016; Columna et al., 2017). By utilizing both quantitative and qualitative research designs, as well as mixed designs, these studies offer a comprehensive outlook on parent perspectives.

There have been significant parallels between APE research on teachers, peers, and parents and the broader special education knowledge base. It is common for researchers to initiate a study using variables and theoretical models developed outside APE to examine if findings generalize to PA contexts. This parallel is evident in Kozub and Lienert's (2003) review of the literature on attitude research in APE, as well as work conducted by McKay et al. (2015, 2018a) utilizing contact theory (Allport, 1954).

One general note about the historical perspective of teacher, peer, and parent related research in APE is the overwhelming use of descriptive methodologies in research design. Specifically, survey methodology has dominated teacher attitudes, beliefs, and perceptions since the early work of Jansma and Shultz (1982) and Rizzo (1984). With respect to peer interactions, observational techniques have been fruitful in examining children's interactions in learning contexts for decades (McWilliam & Bailey, 1995; Odom, Hoyson, Jamieson, & Strain, 1985). Peer involvement in research studies dates back to the late 1960s, where the use of peers as models for learning is considered to be an evidence-based practice in special education (Reichow & Volkmar, 2010). Peer attitudes, and the need for research related to changing peer attitudes toward disability was reviewed almost four decades ago (Donaldson, 1980). With respect to parent involvement, Folsom-Meek (1984) examined the results of earlier investigators in special education (Strom, Rees, Slaughter, & Wurster, 1980), where it was found that parents could successfully support students with disabilities in educational and community learning.

What is of considerable imperative is for APE researchers to utilize sound theoretical, as well as methodological, principles when designing research studies related to the educational outcomes of children with disabilities. These outcomes are influenced by teachers, peers, and parents; thus, studying these stakeholders is paramount. Adding to the recommendations from earlier chapters on research approaches, it is important for those examining teacher, peer, and parent variables to understand the past nature of study. Literature reviews conducted by Block and Vogler (1994), Block and Obrusnikova (2007), and Hutzler (2003) looked comprehensively at the attitudes and perspectives of parents, teachers, paraprofessionals, peers, administrators, and individuals with disabilities, providing a context to the breadth of research in the field.

Figure 26.1 is based on the historic overview of where teachers, peers, and parents have been examined in relation to key variables thought to impact on PE programming. The inputs (e.g., training, grouping patterns, learning contexts) represent not only independent variables in descriptive, quasi-experimental, and intervention based designs, but also serve as dependent variables in studies where motor learning, PA behaviors, and attitude change have been studied. These variables are seen as inputs in the current discussion of APE research history, since many studies have examined the training experienced by teachers who were at either the pre- or in-service levels, grouping patterns of children, learning contexts, and activities using descriptive questionnaires. The influence that these variables have had on the actors in teaching contexts informs researchers on teachers, peers, and parents and provides insights into learning outcomes for children. For example, teacher judgements on their willingness to include, accept, and educate children with disabilities is thought to be important in willingness to include children (Hodge, Murata, & Kozub, 2002). Further, parents have been studied in relation to the impact on PA levels and family function (Ayvazoglu et al., 2015). Finally, McKay et al. (2015) examined how peers perceive children with disabilities following interventions designed to reduce bias or prejudice.

There are three major premises in this chapter that can provide better insights into using past research and remaining consistent with current trends in APE and broader special education. First, evidence-based practices are important in the education of children with disabilities. Second, there is a preference for children with disabilities to be educated alongside peers in integrated settings and that educators should focus on how best to include children rather than on the impact of inclusion on learning (Kozub, Sherblom, & Perry, 1999). And, finally, that systems models are useful in identifying important outcomes to study how parents can be involved in the PA behavior of their children with disabilities (An & Hodge, 2013; Kozub, 2001).

Content overview

The following sections provide a brief overview of important topical areas in relation to studies concerning teacher individual functional constraints, peer influences, and parents perspectives. To start, research related to teacher individual functional constraints will be reviewed. Next, an examination of peer related research is provided. Finally, research aimed at examining how parents are an important influence on the learning of children with disabilities in PE settings will be reviewed to provide a backdrop for later discussion of suggested theoretical and conceptual study.

Teacher individual functional constraints

Research on teachers in relation to various attitudes, beliefs, and perceptions has occupied a prominent place in data collection related to the training of highly qualified individuals to work with children with disabilities. Primarily, the key findings have resulted in theoretical models that support the study of teachers, purport that training can influence attitude development, and offer scales used to measure attitude and belief constructs that demonstrate encouraging estimates of validity and reliability (Campbell & Gilmore, 2003; Hodge, Gutierres Filho, Haegle, & Kozub, 2015; Kozub & Porretta, 1998). Attitude study, as pointed out by Kozub and Lienert (2003) continues to fall short of studying the behaviors of teachers in the learning contexts where it can be determined how to improve outcomes for children with disabilities. What has resulted from attitude studies are findings that have supported APE curriculum for training teachers and in theory lead to better learning outcomes for all children.

Research indicates that teacher attitudes about children with disabilities is associated with diversity issues. In this regard, it is felt that teachers' influence of students should be positive and that educators are cultural workers (Columna et al., 2008). However, teacher attitudes can potentially be biased and not support educational outcomes. This is linked to English language development, where children from diverse backgrounds who struggle with the English language in American schools are viewed as less competent, which can have an impact on both placement and programming (Edl, Jones, & Estell, 2008; Tabb & Yun, 2005).

Previous studies of attitudes among PE and APE teachers identified level of disability and grade level as factors to consider in identifying less favorable attitudes. Early research found that more favorable attitudes were reported by responding teachers towards educating children with intellectual disabilities more so than teaching children with physical disabilities, and that increased age (of teachers) predicted less favorable attitudes (Rizzo, 1984). Although studies such as Rizzo's (1984) provided insights into the current status of attitudes, the main impact of such findings have led researchers to think beyond the attitudes to other factors, such as teachers' self-efficacy (Oh & Kozub, 2010; Taliaferro et al., 2015) and actual teacher behaviors (Ammah & Hodge, 2005; Hodge, Ammah, Casebolt, LaMaster, & O'Sullivan, 2004; Kozub & Lienert, 2003).

Peer influences

The major content in relation to the study of peers in APE has been based on inclusive principles that highlight the importance of integrated contexts. The interests and feelings of peers and their impact on the learning of children with disabilities has been a focus of much of the inclusion debate in PE (Block & Vogler, 1994; Hutzler, Fliess-Douer, Avraham, Reiter, & Talmor, 2007; LaMaster, Gall, Kinchin, & Siedentop, 1998; Obrusnikova, Valkova, & Block, 2003). This interest has prompted researchers to recommend less of a focus on testing the efficacy of inclusive environments from a learning outcome standpoint to more closely examining the processes for successful integration as an ethical premise (Kozub et al., 1999). Peer attitude research in APE provides a means to evaluate the thoughts, feelings, and beliefs of peers toward inclusive and integrative practices (Hutzler, 2003). Peer attitude change in PE settings has long been divided between two lines of research: (a) investigating whether cognitive growth through learned information has an effect on attitudes (Hutzler et al., 2007; Loovis & Loovis, 1997), and (b) investigating whether exposure to, and contact with, an attitudinal referent has an effect on attitudes (Hutzler et al., 2007; McKay et al., 2015, 2018a; Reina, Lopez, Jimenez, Garcia-Calvo, & Hutzler, 2011). Researchers have indicated that a combination of these two lines, including combining structured contact, knowledge acquisition, and awareness activities, is an effective method for changing attitudes (Hutzler et al., 2007; McKay et al., 2015; Reina et al., 2011).

From a content perspective, evidence that interactions between children and the use of peers in instructional settings is a potentially fruitful avenue of study in APE (Klavina, 2008). In this regard, peers are better prepared to support the engagement of children with disabilities following training (Block, 2007; Reichow & Volkmar, 2010). Authors such as Reichow and Volkmar (2010) have synthesized the literature on the use of peers for teaching social skills to children with autism spectrum disorders (ASD) and conclude that various peer models of intervention provide an evidence-based practice consistent with earlier studies in APE (Houston-Wilson, Dunn, Van der Mars, & McCubbin, 1997; Webster, 1987).

Parent perspectives

Parents and their influence on the learning of children with disabilities is a prominent feature in special education literature. Parents' roles in the individualized education processes, program development, and service delivery are important content areas in need of continued study. As such, research identifying parent perspectives on the education of children with disabilities in all curricular areas is important. Further, studies examining parent perspectives toward PE over time is important and few, if any, studies have examined the longitudinal outcomes of PA behavior in general on broader family outcomes. Parents are believed to be potential program providers as well as individuals with important information about their child in relation to PA behavior (An & Hodge, 2013; Chaapel, Columna, Lytle, & Bailey, 2012; Columna, Cook, Foley, & Bailey, 2014; Columna et al., 2008; Kozub, 2001). Further, the notion that parent perspectives vary based on the nature of the disability and other factors related to culture and ethnicity is important to consider in current research practices.

The study of parent perspectives shows a lack of research in APE prior to 2000. There has been a slight shift in this, and more recent researchers, such as Columna et al. (2008), identify factors related to communication and parent understanding of schools as important variables to ensure that caregivers can contribute to the education of their children with disabilities. Finally, the use of parents to support PA in their children requires the use of measures to examine variability in beliefs and intentions consistent with teacher studies discussed earlier to examine the role that parents might take in programming in the PA domain (Jeong, Kim, & Lee, 2015).

To explore how parent input can improve outcomes for children with disabilities, researchers such as Columna et al. (2014) have developed measures and focused on communication issues between teachers and parents of children with ASD. Specifically, these authors found the highest levels of agreement to statements related to teachers understanding parent concerns, valuing parent input, and encouraging participation in their child's programming. In general, Columna et al. (2014) support a need to explore parent input more in future studies.

An important issue identified in Burke, Arnold, and Owen's (2018) study relates to the issue of transition. These outcomes are addressed in the *Individuals with Disabilities Education Act of 1990* (IDEA, 1990) through transition planning; however, there are barriers to these processes when parents are surveyed. Specifically, researchers have identified a lack of services, financial challenges, lack of support from family, lack of time, and other issues in need of policy reform (Ayvazoglu et al., 2015; Burke et al., 2018). In a study conducted by Burke et al. (2018), parents responded to a national survey about transition planning. The authors found that responding parents were more educated and had more training on the transition process. Findings supported that these older parents were more likely to engage in future planning and that, as the level of disability increased, this issue of future planning was more of a concern. This study highlighted the need for family support as children aged, and particularly when functional skills in children are lacking. Further, more support is needed when educational programming is required for a child who has needs that exceed what traditional K-12 educational systems typically provide (Burke et al., 2018).

In summarizing the content of teacher, peer, and parent variables in the literature, it is evident that teachers' attitude development has received considerably more examination than peers' and parents' perspectives. This makes the latter two ripe for more study on how peers and parents mediate PE outcomes and create a more holistic successful educational experience for all children. Further, it is clear that research that goes beyond the use of descriptive methods to show the current status of teacher, peer, and parent perspectives is necessary. Furthermore, with the continued development of appropriate measures, more intervention-based studies are needed to further develop the APE content knowledge base.

Theoretical and conceptual frameworks

In moving forward to build on existing literature in the field of APE, researchers are encouraged to utilize theory, construct conceptual frameworks, and develop additional paradigms to drive inquiry and include the factors that contribute to successful learning outcomes, as depicted in Figure 26.1. As indicated by Tripp and Sherrill (1991), a-theoretical studies are problematic and, with this in mind, the current section provides paradigms, theories, and concepts that are necessary to drive research questions. This section is divided into three parts. First, teachers' theoretical and conceptual frameworks are discussed. This is followed by an examination of the ecological perspective as a broader theory to examine the collective perspectives of teachers, peers, and parents, and, finally, how to improve the study of learning for children with disabilities in APE is discussed.

Teachers' theoretical and conceptual frameworks

The major theoretical framework in attitude study of teachers has involved the use of the theory of planned behavior (TPB) (Ajzen & Fishbein, 1980). This includes the development of instruments such as the Attitude Toward Teaching the Handicapped (PEATH) model, derived from Fishbein and Ajzen's model of the theory of reasoned action and used by Rizzo (1984). In APE, the use of the TPB was cited as one of many theories necessary to study and train adapted physical educators (Tripp & Sherrill, 1991). However, studies that have employed TPB as a framework have been criticized because they have tested intentions toward performing a behavior without examining actual teacher behavior (Kozub & Lienert, 2003).

Bandura's self-efficacy theory (Sharpe, 2013) has also shown up in special education literature examining how teachers interact with students with disabilities. This includes how support and resources impact teachers' self-efficacy. Specific to APE, Oh and Kozub (2010) determined that self-efficacy could be measured in physical educators and that the instrument used in the study had encouraging estimates of validity and reliability, which opens the door for future study of teachers working with children with ASD. Additional use of Bandura's construct was also completed by Beamer and Yun (2014), examining both self-efficacy and teachers' beliefs towards including children with ASD. Self-efficacy and Bandura's social–cognitive theory continue to be promising as theoretical foundations for studying educational outcomes for children with disabilities in special education settings (Sharpe, 2013).

With respect to teacher individual functional constraints, what shapes how educators perceive children and, in turn, make educational decisions about children is an area ripe for study. This could be related to teacher perceptions, training, and available resources in economically deprived communities (Cavendish, Artiles, & Harry, 2014). The use of self-efficacy theory has the potential to impact on a major issue in training pre-service physical educators if applied to the concept of perceptions of challenging behavior in children with disabilities (Oh & Kozub, 2010; Oh, Seo, & Kozub, 2010) and combined with variables related to inequality related to the racialization of disability, as discussed in Cavendish et al.'s (2014) paper. This topic of significant disproportionality requires significant discussion, as well as the issue of challenging behavior and how this impacts teacher perceptions, which may be mediated by race. Building race and/or ethnicity as well as socioeconomic status into research designs, if by no other means than accurately reporting sample demographics, allows for a better understanding of significant disproportionality and other biases found in education that potentially impact on outcomes for all children (Hodge, Kozub, Robinson, & Hersman, 2007).

Linking teacher perceptions and self-efficacy to actual teacher decision making requires more attention in the published literature. Oh and Kozub (2010) provide a measure with encouraging estimates of reliability and validity to examine the relationship between teacher self-efficacy and actual teacher behaviors. Ethnicity and race in relation to how teachers perceive challenging behavior and willingness to use behavior supports before referring children for special education services are important educational topics that can be studied in a variety of educational settings, including APE. The use of positive behavioral supports prior to teachers using special education services could fundamentally be linked to teacher self-efficacy and training. Further, teacher decision making along a continuum of services from the use of positive reinforcers to more restrictive behavioral interventions is potentially linked to teacher knowledge and self-efficacy, as well as other race-, ethnic-, socioeconomic-, and disability-related factors.

Behaviorist theory continues to be a viable option in providing ecologically valid educational experiences for children with disabilities (Cooper, Heron, & Heward, 2007). Although not specifically systems based, behaviorist theory provides the backdrop for behavioral interventions used in educational settings. The use of functional behavior assessment and other positive behavior supports continue to be the basis for training of teachers and also the study of peer interactions in special education literature. The impact of behavioral intervention training is an important factor when examining how teachers react to challenging learner behavior (Oh et al., 2010) and also how children react to various environmental stimulations. The use of behaviorist theory and applied behavior analysis designs continues to be a feasible mechanism for examining how children with disabilities respond to interventions, as well as how important peer interactions impact on learning (Cooper et al., 2007).

For future APE researchers and others interested in developing evidence-based practices for training teachers, we support the use of theories. Past researchers such as Tripp and Sherrill (1991) identify many theories that may still be relevant today, such as contact theory. Further, broader systems-based theories as outlined by Kozub and Lienert (2003) are also highly relevant for current researchers. Attitudes, beliefs, perceptions, and emotional reactions provide important variables and potential mediators to instructional practices that positively impact student learning. It is imperative to identify which factors contribute to effective teaching. Theoretical and conceptual frameworks can assist with this task. Further, from a training standpoint, systems-based models continue to provide frameworks for teacher and professional training (Turnbull, Turnbull, Erwin, Sondak, & Shogun, 2014).

Peers

In relation to the study of peers and children with disabilities, the use of inclusive principles such as a comparative paradigm is recommended by adapted physical educators (Kozub et al., 1999). This is based on the premise that it is ethical to educate all children together. Inclusion movements have traditionally been at odds with integration processes, based on a lack of resources provided. Similar to the research on teachers, scholars have used the TPB to study the belief of children with disabilities and their peers about inclusion (Obrusnikova et al., 2010). There have also been studies examining the theoretical foundations of contact theory (Allport, 1954) as a means to justify inclusion principles as a mechanism to help all children learn to accept differences among peers (McKay et al., 2015, 2018a; McKay, Park, & Block, 2018b, 2018c; Tripp & Sherrill, 1991).

Contact theory (Allport, 1954) is a tenable theoretical framework to study how relationships between children with and without disabilities evolve. Contact theory proposes that social contact will improve relationships between diverse groups, leading to diminished prejudiced ideas, when contact is presented under the right conditions. The conditions include equal status contact; intimate (meaningful) interactions; pursuing cooperative, common goals; and support from program leaders. Researchers identified the Paralympic

School Day (PSD) awareness program (IPC, 2007) as rooted in contact theory, and specific to raising awareness about Paralympic sport, individual differences, and acceptance (McKay, 2013; McKay et al., 2015, 2018a, 2018c). McKay et al. (2018b) addressed contact theory as the theoretical basis of PSD, using a fidelity criteria instrument to control and explain the manner in which PSD met the four components of contact theory. This research addressed the fidelity of implementation to contact theory, instead of simply addressing contact settings (McKay et al., 2018b). Contact theory, along with the ideas found in Silva and Howe's (2012) work related to the capabilities approach, brings a focal point to social justice, socio-cultural attitude change, and providing opportunities for persons of all abilities to know, understand, and find value in adapted sport.

An additional factor related to the contact between children with and without disabilities is the impact on children with serious disabilities where interest in others is found when peers without disabilities are educated in close proximity. Nijs, Pene, Vlaskump, and Maes (2015) found that social interest is increased in persons with serious disabilities as a function of proximity to learners without disabilities. This, combined with the findings of McKay et al. (2015), posit that measures can be developed to examine changes in learners as a function of positive peer interactions in the PE setting.

Parents of children with disabilities

With respect to parents, systems-based models provide a solid theoretical foundation for the study of families and the impact of disability on broader outcomes (An & Hodge, 2013; Ayvazoglu et al., 2015; Ayvazoglu, Oh, & Kozub, 2006; Kozub, 2001). In the following section, we elaborate on the use of these theoretical frameworks in relation to studies focusing on parents.

The use of systems theory is found extensively in the special education literature (Turnbull et al., 2014). This model examines how families where children with disabilities grow up progress through stages in the life cycle and are influenced by inputs such as characteristics of the family, extended family, economics within the family, and a host of other constraints that impact how the family functions (Turnbull et al., 2014). The application of family systems theory is proposed by Kozub (2001) and was the foundation for additional studies by Ayvazoglu et al. (2006); (2015)). An and Hodge (2013) also support systems models in their themes emerging from the study of parents who are advocating for partnerships between physical educators and feel that parent input is important in successful programming. Findings from these authors and the continued emphasis in federal legislation to include parent input as well as consider family factors in special education programming create a sound rationale for using family systems models in future APE research where parents are a focal point.

Ecological perspective

The ecological model of human development has also been used in the APE field. Systems-based models have served as the theoretical framework for studies related to parent perceptions toward PE (Columna et al., 2008). This model proposes that a person develops his/her understanding through interaction with his/her social environment on four levels of inter-action (microsystem, mesosystem, exosystem, and macrosystem). Columna et al. (2008) asserted in this regard that microsystem represents the relationship between an individual and his/her immediate setting (e.g., parents, siblings, family members). The second level, mesosystem, is considered the connections of the child to the broader community (e.g., school, sports league, after-school programs, church). Exosystems, the third level, are the social settings in which a child does not directly participate, but which impact their lives nonetheless (e.g., parental work, family stress). The final level is the macrosystem, which includes different societal rules, customs, principles, beliefs, and values. The study of how environmental constraints at the different levels identified above could potentially provide information on how to set up interventions within specific locales aimed at improving life-time PA outcomes for children with disabilities. This can potentially impact on broader parent satisfaction in APE transition services for parents whose needs may differ based on what part of the country services are being delivered in. According to Columna et al. (2008), families of children with disabilities may develop expectations concerning their children, their role as parents, and their interactions with professionals in relationship to the well-being of their children. As such, the assistance of APE teachers is critical for meeting parent expectations in relation to PA skill development needed for broader community use following secondary education of children with disabilities.

A review/summary of current scholarship

This section builds on the above content overview and theoretical framework section by proposing how research on teachers, peers, and parents can be used to develop evidence-based practices helping to move APE forward through successful learning outcomes for all children.

Pre- and in-service physical educators

Findings support that constructs related to teachers' attitudes, beliefs, perceptions, and other factors (Hodge et al., 2015) can be measured; however, there are some considerations for researchers designing future studies related to these variables. First, there continues to be a need to link teachers' perceptions, beliefs, and attitudes to actual teacher behaviors and perhaps even students' learning. From a theoretical standpoint, it is important to examine how the outcome is produced which is referred to by Caldwell (2001) as the theory of action. It is important to examine and reflect on why outcomes occurred in intervention based studies in order to link the findings to the actual theory used in the study, or develop additional theory to help create future evidence-based practices.

What is also known about the study of individual functional constraints (e.g., attitudes) related to teachers is that the constructs of perceptions, beliefs, attitudes, perceived behavioral control, and self-efficacy are not synonymous terms. This has prompted a broadening of study beyond the original descriptive teacher attitude research. Further, it is known that these constructs can change with training. Specifically, pre-service teachers' self-efficacy has been found to improve over time with coursework (Taliaferro et al., 2015). However, findings such as these are mitigated by the low explained variance that commonly result from responses to questionnaires related to teacher individual functional constraints such as beliefs (Hodge et al., 2015). Another issue is that even though researchers are able to link teacher training and experiences to beliefs, the link to teacher behaviors is difficult to establish (Beamer & Yun, 2014). The notion that beliefs, attitudes, and other related constructs are significant predictors of teacher behavior is still unclear. The reason for this is a lack of research that examines how attitudes and other similar constructs (e.g., motivation) develop and impact teacher behaviors. Some of this is due to the nature of samples used, where many researchers rely on cross-sectional samples of either pre-service or in-service teachers. The low explained variance related to factors such as coursework, or years of experience, and how attitudes can change over time as result of teachers' experiences within their teaching setting, is in need of further study (Kozub & Lienert, 2003).

With respect to teachers and the concept of diversity, Edl et al., (2008) found that in bilingual classrooms where children from Latinx and other backgrounds are educated, teachers consistently rate these students lower in interpersonal competence, including areas related to ability. This demonstrates additional factors that bring complexity to the study of teachers in relation to their attitudes, beliefs, and judgements about children with disabilities. Further, Tabb and Yun (2005) analyzed the attitudes and knowledge of PE teachers about including Mexican-American students in their classes. Tabb and Yun (2005) indicated that experienced teachers, or those who spoke Spanish, demonstrated more positive attitudes toward working with Mexican-American students. On the other hand, those teachers who lacked the ability to communicate in their students' native language faced barriers to integrating them into their classes. In another study, conducted by Culp, Chepyator-Thomson, and Hsu et al. (2009), written journal reflections of teacher candidates during field experiences were analyzed. The authors found that 60% of the journal entries had specific content about barriers in communicating with diverse groups because of their lack of understanding about their styles of linguistic expression and non-verbal behaviors.

PE teachers have experienced difficulties communicating not only with children for whom English is not the primary language, they also experienced challenges communicating with these children's parents (Burden, Columna, Hodge, & Martínez -De la Vega, 2013; Columna, Senne, & Lytle, 2013). The link to parents comes from Columna et al. (2008), who demonstrate that Hispanic families are not as aware and knowledgeable about APE services as White families. Differences in preferences of modes of communication, biases by teachers, and additional cultural factors make diversity an important issue to study along with parent perspectives on APE.

The nature of complexity in the study of teacher-related factors such as beliefs and self-efficacy is found in Beamer and Yun (2014) where teacher training and years of experience were significant predictors of self-reported teacher behaviors related to including children with ASD. However, the key study variables of beliefs and self-efficacy did not remain significant in the regression equations by these researchers. Thus, understanding teacher functional constraints in relation to teacher behavior is very complex. Even though self-efficacy, perceived behavioral control, beliefs, and other factors may correlate to key study variables deemed important to teaching (such as intentions to include), there is a dynamic process inherent in actual behaviors that lend themselves to systems-based theories (Haegger, Chatzisarantis, & Biddle, 2002). Researchers need to continue to examine the constructs, beliefs, attitudes, and other individual functional constraints using systems-based models and over periods of time to explore how these constructs, and other factors (e.g., age, past experiences), are manipulated by training and then how these factors relate to actual teaching behaviors and subsequent student learning.

Children with disabilities and peers

Research on peers and their contribution to the learning of children with disabilities has been found to be the most encouraging in determining how best to educate children with disabilities. Taken collectively, advocates for inclusion have been able to determine that programming alongside peers without disabilities holds significant advantages for the learner with a disability (Block, 2007; Houston-Wilson et al., 1997; Klavina, 2008; Nijs et al., 2015). It has been demonstrated that when educating in inclusive settings, children with disabilities have shown an increase in engagement and learning, and, also, have experienced a decrease in challenging behavior (Rahn, Coogle, Hanna, & Lewellen, 2017). In this regard, there are successful models for including children with disabilities, using peer mediated supports in segregated settings, and support for integrated programs (Reichow & Volkmar, 2010).

The attitude of the peer group is one of the most important variables in successful inclusion practice (McKay et al., 2015, 2018a; Sherrill, 1998; Sherrill, Heikinaro-Johansson, & Slininger, 1994; Tripp & Sherrill, 1991). As such, preparing peers without disabilities for the inclusion of peers with disabilities is critical (Houston-Wilson et al., 1997; Loovis & Loovis, 1997), and this can be achieved through utilizing programs and curricula that impact peer group attitude change (McKay et al., 2018a). One such program, the International Paralympic Committee's PSD program, (IPC, 2007) has proved fruitful for field-based research on peer attitudes (Liu, Kudlacek, & Jesina, 2010; McKay et al., 2015, 2018a, 2018c; Panagiotou, Evaggelinou, Doulkeridou, Mouratidou, & Koidou, 2008; Xafopoulos, Kudlacek, & Evaggelinou, 2009). Research conducted by Grenier and Kearns (2012), and Grenier et al. (2014) also supports school-based disability sport awareness and education activities to increase peer understanding of diversity, and to expand perceptions.

Multiple non-intervention studies have focused on measuring and describing the attitudes of students in PE or PA programs towards peers with disabilities. Overall attitudes about disability and inclusion were positive, with peers responding favorably to including a peer with a disability in their league or PE class, participating alongside a peer with a disability, and co-existing with them in class or on a team (Archie & Sherrill, 1989; Block & Malloy, 1998; Murata, Hodge, & Little, 2000; Obrusnikova et al., 2010; Townsend & Hassall, 2007; Verderber, Rizzo, & Sherrill, 2003).

Multiple intervention studies have focused on measuring and describing the attitudes of students in PE or PA programs towards peers with disabilities, with a number of variables being considered. Early exposure and amount of exposure were found to have a significant positive impact on attitudes (Hutzler et al., 2007), and longer awareness programs compared to shorter awareness programs were found to impact cognitive attitudes positively (Reina et al., 2011). Looking at the impact of grade and age showed differing findings, as Loovis and Loovis (1997) found that grade and age did not have a significant impact on attitudes, and Kalyvas and Reid (2003) found that grade and age did have a significant impact, with older students having less favorable attitudes towards inclusion modifications. Gender also showed differentiated results. Attitudes were shown to be more positive in girls in contrast to boys, as a result of an awareness intervention (Liu et al., 2010; Loovis & Loovis, 1997; Reina et al., 2011; Xafopoulos et al., 2009), but were not shown to be associated with gender in the McKay et al. (2018c) intervention study.

Parents of children with disabilities

The parent perspective in relation to research findings in APE can be examined from two angles. First, how parents perceive PE and, second, the broader role that PA skills contribute to their children's overall independence (Columna et al., 2008). The issue of what parents expect, as well as perceive, have been studied in relation to APE programming. Expectations have been examined in diverse families for APE by Columna et al. (2008) and with respect to different disability classifications by other researchers (Ayvazoglu et al., 2015; Columna et al., 2017), with findings supporting a desire for parents to be included in the decision-making processes for their children with disabilities.

The types of values or beliefs parents hold regarding PA programming in general is an important mediating variable in examining the role that caregivers play in children's PE outcomes. This is of interest because parents may value PA programming but have legitimate concerns about it (Columna et al., 2008). Specifically, parents may have safety fears concerning their child's participation in both school- and community-based programming. Ayvazoglu et al. (2015) found that bullying of children with ASD was a factor in both PA programming and school activities in general. In a previous study, Ayvazoglu et al. (2006) found that parents of children with visual impairments had a general fear of injury for their child during PA programming. It is likely that concerns over the safety of children with disabilities in motor programming could result in less PA behavior outside of school, and this topic needs additional study. This may interact with training of teachers and professionals in general to alleviate parent concerns over this safety issue (An & Hodge, 2013; Chaapel et al., 2012; Columna et al., 2008, 2013).

Parents' skills related to PA and PE is important if they are to provide programming to support their children and, in some cases, the APE program (Kozub, 2001). Columna et al. (2017) found that parents of children with visual impairments lacked skills to engage children in PA. This means that studies aimed at increasing PA behavior in children should focus on both child and parent skills. Columna et al. (2017) showed that parents have a desire to provide physical activities for their children. Therefore, parents voiced the need for PA programs for their children. This concept of parents being program providers in APE has been supported by experts in APE (Folsom-Meek, 1984; Kozub, 2001). In reference to the information presented above, teachers should design, and take the time to share information with parents about, the concepts their students are learning during the PE class. This can be used as an opportunity to provide parents with ideas of games and physical activities they can practice at home and in the community with their children. Also, the activities and games shared with parents must be culturally sensitive, while addressing the needs of the child and his/her family (Columna et al., 2013). The issue of diversity in relation to children, teachers, and parents links the concepts highlighted in this chapter (Columna et al., 2008).

Current trends

Current trends related to teacher, peer, and parent perspectives discussed in this chapter parallel the special education field. Prior to discussing trends related to teacher accountability, inclusion-based programming, technology, significant disproportionality, and parent input, a model for designing future studies is provided. This model found in Figure 26.2 prioritizes the links between different aspects of a child's learning environment.

A reticulation model for study

While discussing the trends in the broader field, the reader is encouraged to consider the model found in Figure 26.2. This model has three major assumptions. First, the child with a disability has to be the center of the study and, in this regard, outcome variables related to learning have to be considered in conjunction with teacher, peer, and parent perspectives. Second, networking is critical and, therefore, the concept of reticulation is the

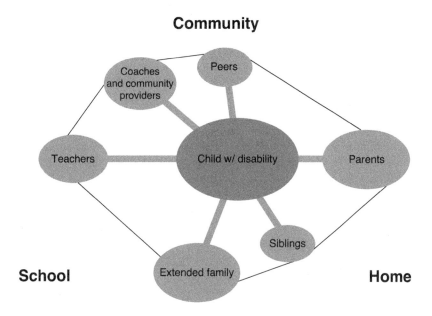

Figure 26.2 Reticulation model for understanding the importance of creating networks to support individuals with disabilities throughout the lifespan

term adopted to highlight a critical need for educational teaming in relation to PE programming as part of the broader special education program, and support for integration into adult community settings. The model found in Figure 26.2 is named based on the need for a pattern of connectivity between individuals similar to a web. The various persons associated with the learning network of children interlace through consistent communication and program planning that forms a learning network for the child and the family. This network includes teachers connecting with parents, extended family, siblings, peers, and other community leaders, such as coaches or recreation providers. The teacher is a critical player in this connection because he/she has the resources provided through educational legislation to facilitate the networking. Finally, the home, school, and community are equally important contexts and researchers should strive to generalize evidence-based practices to identify which interventions work, and in what settings. The cooperation of different individuals working with and alongside learners with disabilities is critical and has to be accounted for in APE given the social nature of PE programming.

Teacher accountability

Teacher accountability has been an issue in the broader educational climate since the signing of *No Child Left Behind Act* in 2001. Currently, the revision to this original legislation is referred to as the *Every Student Succeed Act* (ESSA), signed in 2015. How this affects study of peers, teachers, and parents of children with disabilities continues to be related to accountability of school districts. Further, the ESSA has created aggregate groups related to disability, English language learners, and race/ethnicity, insuring that vulnerable populations of learners are addressed in accountability standards (Sharpe, 2016). Issues related to how teachers continue to be evaluated in relation to learning for all children will be reflected in beliefs, attitudes, and other functional constraints (e.g., self-efficacy) based on how teachers perceive their role in both student learning and student outcomes.

Inclusion based programming

Trends related to peer attitudes, perceptions, and feelings indicate the need for qualitative research to showcase in-depth exploration of the nature and extent to which participants experience inclusive PE environments and/or disability sport awareness programs. McKay et al. (2018a) explored the experiences of sixth grade students, ages 11 and 12, taking part in the PSD program in relation to shaping attitudes and perceptions of disability and disability sport. This study responded to the trend in quantitative PSD research that indicated a significant impact on attitudes, but with very small effect sizes and mean differences (McKay et al., 2015). In general, trends in research relating to peer attitudes show that scores start at relatively positive positions, and move to even more positive positions. With this in mind, the exploration of research utilizing new and different measures may address this trend, along with incorporating mixed method and qualitative research designs.

Technology

Technology advances, including social media and other forms of computer-based resources, are socially linked. With this in mind, teachers, children, and parents have access to more information than at any other time, historically. This information, coupled with the ability to measure constructs at a more objective level, is an important consideration for adapted physical educators. With respect to teachers, the ability to communicate with parents efficiently and in a way that is sensitive to the busy lives of parents with children with disabilities impacts on the nature of study variables related to teacher functional constraints.

Significant disproportionality

The statistical reality that children from different racial and ethnic backgrounds are overrepresented in special education is an important topic in special education today (Cavendish et al., 2014). It continues to be a topic in the Office of Special Education Programming that provides external funding for researchers interested in improving outcomes for children with disabilities (Office of Special Education Programming, 2018). What this means for APE researchers is a need to clearly identify samples in studies, and the need to seek out mediating factors that impact outcomes for children in relation to learning (Hodge et al., 2007). If race and ethnicity, and/or socioeconomic status, are factors that influence identification of children more so than learner needs, the potential influence on APE outcomes requires further study.

Parent involvement

Special education today continues to focus on parents' involvement. In this regard, the notion of parents' involvement in the educational planning for their children is not a new trend. What is new is that parents today have more access to information than ever before. The amount of information on disability, interventions, and potential resources is widespread on the internet. This overlaps with the technology trend, and also impacts the amount of information parents can bring to an individualized education plan (IEP) meeting. With respect to PA planning and programming, parents have access to information from various resources, such as the National Center on Health, Physical Activity and Disability (NCHPAD) (Centers for Disease Control and Prevention, 2018). Training parents on how to teach and promote PA for their children/family is paramount. Research that supports this assertation includes Columna and colleagues (Columna et al., 2018, 2019), who introduced a PA program for parents of children with visual impairments, and Davis et al. (2017), where a program training parents to support PA for children with ASD was the focus of study. In these studies, the specialist provides parents with PA equipment, along with the skills to teach a variety of games and physical activities for their children.

A final thought on current trends is the need to use the findings of researchers related to parent communication, expanding on An and Hodge's (2013) and Columna et al.'s (2014) work reporting that parents want to communicate with practitioners. Researchers interested in finding answers to inactivity, appropriate integration practices, and other important APE topics should focus on networking and the possibilities that exist in helping parents create networks as depicted in Figure 26.2. The idea of networking in relation to parents, within schools and in the communities, is an important process if children with disabilities are going to integrate into the broader community and successfully engage in meaningful PA following their years in public education settings.

Implications for practice

The implications for practice based on the findings discussed in this chapter are multi-faceted. These include practices in relation to how teachers are trained, how children are grouped, how parents receive the skills to engage their children in PA, and how parents are included in the educational processes of their children as it relates to PE. There are also gaps in the literature that indicate a need to examine teacher, peer, and parent variables in a dynamic manner.

Best practice related to the findings used in this chapter include a continued need to study how best to train and evaluate teachers working in integrated teaching settings. Teacher training is linked to beliefs, attitudes, and judgements (Mulholland & Cummings, 2016). In this regard, teacher educators need to examine what types of knowledge lead to both the development of appropriate beliefs and attitudes, and to successful learning outcomes for children with disabilities.

The use of segregated programs for the education of children with disabilities in special education programs is a decision based on legal mandates. Both inclusive and segregated programs still exist. However, the findings used in this chapter continue to support the use of integrated programming and the values of having children with and without disabilities educated together (McKay et al., 2015; Nijs et al., 2015).

With respect to parents, there is a gap in the literature in terms of how to better prepare teachers to work in collaboration with parents. It is clear that parents desire communication with PE and activity providers (An & Hodge, 2013; Chaapel et al., 2012). Parents of children with disabilities should be included in programming for their children based on two important factors. First, parents show an interest in providing programming (An & Goodwin, 2007; Columna et al., 2019, 2018). Second, parents have considerable knowledge about their children with disabilities that can help program providers and support the physical activity participation of their children. This is made possible by practitioners helping to create, and taking part in, the networking described in Figure 26.2.

The issue of parent input and communication is an important factor in APE research as well as in special education programming. Connor and Cavendish (2018) provide a recommendation to measure communication and assess parent input which we believe is very important in both research and programming. Further, Connor and Cavendish (2018) highlight the need to differentiate between parents, considering background, experience, and other differences that might influence how practitioners support learning in children with disabilities. Both parents and children with disabilities are mandated participants in the IEP process, but practitioners are still in need of information on how to best include parents from different backgrounds in the decision-making process (Columna et al., 2014).

Based on findings from existing literature and the perspective that teachers, peers, and parents interact dynamically, we propose a framework for study that highlights the need for networking of practitioners, families, and children to provide evidence-based practices for increasing PA behavior and improving life outcomes for individuals with disabilities (Figure 26.2). Creating interventions that are family and child specific are paramount if long term learning and adoption of PA habits are desired. Finally, the dynamic nature of community-based PA requires that studies consider ecologically friendly skills. This begins with appropriate movement skills, but also needs to include the study of factors that lead to independence in learners with disabilities outside of the family unit to ensure that learning generalizes to the broader setting of the community.

Summary of key points

- The individual needs of children with disabilities are the most important factor to consider in providing meaningful instruction and supporting parents at home who are interested in increasing PA levels in their child. Parent perspectives are a key factor in both the research found in this chapter (Figure 26.1) and in the reticulation model proposed in Figure 26.2 to guide future programming models for children with disabilities.
- Parent input in PE for children with disabilities is important to remain consistent with family systems models.
- Teacher training remains an important issue in providing future physical educators with the necessary tools to effectively program for children with disabilities.
- Peers of children with disabilities are an important part of the learning environment for their children participating in social activities such as PA. Both Figures 26.1 and 26.2 support peers as both a mediating variable in successful outcomes in educational interventions and a key component in the networking needed to insure that children with disabilities benefit from PE instruction. Specifically, in broader PA settings and the networking proposed in Figure 26.2, peers are a potential constant in home, school, and community environments. Peers are a constant in the lives of children with disabilities, as they successfully transition from school-based programming to adult community living and PA is an excellent way to teach appropriate social skills.
- Home and school are equally important environments for children to engage in meaningful PA programming.
- The networks between teachers, parents, and children is an important part of educational programming in PE.
- Dynamic study of the interrelationship between teachers, parents, and peers are needed to examine the long-term functional outcomes of PE programming on children with disabilities.

Reflective questions

1. Identify the extent to which attitude study explained teacher behavior in PE when working with children with disabilities?
2. Can you apply the literature on teacher attitudes, beliefs, and self-efficacy to explain successful learner outcomes, as identified in Figure 26.1, based on published research literature?
3. How would you identify and then apply evidence-based practices in relation to the use of peers in supporting the education of children with disabilities in PE?
4. How has inclusion research supported the need for providing PE programming that involves the engagement of children with disabilities with their same age peers?
5. What role might significant disproportionality play in APE research examining teacher, parent, or peer perspectives?
6. To what extent is learner diversity an important factor in providing appropriate PE for children with disabilities based on this chapter? List any recommendations for how researchers design studies in the future?
7. How would you design networks, as proposed in Figure 26.2, to support individuals with disabilities in relation to PA programming?
8. What are the implications of including parents in your PE program?

References

Ajzen, I., & Fishbein, M. (1980). *Understanding attitude and predicting social behavior.* Englewood Cliffs, NJ: Prentice Hall.

Allport, G. W. (1954). *The nature of prejudice.* Reading, MA: Addison-Wesley.

Ammah, J. O. A., & Hodge, S. R. (2005). Secondary physical education teachers' beliefs and practices in teaching students with severe disabilities: A descriptive analysis. *The High School Journal,* 89(2), 40–54.

An, J., & Hodge, S. R. (2013). Exploring the meaning of parental involvement in physical education for students with developmental disabilities. *Adapted Physical Activity Quarterly, 29,* 147–163.

An, J., & Goodwin, D. L. (2007). Physical education for students with spina bifida: Mothers' perspectives. *Adapted Physical Activity Quarterly, 24*(1), 38–58.

Archie, V. W., & Sherrill, C. (1989). Attitudes toward handicapped peers of mainstreamed and nonmainstreamed children in physical education. *Perceptual and Motor Skills, 69*(1), 319–322.

Ayvazoglu, N. R., Kozub, F. M., Butera, G., & Murray, M. J. (2015). Determinants and challenges in physical activity participation in families with children with high functioning autism spectrum disorders from a family perspective. *Research in Developmental Disabilities, 47,* 93–105.

Ayvazoglu, N. R., Oh, H., & Kozub, F. M. (2006). Explaining physical activity in children with visual impairments: A family systems approach. *Exceptional Children, 72,* 235–248.

Beamer, J. A., & Yun, J. K. (2014). Physical educators' beliefs and self-reported behaviors toward including children with autism spectrum disorder. *Adapted Physical Activity Quarterly, 31,* 362–376.

Block, M. E. (2007). *A teacher's guide to including students with disabilities in general physical education* (3rd ed.). Baltimore, MD: Paul H. Brookes.

Block, M. E., & Malloy, M. (1998). Attitudes on inclusion of a player with disabilities in a regular softball league. *Mental Retardation, 36*(2), 137–144.

Block, M. E., & Obrusnikova, I. (2007). Inclusion in physical education: A review of the literature from 1995–2005. *Adapted Physical Activity Quarterly, 24,* 103–124.

Block, M. E., & Vogler, E. W. (1994). Inclusion in regular physical education: The research base. *Journal of Physical Education, Recreation and Dance, 65*(1), 40–44.

Buchanan, A. M., Miedema, B., & Frey, G. (2017). Parents' perspectives of physical activity in their adult children with autism spectrum disorder: A social-ecological approach. *Adapted Physical Activity Quarterly, 34,* 401–420.

Burden, J., Columna, L., Hodge, S., & Martínez -De la Vega, P. (2013). Ethnolinguistically relevant pedagogy: Empowering English language learners in physical education. *Quest, 65*(2), 169–185.

Burke, M., Arnold, C., & Owen, A. (2018). Identifying the correlates and barriers of future planning among parents of individuals with intellectual disabilities. *Intellectual and Developmental Disabilities, 56*(2), 90–100.

Caldwell, L. (2001). The role of theory in therapeutic recreation: A practical approach. In N. J. Stumpo (Ed.), *Professional issues in therapeutic recreation: On competence and outcomes* (pp. 349–364). State College, PA: Venture.

Campbell, J., & Gilmore, L. (2003). Changing student teachers' attitudes towards disability and inclusion. *Journal of Intellectual & Developmental Disability, 28*, 369–379.

Cartwright, L., Reid, M., & Hammersley, R. (2016). Barriers to increasing the physical activity of people with intellectual disabilities. *British Journal of Learning Disabilities, 45*, 47–55.

Cavendish, W., Artiles, A. J., & Harry, B. (2014). Tracking inequality 60 years after brown: Does policy legitimize the racialization of disability? *Multiple Voices for Ethnically Diverse Exceptional Learners, 14*(2), 30–40.

Centers for Disease Control and Prevention. (2018, August 29). *National Center on Health, Physical Activity and Disability (NCHPAD)*. Retrieved from www.nchpad.org/.

Chaapel, H., Columna, L., Lytle, R., & Bailey, J. (2012). Parental expectations about adapted physical education services. *The Journal of Special Education, 47*(3), 186–196.

Columna, L., Cook, A., Foley, J. T., & Bailey, J. (2014). Survey development to assess parental satisfaction with adapted physical education teachers' abilities working with children with autism. *Physical Education and Sport Pedagogy*. downloaded on July 27, 2018 from. doi: 10.1080/174089.2014.907888.

Columna, L., Dillon, S. R., Dolphin, M., Streete, D. A., Hodge, S. R., Myers, B., … Heffernan, K. S. (2017). Physical activity participation among families of children with visual impairments and blindness. *Disability and Rehabilitation*. doi: 10.1080/09638288.2017.1390698.

Columna, L., Pyfer, J., Senna, T., Velez, L., Bridenthrall, N., & Canabal, M. Y. (2008). Parental expectations of adapted physical educators: A hispanic perspective. *Adapted Physical Activity Quarterly, 25*, 228–246.

Columna, L., Senne, T. A., & Lytle, R. (2013). Communicating with hispanic parents of children with and without disabilities. *Journal of Physical Education, Recreation, and Dance, 80*(4), 48–54.

Columna, L., Streete, D., Hodge, S. R., Dillon, S., Hodge, S. R., Prieto, L., … Heffernan, K. (2019). Parents' intentions toward including their children with visual impairments in physical activities. *Disability and Rehabilitation*. doi:10.1080/09638288.2018.1505969.

Columna, L., Streete, D., Hodge, S. R., Dillon, S., Myers, B. A., Norris, M., … Heffernan, K. (2018). Parents' beliefs about physical activity for their children with visual impairments. *Adapted Physical Activity Quarterly, 35*(4), 361–380.

Connor, D. J., & Cavendish, W. (2018). Sharing power with parents: Improving educational decision making for students with learning disabilities. *Learning Disability Quarterly, 41*(2), 79–84.

Cooper, J. O., Heron, T. E., & Heward, W. L. (2007). *Applied behavior analysis* (2nd ed.). New York: Pearson.

Culp, B., Chepyator-Thomson, J. R., & Hsu, S. (2009). Pre-service teachers' experiential perspectives based on a multicultural learning service practicum. *The Physical Educator, 66*(1), 23–37.

Davis, T. D., Columna, L., Abdo, A. L., Russo, N., Toole, K., & Norris, M. L. (2017). Using sensory motor activities and training for families of children with autism spectrum disorders. *Palaestra, 31*(4), 35–40.

Donaldson, J. (1980). Changing attitudes toward handicapped persons: A review and analysis of research. *Exceptional Children, 45*, 504–514.

Edl, H. M., Jones, M. H., & Estell, D. B. (2008). Ethnicity and English proficiency: Teacher perceptions of academic and interpersonal competence in European American and Latino students. *School Psychology Review, 37*, 38–45.

Folsom-Meek, S. L. (1984). Parents forgotten teachers aids in adapted physical education. *Adapted Physical Activity Quarterly, 1*, 275–281.

Grenier, M., Collins, C., Wright, S., & Kearns, C. (2014). Perceptions of a disability sport unit in general physical education. *Adapted Physical Activity Quarterly, 31*, 49–66.

Grenier, M., & Kearns, C. (2012). The benefits of implementing disability sports in physical education: A model for success. *Journal of Physical Education, Recreation & Dance, 31*, 49–66.

Haegger, M. S., Chatzisarantis, N. L. D., & Biddle, S. J. H. (2002). A meta-analytic review of the theories of reasoned action and planned behavior in physical activity: Predictive validity and the contribution to additional variables. *Journal of Sport & Exercise Psychology*, *24*, 3–32.

Hodge, S. R., Ammah, J. O. A., Casebolt, K., LaMaster, K., & O'Sullivan, M. (2004). High school general physical education teachers' behaviors and beliefs associated with inclusion. *Sport, Education and Society*, *9*(3), 395–419.

Hodge, S. R., Gutierres Filho, P. J. B., Haegle, J. A., & Kozub, F. M. (2015). Underlying dimensions of the physical educators' judgements about inclusion instrument: Brazilian-Version. *Journal of Curriculum and Teaching*, *2*, 96–103.

Hodge, S. R., Kozub, F. M., Robinson, L. E., & Hersman, B. L. (2007). Reporting gender, race, ethnicity, and sociometric status: Guidelines for research and professional practice. *Adapted Physical Activity Quarterly*, *24*, 21–37.

Hodge, S. R., Murata, N. M., & Kozub, F. M. (2002). Physical educators' judgments about inclusion: A new instrument for preservice teachers. *Adapted Physical Activity Quarterly*, *19*, 435–452.

Houston-Wilson, C., Dunn, J. M., Van der Mars, H., & McCubbin, J. (1997). The effect of peer tutors on motor performance in integrated physical education classes. *Adapted Physical Activity Quarterly*, *14*, 298–313.

Hutzler, Y. (2003). Attitudes toward the participation of individuals with disabilities in physical activity: A review. *Quest*, *55*, 247–373.

Hutzler, Y., Fliess-Douer, O., Avraham, A., Reiter, S., & Talmor, R. (2007). Effects of short-term awareness interventions on children's attitudes toward peers with a disability. *International Journal of Rehabilitation Research*, *30*, 159–161.

Individuals with Disabilities Education Act (IDEA) of 1990. U.S.C., Title 20, §§ 1400 *et seq.*

International Paralympic Committee. (2007). *Paralympic school day manual.* Bonn, Germany: Author.

Jansma, P., & Shultz, B. (1982). Validation and use of a mainstreaming attitude inventory with physical educators. *American Corrective Therapy Journal*, *36*, 150–158.

Jeong, M., Kim, S., & Lee, E. (2015). Parents' beliefs and intentions toward supporting physical activity participation for their children with disabilities. *Adapted Physical Activity Quarterly*, *32*, 93–105.

Kalyvas, V., & Reid, G. (2003). Sport adaptation, participation, and enjoyment of students with and without physical disabilities. *Adapted Physical Activity Quarterly*, *20*(2), 182–199.

Klavina, A. (2008). Using peer-mediated instruction for students with severe and multiple disabilities in inclusive physical education: A multiple case study. *European Journal of Adapted Physical Activity*, *1*(2), 7–19.

Kozub, F. M. (2001). Adapted physical activity within the family: The family systems theory. *Palaestra*, *17*(3), 30–38.

Kozub, F. M., & Lienert, C. (2003). Attitudes towards teaching children with disabilities: Review of literature and research paradigm. *Adapted Physical Activity Quarterly*, *20*, 323–346.

Kozub, F. M., & Porretta, D. L. (1998). Interscholastic coaches' attitudes toward integration of adolescents with disabilities. *Adapted Physical Activity Quarterly*, *15*(4), 328–344.

Kozub, F. M., Sherblom, P. R., & Perry, T. L. (1999). Inclusion paradigms and perspectives: A stepping-stone to accepting learner diversity in physical education. *Quest*, *51*, 346–354.

LaMaster, K., Gall, K., Kinchin, G., & Siedentop, D. (1998). Inclusion practices of effective elementary specialists. *Adapted Physical Activity Quarterly*, *15*, 64–81.

Liu, Y., Kudlacek, Y., & Jesina, O. (2010). The influence of paralympic school day on children's attitudes towards people with disabilities. *Acta Universitatis Palackianae Olomucensis. Gymnica*, *40*(2), 63–69.

Loovis, E. M., & Loovis, C. L. (1997). A disability awareness unit in physical education and attitudes of elementary school students. *Perceptual & Motor Skills*, *84*, 768–770.

McKay, C. (2013). Paralympic school day: A disability awareness program. *Palaestra*, *27*(4), 14–19.

McKay, C., Block, M. E., & Park, J. Y. (2015). The impact of paralympic school day on student attitudes toward inclusion in physical education. *Adapted Physical Activity Quarterly*, *32*(4), 331–348.

McKay, C., Haegele, J., & Block, M. E. (2018a). Lessons learned from paralympic school day: Reflections from the students. *European Physical Education Review*, *20*, 1–16.

McKay, C., Park, J. Y., & Block, M. E. (2018b). Fidelity criteria development: Aligning paralympics school day with contact theory. *Adapted Physical Activity Quarterly*, *35*(2), 233–242.

McKay, C., Park, J. Y., & Block, M. E. (2018c). Exploring the variables associated with student attitudes toward inclusion in physical education after taking part in the paralympic school day programme. *International Journal of Inclusive Education.* doi:*10.1080/13603116.2018.1550117*

McWilliam, R. A., & Bailey, D. B. (1995). Effects of classroom social structure and disability on engagement. *Topics in Early Childhood Special Education, 15*, 123–147.

Mulholland, S., & Cummings, T. M. (2016). Investigating teacher attitudes of disability using a non-traditional theoretical framework of attitude. *International Journal of Educational Research, 80*, 93–100.

Murata, N. M., Hodge, S. R., & Little, J. R. (2000). From the field-students' attitudes, experiences, and perspectives on their peers with disabilities. *Clinical Kinesiology, 54*(3), 59–66.

Nijs, S., Pene, A., Vlaskump, C., & Maes, B. (2015). Peer interactions among children with profound intellectual and multiple disabilities during group activities. *Journal of Applied Research in Intellectual Disabilities, 29*, 366–377.

Obrusnikova, I., Block, M., & Dillon, S. (2010). Children's beliefs toward cooperative playing with peers with disabilities in physical education. *Adapted Physical Activity Quarterly, 27*(2), 127–142.

Obrusnikova, I., Valkova, H., & Block, M. E. (2003). Impact of inclusion in general physical education on students without disabilities. *Adapted Physical Activity Quarterly, 20*(3), 230–245.

Odom, S., Hoyson, M., Jamieson, B., & Strain, P. S. (1985). Increasing handicapped preschoolers' peer social interactions: Cross-setting and component analysis. *Journal of Applied Behavior Analysis, 18*, 3–16.

Office of Special Education Programming. (2018, August 29). Ideas that work: Significant disproportionality. Retrieved from https://osepideasthatwork.org/osep-meeting/significant-disproportionality.

Oh, H., & Kozub, F. M. (2010). The psychometric properties of a scale to measure physical educator self-efficacy towards challenging behavior of students with autism in physical education. *Adapted Physical Activity Quarterly, 27*, 191–207.

Oh, H., Seo, D., & Kozub, F. M. (2010). The emotional reactions to challenging behavior scale: Modification and validation. *Adapted Physical Activity Quarterly, 27*, 17–31.

Panagiotou, A. K., Evaggelinou, C., Doulkeridou, A., Mouratidou, K., & Koidou, E. (2008). Attitudes of 5th and 6th grade Greek students toward the inclusion of children with disabilities in physical education classes after a paralympic education program. *European Journal of Adapted Physical Activity, 1*(2), 31–43.

Rahn, N. L., Coogle, C. G., Hanna, A., & Lewellen, T. (2017). Evidence based practices to reduce challenging behaviors of young children with autism. *Young Exceptional Children, 20*(4), 166–177.

Reichow, B., & Volkmar, F. R. (2010). Social skills interventions for individuals with autism: Evaluation for evidence-based practices within a best evidence synthesis framework. *Journal of Autism and Developmental Disorders, 40*, 149–166.

Reina, R., López, V., Jiménez, M., García-Calvo, T., & Hutzler, Y. (2011). Effects of awareness interventions on children's attitudes toward peers with a visual impairment. *International Journal of Rehabilitation Research, 34*(3), 243–248.

Rizzo, R. L. (1984). Attitudes of physical educators toward teaching handicapped pupils. *Adapted Physical Activity Quarterly, 1*, 267–274.

Sharpe, L. A. (2016). ESEA reauthorization: An overview of the every student succeed act. *Texas Journal of Literacy Educational, 4*(1), 9–12.

Sharpe, T. Y. (2013). Educational outcomes for students with special needs: The impact of support and resources on teachers' perceptions. *Journal of the American Academy of Special Education Professionals,132* Spr-Sum. 132–138.

Sherrill, C. (1998). *Adapted physical activity, recreation, and sport: Crossdisciplinary and lifespan* (5th ed.). Boston, MA: WCB/McGraw-Hill.

Sherrill, C., Heikinaro-Johansson, P., & Slininger, D. (1994). Equal-status relationships in the gym. *Journal of Physical Education, Recreation and Dance, 65*(1), 27–31.

Silva, C. F., & Howe, P. D. (2012). Difference, adapted physical activity and human development: Potential contribution of capabilities approach. *Adapted Physical Activity Quarterly, 29*, 24–43.

Strom, R., Rees, R., Slaughter, H., & Wurster, S. (1980). Role expectations of parents of intellectually handicapped children. *Exceptional Children, 47*, 144–147.

Tabb, J. K., & Yun, J. K. (2005). Physical educators' attitudes and knowledge about working with Mexican Americans. *ICHPER–SD Journal, 41*(3), 16–21.

Taliaferro, A. R., Hammond, L., & Wyant, K. (2015). Preservice physical educators' self-efficacy beliefs toward inclusion: The impact of coursework and practicum. *Adapted Physical Activity Quarterly, 32*, 49–67.

Tripp, A., & Sherrill, C. (1991). Attitude theories of relevance in adapted physical education. *Adapted Physical Activity Quarterly, 8*, 12–27.

Townsend, M., & Hassall, J. (2007). Mainstream students' attitudes to possible inclusion in unified sports with students who have an intellectual disability. *Journal of Applied Research in Intellectual Disabilities*, *20*(3), 265–273.

Turnbull, A., Turnbull, R., Erwin, E. J., Sondak, L. C., & Shogun, K. A. (2014). *Families, exceptionality, and professionals: Positive outcomes through partnerships and trust*. New York: Pearson.

Verderber, J. M., Rizzo, T. L., & Sherrill, C. (2003). Assessing student intention to participate in inclusive physical education. *Adapted Physical Activity Quarterly*, *20*(1), 26–45.

Webster, G. E. (1987). Influence of peer tutors upon academic learning time – Physical education of mentally handicapped children. *Adapted Physical Activity Quarterly*, *6*, 393–403.

Xafopoulos, G., Kudlacek, M., & Evaggelinou, C. (2009). Effect of the intervention program "paralympic school day" on attitudes of children attending international school towards inclusion of students with disabilities. *Acta Universitatis Palackianae Olomucensis. Gymnica*, *39*(4), 63–71.

27

According to the kids

Research from the perspective of children with disabilities

Jennifer Leo and Niamh-Elizabeth Mourton

Introduction

The aim of this chapter is to provide global insight into the research that has been conducted from the perspective of children and youth with disabilities about their experiences in physical education (PE) and adapted physical education (APE). PE is defined as instruction focusing on the development of students' physical and motor fitness, fundamental motor skills, and patterns, skills in aquatics, dance, individual and group games, and sports to promote and maintain a physically active, as well as healthy, lifestyle. Instruction must be conducted in the least restrictive environment and adapted to meet each student's unique needs when necessary (IDEA-IA, 2004; Sato & Haegele, 2017). APE is defined as individualized programs related to activities within PE such as physical fitness, motor skill learning, sport skill acquisition and games that meet the unique needs of individuals. It is generally designed to meet the long-term unique needs of individuals with disabilities (Winnick & Porretta, 2016).

Despite the persistent recommendation to address the research gap in this area, there is little research to draw on that places significant emphasis on the perspectives of children with disabilities (Spencer-Cavaliere & Watkinson, 2010). This chapter explores the research that has been conducted to date, identifies trends, such as the primarily qualitative approaches used to gather the genuine perspectives of children and young people with disabilities within PE settings, and proposes recommendations for future research. This chapter presents an international perspective by examining research from countries in North America, Europe, Australasia, and Asia.

To situate the discussion of research from the perspective of children and youth with disabilities, we begin with a historical overview of the PE experience shifting from segregated to primarily general PE settings. We then discuss the value and importance of capturing the perspective of children and youth to illustrate why this matters. An overview of the theoretical and conceptual frameworks that have been used is presented, followed by a discussion of the current literature related to experiences of PE from the perspective of children and youth with disabilities. Finally, trends and implications for practice are highlighted to ensure the perspective of children and youth with disabilities continues to be valued within future research studies.

Historical overview

To gain the authentic views of children with disabilities toward their experiences with PE, it is important to note how far we have come in society in relation to general PE and APE. The PE experience for children with disabilities used to be very much non-existent or in segregated environments separate from their peers (Haegele & Sutherland, 2015). It is important that we preface the following discussion by saying that some families that include children and youth with disabilities may choose segregated schools, which provide services only for students with disabilities. Students in Curtin and Clarke (2005) described positive experiences at their specialized schools, which included feeling supported by teachers, establishing lifelong friends, and building independence. Decisions about education can be very personal to each family and it is important that we recognize that families have a right to choice in their access to the educational experience that works for each individual child.

The UN Convention on the Rights of Persons with Disabilities was adopted in December 2006 and states that individuals with disabilities hold the same rights and should have the same opportunities as those without disabilities. Some countries have been paving the way for inclusion within education. For example, in the UK there is the *Equality Act* (2010), in the USA there is the *Individuals with Disabilities Education Act* (2004), in Australia they have the *Disability Standards for Education* (2005), and in Japan the *Basic Act on Education—Kyōiku kihon-hō* (2006). The UN convention has further impacted national legislation related to education and physical activity globally, as more countries seek to become more inclusive in their policy and their practice.

Over the past 30 years or so, inclusion has become the paradigm of choice for educating students with disabilities (Block, 2000; Block & Obrusnikova, 2007). Inclusion has been narrowly defined as the placement of students with disabilities in general, mainstream, or regular education (DePauw & Doll-Tepper, 2000). However, the placement of students within the learning environment is just one aspect of an inclusive setting. Rather, inclusive education calls for educators to provide content in ways that encourages diverse learning and promotes the abilities of all students, therefore taking the pressure away from the individual child for adapting his/her own learning style (Coates, 2012). More broadly, our definition of inclusion has been viewed as an attitude, a process, and a "philosophical approach to implementing social justice in our schools and in society so that all persons are valued as unique contributing members of society" (DePauw & Doll-Tepper, 2000, p. 139). Although several benefits are expected to be achieved by both students with disabilities and their classmates without disabilities, research questioning the nature and effectiveness of inclusive programming was not initially viewed positively, in part because the placement of children with disabilities in general education was promoted as a human rights issue (Stainback, Stainback, & Bunch, 1989). Over the years, however, research topics related to inclusion in schools have become increasingly acceptable, including those focused on the evaluation of inclusion in PE. The placement of students with disabilities alongside their peers without disabilities has continued across North America and in many European and Asian countries (Block & Obrusnikova, 2007; Fitzgerald & Stride, 2012; Wang, 2019).

According to Goodwin, Watkinson, and Fitzpatrick (2003, p. 193), inclusion in PE is,

> providing all students with disabilities the opportunity to participate in regular PE with their peers, with supplementary aides and support services as needed to take full advantage of the goals of motor skill acquisition, fitness, knowledge of movement, and psycho-social well-being, toward the outcome of preparing all students for an active lifestyle appropriate to their abilities and interests.

However, in the UK, the Sainsbury's Active Kids for All Inclusive PE Training Programme Final Report (Makopoulou & Neville, 2016) stated that, in the pre-program report from 2009, 84% of recently qualified PE teachers and 43% of trainee PE teachers felt that their initial teacher training had not sufficiently prepared them to work with children with disabilities. From 2013 to 2016, over 5,500 participants involved in PE delivery in schools in England received inclusive PE training that yielded positive results. Despite all of this, teachers in PE classes still continue to face problems promoting effective participation of students with disabilities (Tanure Alves, Grenier, Haegele, & Duarte, 2018).

Need for student voice

Having a disability does not define that individual and their experiences. People with disabilities, including students, have valuable insights to share and experiences that are worth hearing and understanding (Fitzgerald, Jobling, & Kirk, 2003; Nind, 2008). In line with the UN Convention on the Rights of Persons with Disabilities (2006), which states that individuals with disabilities hold the same rights and should have the same opportunities as those without disabilities, we need to encourage and promote the meaningful participation for persons with disabilities and equal access to participation in play, recreation, leisure, PE, and sporting activities. It has been shown that the participation barriers for children with disabilities is a complex phenomenon because children report different barriers compared to the ones reported by their parents and professionals (SEDY, 2017). There is a perceived difference among the views from professionals, parents, and children related to this topic, which leads to questioning the need for meaningful communication between all parties to understand each other's expectations and realities related to inclusion. Clemente (2017) states this importance as, "it's the child who takes part in the activity so it is their perspective and feelings that are most important and should be taken into account" (p. 24).

When it comes to PE settings, students are likely to interpret their experiences and interactions differently from adults, as they comprehend the world in a unique way. Therefore, if teachers are going to create rich learning environments that meet the needs of all students, including those with disabilities, it is critical that the perspective of students with disabilities be captured and integrated into the development and delivery of curricular activities (Sanders, 1996). Examining PE experiences from the perspective of students with disabilities offers the opportunity to give voice to students with disabilities through research practice. According to McLeod (2011), there are four common uses of voice within educational settings: "voice-as-strategy (to achieve empowerment, transformation, equality); voice-as-participation (in learning, in democratic processes); voice-as-right (to be heard, to have a say); and voice-as-difference (to promote inclusion, respect diversity, and indicate equity)" (McLeod, 2011, p. 181). General PE classes include a diverse group of learners; as such, teachers will be better suited to respond to and reflect these diverse needs by taking the time to value the difference across students. In practice, participatory projects, such as youth forums, youth leadership, or youth global citizen projects offer examples of how to prioritize student voice beyond the traditional scope of conducting research (Mitchell & Parker, 2008). By reflecting on, and learning from the perspective of students with disabilities in PE settings, educators can shift the role of who has expertise when it comes to learning (McLeod, 2011).

While student voice-as-participation and as-difference are mobilized in self-consciously participatory initiatives and innovative programs that aspire to reflect the diversity of the student body, the authority of student voice-as-strategy is also evident in quality assurance discourses and the status accorded to student evaluations of teaching and course satisfaction.

(McLeod, 2011, p. 181)

Interestingly, in higher education, the participation of students in expressing their views is adopted as a strategy to promote student engagement. Students with disabilities make the best informants to speak of their lives and experiences (Fitzgerald & Stride, 2012). Engaging in research that focuses on the voice of students with disabilities within PE settings is a way to encourage meaningful and authentic participation.

Voice is about speaking and listening (McLeod, 2011). To negotiate the tensions that may have occurred within general education settings, in which students with disabilities perceive the environment differently from their teachers (i.e., students say the teacher is not adapting the environment according to the students' preferred way, whereas the teacher reports a responsibility to deliver the curriculum as is), it may be valuable to encourage teachers to rethink their notion of what it means to listen (Sanders, 1996). Perhaps this approach may help to break down the perceived differences between students and adults. Finally, student voice matters because "it can mean not only recognizing 'difference' but also acting appropriately to make education more inclusive" (McLeod, 2011, p. 186).

Uniqueness of PE setting

Compared to the regular classroom, the learning environment for PE is unique, as it is the only "subject area where the physicality of students is publicly exposed to others" (Fitzgerald & Stride, 2012, p. 283) and there is a "heightened awareness of their bodies" (Goodwin & Watkinson, 2000, p. 156). For this reason, particular attention is needed to better understand how students with disabilities experience PE. To illustrate the uniqueness of the PE environment, students with disabilities reported experience of being stared at by their peers, as participation is done in a public forum. Molton (2014) speaks to the gaze in the PE environment, with her work focusing on the gendered experiences of male and female students that are reflected through "observing, judging, and examining performances of the body during PE lessons" (p. 146). There are parallels for students with disabilities, as the nature of PE lessons (e.g., performing activities in front of, or among, fellow students) may result in others observing, judging, or examining one's performance. In some instances, students with disabilities were tasked with evaluating the costs of participation (e.g., being stared at, feeling excluded; Fitzgerald & Stride, 2012) with the potential benefits (e.g., receiving encouragement from others; Goodwin & Watkinson, 2000).

There is opportunity within the PE environment to foster understanding and inclusion through active, hands-on activities, such as the introduction of disability or parasport activities (e.g., goalball, boccia, or sitting volleyball). Current research on Paralympic School Days or disability awareness events have focused primarily on attitudes of students without disabilities towards the inclusion of students with disabilities, using hypothetical scenarios (Campos, Ferreira, & Block, 2014; McKay, Block, & Park, 2015; Wilhite, Mushett, Goldenberg, & Trader, 1997). Following participation of students without disabilities in a variety of parasport activities, positive attitudes towards students with disabilities were reported (McKay et al., 2015); however, the assessment of attitudes focused on hypothetical scenarios of inclusion. The perspective of students with lived experience of disability is absent from the research on disability awareness and Paralympic activity days. Authentic experiences, in which students with disabilities actively participate in parasport activities alongside their peers, warrant further study. These interactions, which take place outside of the traditional classroom environment, offer unique opportunities for students with disabilities to demonstrate competence as legitimate participants alongside their peers (Spencer-Cavaliere & Watkinson, 2010).

Therefore, it is necessary that we ascertain the views of children with disabilities so that we can create personalized pathways to guide children towards PE and sports activities that they find meaningful in order to take their personal wishes, abilities, and opportunities into account and support sustainable, lifelong physical activity engagement.

Literature overview

In 1994, there were only ten studies that had examined inclusion in PE or APE settings (Block & Vogler, 1994). In a 2007 review of the literature on inclusion in PE, a range of topics received attention, including experiences of students with disabilities and the impact of inclusion on those without disabilities, attitudes of students without disabilities and teachers towards inclusion, and the effect of different forms of support, such as peer tutors, teacher assistants, and APE specialists. Research was presented that reflected multiple perspectives, including those of the teachers and students with and without disabilities (Block & Obrusnikova, 2007).

One emerging theme from Block and Obrusnikova (2007) was that the research examining the perspective of students with disabilities focused on the reportedly limited social interactions (Place & Hodge, 2001). There is a cluster of studies from the early 2000s (Blinde & McCallister, 1998; Goodwin, 2001; Goodwin & Watkinson, 2000; Hutzler, Fliess, Chacham, & Van Den Auweele, 2002; Place & Hodge, 2001) which examined inclusion experiences from the perspective of students with disabilities. Overall, these studies reported mixed results, as students were likely to face both good days and bad days (Goodwin & Watkinson, 2000), and their interactions were described as both self-supporting and self-threatening (Goodwin, 2001). However, Blinde and McCallister (1998), in one of the earliest studies examining the experience of students with disabilities from their perspective, reported mostly negative experiences as students received little support or accommodations, were excluded from PE activities, and ridiculed by their teachers. Looking beyond North America, Hutzler et al. (2002) offered insight into the experiences of youth with disabilities in Israel. They also reported both positive and negative experiences during their PE classes. Hutzler et al. (2002) identified the lack of individualized support and appropriate instruction from the teacher, along with a culture that did not discourage the peers without disabilities from teasing or ridiculing their peers with disabilities. Li and Chen (2012) offered insights from their research in Asia, which further supported the important role of the physical educator as a key factor in determining the successful participation of students with disabilities. Finally, in the first study of inclusion from the perspective of students with disabilities in China, the mostly negative experiences were characterized in terms of personal factors and the physical and social context that either facilitated or inhibited inclusion (Wang, 2019).

Most recently, Pocock and Miyahara (2018) conducted a qualitative meta-analysis to synthesize qualitative research focused on the inclusion of students with disabilities in PE. Of the 12 articles that met their inclusion criteria, only two gathered information from the perspective of students with disabilities, both of which were published in the early 2000s (Fitzgerald, 2005; Goodwin & Watkinson, 2000). Finally, the perspective of students with disabilities received attention in a review by Haegele and Sutherland (2015), which focused on qualitative inquiry. These 13 qualitative studies focused on students' perspectives towards their peers without disabilities, PE teachers, and the concepts of inclusion and exclusion. There is clearly a need to further examine the voice of children and youth with disabilities when it comes to their actual experiences of PE. After all, it is their unique lived experiences of having a disability and their varied experience of what it is like to take part in PE in their school setting.

Theoretical frameworks

Across these reviews (Block & Obrusnikova, 2007; Haegele & Sutherland, 2015; Pocock & Miyahara, 2018), there is a consistent trend that the experiences of students with disabilities have been examined using qualitative research approaches. Qualitative research methods such as interviewing and focus groups offer children and youth with disabilities opportunities to meaningfully take part in research and for researchers to learn from their perspectives on what is working for those with lived experience of disability and how we can improve practice (Batters & Reilly, 2015). Focus groups can be used to explore a variety of different issues, to test solutions, to explore the group's perspective, and to generate ideas; however, not all students with disabilities are able to contribute and communicate in the same way. Focus on Me is an inclusive focus group resource that uses visual and communication aids to collect information that reflect the authentic views, wishes and feelings of young people with disabilities, including those with profound disabilities and complex communication support needs (Mourton & Batters, in preparation). Meaningfully incorporating these tools into a focus group session can enable all participants to communicate effectively, as they can utilize their preferred modes of communication and it can foster an optimal environment for all respondents (Owens, 2007; Whitehurst, 2007; Wilson et al., 2013). In a UK study of PE experiences from the perspective of students with disabilities that used Focus on Me to guide the focus group interviews, findings revealed that young people of all abilities felt listened to and felt their views were heard (SEDY, Focus on Me report). Prout (2001) stated that to include children as research subjects, rather than objects of enquiry, can reveal many novel aspects of the situations, settings, and issues they experience but that these remain invisible when research relies only on adult accounts.

The role of theory in qualitative research shifts seamlessly across the boundaries from outside to inside, which means that theory can be used to guide decisions surrounding the research design to framing the organization and interpretation of the research findings (Sandelowski, 1993). Of those studies that identified a theoretical framework, phenomenology (see Bredahl, 2013; Goodwin & Watkinson, 2000), narrative (see Fitzgerald & Stride, 2012), and grounded theory (see Moola, Fusco, & Kirsh, 2011) were among those found most often to examine the PE experiences of students with disabilities. The available literature is primarily descriptive, which is useful and appropriate for an area of inquiry with a limited research base (Haegele & Sutherland, 2015). However, there is an opportunity for researchers to examine the experience of students with disabilities from a broader variety of theoretical frameworks. For example, using a critical disability studies approach to examine power relationships that exist within a PE class setting (i.e., students with and without disabilities, teacher) would provide further insight into the complexity of PE for students with disabilities.

Despite the primarily descriptive nature of the research on perspectives of students with disabilities in PE, there are a few examples of studies that have utilized conceptual frameworks. Goodwin and Watkinson (2000) used an ecological approach, specifically, Gibson's ecological approach to perception (1979), to interpret the experiences of the students with disabilities within their environment. Similarly, Li and Chen (2012) focused on the PA behavior of students with cerebral palsy (CP) from a segregated school using the Physical Activity for People with a Disability (PAD) model (van der Ploeg, van der Beek, van der Woude, & van Mechelon, 2004). This systems approach offered a framework to examine the students' experiences within the context of personal and environmental influences. Finally, Wang (2019) utilized a social-relationship model of disability to explore experiences of inclusion among Chinese students with disabilities, which also highlighted the interaction of personal, environmental, and social factors. Considering the uniqueness of the PE setting, ecological frameworks such as those mentioned above are appropriate to examine the various factors that interact to create the PE experience for students, including those with disabilities. There is tremendous opportunity to examine the experiences of students with disabilities within PE using multiple approaches and frameworks.

Fostering quality participation

Teachers are influential in supporting or hindering students' participation, as they encourage students to increase participation and raise the social value of disability within the class. Goodwin, Watkinson, and Fitzpatrick (2003) speak of the importance of participation in PE activities in their definition of inclusion in general PE settings. As the adult leaders in the classroom, teachers play a critical role in supporting or hindering the participation of students with disabilities, as they select activities and determine the parameters for modifications or adaptations (Bertills, Granlund, Dahlström, & Augustine, 2018). In one of the few quasi-experimental studies (i.e., non-qualitative) that included the perspective of the students with disabilities, Kalyvas and Reid (2003) examined the enjoyment of students with and without disabilities during an adapted version of Newcomb volleyball. Kalyvas and Reid (2003) found that both the regular and adapted games resulted in increased participation across all students, and was enjoyed by those with and without disabilities, with the exception of some older students without disabilities reporting lower levels of enjoyment with the adapted version of the game. This study highlights the potential for successful participation as perceived by students with disabilities within regular classroom settings, using modified or adapted activities. Unpacking the meaning of participation according to students with disabilities is warranted to better understand how it is conceptualized within studies such as Kalyvas and Reid (2003). Martin Ginis, Ma, Latimer-Chueng, and Rimmer (2016) identified six criteria for meaningful participation, including autonomy, belongingness, challenge, engagement, mastery, and meaning. Conceptualized using literature on the physical activity and exercise experiences of adults with disabilities, these criteria could be used to better understand how students with disabilities define and interpret the meaning of participation. In addition to planning and delivering the curriculum-based activities, teachers have the opportunity to influence how disability sport is viewed by all of the students (Li & Chen, 2012).

Peer relationships

Findings about peer relationships from the perspective of children and youth with disabilities tend to reveal mixed experiences, which included both positive and negative interactions (Haegele & Sutherland, 2015). The PE setting provides students with disabilities an opportunity to demonstrate competence at particular skills (e.g., during a swimming class; or successfully making a basket while seated in a wheelchair), which is critical towards gaining social acceptance (Goodwin & Watkinson, 2000). According to Svendby and Dowling (2013), being able to participate with peers in the same activities in the same space can contribute to feelings of mastery and inclusion for a participant with a disability.

Peer relationships are important to foster feelings of inclusion and have been found to be positive when the interactions are caring, supportive, and consensual (Goodwin, 2001). More specifically, these interactions involve students without disabilities offering meaningful support and assistance that is offered with the consent of the student experiencing disability to enhance participation (Goodwin, 2001). In one of the few studies examining the perspective of students with autism spectrum disorder (ASD) in PE, Healy, Msetfi, and Gallagher (2013) highlight the critical role of positive peer interactions. Participants with ASD viewed the PE environment as a potential place to build friendships with their classmates (Healy et al., 2013). For example, one participant described the direct connection he perceived between PE participation and friendship building: "you can make loads of friends … When I'm running and playing with a ball and passing, they say thanks and after that they say do you want to sleep over or something like that" (Healy et al., 2013, p. 224). Positive peer interactions such as receiving encouragement or help with equipment were used to describe how a sense of belongingness was fostered as students experienced good days in PE (Goodwin & Watkinson, 2000; Wang, 2019). Spending time with peers was a fundamental, desirable element of the PE experience, as students with disabilities in a Norwegian study expressed a desire to be more involved with the other children (Asbjornslett, Engelsrud, & Helseth, 2015). Considering that children and youth with disabilities often have difficulty making friends, it is vital that adults in leadership positions (e.g., teachers) use PE settings to support students to foster friendships with their peers (Baker & Donelly, 2001).

However, not all interactions in general PE settings are positive, as students across various disability types have reported negative interactions with their peers. Characterized primarily as bullying (Fitzgerald, 2005; Haegele & Sutherland, 2015; Healy et al., 2013; Moola et al., 2011), these intimidating behaviors often take place beyond the gymnasium (e.g., in the locker rooms) as students prepared for their PE class (Coates & Vickerman, 2010; Haegele & Kirk, 2018). Experiences of bullying were characterized as hinging on perceptions of difference between peers with and without disabilities. For example, in a discussion of PE as a male student with a visual impairment, Brandon described the following,

> I didn't like when people would point it out like 'Hey go over to the moving eye guy.' I mean, they had a lot of stupid nicknames concerning my eyes. … I think people just picked my eyesight because it was an easy target.
>
> *(Haegele & Kirk, 2018, p. 207)*

Negative peer interactions such as these, along with feelings of frustration and isolation, led to negative perceptions of PE (Haegele & Kirk, 2018). To illustrate how they were able to cope with these behaviors, participants in Fitzgerald (2005) offered strategies to manage bullying, ranging from ignoring the offensive behavior to retaliating with further name-calling. Little is known about the long-term impact of negative experiences such as bullying. In Haegele and Zhu's (2017) retrospective study of PE experiences among adults with visual impairments, specific examples of bullying were difficult for participants to describe, which may speak to the emotional impact of these instances when they occurred. Therefore, the long-term impact of these negative experiences within PE warrants further examination.

Students with disabilities have also reported feeling socially isolated from their peers as they experienced rejection, neglect, and a heightened awareness that their peers viewed their bodies differently (Goodwin & Watkinson, 2000). In the PE environment, this may be a result of students with disabilities being excluded from activities or made to feel they were undesirable participants or partners by their peers (Fitzgerald, 2005; Goodwin & Watkinson, 2000; Haegele & Sutherland, 2015; Wang, 2019). Feelings of exclusion and marginalization have emerged when students with disabilities are physically separated from classmates to complete other, undesirable tasks, such as riding an exercise bike or completing physiotherapy appointments in separate locations (Svendby & Dowling, 2013). The experience of exclusion can have social implications, as students with disabilities are left out of the more socially desirable PE activities to complete activities on their own, which may be perceived to have less social value (Fitzgerald, 2005). To illustrate this desire to be with their peers, one participant in Bredahl (2013) shared,

> The fact that you constantly had to be taken away from the class to go swimming meant that I had to leave my classmates, which was irritating ... and exactly in the seventh, eighth, and ninth grade where you actually need to be together with your friends.
>
> *(p. 48)*

According to students with disabilities, the perceptions of their peers led to lack of engagement and restricted participation opportunities. Students with disabilities have reported that their competence was questioned when they were unable to meet the performance standards of their peers without disabilities, which often resulted in experiences of failing (Bredahl, 2013; Goodwin & Watkinson, 2000). Coates and Vickerman (2010) also reported that perceptions of peers influenced the experiences of students with disabilities, as the students with disabilities reported lower scores from the perspective of their peers, despite their own perceptions of being good at sport. Negative social interactions were first described by Blinde and McCallister (1998) in which students with disabilities were predominantly excluded from participation in their PE classes and they experienced negative emotions such as feeling unwanted and left out.

The implications of these negative interactions suggest that the proposed positive interactions that results from all peers being educated together may not be the reality (Haegele & Sutherland, 2015; Place & Hodge, 2001). Despite the negative aspects, overall, students with disabilities from around the world (including Canada, the US, Norway, and the UK) expressed a desire to participate in PE classes with their peers without disabilities (Asbjørnslett et al., 2015; Coates & Vickerman, 2010; Goodwin & Watkinson, 2000; Place & Hodge, 2001; Svendby & Dowling, 2013).

Role of teachers

Makopoulou and Thomas (2017) state that "Inclusion is about the child's right to participate and the school's duty to accept – and adapt – by making learning more meaningful and relevant for all, particularly those learners most vulnerable to exclusionary pressures" (p. 473). As the adult leader in PE settings, teachers play a critical role in setting the climate of inclusion, as they have the power to afford or restrict opportunities for participation (Goodwin & Watkinson, 2000). While encouragement from teachers plays an important role in motivating students with disabilities to participate in PE (Li & Chen, 2012), restrictions from teachers have been described in terms of hesitation, as they were uncertain how best to support the participation of students with disabilities (e.g., identifying appropriate activity adaptations or determining expectations for performance) (Wang, 2019). Understanding more about the role of teachers from the perspective of students with disabilities offers important insights into how the actions and decisions of adult leaders are interpreted and perceived in practice. For example, participants with physical disabilities in a study by Goodwin and Watkinson (2000) reported, "My teachers won't let me do anything" and "He's like, go pump up balls in the storage room. And they're playing volleyball and I'm like—grrrr!" (p. 152). Similarly, students with visual impairments have reported a lack of appropriate modifications, such as equipment that was larger sized or used sound to help with tracking to facilitate participation in PE classes (Lieberman, Robinson, & Rollheiser, 2006). It is possible that participation hindered by restrictions or lack of modifications stem from a lack of professional knowledge, which could be countered by continuing to develop and support APE professionals (Li & Chen, 2012; Wang, 2019).

To prevent adults from interfering and to promote independence, students with disabilities in Norway have reported a preference for assistance that is provided on their own terms (for example, in specific situations that were selected by the individual child) (Asbjornslett et al., 2015). Teachers are responsible for creating a climate that supports all students, which includes determining the social value of different sports within the PE class and among students (Fitzgerald, 2005). Their decisions (for example, activity and equipment selections) have implications on the actions, behaviors, and attitudes of students, which influences the participation of students with disabilities.

In creating a positive learning environment, it is important that teachers have access to the necessary information about their students. Haegele and Sutherland (2015) spoke to disclosure and its importance in determining the experience of students with disabilities. For example, students with hidden disabilities, such as coronary heart disease (CHD) have expressed concern that disclosing their disability would result in consequences such as exclusion from PE activities (Moola et al., 2011). From the students' perspective, it was better to keep their CHD from the teacher, which afforded them the opportunity to participate alongside their peers to meet the same standard, even though this often resulted in increased exhaustion and the risk of potential negative health consequences (Moola et al., 2011). In contrast, some students in this same study viewed disclosure as a way to ensure their health and safety. This example highlights the value in accessing the perspective of the students with disabilities themselves. A teacher may want to keep a student "healthy" and safe by restricting participation; however, when you hear from the students themselves, it actually makes them feel left out and marginalized. In this case, conducting research into the perspective of the students with disabilities would be of tremendous value in promoting and encouraging meaningful conversations with teachers. However, both sides would need to be cognizant of the roles and responsibilities of one another: for example, the teacher's role to protect and keep the students safe, and the student's responsibility to participate alongside peers.

Despite this recommendation to encourage meaningful conversation between students and teachers, there is evidence to suggest that this can be difficult in practice. For example, students have expressed feeling dismissed by their teachers upon making suggestions that would improve their PE experience (Bredahl, 2013). These instances revealed the teacher's commitment to delivering the curriculum in the same way for all students, without being flexible to adapt or modify to meet the individual needs of students (e.g., refusing a student recommended modification to complete an exam on aerobics class instruction or ignoring a student's request to modify ball activities due to a visual impairment). For example, the lack of modifications within PE activities in a Chinese school resulted in a student no longer participating as they stated,

No, the teacher did not change the game rules for me. I would say these games are not appropriate for me. My teammates do not pass a ball to me because they feel I will lose the ball. I always run and have no chance to touch a ball. There is no fun. Thus, I do not play games with them anymore.

(Wang, 2019, p. 255)

Teachers can positively affect students' experiences when provided with the appropriate training that will help them build their confidence in their ability to be inclusive practitioners. Makopoulou and Neville (2016) found that the National Sainsbury's Active Kids for All Inclusive PE Training in England provided teachers with tangible tools to allow them to go back into their PE lessons and make some sustainable inclusive changes. After receiving this inclusive PE training, teachers found that their skills to include all young people and positively enhance individual PE journeys for young people with disabilities. "She [student with a disability] has gone from no PE, to accessing just a little bit, due to her short attention span, to doing the full PE lessons and engaging in everything" (Teacher) (Makopoulou & Neville, 2016, p. 30).

Within the PE environment

Attention to the PE environment is relevant, as pedagogical inclusion is about the structure of the PE environment, giving consideration to whether the setting is organized in a way that fosters participation, promotes learning and engagement, and children with disabilities have opportunities to use their abilities (Wilhelmsen, Sorensen, & Seippel, 2019). Regardless of the success or challenges associated with its implementation, research on PE experiences from the perspectives of students with disabilities has focused primarily on general PE settings (Coates, 2012; Fitzgerald & Stride, 2012; Goodwin & Watkinson, 2000; Healy et al., 2013; Moola et al., 2011; Spencer-Cavaliere & Watkinson, 2010; Wang, 2019). Therefore, it is worth spending time examining what inclusion looks like from the perspective of students with disabilities. In their review, Haegele and Sutherland (2015) described inclusion from the perspective of students with disabilities using three themes, forced exclusion, self-exclusion, and forced inclusion.

Forced exclusion was used to describe examples of participation that were perceived to be restricted by external measures (e.g., constraints within the physical space or inaccessibility) (Haegele & Sutherland, 2015). Examples of forced exclusion within the environment were apparent in studies by Goodwin and Watkinson (2000), Place and Hodge (2001), and Wang (2019) during which PE activities took place outdoors on inaccessible surfaces, such as grassy fields, rather than the pavement, or gym spaces with stairs and no lifts, which would have afforded participation. Students with visual impairments were asked to complete activities in parallel to their classmates, which means they participated in similar activities, in a separate space (Haegele & Zhu, 2017). Regardless of whether the exclusion was the result of decisions made by the teacher or an inaccessible environment, engaging in activity in a separate space was perceived negatively by students with disabilities. Furthermore, students with disabilities attached negative social value to their perceived experience of exclusion as they felt a lack of support and encouragement from their teacher (Fitzgerald, 2005). Restricted access by the teacher and inaccessibility of the environment may be difficult to separate, as the teacher makes decisions during lesson planning about what activities to do and where. Recognizing that the teacher may be constrained by the spaces afforded within a given school, the teacher has an opportunity to create a positive learning environment by making activity decisions that will meet the needs of their students. Layered within this discussion of the PE environment, Wilhelmsen, Sorensen, and Seippel (2019) worked with children with disabilities to offer a description of the environment based on the motivational climate perceptions of children with disabilities. For children with disabilities to feel included in PE, physical inclusion or "the degree to which children with disabilities participate in PE with peers" is critical (Wilhelmsen et al., 2019, p. 21). However, it is not enough, as students with disabilities also need a mastery-oriented climate in which success is defined according to criteria associated with mastery and effort and mistakes are considered to be a key element to learning, rather than a performance-oriented climate in which normative conceptions of ability are used to determine the criteria for performance within the PE class. Integrating the perspectives of students with disabilities offers important insights to establishing and fostering a PE environment that will work.

From a research perspective, we need to examine the key supports that teachers require to ensure they are able to create an inclusive learning environment, thereby mitigating the impact of situations of forced inclusion. Forced inclusion refers to instances when students with disabilities were required to participate in their PE class without the support of modifications or adaptations to meet their needs (Haegele & Sutherland, 2015). Issues arose because, without the modifications, classmates without disabilities set socially constructed standards for performance that the students with disabilities could not perform (Goodwin & Watkinson, 2000). For example, a participant in the Goodwin and Watkinson (2000) study stated, "they say uhm, you can't do this, you're disabled. And I say back, I can to do this, I'm not that disabled" (p. 152). These socially constructed standards were also evident when choosing partners, as students with disabilities were selected last by their classmates (Fitzgerald & Stride, 2012).

When students with disabilities are expected to participate in classes without modification, many of these students question their perceived competence and abilities as the unmodified classes are too challenging (Healy et al., 2013; Wang, 2019). For example, the speed of regular activities can be too fast to enable students with disabilities to participate (Bredahl, 2013; Healy et al., 2013). Teachers who modify activities or offer variations can mitigate the effects of forced inclusion, thereby fostering meaningful participation as students contribute to the overall class success (Spencer-Cavaliere & Watkinson, 2010). According to Wilhelmsen and colleagues (2019), these efforts by teachers to foster a climate that is autonomy supportive play an important role in positive perceptions of inclusion, according to children with disabilities. Specifically, "the PE teacher should be engaged, respectful of children's perspectives, provide information-rich feedback on children's competence, and promote choice and initiative within a structured learning environment" (Wilhelmsen et al., 2019, p. 22).

Finally, self-exclusion was used to describe situations where students with disabilities self-selected to complete PE activities in a separate space. Building on some of the negative perceptions from forced inclusion, some students requested separation due to fear of injury, sensory issues, and/or the perceived ability divide between those with and without disabilities (Healy et al., 2013). This perceived ability divide may lead to feelings of difference when students with disabilities make comparisons with their peers (Moola et al., 2011). Teachers who foster a mastery-based motivational climate may reduce situations of self-exclusion, as students with disabilities may be more inclined to participate alongside peers without disabilities as success within the environment is not based on performance-oriented criteria (Wilhelmsen et al., 2019). Further research is warranted to better understand how students make decisions about if and when to participate in the same or separate activity space.

Conclusions and future directions

There is no single way to describe the experience of participating in PE from the perspective of students with disabilities. The experiences and perspectives are complex and varied, as students have described a multitude of positive and negative situations that have both hindered and fostered participation in PE. Listening to, and learning from, the voice(s) of students with disabilities is a key component to understanding more about how PE is experienced, particularly in general PE settings. From the perspective of students with disabilities, this complex interaction of activities, teachers, and students with and without disabilities have primarily been captured using qualitative approaches.

Teachers play a critical role in fostering inclusion in PE, yet they are inconsistent in their implementation of activity modifications or willingness to adapt the curriculum. The experiences and practices of teachers vary across schools and geographical settings. Examining research from global perspectives is important, along with considering the use of critical theory (e.g., disability studies) to explore the influence of potential cultural differences on PE experiences of students with disabilities. Finally, little is known about the communication between students with disabilities and their teachers, especially from the perspective of those students with disabilities who expressed a desire to share more about their individual needs and abilities with their teacher.

Positive peer interactions are key, and adults play an important role in fostering them. Negative peer interactions can lead to frustration and isolation; however, positive ones are supportive and improve the general PE experience. Exclusive experiences can lead to being left out of more socially desirable activities, which may impact opportunities for social engagement. Despite negative experiences, the majority of students with disabilities globally have expressed a desire to participate in PE classes with peers with and without disabilities. Requesting and receiving assistance and support was important for students with disabilities; however, it was most successful when provided according to the students' own terms. Students want to be involved and share their needs with their teachers, but better communication is needed. Further research into how to enhance communication, including encouraging teachers to re-think their notion of what it means to listen, is warranted.

Within the general PE setting, disability awareness days or Paralympic activity discovery days have been widely used to increase attitudes of students without disabilities towards the inclusion of their peers with disabilities; however, the perspective of students with disabilities is absent from this literature. Peer relationships have the potential to become positive or negative influences on the PE experiences of students with disabilities. Given the variety of experiences shared throughout the literature, further research is needed to unpack the factors that influence these interactions and identify criteria that can foster positive social interactions within PE. Allport's contact theory may be a useful framework to begin to examine these interactions and the qualities that impact the outcomes (McKay, 2018).

Children and youth report different barriers and experiences compared to adults, including parents and teachers. Considering there are perceived differences identified between children and adults, it is critical that we capture the perspectives of children and youth with disabilities. The views of children with disabilities are important to create personalized pathways to guide children towards PE and sport activities that meaningfully promote lifelong participation. Overall, experiences of inclusion were reported as being mixed, including both positive and negative aspects. An ecological framework or systems approach may be useful to examine the complex interaction of various factors that influence general PE experience. Qualitative research approaches are most commonly used to document the experiences of children and youth with disabilities. Focus on Me is an inclusive focus group resource that has been shown to enhance data collection to include authentic views of participants with disabilities (including those with complex communication needs).

Considering the complexity of the general PE setting, a number of conceptual frameworks were used to examine the intersection of personal and environmental factors, including ecological frameworks (Goodwin & Watkinson, 2000), and the social-relational model of disability (Wang, 2019). An ecological approach can be used to situate comments from students with disabilities within the context of the general PE setting. This would be valuable to help with understanding the voices of students with disabilities as they relate to, and interact with, other elements in the environment. Specifically, the use of a systems or ecological approach is recommended to examine the complex interaction of individual and environmental factors, including attitudes and behaviors of teachers, students without disabilities, self-perceptions of those with disabilities, environmental conditions, activity demands, and overarching policies and curricular requirements. Beyond PE settings, an ecological framework was successfully applied to understand the transition pathways of youth with physical disabilities as they navigated their transition to post-secondary education (Lindsay et al., 2018).

There is a need to further explore how PE is experienced by students with a wide range of disabilities, specifically in terms of using research methods that focus on gathering the perspective of students with a wide range of communication approaches (e.g., for those who communicate non-verbally). The inclusion of resources such as Focus on Me, may offer a way for researchers to engage with participants whose perspectives have been absent from the literature due to perceived communication difficulties. Finally, an examination of how to effectively integrate the knowledge and experiences we learn from the perspectives of students with disabilities to ensure that it is valued within the education system, including the preparation of pre-service teachers, is important.

Summary of key points

1. Inclusion in general PE has become the paradigm of choice for educating students with disabilities over the past 30 years, which is reflected in the research on perspective of students with disabilities. With an emphasis on general PE settings thus far, there is a need to further explore the meaning of inclusion and what it looks like to students with a wide range of disabilities.
2. Children and youth report different barriers and experiences compared to adults, including parents and teachers. Considering there are perceived differences identified between children and adults, it is critical that we capture the perspectives of children and youth with disabilities.
3. The views of children with disabilities are important to create personalized pathways to guide children towards PE and sport activities that meaningfully promote lifelong participation.
4. Overall, experiences of inclusion were reported as being mixed, including both positive and negative aspects. An ecological framework or systems approach may be useful to examine the complex interaction of various factors that influence general PE experience.
5. A qualitative research approach is the most commonly used to document the experiences of children and youth with disabilities.
6. Despite negative experiences, the majority of students with disabilities globally have expressed a desire to participate in PE classes with peers without disabilities.

7. When it comes to assistance and support in PE, students with disabilities have expressed preference for assistance that is provided on their own terms. Students want to be involved and share their needs with their teachers.
8. Better communication between students and teachers may result in better clarity and understanding between the roles and responsibilities of students and teachers.
9. Encouraging teachers to re-think their notion of what it means to listen as a way to address perceived misunderstanding between students and adults is valuable.

Reflective questions

1. Given all of the literature on the perspective of students with disabilities in PE settings, there are many different possible outcomes for a given PE class (e.g., both good days and bad days have been described). What advice would you have for a new teacher who will be instructing PE in an inclusive class setting? Specifically, what would you recommend to help them foster positive social interactions?
2. To advance research in the field of APE, what theoretical or conceptual frameworks may be useful to better understand how PE is experienced by students with disabilities?
3. You have been asked to design a new research study about APE. Who will you speak to? Which perspectives are important in the design of your study and why?
4. An experienced teacher at your school has indicated that they will continue to deliver the curriculum exactly as delivered (i.e., without modification) because that is what they are supposed to do. You believe there are situations that call for adaptation, depending on the needs of the students. Based on what you have learned about the perspectives of students with disabilities, how will you convince this teacher to change their behavior? Or can you?

References

Asbjornslett, M., Engelsrud, G. H., & Helseth, S. (2015). Inclusion and participation in everyday school life: Experiences of children with physical (dis)abilities. *International Journal of Inclusive Education, 19*, 199–212.
Baker, K., & Donelly, M. (2001). The social experiences of children with disability and the influence of environment: A framework for intervention. *Disability & Society, 16*, 71–85.
Batters, R., & Reilly, N. (2015). Investigation the attitudes and perceptions of athletes with an intellectual disability on the utilisation of sports questionnaires. (Dissertation thesis, University of Derby).
Bertills, K., Granlund, M., Dahlström, Ö., & Augustine, L. (2018). Relationships between physical education (PE) teaching and student self-efficacy, aptitude to participate in PE and functional skills: With a special focus on students with disabilities. *Physical Education and Sport Pedagogy, 23*(4), 387–401.
Blinde, E. M., & McCallister, S. G. (1998). Listening to the voices of students with physical disabilities: Experiences in the physical education classroom. *Journal of Physical Education, Recreation & Dance, 69*(6), 64–68.
Block, M. E. (2000). *A teacher's guide to including students with disabilities in regular physical education* (2nd ed.). Baltimore: Paul H. Brookes.
Block, M. E., & Obrusnikova, I. (2007). Inclusion in physical education: A review of the literature from 1995–2005. *Adapted Physical Activity Quarterly, 24*, 103–124.
Block, M. E., & Vogler, E. W. (1994). Inclusion in regular physical education: The research base. *Journal of Physical Education, Recreation & Dance, 65*(1), 40–44.

Bredahl, A. (2013). Sitting and watching the others being active: The experienced difficulties in PE when having a disability. *Adapted Physical Activity Quarterly, 30*, 40–58.

Campos, M. J., Ferreira, J. P., & Block, M. E. (2014). Influence of an awareness program on Portuguese middle and high school students' perceptions toward peers with disabilities. *Psychological Reports, 115*, 897–912.

Clemente, I. (2017). Barriers and facilitators to participation in physical activity for children with disabilities.: A systematic literature review. (Dissertation thesis, Jönköping University). Retrieved from www.diva-portal.org/smash/get/diva2:1107967/FULLTEXT01.pdf

Coates, J. (2012). Teaching inclusively: Are secondary physical education student teachers sufficiently prepared to teach in inclusive environments? *Physical Education and Sport Pedagogy, 17*, 349–365.

Coates, J., & Vickerman, P. (2010). Empowering children with special educational needs to speak up: Experiences of inclusive physical education. *Disability and Rehabilitation, 32*(18), 1517–1526.

Curtin, M., & Clarke, G. (2005). Listening to young people with physical disabilities' experiences of education. *International Journal of Disability, Development and Education, 52*(3), 195–214.

DePauw, K. P., & Doll-Tepper, G. (2000). Toward progressive inclusion and acceptance: Myth or reality? The inclusion debate and bandwagon discourse. *Adapted Physical Activity Quarterly, 17*(2), 135–143.

Fitzgerald, H. (2005). Still feeling like a spare piece of luggage? Embodied experiences of (dis)ability in physical education and school sport. *Physical Education & Sport Pedagogy, 10*, 41–59.

Fitzgerald, H., Jobling, A., & Kirk, D. (2003). Listening to the 'voices' of students with severe learning difficulties through a task-based approach to research and learning in physical education. *Support for Learning, 18*(3), 123–129.

Fitzgerald, H., & Stride, A. (2012). Stories about physical education from young people with disabilities. *International Journal of Disability, Development, and Education, 59*, 283–293.

Gibson, J. J. (1979). *The ecological approach to visual perception.* Boston, MA: Psychology Press.

Goodwin, D. L. (2001). The meaning of help in PE: Perceptions of students with physical disabilities. *Adapted Physical Activity Quarterly, 18*, 189–303.

Goodwin, D. L., & Watkinson, J. E. (2000). Inclusive physical education from the perspective of students with physical disabilities. *Adapted Physical Activity Quarterly, 17*, 144–160.

Haegele, J. A., & Kirk, T. N. (2018). Experiences in physical education: Exploring the intersection of visual impairment and maleness. *Adapted Physical Activity Quarterly, 35*(2), 196–213. doi:10.1123/apaq.2017-0132

Haegele, J. A., & Sutherland, S. (2015). Perspectives of students with disabilities toward physical education: A qualitative inquiry review. *Quest, 67*, 255–273.

Haegele, J. A., & Zhu, X. (2017). Experiences of individuals with visual impairments in integrated physical education: A retrospective study. *Research Quarterly for Exercise and Sport, 88*(4), 425–435. doi:10.1080/02701367.2017.1346781

Healy, S., Msetfi, R., & Gallagher, S. (2013). 'Happy and a bit nervous': The experiences of children with autism in physical education. *British Journal of Learning Disabilities, 41*, 222–228.

Hutzler, Y., Fliess, O., Chacham, A., & Van Den Auweele, Y. (2002). Perspectives of children with physical disabilities on inclusion and empowerment: Supporting and limiting factors. *Adapted Physical Activity Quarterly, 19*(3), 300–317.

Individuals with Disabilities Education Improvement Act (IDEA-IA). (2004) Public Law No. 108-446, Federal Register (2004).

Kalyvas, V., & Reid, G. (2003). Sport adaptation, participation, and enjoyment of students with and without physical disabilities. *Adapted Physical Activity Quarterly, 20*(2), 182–199.

Li, C., & Chen, S. (2012). Exploring experiences of physical activity in special school students with cerebral palsy: A qualitative perspective. *European Journal of Adapted Physical Activity, 5*(1), 7–17.

Lieberman, L. J., Robinson, B. L., & Rollheiser, H. (2006). Youth with visual impairments: Experiences in general physical education. *Rehabilitation and Education for Blindness and Visual Impairment, 38*(1), 35–48.

Lindsay, S., Duncanson, M., Niles-Campbell, N., McDougall, C., Diederichs, S., & Menna-Dack, D. (2018). Applying an ecological framework to understand transition pathways to post-secondary education for youth with physical disabilities. *Disability and Rehabilitation, 40*, 277–286. doi:10.1080/09638288.2016.1250171

Makopoulou, K., & Neville, R. (2016). Sainsbury's Active Kids for All Inclusive PE Training Programme —Final Report. Retrieved from: http://epapers.bham.ac.uk/3172/1/The_Sainsbury's_Inclusive_Phy sical_Education_CPD_-_Final_Report_of_UoB_Evaluation_Team.pdf

Makopoulou, K., & Thomas, G. (2017). Educating teachers for effective inclusive pedagogies. In C. D. Ennis (Ed.), *Routledge handbook of physical education pedagogies* (pp. 473–484). London: Routledge.

Martin Ginis, K. A., Ma, J. K., Latimer-Cheung, A. E., & Rimmer, J. H. (2016). A systematic review of review articles addressing factors related to physical activity participation among children and adults with physical disabilities. *Health Psychology Review*, 10(4), 478–494.

McKay, C. (2018). The value of contact: Unpacking Allport's contact theory to support inclusive education. *Palaestra*, 32, 21–25.

McKay, C., Block, M. E., & Park, J. Y. (2015). The impact of Paralympic School Day on student attitudes toward inclusion in physical education. *Adapted Physical Activity Quarterly*, 32, 331–348.

McLeod, J. (2011). Student voice and the politics of listening in higher education. *Critical Studies in Education*, 52, 179–189.

Mitchell, K., & Parker, W. (2008). I pledge allegiance to … Flexible citizenship and shifting scales of belonging. *Teachers College Record*, 10(4), 775–804.

Molton, E. (2014). Physical education, power, and the cultural politics of the young Turkish body. (Doctoral dissertation, University of Bath). Retrieved from https://core.ac.uk/download/pdf/38146216.pdf

Moola, F., Fusco, C., & Kirsh, J. A. (2011). 'What I wish you knew': Social barriers toward physical activity in youth with congenital heart disease (CHD). *Adapted Physical Activity Quarterly*, 28(1), 56–77.

Mourton & Batters (In preparation). Focus on Me: an inclusive focus group framework development. Youth sport trust and sport empowers disabled youth SEDY. European Union Erasmus+.

Nind, M. (2008). Conducting qualitative research with people with learning, communication and other disabilities: Methodological challenges. ESRC National Centre for Research Methods Review Paper, Economic & Social Research Council, Swindon. Retrieved from http://eprints.ncrm.ac.uk/491/1/MethodsReviewPaperNCRM-012.pdf.

Owens, J. (2007). Liberating voices through narrative methods: The case for an interpretive research approach. *Disability & Society*, 22(3), 299–313.

Place, K., & Hodge, S. R. (2001). Social inclusion of students with physical disabilities in general physical education: A behavioral analysis. *Adapted Physical Activity Quarterly*, 18, 389–404.

Pocock, T., & Miyahara, M. (2018). Inclusion of students with disability in physical education: A qualitative meta-analysis. *International Journal of Inclusive Education*, 22(7), 751–766.

Sandelowski, M. (1993). Theory unmasked: The uses and guises of theory in qualitative research. *Research in Nursing & Health*, 16(3), 213–218.

Sanders, S. W. (1996). Children's physical education experiences: Their interpretations can help teachers. *Journal of Physical Education, Recreation, and Dance*, 67, 51–56.

Sato, T., & Haegele, J. A. (2017). Graduate students' practicum experiences instructing students with severe and profound disabilities in physical education. *European Physical Education Review*, 23(2), 196–211.

SEDY (2017). The Sport Empowers Disabled Youth project. European Union Erasmus+. Retrieved from www.hva.nl/kc-bsv/gedeelde-content/contentgroep/sedy-project/sedy-project.html

Spencer-Cavaliere, N., & Watkinson, E. J. (2010). Inclusion understood from the perspectives of children with disability. *Adapted Physical Activity Quarterly*, 27(4), 275–293.

Stainback, W., Stainback, S., & Bunch, G. (1989). *Educating all students in the mainstream of regular education*. Baltimore: Paul H. Brookes.

Svendby, E. B., & Dowling, F. (2013). Negotiating the discursive spaces of inclusive education: Narratives of experience from contemporary physical education. *Scandinavian Journal of Disability Research*, 15(4), 361–378.

Tanure Alves, M. L., Grenier, M., Haegele, J. A., & Duarte, E. (2018). 'I didn't do anything, I just watched': Perspectives of Brazilian students with physical disabilities toward physical education. *International Journal of Inclusive Education*, 1–14. DOI: 10.1080/13603116.2018.1511760

van der Ploeg, H. P., van der Beek, A. J., van der Woude, L. H., & van Mechelen, W. (2004). Physical activity for people with a disability. *Sports Medicine*, 34(10), 639–649.

Wang, L. (2019). Perspectives of students with special needs on inclusion in general physical education: A social-relational model of disability. *Adapted Physical Activity Quarterly*, 36, 242–263. doi:10.1123/apaq.2018-0068

Whitehurst, T. (2007). Liberating silent voices–Perspectives of children with profound & complex learning needs on inclusion. *British Journal of Learning Disabilities, 35*(1), 55–61.

Wilhelmsen, T., Sorensen, M., & Seippel, O. N. (2019). Motivational pathways to social and pedagogical inclusion in physical education. *Adapted Physical Activity Quarterly, 36,* 19–41. doi:10.1123/apaq.2018-0019

Wilhite, B., Muschett, C. A., Goldenberg, L., & Trader, B. R. (1997). Promoting inclusive sport and leisure participation. *Adapted Physical Activity Quarterly, 17,* 161–175.

Wilson, E., Campain, R., Moore, M., Hagiliassis, N., McGillivray, J., Gottliebson, D., … Graffam, J. (2013). An accessible survey method: Increasing the participation of people with a disability in large sample social research. *Telecommunications Journal of Australia, 63*(2), Article 411.

Winnick, J., & Porretta, D. (Eds.). (2016). *Adapted physical education and sport, 6E.* Champaign, IL: Human Kinetics.

28

Motor competence within the discipline of adapted physical education

Megan MacDonald, Byungmo Ku, Samuel W. Logan, and Jodi Stinson

Motor development is defined as "… the changes in motor behavior over the lifespan *and* the process(es) which underlie these changes" (Clark & Whitall, 1989, p. 194). While development specifically refers to change over time, motor competence is often the term used to describe the motor domain. In contrast to motor development, motor competence represents performance at one point in time, and is typically measured by an appropriate motor assessment (Robinson et al., 2015). For the purpose of this chapter, motor competence is used as a general term intended "… to reflect the various terminologies that have been used in previous literature (i.e., motor proficiency, motor performance, fundamental movement/motor skill, motor ability, and motor coordination" (Robinson et al., 2015, p. 1274). The term motor competence is intended to encompass the different skills and abilities within the motor domain. One aspect of motor competence that will be discussed throughout this chapter is fundamental movement skills (FMS). When the specific term of FMS is used, it is defined as object control (e.g., throwing, catching, kicking), locomotor skills (e.g., running, jumping, hopping) and non-locomotor balance/stability skills (e.g., one-foot balance, bending, twisting) that serve as foundational skills to more advanced and complex movement skills required for participation in sports, games, and context specific physical activity (Ulrich, 2001).

The field of motor development has strong roots in the measurement of cognition and other social behaviors, especially in early childhood. While these roots have a strong historical context (e.g., Piaget), more recent empirical research examining the underlying mechanisms of motor competence on other aspects of child development has emerged. Although our chapter will not extensively focus on these associations, this emerging, yet historically relevant, relationship is discussed within this chapter.

Historical overview

The study of motor development originated in biology and psychology (Clark & Whitall, 1989). There are four periods that are identified as the historical foundations of motor development (see Clark & Whitall, 1989 for a detailed discussion of all four periods). The Precursor

Period (1787–1928) is most closely identified with the emergence of "baby biographies" that were detailed observations, including motor behaviors, of infants over a period of years. The contributions of Charles Darwin are also notable during this period, due to his emphasis on how the environment shapes behavior and an interest in developmental processes within and across generations. The Maturational Period (1928–1946) is associated with the work of Arnold Gesell and Myrtle McGraw, who emphasized the role of biological contributions to motor development. The Normative/Descriptive Period (1946–1970) is defined by the contributions of three physical educators; Anna Espenschade, Ruth Glassow, and G. Lawrence Rarick (Motor Development Academy, 1980). Their collective research emphasized school-aged children's movement skills and research focused on "… understanding motor development rather than cognitive development, or development in general" (Clark & Whitall, 1989, p. 188). Research during this time period focused on the product or outcome of movements. The Process-Oriented Period (1970–present) marked the shift to a systematic inquiry of the underlying processes of how movement emerges, with a particular focus on children's fundamental motor patterns (Seefeldt & Haubenstricker, 1982). Motor development is firmly situated within the broader field of kinesiology as a sub-discipline area of study.

Theoretical/conceptual frameworks

The field of motor development has various theoretical and conceptual frameworks that have been associated with work in the discipline of adapted physical education (APE). Motor development researchers with interest in APE have prominently focused on theoretical frameworks that emphasize inclusivity, and for the most part the field rejects theoretical perspectives solely dedicated to maturation (e.g., theoretical perspectives that are focused on the genetic/growth influence on motor development [thus not considering how the environment, both social and built, influence a person's motor competence]) (Thelen, 2000). Common theoretical perspectives subscribed to by motor development researchers interested in focusing on those with disabilities include, but are not limited to, dynamic systems theory (Thelen, 2005), Newell's constraint model (Newell, 1984, 1986) and Stodden et al.'s developmental perspective (Stodden et al., 2008).

Dynamic systems theory

Dynamic systems theory provides a framework for motor development and APE researchers to approach FMS development. Esther Thelen (2005) outlined three principles of dynamic systems theory: complexity, continuity of time, and dynamic stability. The first principle, complexity, suggests that human movement is the result of complex, interacting constraints that produce self-organized motor patterns. Self-organization refers to the concept that movement is not prescribed simply by maturation of the central nervous system, but, rather, is the result of many systems working together in real time to encourage movement patterns. The second principle, continuity in time, suggests that the process related to motor development is influenced by the cumulative past experiences of an individual and that changes occur in real time and over time at all levels of the individual (from cellular changes to behavioral changes). The third principle, dynamic stability, suggests that human movement patterns have varying degrees of stability and flexibility. Specific movements may be very stable for skilled individuals who have learned and practiced an FMS. However, this skill is still flexible, depending upon the interaction of constraints that influence how the movement will be performed at any point in time in a specific context.

Newell's constraints model

Newell's constraints model (Newell, 1984, 1986) was influenced by Esther Thelen's work on constraints and the coordinative structure theory put forth by Kugler, Kelso, and Turvey (1982). Newell's constraints model offers a valuable framework to APE and identifies three types of constraints (i.e., environmental, organism, and task constraints) that interact to encourage an "… optimal pattern of coordination and control for any activity" (Newell, 1984, p. 348).

Environmental constraints are external to an individual and may be physical, such as temperature, amount of light, conditions of the surface one is moving on, or social, such as cultural influences or stereotyping that influences the type of motor behaviors children have access to during movement experiences. For some children with disabilities, the space an activity is taking place in might be too stimulating (e.g., a loud gymnasium, or distracting overhead florescent lights), in this example the environmental constraint may negatively impact the child's motor competence. On the other hand, an APE environment where diversity is valued by the physical educator, educational assistants and students, and where equipment, game play, and instruction is adapted for inclusivity, may positively impact the motor competence of all students, including students with disabilities.

Organism (i.e., individual) constraints include two subtypes: structural and functional. Structural constraints relate to physical aspects of an individual, such as weight, height, and biological and physiological systems and typically develop gradually over time. Functional constraints relate to psychological aspects of an individual, such as motivation that may change on shorter time scales, depending upon the constraint. APE teachers are specifically trained to understand the needs and best practices related to individuals with varying disabilities. Depending upon the disability, the presentation of individual constraints will be vastly different, requiring careful consideration in the planning and implementation of research studies and lesson plans designed to promote the development of FMSs.

Task constraints are especially relevant to APE researchers. Task constraints include the goal, rules, and equipment related to a specific task and are often manipulated for the purpose of encouraging or discouraging certain types of movements. For example, consider the task of throwing. The objective of a game of darts is to throw the dart as accurately as possible (goal), from a specified distance to the target (rules), using an object with a pointed end that is shaped in such a way that encourages holding via the fingertips (equipment). This tends to produce a movement where an individual aligns their throwing hand with their leg on the same side of the body and "pushes" the dart forward using a straight forward motion and release. In contrast, the objective of throwing as hard as possible (goal), with no specific target (rules), using an object that is round and easily grasped with the whole hand (equipment) results in a different movement pattern. This tends to produce a movement where an individual steps forward with the opposite foot to the throwing hand, the arm reaches behind the body in a wind-up motion, and the individual releases the ball and the arm follows through down and across the front of the body. Successful manipulation of task constraints, to scaffold developmental progress of FMS development, is one of the core responsibilities of APE teachers. Thus, research focused on the constraints model and the manipulation of constraints may have immediate relevance to practitioners (APE teachers) in the field.

Stodden et al.'s (2008) developmental perspective

Stodden et al.'s (2008) developmental perspective is one we strongly believe has direct relevance to the field of APE. Stodden and colleagues (2008) proposed a developmental perspective on the role of motor competence on physical activity engagement. This perspective holds that the relationship between the development of motor competence and physical activity engagement is dynamic and reciprocal, suggesting that one does not occur without the other. Within this model, perceived motor competence, health-related fitness, and obesity serve as mediating factors to the relationship between motor competence and physical activity. This perspective proposes that the relationship strengthens across developmental time, resulting in three specific hypotheses for early childhood, middle childhood, and late childhood and adolescence.

Early childhood

During early childhood (2–5 years old), it is hypothesized that the relationship between motor competence and physical activity will be weak, due to differences in previous experience as a result of several influences such as environmental circumstances, parental factors, and access to structured physical education, and that physical activity engagement may drive motor experiences that contribute to motor competence. Perceived motor competence (i.e., how a child views their own motor competence) is not hypothesized to contribute to physical activity engagement, due to children's inability at a young age to accurately assess their motor competence relative to peers.

Middle childhood

During middle childhood (6–9 years old), it is hypothesized that the relationship between motor competence and physical activity will strengthen and become moderate during this timeframe. As children develop motor competence and gain proficiency in a variety of FMS, they will experience more movement options to participate in more complex sports and games, resulting in increased physical activity. Perceived motor competence begins to play a role during this developmental period because children are developing the cognitive skills to accurately assess their motor competence relative to peers. Therefore, low-skilled children are able to perceive they are low skilled and may choose to engage less in physical activity; in contrast, high-skilled children are more able to perceive they are highly skilled and thus may choose to engage in more physical activity. Furthermore, high-skilled children who engage in more physical activity will be more likely to develop health-related fitness that continues to encourage motor competence and physical activity engagement.

Late childhood and adolescence

During late childhood (10–13 years old) and adolescence (14–18 years old), it is hypothesized that the relationship between motor competence and physical activity will become strong as a result of the compounding and cumulative effect of previous factors that influence the relationship. Finally, it is suggested that the relationship between motor competence and physical activity may lead to positive or negative spirals of engagement that either encourages a healthy weight, or an unhealthy weight, respectively.

The relationship between motor competence and physical activity is important due to the potential health implications. A review article by Robinson and colleagues (2015) provided support for the developmental perspective outlined by Stodden et al. (2008) and indicated a positive relationship between motor competence and physical activity engagement in children without disabilities. As a result of the review, Robinson and colleagues (2015) support that motor competence is related to positive developmental trajectories of health, including perceived motor competence, health-related fitness, and weight status.

The vast majority of research on the relationship between motor competence and physical activity engagement has been conducted in populations of children without disabilities (Robinson et al., 2015). This previous work highlights the importance of motor competence and provides a foundation for understanding its role on the development of positive health outcomes, such as improved physical activity behaviors. It might be hypothesized that children with disabilities follow a similar trend based on Stodden et al.'s (2008) perspective, yet empirical research suggests that the starting point (e.g., motor skill competence and/or physical activity behavior) is lower than that of peers without disabilities (Staples & Reid, 2010). To that end, the benefits of motor competence or physical activity-based interventions might be hypothesized to have amplified benefits for children with disabilities, providing critical skills for peer engagement (e.g., skills to participate in childhood games). This exemplifies the importance of APE, where equitable opportunities to develop motor skill competence and positive physical activity behaviors take place.

A review of motor competence scholarship focusing of children with disabilities

Proficient motor competence provides the foundational skills needed for aspects of daily living as well as advanced sport-specific skills (Ulrich, 2000). Early in life, motor skill development is linked to more general aspects of child development. For example, gross motor skills act upon our gait, an important ambulatory skill which, at an early age, impacts aspects of independence and, more generally, participation in activities. The field of APE has positively impacted the motor competence of children with disabilities through empirical research, including interventions focused on improving motor competence.

Research demonstrates clear disparities in motor competence between children with disabilities and peers without disabilities. For example, school-aged children with autism spectrum disorder (ASD) have been found to perform motor skills similarly to children without disabilities who were about half of their age (Staples & Reid, 2010). While disparities in motor competence have been clearly established, methods to improve motor competence (e.g., interventions) and learn sport-specific skills to optimally participate in daily activities, physical activities, and sport, remains an active area of research.

Thus, the purpose of this summary of current scholarship is to identify some of the more recent motor skill and motor competence-based research in APE for pre-school and school-aged children with disabilities.

The motor skills of pre-school-aged children

The opportunity to engage in physical activity has been asserted as a fundamental human right across the lifespan (Logan, Feldner, Galloway, & Huang, 2016). Rather than waiting for motor development disparities to emerge, early childhood is a critical period for intervention to prevent unnecessary developmental delay in children with disabilities. At a young age, early intervention services are often offered to children with disabilities and children at risk for disabilities. Some disabilities present themselves during childhood and not necessarily at birth (e.g., attention deficit hyperactivity disorder [ADHD], ASD, cerebral palsy [CP]). Delayed development is defined as a score of 1.5 standard deviations or more from the norm on a developmental outcome measure (Bellman, Byrne, & Sege, 2013; Shevell, Majnemer,

Platt, Webster, & Birnbaum, 2005). For example, a developmental delay would be issued in speech if a child scores more than 1.5 deviations from the speech norm, based on their chronological age. In the US, children who experienced delayed development also qualify for special education services (e.g., an Individualized Family Service Plan). Thus, studies in this section include children with disabilities and children who qualify for early special education services (e.g., children at risk for disabilities).

Researchers in APE have been influential in testing novel early interventions such as infant treadmill training to close the gap in known motor skill delays (Ulrich, Ulrich, Angulo-Barroso, & Yun, 2001). For example, young children with Down syndrome typically walk about a year later than their peers without disabilities (Pagani & Messier, 2012). Researchers have demonstrated that the use of a small motorized treadmill by infants with Down syndrome can lead to an earlier onset of independent walking (Ulrich et al., 2001). Similarly, young children with physical disabilities are disadvantaged in that powered mobility devices, such as electric wheelchairs, are not typically available for their use until around the age of 5–6 years. Thus, independent exploration before this age is limited and may set children even further behind in respect to other aspects of child development, including motor competence. To address this gap, researchers have modified battery-operated ride-on toy cars to provide greater access to the activation switch and individualized seating support to afford a means of mobility and play to children as young as seven months-old (Logan et al., 2019), well before access to a standard powered mobility device (Logan et al., 2016; Logan, Huang, Stahlin, & Galloway, 2014). Evidence demonstrates that use of a modified ride-on car provides young children with developmental disabilities the opportunity for self-directed mobility and, in turn, provides opportunities for participation (aspects of daily living) and to explore the environment (Logan et al., 2016, 2014). While research with modified ride-on cars has primarily taken place in the US, this practice has been adopted internationally (see https://sites.udel.edu/gobabygo/for additional international information).

Early group-based motor skill interventions

Researchers in APE have been successful at implementing successful interventions for pre-school children with, or at risk for, disability (Logan, Robinson, Wilson, & Lucas, 2012). One such intervention is the Successful Kinesthetic Instruction for Preschoolers (SKIP) motor skill intervention, which took place in the US. SKIP focuses on the motor skills of kicking, throwing, catching, striking, bouncing, and rolling. Each session is ~30 minutes and includes a warm-up, infusing the primary motor skills, 24 minutes rotating through the primary skills, and a three-minute closure. The SKIP motor skill intervention was implemented with at risk pre-school children, including children with disabilities, who were 3–5 years of age ($n = 72$). The SKIP motor skill intervention was specifically administered on two out of five days to two different motor skill-based intervention groups (one with and one without parental involvement). Object control skills were assessed using the Test of Gross Motor Development – 2nd Edition (TGMD-2; Ulrich, 2000). Both intervention groups had significant improvements compared to the control group, who did not experience an intervention. There were no statistically significant differences between the two intervention groups in respect to object control outcomes (Altunsöz & Goodway, 2016). The children in both intervention groups had retained the learned skills at one month post intervention. Thus, the SKIP intervention had long-term positive impacts on the object control skills of young children with disabilities.

Another motor skill based intervention focused on at risk pre-schoolers in the US, including young children with disabilities, was implemented over the course of 18 weeks, four days per week for ~15– 20 minutes each day and included lessons focused on specific FMSs (Bellows et al., 2017). The intervention group *n* = 147) had significantly better object control skills compared to the control group (*n* = 103), but there were no statistically significant differences in locomotor or balance skills. Improved object control skills persisted when the intervention group was compared to the control group twoyears post intervention (Bellows et al., 2017). Long-term intervention impacts are less known within the field of APE, as demonstrated in the above two studies. This is an important direction for consideration in future APE research.

A smaller scale study (*n* = 10), focused on the motor skills of 5–7-year-old children with coordination difficulties in Canada, implemented a motor skill-based intervention (Kane & Staples, 2016). The intervention was implemented three times per week for about two weeks and each session was two hours in length. Object control and locomotor skills showed statistically significant improvements in nine of the participants over the course of the intervention. Thus, early on, evidence strongly suggests that motor skills are malleable and that targeted interventions are important in respect to improving the motor skills of young children with disabilities.

Early group motor skill-based interventions focused on specific disabilities

Motor skill interventions focused on specific, rather than broader, disability groups (e.g., young children with disabilities and developmental delays) have also been implemented. This has included testing the effects of a motor skill intervention in young children with ASD and children with CP. Bremer, Balogh, and Lloyd (2015) implemented a 12-hour motor skill intervention for young four-year-old children with ASD in Canada, focused on targeted instruction on one motor skill per session, with each session ending with free play. The intervention group had better object manipulation skills and a better total motor quotient score compared to the control group. Motor skill improvements were also evident when an eight-week motor skill intervention, based on techniques from *Purposeful Play* (McCall & Craft, 2004), was implemented for five pre-school-aged children with ASD in the Czech Republic (Duronjic & Valkova, 2010).

Another motor skill intervention targeted young children with ASD between the ages of four and six years (Ketcheson, Hauck, & Ulrich, 2017) and this eight-week intensive motor skill intervention, led by an adapted physical educator, took place for approximately four hours per day, five days per week. The intervention consisted of 25 minutes of free play, direct motor skill instruction for two 50-minute blocks and small group lessons for two 50-minute blocks. The control group consisted of no intervention. The intervention group (*n* = 20) improved their locomotor and object control skills compared to the control group (*n* = 9) To date, this pilot study is one of the more intensive motor skill interventions targeted at young children with ASD in the US (Ketcheson et al., 2017).

Collectively, these early interventions focused on young children with disabilities and developmental delays display that motor skills can improve at a young age, with the right interventions. In addition to the interventions that were highlighted, motor skill interventions have successfully improved the motor skills of young children with low vision (Aki, Atasavun, Turan, & Kayihan, 2007). Although there is a relative paucity of research focused on targeted interventions, findings clearly indicate that positive improvements in motor competence can occur with disability populations. Of note, there is limited research in APE that has implemented randomized control trials. As the field of APE moves forward, study designs implementing randomized control trials (or stratified randomized control trials) need to be considered. This type of study design would permit causal explanation of motor skill interventions and would allow researchers to thoroughly examine whether certain interventions are more effective than others.

Motor skills and cognitive behaviors

The importance of motor skill development in young children is undeniable, given the role that motor skills have on active independence and a child's ability to explore their surroundings. While much of the work represented in this chapter is from the US, some projects represent international work beyond North America. Thus, our collective ability, in the field of APE, to provide substantial programs that ultimately improve motor skills is global. Based on work to date, less is known about which motor skill interventions work best or how timing and dose (e.g., time in session) play a role in best outcomes. Research findings indicate that there are strong associations with better motor skills and other salient child behaviors, such as executive function, social skills, communication skills, as well as early academic achievement (e.g., MacDonald, Lord, & Ulrich, 2014; MacDonald, Ross, McIntyre, & Tepfer, 2017). In short, evidence suggests that motor skills have strong associations with other aspects of child development. Thus, the known motor skill delays faced by children with disabilities and children at risk for disability may, in fact, negatively impact other salient childhood behaviors, all of which are important for healthy childhood development, including motor skills. Intervening early is critical towards positive outcomes, as it relates to early motor skill development.

More recently, early initiatives focused on school readiness have gained attention. Within school readiness initiatives, motor competence has received less attention compared to other school readiness outcomes (e.g., social behaviors). Researchers in APE in the US have studied the effects of a motor skill intervention for young at risk children (mean age 5.14 years) and found that participation in the motor skill intervention significantly improved executive function skills compared to the control group (Mulvey, Taunton, Pennell, & Brian, 2018). In this study, young children were randomly assigned to the intervention (n = 50) or control group (n = 57). Children who were assigned to the intervention group participated in the SKIP program (Brian, Goodway, Logan, & Sutherland, 2017), twice weekly for 30 minutes each session for six weeks. Children in the control group participated in their regular recess activities, without a specific intervention. The findings from this study exemplify the strong relationship of motor competence with other aspects of child development, including aspects highly correlated with school readiness (e.g., executive function). Thus, how early motor skill interventions correlate with, or enhance, the school readiness skills of children with disabilities is an area of research that needs further exploration.

Broadly, the empirical studies indicated above highlight the successes of early motor skill interventions focused on young children with disabilities. The benefits of acting early are well documented, yet there is more to examine in respect to the best types of interventions (e.g., in physical education settings, natural environments with or without parent involvement) and dose (e.g., how often and for how long intervention should take place).

The motor skills of school-aged children

Proficient motor skills provide the foundation for sport specific skills as well as foundational skills needed to participate in many physical activities. For example, students may be interested in participating in school playground games, such as four-square, which requires relatively proficient object control skills (e.g., catching and passing) as well as coordination skills to direct the ball and move within and around the allotted space (i.e., the square). The compounded effect of motor skill difficulties, often experienced by children with disabilities, can negatively impact participation in physical activity. Unfortunately, as school-aged children with disabilities age, physical activity behaviors tend to decline (Esposito, Nakazawa, Venuti, & Bornstein, 2012; MacDonald, Esposito, & Ulrich, 2011; Rimmer & Rowland, 2009), and the gap in physical inactivity widens compared to peers without disabilities (Sanson, Hemphill, & Smart, 2004; Staples & Reid, 2010; Tyler, MacDonald, & Menear, 2014). School-based physical education is the most logical place for all students to receive motor competence training, which may also lead to more opportunities to participate in physical activity (see Stodden et al., 2008).

Although much effort in recent years has focused on improving the physical activity behaviors of school-aged children (with and without disabilities), we believe that improving motor competence will provide unique opportunities for children with disabilities to participate in physical activities. Our review of motor skill-based interventions ultimately supports unique links between motor skill development and physical activity, relationships which are highlighted in Stodden et al's., 2008 developmental perspective. In additional to motor development outcomes (such as better motor skills), researchers in motor development are also focused on intervention techniques and their respective impact on outcomes such as physical activity behaviors.

Physical activity outcomes

The relationship between motor competence and physical activity strengthens as children enter middle childhood and beyond (Robinson et al., 2015; Stodden et al., 2008). Thus, many APE programs are focused on improving physical activity behaviors. Researchers in Japan studied the effects of an exercise training program for children with intellectual disabilities, implemented by physical educators, on the outcome of walking speed (Hayakawa & Kobayashi, 2011). Participants took part in a 12-week intervention once per week for 30 minutes. Intervention sessions consisted of training with specialized equipment, including a spring training machine, a bicycle ergometer with pedals that moved in an elliptical orbit, and a hand and foot ipsilateral machine. Improvements occurred, including reduced/faster times in the 50-meter dash, the 10-meter walk time and in a 10-meter obstacle course walk. Researchers in Greece studied the effects of a 12-week trampoline exercise intervention on motor performance in adolescents with intellectual disabilities (Giagazoglou et al., 2013). The participants ($n = 18$) were assigned to a 12-week trampoline exercise intervention or a control group. The intervention consisted of 20 minutes of trampoline exercises and regular physical education participation and the control group participated in typical physical education only. The participants assigned to the intervention group had positive improvements in balance and their jumping ability, including their broad and vertical jump distance.

Motor skill outcomes

Researchers in Holland implemented an APE intervention to target the improvement of ball skills for children with learning disabilities (Westendorp et al., 2014). The intervention was focused on learning balls skills (e.g., striking, dribbling, catching, kicking, throwing, and rolling). The first four weeks of the intervention targeted simple ball exercises, followed by 12 weeks where the simple exercises were repeated and then followed by more complex ball related exercises (e.g., games). Statistically significant improvements of object control skills were found for the intervention group compared to the control group at pre- and post-intervention.

Researchers in South Africa examined the intervention effects of a motor skill intervention for children with developmental coordination disorder (DCD; Peens, Peinaar & Nienaber, 2008). Participants between the ages of seven and nine years old (n = 58) with DCD were assigned to one of four possible conditions, including a psychological intervention, a motor skill-based intervention, a combined psycho-motor intervention, or control group (no intervention). The motor-skill based intervention involved the integration of a task-specific, kinesthetic and sensory integration curriculum (eight weeks, twice per week, 30mins per session). The psychological intervention was focused on "discovering the self" and answering the question "who am I?"; the psycho-motor intervention program involved both a psychological intervention and a motor-skill based intervention (eight weeks, twice motor and twice psycho per week, motor [30mins per session] and psycho [45mins/session]). Children's motor skill proficiency was measured using the Movement Assessment Battery for Children (Henderson, Sugden, & Barnett, 2007). Motor skill improvements occurred in the motor skill intervention group, psycho-motor intervention group, and control group. There were no improvements based on participation in the psychological intervention group. Motor skill improvements were expected in the motor skill intervention group and psycho-motor intervention group, but, surprisingly, the control group also experienced motor skill improvements. The improvements in the control group shed light on the possibility that some of these improvements were the result of growth and maturation, rather than specific to the intervention protocols. More research, comparing various types of interventions, is important in respect to learning which interventions are the most successful. Collectively, these studies focused on implementing different types of motor skill interventions, using different techniques and across different countries. Similarly, study outcomes vary, but are focused on the child outcomes of physical activity behaviors or motor skill outcomes.

The pedagogy of motor skill-based interventions

There are a variety of approaches to motor skill interventions as it relates to content (e.g., the types of motor skills targeted in the intervention); however, other components of the intervention, such as pedagogical techniques, are also important to study and understand. Adapted physical educators are often adapting teaching methods, changing equipment, and adapting rules to teach some aspects of motor skill development, including teaching sport-specific motor skills to many children with disabilities. When two different types of fundamental motor skill interventions were implemented by adapted physical educators comparing the motor skills of children with intellectual disabilities, one intervention stood out (Capio, Poolton, Sit, Eguia, & Masters, 2013). When an error-reduced motor skill intervention was compared to an error-strewn motor skill intervention, the error-reduced motor skill intervention had more positive effects on the motor skills of school-aged children with intellectual disabilities. The error-reduced approach used common techniques used by physical educators and adapted physical educators, including progressively reducing the size of equipment (including targets) in each subsequent session. Conversely, the error-strewn approach worked by progressively increasing the size of the equipment. This specific intervention was focused on ball skills, thus the error-reduced group started with larger equipment, including large-sized target square and balls, which were progressively reduced. In contrast, the error-strewn group started with regular (smaller) equipment that was progressively increased in size over the course of the intervention. Following the six-week intervention, children who participated in the error-reduced intervention improved their fundamental motor skills more than children who took part in the error-strewn intervention. Not surprisingly, the error-reduced intervention is more comparable to the pedagogy commonly used for skill practice among adapted physical educators.

Similarly, which pedagogical techniques are most salient within motor skill interventions for young children with disabilities is also an important area of research for adapted physical educators. Robinson and Goodway (2009), researchers in the US, tested the effects of two motor skill interventions using a randomized control trial. There were three groups: (1) low autonomy instruction. This is an instructor-centered approach where the instructor makes engagement-related decisions of how children experience the learning environment, such as which skills to practice and for how long; (2) mastery motivational instruction. This is a child-centered approach where the child makes engagement-related decisions of how to experience the learning environment; (3) control group. This group experienced unstructured recess. The sessions of all groups lasted for 30 minutes, two times per week for nine weeks. Both intervention groups (low autonomy and mastery) improved their motor skills compared to the control group at posttest, and these positive changes were maintained following a nine-week retention test. The researchers highlight more closely identifying pedagogical techniques as an important area of future research.

Current and future trends

APE researchers have successfully implemented interventions which have improved the motor competence and physical activity behaviors of children with disabilities. However, there are several directions for future research that would inform evidence-based practice in APE. Stodden et al.'s (2008) developmental perspective has been used as a framework to design and interpret many studies on motor competence and physical activity with children without disabilities over the past ten years (see Robinson et al., 2015 for a review). However, there is a paucity of research with children with disabilities using Stodden et al.'s (2008) developmental perspective. Motor skill competence and physical activity behavior is lower for children with disabilities compared to peers without disabilities (Staples & Reid, 2010). Therefore, it is important to understand how Stodden et al.'s (2008) developmental perspective may be applied to disability populations and how the relationship between motor competence and physical activity may be different, depending upon disability group. Knowledge gained from research in this area would inform the design of interventions aimed to facilitate motor competence and physical activity outcomes across childhood for children and youth with disabilities.

Another future direction of research includes using research designs that allow causal interpretations to understand the optimal characteristics of motor skill interventions, including pedagogical strategies that advance motor competence for disability populations. It is always important for researchers to consider their research questions carefully and determine the most appropriate study design. There may be instances when single-case research designs or randomized controlled trials (RCTs) are most appropriate, depending upon the research question. RCTs need to be considered on a larger scale as the field of APE moves forward. RCTs are often considered a gold standard of research design and results can inform evidence-based practices with a strong level of evidence. In general, there has been a lack of RCTs in the field of APE, preventing widespread adoption of effective intervention strategies.

There are many characteristics and pedagogical strategies of motor skill interventions that warrant further investigation. This is also an issue for intervention studies with children without disabilities (Van Capelle et al., 2017). A recent review found that 20 of 21 studies that implemented a motor skill intervention for children with disabilities found significant effects (Bishop & Pangelinan, 2018). However, due to the varying sample types across disability diagnoses, research designs used, and pedagogical approaches, many aspects about how best to implement motor skill interventions remains unclear. For example, research is warranted that aims to further understand the dose–response relationship between total instruction time and improvement in FMSs, optimal duration of instructional sessions (i.e., minutes per session), and delivery schedule of instruction (i.e., number of days per week). Knowledge gained as a result of pursuing these potential directions for future research would provide adapted physical educators with evidence-based practices to implement motor skill interventions with children with disabilities and foster lifelong engagement in physical activity.

Summary of key points

- Motor development originated in the fields of biology and psychology.
- Dynamic systems theory informs the field of APE and highlights the complexity of change of motor competence over time.
- Newell's constraints model includes environmental, individual, and task constraints.
- APE teachers can manipulate constraints to encourage optimal motor behaviors that facilitate change over time.
- Stodden et al.'s (2008) developmental perspective suggests that the relationship between motor competence and physical activity is dynamic and reciprocal, is influenced by perceived motor competence, health-related fitness and obesity, and strengthens across developmental time.
- Motor skill interventions are effective in promoting advances of fundamental motor skills for pre-school-aged children with and without disabilities
- Motor skill interventions are effective in promoting advances of fundamental motor skills for school-aged children with and without disabilities
- Theory-based research, intervention type, sample size, and study design are important considerations of future research on fundamental motor skills of children with disabilities

Reflective questions for discussion

- What is the role of APE teachers in the promotion of fundamental motor skills and physical activity during physical education classes?
- What are potential directions for APE research in regard to motor skill interventions?
- What are your predictions for how Stodden et al.'s (2008) developmental perspective may or may not hold up for children with different abilities across the early, middle, and late periods of childhood?

Reference

Aki, E., Atasavun, S., Turan, A., & Kayihan, H. (2007). Training motor skills of children with low vision. *Perceptual and Motor Skills, 104*(3_suppl), 1328–1336. doi:10.2466/pms.104.4.1328-1336

Altunsöz, I. H., & Goodway, J. D. (2016). SKIPing to motor competence: The influence of project successful kinesthetic instruction for preschoolers on motor competence of disadvantaged preschoolers. *Physical Education and Sport Pedagogy, 21*(4), 366–385. doi:10.1080/17408989.2015.1017453

Bellman, M., Byrne, O., & Sege, R. (2013). Developmental assessment of children. *British Medical Journal, 346*, e8687. doi:10.1136/bmj.e8687

Bellows, L. L., Davies, P. L., Courtney, J. B., Gavin, W. J., Johnson, S. L., & Boles, R. E. (2017). Motor skill development in low-income, at-risk preschoolers: A community-based longitudinal intervention study. *Journal of Science and Medicine in Sport, 20*(11), 997–1002. doi:10.1016/j.jsams.2017.04.003

Bishop, J. C., & Pangelinan, M. (2018). Motor skills intervention research of children with disabilities. *Research in developmental disabilities, 74*, 14–30.

Bremer, E., Balogh, R., & Lloyd, M. (2015). Effectiveness of a fundamental motor skill intervention for 4-year-old children with autism spectrum disorder: A pilot study. *Autism, 19*(8), 980–991. doi:10.1177/1362361314557548

Brian, A., Goodway, J. D., Logan, J. A., & Sutherland, S. (2017). SKIPing with head start teachers: Influence of T-SKIP on object-control skills. *Research Quarterly for Exercise and Sport, 88*(4), 479–491. doi:10.1080/02701367.2017.1375077

Capio, C. M., Poolton, J. M., Sit, C. H. P., Eguia, K. F., & Masters, R. S. W. (2013). Reduction of errors during practice facilitates fundamental movement skill learning in children with intellectual disabilities: Error-reduced FMS training in children. *Journal of Intellectual Disability Research, 57*(4), 295–305. doi:10.1111/j.1365-2788.2012.01535.x

Clark, J. E., & Whitall, J. (1989). What is motor development? The lessons of history. *Quest, 41*, 183–202. doi:10.1080/00336297.1989.10483969

Duronjić, M., & Válková, H. (2010). The influence of early intervention movement programs on motor skills development in preschoolers with autism spectrum disorder (case studies). *Acta Gymnica, 40*(2), 37–45.

Esposito, G., Nakazawa, J., Venuti, P., & Bornstein, M. H. (2012). Perceptions of distress in young children with autism compared to typically developing children: A cultural comparison between Japan and Italy. *Research In Developmental Disabilities, 33*(4), 1059–1067. doi:10.1016/j.ridd.2012.01.014

Giagazoglou, P., Kokaridas, D., Sidiropoulou, M., Patsiaouras, A., Karra, C., & Neofotistou, K. (2013). Effects of a trampoline exercise intervention on motor performance and balance ability of children with intellectual disabilities. *Research in Developmental Disabilities, 34*(9), 2701–2707. doi:10.1016/j.ridd.2013.05.034

Hayakawa, K., & Kobayashi, K. (2011). Physical and motor skill training for children with intellectual disabilities. *Perceptual and Motor Skills, 112*(2), 573–580. doi:10.2466/06.13.15.PMS.112.2.573-580

Henderson, S. E., Sugden, D. A., & Barnett, A. L. (2007). *Movement assessment battery for children-2 second edition (movement ABC-2)*. London, UK: The Psychological Corporation.

Kane, K. J., & Staples, K. L. (2016). A group motor skills program for children with coordination difficulties: Effect on fundamental movement skills and physical activity participation. *Physical & Occupational Therapy In Pediatrics, 36*(1), 28–45. doi:10.3109/01942638.2014.978934

Ketcheson, L., Hauck, J., & Ulrich, D. (2017). The effects of an early motor skill intervention on motor skills, levels of physical activity, and socialization in young children with autism spectrum disorder: A pilot study. *Autism, 21*(4), 481–492. doi:10.1177/1362361316650611

Kugler, P., Kelso, J., & Turvey, M. (1982). On the control and coordination of naturally developing systems. *The Development of Movement Control and Coordination, 5*, 1–78.

Logan, S. W., Catena, M. A., Sabet, A., Hospodar, C. M., Yohn, H., Govindan, A., & Galloway, J. C. (2019). Standing tall: Feasibility of a modified ride-on car that encourages standing. *Pediatric Physical Therapy, 31*(1), E6-E13.

Logan, S. W., Feldner, H. A., Galloway, J. C., & Huang, -H.-H. (2016). Modified ride-on car use by children with complex medical needs. *Pediatric Physical Therapy, 28*(1), 100–107. doi:10.1097/PEP.0000000000000210

Logan, S. W., Huang, -H.-H., Stahlin, K., & Galloway, J. C. (2014). Modified ride-on car for mobility and socialization: Single-case study of an infant with down syndrome. *Pediatric Physical Therapy, 26*(4), 418–426. doi:10.1097/PEP.0000000000000070

Logan, S. W., Robinson, L. E., Wilson, A. E., & Lucas, W. A. (2012). Getting the fundamentals of movement: A meta-analysis of the effectiveness of motor skill interventions in children: Effectiveness of motor skill interventions. *Child: Care, Health and Development, 38*(3), 305–315. doi:10.1111/j.1365-2214.2011.01307.x

MacDonald, M., Esposito, P., & Ulrich, D. (2011). The physical activity patterns of children with autism. *BMC Research Notes, 4*(1), 422. doi:10.1186/1756-0500-4-422

MacDonald, M., Lord, C., & Ulrich, D. A. (2014). Motor skills and calibrated autism severity in young children with autism spectrum disorder. *Adapted Physical Activity Quarterly, 31*(2), 95–105. doi:10.1123/apaq.2013-0068

MacDonald, M., Ross, S., McIntyre, L. L., & Tepfer, A. (2017). Relations of early motor skills on age and socialization, communication, and daily living in young children with developmental disabilities. *Adapted Physical Activity Quarterly, 34*(2), 179–194. doi:10.1123/apaq.2016-0028

Motor Development Academy. (1980). Journal of physical education and recreation (p. 38). Author.

Mulvey, K. L., Taunton, S., Pennell, A., & Brian, A. (2018). Head, toes, knees, SKIP! Improving preschool children's executive function through a motor competence intervention. *Journal of Sport and Exercise Psychology, 40*(5), 233–239. doi:10.1123/jsepp.2018-0007

Newell, K. (1986). Constraints on the development of coordination. *Motor development in children : Aspects of coordination and control.* Retrieved from https://ci.nii.ac.jp/naid/10016683819

Newell, K. M. (1984). Physical constraints to development of motor skills. *Motor development during childhood and adolescence/Edited by Jerry R. Thomas.* Retrieved from http://agris.fao.org/agris-search/search.do?recordID=US201301458927

Pagani, L., & Messier, S. (2012). Links between motor skills and indicators of school readiness at kindergarten entry in urban disadvantaged children. *Journal of Educational and Developmental Psychology, 2*(1), 95.

Peens, A., Pienaar, A. E., & Nienaber, A. W. (2008). The effect of different intervention programmes on the self-concept and motor proficiency of 7- to 9-year-old children with DCD. *Child: Care, Health and Development, 34*(3), 316–328. doi:10.1111/j.1365-2214.2007.00803.x

Rimmer, J. A., & Rowland, J. L. (2009). Physical activity for youth with disabilities: A critical need in an underserved population. *Developmental Neurorehabilitation, 11*, 141–148. doi:10.1080/17518420701688649

Robinson, L. E., & Goodway, J. D. (2009). Instructional climates in preschool children who are at-risk. Part I: Object-control skill development. *Research Quarterly for Exercise & Sport, 80*(3), 533–542. doi:10.5641/027013609X13088500159480

Robinson, L. E., Stodden, D. F., Barnett, L. M., Lopes, V. P., Logan, S. W., Rodrigues, L. P., & D'Hondt, E. (2015). Motor competence and its effect on positive developmental trajectories of health. *Sports Medicine, 45*(9), 1273–1284. doi:10.1007/s40279-015-0351-6

Sanson, A., Hemphill, S. A., & Smart, D. (2004). Connections between temperament and social development: A review. *Social Development, 13*(1), 142–170. doi:10.1046/j.1467-9507.2004.00261.x

Seefeldt, V., & Haubenstricker, J. (1982). Patterns, phases, or stages: An analytical model for the study of developmental movement. *The Development of Movement Control and Coordination, 309*, 318.

Shevell, M., Majnemer, A., Platt, R. W., Webster, R., & Birnbaum, R. (2005). Developmental and functional outcomes at school age of preschool children with global developmental delay. *Journal of Child Neurology, 20*(8), 648–654. doi:10.1177/08830738050200080301

Staples, K. L., & Reid, G. (2010). Fundamental movement skills and autism spectrum disorders. *Journal of Autism and Developmental Disorders, 40*(2), 209–217. doi:10.1007/s10803-009-0854-9

Stodden, D. F., Goodway, J. D., Langendorfer, S. J., Roberton, M. A., Rudisill, M. E., Garcia, C., & Garcia, L. E. (2008). A developmental perspective on the role of motor skill competence in physical activity: An emergent relationship. *Quest, 60*(2), 290–306. doi:10.1080/00336297.2008.10483582

Thelen, E. (2000). Motor development as foundation and future of developmental psychology. *International Journal of Behavioral Development, 24*(4), 358–397.

Thelen, E. (2005). Dynamic systems theory and the complexity of change. *Psychoanalytic Dialogues, 15*, 255–283. doi:10.1080/10481881509348831

Tyler, K., MacDonald, M., & Menear, K. (2014). Physical activity and physical fitness of school-aged children and youth with autism spectrum disorders. *Autism Research and Treatment, 2014*, 1–6. doi:10.1155/2014/312163

Ulrich, D. A. (2000). *Test of gross motor development.* Austin, TX: PRO-ED.

Ulrich, D. A. (2001). *Test of gross motor development* (2nd ed.). Austin, TX: PRO-ED.

Ulrich, D. A., Ulrich, B. D., Angulo-Kinzler, R. M., & Yun, J. (2001). Treadmill training of infants with down syndrome: Evidence-based developmental outcomes. *Pediatrics, 108*(5), e84–e84. doi:10.1542/peds.108.5.e84

Van Capelle, A., Broderick, C. R., van Doorn, N., Ward, R. E., & Parmenter, B. J. (2017). Interventions to improve fundamental motor skills in pre-school aged children: A systematic review and meta-analysis. *Journal of Science and Medicine in Sport, 20*(7), 658–666.

Westendorp, M., Houwen, S., Hartman, E., Mombarg, R., Smith, J., & Visscher, C. (2014). Effect of a ball skill intervention on children's ball skills and cognitive functions. *Medicine & Science in Sports & Exercise, 46*(2), 414. doi:10.1249/MSS.0b013e3182a532b3

29

Public health research

Physical inactivity

Byron Lai and Heidi Stanish

Introduction

In this chapter, we discuss physical inactivity as a significant public health issue that disproportionately affects children and youth with disabilities around the globe, as well as the role of adapted physical education (APE) in addressing this issue. To support this discussion, the first section of this chapter reviews current public health and physical education research regarding physical inactivity and sedentary behavior for children with and without disabilities. The second section reviews current adapted physical activity and education scholarship. The final section lists examples of interventions for children with disabilities that can be implemented by adapted physical educators, along with a public health strategy on how to evaluate the impact of such programs in larger, real-world settings.

A key focus of this chapter is the role of schools in addressing physical inactivity. In particular, the important contribution of physical education in assisting youth to achieve national and international physical activity recommendations is highlighted. We acknowledge that APE continues to be an emerging discipline and that less is known about the school-based physical activity of children with disabilities compared to their typically developing peers. Yet, ample evidence supports that it is time to take action. We offer some theoretical underpinnings of behavior that may assist APE professionals in serving as agents of change.

The aim of this chapter is to provide an overview of the published scholarship that has established our current understanding of health-promoting physical activity among children with disabilities. We also identify gaps in the knowledge base and offer implications for practice. While this chapter draws attention to the concerning levels of physical inactivity among children with disabilities, we also endeavor to celebrate the advances made by dedicated scholars in adapted physical activity who are committed to ensuring that children with disabilities have equal opportunities for achieving good health via enjoyable physical activity.

Public health, physical inactivity, and physical education

Introduction to public health and physical inactivity

Public health is commonly defined as "the science and art of preventing disease, prolonging life, and promoting health through the organized efforts and informed choices of society, organizations, public and private communities, and individuals" (Winslow, 1920, p. 30). A critical public health issue that has summoned a global call to action is physical inactivity (Kohl et al., 2012), now identified as the fourth leading risk factor for global mortality (World Health Organization, 2009). An individual is best classified as physically inactive when they do not engage in sufficient physical activity to obtain health-enhancing benefits as recommended by current guidelines (Tremblay et al., 2017). Sedentary behavior, defined as any waking behavior characterized by an energy expenditure ≤1.5 metabolic equivalents while in a sitting, reclining, or lying posture, is also associated with adverse health outcomes but is not synonymous with physical inactivity (Tremblay et al., 2017). Physical inactivity was responsible for 5.3 million of the 57 million deaths (9.3%) that occurred within the year 2008 and was linked with a variety of non-communicable diseases, including type 2 diabetes and cancers (Lee et al., 2012). This was similar to a more recent estimate of 8.3%, which was drawn from longitudinal data from an adult sample that was included within both the National Health Interview Survey in 1990 to 1991 and the National Health Index in 2011 (Carlson, Adams, Yang, & Fulton, 2018). The global consequence of this unhealthy behavior on healthcare systems has been estimated at $53.8 billion (Ding et al., 2016). Worldwide, 81% of adolescents aged 11–17 years were insufficiently physically active in 2010 (Sallis et al., 2016). The World Health Organization (WHO) Global Action Plan on Physical Activity 2018–2030 (World Health Organization, 2018), targets a 10% relative reduction in the global prevalence of physical inactivity by 2025 to improve the prevention and treatment of non-communicable diseases worldwide (Guthold, Stevens, Riley, & Bull, 2018).

Based upon the evidence supporting the strong link between physical activity and risk for non-communicable diseases, the WHO published the Global Recommendations on Physical Activity for Health (World Health Organization, 2010). For children ages 5–17 to improve components of health-related fitness, bone health, cardiovascular, and metabolic health bio-markers and reduce symptoms of anxiety and depression, the WHO recommends that: (a) children should accumulate at least 60 minutes of moderate to vigorous intensity physical activity daily, (b) amounts of physical activity greater than 60 minutes provide additional health benefits, and (c) most of the daily physical activity should be aerobic. Vigorous intensity activities should be incorporated, including those that strengthen muscle and bone, at least three times per week. These global recommendations state that physical activity should be performed daily "as part of play, games, sports, transportation, recreation, physical education, or planned exercise, in the context of family, school, and community activities" (World Health Organizaiton, 2010, p. 18). Children with disabilities should achieve these same guidelines.

Similar to many countries around the world, the United States (US) established its own federal guidelines. In 2008, the Department of Health and Human Services published the Physical Activity Guidelines for Americans and the second edition of the guidelines was released in 2018 (U.S. Department of Health and Human Services, 2008). The US guidelines recommend that children ages 6–17 strive to achieve a minimum of 60 minutes of moderate to vigorous intensity aerobic physical activity per day, and these minutes should also include muscle- and bone-strengthening activities on at least three days of the week. Toddlers and pre-schoolers ages 3–5 years are recommended to be physically active throughout the day to support growth and development. It is suggested that, whenever possible, children and adolescents with disabilities should meet the guidelines and, if unable to participate in the appropriate types or amounts of physical activities to meet the guidelines, then they should be as active as possible.

The pandemic of physical inactivity: surveillance research

Globally, prevalence data demonstrate that children are physically inactive. An excellent resource that demonstrates the global physical inactivity epidemic is the Global Matrix 3.0 (Aubert et al., 2018). The Global Matrix initiative began in 2014 and created a harmonized process for work groups around the world to gather and assess the best data available regarding physical inactivity among children, to generate report cards in a standard format that includes letter grades on ten common indicators (e.g., overall physical activity, active transportation, schools, active play, community and environment) (Aubert et al., 2018; Tremblay et al., 2014). Work groups comprise researchers, health professionals, and other stakeholders who synthesize evidence, primarily data from national surveillance surveys, to develop the physical activity report cards. The 2018 Global Matrix 3.0 included reports from 49 countries, up from 38 countries in 2016 and 15 countries in 2014 (Aubert et al., 2018). Average grades across all indicators of "C-," "D+," and "C-," respectively, were reported for countries classified as "low or medium," "high," and "very high" on the United Nations' human development index in the 2018 matrix. As an example, 2005–2006 data from the National Health and Nutrition Examination Survey (NHANES) conducted in the US were used by the National Physical Activity Plan Alliance (NPAP) to report in 2018 that "a significant drop in physical activity occurs with increasing age: 42.5%, 7.5% and 5.1% of 6–11 year olds, 12–15 year olds and 16–19 year olds meet physical activity recommendations, respectively, using objective physical activity measurement by accelerometry" (National Physical Activity Plan Alliance, 2018, p. 12; Katzmarzyk et al., 2018). The NPAP is a non-profit organization, comprising physical activity experts, that is responsible for creating the bi-annual *United States Report Card on Physical Activity in Children and Youth*, summarizing physical inactivity of children and youth within the US. There has been little to no improvement in grades on the ten indicators in the US report; the 2014, 2016, and 2018 iterations all indicated a letter grade of "D-" for overall physical activity, which means that only 20–26% of children within the US are achieving the physical activity guidelines (National Physical Activity Plan Alliance, 2018).

Children with disabilities have generally been underrepresented in national surveillance and, as such, public health goals and priorities that draw from the data may not reflect the needs of this pediatric population. In recent years, however, an emergence of secondary data analyses of national surveys has helped to identify the health inequities experienced by children with a variety of disabling conditions, as well as disparities in physical activity and fitness. One analysis of the NSCH 2007 data found that children with functional limitations had approximately two times higher odds of not achieving 60 minutes of vigorous intensity physical activity per week (goals set by Healthy People 2010) than children without special health care needs (Kim & Greaney, 2014). Only 32% of children with functional limitations were found to achieve this level of physical activity. An analysis of these same NSCH data found that youth with learning disabilities, youth with attention deficit hyperactivity disorder, and youth with comorbid learning disability and attention deficit hyperactivity disorder were 33%, 57%, and 39% less likely to be physically active than their peers without these conditions, respectively (Cook, Li, & Heinrich, 2015). Youth with learning disabilities were also 40% more likely to be sedentary than those without. Data from the 1999–2010

NHANES demonstrated that adolescents with a disability were less likely to be engaged in physical activity and more likely to be obese compared to adolescents without a disability (Kim, Conners, Hart, Kang, & Kang, 2013). Several analyses of data from the NSCH between 2003 and 2016 have indicated that, overall, children with autism spectrum disorder were more likely to be overweight and obese than typically developing children and were less likely to be physically active (Corvey, Menear, Preskitt, Goldfarb, & Menachemi, 2016; Healy, Aigner, Haegele, & Patterson, 2019; McCoy, Jakicic, & Gibbs, 2016; Ratcliff, Hong, & Hilton, 2018; Tybor et al., 2019). Similar findings were reported in a nationally representative data set of Irish youth, where those with autism spectrum disorder participated in less physical activity than those without, and rates of overweight and obesity were higher (Healy, et al., 2017). Data from the NSCH also indicated that children with severe visual impairments were less physically active than children without impairments (Haegele, Aigner, & Healy, 2019), and that children with intellectual disabilities had a higher prevalence of obesity compared to children without intellectual disabilities and participate in physical activity less frequently (Segal et al., 2016). These, and other analyses of nationally representative data of children with disabilities, conducted worldwide, have helped to inform the global matrices of physical activity report cards for children and youth that are vital to advocacy and intervention efforts.

Physical inactivity and sedentary behavior among children with disabilities

In addition to surveillance studies, an existing body of research demonstrates that (in general) children with disabilities exhibit low levels of physical activity and may lag further behind their typically developing peers. Despite challenges associated with obtaining sufficient sample sizes and accurately measuring physical activity and sedentary behavior of children with disabilities, many APE or physical activity researchers have been dedicated to conducting rigorous studies that have produced robust findings. We can now turn to several review papers that summarize the evidence, identify trends, and provide clear paths and priorities for future research. It is encouraging that recent publications are derived from work done around the world and that researchers internationally have taken an interest in understanding physical activity and, more recently, sedentary behavior among children with disabilities. Interest in examining sedentary behavior has grown in the field as the link between excessive sedentary time and unfavorable health becomes more apparent. The use of accelerometers to quantify physical activity and sedentary time has advanced the research by increasing the accuracy and objectivity of measurement, as well as removing the cognitive demand and reducing burden associated with recall questionnaires. Accelerometry has facilitated direct comparisons between children with disabilities and their peers without disabilities, as well as across disability groups.

Accelerometer studies indicate that children and adolescents with intellectual disabilities, including Down syndrome, generally exhibit low levels of physical activity (with varying results). For example, descriptive studies out of the US, United Kingdom (UK), Spain, and Iceland have reported daily moderate and vigorous physical activity (MVPA) ranging from approximately 30 to 57 minutes per day and 0–43% of children with intellectual disabilities meeting the guideline (Downs, Fairclough, Knowles, & Boddy, 2016; Einarsson et al., 2015; Esposito, MacDonald, Hornyak, & Ulrich, 2012; Izquierdo-Gomez et al., 2014). Among children with autism spectrum disorders, estimates of time in MVPA are higher and range from approximately 29 to 166 minutes per day, and 14–100% achieving the guideline

(Bandini et al., 2013; MacDonald, Esposito, & Ulrich, 2011; Obrusnikova & Cavalier, 2011; Stanish et al., 2017; Tyler, MacDonald, & Menear, 2014). One study of children and adolescents with cerebral palsy found that participants averaged 43 minutes per day of MVPA and were inactive for 8.26 hours per day (Mitchell, Ziviani, & Boyd, 2015).

Research undertaken to compare physical activity and/or sedentary time between children with and without disabilities have also produced mixed results. There is evidence to indicate that children with autism spectrum disorder engage in less physical activity than their typically developing peers (Pan et al., 2016; Stanish et al., 2017; Tyler et al., 2014), and similar findings have been reported for children with intellectual disabilities (Einarsson et al., 2015; Foley, Bryan, & McCubbin, 2008) and Down syndrome (Matute-Llorente, González-Agüero, Gómez-Cabello, Vicente-Rodríguez, & Casajús, 2013). However, other studies have found no differences in accelerometer-measured physical activity engagement between young children with autism spectrum disorder and typically developing children (Bandini et al., 2013; Thomas, Hinkley, Barnett, May, & Rinehart, 2019). A recent comparative study from Sweden found that children from four disability groups spent significantly less time overall in physical activity and more time sedentary than their typically developing counterparts (Lobenius-Palmer, Sjoqvist, Hurtig-Wennlof, & Lundqvist, 2018). Children with physical/visual impairment, intellectual disability, autism spectrum disorder, and hearing impairment engaged in 63, 80, 79, and 111 minutes per day of MVPA, respectively, compared to 142 minutes per day for typically developing children. The proportion of children with disabilities meeting the physical activity guidelines was 31%, 52%, 40%, and 84%, respectively, compared to 83% of typically developing children. Daily minutes of sedentary time ranged from 417 to 458 minutes per day among the children in the four disability groups, compared to 350 minutes per day in children with typical development. These findings are supported by accelerometer studies of physical activity and sedentary time among youth with cerebral palsy from Canada and the Netherlands. In a 24-hour period, adolescents and young adults with cerebral palsy engaged in 48 minutes less of physical activity and 80 minutes more of sedentary time compared to an able-bodied control group (Nooijen, Slaman, Stam, Roebroeck, & Van Den Berg-Emons, 2014). Children and adolescents with cerebral palsy accumulated significantly more time in sedentary behavior than a matched group of typically developing youth, 47.5 versus 43.6 minutes per hour, and took less frequent/fewer breaks that interrupted sedentary time (Obeid, Balemans, Noorduyn, Gorter, & Timmons, 2014). A comparative study of young children with and without cerebral palsy aged 6–10 years derived similar results (Ryan, Forde, Hussey, & Gormley, 2015). Children with cerebral palsy spent significantly more time in sedentary behavior (193 minutes per day) than typically developing children (123 minutes per day), and accumulated less moderate, vigorous, and total physical activity. Children with visual impairments were also found to spend less time in physical activity and more time in sedentary behaviors than children without visual impairments, accumulating about 18 minutes per day in MVPA (Houwen, Hartman, & Visscher, 2009). A recent analysis of NHANES accelerometer data found that children and adolescents with visual impairments did not accumulate more sedentary time or less physical activity than those with normal vision (Smith et al., 2019), which further supports the need for more research within this area.

Systematic reviews of the physical activity research involving children with disabilities have helped to identify gaps and limitations in previous research and provide directions for future work. Children with intellectual disabilities and autism spectrum disorder have been studied quite frequently, but review papers also exist on physical activity research involving children with cerebral palsy, visual impairments, and mixed disability groups (Augestad et al.,

2015; Carlon, Taylor, Dodd, & Shields, 2013; Frey, Stanish, & Temple, 2008; Haegele & Porretta, 2015; Hinckson & Curtis, 2013; Jones et al., 2017; McGarty, Penpraze, & Melville, 2014). There are some common conclusions and recommendations for future work derived from the published systematic reviews, including concerns regarding valid and reliable measures of physical activity and sedentary behavior, small and heterogeneous samples of children, inconsistent study designs, most studies conducted in the US, the need for large collaborative efforts, the need to examine health outcomes that are associated with physical activity, and better characterization of children and disability. Most importantly, children with disabilities require interventions that can effectively engage them in a lifestyle of physical activity, to impact the aforementioned reports of physical inactivity.

Physical education and public health

In 1991, Sallis and McKenzie (1991) published a pivotal paper entitled "Physical education's role in public health" that highlighted the importance of physical education as a medium for tackling the issue of physical inactivity. This paper marked a major paradigm shift from a focus on promoting competitive sports and teaching sport-related skills to a focus on promoting physical activity as a method of improving health-related fitness behaviors that transfer into adulthood. In other words, physical education previously emphasized competitive sports, but physical education now focuses on teaching health-enhancing physical activity behaviors. Sallis and McKenzie reported three key take-home messages: (a) physical education should promote physical activity skills that can transfer into adulthood; (b) programs should include moderate intensity physical activity; and (c) physical education is an ideal environment to deliver nationwide programs that improve health-related fitness.

Physical education is viewed as an important channel for promoting physical activity among children because it is a core requirement of most school systems in many countries. Sallis and colleagues (2012) reviewed major advances in physical education research and public health initiatives since their 1991 paper. They concluded that there had been several accomplishments, including further evidence of the health benefits of physical education and acceptance of physical education as a public health resource. Yet, they acknowledged that further efforts were required to embed the public health goals from 1991 within physical education practice. The 2012 report identified several recommendations for increasing MVPA, as well as two evidence-based physical education programs (SPARK and CATCH) that have been, and still are, implemented on a national level. These authors introduced and created momentum for health optimizing physical education (HOPE) that they defined as:

> physical education that encompasses curriculum and lessons focused on health-related physical activity and fitness; keeps students active for at least 50% of class time; engages all students, regardless of physical ability; and significantly contributes to students' overall physical activity participation, thereby improving their health.
>
> *(Sallis et al., 2012, p. 131)*

In 2013, the Institute of Medicine (IOM; now the Heath and Medicine Division) published *Educating the Student Body: Taking Physical Activity and Physical Education to School* in response to the growing prevalence and health impacts of physical inactivity among children and adolescents (Committee on Physical Activity and Physical Education in the School Environment, 2013). The IOM report emphasized the importance of schools in providing opportunities for physical activity and helping children and adolescents to meet the physical activity guidelines. The report stated that physical education had a pivotal role in addressing the pandemic issue of physical inactivity and proposed that whole-school involvement, equity in access, and professional development were potential mechanisms of change.

APE and public health

The field of APE does not appear to have widely accepted the public health goals around physical inactivity. Yun and Beamer (2018) recently published an insightful paper with the aim of illustrating how to integrate physical activity promotion within APE requirements. The authors drew attention to the traditional goals of APE programming and teacher preparation that focus on modifying games, sports, and activities to maximize the involvement of children with disabilities, as well as skill development. They noted that increasing MVPA within physical education classes is not addressed in most APE textbooks or in APE course offerings in teacher education programs (Piletic & Davis, 2010). In light of the significant health risks associated with physical inactivity, there is a justified need to make physical activity engagement a goal for APE and link program delivery to public health goals. This can be achieved if APE teachers and researchers embrace the paradigm shift that has occurred in general physical education and advocate the same practices and expectations for students with disabilities. Yun and Beamer asserted that promoting engagement in physical activity among all children with disabilities can be achieved by including physical education goals in the individualized education program; considering content, location, and instructional methods that maximize participation; and collaborating with other school-based programs to encourage physical activity in and outside of APE/physical education classes. Unfortunately, there is a lack of research to support the health benefits of APE and the extent to which APE is preparing children with disabilities for a physically active life.

Dr. Jeffrey McCubbin, an international scholar and pioneer in adapted physical activity, contemplated the impact that our field of study has had on the health trajectory of people with disabilities in his thoughtful commentary entitled "Adapted physical activity: Influential impacts to establish a field of study" (McCubbin, 2014). McCubbin acknowledged several advances in research that have helped us better understand the differences in motor performance, physical activity, and fitness of children and adults with disabilities. However, he asserted that there is much more we need to know. McCubbin suggested that adapted physical activity is challenged by being too broad and lacking depth, and he respectfully stated that "perhaps we have looked in too many directions, started down too many paths, left too many ideas unfinished, and failed to communicate outcomes that really matter" (McCubbin, 2014, p. 54). Future directions for work in our field include new research, particularly long-term intervention approaches, that impact health outcomes and reduce secondary conditions in people with disabilities. Secondary conditions are health conditions (both physical and mental) that occur as a result of a disability from prolonged physical inactivity or deconditioning (Rimmer, Chen, & Hsieh, 2011). APE has a vital role to play in decreasing the disparities in health and fitness experienced by children with disabilities, yet there is considerable work to be done in both research and educational practice. We can gain direction and energy from the accomplishments of the general physical education field in aligning with public health goals to ensure that children with disabilities who receive APE services also benefit from targeted efforts and opportunities for increased physical activity.

Summary of current scholarship: physical inactivity and children with disabilities

Understanding physical inactivity in children with disabilities

A decade ago, Rimmer and Rowland (2008) published a pivotal paper that was among the first to highlight the disparities in physical activity participation among youth with and without disabilities. The authors drew attention to the barriers known to restrict physical activity, successful fitness interventions that targeted youth with disabilities, and, most importantly, proposed a conceptual model for promoting physical activity among youth with disabilities. The paper strongly stated the importance of physical activity and fitness for promoting health and minimizing secondary conditions among youth with disabilities, and was a call to action to researchers, educators, and health care providers. Since that time, new studies have provided a greater understanding of physical activity, and inactivity, among children with various disability types as well as the factors that influence their behavior. The body of knowledge in this area continues to grow, yet there remains much to learn.

Physical activity within schools

As previously stated, schools are considered to be important settings for health-promoting physical activity among children. Physical education, recess, active transportation, and before- and after-school offerings provide valuable opportunities to engage children in MVPA and to contribute to the recommended 60 minutes per day. Children with disabilities are no exception and should have equal access to all school-based physical activity programs. Further, because children with disabilities often face obstacles to accessing community opportunities for sports and exercise, and may experience exclusion, schools may be the primary provider of physical activity programming. Adapted physical educators have an important role to play in promoting physical activity participation by children with disabilities, within and outside of school settings. Unfortunately, there is scarce research available to guide school- and physical education-based efforts to reduce physical inactivity among students with disabilities. While we know much more about the overall physical activity levels of children with disabilities than we once did, studies on behavior within school settings, including during physical education classes, are limited in number and scope. The US Department of Health and Human Services recommends that students engage in MVPA for at least 50% of the time spent in physical education class, and others suggest that 40% of recess time should be spent active as a health promotion target (Ridgers, Stratton, & Fairclough, 2005). However, it is unclear what percentage of students with disabilities are achieving these standards.

In an effort to understand the behavior of children with disabilities during school time, Sit and colleagues (2017) measured physical activity and sedentary time via accelerometry during physical education, recess, and lunchtime among children with five different disability types. Children with visual impairments, hearing impairments, intellectual disabilities, physical disabilities, and social development problems from special education schools in Hong Kong participated and, overall, accumulated 17 minutes (or 4.2% of the school day) of MVPA. On average, children spent 7.2 minutes (13.2%) of physical education class engaged in MVPA and 3.0 minutes (9.4%) of recess. Approximately 70% of the entire school day was spent sedentary, and 50% of both physical education and recess were spent sedentary. A comparative study of physical activity during physical education classes (integrated versus self-contained) and recess among Taiwanese adolescents with and without intellectual disabilities found that all students accumulated very few minutes of MVPA in both activity settings (Pan, Liu, Chung, & Hsu, 2015). Regardless of educational placement, adolescents with intellectual disabilities engaged in an average of 11 minutes of moderate activity during physical education; about 25% of class time. Students, depending on education placement, spent 3–8 minutes of recess engaged in moderate physical activity which was 9–18% of the time. Similarly, Foley and colleagues (2008) compared the physical activity levels of elementary school-aged children with and without intellectual disabilities in school, after-school, and on weekends in the US. Although time spent in MVPA was not reported, accelerometer activity count data supported that students with intellectual disabilities were significantly less active during integrated physical education classes and recess compared to their peers without intellectual disabilities. The disparities between groups is concerning in light of the importance of physical education as a vehicle for promoting physical activity across students of all abilities. Recent work in Iceland reported similar differences in school-based physical activity among children with and without intellectual disabilities aged 6–16 years (Einarsson, Jóhannsson, Daly, & Arngrímsson, 2016). Compared to the children with intellectual disabilities, the typically developing children accumulated 15.1 more minutes of MVPA during school hours. However, children with intellectual disabilities were 6% less sedentary than their peers during school. A notable finding of this study was that children with intellectual disabilities accumulated significantly more minutes of MVPA during school than after school, and the differences between the groups in both physical activity and sedentary time was more pronounced in the after-school hours. This supports that children with disabilities spend more of their free time sedentary, perhaps due to fewer community-level opportunities for sports and exercise, and that schools play a critical role in assisting students with disabilities to achieve the physical activity guidelines.

Pan compared physical activity levels of students with and without autism spectrum disorder during inclusive recess periods at schools in Taiwan (Pan, 2008). Overall, children with autism spectrum disorder engaged in approximately 28 minutes of MVPA across all recess periods which equated to 27.7% of total recess time. The author noted that school recess contributed a good proportion (almost half) of the recommended 60 minutes per day of MVPA, which is very encouraging. However, children with autism spectrum disorder were not active for the recommended 40% of recess time, suggesting a missed opportunity for health-promoting physical activity. Interventions for increasing physical activity among children with disabilities during recess are warranted, yet, the challenge is to intervene without imposing too much structure and eliminating the creativity and spontaneity associated with free play. A study of objectively-measured physical activity patterns among Iranian children with autism spectrum disorder ages 7–14 found that children were significantly less active in school compared to after school (Memari et al., 2013). The authors offered possible explanations for this, including overprotective teachers/coaches that limit participation due to concerns around injury and a focus on academic performance over physical activities. A steep age-related decline in physical activity was also reported, consistent with other studies involving youth with autism spectrum disorder (MacDonald et al., 2011), which adds to the urgency of addressing the physical inactivity observed in children with disabilities.

Physical activity promotion outside of the school setting

Adapted physical educators are excellently positioned to tackle the growing issue of physical inactivity (Yun & Beamer, 2018). They are embedded within a sustainable system (the school), have direct access to students and parents, and relevant training. In addition to providing a supportive physical activity environment during recess and physical education, adapted physical educators can encourage students and their parents to engage in physical activity outside of the school setting. Reviews have identified several physical activity options that can accommodate children and youth with disabilities within their community (O'Brien et al., 2016; Verschuren, Peterson, Balemans, & Hurvitz, 2016). These programs should be reviewed in detail for information regarding frequency, intensity, time, and type, so that they can be implemented by physical educators. A more detailed summary of successful interventions is described in the next major section. Of note, these programs are often tested within researcher-controlled conditions. Thus, adapted physical educators should anticipate challenges with the implementation and overall impact of clinically successful physical activity programs in real-world settings.

Factors influencing physical activity among children with disabilities

Theories of behavior can be used to explain and promote physical activity behavior in people with disabilities. Common behavioral theories among the extant physical activity literature for people with disabilities include the theory of reasoned action, transtheoretical model, supportive accountability theory and, the most commonly applied theory, social cognitive theory (Lai, Young, Bickel, Motl, & Rimmer, 2017). Social cognitive theory posits that there are four primary constructs that explain why people with disabilities are physically inactive, namely, exercise confidence (i.e., self-efficacy), goals, outcome expectations (i.e., the physical or social outcomes that a person expects to receive from the intervention), and barriers or facilitators (i.e., socio-structural factors) (Bandura, 1998; Ellis & Motl, 2013). These four constructs can guide the implementation of various behavioral change techniques that enhance physical activity behavior, and these techniques are critical because theory-based interventions have demonstrated larger effects on physical activity than those that were not theory based in people with disabilities (Ma & Martin Ginis, 2018).

Michie and colleagues (2013) have identified 93 behavioral change techniques that they have categorized into a taxonomy that health professionals can use for "specifying, evaluating, and implementing behavioral change interventions". Potentially effective techniques for enhancing physical activity behavior in people with disabilities, as demonstrated by a meta-analysis, include those related to self-regulation, namely, intention formation, specific goal-setting, feedback on performance, and review of goals (Ma & Martin Ginis, 2018). Despite the importance of these various techniques, health professionals often emphasize the elimination of barriers that prevent people with disabilities from engaging in physical activity.

Barriers and facilitators to participation

Attempts to elucidate the individual, social, and environmental influences on physical activity participation among children with disabilities have intensified with the growing problem of inactivity. This work is particularly challenging because of the complex and multi-faceted nature of physical activity behavior. Yet, the importance of this research for informing the development of effective interventions to increase physical activity and reduce sedentary time cannot be overstated. Researchers and clinicians are encouraged to thoughtfully consider the known correlates and determinants of physical activity as they aim to reduce the existing health disparities faced by children with disabilities.

Researchers have used questionnaires, interviews, and focus groups to discern the physical activity barriers and facilitators experienced by children with different disability types. For example, some cited barriers for children with autism spectrum disorder include limited skills of service providers, fear of social exclusion, lack of enjoyment of physical activity, requirement of additional supervision, reduced skills for physical activity, and preference for sedentary pursuits such as television and video games (Must, Phillips, Curtin, & Bandini, 2015; Obrusnikova & Cavalier, 2011; Stanish et al., 2015). These barriers are similar to those reported for children with intellectual disabilities and Down syndrome, in addition to lack of accessible programs, disability-related functional limitations, not having someone to participate with, and activities being difficult to learn (Lin et al., 2010; Stanish et al., 2016). Some facilitators of physical activity behavior among children with autism spectrum disorder, intellectual disabilities, and/or Down syndrome were also reported and include positive role of the family/parent preference for physical activity, social opportunities, perceived competence in physical activity, feeling rewarded, playing team sports, enjoyment of physical activity. Parents of children with special needs, including learning disabilities, autism spectrum disorder, and attention deficit hyperactivity disorder, reported that the child's lack of interest, lack of appropriate programs, behavioral problems, and lack of time restricted their child's participation in physical activity (Yazdani, Yee, & Chung, 2013). A recent mixed methods systematic review of parent perceived barriers and facilitators for children with intellectual disabilities reported that family, child factors, inclusive programs and facilities, social motivation, and children's experiences in physical activity are relevant factors (McGarty & Melville, 2018). Further, these factors may be facilitators or barriers to physical activity, depending on the education and information of others relevant to the child's experience.

Factors that influence physical activity among children with physical disabilities have also been systematically reviewed (Bloemen et al., 2015; Li et al., 2016; Shields, Synnot, & Barr, 2012). Some frequently reported barriers to physical activity included inaccessible facilities, lack of transportation, untrained program providers, negative attitudes, lack of friends, and poor physical skills. Factors that correlate positively to physical activity included preference for/enjoyment of physical activity, perceived physical competence, motivation, and parental support. Perceived competence was also found to be significantly related to participation in physical activity of children with spina bifida (Marques, Maldonado, Peralta, & Santos, 2015).

Indeed, barriers to physical activity are vast and complex. In an effort to make sense of these barriers, a systematic review of over thirty years of research demonstrated that physical activity barriers can be categorized within the socio-ecological model (Martin Ginis, Ma, Latimer-Cheung, & Rimmer, 2016). Barriers can include those experienced at the level of the individual, the individual's relationships with peers, family, or the physical educator, or those experienced in the school, community, or policy level. For example, children with disabilities might have mobility limitations that are not accommodated by accessible or adaptable equipment, programs, or facilities at school; they might not be supported by friends or parents who support physical activity behavior; and few schools and policies enforce or support physical activity behavior for people with disabilities, both inside and outside of the school setting. Resolving these barriers is critical towards creating successful physical activity programs for children and youth with disabilities.

Physical activity interventions

After understanding and explaining the problem of physical inactivity and the factors known to influence behavior, it will be important to understand what type of interventions can be delivered by adapted physical educators to promote physical activity behavior. Although the primary focus of adapted physical educators is to adapt school-based activities so that they are suitable for all individuals, ideally, adapted physical educators will implement strategies to promote physical activity both inside and outside of the school setting (i.e., the home or nearby parks and recreation facilities). Promotion of physical activity outside of the school setting is critical, because time allotted for physical education classes may not be sufficient for youth with disabilities to achieve the physical activity guidelines. Within this section, we summarize four review articles to address the following questions: (a) what physical activity interventions are available to children and youth with disabilities? and (b) what are some of the limitations and methodological concerns regarding these published studies? After understanding what interventions are out there to address the public health issue of physical inactivity, it will be important to translate successful clinical studies into larger real-world settings. Thus, the second part of this section describes how to evaluate the real-world impact of research-based physical activity programs.

One systematic review by O'Brien and colleagues (O'Brien et al., 2016) found 30 published studies that implemented physical activity interventions for youth who used wheelchairs. Intervention types included functional exercises, progressive resistance training, sports and game-based activities, active video games, and education or behavior-based programming. The results demonstrated that youth who use wheelchairs can participate safely in a variety of activities. However, the effects of these various activities on health and function outcomes were less convincing. Most outcomes demonstrated no improvements post-intervention. This lack of improvements was suggested to be due to either insufficient doses of physical activity or poor (i.e., inaccurate or precise) methods of evaluating the outcomes of the interventions.

In a broader scoping review by Arbour-Nicitopoulos and colleagues (2018) that aggregated out-of-school physical activity programs for children and youth with physical disabilities, it was reported that 17 studies included either adapted dance, wheelchair sports, recreational gymnastics, swim programs, tennis, and summer camp or recreational facility activities. Arbour-Nicitopoulos and colleagues qualitatively appraised the 17 included studies and concluded that instructor training was a critical component of all studies. Of note, most studies were conducted and implemented by therapists. Few interventions were implemented by researchers from either adapted physical activity or education.

A scoping review by McPherson, Keith, and Swift (2014) found 34 obesity prevention interventions for children with physical disabilities. Interventions included aerobic and strength training, coaching dietary or nutritional strategies (often combined with physical activity and various behavior coaching strategies), aquatic exercise, active video gaming, parental education, and group-based activities. Eighteen of the 34 studies reported positive effects on obesity (52.9%) after the intervention, but no studies had "long-term" effects. These findings indicate that more research is necessary within this area.

A review of physical activity intervention literature by Frey, Temple, and Stanish (2017) identified 11 studies that implemented an intervention for youth with intellectual disabilities. Intervention types included a bicycle riding training camp, treadmill training, strength training, walking and snow shoeing, and a combination of strength and aerobic activities. Although 81.8% of studies ($n = 9/11$) reported an increase in physical activity after the intervention, studies recruited small samples of participants and only four of the included studies implemented randomized controlled trials (arguably the highest quality intervention design). Frey and colleagues reported some key research limitations: "Conclusions cannot be made regarding intervention components that impacted outcome variables, if the observed effects were specifically due to the intervention or if interventions could be maintained long-term" (Frey et al., 2017, p. 444).

In summary, the four review articles identified various interventions and methods of physical activity promotion among youth with disabilities. Nevertheless, most interventions included small samples and the long-term effects of interventions on outcomes was questionable. Much more research is warranted before these research-based interventions have sufficient evidence for translation into real-world physical education settings. Interventions will have to be rigorously tested across multiple school settings to ensure that they can be easily implemented (i.e., interventions are feasible) and the effects of interventions on outcomes can be maintained.

Implications for practice and research priorities

A considerable amount of research has been done to identify and understand the problem of physical inactivity. While there have been an encouraging number of intervention studies for children with disabilities, far more work needs to be done to identify effective strategies that can reach and impact children on a larger scale. Intervention research typically includes small samples that study research efficacy (i.e., clinically successful studies under tightly controlled conditions). Programs are rarely (if at all) replicated on a larger scale within real-world settings. There is a need for effective programs and strategies that can engage children with disabilities in health-enhancing physical activity both within and outside of the school setting. To aid this pursuit, this chapter summarized physical inactivity as a public health issue in children with disabilities, pivotal studies within adapted physical activity and education, and described examples of interventions that can be implemented. Below, we describe a potential method for testing the impact of successful research-based interventions within larger real-world settings.

Evaluating the impact of physical activity programs

This section focuses on how to evaluate the public health impact of physical activity interventions through the reach, effectiveness, adoption, implementation, and maintenance (RE-AIM) framework. The first RE-AIM publication was in the *American Journal of Public Health* in 1999 (Glasgow, Vogt, & Boles, 1999). Since inception, RE-AIM has been used extensively within public health research, and has undergone minimal revisions. The purpose of RE-AIM is to evaluate the impact of interventions within complex real-world settings, particularly interventions that have already been tested successfully under optimal research-controlled conditions (i.e., tested for efficacy).

As denoted within the acronym, RE-AIM is simply defined and evaluated through four components (Glasgow et al., 1999). Reach is the extent to which the intervention is received by the target population. Reach can be measured by dividing the number of people enrolled within the intervention by the total number of people within the desired setting or demographic. Effectiveness is the extent to which the intervention improves the desired health or behavioral outcomes, as traditionally measured in clinical studies. Adoption refers to the success at which people within the community can implement the intervention. Regarding physical activity interventions for children with disabilities in a school setting, adopters could refer to physical educators, classrooms, or schools that implement the program. Since adopters are the individuals within the community who will be implementing the intervention under real-world conditions, adoption of the intervention is critical for evaluating the longevity of a program. Implementation refers to the extent to which the fidelity of the intervention can be maintained when delivered within the desired community system. Maintenance refers to how well the intervention can be sustained by either community organizations or the individual. Further details on how RE-AIM has been applied within interventions from inception (1999) to the year 2010 and how to measure each RE-AIM domain can be found elsewhere (Gaglio, Shoup, & Glasgow, 2013).

Summary of key points/conclusion

- Physical inactivity is a global pandemic public health issue, and is arguably more important to address among children with disabilities.
- Adapted physical educators are excellently positioned to address the public health issue of physical inactivity, by promoting physical activity both within and outside of the school setting.
- Adapted physical educators can review successful research-based interventions (such as those reviewed in this chapter) to identify strategies that might successfully promote physical activity participation and enhance the health and function of their students.
- While there has been tremendous growth in physical activity research among children with disabilities, we would encourage adapted physical educators to enhance their involvement within physical activity research to address some of the lingering issues and knowledge gaps within this area.

Reflective questions

1. Sample sizes are typically low within research-based interventions. How should researchers consider tackling this issue, given that research studies are typically limited by resources such as funding and staffing?
2. Given the same limitations as noted in the previous question, what strategies may enhance the likelihood that a physical activity program can be replicable across different school settings?
3. Within this chapter, we presented RE-AIM as a method to evaluate the real-world impact of research-based interventions and described some potential metrics. However, what threshold or values for each metric are required for a metric to be considered successful? For example, in typical clinical research metrics/measures, minimal clinically important differences are research-established values/thresholds that are deemed successful if achieved. These recommendations do not exist for implementation science, which has not yet been explored in physical activity research for children with disabilities.
4. As a physical educator, how might you ensure that a research-based intervention you implement for your students will result in the same benefits as demonstrated from the research paper?

References

Arbour-Nicitopoulos, K. P., Grassmann, V., Orr, K., McPherson, A. C., Faulkner, G. E., & Wright, F. V. (2018). A scoping review of inclusive out-of-school time physical activity programs for children and youth with physical disabilities. *Adapted Physical Activity Quarterly*, *35*(1), 111–138.

Aubert, S., Barnes, J. D., Abdeta, C., Abi Nader, P., Adeniyi, A. F., Aguilar-Farias, N., … Tremblay, M. S. (2018). Global matrix 3.0 physical activity report card grades for children and youth: Results and analysis from 49 countries. *Journal of Physical Activity and Health*, *15*(S2), S251–S273. doi:10.1123/jpah.2018-0472

Augestad, L. (2015). Physical activity, physical fitness, and body composition among children and young adults with visual impairments: A systematic review. *British Journal of Visual Impairment*, *33*(3), 167–182.

Bandini, L. G., Gleason, J., Curtin, C., Lividini, K., Anderson, S. E., Cermak, S. A., … Must, A. (2013). Comparison of physical activity between children with autism spectrum disorders and typically developing children. *Autism*, *17*(1), 44–54. doi:10.1177/1362361312437416

Bandura, A. (1998). Health promotion from the perspective of social cognitive theory. *Psychology and Health*, *13*(4), 623–649.

Bloemen, M. A., Backx, F. J., Takken, T., Wittink, H., Benner, J., Mollema, J., & De Groot, J. F. (2015). Factors associated with physical activity in children and adolescents with a physical disability: A systematic review. *Developmental Medicine & Child Neurology*, *57*(2), 137–148.

Carlon, S. L., Taylor, N. F., Dodd, K. J., & Shields, N. (2013). Differences in habitual physical activity levels of young people with cerebral palsy and their typically developing peers: A systematic review. *Disability and Rehabilitation.*, *35*(8), 647–655. doi:610.3109/09638288.09632012.09715721

Carlson, S. A., Adams, E. K., Yang, Z., & Fulton, J. E. (2018). Percentage of deaths associated with inadequate physical activity in the United States. *Preventing Chronic Disease*, *15*, E38. doi:10.5888/pcd18.170354

Committee on Physical Activity and Physical Education in the School Environment.In Kohl, H. W., III, & Cook, H. D. (Eds.). (2013). *Educating* the student body: Taking physical activity and physical education to school. Washington, DC: National Academies Press (US).

Cook, B. G., Li, D., & Heinrich, K. M. (2015). Obesity, physical activity, and sedentary behavior of youth with learning disabilities and ADHD. *Journal of Learning Disabilility*, *48*(6), 563–576. doi:10.1177/0022219413518582

Corvey, K., Menear, K. S., Preskitt, J., Goldfarb, S., & Menachemi, N. (2016). Obesity, physical activity and sedentary behaviors in children with an autism spectrum disorder. *Maternal and Child Health Journal*, *20*(2), 466–476. doi:10.1007/s10995-015-1844-5

Ding, D., Lawson, K. D., Kolbe-Alexander, T. L., Finkelstein, E. A., Katzmarzyk, P. T., van Mechelen, W., & Pratt, M. (2016). The economic burden of physical inactivity: A global analysis of major non-communicable diseases. *Lancet*, *388*(10051), 1311–1324. doi:10.1016/s0140-6736(16)30383-x

Downs, S. J., Fairclough, S. J., Knowles, Z. R., & Boddy, L. M. (2016). Physical activity patterns in youth with intellectual disabilities. *Adapted Physical Activity Quarterly*, *33*(4), 374–390. doi:10.1123/apaq.2015-0053

Einarsson, I. O., Olafsson, A., Hinriksdottir, G., Johannsson, E., Daly, D., & Arngrimsson, S. A. (2015). Differences in physical activity among youth with and without intellectual disability. *Medicine and Science in Sports and Exercise*, *47*(2), 411–418. doi:10.1249/mss.0000000000000412

Einarsson, I. Þ., Jóhannsson, E., Daly, D., & Arngrímsson, S. Á. (2016). Physical activity during school and after school among youth with and without intellectual disability. *Research in Developmental Disabilities*, *56*, 60–70. doi:10.1016/j.ridd.2016.05.016

Ellis, T., & Motl, R. W. (2013). Physical activity behavior change in persons with neurologic disorders: Overview and examples from Parkinson disease and multiple sclerosis. *Journal of Neurologic Physical Therapy*, *37*(2), 85–90.

Esposito, P. E., MacDonald, M., Hornyak, J. E., & Ulrich, D. A. (2012). Physical activity patterns of youth with Down syndrome. *Intellectual and Developmental Disabilities*, *50*(2), 109–119. doi:10.1352/1934-9556-50.2.109

Foley, J. T., Bryan, R. R., & McCubbin, J. A. (2008). Daily Physical activity levels of elementary school-aged children with and without mental retardation. *Journal of Developmental and Physical Disabilities*, *20*(4), 365–378. doi:10.1007/s10882-008-9103-y

Frey, G. C., Stanish, H. I., & Temple, V. A. (2008). Physical activity of youth with mental retardation: Review and research agenda. *Adapted Physical Activity Quarterly*, *25*, 95–117.

Frey, G. C., Temple, V. A., & Stanish, H. I. (2017). Interventions to promote physical activity for youth with intellectual disabilities. *Salud Pública De México*, *59*, 437–445.

Gaglio, B., Shoup, J. A., & Glasgow, R. E. (2013). The RE-AIM framework: A systematic review of use over time. *American Journal of Public Health*, *103*(6), e38-e46. doi:10.2105/AJPH.2013.301299

Glasgow, R. E., Vogt, T. M., & Boles, S. M. (1999). Evaluating the public health impact of health promotion interventions: The RE-AIM framework. *American Journal of Public Health*, *89*(9), 1322–1327.

Guthold, R., Stevens, G. A., Riley, L. M., & Bull, F. C. (2018). Worldwide trends in insufficient physical activity from 2001 to 2016: A pooled analysis of 358 population-based surveys with 1· 9 million participants. *The Lancet Global Health*, *6*(10), e1077-e1086.

Haegele, J. A., Aigner, C. J., & Healy, S. (2019). Physical activity, body mass index, and health status among youth with severe visual impairments aged 13-17 years in the United States. *Disability and Health Journal, 12*(1), 24–28. doi:10.1016/j.dhjo.2018.07.001

Haegele, J. A., & Porretta, D. (2015). Physical activity and school-age individuals with visual impairments: A literature review. *Adapted Physical Activity Quarterly, 32*(1), 68–82. doi:10.1123/apaq.2013-0110

Healy, S., Aigner, C. J., Haegele, J. A., & Patterson, F. (2019). Meeting the 24-hr movement guidelines: An update on US youth with autism spectrum disorder from the 2016 National Survey of Children's Health. *Autism Research, 12*(6), 941–951. doi:10.1002/aur.2095

Healy, S., Haegele, J. A., Grenier, M., & Garcia, J. M. (2017). Physical activity, screen-time behavior, and obesity among 13-year olds in Ireland with and without autism spectrum disorder. *Journal of Autism and Developmental Disorders, 47*(1), 49–57. doi:10.1007/s10803-016-2920-4

Hinckson, E. A., & Curtis, A. (2013). Measuring physical activity in children and youth living with intellectual disabilities: A systematic review. *Research in Developmental Disabilities, 34*(1), 72–86.

Houwen, S., Hartman, E., & Visscher, C. (2009). Physical activity and motor skills in children with and without visual impairments. *Medicine and Science in Sports and Exercise, 41*(1), 103–109.

Izquierdo-Gomez, R., Martinez-Gomez, D., Acha, A., Veiga, O. L., Villagra, A., & Diaz-Cueto, M. (2014). Objective assessment of sedentary time and physical activity throughout the week in adolescents with Down syndrome. The UP&DOWN study. *Research in Developmental Disabilities, 35*(2), 482–489. doi:10.1016/j.ridd.2013.11.026

Jones, R. A., Downing, K., Rinehart, N. J., Barnett, L. M., May, T., McGillivray, J. A., ... Hinkley, T. (2017). Physical activity, sedentary behavior and their correlates in children with autism spectrum disorder: A systematic review. *PloS One, 12*(2), e0172482.

Katzmarzyk, P. T., Denstel, K. D., Beals, K., Carlson, J., Crouter, S. E., McKenzie, T. L., ... Wright, C. (2018). Results from the United States 2018 report card on physical activity for children and youth. *Journal of Physiscal Actitivity and Health, 15*(Suppl 2), S422–S424. doi:10.1123/jpah.2018-0476

Kim, J., & Greaney, M. L. (2014). Prevalence of physical activity, screen time, and obesity among US children by the service type of special health care needs. *Disability and Health Journal, 7*(3), 318–324. doi:10.1016/j.dhjo.2014.02.005

Kim, Y., Conners, R. T., Hart, P. D., Kang, Y. S., & Kang, M. (2013). Association of physical activity and body mass index with metabolic syndrome among U.S. adolescents with disabilities. *Disability and Health Journal, 6*(3), 253–259. doi:10.1016/j.dhjo.2013.01.002

Kohl, H. W., III, Craig, C. L., Lambert, E. V., Inoue, S., Alkandari, J. R., & Leetongin, G. Lancet Physical Activity Series Working Group. (2012). The pandemic of physical inactivity: Global action for public health. *The Lancet, 380*(9838), 294–305.

Lai, B., Young, H. J., Bickel, C. S., Motl, R. W., & Rimmer, J. H. (2017). Current trends in exercise intervention research, technology, and behavioral change strategies for people with disabilities: A scoping review. *American Journal of Physical Medicine & Rehabilitation, 96*(10), 748–761.

Lee, I. M., Shiroma, E. J., Lobelo, F., Puska, P., Blair, S. N., & Katzmarzyk, P. T. (2012). Effect of physical inactivity on major non-communicable diseases worldwide: An analysis of burden of disease and life expectancy. *Lancet, 380*(9838), 219–229. doi:10.1016/s0140-6736(12)61031-9

Li, R., Sit, C. H., Jane, J. Y., Duan, J. Z., Fan, T. C., McKenzie, T. L., & Wong, S. H. (2016). Correlates of physical activity in children and adolescents with physical disabilities: A systematic review. *Preventive Medicine, 89*, 184–193.

Lin, J. D., Lin, P. Y., Lin, L. P., Chang, Y. Y., Wu, S. R., & Wu, J. L. (2010). Physical activity and its determinants among adolescents with intellectual disabilities. *Research in Developmental Disabilities, 31*(1), 263–269.

Lobenius-Palmer, K., Sjoqvist, B., Hurtig-Wennlof, A., & Lundqvist, L. O. (2018). Accelerometer-assessed physical activity and sedentary time in youth with disabilities. *Adapted Physical Activity Quarterly, 35*(1), 1–19. doi:10.1123/apaq.2015-0065

Ma, J. K., & Martin Ginis, K. A. (2018). A meta-analysis of physical activity interventions in people with physical disabilities: Content, characteristics, and effects on behaviour. *Psychology of Sport and Exercise, 37*, 262–273. doi:10.1016/j.psychsport.2018.01.006

MacDonald, M., Esposito, P., & Ulrich, D. (2011). The physical activity patterns of children with autism. *BMC Research Notes, 4*, 422. doi:10.1186/1756-0500-4-422

Marques, A., Maldonado, I., Peralta, M., & Santos, S. (2015). Exploring psychosocial correlates of physical activity among children and adolescents with spina bifida. *Disability and Health Journal, 8*(1), 123–129. doi:10.1016/j.dhjo.2014.06.008

Martin Ginis, K. A., Ma, J. K., Latimer-Cheung, A. E., & Rimmer, J. H. (2016). A systematic review of review articles addressing factors related to physical activity participation among children and adults with physical disabilities. *Health Psychology Review, 10*(4), 478–494. doi:10.1080/17437199.2016.1198240

Matute-Llorente, A., González-Agüero, A., Gómez-Cabello, A., Vicente-Rodríguez, G., & Casajús, J. A. (2013). Physical activity and cardiorespiratory fitness in adolescents with Down syndrome. *Nutricion Hospitalaria, 28*(4), 1151–1155.

McCoy, S. M., Jakicic, J. M., & Gibbs, B. B. (2016). Comparison of obesity, physical activity, and sedentary behaviors between adolescents with autism spectrum disorders and without. *Journal of Autism and Developmental Disorders, 46*(7), 2317–2326.

McCubbin, J. (2014). Adapted physical activity: Influential impacts to establish a field of study. *Kinesiology Review, 3*(1), 53–58.

McGarty, A. M., & Melville, C. A. (2018). Parental perceptions of facilitators and barriers to physical activity for children with intellectual disabilities: A mixed methods systematic review. *Research in Developmental Disabilities, 73*, 40–57.

McGarty, A. M., Penpraze, V., & Melville, C. A. (2014). Accelerometer use during field-based physical activity research in children and adolescents with intellectual disabilities: A systematic review. *Research in Developmental Disabilities, 35*(5), 973–981. doi:10.1016/j.ridd.2014.02.009

McPherson, A. C., Keith, R., & Swift, J. A. (2014). Obesity prevention for children with physical disabilities: A scoping review of physical activity and nutrition interventions. *Disability and Rehabilitation, 36*(19), 1573–1587.

Memari, A. H., Ghaheri, B., Ziaee, V., Kordi, R., Hafizi, S., & Moshayedi, P. (2013). Physical activity in children and adolescents with autism assessed by triaxial accelerometry. *Pediatric Obesity, 8*(2), 150–158.

Michie, S., Richardson, M., Johnston, M., Abraham, C., Francis, J., Hardeman, W., … Wood, C. E. (2013). The behavior change technique taxonomy (v1) of 93 hierarchically clustered techniques: Building an international consensus for the reporting of behavior change interventions. *Annals of Behavioral Medicine, 46*(1), 81–95.

Mitchell, L. E., Ziviani, J., & Boyd, R. N. (2015). Habitual physical activity of independently ambulant children and adolescents with cerebral palsy: Are they doing enough?. *Physical Therapy, 95*(2), 202–211. doi:10.2522/ptj.20140031

Must, A., Phillips, S., Curtin, C., & Bandini, L. G. (2015). Barriers to physical activity in children with autism spectrum disorders: Relationship to physical activity and screen time. *Journal of Physical Activity and Health, 12*(4), 529–534.

National Physical Activity Plan Alliance. (2018). *The 2018 United States report card on physical activity for children and youth.* Washington, DC: National Physical Activity Plan Alliance.

Nooijen, C. F., Slaman, J., Stam, H. J., Roebroeck, M. E., & Van Den Berg-Emons, R. J. (2014). Inactive and sedentary lifestyles amongst ambulatory adolescents and young adults with cerebral palsy. *Journal of Neuroengineering and Rehabilitation, 11*(1), 49.

O'Brien, T., Noyes, J., Spencer, L. H., Kubis, H. P., Hastings, R. P., & Whitaker, R. (2016). Systematic review of physical activity and exercise interventions to improve health, fitness and well-being of children and young people who use wheelchairs. *BMJ Open Sport & Exercise Medicine, 2*(1), e000109.

Obeid, J., Balemans, A. C., Noorduyn, S. G., Gorter, J. W., & Timmons, B. W. (2014). Objectively measured sedentary time in youth with cerebral palsy compared with age-, sex-, and season-matched youth who are developing typically: An exploratory study. *Physical Therapy, 94*(8), 1163–1167. doi:10.2522/ptj.20130333

Obrusnikova, I., & Cavalier, A. R. (2011). Perceived barriers and facilitators of participation in after-school physical activity by children with autism spectrum disorders. *Journal of Developmental and Physical Disabilities, 23*(3), 195–211.

Pan, C. Y. (2008). Objectively measured physical activity between children with autism spectrum disorders and children without disabilities during inclusive recess settings in Taiwan. *Journal of Autism and Developmental Disorders, 38*(7), 1292.

Pan, C. Y., Liu, C. W., Chung, I. C., & Hsu, P. J. (2015). Physical activity levels of adolescents with and without intellectual disabilities during physical education and recess. *Research in Developmental Disabilities, 36c*, 579–586. doi:10.1016/j.ridd.2014.10.042

Pan, C. Y., Tsai, C. L., Chu, C. H., Sung, M. C., Ma, W. Y., & Huang, C. Y. (2016). Objectively measured physical activity and health-related physical fitness in secondary school-aged male students with autism spectrum disorders. *Physical Therapy, 96*(4), 511–520.

Piletic, C. K., & Davis, R. (2010). A profile of the Introduction to adapted physical education course within undergraduate physical education teacher education programs. *ICHPER-SD Journal of Research, 5*(2), 26–32.

Ratcliff, K., Hong, I., & Hilton, C. (2018). Leisure participation patterns for school age youth with autism spectrum disorders: Findings from the 2016 National Survey of Children's Health. *Journal of Autism and Developmental Disorders, 48*(11), 3783–3793. doi:10.1007/s10803-018-3643-5

Ridgers, N. D., Stratton, G., & Fairclough, S. J. (2005). Assessing physical activity during recess using accelerometry. *Preventative Medicine, 41*(1), 102–107. doi:10.1016/j.ypmed.2004.10.023

Rimmer, J. A., & Rowland, J. L. (2008). Physical activity for youth with disabilities: A critical need in an underserved population. *Developmental Neurorehabilitation, 11*(2), 141–148.

Rimmer, J. H., Chen, M.-D., & Hsieh, K. (2011). A conceptual model for identifying, preventing, and managing secondary conditions in people with disabilities. *Physical Therapy, 91*(12), 1728–1739. doi:10.2522/ptj.20100410 %J Physical Therapy

Ryan, J. M., Forde, C., Hussey, J. M., & Gormley, J. (2015). Comparison of patterns of physical activity and sedentary behavior between children with cerebral palsy and children with yypical development. *Physical Therapy, 95*(12), 1609–1616. doi:10.2522/ptj.20140337

Sallis, J. F., Bull, F., Guthold, R., Heath, G. W., Inoue, S., & Kelly, P. Lancet Physical Activity Series 2 Executive Committee. (2016). Progress in physical activity over the Olympic quadrennium. *Lancet, 388*(10051), 1325–1336.

Sallis, J. F., & McKenzie, T. L. (1991). Physical education's role in public health. *Research Quarterly for Exercise and Sport, 62*(2), 124–137.

Sallis, J. F., McKenzie, T. L., Beets, M. W., Beighle, A., Erwin, H., & Lee, S. (2012). Physical education's role in public health: Steps forward and backward over 20 years and HOPE for the future. *Research Quarterly for Exercise and Sport, 83*(2), 125–135.

Segal, M., Eliasziw, M., Phillips, S., Bandini, L., Curtin, C., Kral, T. V., … Must, A. (2016). Intellectual disability is associated with increased risk for obesity in a nationally representative sample of U.S. children. *Disability and Health Journal, 9*(3), 392–398. doi:10.1016/j.dhjo.2015.12.003

Shields, N., Synnot, A. J., & Barr, M. (2012). Perceived barriers and facilitators to physical activity for children with disability: A systematic review. *British Journal of Sports Medicine, 46*(14), 989–997.

Smith, L., Jackson, S. E., Pardhan, S., Lopez-Sanchez, G. F., Hu, L., Cao, C., … Yang, L. (2019). Visual impairment and objectively measured physical activity and sedentary behaviour in US adolescents and adults: A cross-sectional study. *BMJ Open, 9*(4), e027267. doi:10.1136/bmjopen-2018-027267

Stanish, H., Curtin, C., Must, A., Phillips, S., Maslin, M., & Bandini, L. (2015). Enjoyment, barriers, and beliefs about physical activity in adolescents with and without autism spectrum disorder. *Adapted Physical Activity Quarterly, 32*(4), 302–317.

Stanish, H. I., Curtin, C., Must, A., Phillips, S., Maslin, M., & Bandini, L. G. (2016). Physical activity enjoyment, perceived barriers, and beliefs among adolescents with and without intellectual disabilities. *Journal of Physical Activity and Health, 13*(1), 102–110.

Stanish, H. I., Curtin, C., Must, A., Phillips, S., Maslin, M., & Bandini, L. G. (2017). Physical activity levels, frequency, and type among adolescents with and without autism spectrum disorder. *Journal of Autism and Developmental Disorders, 47*(3), 785–794.

Thomas, S., Hinkley, T., Barnett, L. M., May, T., & Rinehart, N. (2019). Young children with ASD participate in the same level of physical activity as children without ASD: Implications for early intervention to maintain good health. *Journal of Autism and Developmental Disorders, 49*(8), 3278–3289. doi:10.1007/s10803-019-04026-9

Tremblay, M. S., Aubert, S., Barnes, J. D., Saunders, T. J., Carson, V., & Latimer-Cheung, A. E.; Sedentary Behavior Research Network Terminology Consensus Project Participants. (2017). Sedentary Behavior Research Network (SBRN) – Terminology Consensus Project process and outcome. *International Journal of Behavioral Nutrition and Physical Activity, 14*(1), 75.

Tremblay, M. S., Gray, C. E., Akinroye, K., Harrington, D. M., Katzmarzyk, P. T., Lambert, E. V., … Tomkinson, G. (2014). Physical activity of children: A global matrix of grades comparing 15 countries. *Journal of Physical Activity and Health, 11*(Suppl 1), S113-1125. doi:10.1123/jpah.2014-0177

Tybor, D. J., Eliasziw, M., Kral, T. V. E., Segal, M., Sherwood, N. E., Sikich, L., … Must, A. (2019). Parental concern regarding obesity in children with autism spectrum disorder in the United States:

National Survey of Children's Health 2016. *Disability and Health Journal, 12*(1), 126–130. doi:10.1016/j.dhjo.2018.09.004

Tyler, K., MacDonald, M., & Menear, K. (2014). Physical activity and physical fitness of school-aged children and youth with autism spectrum disorders. *Autism Research & Treatment, 2014*, 312163. doi:10.1155/2014/312163

U.S. Department of Health and Human Services. (2008). 2008 physical activity guidelines for Americans. Washington, D.C: U.S. Department of Health and Human Services.

Verschuren, O., Peterson, M. D., Balemans, A. C. J., & Hurvitz, E. A. (2016). Exercise and physical activity recommendations for people with cerebral palsy. *Developmental Medicine & Child Neurology, 58*(8), 798–808. doi:10.1111/dmcn.13053

Winslow, C. E. (1920). The untilled fields of public health. *Science, 51*(1306), 23–33.

World Health Organization. (2009). *Global health risks: Mortality and burden of disease attributable to selected major risks*. Geneva: Author.

World Health Organization (2010). *Global recommendations on physical activity for health*. World Health Organization. Retrieved from https://who.int/dietphysicalactivity/global-PA-recs-2010.pdf

World Health Organization. (2018). *Global action plan on physical activity 2018–2030: More active people for a healthier world.*. Geneva, Switzerland: World Health Organization.

Yazdani, S., Yee, C. T., & Chung, P. J. (2013). Factors predicting physical activity among children with special needs. *Preventing Chronic Disease, 10*, E119. doi:10.5888/pcd10.120283

Yun, J., & Beamer, J. (2018). Promoting physical activity in adapted physical education. *Journal of Physical Education, Recreation & Dance, 89*(4), 7–13. doi:10.1080/07303084.2018.1430628

Index

Page locators in *italics* and in **bold** refer to figures and tables, respectively.

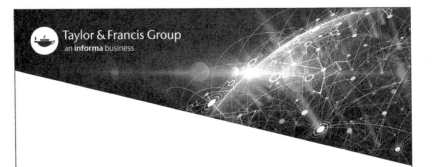